PERVASIVE COLLABORATIVE NETWORKS

IFIP – The International Federation for Information Processing

IFIP was founded in 1960 under the auspices of UNESCO, following the First World Computer Congress held in Paris the previous year. An umbrella organization for societies working in information processing, IFIP's aim is two-fold: to support information processing within its member countries and to encourage technology transfer to developing nations. As its mission statement clearly states,

> *IFIP's mission is to be the leading, truly international, apolitical organization which encourages and assists in the development, exploitation and application of information technology for the benefit of all people.*

IFIP is a non-profitmaking organization, run almost solely by 2500 volunteers. It operates through a number of technical committees, which organize events and publications. IFIP's events range from an international congress to local seminars, but the most important are:

• The IFIP World Computer Congress, held every second year;
• Open conferences;
• Working conferences.

The flagship event is the IFIP World Computer Congress, at which both invited and contributed papers are presented. Contributed papers are rigorously refereed and the rejection rate is high.

As with the Congress, participation in the open conferences is open to all and papers may be invited or submitted. Again, submitted papers are stringently refereed.

The working conferences are structured differently. They are usually run by a working group and attendance is small and by invitation only. Their purpose is to create an atmosphere conducive to innovation and development. Refereeing is less rigorous and papers are subjected to extensive group discussion.

Publications arising from IFIP events vary. The papers presented at the IFIP World Computer Congress and at open conferences are published as conference proceedings, while the results of the working conferences are often published as collections of selected and edited papers.

Any national society whose primary activity is in information may apply to become a full member of IFIP, although full membership is restricted to one society per country. Full members are entitled to vote at the annual General Assembly, National societies preferring a less committed involvement may apply for associate or corresponding membership. Associate members enjoy the same benefits as full members, but without voting rights. Corresponding members are not represented in IFIP bodies. Affiliated membership is open to non-national societies, and individual and honorary membership schemes are also offered.

PERVASIVE COLLABORATIVE NETWORKS

IFIP TC 5 WG 5.5 Ninth Working Conference on VIRTUAL ENTERPRISES, September 8-10, 2008, Poznan, Poland

Edited by

Luis M. Camarinha-Matos
New University of Lisbon
Portugal

Willy Picard
The Poznan University of Economics
Poland

 Springer

Pervasive Collaborative Networks

Edited by Luis M. Camarinha-Matos and Willy Picard

p. cm. (IFIP International Federation for Information Processing, a Springer Series in Computer Science)

ISSN: 1571-5736 / 1861-2288 (Internet)

ISBN: 978-1-4419-4654-6   e-ISBN: 978-0-387-84837-2

Printed on acid-free paper

9 8 7 6 5 4 3 2 1

springer.com

TABLE OF CONTENTS

TECHNICAL SPONSORS:

IFIP WG 5.5 COVE
Co-Operation infrastructure for Virtual Enterprises and electronic business

Society of Collaborative Networks

ORGANIZATIONAL CO-SPONSORS

Poznan University
of Economics

New University of Lisbon

PRO-VE'08 – 9th IFIP Working Conference on VIRTUAL ENTERPRISES
Poznan, Poland, 8-10 September 2008

General Chair: Willy Picard (PL)

Program Committee Chair: Luis M. Camarinha-Matos (PT)

Program Committee Co-chairs:
Hamideh Afsarmanesh (NL) - VO Breeding Environments
Dimitris Assimakopoulos (FR) - Professional Virtual Communities
Xavier Boucher (FR) - Evolutionary Supply Chains and VOs
Myrna Flores (CH) - Networking and Innovation
Alexandra Klen (BR) - CNO coordination and Management
Ricardo Rabelo (BR) - CNO Knowledge Management
Klaus-Dieter Thoben (DE) - Industrial CNO Applications

REFEREES FROM THE PROGRAMME COMMITTEE

Witold Abramowicz (PL)
António Abreu (PT)
Cesar Analide (PT)
Samuil Angelov (NL)
Américo Azevedo (PT)
Eoin Banahan (UK)
José Barata (PT)
Ron Beckett (AU)
Peter Bertok (AU)
Jim Browne (IE)
Jorge Cardoso (DE)
Wojciech Cellary (PL)
Schahram Dustdar (AT)
Elsa Estevez (AR)
Rosanna Fornasiero (IT)
Cesar Garita (CR)
Ted Goranson (USA)
Paul Grefen (NL)
Fernando Guerrero (ES)
Jairo Gutierrez (NZ)
Tarek Hassan (UK)
Tomasz Janowski (CN)
Toshiya Kaihara (JP)
Iris Karvonen (FI)
Bernhard Koelmel (DE)
Kurt Kosanke (DE)
Adamantios Koumpis (GR)
George Kovacs (HU)

John Krogstie (NO)
Andrew Kusiak (US)
Celson Lima (FR)
István Mézgar (HU)
Arturo Molina (MX)
Mieczyslaw Muraszkiewicz (PL)
Paulo Novais (PT) (Org Chair)
Martin Ollus (FI)
Angel Ortiz (ES)
Luis Osório (PT)
Adam Pawlak (PL)
Michel Pouly (CH)
Goran Putnik (PT)
Yacine Rezgui (UK)
Rainer Ruggaber (DE)
Raimar Scherer (DE)
Weiming Shen (CA)
Waleed W. Smari (US)
Riitta Smeds (FI)
António L. Soares (PT)
Jorge P. Sousa (PT)
Volker Stich (DE)
Lorna Uden (UK)
Antonio Volpentesta (IT)
Peter Weiß (DE)
Lai Xu (AU)

FOREWORD

COLLABORATIVE NETWORKS
Becoming a pervasive paradigm

In recent years the area of collaborative networks is being consolidated as a new discipline (Camarinha-Matos, Afsarmanesh, 2005) that encompasses and gives more structured support to a large diversity of collaboration forms. In terms of applications, besides the "traditional" sectors represented by the advanced supply chains, virtual enterprises, virtual organizations, virtual teams, and their breading environments, new forms of collaborative structures are emerging in all sectors of the society. Examples can be found in e-government, intelligent transportation systems, collaborative virtual laboratories, agribusiness, elderly care, silver economy, etc. In some cases those developments tend to adopt a terminology that is specific of that domain; often the involved actors in a given domain are not fully aware of the developments in the mainstream research on collaborative networks. For instance, the grid community adopted the term "virtual organization" but focused mainly on the resource sharing perspective, ignoring most of the other aspects involved in collaboration. The European enterprise interoperability community, which was initially focused on the intra-enterprise aspects, is moving towards inter-enterprise collaboration. Collaborative networks are thus becoming a **pervasive paradigm** *giving basis to new socio-organizational structures.*

In terms of research, in addition to the trend identified in previous years towards a sounder consolidation of the theoretical foundation of the discipline, there is now a clear line of developments focused on modeling and reasoning about the so called "soft issues", including social capital, cultural aspects, ethics and value systems, trust, emotions, behavior, etc. Computational intelligence, qualitative modeling, and reasoning methods are more and more used. A recent addition to the research agenda of collaborative networks is the attempt to apply affective computing principles in order to better understand the behavior of a collaborative community and better support the interactions of its members.

The **PRO-VE '08** *held in Poznan, Poland, is the 9th event in a series of successful conferences, including PRO-VE '99 (held in Porto, Portugal), PRO-VE 2000 (held in Florianopolis, Brazil), PRO-VE '02 (held in Sesimbra, Portugal), PRO-VE '03 (held in Lugano, Switzerland), PRO-VE '04 (held in Toulouse, France), PRO-VE '05 (held in Valencia, Spain), PRO-VE '06 (held in Helsinki, Finland), and PRO-VE'07 (Guimarães, Portugal).*

This book includes a number of selected papers from the PRO-VE '08 Conference, providing a comprehensive overview of recent advances in various CN domains and their applications. There is a special emphasis on the CN topics related to performance and value systems, VO breeding environments, VO creation and management, negotiations, collaboration platforms, collaborative problem solving, complex systems, business benefits, affective computing, cultural issues, and case studies and applications in industry and services.

Like in previous editions of PRO-VE, the book itself is the result of cooperative and highly distributed work among the authors of the articles and the International Program Committee members, thus constituting a valuable tool for all those interested in the emerging applications, research advances, and challenges of the collaborative networks. We would like to thank all the authors both from academia/research and industry for their contributions. We appreciate the dedication of the PRO-VE Program Committee members who helped both with the selection of articles and contributed with valuable comments to improve their quality.

The editors,

Luís M. Camarinha-Matos
Faculty of Science and Technology, New University of Lisbon, Portugal

Willy Picard
The Poznan University of Economics, Poland

Camarinha-Matos, L.M.; Afsarmanesh, H. (2005). Collaborative networks: A new scientific discipline, J. Intelligent Manufacturing, vol. 16, N° 4-5, pp439-452, ISSN: 0956-5515.

PART 1

VBE MANAGEMENT

COMPETENCY MODELING TARGETED ON PROMOTION OF ORGANIZATIONS TOWARDS VO INVOLVEMENT

Ekaterina Ermilova, Hamideh Afsarmanesh
University of Amsterdam, THE NETHERLANDS
{ermilova, hamideh}@science.uva.nl

During the last decades, a number of models is introduced in research, addressing different perspectives of the organizations' competencies in collaborative networks. This paper introduces the "4C-model", developed to address competencies of organizations, involved in Virtual organizations Breeding Environments (VBEs), from a new perspective. Design of the 4C-model aims at modeling those characteristics of organizations' competencies that are directly related to the criteria demanded in collaborative opportunities. As such, the 4C-model directly promotes these organizations for invitation / involvement in potential Virtual Organizations (VOs). The main components in the 4C-model include: Capabilities, Capacities, Costs, and Conspicuities, that constitute the 4C in this model. The paper further illustrates the applicability / validity of this approach to the context of VO creation. The introduced approach for competency-based creation of VOs in this paper also benefits from the introduction of other related concepts, namely "aggregate competency" and "collective competency".

1. INTRODUCTION

In earlier definitions, organization's competency is mainly addressing its capabilities, for example Gallon (Gallon et al, 1995) defines competency as "aggregation of capabilities, where synergy that is created has sustainable value and broad applicability". However participation of VBE members in general VBE activities such as the VO configuration, training, marketing, and trust establishment, require prior submission and analysis of their detailed competencies (Afsarmanesh & Camarinha-Matos, 2005). For example, in order to promote itself towards the invitation / involvement for new VOs, a VBE member must provide detailed and up-to-date information about its competencies. For this purpose, the information needed for an organization typically includes an accurate description of the member's capabilities, its free resources' capacities, the production costs for each of its product, as well as any conspicuous proof of the validity of the provided information. Based on the analysis of such competency information provided by all members, the VO broker selects the best-fit partners for a new VO.

In small VBEs (having less than 10 members), the competency information can perhaps be even transmitted orally from the VBE members to the VBE administrator and/or the VBE coach. However in medium and large VBEs depending on organization's complexity and especially in dynamic VBEs - continuously adjusting

Please use the following format when citing this chapter:

Ermilova, E. and Afsarmanesh, H., 2008, in IFIP International Federation for Information Processing, Volume 283; *Pervasive Collaborative Networks*; Luis M. Camarinha-Matos, Willy Picard; (Boston: Springer), pp. 3–14.

their competencies to the changing conditions in the market/society - the collection and analysis of competency information by a human actor in the VBE is not anymore effective. In such VBEs, computer-based mechanisms for competency management are required.

Competency is generally considered as a "tacit knowledge", which is hard to comprehensively capture, model and represent. Furthermore, in different disciplines, competency is associated with different types of characteristics, e.g. from some intangible characteristics such as "knowledge" (HR-XML, 2001) and "attitude" (Andros Consultants, 2000) to tangible characteristics such as "resource" (Javidan, 1998) and "product" (Molina & Flores, 1999).

The competency model introduced in this paper and called the "4C-model" includes 4 main components, namely: capability, capability, cost, and conspicuity.

In this paper, we state and discuss that the definition, modeling and representation of organizations' competencies depend on the targeted objectives for this task and especially the target of promoting the VO creation in VBEs which is considered in this paper. In section 2, we address an overview of different competency models developed during the last decades, as well as their different objectives. Then in section 3, we introduce the objective of our research on competency modeling and management; namely the "promotion of the VBE member organizations towards their VO involvement". We also address some specific VBE requirements, related to competency modeling and management, for which our solution approach is presented in section 4. Further in section 5, we extend the 4C competency model and introduce new concepts of "aggregate competency" and "collective competency". Section 6 concludes this paper.

2. STATE OF THE ART IN ORGANIZATION COMPETENCY

This section subsequently presents several existing definitions and models for organization's competency, as being addressed in three disciplines of (1) intra-organization managerial sciences and industrial engineering, (2) inter-organization managerial sciences, and (3) networks managerial sciences. These disciplines although are related to each other, have different position in regards to the competency model, and thus the models defined in these disciplines also differ. The main objective for this section is to provide a comprehensive overview of different developed competency models in order to further position our 4C-model of competency, described in section 4, among the related research on competency models.

While the detailed description of all addressed state-of-the-art competency models is outside the scope of this paper, below Table 1 represents a survey of the main referenced models, specifically addressing their main objectives, competency definitions, and fundamental competency components. The main conclusion made out of the study is the following: Although the competency models are not uniform, they correspond to and inter-relate with each other via similar components. Depending on the context, where the competency is modeled, and depending on the purpose for modeling, similar components are extended with some more specific components.

Table 1 – State of the art works on organization's competency modeling

Ref.	Name of the model	Objective for competency modeling	Competency definition and/or fundamental components in the competency model
		(1) Intra-organization managerial sciences	
(Prahalad & Hamel, 1990)	Core competence notion	Strategic planning and providing means for achieving better synergies among its various business units in a multi-business corporation.	"the collective learning in the organization, especially how to co-ordinate diverse production skills and integrate multiple streams of technologies" – Production skills – Technologies
(Javidan, 1998)	Core competence hierarchy	Extension of the core competency notion.	– Resources (physical resources, human resource, organizational resources Capabilities (organization abilities to exploit resources) – Competencies (cross-functional integration and coordination of capabilities) – Core competencies (skills and areas of knowledge that are shared across business units and result from integration and harmonization of SBUs' competencies)
		(2) Inter-organization managerial sciences	
(HR-XML, 2001)	HR-XML competencies schema	Providing trading partners standardized and practical means to exchange information about competencies within a variety of business contexts	"a specific, identifiable, definable, and measurable knowledge, skill, ability and/or other deployment-related characteristic (e.g. attitude, behavior, physical ability) which a human resource may possess and which is necessary for, or material to, the performance of an activity within a specific business context" – Taxonomy Id – Competency Id – Competency Evidence – Competency Weight – Competency (resulted from the decomposition the "top-level" competency)
		(3) Networks managerial sciences	
(Molina & Flores, 1999)	Core Competencies in the manufacturing clusters	Matching of fulfilling the tasks defined for a new VO against the constituent skills provided by the cluster of organizations	– Products – Processes (Business Processes) – Skills (Technology) – Task (set of activities/operations) service
(SFB457, 1999), (Mueller, 2006)	Competence cells	Planning of production system in the competence cell-based networks	"the smallest autonomous performance unit able to create value, be indivisible and able to exist independently" – Competence of humans – Resources (production areas, stocks, personnel, work equipment and auxiliary equipment, organizational and financial means) – Fulfilled task or executed function
(Boucher et al, 2005)	s-a-r-C model	Competence increase for individual firms within a network of firms	"the interaction between three components: the professional situations, the actors, and the resources" – Professional Situation (tasks and problems) – Actor (human resources of the firm) – Resource (material capabilities)

A summary of our main observations follow:

a. The competency definitions and models differ from one model to another, depending on the purpose for competency modeling.
b. There are two competency components that are common in all models, namely *(i) "resource"*, including "human resource" (also called "actor"), "physical resources", "ICT resources" (also called "technologies" or "skills") and a few other types of resources, and *(ii) "activity"* (also called "process", "production skill", "capability", "professional situation", "task" or "problem"). The absence of uniformity of naming of the same competency components is caused by difference in the context, where competency is being modeled.
c. Different models provide different extensions to the two-components-base addressed above in (b), such as the "taxonomy" and "classification" of competencies, as well as "competency weight" and "competency evidence" in (HR-XML, 2001).
d. The structure and level of details addressed in competency models depend on further intentions of using this specific model. Models, used for further creation of competency repositories, structuring and processing of competencies, such as in (HR-XML, 2001) are typically more detailed.

3. REQUIREMENTS FOR VBE COMPTETENCY

As specified in (Afsarmanesh & Camarinha-Matos, 2005), the main objective for competency definition, identified in the research on VBEs, is to support **competency-based configuration of VOs**, namely: (i) specific matching the VBE's competency collection against descriptions of the arisen Collaborative business Opportunities (COs) in the market / society and (ii) the selection of best-fit VO partners based on their competencies.

Our experimental study on the requirements for competencies in VBEs is performed in collaboration with several industrial VBE networks from Europe and Latin America, for example the SwissMicroTech (Switzerland), HELICE (Spain), CeBeNetwork (Germany), and IECOS (Mexico) within the IP-ECOLEAD project.

On the *first stage* of our study, we prepared and distributed a set of questionnaires, aimed to collect all requirements in relation to competency models and basic functionality for competency management. Responses from more than ten VBEs were gathered. The results generated from the analysis of this experimental study constitute the main criteria for our approach to modeling and management of organizations' competencies in VBEs. These criteria follow:

• In VBEs, organizations' competencies are required mainly for promotion of the VBE members towards involvement in potential VOs.

• Organizations' competencies are associated with a variety of elements in different VBEs, such as their ability to perform: tasks, business processes, job, core business activities and practices, and when applying a merge of human/physical/ICT resources (e.g. the knowledge, skills, and even attitude of the personnel, or the machinery available at the organization), and furthermore aimed at offering different products and/or services in the market/society.

- Availability/capacity of the VBE member organization's competency, which can be offered to potential new VOs, should be provided with a high level of details.
- Validity of the provided competency information needs to be properly addressed in the VBE. For example, customers' letters of satisfaction/recommendation can be made available to VBEs, with the contact information of the person who signed this letter. Furthermore, a strict system (e.g. certificates) shall exist, with which VBEs can evaluate the data provided by organizations in order to assure information accuracy, so that organizations do not claim false competencies at the VBE level.
- New competencies may be generated in VOs.
- Competencies held by the VBE and that can be offered to the market/society are represented by the collection of the VBE members' competencies.

In the *second stage* of our study, we designed the 4C competency model and developed a software system to manage the organizations' competency related information. This system, called PCMS (Profile and Competency Management System) (Ermilova & Afsarmanesh, 2007), offers specific functionality and services for competency management based on the prepared competency model. These aim to process different aspects of the competency, introduced in the 4C-model, as well as to provide effective web-interfaces and web-services for both human and software access and processing of competency related information.

In the *third stage*, the 4C-model and the PCMS went through a series of trial evaluation and finally validation at running VBE networks associated with the ECOLEAD project. During this stage the competency model was improved and evolved. Another objective for the development of the VBE competency model was its proper alignment with the concepts introduced by previous research in this area as addressed in section 2. The final stage of the 4C competency model is presented in the next section.

4. 4C-MODEL OF COMPETENCY

The main objective of the "4C-model of competency" is the "promotion of the VBE member organizations towards their participation in future VOs". The four fundamental components of competency in this model represent: "Capability", "Capacity", "Cost" and "Conspicuity". A description, as well as a motivation for the appearance of each component in this model, is further addressed below. We provide the following definition of competency.

Organizations' competencies in VBEs represent up-to-date information about their capabilities, capacities, costs, as well as conspicuities, illustrating the accuracy of their provided information, all aimed at qualifying organizations for VBE participation, and mostly oriented towards their VO involvement.

The main features that make the 4C-model unlike other models (as addressed in section 2) are the following:

- The 4C-model is developed in the context of VO creation within VBEs. Thus, the competency structure and main elements primarily intend to meet the specific VBE requirements (as addressed in section 3).
- The 4C-model is the base for development of a competency database, as well as the system for cataloguing and processing of competencies (i.e. the PCMS). Thus, the competency structure shall be detailed, and shall support further structuring and processing of the competencies.

4.1 Why 4 Cs?

Similar to other competency models addressed in section 2, the 4C competency model needed in VBEs has a compound structure. However, the primary emphasis in this model goes to the four following components, which are identified through our experimental study as necessary and sufficient components. The reasons why these elements are introduced as prerequisites for the 4C-model are addressed below:

1. **Capabilities** represent the capabilities of organizations, e.g. their processes and activities. When collective business processes are modeled for a new VO, the VO planner has to search for specific processes or activities that can be performed by single organizations, an order to instantiate the model.

2. **Capacities** represent free capacities of resources needed to perform one capability. Specific capacities of organizations are needed to fulfill the quantitative values of capabilities, e.g. amount of production units per day. If capacity of one member for a specific capability is not enough for a new VBE, another member (or a group of members) who has the same capability can be also invited.

3. **Costs** represent the costs of products/services provision in relation to one capability. They are needed to estimate if invitation of a specific group of members to a VO does not exceed the planned VO budget.

4. **Conspicuities** represent means for the validity of information provided by the VBE members about their capabilities, capacities and costs. The conspicuities in VBEs mainly include certified or witnessed documents, such as certifications, licenses, recommendation letters, etc.

4.2 Generic 4C-model of competency

An illustration of the generic 4C-model of competency, applicable to all variety of VBEs, is addressed in Figure 1.

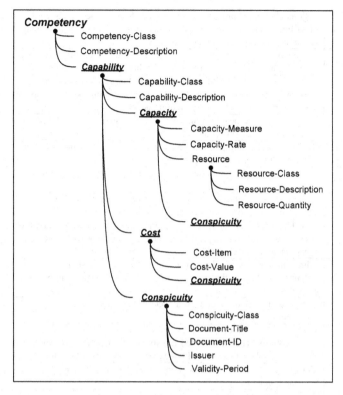

Figure 1 - Generic 4C-model of competency

Further, detailed definitions of all competency components are provided in Table 2. Please note that in the third column of this table we address if there is any correspondence/match between aspects introduced in the 4C-model of competency in comparison to other competency models, described in section 2.

Table 2 – Definitions of concepts represented in the 4C-model of competency

Concept:	Definition:	Match:
Competency	Competency is a compound object that cannot be represented by one textual value. The same as in (Javidan, 1998), in 4C-model, competency is associated with a set of specific capabilities.	(Javidan, 1998),
Competency-Class	Competency can be classified by domains and their specific sectors, e.g. "metalworking competency", "health-care competency", etc. Competency can also belong to two or several classes.	(HR-XML, 2001)
Competency-Description	Although a Competency-Class in general identifies a competency, a more extensive textual definition of each competency can be also provided.	
Capability	The capability is defined as an ability "to perform a task or activity". In our model Capability further refer to Capacity, which in fact represents Free Capacity of all Resources exploited within that Capability. Furthermore, we define two main types of capabilities, such as process (mainly for manufacturing domain) (Molina & Flores, 1999) and activity (for service-oriented domain).	(Javidan, 1998), (Molina & Flores, 1999)
Capability-	Capabilities can be classified. First, they can be divided into two	

Class	disjoint classes of "process" and "activity". Second, they can be further classified by the domain or a specific sector. Capability can also belong to two or several classes at the same time.	
Capability-Description	Although a Capability-Class in general identifies a capability, a more extensive textual definition of each capability can be also provided.	
Capacity	Capacity is described as the current availability of resources needed to perform one specific capability. The capacity component is mainly resulted from our study of VBE requirements.	-
Capacity-Measure	This represents a measure unit for a specific capacity, e.g. "thousands units per hour", or "hours a day".	
Capacity-Rate	This is a specific numeric value for capacity related to its measure unit, e.g. e.g. "20 thousands units per hour"	
Resource	The resource class represents the elements applied to business processes in the organizations.	
Resource-Class	Resources can be classified. First, they can be divided into four disjoint classes of "Human resources", "Physical resources", "ICT resources", and "Organizational resources" (e.g. brand and reputation). Further, for each class, the domain-specific sub-classes can be provided, such as "manufacturing machinery" for the "Physical resource" class.	(Molina & Flores, 1999)
Resource-Description	Although a Resource-Class in general identifies a resource, a more extensive textual definition of each specific resource can be also provided.	
Resource-Quantity	This is a number or amount of a specific resource, owned by a VBE member organization.	
Cost	Costs represent the costs of products/services provision in relation to one capability. They are needed to estimate if invitation of a specific group of members to a VO will not exceed the planned VO budget.	-
Cost-Item	This is an item, for that the cons is provided, for example "100 thousands units a day".	
Cost-Value	This is a monetary prize for a Cost-Item.	
Conspicuity	This knowledge class is introduced to represent the indication / proof of validity of the competency information provided by the organization. A conspicuity can either be an on-line document or some web accessible information, e.g. organization's brochures, web-site, etc. Conspicuity documents can indicate the product quality, financial stability, etc., and they will be maintained in the VBE when provided by the VBE entities. The main reason for introducing the conspicuity documents in the VBE is to avoid baseless claims of competencies by organizations. Therefore the issue of verification/validation of the competency data is also necessary to be addressed. The conspicuity component of competency mainly resulted from our study of VBE requirements.	(HR-XML, 2001)
Conspicuity-Class	The conspicuity of information validity, can be of two different kinds including: the "witnessed conspicuity" documents (e.g. a letter of recommendation or an article in a magazine/news section), and the "authorized / certified conspicuity" documents (e.g. accreditation statements, financial ratings, licenses, certificates, patents and awards).	
Document-Title	This is a title of a specific conspicuity document.	
Document-ID	This is a specific identifier (e.g. license number) of a conspicuity document.	
Issuer	This is the name of an organization, or a person, that issued a specific conspicuity document.	
Validity-Period	This is a validity period (e.g. March 2000 - March 2010) of a conspicuity document.	

4.3 Domain extension of the generic 4C-model of competency

Further to the elements of the generic 4C-model that are shared by all VBEs (as addressed in section 4.2) independent of their domain area application, there is a number of competency elements that are VBE domain (business area) dependent and/or specific VBE application dependent. To address the specifities of competencies in different VBE domains and application environments, while supporting the reusability and replicability of the model in different VBE domains/applications, the 4Cs-model of competency has three following levels:

▪ **Core level** that represents the generic competency model, applied to all VBEs (as addressed in section 4.2).

▪ **Domain level** that represents an extension of the core level with specific components related to each domain or business area of the VBEs. Many domain extensions can be defined for the competency model, depending on the number of different VBE activity/business domains existing in the market and society. All VBEs from the same domain can share the same domain extension. At the domain level, the domain extension is integrated to the object-classes (e.g. Competency-Class, Capability-Class) in the generic competency model of the core level (see Figure 1). For instance, as illustrated in Figure 2, the Capability-Class definition of the generic 4C-model at the core level is extended at the domain level with a number of domain specific capability classes (e.g. Metalworking, Product design, etc.). Please note that for the "Capacity" element in the 4C-model, the domain extension is applied to the Capacity-Measure element (see Figure 1).

▪ **Application level** that represents an extension of the domain level with new components related to every specific application environment of the VBE. Namely, each VBE has its own application extension. The application extension is also directly integrated to the domain extension of the generic competency model as the specific sub-classes of domain classes, e.g. for the capabilities, resources, etc.

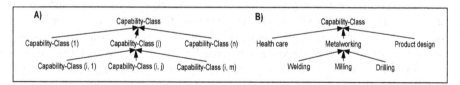

Figure 2 – Domain extension of the 4-C model of competency: A) generalized representation of domain capability extension and B) some exemplified domain capability extensions

Based on the domain and application classifications introduced in each VBE, the PCMS will organize/collect/group competencies and their components.

During the creation stage of every VBE's life cycle (Afsarmanesh & Camarinha-Matos, 2005), the domain and application level extensions for its competency model shall be created, while during the VBE's operation and evolution stage these extensions may further evolve.

Development of the domain/application extensions from scratch is a time-consuming task. However some "prototypes" of domain extensions exit and can be applied. For example, the activity classifications provided in the NACE codes

(NACE, 2008) represent a "prototype" for domain-dependent classifications of competencies and capabilities that can be used for VBEs.

5. AGGREGATE AND COLLECTIVE COMPETENCY

To properly support the competency-based VO creation in VBEs, this section introduces two new concepts of "aggregate competency" and "collective competency", as also illustrated in Figure 3.

An **aggregate competency** represents a *total* aggregation/merge of competency definitions of one, several, or of all members inside a VBE. This aggregation is primarily focused on (1) evaluation of the ability of a group of VBE members, or of all its members to address the criteria demanded through COs, (2) identification of the general competency gaps in the entire VBE while compared against most COs related to the VBE domain and application, as well as (3) preparation of VBE's aggregate competency catalog for the VBE customers as a part of VBE marketing activities.

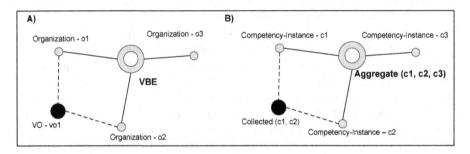

Figure 3 - A) Example VBE structure and B) Competency dissemination in the VBE

Competency aggregation is performed only at the level of "competency instances" (actual existing competencies in VBE), but not on the level of the "competency model". The main rules for aggregation of several object-instances (e.g. competency-instances, resource-instances, capability-instances) are the following:

a. If two or more object-instances belong to the same class (e.g. Competency-Class, Capability-Class, as well as Capacity-Measure), they are merged into one aggregate object-instance. For example, if competencies c_1, c_2 and c_3 (see Figure 3) belong to the same "Welding" class (see Figure 2), they become one aggregate competency-instance. If all of them belong to different classes, they remain separate instances. If two of them, e.g. c_1 and c_2, belong to the same Competency-Class, while c_3 does not, the c_1 and c_2 instances become one aggregate competency instance, while the c_3 instance remains a separate instance.

b. If the values for the same attribute of two or more aggregated object-instances (see a. above) are strings, they all become values of the same attribute of the aggregate object-instance. For example, if the competency-instances c_1, c_2, and c_3 are aggregated in one instance, the Competency-Description attribute (see

Figure 1) of the resulted aggregate competency instance has 3 values that are equal to Competency-Descriptions of c1, c2, and c3.

c. If the values for the same attribute of two or more aggregated object-instances (see a. above) are numeric, they are summarized. For example, the capacity-rate of an aggregation of two capacity-instances is a sum of capacity-rates of these capability-instances.

d. If the values for the same attribute of two or more aggregated competency-instances (see a. above) are objects-instances (e.g. capability-instances), they are processed the same as competency-instances (i.e. from a. to e. above). For example, if the competency-instances c1, c2, and c3 are aggregated, the Capability attribute (see Figure 1) of the resulted aggregate competency is equal to the aggregation of all capabilities associated with c1, c2, and c3.

A **collective competency** represents a *partial* aggregation/merge of competencies of a group of VBE members that constitute the (candidate) partners to form a specific VO. In other words, the collective competency represents a VO Broker's predefined "competency plan" for VO, that needs to be fulfilled by the selected group of VBE members. The *predefined* collective competencies are primarily needed in order to (1) get matched against the aggregate competency of the same group of VBE members, (2) calculate the remaining free capacities of each VBE member in addition to those which are currently occupied by its involvement in the VOs, and (3) develop the VO's profile.

Definitions of all collective competencies shall be prepared manually matching VO Brokers' plans, based on COs, during the creation phase of each VO.

6. CONCLUSION

The main contribution of this research is the development of the "4C-model" for characterization of organizations' competencies. The model is specifically designed to addresses competencies of member organizations in Virtual organizations Breeding Environments (VBEs). It is targeted at the promotion of these organizations towards their invitation / involvement in potential Virtual Organizations (VOs).

This paper addresses several existing state-of-the-art competency models for organizations. It further positions the 4C-model of organization's competency among the other addressed models and illustrates its applicability/validity for the context of VO creation.

To better address the competency-based creation of VOs, the new concepts of "aggregate competency" and "collective competency" are introduced. The aggregate competency represents the aggregation/merging of all members' competencies within VBE. Aggregate competency is needed for performing activities such as identification of competency gaps in the entire VBE when considering the demands identified through the existing opportunities in the market/society. Similarly, VBE's aggregate competencies are required for the purpose of marketing of VBEs. The collective competency represents a partial merging of specific competency components of VO partners, that fulfill the criteria specified in the VO's collaborative opportunity. As such, collective competencies of VO partners address and evaluate the ability of a group of VBE members to satisfy the VO requirements and thus to form a new VO. It is also required for calculation of remaining free capacities of each VBE member after its involvement in VOs. This paper also presents the approaches for derivation of aggregate competencies and collective competencies.

In the EC founded ECOLEAD project (ECOLEAD, 2008), based on the 4C-model of competencies, a database system is developed to manage the VBE members' competencies. Furthermore, a VBE competency management system is developed called PCMS to support the collection, cataloguing, and processing of different competencies in this environment. The description of this database and the management system of PCMS are the subject of a forthcoming paper.

Acknowledgements

The work on this paper is partially supported by the FP6 IP project ECOLEAD, funded by the European Commission.

REFERENCES

Afsarmanesh H., Camarinha-Matos L.M., A framework for management of virtual organization breeding environments, in Collaborative Networks and their Breeding Environments, Springer, 2005, pp. 35-49

Allen, C. (2007): Competencies (Measurable Characteristics) Recommendation, 2007 April 15, http://ns.hr-xml.org/2_5/HR-XML-2_5/CPO/Competencies.html, viewed 12-11-2007

Andros Consultants (company) (2000): Selecting the best – the roles of competencies, http://www.andros.org/intouch/SiT_0602_SelectBest_competencies.pdf (viewed 02/2007)

Boucher, X., Peillon, S., Burlat, P. (2005): Towards a decision support for a collaborative increase of competencies within networks of firms. Research Report G2I-EMSE 2005-600-009, Septembre 2005, Ecole des Mines de Saint-Etienne

Camarinha-Matos, L.M.; Afsarmanesh, H. (2004): The emerging discipline of collaborative networks, in Virtual Enterprises and Collaborative Networks (L.M. Camarinha-Matos, Editor), Kluwer Academic Publishers

ECOLEAD project, www.ecolead.org [viewed 28.04.2008]

Ermilova, E., Afsarmanesh, H. (2007): Modeling and management of Profiles and Competencies in VBEs. Journal of Intelligent Manufacturing, Springer.

Gallon, M. R., Stillman, H. M., Coates, D. (1995): Putting core competency thinking into practice, in Research Technology Management, Vol. 38 No. 3, May–June 1995

HR-XML consortium, http://www.hr-xml.org, viewed 12-11-2007

Javidan, M. (1998): Core Competence: What does it mean in practice? Long Range planning. 31(1), 60 - 71

Molina, A., Flores, M. (1999): A Virtual Enterprise in Mexico: From Concepts to Practice. Journal of Intelligent and Robotics Systems, 26, 289-302.

Mueller, E. (2006): Production planning and operation in competence0cell based networks, in Production Planning & Control, Vol. 17, No. 2, march 2006, pp. 99-112

NACE codes, http://europa.eu.int/comm/competition/mergers/cases/index/nace_all.html [viewed viewed 28/02/2008]

Prahalad, C.K., Hamel, G. (1990): The core competence of the corporation. Harvard Business Review, May-June, 68(3), 79-90.

SFB457 (1999): Sonderforschungbereich 457 Hierarchielose regionale Produktionsnetze, Finanzierungsantrag 2000, 2001, 2002, TU Chemnitz

2 | A VIRTUAL BREEDING ENVIRONMENT REFERENCE MODEL AND ITS INSTANTIATION METHODOLOGY

David Romero[1], Nathalie Galeano[1], Arturo Molina[2]

[1]*CIDYT - ITESM Campus Monterrey, Monterrey, MEXICO*
david.romero.diaz@gmail.com, ngaleano@itesm.mx
[2]*VIDT - ITESM Campus Monterrey, Monterrey, MEXICO*
armolina@itesm.mx

Virtual Breeding Environments (VBEs) are long-term strategic alliances of organisations aimed at offering the conditions to support the rapid and fluid configuration of Virtual Organisations (VOs). VBE reference models play a guiding role to conceptualise a set of business processes to enhance the responsiveness and flexibility of networks to react to a collaboration opportunity through a collection of collaborative drivers and enablers. VBE reference models serve as a reference guide for the implementation of breeding environments in different domains and application environments. This paper presents an instantiation methodology as a controlled process, addressing systematically a set of steps, supported by different mechanisms and methodologies needed to establish and characterize the management functionalities and running of a VBE that also addresses activities during its entire lifecycle based-on a VBE reference model proposed.

1. INTRODUCTION

Virtual Breeding Environments (VBEs) also known as source networks or clusters, are long-term strategic alliances of organisations aimed at offering the necessary conditions (e.g. human, financial, social, infrastructural and organisational) to support the rapid and fluid configuration of Virtual Organisations. VBEs mainly focus on creating an adequate environment for the establishment of cooperation agreements, common operation principles, common interoperable infrastructures, common ontologies, and mutual trust among others, with the objective of preparing their members (organisations and support institutions) to be ready to collaborate in potential VOs that will be established when a collaboration (business) opportunity arises. *Virtual Organisations (VOs)* are short-term and dynamic coalitions of organisations that may be tailored within a VBE to respond to a single collaboration opportunity, through integrating the core-competencies and resources required to meet or exceed the quality, time and cost frames expected by the customer, and that dissolve once their mission/goal has been accomplished, and whose cooperation is supported through computer networks (Camarinha-Matos & Afsarmanesh, 2007b).

This paper presents an instantiation methodology as a controlled process, addressing systematically a set of steps, supported by different mechanism and methodologies needed to establish and characterize the management functionalities

Please use the following format when citing this chapter:

Romero, D., Galeano, N. and Molina, A., 2008, in IFIP International Federation for Information Processing, Volume 283; *Pervasive Collaborative Networks*; Luis M. Camarinha-Matos, Willy Picard; (Boston: Springer), pp. 15–24.

and running of a VBE that also addresses activities during its entire lifecycle based-on a VBE reference model proposed.

2. BASIC CONCEPTS ON INSTANTIATION

Enterprise instantiation process has been conceptualised as a supporting process for specific description/modelling of a particular organisation, or network, based-on a specific reference model or architecture. A *reference model* or *architecture* serves as a reference guide in the creation and maintenance process of an entity to obtain and maintain a consistent list of requirements to define, prototype, design, implement, and execute business processes according to certain requirements. Instantiation concept is traditionally associated with enterprise modelling, mainly with enterprise reference models and architectures like CIMOSA (CIM Open System Architecture) and GERAM (General Enterprise Reference Architecture and Methodology).

An *instantiation process* serves as a controlled approach to guide an organisation, or network, in the derivation process of a reference model or architecture through three modelling levels (general, partial and particular) allowing the detailing of business requirements in each level: from *general* business requirements (requirements definition), through the optimisation and specification of *partial* requirements (design specification), to their *particular* implementation in a specific domain (implementation description). Each modelling level analysed from different modelling points of view: function, information, resources, and organisation.

For the purpose of this paper a *VBE instantiation process* can be referred as a controlled process characterizing a new breeding environment based-on a *VBE reference model* and the *VBE domain specificities*. The *VBE instantiation process* addresses systematically a set of steps, which are supported by mechanisms and methodologies, for the specification and/or generation of a customized VBE model, describing its components to characterize a specific VBE typology, and these components together represent an instance of the VBE reference model.

3. VBE REFERENCE MODEL

VBE reference model aims to synthese and formalize the base concepts, principles and practices for long-term collaborative networks. The VBE reference model proposed in this paper intends to provide a common framework for traditional breeding environments (production/service oriented) such as: industrial clusters, industry districts & business ecosystems, and new emerging ones like: disaster rescue networks & virtual laboratory networks (Camarinha-Matos & Afsarmanesh, 2006).

The *VBE reference model* focuses on providing a comprehensive overview of the key elements/components of a breeding environment and the main requirements to create and manage one during its entire lifecycle. Table 1 presents a model-based VBE reference model derived from the ARCON[*] modelling framework (Camarinha-Matos & Afsarmanesh, 2007a) defining two sub-spaces, each one with four modelling views, providing an abstract representation of a VBE from its inside (endogenous elements) and its outside (exogenous interactions).

---

[*]ARCON (A Reference Model for COllaborative Networks)

Table 1 – VBE Reference Model based-on ARCON Modelling Framework

VBE Endogenous Elements				VBE Exogenous Interactions			
Structural	Componential	Functional	Behavioural	Market	Support	Societal	Constituency

Actors:
• Private Organisations
• Public Organisations
• NGOs
Roles:
• VBE Member(s)
• VO Support Provider
  o Opportunity Broker
  o VO Planner
  o VO Coordinator
• VBE Administrator
• VBE Support Provider
  o Ontology Provider
  o Service Provider
  o Support Institution
• Public (Guests)
• VBE Advisor(s)
Relationships:
• Networking
• Coordination
• Cooperation
• Collaboration
Network:
• Virtual Breeding Environment (VBE)
  o Size
  o Typology
  o Location
  o --
	Physical Resources:
	• Machinery
	ICT Resources:
	• Hardware
	  o ICT-Infrastructure
	• Software
	  o VBE Management System
	Human Resources:
	• VBE Staff
	Info./Knowledge Resources:
	• VBE-Itself, VOs & VBE Members Profile & Competency Information
	• VBE Governance Information
	• VBE Value System Information
	• VBE Support Institutions Information
	• VOs Information
	• VBE Bag of Assets Information
	• VBE & VO Inheritance Information
	Ontology Resources:
	• VBE Ontology (Top, Core & Domain Levels)
		Fundamental Processes:
		• Membership & Structure Management
		• Profiling & Competency Management
		• Trust Management
		• Performance Management
		• Decision Support Management
		• VO Creation Management
		  o CO Identification
		  o CO Characterization & Rough Planning
		  o Partners Search & Selection
		  o Agreements/Contracts Negotiation Wizard
		• VO Information Management
		• VO Registration Management
		• VO Inheritance Information Management
		Background Processes:
		• Strategic Management
		• Marketing Management
		• Financial Management
		• Accounting Management
		• Resources Management
		• Governance Management
		• VBE Bag of Assets Management
		• Value System Info. Management
		• Ontology Management
		• ICT Management
		• Support Institutions Management
		Procedures
		Methodologies
			Prescriptive Behaviour:
			• Cultural Principles:
			  o Regional Traditions
			  o Business & NGO Culture
			  o VBE Culture
			• Governance Principles:
			  o Performance Orientation
			  o Responsibility & Accountability
			  o Commitment to VBE
			  o Membership Eligibility
			  o Leadership Role
			  o Contract Enforcement Policy
			  o Brokering Principles
			  o Decision-Making Principles
			Obligatory Behaviour:
			• Bylaws:
			  o Rights & Duties Policies
			  o Membership Policies
			  o Security Issues
			  o Conflict Resolution Policy
			  o Financial Policies
			  o Amendments to Bylaws
			  o IPR Policies
			• Internal Regulations:
			  o ICT User Guidelines
			Constrains & Conditions:
			• Adhesion Agreement
			• Agreement Amendments
			Contracts & Agreements:
			• Confidentiality Constrains
			• Legal Constrains (Contracts)
			• Internal Normative Constrains
			Incentives & Sanctions:
			• Incentives & Sanctions Policies
				Network Identity
				Statement:
				• VBE Mission
				• VBE Vision
				• VBE Strategy
				• VBE Goals
				References/Testimonials:
				Network Profile:
				• Who are we?
				• How to contact us?
				Market & Branding Strategy:
				• Marketing/Advertisement Strategy
				  o Broadcast & Direct
				  o Branding Strategy
				Market Interactions:
				• VBE & VO Customers:
				  o Strategic Customers
				  o Potential Customers
				• Competitors:
				  o Direct Competitors
				  o Indirect Competitors
				• (Potential) Suppliers
				• Substitutors
				• Complementors
				Interactions/Transactions:
				• Bidding
				• Handling Inquiries
				• Contracting
					Network Social Nature:
					• Profit/Not-Profit
					• Governmental
					• NGO
					Support Entities:
					• Certification Entities
					• Insurance Entities
					• Logistics Entities
					• Standard Registries:
					  o Clearing Centers
					  o Mater Data Providers
					• Financial Entities:
					  o Banks
					  o Investors & Sponsors
					• Coaching Entities:
					  o Advisers & Experts
					• Training Entities:
					  o Advisers & Experts
					• Professional Associations
					• Research Entities:
					  o Universities
					  o Research Institutes
					Service Acquisition:
					• Financial Relation
					• Technological Service
					• Training Action
					• Coaching Action
					• Guarantee Action
					• Knowledge Transfer
					• Consulting Service
					Agreement
					Establishment
						Network Legal Identity:
						• Legal Status
						  o Legal Entity
						  o Informal Entity
						• Values & Principles
						Impacts:
						• Advertising VBE Competency Domain
						• VO Creation
						Legal Issues:
						• Conflict Resolutions
						• Intellectual Property Rights
						Public Interactions:
						• Governmental Organisations:
						  o Social Security
						  o City Hall
						  o Civil Defence
						• Associations
						• Interest Groups
						• Supporters
						• Opponents
						• Regulatory Boundaries
						• Other Entities
						Public Relations:
						• Political Relations
						• Seeking Support
						• Information Transfer
						  o Broadcast & Direct
						• Social Relations
						  o Cultural & Patronage
						• Building Reputation
						• Building Success Cases
							Attracting Factors:
							• VBE Reason for Existence
							• Attracting & Recruiting Strategy
							  o Advertising
							  o Industrial Fairs
							• Motivating Community Participation
							• Incentives
							Rules of Adhesion:
							• Charter of Foundation
							• Rewards mechanism for Enrolment
							• Notice of Termination of Business
							Potential Members:
							• Business Organisations
							  o Private Institutions
							  o Individual Experts
							  o Public Institutions
							Sustainability Factors:
							• Members Searching:
							  o Invitation
							  o Solicitation
							• Rewarding

The *VBE endogenous elements* aim at identifying a set of characteristic properties that can together capture the VBE constituting elements. Modelling views proposed by ARCON modelling framework for this sub-space are: (1) *Structural* - addressing the VBE network structure in terms of its constituent elements such as actors, roles and their relationships, as well as the network topology; (2) *Componential* - focusing on the VBE resources composition such as human, technological, information, knowledge, and ontologies; (3) *Functional* - attending the VBE processes, procedures and methodologies as the base functions/operations related to the different VBE lifecycle stages; and (4) *Behavioural* - covering the VBE principles, policies and governance rules that drive and constrain the VBE and its members behaviour.

The *VBE exogenous interactions* aim to reveal the VBE interactions with its surrounding environment. Modelling views proposed by ARCON modelling framework for this sub-space are: (1) *Market* - addressing the interactions with customers and competitors; (2) *Support* - attending the support services provided by third party institutions; (3) *Societal* - capturing the interactions between the VBE and the society in general; and (4) *Constituency* - focusing on the interaction with the potential VBE members.

4. VBE MANAGEMENT FRAMEWORK

Making a zoom-in the *VBE reference model functional modelling view,* a set of fundamental and background processes can be defined as important catalysts for ensuring the success of all VBE management activities. Table 2 and 3 intent to provide a widespread overview of the key business processes (management functionalities) required to support and facilitate the VBE management activities needed to be performed during the VBE lifecycle, under a three division classification: VBE actors, VO creation and VBE general management.

VBE fundamental processes, also known as main processes, are those business processes that fundamentally affect the VBE performance and influence how well other processes are executed to increase the VBE competitiveness.

Table 2 – VBE Fundamental Processes

	Functionality	Description
VBE Actors' management	Membership & Structure Management	Set of management activities and supporting tools allowing integration, accreditation, disintegration, rewarding, and categorization of members within the VBE. It is separated into mechanisms for members' registration, members' rewarding, and assignment of roles, rights and responsibilities to VBE members (Afsarmanesh & Camarinha-Matos, 2005; Sitek et al, 2007).
	Profiling & Competency Management	Set of management activities and supporting tools for creating and maintaining profiles for VBE members, for the VBE itself, and for the VOs registered within the VBE; as well as for the competency-based assessment of new VBE members and discovery of new competencies out of the collective competencies of all VBE members in the breeding environment (Ermilova & Afsarmanesh, 2006).
VO Creation Management	Collaboration Opportunity Identification	Set of management activities and supporting tools that will support the identification of new collaboration opportunities that will trigger the formation of new VOs. Collaboration opportunity detection will be according to the VBE competency domain. A collaboration opportunity might be external, originated by a (potential) customer or internal detected by a VBE member acting as a broker (Demšar et al, 2007; Camarinha-Matos et al, 2007).
	Collaboration Opportunity Characterization & VO Rough Planning	Set of management activities and supporting tools for identifying the required competencies, capabilities and capacities needed to respond to the collaboration opportunity identified, as well as for defining a rough structure for the potential VO, including its organisational form and the VO partners corresponding roles. At this stage it is important to define the VO partnership form which is typically regulated by contracts and cooperation agreements (Concha et al, 2008; Camarinha-Matos et al, 2007).

VO Creation Management	Partners Search & Selection	Set of management activities and supporting tools devoted to the identification of potential VO partners, their assessment and intelligent selection by matching their competencies with the competencies required to respond to the collaboration opportunity identified. Some elements for search and selection could be: technical, economical, reliability indicators, preferences, etc. (Baldo et al, 2007; Camarinha-Matos et al, 2007).
	Agreement/ Contract Negotiation Wizard	*Agreement Negotiation:* Set of management activities and supporting tools that will assist human actors (VO partners) during the negotiation processes (iterative process to reach agreements and align needs with offers) towards the VO constitution. Management activities include formulation and modelling of contracts and agreements, as well as the contracting process itself. Important issues to consider at this process include: determination of the objects of negotiation; negotiation protocols; decision-making process and corresponding parameters; representation of agreements (Camarinha-Matos & Oliveira, 2006; Camarinha-Matos et al, 2007). *Contracting:* As a set of management activities and supporting tools that will assist the contracting process through the formulation and modelling of contracts and agreements as well as the contracting process itself, before a VO can effectively be launched (Camarinha-Matos & Oliveira, 2006; Camarinha-Matos et al, 2007).
	Virtual Organisations Information Management	Set of managing activities and supporting tools to manage the information related to the VOs registered within the VBE. (1) *VO Registration:* This task comprises the process of registering a newly created VO in the VBE; and (2) *VO Inheritance Information:* This task comprises the management of inheritance information after VO dissolution; information feeds back into the VBE to create sustainable effects and to provide the VBE members with lessons learned from previous VOs (Loss et al, 2006; Karvonen et al, 2007).
VBE General Management	Trust Management	Set of management activities and supporting tools for basic trust assessment of VBE membership applicants, and subsequent dynamic trust appraisal and monitoring during their ongoing VBE membership (Msanjila & Afsarmanesh, 2006).
	Performance Management	Set of management activities and supporting tools based-on a systematic procedure of planning, monitoring, rating and rewarding VBE actors' performance based-on the definition of key performance indicators (Camarinha-Matos & Abreu, 2005).
	Decision Support Management	Set of management activities and supporting tools for monitoring key performance indicators in the VBE and issuance of notifications and warnings. It is separated into mechanisms for VBE competency gap analysis, lack of performance warning, and low trust level warning (Afsarmanesh & Ermilova, 2007).

VBE background processes, also known as supporting processes, are those business processes that run basic but relevant business processes in charge of supporting the VBE effective management during its lifecycle. The supporting processes are characterized for its necessity for maintaining, leverage and optimizing daily VBE business operations.

Table 3 – VBE Background Processes

	Functionality	**Description**
VBE General Management	Strategic & Marketing Management	Set of management activities and supporting tools that will support the strategic formulation process, including the marketing and branding activities, for promoting the VBE competencies among its potential VBE members and potential VO customers (Strum et al, 2004).
	Financial, Accounting & Resource Management	Set of management activities and supporting tools based-on accounting procedures to guarantee the VBE financial health and ensure the effective, efficient and equitable use of the VBE resources (Romero et al, 2006; 2007a).
	Governance Management	Set of management activities and supporting tools that refer to the VBE policy management, including internal operational rules and bylaws, for supporting the operation, regulation, and control of the VBE network structure: actors, positions, authorities, roles, rights, responsibilities and relationships between them (Romero et al, 2006; 2007b).
	VBE Bag of Assets Management	Set of management activities and supporting tools for handling the VBE assets, including: documents to share, software tools to share, lessons learned, VBE governance policies, etc. It is separated into mechanisms for enforcing proper access rights (public, restricted, private) for all VBE stakeholders, and announcement of news (dashboard) (Afsarmanesh & Ermilova, 2007).
	Value System Information Management	Set of management activities and supporting tools that will provide features for supporting and handling both, material and immaterial values, within the VBE (Romero et al, 2007a).

VBE General Management	Ontology Management	Set of management activities and supporting tools for VBE ontology adaptation into a specific VBE domain sector, VBE ontology evolution during the VBE lifecycle, as well as for VBE ontology learning process (e.g. in the form of a dictionary of the VBE related concepts) (Afsarmanesh & Ermilova, 2007; Plisson, 2007).
	ICT Management	Set of management activities and supporting tools for managing a low cost, easy-to-access and operational ICT-infrastructure that will allow VBE actors with different distributed/heterogeneous applications to communicate with each other transparently and seamlessly, in order to support collaboration (businesses) between them over the Internet (Rabelo et al, 2006).
	Support Institutions Information Management	Set of management activities and supporting tools for identifying and integrating Support Institutions into the VBE. Support Institutions information will be entered through registration mechanism, like the one applied to the VBE members' registration process (Romero et al, 2006).

5. VBE INSTANTIATION METHODOLOGY

The *VBE instantiation process* happens only once for every specific breeding environment - a priori to its creation. As such, different VBE characteristics are needed to be identified at this time, independently of the VBE lifecycle stages during which they may be activated or applied.

The *VBE instantiation methodology* aims to identify the necessary components and functionalities required during all the VBE lifecycle stages to support its actors (stakeholders) towards the successful creation of a breeding environment and its effective and efficiently management (operation) towards the achievement of the VBE strategic goals. Figure 1 presents an overview of the main steps to be followed to create and manage a VBE during its lifecycle, based-on UML notation.

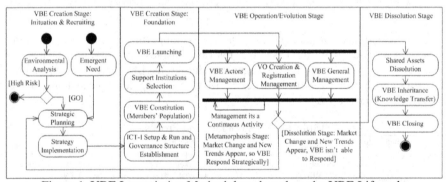

Figure 1. VBE Instantiation Methodology based-on the VBE Lifecycle

As depicted in Figures 2 and 3, the *VBE creation stage* is divided in two sub-stages: (1) *VBE initiation and recruiting* - referring to the processes of planning the creation of a new breeding environment by following a number of preparation steps to facilitate the execution of all operational activities; and (2) *VBE foundation* - referring to the processes of set-up and running an ICT-infrastructure to support the VBE operation, establishing the VBE governance structure, and populating the VBE by registering founding members and their related support institutions to allow the breeding environment initiate its operations.

During the VBE initiation and recruiting sub-stage, three processes should be performed: (1) *Environmental analysis* - focusing in the VBE creation drivers and the identification of the attractors (reasons) for organisations to join the VBE. The expected results from this process are the identification of the critical success factors for the VBE business model in a specific domain sector; (2) *Strategic planning* -

addressing the VBE goal setting, strategy analysis and strategy formulation towards the VBE business model definition. Expected results: VBE identity statements (e.g. mission, vision, goals) and first draft of the business plan including marketing, operational, organisational, financial and legal aspects; and (3) *Strategy implementation* - covering the VBE strategy implementation plan at business processes, ICT-infrastructure and governance levels. Expected results: Business processes required to enable a successful VBE management framework, an interoperable ICT-infrastructure for supporting the information systems and repositories related to the VBE business processes, and a VBE governance structure.

Going through the VBE foundation sub-stage, four processes should be carried out: (1) *VBE ICT-infrastructure set-up & run + governance structure establishment* - attending the implementation of the ICT-infrastructure, including the parameterization of all information systems and repositories, and the creation of the VBE steering committee and the publication of the VBE governance principles, rules and bylaws. Expected results: Running ICT-infrastructure and VBE actors acknowledge of the breeding environment regulations and authority; (2) *VBE constitution* - addressing the population of the VBE by following a members' registration process. Expected results: A catalogue with a complete profile of the founding VBE members' competencies and their roles, rights and responsibilities assigned; (3) *Support institutions selection* - covering the recruitment of supporting entities and service acquisition from third party institutions to support different VBE requirements. Expected results: A catalogue of the support institutions associated to the VBE; and (4) *VBE launching* - focusing on starting the VBE operation. Expected results: Public announcement to the media that the VBE is beginning its operation.

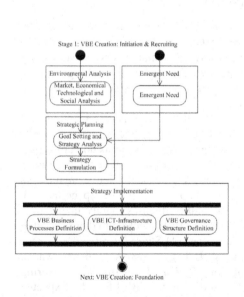

Figure 2. VBE Initiation & Recruiting

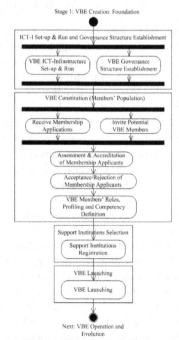

Figure 3. VBE Foundation

VBE operation stage (see Figure 4) compromises the processes of running, executing and adapting the VBE management activities to support the breeding environment reaching its objectives. A detail description of these business processes is presented in Tables 2 and 3. *VBE actors' management* activities will focus on creating a full profile of the VBE actors and managing their competencies towards VO creation process; *VO creation management* will support all activities related to VO creation process in order to respond to the collaboration opportunities identified, and *VBE general management* will assist common network management activities.

Moreover, *VBE evolution stage* (see Figure 4) compromises a set of feedback activities carried out through the VBE performance management process to develop improvement proposal which could include: (1) design, operation and control of new management approaches, (2) recruitment, assessment and selection of new VBE members and support institutions, (3) re-definition and assessment of VBE actors' roles, etc.

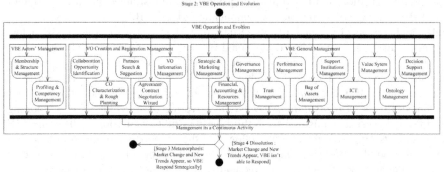

Figure 4. VBE Operation/Evolution

During *VBE operation stage,* two actions could take place as result of market changes and new trends appearances: *metamorphosis* or *dissolution.* VBE could go into a *metamorphosis stage* to respond to these environmental factors and survive by adapting its structure to these new competitive factors, or it could go into a *dissolution stage*, if the adaptation is not possible and a closure is necessary to completely re-structure the breeding environment.

VBE metamorphosis stage (see Figure 5) refers to the VBE nature adaptation by changing its strategy, business processes and structure to tactically respond to new market changes and trends, allowing VBE to remain competitive in its domain sector.

VBE dissolution stage (see Figure 6) refers to a closure stage where total activities in the VBE will cease. Dissolution happens when a VBE cannot achieve anymore its objectives, and even its metamorphosis cannot help the VBE to keep going with the new market changes and trends. VBE dissolution focuses mainly in planning the transfer of collected knowledge during the entire VBE lifecycle to other breeding environments. It is divided in three main processes: (1) *Shared assets dissolution* - aimed at returning the belongings on the VBE bag of assets to their owners. Expected results: VBE bag of assets dissolution; (2) *Knowledge transfer* - covering the capture and transfer of knowledge collected during the VBE lifecycle. Expected results: VBE knowledge base legacy; and (3) *VBE closing* - addressing the ending affairs and contracts with all VBE actors (including customers), shutting down ICT-infrastructure and announcing the VBE closing. Expected results: Contracts ended, information systems and repositories shutdown and public announcement to the media that the VBE is closing its operation.

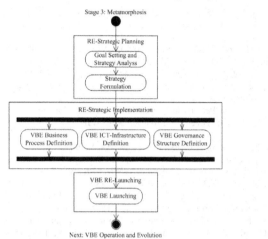

Figure 5. VBE Metamorphosis

Figure 6. VBE Dissolution

6. CONCLUSIONS

The *VBE instantiation methodology* presented in this paper aims to serve as a systematic and standardized guideline for supporting the processes and activities involved in the creation and management of new breeding environments. As such, the *VBE reference model* proposed aims at understanding the requirements as well as provision of mechanisms and functionalities for VBEs through adequate organisational models, operating principles, as well as through provision of ICT tools to support the entire VBE lifecycle and its actors.

As the base, the proposed *instantiation methodology* uses the *VBE reference model* to provide a comprehensive overview of the key generic elements, components and features of VBEs and their main requirements that must be addressed while creating and managing VBEs throughout their entire lifecycle. A detailed description of each processes and its activities is available as part of ECOLEAD project results, this detail was not presented in this paper due to the limitation of space.

The presented *VBE reference model* and its *instantiation methodology* represent a fundamental step and an effort towards defining a set of standardized guidelines which will support the instantiation (principle of replicability) of the *VBE reference model* into different domains and application environments, and thus support covering all activities required to customize a specific VBE model.

7. ACKNOWLEDGMENT

The information presented in this document is part of the results of the ECOLEAD Project (European Collaborative Networked Organizations Leadership Initiative), funded by the European Community, FP6 IP 506958. Document D22.5 - "Guidelines for VBE Instantiation in Different Domains" presents in detail results about this topic. The authors wish to acknowledge all partners in the project, especially Ekaterina Ermilova, Simon Msanjila & Hamideh Afsarmanesh from UvA.

8. REFERENCES

1. Afsarmanesh, H. and Camarinha-Matos, L.M. (2005). "A Framework for Management of Virtual Breeding Environments", in Collaborative Networks and their Breeding Environments, IFIP, NY: Springer Publisher, pp. 35-48.
2. Afsarmanesh, H.; Camarinha-Matos, L.M. and Msanjila, S.S. (2007). "Virtual Organizations Breeding Environment: Key Results from ECOLEAD", IFAC-CEA'07, Monterrey, Mexico.
3. Baldo, F.; Rabelo, R.J. and Vallejos R.V. (2007). "An Ontology-based Approach for Selecting Performance Indicators for Partners Suggestion", in Establishing the Foundation of Collaborative Networks, IFIP, Vol. 243, NY: Springer Publisher, pp. 187-196.
4. Camarinha-Matos, L.M. and Abreu, A. (2005). "Performance Indicators based-on Collaboration Benefits", in Collaborative Networks and their Breeding Environments, IFIP, NY: Springer Publisher, pp. 273-282.
5. Camarinha-Matos, L.M. and Afsarmanesh, H. (2006). "Collaborative Networks: Value Creation in a Knowledge Society", in Knowledge Enterprise, IFIP, Vol. 207, pp. 26-40, NY: Springer Publisher.
6. Camarinha-Matos, L.M. and Oliveria, A.I. (2006). "Contract Negotiation Wizard for VO Creation", 3rd International Conference in Digital Enterprise Technology, EST Setúbal Press.
7. Camarinha-Matos, L.M. and Afsarmanesh, H. (2007a). "A Comprehensive Modelling Framework for CNOs", in Journal of Intelligent Manufacturing, Springer Publisher, Vol. 18, No. 5, pp. 529-542.
8. Camarinha-Matos, L.M. and Afsarmanesh, H. (2007b). "A Framework for VO Creation in a Breeding Environment", in IFAC International Journal Annual Reviews in Control, Elsevier Publisher, Vol. 31, No. 1, pp. 119-135.
9. Camarinha-Matos, L.M.; Oliveira, A. I.; Ratti, R.; Demšar, D.; Baldo, F. And Jarimo, T. (2007). "Computer-Assisted VO Creation Framework", in Establishing the Foundation of Collaborative Networks, IFIP, NY: Springer Publisher, pp. 163-178.
10. Concha, D.; Romero, T.; Romero, D.; Galeano, N.; Jimenez, G. and Molina, A. (2008). "Analysis & Design of a CO-Characterization Tool for VO Creation", 17th IFAC World Congress, Seoul, Korea.
11. Demšar, D.; Mozetič, I. and Lavrač, N. (2007). "Collaboration Opportunity Finder", in Establishing the Foundation of Collaborative Networks, IFIP, Vol. 243, NY: Springer Publisher, pp. 179-186.
12. Ermilova, E. and Afsarmanesh, H. (2006). "Competency and Profiling Management in Virtual Organization Breeding Environments", in Network-Centric Collaboration and Supporting Frameworks, IFIP, NY: Springer Publisher, pp. 131-142.
13. Karvonen, I; Salkari, L. and Ollus, M. (2007). "Identification of Forms and Components of VO Inheritance", in Establishing the Foundation of Collaborative Networks, IFIP, Vol. 243, NY: Springer Publisher, pp.253-262.
14. Loss, L.; Rabelo, R.J. and Pereira-Klen, A.A. (2006). "VO Management: An Approach based-on Inheritance Information", 4th Global Conference on Sustainable Product Development and Lifecycle Engineering, São Carlos, São Paulo, Brazil.
15. Msanjila, S.S. and Afsarmanesh, H. (2006). "Assessment and Creation of Trust in VBEs", in Network-Centric Collaboration and Supporting Frameworks, IFIP, NY: Springer Publisher, Vol. 224, pp. 161-172.
16. Plisson, J.; Ljubi, P.; Mozeti, I. and Lavra, N. (2007). "An Ontology for Virtual Organization Breeding Environments", in IEEE Transactions on Systems, Man, and Cybernetics, Vol. 37, No. 6.
17. Rabelo, R.J.; Gusmeroli, S.; Arana, C. and Nagellen, T. (2006). "The ECOLEAD ICT-Infrastructure for Collaborative Networked Organizations", in Network-Centric Collaboration and Supporting Frameworks, IFIP, NY: Springer Publisher, Vol. 224, pp. 451-460.
18. Romero, D.; Galeano, N.; Giraldo, J. and Molina, A. (2006). "Towards the Definition of Business Models and Governance Rules for Virtual Breeding Environments", in Network-Centric Collaboration and Supporting Frameworks, IFIP, NY: Springer Publisher, Vol. 224, pp. 103-110.
19. Romero, D.; Galeano, N. and Molina, A. (2007a). "A Conceptual Model for Virtual Breeding Environments Value Systems", in Establishing the Foundation of Collaborative Networks, IFIP, NY: Springer Publisher, Vol. 243, pp. 43-52.
20. Romero, D.; Giraldo, J.; Galeano, N. and Molina, A. (2007b). "Towards Governance Rules and Bylaws for Virtual Breeding Environments", in Establishing the Foundation of Collaborative Networks, IFIP, NY: Springer Publisher, Vol. 243, pp. 93-102.
21. Sitek, P.; Seifert, M. and Graser, F. (2007). "Partner Profiling to support the Initiation of Collaborative Networks", 13th International Conference on Concurrent Enterprising, pp. 213-220.
22. Sturm, F., Kemp, J., Wendel de J. and Ruven, V. (2004), "Towards Strategic Management in Collaborative Network Structures", in Collaborative Networked Organizations: A Research Agenda for Emerging Business Models, pp. 131-138, Springer Science Publisher, 2004.

3 SYSTEMIC STRATEGIC MANAGEMENT FOR VBEs IN THE MANUFACTURING SECTOR

Heiko Duin

BIBA – Bremer Institut für Produktion und Logistik GmbH, GERMANY
du@biba.uni-bremen.de

The concept of Virtual Organisation Breeding Environment (VBE) is now understood as a fundamental entity to enable the formation of dynamic collaborative organisations especially Virtual Organisations (VOs).
System theory fits well when dealing with dynamic and complex systems such as organisations. Therefore, the system theoretic or systemic view is adequate for analysing the internal and external challenges as well as the manoeuvring spaces for VBEs under dynamic circumstances. The VBE can be considered as a system of members who form a larger unit – the VBE itself – and which is embedded in a larger system, i.e. the market. The single members of a VBE which are normally companies can also be seen as (sub-) systems which build up the VBE. Strategic management has the function to identify the mid- and long-term objectives of the VBE including supportive strategic programmes (actions) to ensure the evolution of the network.
Based on a requirements analysis of a theoretic VBE, this paper provides a short state of the art on systemic approaches used in strategic management of manufacturing enterprises and how they can be transferred to collaborative organisations like VBEs. The result is a proposal of a strategic management process for VBEs supported by systemic methods and tools.

1. INTRODUCTION

Today, many manufacturing systems are subject to enormous pressures because of the ever changing market environments showing e.g. discontinuities in trends and globalisation. Manufacturers have responded to these conditions by forming collaborative relationships to suppliers, distributors and even customers (e.g. Jagdev and Thoben, 2001; p. 31). When two or more enterprises collaborate, they form a collaborative (enterprise) network.

Collaborative networks can be divided into long-term strategic networks and goal-oriented networks. Examples for long-term networks are Professional Virtual Communities or Industrial Clusters, while goal oriented networks may be further divided into grasping-opportunity driven (e.g. Virtual Enterprise, Extended Enterprise) and continuous-production driven networks like Supply Chains (Camarinha-Matos and Afsarmanesh, 2006)

Two basic types of collaborative networks are represented by Virtual Organisations (VOs) and by Source Networks (Kürümlüoglu et al., 2005):

Please use the following format when citing this chapter:

Duin, H., 2008, in IFIP International Federation for Information Processing, Volume 283; *Pervasive Collaborative Networks*; Luis M. Camarinha-Matos, Willy Picard; (Boston: Springer), pp. 25–32.

- A **Virtual Organisation** (VO) is a temporary consortium of partners from
  different organisations established to fulfil a value adding task, for example
  a product or service to a customer. The lifetime of a VO is typically restricted: it is created for a definite task and dissolved after the task has been
  completed. A synonym for VO is the term *Virtual Enterprise*.
- A **Source/Support Network** is a more stationary, though not static, group
  of organisational entities which has developed a preparedness to collaborate
  in case of a specific task / customer demand. Another name for such a network is *Breeding Environment*.

The relationship between these two forms is that the Breeding Environment prepares the instantiation of VOs. It acts as an incubator for a VO. From the VO point
of view, the VO is created when a business opportunity occurs. In order to perform
the actual value creation task, the VO can be created from scratch (collecting cooperating partners from an "open universe" of enterprises) or through a *VO Breeding
Environment* (VBE).

This paper proposes a strategic management approach for such strategic alliances, especially VBEs, based on a systemic point of view.

2. RELATION TO EXISTING THEORIES AND WORK

2.1 The Systemic View

The idea to develop a theory of systems – or a general systems theory – has been
introduced by Bertalanffy in the 50ies of last century. His efforts were published in
his very well regarded book *General Systems Theory – Foundations, Development,
Applications* (Bertalanffy, 1968). It can be seen as an interdisciplinary field of science and the study of the nature of complex systems in nature, society, and science.

In Europe, the principles of systems have been applied to the management of organisations by Hans Ulrich resulting in the St.-Gallener Management Model (e.g.
Ulrich and Krieg, 1972). Ulrich considered an organisation as a *goal-oriented social
system*. Management is the *shaping* and *directing* of such systems on any level (strategic, tactical, and operational) resulting in a *system-oriented management science*
(Ulrich, 1984; p. 11).

In the US, Jay Forrester created the field of *Systems Dynamics*, where he introduced the modelling socio-economic inter-relationships within organisations by systems of differential equations (e.g. Forrester, 1968). Peter Senge based his work on
learning organisations also on the systems approach. where people continually expand their capacity to create the results they truly desire, where new and expansive
patterns of thinking are nurtured, where collective aspiration is set free, and where
people are continually learning to see the whole together (Senge, 1990).

Some basic concepts of systems are shown in Figure 1. The structure of a system
is described by its elements and their relations between each other. An element or a
subset of elements of a system can form another system – a sub-system. Furthermore, the considered system is embedded into a larger system – the super-system –
to which it is a sub-system.

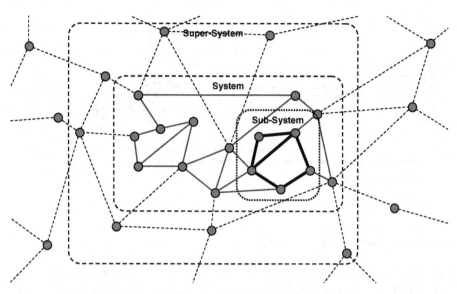

Figure 1: Structural Concepts of Systems

Ropohl proposes three different aspects (or concepts) to better understand systems (Ropohl, 1999):

- **Structural system concept**: Within this concept, the analysis of systems focuses on the single elements and the relations between them.
- **Functional system concept**: The functional concept focuses on the behaviour emerging from the system structure. As behaviour only occurs over time, this concept also considers the dynamics of the system.
- **Hierarchical system concept**: This concept analyses the hierarchical structure of the system, i.e. what is included, what are the sub-systems and what is the system environment (super-system).

Further, there are four basic principles of general systems theory:

- A system is more than the simple sum of its parts (elements and relations). The system is a holistic unit. The number of relations describes the character of the system.
- The structure of the system which is defined by the elements and their relations determines the function (behaviour) of the system.
- The function of the system can be created by different structures. Different structures might show the same behaviour (structural equivalence).
- It is impossible to fully describe a system with only one of three concepts (impossible reductionism).

Systems show some characteristics like openness, complexity, ordered structure, steerability, self organisation, and meaningfulness (Wegehaupt, 2004; p. 31).

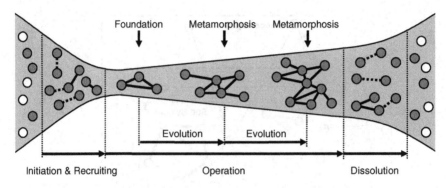

Figure 2: VBE Life Cycle

2.2 VO Breeding Environments (VBEs)

VBEs have been described in recent literature (e.g. Klen et al., 2006; Afsarmanesh and Camarinha-Matos, 2005). Within the VBE several actors and their roles have been identified so far: Members, VBE Administrator, Broker, VO Planner, and VO Coordinator. Duin suggests to also establish a Steering Committee headed by the VBE Administrator (Duin, 2007).

The life cycle of a VBE as shown in Figure 2 consists of three main phases: Initiation and Recruiting, Operation and Dissolution. The dissolution of the VBE is a rare event, instead a VBE changes by metamorphosis (Afsarmanesh and Camarinha-Matos, 2005).

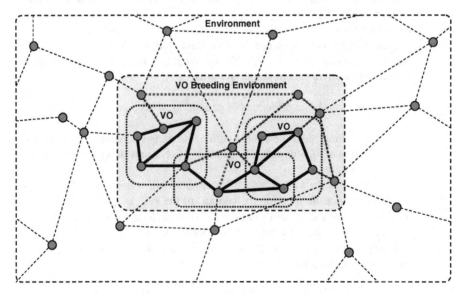

Figure 3: A Systemic View on the VBE

For a better understanding of the systemic approach applied to view the VBE concept, the following observations can be made:

- The existence of a VBE is generally long-term and therefore needs some kind of strategic management. The points in time, when strategic decisions have to be made are the foundation and each of the metamorphosis steps.
- The VBE is a non- focal CNO. This means, it follows a heterarchic concept. Ideally all members are involved in strategy development.
- Dynamics occurs in evolution once the system as a stable phase. Instability can be solved by metamorphosis, which is a radical change of the structure of the system with the goal to become stable again.
- Each single VBE is focussed on a specific domain, sector or market. In this paper, the focus is set to manufacturing, i.e. the production of goods and/or services.
- VBEs can be of different size ranging from a few members to several thousands. This paper addresses small/medium sized VBEs (3 to 100 members).

An application of the concepts and principles mentioned in chapter 2.1 to VBEs reveals some basic observations, which are given in Table 1.

Concepts	Observations
Structural Concept	The structure of the system consists of the members and their relations. The relations include issues resolved in a cooperation agreement, a common infrastructure and the sharing principles.
Functional Concept	The main function of the VBE is to enhance the preparedness of its members to form a VO on the appearance of business opportunities.
	This implies, that the success of the VBE might be measured in the turnover generated by VOs created from the VBE.
Hierarchical Concept	The system under consideration is the VBE itself.
	The elements are the members of the VBE. The relations are the exchange of information, physical goods and trust. Each member can be seen as a sub-system (as it is normally an organisation, which is a system in itself). But, also the VOs created in the context of the VBE are sub-systems.
	The super-system, where the VBE is embedded in, consists of the specific market, the different national societies, and last but not least the eco-system world.

Principle	Observations
Holistic Unit	The VBE itself is something new and can be viewd as a unit. Viewed from the outside, a VBE seems to be an (networked) organisation.
System Function	As the objective of a VBE is to respond to occurring business opportunities by creating appropriate VOs, the structure of its membership must be adequate, i.e. the competencies not only for working in an networked organisation but also for the selected domain must be present.
Structural Equivalency	The exchange (inclusion and/or exclusion) of members changes the structure but may not affect the function. Different settings may show different efficiency and/or effectiveness. If the system function (e.g. by defining new strategic objectives like the addressed sector) needs to be changed, this has to be done changing the structure.
Impossible Reductionism	N/A

Table 1: Application of System Concepts and Principles to a VBE

3. REQUIREMENTS WITHIN STRATEGIC MANAGEMENT

3.1 The Strategic Management Process

The strategic management process consists of strategy planning, implementation and controlling. Strategy planning is driven by normative management, i.e. the management of vision, mission and long-term objectives (e.g. Duin, 2007).

This process needs to be applied to the networked organisation type VBE which implies, that methods and tools to support the process need to provide the ability to model adequately the system "VBE", the sub-systems "VOs" and Members and the super-system Environment in order to analyse the behaviour in a holistic way.

3.2 Requirements Analysis

The identification of requirements for a strategic management system for a VBE needs to support the whole process and its supporting methods and tools. Table 2 provides an overview on the requirements by applying the systemic view.

Area	Requirements
General Requirements	The approach needs to support systemic characteristics like complexity, modelling of inter-relationships, and the simulation of behaviour (or dynamics).
	Hierarchic decomposition, i.e. the composition of a system by sub-systems etc. This includes the differentiation between internal and external view.
	The modelling approach should support the reduction of complexity revealing the main structure and driving forces within the system. Often detailed structures which have only marginal effects are not important for strategic decisions.
	A simulation component should be available to generate scenarios reflecting the effects of the implementation of strategic decisions.
	Scenarios should be comparable.
	A component which explains simulation results should be available. Humans often have difficulties to explain the behaviour of a system by just knowing the structure.
Internal View	Indicators or measures reflecting the goals and the structure of the VBE should be identified and modelled including their inter-relationships.
	Action plans which represent the implementation of strategic decisions need to be modelled.
External View	External factors which might influence the functions of the systems need to be taken into account. These could be events which have a strong influence on the success of the VBE. Typically such influences come from legislation, society or technological developments.
	Market factors including suppliers, competitors and customers need to be addressable. This may include the modelling of competing actors including their action plans.

Table 2: Requirements for Supporting Strategic Management in VBEs

4. SYSTEMIC APPROACHES FOR STRATEGIC MANAGEMENT

Strategic management is the art and science of formulating, implementing and evaluating cross-functional decisions that will enable an organisation (and we can view a VBE as an organisation) to achieve its objectives (e.g. Mintzberg, 1994).

Strategic management and strategic planning can be supported by a variety of approaches developed during the last decades. Most of them focus on specific tasks like the analysis of internal and external factors, product-market-mix (portfolio analysis), product life cycle analysis etc. (e.g. Hungenberg, 2006).

4.1 Systems Thinking

Many philosophers, scientists and management gurus advocate the development of systems thinking – the ability to see the world as a complex system in which it is understood that "you just can't do one thing" and "everything is connected to everything else" (e.g. Sterman, 2000). Therefore, systems thinking is the principle to view our world (or parts of this wolrd like human beings, organisations, nations, etc.) as a system with a structure, function and behaviour.

4.2 Scenario Techniques

Scenario techniques are based on two principles (e.g. Gausemeier et al., 1998):

- **Systems thinking**: Organisations must perceive their environment as a complex network of inter-related (external as well as internal) factors.
- **Multiple futures**: Organisations should not reduce their strategic thinking to one exact prognosticated future. Instead, alternative future scenarios should be created and considered during strategic planning.

A scenario can be seen as a generally intelligible description of a possible situation in the future, based on a complex network of influence factors. Most scenario techniques use some kind of formalisms to model the system and to generate more or less probable scenarios. They are then used to generate and evaluate strategic plans against these scenarios.

4.3 Simulation Approaches

Simulation is always done with an underlying model to be simulated. There are various kinds of simulation approaches, e.g. Monte-Carlo-based, discrete, or continuous simulation, Petri nets, and agent based simulations.

The underlying model provides the structure of the system while the simulation results describe the system dynamics – the system behaviour.

5. CONCLUSIONS

This paper introduced the concepts and principles of systems based on the general systems theory. It then explained the emerging concept of the VBE as a source network for VOs. The systemic view is applied to the VBE concept and requirements concerning the strategic management of such kind of networks have been addressed.

6. ACKNOWLEDGEMENS

The author thanks the partners and the European Commission for support in the context of the ECOLEAD project, funded under contract number FP6-506958.

7. REFERENCES

Afsarmanesh, H. and Camarinha-Matos, L.: A Framework for Management of Virtual Organization Breeding Environments. In: *Collaborative Networks and Their Breeding Environments - IFIP TC 5 WG 5.5 Sixth IFIP Working Conference on Virtual Enterprises, 26-28 September 2005, Valencia, Spain*. 2005. pp 35-48.

Bertalanffy, L. v.: *General System Theory: Foundations, Development, Applications*. George Braziller. New York 1968.

Camarinha-Matos, L. and Afsarmanesh, H.: Collaborative Networks: Value Creation in a Knowledge Society. In: *Knowledge Enterprise: Intelligent Strategies in Product Design, Manufacturing, and Management.Proceedings of PROLAMAT 2006, IFIP TC5 International Conference, June 15-17, 2006, Shanghai, China*. Boston 2006. pp 26-40.

Duin, H.: Causal Cross-Impact Analysis as Strategic Planning Aid for Virtual Organisation Breeding Environments. In: *Establishing the Foundation of Collaborative Networks - IFIP TC 5 Working Group 5.5 Eighth IFIP Working Conference on Virtual Enterprises, 10-12 September 2007, Guimaraes, Portugal*. 2007. pp 147-154.

Forrester, J.: *Principles of Systems*. MIT Press. Cambridge (Massachusetts) 1968.

Gausemeier, Jürgen, Fink, Alexander and Schlake, Oliver: Scenario Management: An Approach to Develop Future Potentials. In: *Technological Forecasting and Social Change*. 59 (1998) 2, pp 111-130.

Hungenberg, H.: *Strategisches Management im Unternehmen. Ziele - Prozesse - Verfahren*. Gabler. 2006.

Jagdev, Harinder S. and Thoben, Klaus-Dieter: Anatomy of Enterprise Collaborations. In: *Production Planning and Control*. 12 (2001) 5, pp 437-451.

Klen, E. R., Pereira-Klen, A. and Gesser, C. E.: Towards the Sustainability of Virtual Organization Management. In: *Proceedings of GCSM2006 - IV Global Conference of Sustainable Product Development and Life Cycle Engineering, Sao Carlos, Spain*. 2006.

Kürümlüoglu, M., Nostdal, R. and Karvonen, I.: Base Concepts. In: Camarinha-Matos, L.; Afsarmanesh, H.; Ollus, M. (Eds.): *Virtual Organizations. Systems and Practices*. Springer. New York 2005, pp 11-28.

Mintzberg, H.: *The Rise and Fall of Strategic Planning*. 1994.

Ropohl, Günter: Philosophy of Socio-Technical Systems. In: *Society for Philosophy and Technology*. 4 (1999) 3, pp 59-71.

Senge, P.: *The Fifth Discipline: The Art and Practice of the Learning Organization*. Currency Doubleday. 1990.

Sterman, J.: *Business Dynamics - Systems Thinking and Modeling for a Complex World*. McGraw-Hill. 2000.

Ulrich, H.: *Management*. Verlag Paul Haupt. Bern 1984.

Ulrich, H. and Krieg, W.: *Das St. Galler Management Modell*. Verlag Paul Haupt. Bern 1972.

Wegehaupt, P., 2004, Führung von Produktionsnetzwerken, WWW-Seite, <http://www.werkzeugbau-aachen.de/de/563d2e5c6b82304ac12570340024caa9/Patrick_2004.pdf>, Accessed February 12, 2007.

4

NETWORKING AGRIFOOD SMEs AND CONSUMER GROUPS IN LOCAL AGRIBUSINESS

Antonio P. Volpentesta, Salvatore Ammirato
Università della Calabria, volpentesta@deis.unical.it, ammirato@deis.unical.it, ITALY

How could a cluster of high quality agrifood SMEs face global competition? How could a local group of consumers purchase trusted quality goods at reduced prices? To address these issues, we present a model of local trade networks that specifies relationships and links between and within consumer groups and agrifood producer clusters, where exchange can take place only if formal relationships between them exist. An application of the model has been trialed in an EU funded project, SADECAL, aimed at creating a collaborative network in the agrifood sector.

1. INTRODUCTION

Over recent years, the European agribusiness sector has been facing new challenges due to deregulation and globalisation of the markets, increased customer quality requirements in agrifood products and the development of new technologies.

Growing competitive pressures drive agrifood producers to search for new ways of doing business able to guarantee competitive advantages, to improve farm revenue streams and to develop new consumer market niches. Different studies (Volpentesta & Ammirato, 2007; Bowler et al, 1996; Weaver & Fennell, 1997) show that ways to realise agribusinesses' expectations consist in operating on:

- agrifood products, setting them with high "typical and quality" features (i.e. strictly related with local territory);
- production/distribution processes, making the long and complex agrifood supply chains shorter;
- technological platforms, supporting adequate e-business solutions for SMEs (European Commission, 2007).

In this paper, we introduce results of an EU funded project, SADECAL, aimed at creating a collaborative network in the agrifood sector. In particular, we refer to a regional scenario where *agribusiness clusters* (coalitions of SMEs producing high "typical and quality" agrifood goods) and *consumer groups*; (individuals clustered into virtual communities of common interests for purchasing) are involved in a trade network (Mathewson & Winter, 1996; Schotanus & Telgen, 2007; Wang & Watts, 2003).

For such a network, we propose an organisational framework and an open-source e-business platform aimed to:

- support the 'Relocalisation' process, i.e. the identification and valorisation of local resources;

Please use the following format when citing this chapter:

Volpentesta, A.P. and Ammirato, S., 2008, in IFIP International Federation for Information Processing, Volume 283; *Pervasive Collaborative Networks*; Luis M. Camarinha-Matos, Willy Picard; (Boston: Springer); pp. 33–40.

- foster the emergence of 'alternative agrifood networks';
- maximize returns and reduce costs within groups by-passing the large-scale retail trade;
- create sustainable relationships between agribusiness clusters and consumer groups;
- provide Internet-based 'electronic trade platforms' for agribusiness[i].

The paper is organized as follows. Section 2 introduces the theoretical background. Section 3 outlines the organizational model. Section 4 presents an application of the model in a regional economic context. Lastly, section 5 is devoted to the conclusion.

2. THEORETICAL BACKGROUND

In the last decade the agribusiness industry has been undergoing major restructuring. Factors like technological innovations, increased customer quality requirements, new labor practices, poor agriculture commodity prices, emergence of international retail giants and rise of massive superstores, have revolutionized the industry from top to bottom (Vias, 2004).

In the retail sector, concentration is taking place with fewer firms controlling ever-increasing portions of the retail market (Hollingsworth, 2004). This leads agrifood SMEs to face a pressing request for "new ways" of doing business in order to obtain competitive advantages. Some of these ways rely on joint initiatives and new approaches for cooperation (Schiefer, 2004).

Different studies (Bowler et al., 1996; Volpentesta & Ammirato, 2007; Weaver & Fennell, 1997) show how successful initiatives in supporting agribusiness industry challenges point to foster 'relocalisation' of agrifood systems, the emergence of 'alternative agrifood networks' and to introduce eBusiness practices and instruments through the industry. "Relocalisation" refers to the identification and valorization of local resources –including cultural identity – through the rediscovery of local traditions as a means to improve wellbeing, genuineness and, in a more general sense, quality of life. It has been suggested that one means of doing so is by protecting distinctive products that claim historical associations with a specific area and by securing Protected Designation of Origin (PDO) and Protected Geographical Indication (PGI) status for 'typical' regional foods (De Roest & Menghi, 2000; Ilbery & Kneafsey, 1998). The ability of typical agrifood producers to access "alternative agrifood networks" is strictly interconnected with relocalisation. These kinds of networks tend to minimize links in the chain and the involvement with conventional, multinational food supply chain and large retail chains (Volpentesta & Ammirato, 2007; Watts et al., 2005). They may be supported by collaborative commerce platforms in order to improve food quality and safety control, traceability, efficient consumer response, transaction efficiency, consumer trust, and supply chain cooperation (Schiefer, 2004).

A sustainable way to exploit the advantages of relocalisation, is, thus, the creation of alternative food networks where exchanges can take place among coalitions of consumers and clusters of agrifood producers in order to by-pass the tight tie-in with the large-scale retail chains. These kinds of arrangements are stable, non-equity based and collaborative and they have become increasingly important as a means of reducing cost (Contractor & Lorange, 1988; Zajac & Oslen, 1993), increasing revenue (Contractor & Lorange, 1988), or mitigating risk in response to economic factors (Ebers, 1997).

An interesting case of alternative food networks is represented by trade networks characterized by a close relationship between buyers and sellers/producers of goods/services of differentiated quality (Wang and Watts, 2006). Such a network comprises *purchasing groups, agrifood producers clusters* and sometimes an intermediary between them.

The notion of a purchasing group refers to the idea of an agreement between two or more entities which "is often motivated by the expectations of improved efficiency and better effectiveness due to economies of scale and economies of scope" (Rozemeijer, 2000). Nolleta and Beaulieu (2003) define a purchasing group "as a formal or virtual structure which makes the consolidation of purchases for many organisations possible. Consolidation is a procurement practice used by local entities to transfer activities such as: bidding, supplier evaluation, negotiation, and contract management to a central entity. For Schotanus and Telgen (2007) a purchasing group "consists of dependent or independent organisations that share and/or bundle together in order to achieve mutually compatible goals that they could not achieve easily alone".

A producers cluster is a firms' aggregation that is based on a "long-term purposeful arrangement among distinct but related for profit organisations that allow the firms in them to gain or sustain competitive advantage vis-à-vis their competitors outside the network" (Jarillo,1988).

Lockett and Brown (2006) state that intermediaries are necessary for online aggregations of SMEs to function. In particular, they have shown that an intermediary can have "a critical role in gaining the commitment of potential participants to enter the e-aggregation and can be considered as a trusted third party".

3. THE ORGANIZATIONAL MODEL

The economic context where the model could be applied is characterized by the presence in a limited geographical area of:
- many agrifood SMEs, possibly organized in clusters, manifesting a common strategic goal to cross over the large retail scale and directly control the distribution channel;
- a community of potential consumers, who need to purchase "secured" goods at lower prices;
- ICT infrastructures necessary for e-commerce solutions, timely, economy and high-efficient communication and means to agrifood producers and consumers.

But, even if the adoption of a group commerce ICT solution allows to purchase and/or sell agrifood products more cost-effectively and efficiently, the main enabling factor to consider is "trust". It is widely recognized that trust is a key facilitator of eCommerce (Bhattacherjee, 2002) and that lack of trust is one of the most frequently reasons for customers to not purchase from the Internet (Lee & Turban, 2001). From the perspective of buyers, trust in sellers is necessary but not sufficient for an online transaction to take place. Buyers must also trust the intermediary; Myoung-Soo and Jae-Hyeon (2005) surveyed that buyers base their trust on the reputation of the intermediary as well as web usability and transaction security. In this sense, intermediary should not only guarantee completion of the transaction process but also qualify the sellers.

In the model we introduce, different roles need to be played. In what follows we describe main organizational roles for the management of collaborative trading processes in a trustworthy environment.

The trusted third party (TTP) refers to an organization unit which enjoys equal trust from both the agrifood producers and consumers. It is aimed to influence innovation decisions, facilitate transactions, organize the agrifood trade network and, above all, provide and manage the 'trust platform', where e-business engagement by agrifood producer clusters and consumer groups can be effectively supported (Swan & Newell, 1995; Newell et al., 2000).

In our model, the TTP plays a triple role in intermediation between producers and consumers groups:
- technology intermediary, whose role is to provide the ICT platform including hardware, security and communication;
- transaction intermediary, which provides services including applications software, hosting and consultancy. Among its roles, there are the coordination and management of information flows (from agribusiness to consumers and vice-versa) and the logistic chain (from agribusinesses to consumers groups). Operatively, it collects cumulative purchase orders from consumers groups and processes them in order to form single purchase orders for each agrifood producers cluster. Once goods arrive from clusters, it packs them with respect to each consumers group order and sends them to the consumers group pick-up point;
- guarantee authority, that defines an "ethical code" and behavioural rules in transaction processes.

In addition TTP has a critical role in gaining the commitment of potential participants, both as individuals and groups, to enter the aggregation. This means it provides a broad governance function, enables the promotion of cooperation among groups and controls transactions to ensure behavioural correctness of members interactions in the network.

The consumers group (CG): it is a particular kind of no-profit purchasing group that is self-organized. Its members are final consumers, typically households, who want to purchase agrifood goods at reduced prices. Moreover, following the increasing movement towards rediscovery of local traditions as means to trust the quality and origin of products, consumers want to first purchase secured typical regional foods, where traceability and producers reputation, usually based on EU certifications, can assure the required trust. In order to achieve enough purchasing power able to gain the desired trade discounts, consumers decide to share their "shopping lists" to create a unique order for an heterogeneous bundle of products. In creating and submitting the cumulative order to the TTP, the CG is required to follow the ethical code and behavioural rules previously established.

The agrifood producers cluster (AC): it is a for-profit organization whose members are SMEs or simple farms, all placed in the same territory, producing high quality agrifood goods. Members in a cluster are characterized by offering the same type of products, but their products differ from each other in terms of characteristics as designation of origin, quality, manufacturing methods, etc. For instance, one cluster can offer different kinds of olive oil, another cluster sells different kinds of milk packets and dairy products, etc. Once a cluster receives purchasing orders, it sends the requested goods to the TTP collection point. In its behaviour, an AC adopts the ethical code and follows the rules established by the TTP. A representation of the organizational model is presented graphically in Figure 1.

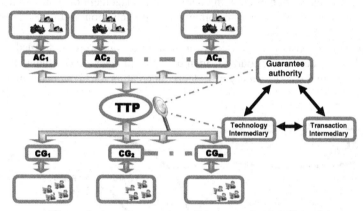

Figure 1. A representation of the organizational model

4. AN APPLICATION OF THE MODEL

The model was implemented during the execution of an EU founded project, SADECAL, aimed to create a collaborative trade network in the agrifood sector in Calabria[ii]. In particular, the economic context we have taken into account is the District of High Quality Productions placed in Sibari, namely, the *DAQ-Sibari* [iii] (see. Figure 2).

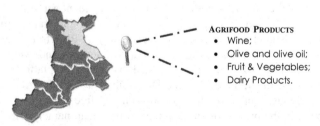

Figure 2: The DAQ-Sibari territory and its main agrifood production.

After a public call to join the project, nine ACs, operating in the four main agricultural sectors (wine, olive, fruit and vegetable and dairy productions), were selected. Their products are all secured by PDO and PGI status for typical regional foods.

The task of TTP was assigned to the 'District Centre' of the "Società di Distretto" (a consortium of 92 organizations among the ones belonging to the DAQ-Sibari). In particular, a Project Management Board, constituted by designated members of DEIS (Department of Electronics, Computer Science and Systems at University of Calabria), District Centre, ACs and CG, was charged with the role of guarantee authority. A technical staff of the District Centre was supported to play the role of technology intermediary by some researchers of the DEIS that, as technological partners, provided ICT platform and training to users. Another staff of the District Center was charged with operational management of transactions so that goods were shipped on time and in compliance with behavioural rules established by the Project Management Board.

In relation to consumers, awareness/promotion actions were performed by DEIS personnel in order to encourage members (employees and students) of the community around the University of Calabria in creating a CG, named Unical-*CG*. [iv] (see Figure 3).

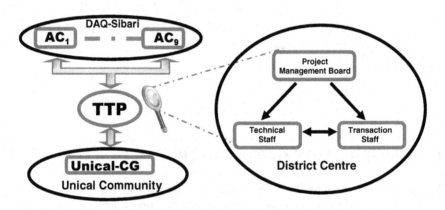

Figure 3. The organizational model in the project

A web-based collaborative commerce platform was developed by DEIS researchers and it was used by the District Centre to support management activities (Unical-*CG* data management, ACs data management, selling catalogue management, order processing and logistic chain management, e-payment). A PHP framework (namely P4A, an open source software containing libraries, modules and widgets), a web server Apache and a MySQL database were used to develop the platform.

To increase trust in the model, in the DAQ-Sibari and in the ACs, a series of presentation meetings, typical products exposition and free tasting were organized. The involvement in the project of an university department, namely DEIS, has been considered a key factor to persuade community members to agree to the Unical-CG.

5. CONCLUSION

Following directions by the European Commission (2007), we have proposed an organizational model of a trustable platform where potential consumers groups and agribusinesses clusters can meet to trade high quality agrifood goods in a regional scenario.

An application of the model in an economic regional context has allowed us to observe some typical advantages for both consumers (lower purchasing prices, higher goods quality, lower transaction costs, satisfaction, and learning from each other) and producers (reduced transaction costs, early payments, dealing directly with the customer, opportunity to bypass large regional and national distributors, and raising profitability).

The experience gained during the project execution has shown that the role of the intermediary, acting as TTP, appears to be critical in the formation of buyer-seller agrifood trade networks. In our project, the TTP had to face set-up costs, coordination costs and producers/seller resistance. Moreover, the main difficulty was not the technical part but the organization of appropriate market rules, the provision of appropriate trade information, the design of appropriate trade filters that determine the eligibility of participants and traded goods, and the organization of linkages between different interacting groups .

Further studies are underway in order to define an evaluation model to estimate economic advantages for both agrifood producers and consumers as well as intermediation costs.

5.1 Acknowledgements

This paper reports major findings of the project 'SADECAL: supporting e-Business diffusion in Calabria', financed by EU within the ERDF program. The authors thank Eng. Marco Della Gala for his meaningful contribution in graphic design and modelling suggestions.

6. REFERENCES

1. Bhattacherjee A. Individual trust in online firms: scale development and initial test. Journal of Management Information Systems 2002,: 19(1): 211-241.
2. Bowler I, Clarke G, Crockett A, Iberry B and Shaw A. The Development of Alternative Farm Enterprises: A Study of Family Labour Farms in the Northern Pennines of England. Journal of Rural Studies 1996; 12 (3): 285-295.
3. Contractor F and Lorange P. Cooperative Strategies in International Business. Lexington, MA: Lexington Books, 1988.
4. De Roest K and Menghi A. Reconsidering 'traditional' food: the case of parmigiano reggiano cheese. Sociologia Ruralis 2000; 40 (4): 439–451.
5. Ebers M. The Formation of Inter-Organisational Networks. Oxford: Oxford University Press, 1997.
6. European Commission. eBusiness Watch: The European e-Business Report 2006/07 edition, Luxembourg: Office for Official Publications of the European Communities, 2007.
7. Fritz M, Hausen T and Schiefer G. Developments and Development Directions of Electronic Trade Platforms in US and European Agri-Food Markets: Impact on Sector Organization. International Food and Agribusiness Management Review 2004; 7 (1): 1-21.
8. Hollingsworth A. Increasing retail concentration: evidence from the UK food retail sector, British Food Journal 2004; 106 (8/9): 629-683.

9. Ilbery B and Kneafsey M. Product and place: promoting quality products and services in the lagging rural regions of the European Union. European Urban and Regional Studies 1998; 5: .329–341.
10. Jarillo J. On Strategic Networks. Strategic Management Journal 1988; 9(1): 31–41.
11. Lee MKO and Turban E. A trust model for consumer internet shopping. International journal of Electronic Commerce 2001; 6 (1): 75-91.
12. Lockett N and Brown DH. Aggregation and the Role of Trusted Third Parties in SME E-Business Engagement: A Regional Policy Issue. International Small Business Journal 2006; 24 (4): 379-404.
13. Mathewson F and Winter RA. Buyers Groups, Int J of Industrial Organization 1996; 15: 137-164.
14. Myoung-Soo K and Jae-Hyeon A. A Model for Buyer's Trust in the E-marketplace. Proceedings of ICEC'05, August 15–17, 2005, Xi'an, China
15. Newell S, Swan J and Galliers R. A Knowledge-focused Perspective on the Diffusion and Adoption of Complex Information Technologies: The BPR example. Information Systems Journal 2000; 10(3): 239–259.
16. Nolleta J. and Beaulieu M. The development of group purchasing: an empirical study in the healthcare sector. Journal of Purchasing & Supply Management 2003; 9: 3–10.
17. Raynolds LT. The Globalization of Organic Agro-Food Networks. World Development 2004; 32(5): 725–743.
18. Rozemeijer F. How to manage corporate purchasing synergy in a decentralised company? towards design rules for managing and organising purchasing synergy in decentralised companies. European Journal of Purchasing & Supply Management 2000; 6 (1): 5–12.
19. Schiefer G. New technologies and their impact on the agri-food sector: an economists view. Computers and Electronics in Agriculture 2004; 43: 163–172.
20. Schotanus F and Telgen J. Developing a typology of organisational forms of cooperative purchasing. Journal of Purchasing & Supply Management 2007; 13: 53–68.
21. Swan J and Newell S. The Role of Professional Associations in Technology Diffusion. Organization Studies 1995; 16(5): 847–874.
22. Vias AC. Bigger stores, more stores, or no stores: paths of retail restructuring in rural America. Journal of Rural Studies 2004; 20: 303–318.
23. Volpentesta AP and Ammirato S. Evaluating e-commerce web interfaces of agri-food SMEs in an European lagging behind region. International Journal of Entrepreneurship and Innovation Management 2007; 7 (1): 74–91.
24. Wang P and Watts A. Formation of buyer-seller trade networks in a quality-differentiated product market. Canadian Journal of Economics 2006; 39 (3): 971-1004.
25. Watts DCH, Ilbery B and Maye D. Making reconnections in agro-food geography: alternative systems of food provision. Progress in Human Geography 2005; 29 (1): 22–40.
26. Weaver DB and Fennell DA. The Vacation Farm Sector in Saskatchewan: A Profile of Operations. Tourism Management 1997; 18 (6): 357-365.
27. Zajac E and Olsen C. From Transaction Cost to Transaction Value Analysis: Implications for the Study of Interorganizational Strategies. Journal of Management Studies 1993; 30(1): 131–145.

---

[i] Fritz et al. (2004) define an electronic trade platform as "a support system able to match agribusiness clusters and consumer groups, intermediate trading transactions up to contract conclusion and provide the institutional infrastructure that is in line with the legal and technical environment"

[ii] Calabria is a southern Italy lagging behind region included, by the EU, among the Objective 1 region. In Calabria, the agribusiness sector contributes 7.8% to the aggregate regional product and accounts for 18.9% of the total employment in the region; both of these rates are approximately twice the equivalent national averages.

[iii] The DAQ-Sibari was established with a Calabrian Regional Law in 2004. Its territory is in the northeast of Calabria and it comprises almost 200,000 hectare divided in 32 municipal districts. More than a thousand organizations (farms, agrifood SMEs, manufacturers, clusters of them, etc.) belongs to the DAQ-Sibari.

[iv] The University of Calabria is a university of southern Italy, consists of six faculties, 42 undergraduate degrees, 36 specialisations, 23 departments and 170 classrooms. We have the largest library system in Italy and over 40,000 students and about 2,000 employees including professors and researchers. The University is the first and the largest Italian university campus and includes 3,000 student residence.

PART 2

SOCIAL CAPITAL, VALUE SYSTEMS
AND SOFT ISSUES

COLLABORATIVE NETWORKS AND SOCIAL CAPITAL: A THEORETICAL AND PRACTICAL CONVERGENCE

5

Rolando Vargas Vallejos
University of Caxias do Sul - rvvallej@ucs.br
Janaina Macke
University of Caxias do Sul - jmacke@terra.com.br
Pelayo Munhoz Olea
University of Caxias do Sul - pelayo.olea@gmail.com
Eduardo Toss
University of Caxias do Sul - tosspuc@hotmail.com
BRAZIL

This paper addresses the issue of social capital analysis for collaborative networks. The objective of the research project is to understand how collaborative networks can be influenced considering the perspective of social capital. Initially, the authors identified and analyzed relevant works that were developed in the collaborative network field, focusing on the social capital approach. Therefore, nineteen papers have been selected from well-known journals basically extracted from the Business Source Premier Database. Thereafter, a tool for analyzing those papers has been developed. During evaluation, the authors considered twenty six aspects that can be divided into two major themes: the methodological and characterization approach and the theory of social capital and collaborative networks. As a result of this work, we conclude that a great variety of techniques to collect information exists, but that the difficulty of measuring social capital continues.

1. INTRODUCTION

Social Capital is a component of the Social Theory that is being considered as a key-element for the human and economic development of communities. Some reasons that contribute to the interest in Social Capital are: the value of the social relations in social and economic discussions, the transformations of the society and the role of the State, the importance of network relations to improve economic performances and the necessity of concepts to understand the complexity of human being. Social Capital can be understood as a set of informal norms and values, common to the members of a specific group which allow the cooperation among them. Many authors point to the difficulty to measure that concept; most of the time rather the absence of Social Capital instead of its presence is measured. The task of analyzing some experiences and the construction of new concepts needs refined procedures, with results that are closely tied with its context. Considering this, the main objective of the present research is to analyze some experiences of Social Capital

Please use the following format when citing this chapter:

Vallejos, R.V., Macke, J., Olea, P.M. and Toss, E., 2008, in IFIP International Federation for Information Processing, Volume 283;
Pervasive Collaborative Networks; Luis M. Camarinha-Matos, Willy Picard; (Boston: Springer), pp. 43–52.

generation, in order to find and establish some evaluation metrics. The results will contribute to the research in the socio-organizational field and will provide the managers with a tool to evaluate collaborative networks (intra and inter-groups).

Considering Collaborative Networks (CN) it is important to analyze the impact of the methodologies of development induction and, consequently, to evaluate aspects of their creation, operation and dissolution, as well as, the success/failure in the implementation of this kind of methodology. In other words, the exploitation and, even though, the generation of Social Capital are closely related to the programming of the groups qualification (induction) and to how the responsible agents for the inductive process were capable to implement each phase of that methodologies.

For that reason, Social Capital is here considered to be a necessary dimension to the local development. In fact, the rational and sustainable exploitation of the resources of a place - with emphasis in the endogenous factor - is a function of three mayor characteristics: stimulate the entrepreneurship (to allow a better exploitation of the local enterprising capacity or to stimulate its creation), support and promotion of many forms of Social Capital (enforcing the civil society) and organize and articulate public politics with the identified elements for the local development.

In the near future, the analysis of experiences combined to the local context will allow the creation of theoretical constructs and consequently, the contribution for the social theory. As practical results, it will be possible to generate elements that will allow the optimization of CN formation and operation processes.

2. COLLABORATIVE NETWOKS

The concept of the network is not new, but its use nowadays has been influenced by global changes in politics, society and economics. Some strong arguments may explain the dissemination of the use of network concept. In an economical perspective, a network may constitute an answer to challenges for organizations because of the intense competition caused by a globalized economy (Castells, 1998; Loiola and Moura, 1996). In a political perspective, a network seems to constitute an answer to the fiscal crisis and to the erosion of the contemporaneous Government supremacy (Castells, 1998).

Among the various types of networks, a special relevance is given to Collaborative Networks (CN). The concept of CN has become stronger in recent years within academic and industrial areas. It constitutes an effort to concretize and modernize the traditional concept of cooperation networks among companies. A CN is constituted by several entities (e.g., organizations and people) that are autonomous, geographically distributed, and heterogeneous in terms of their operating environment, culture, social capital, and goals. These entities collaborate to achieve common goals, and their interactions are supported by a computer network. Unlike other networks, in CN collaboration is an intentional property that derives from the shared belief that together the network members can achieve goals that would not be possible or would have a higher cost if attempted by them individually (Camarinha-Matos and Afsarmanesh, 2005).

A large number of research projects in this area are carried out worldwide and a growing number of practical cases on different forms of CNs have been reported.

CNs are complex systems, emerging in many forms in different application domains, and consist of many facets with proper understanding requires the contribution from multiple disciplines. In fact, the various manifestations of CNs have been studied by different scientific disciplines, including the computer science, computer engineering, management, economy, sociology, industrial engineering, law, etc. (Camarinha-Matos and Afsarmanesh, 2005). In order to contribute to the integration of insights by some of those different scientific disciplines, this paper addresses the issue of Social Capital analysis for CNs.

The concept of Social Capital, when measuring the potential of wealth production that flows of the diverse forms of collective association, allows to explore the impacts of the civil society in the economic performance. It is possible to identify four main ways how Social Capital, found in social networks, stimulates the economic growth (Skidmore, 2001, p. 134): (i) high level of social trust and strong reciprocity norms, reduce the transaction costs (Fukuyama, 1995); (ii) social networks attenuate the risks, allowing that their members engage more in innovations; (iii) social networks facilitate fast information dissemination and with this, they reduce the asymmetries; (iv) social networks allow that its members resolve easily their collective problems.

3. SOCIAL CAPITAL: THE FOUNDATION OF THE RELATIONSHIPS IN NETWORKS

The concept of Social Capital has gained interest in the scientific community in significant variety of disciplines. Elements as trust, networks of relationship and share of norms are topics that have been discussed by researchers from different areas.

The notoriety of the concept came from the publication of the book of Robert Putnam, in 1993, entitled "Making Democracy Work: civic traditions in modern Italy". In this work, Putnam relates the results of more than twenty years study about the Italian society, in which the initial topic was to understand the differences of the development of north and south Italy. The author concluded that the disparities between institutional performance and development of the regions are resulting from a mayor presence of Social Capital (in case of the north of the country). The authors conclusions had strong impact in the scientific community and were corroborated by others studies (Fukuyama, 1995, 1999; 2000; Grootaert, 1998; Onyx & Bullen, 2000).

The World Bank, since 1990, distinguishes in its evaluation of development projects four forms of capital: natural capital (natural resources of a country); financial capital (including infrastructure, capital goods, property, etc.); human capital (health, education and nutrition); and social capital (capacity of a society to establish relationships of interpersonal trust and cooperation networks, with the aim to produce collective goods). The World Bank emphasizes that Social Capital is related to the institutions, relations and norms and is a core element for the economic prosperity and the sustainable local development.

The diffusion of the concept is happening following two theoretical approaches. One treats Social Capital as an individual good, being able to be accumulated by a person. The main representatives of this approach are Bourdieu (2003a; 2003b),

Granovetter (1985) and Portes (1998). For these authors, Social Capital can be internalized by a person and can be used by him or her to produce benefits. Social Capital, in this way, is linked to a worthwhile position (status) of an individual inside a workgroup and indicates power aspects.

The other approach treats Social Capital as an element that belongs to a workgroup, community or society, which should be analyzed as a public good and is present in the relations between persons or groups. Coleman (1990), Putnam (1993; 2000) and Fukuyama (1995; 1999) are the main representatives of this approach. For these authors, the Social Capital is the social tissue to story line or the glue that guarantees the cohesion of a group and is based in trustfulness, in norms of reciprocity, in cooperation and in participation systems. The present study is inserted in this second approach.

After the introduction of these two approaches, it is necessary to identify the different units (or axes) of analysis. The units of analysis differ with regards the context relations: one investigates the relationships inside a group (intra-groups relations); another one studies the relationship between groups (inter-groups relations). In the first case, we find studies about Social Capital evaluation in communities, associations or groups. In the second case, we find studies of Social Capital creation among companies, nations, or other organizational forms. In the present project we do consider both approaches, since the theoretical referential is eminently the same, changing only some specific aspects.

Since the concept of Social Capital emerged, it has been used to explain a lot of social phenomena; most of the research have focused on the role of Social Capital in the human capital development (Coleman, 1990; Loury, 1987), in the economic performance (Baker, 1990), in the development of regions (Putnam, 1993) and in the development of countries (Fukuyama, 1995).

In their study of Social Capital and its importance to the creation of intellectual capital, Nahapiet & Ghoshal (1998) proposed three Social Capital dimensions, which are: *structural, relational* and *cognitive*. Although the authors have differentiated analytically Social Capital in dimensions, they point out that a great part of the characteristics studied are highly related, what does not disable the classification, therefore facilitates the construct comprehension.

In the structural dimension of Social Capital the authors analyzed the presence or not of relationships between the actors, the configuration or morphology of the network, describing the standards of connections, through variables as density, connectivity network configuration, stability and ties (Coleman, 1990).

The relational dimension describes the kind of personal relationships, developed through a history of interactions (Granovetter, 1992). This concept focuses on aspects that influence behaviors like respect and friendship, which are going to decide to sociability, acceptance and prestige. Two actors can occupy similar positions in a network, however if their emotional and personal attitudes differ, their actions will be different in many aspects because they are related to a behavioral component, which is revealed through facets as trust and distrust (Fukuyama, 1995; Putnam, 1993; 2000), norms (Coleman, 1990; Putnam, 1993), obligations and expectations (Coleman, 1990; Granovetter, 1992) participation and diversity tolerance (Nahapiet & Ghoshal, 1998).

The third dimension of Social Capital, the cognitive, refers to the resources that emanate shared visions, interpretations and systems of meaning, mainly codes and narratives shared values and other cultural elements. Some authors affirm that this dimension has not been explored in the literature yet (Nahapiet & Ghoshal, 1998).

Figure 1 below represents these three Social Capital dimensions and their essential elements.

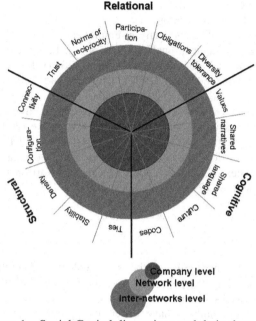

Figure 1 – Social Capital dimensions and their elements.

4. RESEARCH METHOD

Initially, relevant works were identified which were developed in the CN discipline, focusing on the Social Capital approach. Nineteen papers were selected from well-known journals extracted basically from the Business Source Premier Database. Subsequently, a tool was developed in order to analyze these papers considering twenty six items divided in to two major themes; one on methodological and characterization approach and another considering the theories of Social Capital and CNs.

Regarding methodological aspects, the variables analyzed were:

(i)   qualitative, quantitative, qualitative-quantitative approach (Roesch, 1999);

(ii) epistemological paradigm: functionalist, radical structuralist, interpretive and radical humanist (Burrel & Morgan, 1979);

(iii) kind of research: applied, results evaluation, formative evaluation, research-action, proposition of plans and diagnosis research (Patton, 1990);

(iv) strategy of research: case study, survey, action research, ethnography, experiments, phenomenology (Roesch, 1999). The case studies also were analyzed considering: single cases/multiple cases, criteria of choice and unit of analysis;

(v)   nature of the research: exploratory, descriptive, causal/explanatory (Churchill Jr., 1999 *apud* Froemming et al., 2000; Pinsonneault and Kraemer, 1993 *apud* Freitas et al., 2000);

(vi) temporary nature of the research: longitudinal studies, transversal studies (Sampieri et al., 1991);

(vii) conceptual map (present or not);

(viii) techniques of collect and analyses employed.

The authors of the nineteen analyzed papers are: Frank and Yasumoto (1998); Molina-Morales (2005); Valentinov (2004); Rhee (2004); Reagans and Zuckerman (2001); Walker, Kogut and Shan (1997); Duysters and Lemmens (2003); Pollitt (2002); Anand, Glick and Manz (2002); Bellandi (2001); Bellandi (2002); Schuller (2007); Schultze and Orlikowski (2004); Vanhaverbeke, Beerkens, Duysters and Gilsing (2004); Yao, Dingkun and Prescott (2002); Cooke (2007); Grewal, Lilien and Mallapragada (2006); Cross and Sproull (2004); Ikpen and Tsang(2005).

Regarding the already cited theories about Social Capital and CNs it was considered the studies of Macke (2006), Macke and Carrion (2006), Camarinha-Matos and Afsarmanesh (1999) and Vallejos (2005).

5. RESULTS

The nineteen papers analyzed can be separated into theoretical (36,8%) and theoretical-empirical (63,2%) papers. Is possible to state that the most referenced author is Coleman (68,4%) followed by Burt (52,6%), what initially might seem unusual because these authors have different approaches about Social Capital. Coleman defines Social Capital as a "public good" while Burt emphasizes the "personal benefits" associated to the subject. Most of the authors of the analyzed papers use this contrast of theories to reference diverse forms, benefits, dimensions and relations associated to Social Capital. The nature of Social Capital analyzed is predominantly analyzed between groups (inter-groups relations) (63,1%).

Considering the classification of Nahapiet and Ghoshal (1998) we analyzed the occurrence of the three dimensions of Social Capital, which are: cognitive, relational and structural. The dimension that was less cited in the papers was the cognitive, where the elements most discussed were culture (15,8%) and values (10,5%). Taking into account the relational dimension, the elements most discussed were trust (52,6%), norms of reciprocity (42,1%) and obligations and expectations (21%). The structural dimension can be considered as the most cited in the papers and the discussed elements were strong and weak ties (57,9%) and their diverse implications in networks, density of the relations (47,4%), network connectivity (15,8%) and network configuration (15,8%).

Table 1 shows a sample part of one table of the tool developed in order to analyze these papers.

Regarding the research paradigms (Burrel & Morgan, 1979), the authors identified an absolute predominance of the functionalist paradigm (75%), against the interpretive paradigm that was used in 25% remainders papers. The radical structuralism and the radical humanist paradigms did not have any occurrence. This does verify, in that sense, the need of an enrichment of the studies through a more pluralist debate.

Table 1 – Sample of part of one table of the tool developed.

Paper	Cognitive dimension		Relational dimension			Structural dimension			
	Values	Culture	Trust	Norms of reciprocity	Obligations and expectations	ties	density	conectivity	configuration
Frank and Yasumoto (1998)			x	x	x	x	x		
Molina-Morales (2005)		x	x			x	x		
Valentinov (2004)			x	x	x				
Rhee (2004)						x	x		
Reagans and Zuckerman (2001)						x	x		
Walker, Kogut and Shan (1997)				x					
Duysters and Lemmens (2003)	x		x			x	x	x	
Pollitt (2002)			x			x	x		
Anand, Glick and Manz (2002)									
Bellandi (2001)		x	x	x	x	x			
Bellandi (2002)									
Schuller (2007)	x		x	x					
Schultze and Orlikowski (2004)			x		x				
Vanhaverbeke, et.al. (2004)						x	x		x
Yao, Dingkun and Prescott (2002)						x		x	x
Cooke (2007)			x	x					
Grewal, Lilien and Mallapragada(2006)						x			
Cross and Sproull (2004)				x					
Ikpen and Tsang(2005)		x	x	x		x	x	x	x

Despite the difficulties to measure Social Capital, most of the studies have a quantitative approach (75%) and use the survey method for the research (83%). Transversal studies are predominant (75%), it means, the instant image of a phenomenon.

The nature of Social Capital is analyzed predominantly between groups (63%), showing a strong relation with networks, mainly with the relational and structural aspects. The intra-groups Social Capital relation was analyzed in 21% of the studies and other 16% were studies comparing intra and inter-groups analysis. The CNs forms most cited were strategic alliances (36,8%) and industrial districts (26%).

The most organizational variables cited are knowledge transfer (47,4%), organizational behavior (42,1%), innovation (26,3%), cooperation (21%), turn over (21%) and learning (21%). Knowledge transfer is considered as a core element due to benefits that are related to Social Capital development inside a network.

6. CONCLUSIONS

With this study we conclude that:

(i) the issue of Social Capital in the CN context does need further exploration. Although the word "trust" appears most of the time, it is related as an isolated concept and not as an element of Social Capital;

(ii) concerning the dimensions of Social Capital, the cognitive dimension is receiving not much attention. Some papers treat "knowledge transfer" without a link with the cognitive aspects of this process;

(iii) although a predominance of quantitative studies exists, persist methodological difficulties to measure Social Capital, that can be observed in the structural and relational dimensions;

(iv) important variables for the study of Social Capital like participation, commitment and pro-activity were rather not discussed in the studies. *Commitment* appeared only in two papers, while *participation* and *pro-activity*, were not mentioned in any of them.

To cope with these difficulties, we are developing a model to analyze the Social Capital in CNs. In this model we deny the usefulness of endogenous resources like technology in general. Technology is available to most of the companies and, therefore, will not be a long term competitive advantage. We propose that CNs will be more competitive and successfully if they invest in two core elements that are organizational culture and people.

In this way, the model under construction (figure 2), starts with the partners core competencies identification, for the analysis and/or formation of a CN, in order to establish the main processes and expected results for the local development. Relevant organizational variables are investigated and the Social Capital approach that is used as a cement of the relationships among the CN.

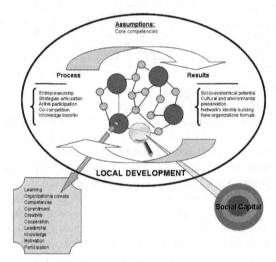

Figure 2 – Social Capital and Collaborative Networks: a proposal of a model "as is" for local development analysis.

As an early result of this work it is possible to conclude that there is a great variety of techniques to collect information, but remains the difficulty to measure Social Capital. The epistemological paradigm is essentially functionalist with emphasis on structural and relational dimensions of Social Capital. The results of this meta-analysis are being considered as background for the discussion and the development of a methodology to study CNs with the Social Capital approach.

In short, the Social Capital concept is very important for the environment of networks. Social Capital is linked to models that influence the performance and productivity of a CN, contributing, in general, to the local development.

Acknowledgements
This work is being supported by the University of Caxias do Sul (UCS) and the Brazilian IFM II project (www.ifm.org.br).

4. REFERENCES

1.   Anand, V.; Glick, W. H.; Manz, C. C. Thriving on the knowledge of the outsiders: Tapping organizational social capital. Academy of Management Executive, 2002, v. 16, n.1.

2. Bellandi, M. Local development and embedded large firms. Entrepreneurship & Regional Development, 2001, v.13.
3. Bellandi, M. Italian Industrial Districts: An Industrial Economics Interpretation. European Planning Studies, 2002, v.10, n.4.
4. Bourdieu, P. O Poder Simbólico. 6 ed. Rio de Janeiro: Bertrand, 2003a.
5. Bourdieu, P. Razões Práticas: sobre a teoria da ação. 4 ed. Campinas: Papirus, 2003b.
6. Burrel, G.; Morgan, G. Sociological Paradigms and Organizational Analysis. London: Heinemann, 1979.
7. Camarinha-Matos, L. M.; Afsarmanesh, H. The Virtual Enterprise Concept. Infrastructures for Virtual Enterprises – Networking Industrial Enterprises. Kluwer Academic Publishers, 1999.
8. Camarinha-Matos, L. M.; Afsarmanesh, H. Collaborative Networks: A new scientific discipline. Journal of Intelligent Manufacturing, Springer. The Netherlands, n. 16, 2005, p.439–452.
9. Coleman, J. S. Foundations of Social Theory. Cambridge: Harvard University Press, 1990.
10. Coleman, J. S. Social Capital in the creation of Human Capital. American Journal of Sociology, 94: 95-120, 1988.
11. Cooke, P. Social Capital, Embeddedness and Market Interactions: An analysis of Firm Performance in UK Regions. Review of Social Economic, 2007, p.79-106.
12. Cross, R.; Sproull, L. More Than an Answer: Information Relationships for Actionable Knowledge. Organizational Science, 2004, v. 15, n.4: 446-462.
13. Duysters, G.; Leemens, C. Alliance Group Formation. Int. Studies of Mgt. & Org., 2003, vol. 33, n.2: 49-68.
14. Frank, K. A.; Yasumoto, J. Y. Linking Association to Social Structure within a System: Social Capital within and between subgroups. AJS, 1998, v .104, n.3: 642-686.
15. Freitas, H. Oliveira, M., Saccol, A. Z. e Moscarola, J. O Método de Pesquisa Survey. Revista de Administração, 2000, v.35, n.3, p. 105-112.
16. Froemming, L. M. S., Luce, F. B., Perin, M. G., Sampaio, C. H., Beber, S. J. N.; Trez, G. Análise da Qualidade dos Artigos Científicos da Área de Marketing no Brasil: As Pesquisas survey na década de 90. RAC, 2000, v.4, n.3, p. 201-219.
17. Fukuyama, F. The great disruption: human nature and the reconstitution of social order. London Profile Books, 1999.
18. Fukuyama, F. Trust: the social creation virtues and the creation of prosperity. New York: Free Press, 1995.
19. Granovetter, M. S. The strength of weak ties. American Journal of Sociology, 78 :1360-80, 1973.
20. Grewal, R.; Lilien, G. L.; Mallapragada, J. Location, Location, Location: How Network Embeddedness Affects Project Success in Open Source Systems. Management Science, 2006, v. 52, n.7: 1043-1056.
21. Grootaert, C. Social capital: the missing link?, Social Capital Iniciative Working Paper N. 3, The World Bank, Washington D.C.
22. Inkpen, A. C.; Tsang, E. W. K. Social Capital, Networks and Knowledge Transfer. Academy of Management Review, 2005, v. 30, n.1: 146-165.
23. Loury, G. Why would we care about group inequality? Social Philosophy & Policy, 1987, 5: 249-271.
24. Macke, J. Programas de Responsabilidade Social Corporativa e Capital Social: contribuição para o desenvolvimento local? 2006. 307 f. Tese (Doutorado em Administração) - Programa de Pós-Graduação em Administração, Escola de Administração, Universidade Federal do Rio Grande do Sul, Porto Alegre, 2006.
25. Macke, J.; Carrion, R. M. Planejamento, Implementação e Avaliação de Programas Sociais: Uma Proposta de Inovação. REAd. Revista Eletrônica de Administração, v. 12, n. 5, set./out. 2006. Available in: http://read.ea.ufrgs.br.
26. Merton, R. K. Social theory and social structure. New York: Free Press, 1968.
27. Molina-Morales, F. X. The Territorial Agglomerations of Firms: A Social Capital Perspective from the Spanish Tile Industry. Growth and Change, 2005, v. 36, n.1: 74-99.
28. Nahapiet, J. e Ghoshal, S. Social capital, intellectual capital and the organizational advantage. Academy of Management Review, 1998, 23(2):242-266.
29. Onyx, J. e Bullen, P. Measuring Social Capital in Five Communities. The Journal of Applied Behavioral Science, 2000, 36 (1), 23-42.
30. Patton, M. Q. How to use qualitative methods in evaluation. London: Sage Publication, 1990.
31. Pollitt, M. The economics of trust, norms and network. Business Ethics: A European Review, 2002, v. 11, n.2: 119-128.

32. Portes, A. Social capital: its origins and application in modern sociology. Annual Review of Sociology, 1998, 24(1), p.1-24.
33. Putnam, R. D. Bowling Alone: the collapse and revival of American community. New York: Simon & Schuster Paperbacks, 2000.
34. Putnam, R. D.; Leonardi, R.; Nanetti, R. Y. Making Democracy Work: civic traditions in modern Italy. Princeton: Princeton University Press, 1993.
35. Reagans, R.; Zuckerman, E. W. Networks, Divesity, and Productivity: The Social Capital Corporate R&D Teams. Organizational Science, 2001, v. 12, n.4: 502-517.
36. Rhee, M. Network Updating and Exploratory Learning Environment. Journal of Management Studies, 2004, p. 933-949.
37. Roesch, S. M. A.. Projetos de estágio e de pesquisa em administração: guia para estágios, trabalhos de conclusão, dissertações e estudos de caso. São Paulo: Atlas, 1999.
38. Sampieri, R., Collado, C., Lucio, P. Metodología de la Investigación. México: McGraw Hill, 1991.
39. Schuller, T. Reflections on the Use of Social Capital. Review of Social Economy, 2007, v. LXV n.1: 11-28.
40. Schultze, U.; Orlikowski, W. J. A Practice Perspective on Technology-Mediated Network Relations: The Use of Internet-Based Self-Service Technologies. Information System Research, 2004, v. 15, n.1.
41. Skidmore, D. Sociedade Civil, Capital Social e Desenvolvimento Econômico. In: Abreu, A. A (org.). Transição em Fragmentos: desafios da democracia no final do século XX. Rio de Janeiro: FGV, 2001. p. 129-152.
42. Valentinov, V. Social Capital and Organizational Performance: a Theoretical Perspective. JIIDT, 2004, v. 8, p. 23-33.
43. Vallejos, R. V. Um modelo para formação de Empresas Virtuais no setor de moldes e matrizes. Tese de doutorado. Universidade Federal de Santa Catarina, 2005.
44. Vanhaverbeke, W.; Beerkens, B.; Duysters, G.; Gilsing, V. Explorative and Exploitative Learning Strategies in Technology-Based Alliance Networks. Academy of Best Conference Paper, 2004.
45. Walker, G.; Kogut, B.; Shan, W. Social Capital, Structural Holes and the Formation of an Industry Network. Organizational Science, 1997, v. 8, n.2: 109-125.
46. World Bank. Social Capital for Development. Available in: http://www1.worldbank.org/prem/ /poverty/scapital/index.htm.
47. Yao, E.; Dingkun, G.; Prescott, J. E. Value Creation Through "Going Together": An Event Study on Market Response to Technology Alliance Formation in Global Pharmaceutical Industry. Academy of Management Proceedings, 2002.

6

ANALYSIS OF CORE-VALUES ALIGNMENT IN COLLABORATIVE NETWORKS

Luis M. Camarinha-Matos
New University of Lisbon, Quinta da Torre – 2829 Monte Caparica, PORTUGAL
cam@uninova.pt
Patrícia Macedo
Escola Superior de Tecnologia de Setúbal, Instituto Politécnico de Setúbal, PORTUGAL
pmacedo@est.ips.pt
António Abreu
New University of Lisbon, Quinta da Torre – 2829 Monte Caparica, PORTUGAL
ajfa@fct.unl.pt

The identification and characterization of core-values in collaborative networks is an important element for the identification of a potential for conflicts. This paper introduces an approach, based on causal models and graph theory, for the analysis of core-values alignment in networked organisations. The potential application of this approach is also discussed in the VO breeding environment context.

1. INTRODUCTION

Most works on Collaborative Networks (CNs) are focused on the (potential) benefits of collaboration. However, participation in a CN also involves risks and often consortia fail due to internal conflicts. Conflicts can be originated by different core-values priorities and different perceptions of outcomes. The perception of outcomes is to some extent subjective in the way that it depends of the preferences of the subject and how exchanges are evaluated. The set of core-values and preferences hold by an individual or organization is defined in its *value system.*

In a collaborative network environment the value system of each network member may influence the success of collaboration. Therefore, when considering a candidate to join a network, it is important to assess this potential member according to the set of core-values that it holds and the network's core-values. Such analysis should provide elements that help managers to detect a potential for conflicts or the likelihood of the new member contributing to add value to the network.

Values in organizations have been studied during the last decades using diverse approaches that are focused essentially on four aspects: creation of organizational core-values taxonomies; development of methodologies to collect organizational core-values; development of frameworks in order to classify organizations according to their core-values; and analysis of the relation between the core-values held by employees and organizational core-values. For instance, the social researchers

Please use the following format when citing this chapter:

Camarinha-Matos, L.M., Macedo, P. and Abreu, A., 2008, in IFIP International Federation for Information Processing, Volume 283; *Pervasive Collaborative Networks*; Luis M. Camarinha-Matos, Willy Picard; (Boston: Springer), pp. 53–64.

Rokeach and Schwartz (Rokeach, 1973; Schwartz, 1992) developed some empirical work to identify core-values. Based on this work they proposed organizational core-values taxonomies. Brian Hall and Richard Barret (Barrett, 2006; Hall, 1995) developed theories about values in organizations, and discussed the importance of values management for the success of organizations. Their works contributed as well to clarify the differences between the core-values hold by organizations and their expected core-values. Richard Barret also studied the alignment between employee's core-values and enterprise's core-values. On the other hand, Eden (Eden, 1992) used causal maps to represent the cognitive structure of core-values. This work establishes the relationships between organizational goals and core-values. Another cognitive approach was proposed by Rekom and his colleagues (Rekom, Riel and Wierenga, 2006) as a methodology to measure core-values based on daily actions.

In recent years some studies have explored the importance of value systems in the context of networked organizations (Abreu and Camarinha-Matos, 2006; Afsarmanesh and Camarinha-Matos, 2005; Macedo, Sapateiro and Filipe, 2006; Zineldin, 1998), however none of them proposed methodologies, approaches or support tools to help network managers to analyze Virtual Organization's (VO) Value System in a Virtual organizations Breeding Environments (VBE) context.

The aim of this paper is to propose an approach based on graph theory and causal maps to analyze the core-values alignment in collaborative networked environments. This work aims at contributing to answer the following main questions:

- How to identify which values can a potential new member add to the VBE core-values?
- How to analyze the alignment between VBE core-values and the set of core-values of a potential new member?
- How to analyze the potential for conflicts among VO members?
- How to analyze the alignment between VO's core-values and VO members' core-values?

2. VALUE SYSTEM BASE CONCEPTS

There is no consensus about the value system definitions among the various disciplines (e.g. economy, sociology, artificial intelligence) that have addressed this topic. In an attempt to provide a "unified" definition, (Camarinha-Matos and Macedo, 2007) proposed a conceptual model for value systems embracing the economic and sociological notions. In order to discuss the core-value concept it is necessary to first summarize the generic conceptual model of value system introduced in previous work (Camarinha-Matos, Macedo, 2007).

This conceptual model identifies as main elements of a value system:
- **Object of Evaluation** – Something (x) that can be evaluated, and have value for the evaluator:

  $x \in S$ where: S is the set of things that can be evaluated.
- **Evaluation Functions** - The functions used to implement an evaluation act.

  $f \in F : F = NF \cup QF$, where NF is the set of numeric functions, and QF the set of qualitative functions.

- **Evaluation Dimensions** - Characteristics of an object that are evaluated. $D = \{d_1, d_2, ...d_n\}$ is the set of evaluation dimensions. Furthermore $f \, \Phi \, d$ means: *the function f permits to evaluate the dimension d.*
- **Evaluation Perspective** - A selected set of evaluation dimensions and the corresponding weights chosen to evaluate an object from a given point of view.

  $ep_x = <dv_x, wv> \in P$,where $x \in S$ and P is the set of evaluation perspectives.

  wv represents the weights-vector and dv_x expresses the set of dimensions of an object that is evaluated (dimensions-vector), where:

  $$dv_x = [d_1, d_2, ...d_n] : d_i \in D \quad wv = [w_1, ...w_n] : w_i \in [0..1] \wedge \sum_{i=0}^{n} w_i = 1$$

  i.e., $wv[i]$ represents the degree of importance of the characteristic $dv_x[i]$

  For each *dimensions-vector* an *evaluation-vector* can be specified as:
  $$fv_d = [f_1, f_2, ...f_n] : f_i \in F \text{ , where } i \in [1..n] \wedge fv_d[i] \Phi dv_x[i]$$

  In order to represent the fact that an object can *be evaluated through different perspectives*, the operator Ξ is defined as: $x \Xi ep$, meaning **x** is evaluated through the perspective *ep*, where $x \in S \wedge ep \in P$.

These elements are further organized in two sub-groups:
- Entities that can be evaluated: Objects of evaluation.
- Evaluation mechanism: Functions, Dimensions, and Perspectives.

Based on these elements, a Value System is thus composed of a set of valuable things for an organization and a set of functions used for its evaluation according to different perspectives, where each perspective is composed of a weighted set of evaluation dimensions.

Value System - $VS = <EVS, RVS>$ where $EVS = <OS, ES>$ is the aggregation of the two subsystems that compose the value system and *RVS* represents the set of relationships between the two sub-systems:

- **Value Objects Subsystem** - OS = <S, RS> where: *S* is the set of valuable things; RS is the set of relationships among the elements of S.

- **Evaluation Subsystem** - *ES=<EF, RE >* where: EF is defined as a triple: $EF = <F, D, P>$ *F* is the set of evaluation functions; *D* is the set *of* evaluation dimensions; *P* is the set of evaluation perspectives; and *RE* is the set of relationships among the elements of *EF*.

Each organization (or network of organizations) considers a set of characteristics as the most important for itself; these characteristics are called **core-values** (Collins and Porras, 1996). The core-values are used as the base for the decision-making processes and they are the elements that motivate and regulate its own behaviour (Hall, 1995; Higgins, 2004). Therefore we can introduce the notion of **Core Value System** to encompass the core-values. This concept is a restricted view of the generic value system model presented above, and can be considered as specialization of it.

This model assumes that *core–values* are the core characteristics of the organisation (or network of organizations) to be evaluated. Thus, a core-value is defined as an evaluation dimension of the Core Value System and the organisation (or network of organizations) as the (sole) object of evaluation (see Figure 1).

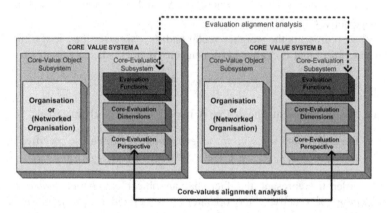

Figure 1 – Core Value System components and alignment analysis.

Core-Value System - $CVS = <CEVS, CRVS>$ where $CEVS = <COS, CES>$ is the aggregation of the two subsystems that compose the core-value system and *CRVS* represents the set of relationships between the two sub-systems:

- **Core Value Objects Subsystem (COS)** is represented by the organisation (or networked organisation) itself.
- **Core Evaluation Subsystem** - *CES=<CEF, CRE >* where: CEF is defined as a triple: $CEF = <CF, CV, CP>$ *CF* is the set of evaluation functions to evaluate the organisation core-values; *CV* is the set of core-values; *CP* is the core-evaluation perspective; and *CRE* is the set of relationships among the elements of *CEF*.

The core-evaluation perspective is defined as:

$$ep_{core} = <dv_{core}, wv_{core}> \in CP \text{ , where:}$$

- dv_{core} expresses the vector of core-values of the organisation.
- wv_{core} represents the weights -vector, where each element defines the degree of importance of the respective core-value. These weights represent the preferences of the value-system's owner.

Example: Let us suppose the core-values held by a Logistic Enterprise are *innovation, reliability*, and *profit* and each core-value has a different degree of importance (see Figure 2). This set of core-values is thus part of the Core Value System, and more specifically part of the core-evaluation subsystem (CES).

$CV=\{innovation, profit, reliability\} \in CES$

- $dv_{core}=[innovation, profit, reliability]$
- $wv_{core}=[0.1, 0.5, 0.4]$, representing the enterprise 's preferences.

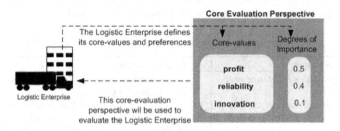

Figure 2- Core values and core evaluation perspective concepts.

According to this approach, the analysis of the alignment between two Core Value Systems has to comprise two main aspects (see Figure 2):

- The analysis of core-values alignment, where the compatibility between the two sets of core-values is analyzed.
- The analysis of evaluation alignment, where it is analyzed whether the evaluation functions of different Core Value Systems, used to evaluate the same characteristic, are similar. Although, two evaluators could hold the same core-value, if they use different evaluation functions, the evaluation results could be distinct.

However, the aim of this paper is to solely discuss the core-values alignment.

3. A META-MODEL TO ANALYZE CORE-VALUES

In order to analyze the core-values of a collaborative network it is necessary to have a model that supports the analysis of the relationships among the following entities: core-values, organizations, and VOs. Therefore, as a first approach, let us consider the following relationships:

1. Core-values and core-values – in order to understand how core-values influence each other.
2. Core-values and organisations – in order to know which core-values are held by each organization.
3. Core-values and VOs – in order to understand which core-values are held by the VO.

These relationships can be modelled using graphs. The main goal is to represent a network in symbolic terms, abstracting reality as a set of linked nodes. In this case each node represents an element (a VO, an organization, or a core-value) and the directed arcs specify the relationships. On the other hand, an extension of graph theory is the Causal Models that naturally emerged due to the need for a sketching technique to support and facilitate reasoning about cause and effect. Causal modelling builds upon a binary relationship, called an *influence relationship*, between two entities that represent named quantitative or qualitative values or value sets. Whereby changes in the influencing entity are conveyed as changes in the influenced entity (Greenland and Brumback, 2002). In this case, the causal modelling method is used to model the causal relations among core-values in order to analyze the influence among them.

Considering the nature of this analysis, as first approach, a combination of these two modelling techniques is suggested, as illustrated in Table 1

Table 1 – Framework to analyze core-values in CNO's.

Core-Values		Organization	VO
	Core-values influence map.	*Organization 's core-values map*	*VO's core-values map*
Core-Values	Use causal maps to show how core-values influence positively or negatively each other.	Use graphs to show the core-values held by each organisation.	Use graphs to show the core-values held by the VO., and the core-values shared by VOs.
	core-value x → core-value y *Positive influence relationship*	Organisation A → core-value x	VOi → core-value x
	core-value x → core-value y *Negative influence relationship*	*Ownership relation*	*Ownership relation*

4. POTENTIAL APPLICATION

In order to detect a potential for conflicts and to promote alignment between (core) Value Systems, this example illustrates how the proposed approach can be used to answer the research questions introduced above. For that, let us assume the existence of a *Reference Core-Values Knowledge Base,* which contains a description about every possible core-value that an organisation can hold. This knowledge base also stores the information about the influence relationship between pairs of core-values. This knowledge can be provided by experts or result of surveys and interviews (see (Rekom, 2006) and (Hall, 1995), as examples). The creation of a *Reference Core-Values Knowledge Base* has two main purposes:

- To allow that the selection of core-values is done from a limited set. This will guarantee the existence of a common terminology.
- To allow that the generation of core-values maps from a subset of core-values is done consistently. This will permit to compare core-value maps of network members and to analyze the influence among core-values of distinct members.

In the proposed example scenario, the existence of a *VO breeding environment* (VBE) is considered which initially contains seven organizations: a bank, two universities, three factories and one logistics operator, as illustrated in Figure 3.

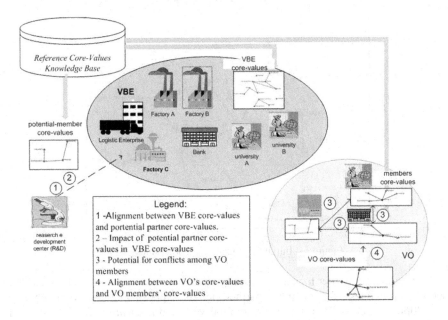

Figure 3 – Example VBE scenario.

In this context, when a VBE is formed, each member can select from the pre-configured list of reference core-values, the ones that it considers as its core-values. The pre-configured list is generated from the data stored in the *Reference Core-Values Knowledge Base*. From these data the following maps can be generated:
1. Core-values map. This causal map shows the influences between VBE's core-values, as illustrated in Figure 4 .
2. Organisation's core-values map. This two-mode graph shows both the core-values held by VBE members and how they are shared, as illustrated in Figure 5.

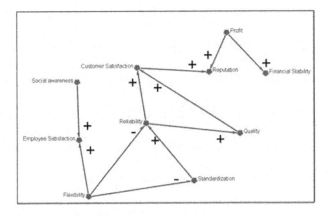

Figure 4 - Core-values influence map

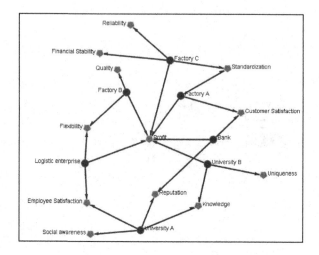

Figure 5 – Initial Organization's core-values map

Furthermore, in order to analyze the alignment between VBE core-values and the set of core-values of a potential partner, let us suppose that the Research and Development Center (RDC) wants to join the VBE and *Innovation, Knowledge,* and *Uniqueness* are its core-values.

In order to analyze the alignment between the core-values of the VBE and the core-values of the Research Center and to identify which values can be added to the VBE core-values, a causal map is generated, as shown in Figure 5. The comparative analysis of these two causal maps (Figure 5 and Figure 6) shows that *Innovation* was added to the map and that it can influence negatively the *Standardization*. This means that there exists a potential for conflicts between the RDC and other VBE members that have *Standardization* as a core-value.

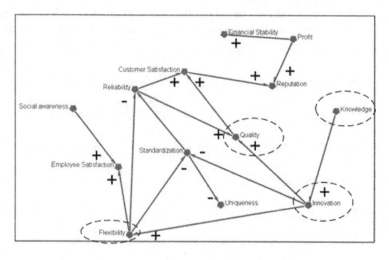

Figure 6 - Core-values influence map after RDC joined the VBE.

On the other hand, the analysis of the causal map shows that *Innovation* influences positively *Quality* and *Flexibility* and it is positively influenced by *Knowledge*. As the *Flexibility* and *Quality* characteristics have a positive influence in other core-values, this means that if the level of *Innovation* increases in the network it is expected that the level of *Flexibility, Quality, Customers' satisfaction, Reputation*, and *Employee's satisfaction* will also increase.

By generating a new Organizations' core-values map that includes the RDC (as illustrated in Figure 7), it is possible to conclude that this potential member shares core-values with University A and B.

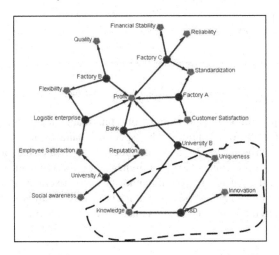

Figure 7 – *Organization 's core-values map* after RDC joined the VBE.

In order to illustrate how to analyze the potential for conflicts among VO members and the alignment between VO's core-values and VO members' core-values, let us suppose that two business opportunities are identified by a broker, and a subset of these organizations are selected to form VOs.

In this case, the two following VOs were created:
- VO1 to develop a specific medicine. In this example VO1 selects Quality, Social awareness, Innovation, Uniqueness, and Profit as core-values.
- VO2 to manufacture pharmaceutical equipment. In this example VO2 selects Standardization, Customer satisfaction, and Profit as core-values.

When a VO is formed inside a VBE and assuming that the VO planner defines the set of core-values that will guide the behaviour of this VO, a VO's core-values map can be generated, which shows the cores values held by this VO. Since, various VOs can coexist at the same time in the context of a VBE, may be useful to analyze the shared values among VOs.

Figure 8 illustrates the core-values held by each VO. This map evidences that these two VOs give importance to distinct sets of core-values, and only the profit core-value is shared.

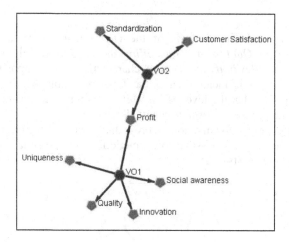

Figure 8 - VO's core-values map.

Since the purpose of VO2 is to manufacture pharmaceutical equipment, a factory that has the capacity to implement the specific manufacture process must be selected. Consequently the VO2 planner cannot choose for instance a Bank to do it, in spite of the Bank core-values having a higher level of alignment with VO's core-values. Therefore, the partner selection cannot be made exclusively based on core-values analysis; competencies fitness is naturally a must. However in the case that competences required are guaranteed, this analysis can be useful.

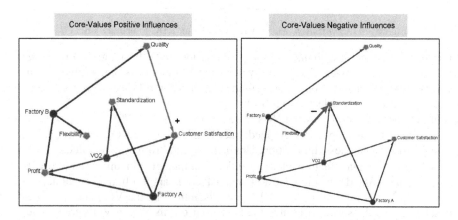

Figure 9-Alignment analysis between VO2 and potential members.

Based on the causal maps of Figure 9 it is possible to analyze the alignment of the VO2 with relation to Factory A and Factory B. Comparing these two potential members, it can be realized that Factory A's core-values fit better the VO2's core-values than Factory B. Furthermore, the Flexibility core-value of Factory B has a negative influence on Standardization. As Standardization is a core-value of VO2, Factory B may have a negative impact in VO2's performance.

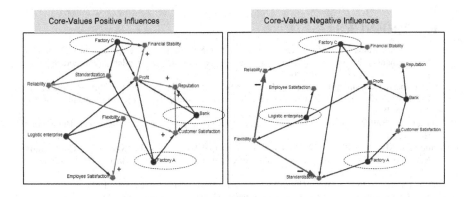

Figure 10 - Alignment analysis among VO2 members.

Let us, now suppose that VO2 is composed of the Bank, the Logistic Operator, the Factory A, and the Factory C. Based on Organization's core-value map for VO2, it is possible to analyze the potential for conflicts among VO members. As illustrated in

Figure 10, a potential for conflict between the Logistic Operator and Factory C can be detected. This potential for conflict is derived from the fact that the Flexibility core-value held by the Logistic Operator has a negative influence on reliability held by Factory C. Identical situation occurs in relation to Factory A and C due to the negative impact of Standardization on the Flexibility core-value.

It shall be noted that the above discussion is only an illustration based on the exemplified reference core-values. Different conclusions could naturally be derived from different causal maps.

5. CONCLUSIONS

Reaching a better characterization and understanding of the core-values role in collaborative processes is an important pre-condition to avoid conflicts and misunderstandings in the operation phase of VOs and VBEs. This understanding is also a base for the establishment of proper analysis methods to support decision making processes at various levels: VBE management, VBE membership, VO brokering, and VO planning.

The suggested approach proposes a model to analyze core-values alignment in a VBE context, inspired in the causal models and graph theories. The proposed model has the advantage of providing a visual/graphical representation which is easy to understand and to promote the communication between partners.

The applicability of the suggested approach was illustrated through the example presented; however the development of a full practical software tool to analyze the core-values in collaborative networks still requires further work.

Acknowledgments – This work as supported in part by the ECOLEAD integrated project funded by the European Commission.

6. REFERENCES

1. Abreu A, Camarinha-Matos LM. "On the Role of Value Systems and Reciprocity in Collaborative Environments." In: Spring, ed. IFIP, Volume 224, Network-Centric Collaboration and Suporting Frameworks: Boston Springer, 2006.
2. Afsarmanesh H, Camarinha-Matos LM. "A framework for Management of Virtual Organization Breeding Environments". In: Collaborative Networks and their Breeding Environments: Springer, 2005: 35-48.
3. Barrett R. Building a Vison-Guided, Values-Driven organization, Paperback ed: Butterworth-Heinemann, 2006.
4. Camarinha-Matos L, Macedo P. "Towards a Conceptual Model of Value Systems in Collaborative Networks". In: Establishing the Foundation of Collaborative Networks: Springer Boston, 2007: 53-64.
5. Collins J, Porras J. Building your Company Vision. In: Havard Business Review, 1996.
6. Eden C. On the Nature of Cognitive Maps. Journal of Managemnet Studies 1992;29.
7. Greenland S, Brumback B. An overview of relations among causal modeling methods. International Journal of Epidemiology 2002.
8. Hall B. Values Shift: A Guide to Personal and Organizational Transformation: Resource Publications, 1995.
9. Higgins ET. An Experience that Creates Value. Journal of Cultural and Evolutionary Psychology ,Akadémiai Kiadó 2004;2:9-22.
10. Macedo P, Sapateiro C, Filipe J. "Distinct Approaches to Value Systems in Collaborative Networks Environments". In: Network-Centric Collaboration and Supporting Frameworks: Springer Boston, 2006: 111-120.
11. Rekom Jv, Riel CBMv, Wierenga B. A Methodology for Assessing Organizational Core Values. Journal of Management Studies 2006;43:175-201.
12. Rokeach M. The nature of human values. New York: Free Press. 1973.
13. Schwartz SH. Universals in the content and structure of values: Theoretical advances and empirical tests in 20 countries. Advances in experimental social psychology 1992:1-65.
14. Zineldin MA. Towards an ecological collaborative relationship management A "co-opetive" perspective. . European Journal of Marketing 1998;32:1138 - 1164.

7 QUANTITATIVE ANALYSIS OF THE SOFT FACTOR "COOPERATION CLIMATE" IN COLLABORATIVE NETWORKS

Hendrik Jähn[1]

[1]*Chemnitz University of Technology, hendrik.jaehn@wirtschaft.tu-chemnitz.de,*
GERMANY

In the following an approach for the quantitative inclusion of the soft-factor cooperation climate in the enterprise oriented performance analysis is presented. This quantitative analysis is realised by an adapted value benefit analysis in combination with the Repertory Grid methodology. Through this a comprehensive model representing value-adding process related and value-adding-process neutral phases has been developed. This framework can be integrated in a model for network management and operation. Although the model is of theoretic nature the result give evidence concerning the behaviour of participants in collaborative networks.

1. MOTIVATION

For the composition of successful and pervasive collaborative networks, the cooperation of all network participants is of fundamental meaning. In this connexion, one has to pay attention to the suitability by choosing the partner on the one hand but otherwise needs to include the soft factors in the evaluation. A meaningful consideration of important soft factors here completes the performance analysis of companies. In the following, the soft factor "Quality of Cooperation" will be presented together with possibilities for its entries within the performance analysis. Performance analysis here implies the entry as well as the validation and evaluation of a work performed by a company within a value-adding process. For this purpose, a comprehensive approach has been designed [Jähn 2005], in which the selected performance parameters are analysed in a quantitative form. By aggregation of the single degrees of performance, the result is a benefit measured value, which represents the total quality of a company's performance. In case of insufficient value performance here, the determined capital gains of a company, within an allocation of profits model belonging to the total approach [Jähn, 2007], can be reduced.

2. OPERATIONALISATION

The soft factor "Quality of cooperation" together with the performance parameter "Cooperation climate", can excellently be described as the totality of characteristics and attributes of a product or operations, which refer to its adequacy to complete given requirements. The product, in this case, is composed out of the cooperation of

Please use the following format when citing this chapter:

Jähn, H., 2008, in IFIP International Federation for Information Processing, Volume 283; *Pervasive Collaborative Networks*; Luis M. Camarinha-Matos, Willy Picard; (Boston: Springer), pp. 65–72.

the companies. The characteristics and attributes will be represented by soft-facts, which describe the quality of the cooperation, while the given requirements represent the target values of the single characteristics. However, a problem of this approach is that the characteristics and attributes of the quality of teamwork are not available in a quantitative form as such attributes describe soft / qualitative factors. Those soft-facts are normally described by linguistic variables which are represented by linguistic expressions like "high", "little" or "middle", alternatively "good" or "bad". Therefore, next to the proper attributes, one has to find a possibility to transfer their qualitative forming into a quantitative value.

Approaches for the integration of soft-facts indeed can be found in different contexts in technical literature, but nevertheless, the quantitative analysis of soft factors always causes problems for scientists. Up to now, some approaches have been identified [Scott, 1991; Burt, 1992], which, however, cannot be used primary, as their evaluation results are unusable in the present case. The here added Repertory Grid methodology counts thereby to the most promising approaches, as there exists a simple proceeding, linked with effective evaluation methods and a high level of acceptance.

Nevertheless, there had to be developed a method, which helps to edit the data, collected by the Repertory Grid methodology, to be able to make a statement with regard to the quality of teamwork between the network participants under the focus of the company, which has to be analysed. For this purpose, the value benefit analysis has been chosen. It makes it possible to determine a weighting aggregated value, according to the meaning of the different aspects, which can directly flow into the weighting function. The next paragraph will focus on the cooperation and successive proceedings of the Repertory Grid method and value benefit analysis, within an investigation of the performance parameter "cooperation climate".

3. PROCEDURE OF THE ANALYSIS

3.1. Overall Concept

First of all, a Repertory Grid questionnaire, including all elements and constructs, which are relevant for the task, needs to be designed. The analysis will eventually take place within the scope of a value benefit analysis, by converting the value benefit into an evaluation function for the performance parameter 'cooperation climate'. Figure 1 shows this procedure. Thus it appears that both used methods can be applied in a neutral or in a specific way concerning the value-adding process. The contents of the single stages of the approach will be explained below.

3.2. Value-Adding-Process Neutral Steps

Determination of Elements
The preparation for the measuring of the performance parameter „cooperation climate" by means of the Repertory Grid method, includes determination of the objects (elements), which need to be evaluated [Fransella, 1977]. It must be pointed out that the number of considered elements should have a reasonable size, as an adequate differentiation will not be possible with a number of elements, which is too low; the evaluation work will be too extensive and the statements will tend to

inconsistencies with a number of elements, which is too high; as a result, the evaluator will lose track. A number between six and twenty-five elements is recommended.

The elements, that need to be considered, involve primarily the companies, which were in direct contact with the analysed enterprises during the value-adding process. This includes all supplying and supplied firms and all administrative companies, which are also necessarily in contact with most producing companies. In order to avoid new identification of relevant elements for every value-adding process and for every company, all firms can be listed in the resources pool, whereas only the contacted firms will be evaluated later on.

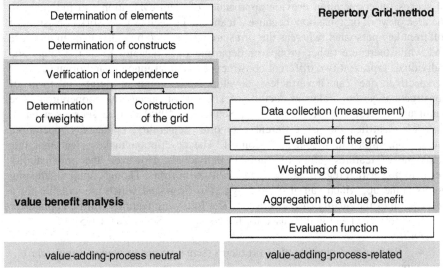

Figure 1: Quantification of the performance parameter 'cooperation climate'

Besides the assessment of the enterprises, the company that needs to be evaluated had contact with during the value-adding process, the Repertory Grid method also provides the opportunity for self-evaluation. From a socio-scientific view, this seems to be absolutely reasonable, as a self-improving process can possibly be initiated through repeating self-reflection. This is especially the case when an enterprise also receives feedback after the evaluation of the questionnaires, containing the information, to which extent its self-evaluation corresponds with the evaluation by the other companies. Additionally, the self-evaluation also provides the opportunity to draw comparisons with the evaluation by other firms and to identify possible mispricing. The self-evaluation can for example be realised through the elements 'me' and 'me – others'.

This possibility does not play a role for the analysis of the 'cooperation climate'. Concluding, one needs to point out the possibility to measure perfection. With a number of elements, which is too high, only the elements with the most intensive contacts should be chosen. For the basic version of a Grid, this option was modified to make a statement regarding the construction of the questionnaires ('Grid') as well as the determination of the planned output possible. This can be achieved through the introduction of the element 'ideal'.

Determination of Constructs

Selected decision makers determine the constructs on their own initiative, herefor for example thetriad method [Fransella, 1977] can be applied. For the measuring of the performance parameter 'cooperation climate', a modified method is necessary, because a comparability with the perfection, the so-called nominal condition, should primarily be achieved through the evaluation. This perfection should basically derive from the strategic orientation of the network and should be determined against this background. On this account, one needs to develop a construct catalogue for the Repertory Grid of the performance analysis at first; on this basis, the quality of the cooperation for all firms can be determined. Indication for the characteristics of successful cooperation provide approaches of team evaluation and judgment in the area of work organisation, because a team can be seen as a network consisting of different key personnel, whereas the firms are represented by individuals in this case and while there are rather groups or departments in a team. Even if groups and individuals represent two different constructs from an ergonomic and organisational perspective, one can nevertheless develop some common points in form of constructs regarding relevant factors of success of successful cooperation. The summary by *Jeserich* [Jeserich, 1991; Schneider, 1995] can be seen as a basis. *Jeserich* identifies the six different categories sensibility, contacts, cooperation, integration, information and self- control. The description makes clear that this catalogue of features refers to (human) individuals. However, the practicability needs to be verified regarding the applicability with firms. Though, some interesting points come up, which can also be assigned to firms and which are suitable for a description of the quality of cooperation. The following features will be applied for the Repertory Grid and will be used for the constructs [Schneider, 1995]:

Sensibility

- Recognizes other people's problems (sensitive for problems \ superficial)

Contacts

- Approaches others on his own initiative (talkative \ uncommunicative)
- Offers consultation (consultative \ denies consultation)

Cooperation

- Helps others, who are in difficulties (selfless \ selfish)
- Does not stand up against others on their expenses (open to compromises \ focused on asserting)
- Informs others of feelings of success (communicates success \ reserved)
- Does not apply instruments of power (convincing \ repressive)

Integration

- Recognizes where and why conflicts develop and looks for solutions (solves conflicts \ creates conflicts)
- Orientates different interests on one aim (oriented on network \ individualist)
- Defines rules (adheres to rules \ expands rules)

Self-control

- Does not react to attacks aggressively (able to accept criticism \ not able to accept criticism)
- Does not create stress with others (aspires harmony \ rebellious)
- His mood can be predicted (predictable \ moody)

One can see that many descriptions have only been summarised to one term. Partly, the descriptions have also been used as an association basis to reason on further important quality features regarding cooperation in the network. If the number of considered constructs seems to be too high, one can aspire a summing up in construct categories. Construct categories unit various similar constructs and will be treated as analog to constructs further on.

Verification of independence of Constructs

A further value-adding process neutral step focuses on the verification of the constructs regarding independence. Both, reciprocal preference independence and difference independence of the constructs is essential due to two points. On the one hand independence must be verified to make an application of the value benefit analysis with the additive model possible; on the other hand will this be the condition for the determination of the weighting with established methods. A consistent Grid is guaranteed additionally. In case independences of constructs could be determined, those must be eliminated with proper methods. The most effective method is a summing up of the construct categories. After the summing up, a new verification on independence will be essential until it can be verified doubtlessly.

Determination of weightings of Construct Categories

To get a significant result regarding the degree of performance of the performance parameter 'cooperation climate', the single constructs respectively if needed the construct categories will be assessed according to their importance. For this, the weighting of the single constructs, respectively construct categories, must be determined. This can be realised with an established method like the Trade-off-method [Eisenführ, 2003]. The identified weightings can be used over a longer time period, but should be checked from time to time regarding plausibility and suitability by means of recalculation and should be corrected if required.

Construction of the Grid

After this verification regarding independence of constructs respectively construct categories, the questionnaire (Grid) can be designed, independent from the determination of the weighting. For this, elements and constructs / construct categories will be brought together in the form of a matrix, whereas the elements will be put into columns and the constructs into rows. In this way, a rough questionnaire of the Repertory Grid is created; an example is displayed in figure 2.

It gets obvious that every construct category is represented by different constructs, whereas dependence within a construct category is unproblematic, because the result will only be considered for the evaluation of the Grid for every construct category in an aggregated form. The central factor of success for the data collection by means of the Grid is the cooperation of all firms, which have participated in a value benefit process in the production network. Basically one must assume that the effort, which is needed for filling in the Grid, will be felt as a negative burden. This relates to the expenditure of time and work, which causes costs. From this perspective, firms must already be convinced at the point of the admission into the resource pool that cooperation is absolutely necessary and that it is normally positive. To keep the effort for the firm low, it is recommended that the number of constructs is minimised to a justifiable amount, as displayed in figure 2. However, the number of constructs automatically results from the number of contacted firms.

It is also important to develop a proper scale for the evaluation of the constructs in terms of characteristic values. Application of three discreet gradations for the feature pole and the antipole of the constructs are common for the Repertory Grid method and also thinkable for the given domain; whereas '3' expresses the strongest value in the feature pole and '-3' expresses the strongest value of the antipole. The possibility of a neutral valuation by using zero must be discussed; if this is not possible, no neutral valuation can be made. However, neutral valuation is permitted in the given case. Therefore, an evaluation scale consisting of seven evaluation possibilities for every construct is designed. It must be emphasized that a valuation with '-3' cannot be automatically considered the worst and „3" cannot be considered the best, but represents a quantified statement regarding the value. Consequently, the feature pole cannot be interpreted as positive and the antipole as negative. The actual aspired valuation will be made possible by the element „ideal". This valuation will be hold by selected decision makers, e.g. by representatives of single firms, also independent from a certain value-adding-process and therefore on a long-term basis. The element „ideal" does not need to be ranked with the extreme valuations '-3' or '3' necessarily; theoretically, every valuation, also a neutral one (0), is possible. With this high degree of flexibility, problems can occur regarding the evaluation, which will be dealt with in detail in the next but one paragraph 'Evaluation of the Grids'.

In this way a Repertory Grid questionnaire ('Grid') is created, which is generated by the network management for every firm, which takes part in a value-adding-process. After the completed formulation of the Grid, all conditions for the value-adding-process related application of this method are fulfilled.

Attribut Pole	Ideal	Actor 1	Actor 2	Actor 3	Actor 4	Network-Coach	Antipole
sensitive for problems							superficial
talkative							uncommunicative
consultative							denies consultation
selfless							selfish
open to compromises							focused on asserting
communicates success							reserved
convincing							repressive
solves conflicts							creates conflicts
oriented on network							individualist
adheres to rules							expands rules
able to accept criticism							unable to accept criticism
aspires harmony							rebellious
predictable							moody

Figure 2: Repertory Grid for 'cooperation climate'

3.3. Value-Adding-Process Specific Steps

Collection of Data

Regarding the operational structuring of the performance analysis in picture 1, the data collection must be assigned to the stage of measuring. The specialty is that a complete automatisation with the soft factors is not possible and therefore, a manual collection is needed. After completion of the value-adding process, the involved firms are supplied online with the Grid, which must be completed within a proper time slot and can be filled in online as well. Representatives of the single firms will complete the matrix with the evaluation numbers for the contacted firms and for all constructs in the given area and afterwards, they will forward this to the network management. Upon receipt of all Grids, the evaluation process can begin.

Evaluation of the Grids

After return of the Grid, detailed information will be available. Normally, evaluations by various firms are available for the analysed elements (firms). It is important to make the figures of the calculation of a firm-specific aggregated performance measured value (value benefit of the performance parameter 'cooperation climate') amenable in a proper way. Different approaches are possible for this. In principle, the evaluation of the Grid can be performed by means of IKT, as all needed data is available. This process represents a pre-stage for the actual performance evaluation.

The most common methods for the evaluation of the Repertory Grid questionnaires are the manual evaluation, the cluster- and principal component analysis [Raeithel, 1993; Fransella 1977]. Those methods primarily focus on the clinical-diagnostic aspect of the Repertory Grid method, as similarities regarding evaluation of elements are identified. In this context, the manual evaluation is the simplest method. As a quantitative consideration is the objective, the manual evaluation cannot be applied. The cluster analysis gives useful motivation through its quantitative orientation for the analysis of the Grid in the given context. Especially the consideration of distances with both methods seems a reasonable approach, although the desired results are different. So the deviation of the nominal output from the actual output regarding the performance analysis with the single constructs respectively construct categories comes to the fore. As this also applies to the soft factors, the nominal output must be defined and the actual output must be compared with the nominal output. The actual output is measured by means of questionnaires; the nominal output can be determined by means of a survey in advance. By contrast, the elements are compared with the mentioned 'classic' evaluation method. Regarding the performance analysis, elements which represent the nominal output, can be compared with elements which represent the actual output. Here, the distance measures play an important role.

Weighting of Constructs respectively Construct Categories

As mentioned before, single construct categories are available for the specific weightings. These weightings can be applied regarding the aggregation into a firm-specific value benefit. The determination of the weightings can take place by using a suitable method (e.g. Trade-off-method) being performed by entitled decision makers [Eisenführ, 2003]. From an operational structuring view of the performance analysis, the determination of weighting of constructs or construct categories can be counted to the evaluation stage.

Aggregation into a Value Benefit

Even the aggregation into a value benefit of the performance parameter 'cooperation climate' belongs to the evaluation stage. Through multiplication of the weightings of the single construct categories with the single characteristic values of the construct categories and through adding together those figures, it is possible to get an overall statement regarding the performance parameter 'cooperation climate'. The result is a numerical value without measurement, which represents the value benefit of the performance parameter 'cooperation climate' of a firm covering all construct categories. This value can be made amenable directly with an evaluation function of the firm-based performance analysis.

3.4. Generation of an evaluation function

After determination of the value benefit, one needs to determine a suitable evaluation function for the 'cooperation climate'. It should be considered, which developing of the value benefit function gives a realistic respectively a desired picture. The interpretation of the value benefits complies with the environmental conditions, the intentions of the decision makers and last but not least with the measure of the available data. As the value benefits can be put into a certain interval depending on the scaling, it stands to reason to takes those values as a proper evaluation, so that a linear relation between the value benefit and the evaluation of this performance parameter seems to be reasonable and so that one only needs to perform a standardisation on values between zero and ten for the evaluation. This value directly goes into the calculation of the overall performance of a firm.

4. CONCLUSION

The consideration of soft factors regarding the performance analysis is essential. Using the example of 'cooperation climate', a theoretical approach is introduced, which allows a quantitative collection, evaluation and analysis of the collected data is possible. The result in the form of an aggregated measured value can be included in an integrated concept of the performance analysis [Jähn, 2005]. For the realisation of the approach, collecting of 'Real-World-data' is indispensable. With the collection of the evaluations of the constructs, assumed as ideal, data is already available. In the next step, the results of the approach must be verified and evaluated by means of assessment of network members. At this stage of work in already can be concluded that applicability within an operator concept for networks is possible.

5. REFERENCES

1. Burt R.S. Structural Holes. New York: Cambridge University Press, 1992.
2. Eisenführ F, Weber M. Rationales Entscheiden. 4th ed. Berlin, Heidelberg, New York: Springer, 2003.
3. Fransella F, Bannister D. A manual for repertory grid technique. London New York San Francisco: Academic Press, 1977.
4. Jähn H, Fischer M, Zimmermann M. An Approach for the Ascertainment of Profit Shares for Network Participants. In Collaborative Networks and their breeding Environments. Camarinha-Matos L.M. et al.,eds. Boston: Springer, 2005; 257-264.
5. Jähn H, Fischer M, Teich T. Distribution of network generated profit by considering individual profit expectations. Camarinha-Matos L.M. et al.,eds. Boston: Springer, 2007; 337-344.
6. Jeserich W. Mitarbeiter auswählen und fördern – Assessment-Center-Verfahren. 6th ed. München, Wien: Hanser, 1991
7. Raeithel A. Auswertungsmethoden für Repertory Grids. In: Einführung in die Repertory Grid Technik, Band I: Grundlagen und Methoden. Scheer J.W. et al., eds. Bern, Göttingen, Toronto, Seattle: Huber, 1993.
8. Schneider H, Knebel H. Team und Teambeurteilung: Neue Trends in der Arbeitsorganisation. Köln: Wirtschaftsverlag Bachem, 1995.
9. Scott J. Social Network Analysis. London: SAGE, 1991.

PART 3

VALUE CREATION IN NETWORKS

VALUE CREATION ELEMENTS IN LEARNING COLLABORATIVE NETWORKED ORGANIZATIONS

Leandro Loss, Alexandra A. Pereira-Klen, Ricardo J. Rabelo
Federal University of Santa Catarina, Department of Automation and Systems
GSIGMA – Intelligent Manufacturing Systems Group, BRAZIL
{loss,klen}@gsigma.ufsc.br
rabelo@das.ufsc.br

Organizations that work in strategic alliances, also known as Collaborative Networked Organizations (CNOs), learn with this experience. The whole learning process in which they are involved with is rich, creates value for the alliance and should be better explored in order to improve the CNO partners' performance when facing new challenges. The core content of this work is related to the characterization of value creation elements that support the learning process in a CNO environment. These elements create value for the entire alliance in the technological, organizational and human perspectives and hence contribute to the learning process and to the preparedness of CNOs.

1. INTRODUCTION

Approximately over the last ten years several researchers have developed frameworks, reference models, techniques, and tools in order to support business in strategic alliances (Child, 2003). The core idea behind the concept of such strategic alliances, also known as Collaborative Networked Organizations (CNO) (Camarinha-Matos and Afsarmanesh, 2006), is that organizations working together are stronger than when working only by themselves or isolated. As a result organizations may share responsibilities, risks, profits, improve their work power, market share and become more competitive.

At the same time, while such studies evolve, new challenges appear. Actually, the scope and the complexity of related activities have achieved a new degree of complexity when considering inter-organizational operations. Innovative approaches have been developed in order to attend to this emergent need. As a consequence of this rapid development and efficiency improvement, adequate resources and knowledge are required. However, very often resources are not available or there is a lack of adequate knowledge for carrying out inter-organizational tasks which are based on distributed and collaborative business processes.

The fact is that it is very hard to succeed in the establishment of strategic alliances where everything happens according to what was originally planned. There are many variables involved in this context and there is not a single way to predict or to be ready to foresee all possible problems. An important but quite few explored research area is related to the **learning** capacity that networked organizations intrinsically have. This learning is not only related to the organizational learning perspective of one single organization, but rather it is also related to the learning

Please use the following format when citing this chapter:

Loss, L., Pereira-Klen, A.A. and Rabelo, R.J., 2008, in IFIP International Federation for Information Processing, Volume 283; *Pervasive Collaborative Networks*; Luis M. Camarinha-Matos, Willy Picard; (Boston: Springer), pp. 75–84.

capacity of all partners involved in the alliance. Additionally, other parameters that should be also taken into account refer to the capacity of the entire network to learn with its own experience and with the experience of others, and, even more relevant, the ability to create value to the entire alliance.

In this sense, it is important to advance the literature about learning in strategic alliances towards elements to foster value creation in those alliances. Such value will help to understand partners' behavior, concepts involved in collaboration opportunities, and in cooperation processes. Value creation may also support stronger foundations and the preparedness required to create dynamic alliances, like Virtual Organizations.

Following the idea of Learning based on value creation, three elements are described in this work. This paper is therefore divided as follows: section two presents the concepts of strategic alliances in general, and of Collaborative Networked Organizations, Virtual Organization Breeding Environments, Professional Virtual Communities, and Virtual Organizations in particular. Section three defines the concept of Learning CNOs as well as the characterization of supporting tools and techniques taking the value creation elements into consideration. Finally, section four presents some preliminary conclusions.

2. STRATEGIC ALLIANCES

One alternative that has arisen in order to help organizations to become more competitive is to join competences, work power, and knowledge. This may become true via alliances. By definition (Oxford, 2000), an alliance is *"an agreement between countries, political parties, etc. to work together in order to achieve something that they all want"*. It means sharing risks and benefits (profits) when facing new collaboration opportunities. Thus, a strategic alliance (also known as business partnering) may be understood as a formal relationship that grows up between two or more parties to pursue a set of agreed goals or to meet a critical business (Lendrum, 1997). It is important to highlight that during a strategic alliance, participants remain as independent organizations (Doz, 1998).

Strategic alliances are not new in society. They have appeared over the years in many areas, including politics, trade, humanitarian support, among others. However, this field has increased its importance nowadays due to its empowerment by the Information and Communication Technologies (ICT) (Castells, 2006). ICT infrastructures have provided more reliable communication channels and higher interconnectivity between organizations (B2B approaches), between organizations and people (B2C approaches) and even among people by ordinary instant messaging tools.

Strategic alliances also may vary from a vast amount of manifestations. According to Child and Faulkner, (1998) and Child (2003), strategic alliances range from contract-based manifestations (like *joint ventures, holdings, consortia*) and *supply chains* (Gaspareto, 2003), to less formal or more dynamic collaboration forms (like Virtual Organizations (VOs) and Virtual Enterprises (Camarinha-Matos *et al.*, 2005).

The discipline that studies such diversity of forms of collaboration is called Collaborative Networks (Camarinha-Matos and Afsarmanesh, 2006), and it comprises a variety of entities that includes people, companies or non-profit organizations that are not necessarily settled in the same country or region. They are also largely autonomous and heterogeneous. This heterogeneity also considers different environments and culture of each involved entity (Camarinha-Matos and Afsarmanesh, 2007). According to Camarinha-Matos and Afsarmanesh, (2006), collaborative networks that have some kind of organization (e.g. ethical code, rules, and roles) are called Collaborative Networked Organizations (CNOs).

In the ECOLEAD Project (2006), three main manifestations of CNOs have been more deeply studied, which are *Virtual Organizations, Virtual Organizations Breeding Environments,* and *Professional Virtual Communities.*

The term **Virtual Organization** (VO) is defined indistinctly by many authors. Wassenaar (1999) relates VOs with theories from electronic commerce (*e-commerce* and *e-business*). Strausak (1998) considers VOs as informal entities with the participation of many organizations. Others, like Kaihara and Fujii (2006), define VOs as agile and reconfigurable organizations. However, definition for VO that has gained more importance in researches is straightforward related to ICTs infrastructures as they allow overcoming barriers of time and distance among organizations (Eversheim *et al.*, 1998). In this sense Rabelo and Pereira-Klen (2004) define VOs as "*temporary alliances among organizations that come together to share skills or core competencies and resources in order to better respond to new collaboration opportunities as well as to produce value-added services and products, and whose cooperation is supported by computer networks*". Nevertheless, VOs cannot be easily created from a vast mount of organizations where there is no commitment and well defined rules. In order to support the VO creation and launching phases, and to also give some level of preparedness to the organizations, the concept of VBE has emerged.

Virtual Organization Breeding Environment (VBE) is seen as long term association of service enterprises or organizations that work together in order to overcome other obstacles of communication and distance among organizations and that may be in the way of the rapid formation of VOs (Camarinha-Matos and Afsarmanesh 2004). These obstacles include aspects as trust building, contract establishment, business roles and duties, and even cultural differences among the organizations willing to work as a VO.

In a complementary perspective, the **Professional Virtual Communities** (PVCs) combine the concepts of virtual teams and professional communities. The former is related to social systems of networks of individuals and the relationships of these individuals are mediated by ICT tools. The latter is related to the ecosystem where the professionals that are taking part of a certain virtual team may share knowledge, have similar working culture, similar values, among others (Camarinha-Matos and Afsarmanesh 2004). It is possible to correlate Virtual Teams with Virtual Organizations, and PVCs with VBEs.

Much has been developed under the umbrella built by these three CNO manifestations. There are the researches related to trust building (Msanjila and Afsarmanesh, 2006), governance rules (Romero *et al.*, 2007), PVCs management (Crave *et al.*, 2006 and Picard, 2007), ICT support (Tramontin-Jr and Rabelo, 2007), and partner search and suggestion (Baldo *et al.*, 2007), VO performance measurement (Westphal *et al.*, 2007), just to mention some approaches.

Despite all efforts, very few of them have been dealing with the learning issue as well as using it as a way to leverage value creation in CNOs. Next section explores some issues that should be considered in Learning CNO (L-CNO).

3. LEARNING CNOs

The concept of Learning Collaborative Networked Organization (L-CNO) is seen as the ability that a CNO has to gather its experience and its existing and new knowledge for value creation along the CNO's life-cycle. This concept fits better to long-term associations like VBEs and PCVs as knowledge produced by short-term manifestations (like VO) are more volatile and hence more difficult to gather. This means that once VOs are dissolved, the knowledge produced by them can be easily lost or simply remain spread over many partners that have worked together. Even though when VOs emerge from VBEs the problem is that knowledge is usually lost if they are not properly gathered and stored.

The area which has tackled this problem has been called *Virtual Organization Inheritance* (VO-I) (Loss *et al.*, 2006, Karvonen *et al.*, 2007). VO-I is seen as the process of gathering the information and knowledge from past VOs, whereas VO-I Management is the process that manages what has been inherent about given VOs, usually supported by computer systems, for enhancing the CNO behavior (VBE or PCV) (Loss *et al.*, 2007b). It comprises a continuous improvement of business processes and rules, as well as the quality of the final products and/or services.

However VO-I is not concerned with the learning aspect, neither with the value creation in CNOs. An initial work towards a framework for L-CNO was proposed in a previous work (Loss *et al*, 2007b), which was based on VO-I foundations combined with Knowledge Management (KM) and Organizational Learning (OL) areas. This framework's goal aimed supporting CNOs to learn and to create value. In that work two main analysis axes were considered: one axe for dealing with organizational value elements, and the other axe with technological value elements.

In the work presented in this paper, this approach is extended with the addition of more aspects as it was restricted to some specific techniques and tools. An extra axe has been incorporated, which is the human value element. **Figure 1** shows the proposed extension, presenting the three main value elements for L-CNO.

This considers that value creation elements can be represented by (a set of) tools or mechanisms that leverage CNO value creation throughout *collaboration*. These three value creation elements are seen as complementary to each other. It means that L-CNO mechanism is more effective if these three elements are applied together. For example, an organizational procedure may be easier to execute when supported by some computational tool. However, tools do not execute tasks alone, they require human interaction instead. In a complementary perspective, individuals may execute tasks in an easier manner when they have well established rules and procedures. Another important point that is covered by the human value element is the social aspect, which is intrinsically involved in all activities and that impact the CNO learning and value creation.

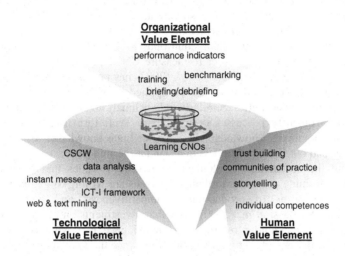

Figure 1 – Value Elements of L-CNO

3.1 Organizational Value Element

In the proposed approach, *briefing* and *debriefing* mechanisms (Loss *et al.*, 2006) are the VO-I instruments used to implement the *Organizational value element*. The former comprises a list of duties and responsibilities that are expected to be executed/done during the VO life-cycle. The latter is a counter-check of this list and it is done either during the life-cycle or at the end of the VO. Milestones are checked during the *debriefing* and the most important issues are recorded. Successful and unsuccessful situations might be noted down for future retrieval. Under the Knowledge Management perspective, *briefing* and *debriefing* cover the distribution, creation and evolution of the knowledge (Loss *et al.*, 2007b). It also supports the creation of economic value by reducing costs when saving time and resources with the results of these mechanisms.

Although *briefing* and *debriefing* are effective, these mechanisms do not gather all the knowledge produced by short-term alliances. In this way, other methods, techniques, and tools shall be taken into account for the L-CNO environment and value creation. These new approaches may be benchmarking, performance indicators, training programs, among others.

According to Vallejos *et al.* (2006), *benchmarking* is a continuous and systematic process used to evaluate enterprises' business processes. It is used in order to establish referential patterns of performance. Likewise *briefing* and *debriefing*, evaluations done in benchmarking processes can be stored and the top ranked can become a referential to the other CNO's partners. In this sense, partners may learn with the knowledge produced by CNO throughout the evolution of practices and processes. Value can then be created when new business processes are executed taking advantage of what has been learnt. Benchmarking can also be applied based on organizations out of the CNO's scope, acting as a target to be reached by the entire CNO. Framing benchmarking to the KM approach, it leads to knowledge creation as every time a new referential pattern emerges (the benchmark) new approaches on how to behave in face to this arise up. As a result, knowledge evolution takes place. Knowledge is also formalized as new practices are written down and made available to other partners.

Another interesting line that can contribute to L-CNOs is the adoption of performance indicators (PIs) in order to measure CNOs performance (Westphal *et al.*, 2007). In a close approach, Baldo *et al*, (2007) has proposed a methodology to select the most suitable PIs that should be applied to VO partners' selection for given collaboration opportunities. Similarly to benchmarking, PIs' values are seen as metrics used to quantify processes or objectives. Well formalized PIs represent formalized and organized knowledge. PIs also facilitate knowledge distribution as they can be spread out CNO's members in a standard terminology.

Still about the organizational element, Steil (2006) argues that organizations which promote training programs to their employees are willing to get back what it was invested in terms of productivity, competitiveness, and higher profits. Researches done by Bassi *et al.* (2000) show that investments on training programs increase the total stockholder return. It is an evidence that what is learned by employees is usually absorbed by the organization since the knowledge gathered by one individual in training activities can be distributed to other partners, fostering the confrontation of experiences and the creation of new knowledge into the CNO. The organizational value element is empowered when supported by tools. Next sub-section brings some tools that can be part of L-CNO environment.

3.2 Technological Value Element

The *technological* value creation element considers the tools that support extraction, storing, access, and distribution of information and knowledge to all interested CNO's members. This leverages the CNO learning by using, spreading, and producing knowledge. In general, the technological creation element comprises ICT Infrastructures (ICT-I). Rabelo *et al.* (2006) presented a distributed ICT-I model where a set of CNO-related services can be accessed on demand, and some of these services can be used as enablers to support the desired information gathering for the CNO learning.

Another approach is data analysis techniques, such as data mining, which can extract hidden patterns from data within CNOs. Despite this approach is valid only for CNOs that store data in structural repositories (e.g. databases), the analysis of a vast amount of data is a powerful ally in several situations, like checking marketing tendencies, which typical have been occurring in the last VOs, which are the most trustful partners according to the different VOs' types of products, and the generation of understandable hypothesis.

In a similar context, there are tools related to Text and Web Mining (Mladenic and Grobelnik, 2003). Text and Web mining techniques are applied in data sources that neither have predefined formats nor are stored in databases. When these techniques are applied to CNOs, they may provide support for retrieving documents and documents' categorization.

Actually, even simple tools for messages exchange like *Windows Live Instant Messenger, Google talk, Skype, Miranda, Pidgn,* among others, shall support the CNO's learning and value creation. Despite their simplicity, they provide peer-to-peer communication hence they are extremely relevant in exchanging knowledge among people instantaneously. Moreover, when history files are stored by users they can be retrieved in the future or also be under analysis of text mining tools (this is, for example, one facility supported by one of the services of that mentioned ICT-I).

A further alternative for fostering CNO learning is the adoption of Computer Supported Cooperative Work (CSCW) tools. These tools are used to coordinate activities among people by the use o computer systems. Besides innumerous applications, these tools can support the creation/elaboration of contracts and facilitate the implementation of electronic contracts (*e-contracts*). *E-contracts* also help in defining business activities that are expected to occur as well as sanctions for any deviation from the prescribed behavior. *E-contracts* are framed in L-CNO because they can be an important type of information from where knowledge can be generated to help in future businesses.

3.3 Human Value Element

According to Jonassen (1996), when dealing with organizations, one should not only take care of technological or organizational aspects, but also of their integration with human aspects regarding that individuals are the core of any organization.

With the aim of encouraging the knowledge exchange in an informal way and the trust building, another part of the research described in Loss *et al.* (2007a) has proposed the use of Communities of Practice (CoPs). The authors argue that CoPs act as a mechanism for trust building among CNO's partners based on the assumption that knowledge is more easily exchanged when done among people who know and trust to each other.

Another interesting strategy is the storytelling technique (Snowden, 2001). It is used for promoting dissemination of knowledge among people, for building trust, and for creating cultural value. Snowden claims that storytelling reveals patterns of culture and behavior about organizations lives and this is a way to manage the communication flow and understanding within an organization. If applied in the context of L-CNO, storytelling can be very useful to disseminate best practices in a CNO due to its easy understanding. According to Brown and Duguid (2001), much of the existing knowledge in working groups (like CNOs) comes from their stories. Brown and Duguid (2001) argue that the constant storytelling about problems, solutions, failures and reasons, and triumphs that happens over breakfast, lunch, and coffee, can also server to a number of purposes and others' situations.

Nevertheless, individual competences shall not be forgotten when considering an L-CNO environment and value creation. Competence is seen a set of knowledge that comprise a certain subject. Competences are extremely linked to the tacit knowledge of each individual, to the individual's abilities (physical or mental) related to certain tasks, to the values, and even to the social relationship with other people around. Whenever people are encouraged to improve their competences, the benefits of this personal growth can reflect in the CNO improvement as well. New forms of acting are absorbed by the CNO throughout people's abilities, knowledge and culture.

As one may note, the human value creation element is closely related to the organizational value creation element, and both are supported by the technological value creation element. These three elements support the value creation in CNOs and are enablers to fostering a Learning CNO environment.

4. CONCLUSIONS

This paper has presented the key elements for supporting CNOs learning. The involved processes consider three complementary perspectives. Extending a previous work, the organizational and technological value creation elements were improved. Methods and tools such *benchmarking*, performance indicators, and training programs were added to the organizational value element. For the technological value creation element, tools such as text and web mining, instant messengers, and CSCW were considered. Besides these two value creation elements, a third one was brought up to light: the human value creation element. Its facilitators are composed by communities of practices, trust building, storytelling, and individual competences.

It is important to highlight that the organizational and technological value creation elements shall be seen as a set of mechanisms that may be used to improve the efficiency in disseminating and combining data. When they are merged and properly used by individuals (human value element) they can support the L-CNO concept and create value in/to the entire CNO.

The proposed model provides methodologies and tools that can be used for managing best practices and spreading them out to all CNOs' members, which creates a virtuous cycle of learning and hence enhance CNO competitiveness.

Next steps of this research include the investigation of the influence of corporate governance in learning; the characterization of environments where knowledge can be easily shared; the investigation of the relation learning and CNO; and an empirical study using the framework in a real case.

4.1 Acknowledgments

This work has been developed in the scope of the Brazilian IFM project (www.ifm.org.br) and the European IST FP-6 IP ECOLEAD project (www.ecolead.org).

5. REFERENCES

1.   Bassi, L.; Ludwig, J.; McMurrer, D.; Buren, M.; 2000. Profiting from Learning: Do Firms' Investments in Education and Training Pay Off? Research White Paper. *American Society for Training and Development*, 2000.
2.   Baldo, F.; Rabelo, R. J.; Vallejos, R. V.; An Ontology-Based Approach for Selecting Performance Indicators for Partners Suggestion. In: Establishing the Foundation of Collaborative Networks. Camarinha-Matos, L. M.; Afsarmanesh, H.; Novais, P.; Analide, C.; (eds) Springer, p 187-196.
3.   Brown J. S; Duguid, P.; Balancing Act: How to Capture Knowledge without Killing It. In: Harvard Business Review on Organizational Learning. *Harvard Business School Publishing* Boston, p 45-60.
4.   Camarinha-Matos, L. M., Afsarmanesh, H.; 2004. Collaborative Networked Organizations: A Research Agenda for Emerging Business Models. Kluwer Academic Publishers, Norwell, MA, USA.
5.   Camarinha-Matos, L. M., Afsarmanesh, H., e Ollus, M.; 2005. Virtual Organizations: Systems and Practices. Springer, Norwell, MA, USA.

6. Camarinha-Matos, L. M. e Afsarmanesh, H.; 2006. Collaborative networks: Value creation in a knowledge society. In PROLAMAT conference, eds. Wang, K., Kovács, G. L., Wozny, M. J., e Fang, M., volume 207 of IFIP, (Boston: Springer) pp 26–40.
7. Camarinha-Matos, L. M., Afsarmanesh, H.; 2007. A Comprehensive Modeling Framework for Collaborative Networked Organizations. *Journal of Intelligent Manufacturing*. 18:529-542.
8. Castells, M.; 2006. A Sociedade em Rede, volume 1. Paz e Terra, 9a. edição.
9. Child, J., Faulkner, D., 1998. *Strategies of Cooperation*. Oxford: Oxford University Press Inc.
10. Child, J.; 2003. Learning Through Strategic Alliances. Eds. Dierkes, M., Antal, A. B., Child, J., e Nonaka, I., Handbook of Org. Learning and Knowledge. Oxford University Press Inc. pp 657-680.
11. Crave, S.; Bouron, T.; Ladame, S.; 2006. Using Social Capital as a Conceptual Framework for Professional Virtual Communites Formalization.. In Camarinha-Matos, L. M., Afsarmanesh, H., e Ollus, M., (eds); Network-Centric Collaboration and Supporting Frameworks. Helsinki, Finland, volume 224. Springer. pp 371-378.
12. Doz Y. L., Hamel G., Alliance Advantage. The art of Creating Value through Partnering, Harvard Business School Press, Boston, 1998.
13. ECOLEAD 2006. European Collaborative Networked Organizations Leadership Initiative. Technical report D21.4a - Characterization of VBE Value Systems and Metrics, March 2006.
14. Eversheim,W., Bauerhansl, T., Bremer, C., Molina, A., Schuth, S., Walz, M.; 1998. Configuration of Virtual Enterprises based on a Framework for Global Virtual Business. In: Sieber, P. and Griese, J., (eds), Organizational Virtualness - VONet - Workshop, pp 77–83, Simowa Verlag. Simowa, Verlag Bern.
15. Gaspareto, V.; 2003. A systematic approach for supply chain performance evaluation [in Portuguese]. PhD Thesis, Department of Production Engineering, Federal University of Santa Catarina, Brazil.
16. Jonassen, D.; 1996. The use of new information technologies in distance education and constructiuve learing [in Portuguese], INEP, pp.16-70.
17. Kaihara, T.; Fujii, S.; 2006. Game theoretic negotiation strategy for virtual enterprise with multiagent systems. In Camarinha-Matos, L. M., Afsarmanesh, H., e Ollus, M., (eds); Network-Centric Collaboration and Supporting Frameworks. Helsinki, volume 224. Springer. pp 439–448.
18. Karvonen, I., Salkari, I., Ollus, M., 2007. Identification of Forms and Components of VO Inheritance. In IFIP International Federation of Information Processing, Volume 243. Establishing the Foundation of Collaborative Networks; eds. Camarinha-Matos, L., Afsarmanesh, H., Novais, P., Analide, C. (Boston: Springer), pp 253-262.
19. Lendrum T., The Strategic Partnering Handbook, A Practice Guide for Managers, McGraw-Hill, Nook Company, 1997.
20. Loss, L., Pereira-Klen, A. A., Rabelo, R. J., 2006. Virtual Organization Management: An Approach Based on Inheritance Information. In: .Global Conference on Sustainable Product Development and Life Cycle Engineering.. Oct 03-06. São Carlos, SP, Brazil.
21. Loss, L.; Schons, C. H.; Neves, R.M.; Delavy, I. L.; Chudzikiewicz, I. S.; Vogt, A. M.; 2007a. Trust Building in Collaborative Networked Organizations Supported by Communities of Practices. In: Establishing the Foundation of Collaborative Networks. Camarinha-Matos, L. M.; Afsarmanesh, H.; Novais, P.; Analide, C.; (eds) Springer, pp 23-30.
22. Loss, L.; Pereira-Klen, A. A., Rabelo, R. J.; 2007b. Towards Learning Collaborative Networked Organizations. In: Establishing the Foundation of Collaborative Networks. Camarinha-Matos, L. M.; Afsarmanesh, H.; Novais, P.; Analide, C.; (eds) Springer, pp 243-525.
23. Mladenic, D.; Grobelnik, M.; 2003. Text and Web Mining. In Mladenic, D., Lavrac, N., Bohanec, M., Moyle, S., (eds); Data Mining and Decision Support: Integration and Collaboration. Kluwer Academic Publishers, The Netherlands. pp 15-22.
24. Msanjila, S. S.; Afsarmanesh, H.; 2006. Assessment and Creation of Trust in VBEs. In: Network-Centric Collaboration and Supporting Frameworks. Camarinha-Matos, L. M.; Afsarmanesh, Ollus, M..; (eds) Springer, pp 161-172.
25. Oxford; 2000. Advanced Learners Dictionary of Current English. Oxford University Press.
26. Picard, W.; 2007. Support For Power in Adaptation of Social Protocols for Professional Virtual Communites. In: Establishing the Foundation of Collaborative Networks. Camarinha-Matos, L. M.; Afsarmanesh, H.; Novais, P.; Analide, C.; (eds) Springer, pp 363-370.
27. Rabelo, R. J., Pereira-Klen, A. A.; 2004. Collaborative Networked Organizations: A Research Agenda for Emerging Business Models, capítulo A Brazilian Observatory on Global and Collaborative Networked Organizations. In Collaborative Networked Organizations: A Research Agenda for Emerging Business Models (eds) Kluwer Academic Publishers, pp 103-112.

28. Rabelo, R. J., Gusmeroli, S.; Arana, C.; Nagellen, T.; 2006. The ECOLEAD ICT Infrastructure for Collaborative Networked Organizations. In: Network-Centric Collaboration and Supporting Frameworks. Camarinha-Matos, L. M.; Afsarmanesh, Ollus, M..; (eds) Springer, pp 451-460.
29. Romero D.; Galeano, N.; Molina, A..; 2007. A Conceptual Model for Virtual Breeding Environments Value Systems. In: Establishing the Foundation of Collaborative Networks. Camarinha-Matos, L. M.; Afsarmanesh, H.; Novais, P.; Analide, C.; (eds) Springer, p 43-52.
30. Snowden, D.; Narrative Patterns: the perils and possibilities of using story in organizations. In: Knowledge Management. Vol 4, Issue 10, 2001. pp. 3-14.
31. Steil, A. V.; 2006. Competences and Organizational Learning: how to plan training programs to empower organizations to learn form individual competences [in Portuguese]. Stella Institute, Florianópolis - Brazil, 1st edition.
32. Strausak, N.; 1998. Resume of VoTalk. In Sieber, P. and Griese, J., (eds), Organizational Virtualness - VONet - Workshop, pp 9–24, Simowa Verlag. Simowa Verlag Bern.
33. Tramontin Jr., R. J.; Rabelo, R. J.; A Knowledge Search Framework for Collaborative Networks. In: Establishing the Foundation of Collaborative Networks. Camarinha-Matos, L. M.; Afsarmanesh, H.; Novais, P.; Analide, C.; (eds) Springer, pp 573-582.
34. Vallejos, R. V.; Lima, C.; Varvais, G.; 2006. A Framework to Create a Virtual Org. Breeding Environment in the Mould and Die Sector. In: Network-Centric Collaboration and Supporting Frameworks. Camarinha-Matos, L. M.; Afsarmanesh, Ollus, M..; (eds) Springer, pp 599-608.
35. Wassenaar, A.; 1999. Understanding and designing virtual organisation forms. VoNet Newsletter. Vol. 3, No 1, Berne.
36. Westphal, I.; Thoben, K.; Seifert, M.; 2007. Measuring Collaboration Performance in Virtual Organizations. In: Establishing the Foundation of Collaborative Networks. Camarinha-Matos, L. M.; Afsarmanesh, H.; Novais, P.; Analide, C.; (eds) Springer, pp 33-42.

9 | SUSTAINABILITY OF VIRTUAL COLLABORATIVE NETWORKS

Malgorzata Pankowska
University of Economics Katowice POLAND, pank@ae.katowice.pl

Sustainability exemplifies the new problem field for managers and project leaders in an emergent network-based organizational world where corporations must maintain consistency of purposes and yet be flexible enough to interact and compete in conditions of constant change and flux. The first part of the paper covers the theoretical framework of sustainability of collaborative networks as the simultaneous effort of balancing economic, social and intellectual development goals. The second part comprises the comparative analysis of 181 FP6 projects and the last part presents discussion on ways to increase sustainability.

1. INTRODUCTION

The etymology of "sustainable" carries interesting and important implications for the way the word is used as it includes several contradictions. The word "sustain" is derived form the Latin "sub-tenere", meaning "to uphold". This carries a passive connotation in it and gives the concept an image of stability, persistence and balance. "Sustainable" is used in a more active sense together with "development". Development means change, progress and growth. So, "sustainable development" can refer to a process which is being upheld or defended at the same time as it implies movement and improvement (Sunden & Wicander, 2005). Sustainability and sustainable development are about actions, interactions, cooperation and collaboration in virtual collaborative networks developed as projects.

2. THEORETICAL FRAMEWORK

Sustainable development is the practice of meeting the needs of society today without compromising the ability of future generations to meet their own needs (Russell et al., 2007). Sustainability is a characteristic of a process or state that can be maintained indefinitely at a certain level. The term in its environmental usage, refers to the potential longevity of vital human ecological support systems, such as the planet's climatic system, systems of agriculture, industry, forestry and fisheries, and human communities in general and the various systems on which they depend.

Understanding sustainability is the simultaneous effort of balancing economic, social and environmental goals for a corporate (Bondy et al., 2007). As such, sustainability is another metaphor for describing corporate social responsibility, corporate citizenship or ethical business conduct and for the purpose of the paper sustainability is used as a synonym of these concepts. Sustainable business strategies and processes are roadmaps to achieve sustainability and it is about understanding and considering the positive and negative impacts and minimising the risk of unintended consequences across sustainability dimensions (Ahmed & Sundaram, 2007).

Please use the following format when citing this chapter:

Pankowska, M., 2008, in IFIP International Federation for Information Processing, Volume 283; *Pervasive Collaborative Networks*; Luis M. Camarinha-Matos, Willy Picard; (Boston: Springer), pp. 85–92.

Models of governance for sustainability need to concentrate more on change than on stability, meaning the existing rules, customs, practices and rights are seen as the subject matter of governance to be influenced, rather than as the main business of governance (Martin et al., 2007). Governance refers to self-organizing of the interorganizational networks characterized by interdependence of resource exchange, business rules and significant autonomy from the state (Kjaer, 2007). Each virtual collaborative network develops their own intellectual resources and capabilities, but they alone do not ensure the sustainable advantage. A competitive advantage is sustainable when it persists despite efforts by competitors or potential entrants to duplicate or neutralize it. For this to occur, there must be persistent asymmetries among the networks. They must possess different resources and capabilities. Resource heterogeneity is the cornerstone of an important framework in strategy: the resource–based theory of the firm, which points out that if all firms in the market have the same stocks of resources and capabilities, no strategy for value-creation is available to one firm that would not also be available to all other firms in the market. To be sustainable, competitive advantage must be followed by resources and capabilities that are scarce and imperfectly mobile (Besanko et al., 2007). Some resources are inherently nontradeable. These include the knowledge an organization has acquired through cumulative experience, or a reputation for toughness in its competition with rivals. Other resources may be tradeable, but because they are relationship specific, they may be far more valuable inside one organization than another. Business organizations implement different isolating mechanisms to ensure sustainability, which are generally divided into two distinguished groups i.e. impediments to imitation and early-mover advantages. Impediments to imitation include legal restrictions (patents, copyright protection, trademarks), governmental control over entry into markets (licensing, certifications) and favourable access to inputs by controlling sources of supply (ownership, long-term exclusive contracts). Early-movers advantages cover pioneers' abilities to cumulate experiences, develop reputation and generate network externalities more quickly than rivals.

3. METHODOLOGY AND FINDINGS

A collaborative network is constituted by a variety of entities (e.g. organizations and individuals) that are largely autonomous, geographically dispersed and heterogeneous in terms of their operating environment, culture, social capital and goals. According to Camarinha-Matos et al. sustainable development of collaborative networks needs to be supported by fundamental research leading to the establishment of collaborative networks as a new scientific discipline (2005).

Virtual organizations are temporary alliances of organizations that come together to share skills or core competencies and resources in order to better respond to business opportunities and produce value-added services in computer supported environment. This temporality is not contradictive to sustainability. The main problem of this paper is to explain how virtual collaborative networks prolong and could prolong their vitality and sustainability. Post-modern virtual organizations move beyond the bureaucratic and hierarchical form of organizing. There is no assumption that they consist of a stable set of structures and rules, but quite the opposite. They are an emergent, semantically constructed phenomena consisting of evolving networks of actors (Rasche, 2008).

In each virtual organization project, sponsors expect long-time results that would constitute knowledge and social capital. They want to know, what results will be achievable in the future after finishing the project and how project partners wish to ensure the results' sustainability. In this research, the FP6 participating organizations are evaluated from the point of their convincing commitment towards a deep and durable integration beyond the period of EC support. In FP6 traditional funding instruments of the scientific research community such as Specific Targeted Research Projects (STREPs), Coordination Actions (CAs), Specific Support Actions (SSAs) were implemented as well as more ambitious projects i.e. Integrated Projects (IPs) and the Networks of Excellence (NoE) (table 1).

Table1 - The Sixth Framework Programme (FP6) Instruments

Instru-ment	Purpose	Target Audience	EU covered activities	Average duration	Flexibility	Partnerships increase
IPs	objective-driven research, sustainable development	industry, SMEs, universities, potential end users	research, demonstrations, training, management	36-60	yearly update of work plan	possible through competitive calls
STREPs	objective – driven research, focused on a simple issue	industry, SMEs, universities, research institutes	research, demonstrations innovation based activities, management	18-36	fixed over all work plan	possible
NoE	durable integration of the partners, research activities, sustainable development	industry, SMEs, universities, research institutes	Joint Programme of Activities (JPA) integration, joint research, spreading of excellence, management	48-60	yearly update of work plan	possible through competitive calls
CAs	coordination networking	industry, SMEs, universities, research institutes	research meeting coordination, events, dissemination, management	18-36	fixed over all work plan	possible
SSAs	preparation of the future action, support policies, results dissemination	industry, SMEs, universities, research institutes	meetings, workshop studies, publications, awards, management	9-30	fixed over all work plan	possible

Source: (Classification of the FP6 instruments, 2004)

Particularly, for NoE and IPs, the scope and degree of the effort to achieve integration and the network's capacity to promote excellences beyond its membership, as well as the prospects of the durable integration of their research capabilities and resources after the end of the periods covered by the EC financial contribution are important (table 1). This is to be achieved through the implementation of a Joint Programme of Activities (JPA) aimed principally at creating a progressive and durable integration of the research capacities of the network partners while, at the same time, advancing knowledge on the topic.

To identify the existing practices of virtual collaborative networks sustainability a comparative analysis was set up for a group of 181 networks (Food, 2007). The projects were funded within FP6 TP5 Food Quality and Safety and drew on expertise from such areas as genomics, medicine, information technologies, ethics, environmental, economic and social sciences to achieve their aims. A total of €751 million in funding was injected in research activities in 2002-2006. The supported research activities contributed to the realisation of European Research Area promoting mobility, cooperation and training of scientists and practitioners through the pooling of know-how and expertise.

All the involved networks identified the need for sustainability assurance, but they had very differently implemented practices to deal it and similar actions planned. Many organizations had practices for systematic collection and saving of experience, but also some of them had informal, verbal exchange of experience between managers of similar networks. Some partners measured their performance during the project for the use of management. In some cases the customer required the recording of quality data. In this comparative analysis the following criteria have been accepted:

- Publications: scientific papers, news, newsletters, lay papers
- Links to related projects, other networks and organizations
- Access to the network for partners, registered users and open for all
- Events
- Access to knowledge base
- Surveys and questionnaires for customers
- Training and courses offline and online
- Jobs offers and scholarships.

Table 2 - FP6 TP5 Food Quality and Safety projects in numbers according to comparative criteria

	Publi-cations	Links	Only for partners network	Open network	Events	Know-ledge base	Surveys	Train-ings	Jobs offers
STREPs (total 59)	26	7	12	2	21	4	4	-	1
NoE (total 12)	12	7	4	3	12	2	2	8	7
CAs (total 7)	3	1	-	1	3	-	1	-	-
IPs (total 31)	31	15	13	8	31	9	6	8	7
SSAs (total 72)	37	15	12	22	48	22	6	2	6

Experiences were shared in the networks most often through different events: cooperation meetings, workshops, conferences, symposia, congresses, discussion forums, seminars, exhibitions, training and mobility programmes, board meetings of partly business and partly social character. These can be used to share knowledge, to introduce new members, present the latest news and to discuss ideas for development. Generally, although the projects were funded in 2002-2006, many have still not developed a website or it has been removed and was not placed in the catalogue "Food Quality and Safety" (i.e. 63 out of all).

The 59 STREPs (33%) were designed to gain knowledge or demonstrate the feasibility of new technologies. Available to small and emerging players, they fulfilled an important function for the scientific community, because they financed research on new technologies that do not necessarily have a direct impact on the market. The project partners are involved in realizing from-fork-to-farm strategy to ensure the purity at every stage of the production process, thereby promoting high quality European products on a sustainable basis (e.g. BEESHOP project). STREPs also helped to create recommendations for lifestyles and healthy habits to improve the quality of life of EU citizens. They communicate project results through publications, different events and in closed communities. The REPRO project ensures direct public dissemination and development of three stakeholder integration platforms: an industrial interaction platform, a consumer integration platform and a co-producent brokerage platform. The STREPs: Qalibra and Beneris were revealed as connected complementary projects financed simultaneously. IRRQUAL project on irrigation model development was observed to declare no need to launch virtual network.

The 7 CAs (4%) covered the definition, organization and management of joint initiatives that aimed to avoid duplication of efforts in different countries and sought to build synergies between existing national and international initiatives so as to better integrate European research. Only some of them were involved in publications and events, there was no need for open trainings, staff mobility and exchange of knowledge in closed community.

The 72 SSAs (39%) helped to prepare and support new research activities, so they are not included in Table 2 as not having specified project theme. They aided in the preparation of FP7, encouraging and facilitating participation in European collaborative research efforts. In particular, FP6 Specific Support Actions were directed at the following seven objectives: achieving ERA objectives, promotion of SME participation, stimulating international cooperation, linking with candidate countries, supporting policy development, stimulating exploitation, and contributing to the EU strategy for life sciences and biotechnology. SSAs are involved in developing closed virtual networks (12 projects) as well as open networks (22 projects) (Table 3). The BIOPOP SSAs project sets up a website featuring a virtual city square to promote further public participation in science. Science agora is open to the public to participate in and comment on. There are music games, animations and genetic toys for young children. The DIVERSEEDS SSAs project aims at establishing a communication platform that makes it possible for European researchers and their Asian counterparts to exchange the results of their research. The authorized access pages provide the project information in Wiki format. The ETNA SSAs project builds a network of researchers all over Europe including third countries. The created virtual collaborative network ensures continuous interactions among scientists, research organizations and research programmes. The GMO-COMPASS SSAs project aims to study genetically modified organisms (GMOs) and to establish a European consumer-oriented website providing easy-to-understand information on the safety of GMOs products. The GMO-COMPASS partners develop marketing strategies (offline and online) such as content cooperation with consumer and commercial food-related websites and consumer websites, offering news, interviews, fact sheets, forums, virtual platforms for open dialogues, moderated online discussions to address risk perceptions and consumer expectations on food quality and the safety of GMOs products. The SAFOODNET SSAs project is to preserve the integrity of the food safety area, building a sustainable network promoting the sharing of knowledge in order to prevent risk and develop pilot actions, seminars, regional meetings and local presentations. The FUNCTIONALFOODNET SSAs project is divided into 2 sub-networks: general network and product-specific network to support cooperation among SMEs and strong companies to support healthy food production and advertising. The EPIPAGRI SSAs project declares the feasibility for joint management of the intellectual property of European PROs (Public Research Organizations) to bring them together and to unify for a strategy of raising interest in a European initiative for harmonizing public intellectual property right policies. The aim is to design guidelines concerning research partnership agreements and licensing policies.

The 31 IPs (17%) were designed to deliver new knowledge, a competitive advantage to European industry, and respond to SME needs by integrating and mobilising the critical mass and research activities and resources. In IPs conferences, country reports, international correspondent networks reporting on progress, annual meetings and workshops, forums, reportages and interviews from the laboratory and the field, insights into projects aims and methods of research are applied (i.e. CO-EXTRA project). The EUROPREVALL IP is to explain the demographic patterns for allergies, so the project publications for people without scientific background (lay state-of-the-art papers) as well as review papers and academic position papers are accessible on the IP website.

The 12 NoE projects (7%) were aimed at strengthening excellence by connecting resources and expertise and supporting effective integration and cooperation in the research activities of the network partners, as well as advancing the overall topics of interest. Their proposition is to reach a durable restructuring and shaping and integration of efforts and institutions or parts of institutions, the success of a NoE is not measured in terms of scientific results but by the extent to which the social fabric for researchers and research institutions in a given field has changed due to the project, and the extent to which the existing capacities become more competitive as a result of this change. Interacting activities include coordinated programming of the partner's activities, sharing of research platforms, tools and facilities, joint management of the knowledge portfolio, staff mobility and exchanges, relocation of staff, teams and equipment, reinforcement of electronic communication systems. The sustainability of the NoE is to be achieved at three different levels of partnership i.e. policy, research and dissemination.

For example, EAPGENE NoE accepts spreading of excellence through trainings, technology transfer and knowledge dissemination to the third countries, cross linking with other collaborative networks, ethics and consumer concerns development, evaluation of public concerns and requests, communications through the website for public and for partners, conferences, workshops, newsletters and leaflets. They offer mobility opportunities and links to Knowledge Database Wiki. The objective of EADGENE is to develop the ATO (animal trait ontology) and to develop future projects to increase the value of an ATO for the animal production industry and research. The EPIZONE NoE consortium agreement defines the development of a management structure based on a virtual institute with clear rules and processes, including mechanism for review and assessment and an appropriate administrative support. The virtual institute activities cover diagnostics, intervention strategies, surveillance, epistemology and risk assessment. In ENDURE NoE a virtual laboratory named the European Pest Control Competence Centre was created as a source of knowledge and expertise for supporting public policy makers, regulatory bodies, extension services and other ways to protect stakeholders.

4. SUSTAINABILITY FRAMEWORK

The FP6 guides for applicants do not directly specify how sustainability must be expressed and measured in projects. Evaluation criteria for the projects cover proposal relevance to the objectives of co-operative research, science and technology excellence, potential impact, excellence of the consortium, quality of management, mobilisation of resources (Horizontal, 2003). Each of these criteria concerns sustainability assurance, so the important problem of sustainability is usually addressed in project work packages. Project stakeholders are demanded to reveal if the project demonstrates the effective plan for spreading excellence, exploitating results and disseminating knowledge, including SMEs and organizations outside the collaborative network

This chapter proposes a normative framework for judging the sustainability effects and makes suggestion on how to create virtual network capable of offering a sustainability contribution. The sustainability model integrates the informational, social and economic dimensions of business that helps to understand the complexities and impact of sustainability issues (Table 3).

Table 3 – Sustainability dimensions

Sustainability dimension	Item description
Virtual collaborative network project strategy	Specification of what, for what needs, why, where, when and how project stakeholders want to achieve in the long run
Wide participation and clear, shared purpose	Development of abundant, long-term, mutually beneficial, collaborative relationships and a shared project vision among partners
Information publicly available and used to improve program and reward effort	Dissemination of information on project results in open networks to determine if activities are worth sustaining, continuous updating and rewards from the customer's point of view
Science and technology resources	Obtaining and utilization of technology, material , personnel resources through products commercialisation or continuous sponsoring
Collaborative complementary skills, knowledge, training and mobility opportunities	Self-organization and self-stimulation to further research as well as continuous upgrading project knowledge involving both internal partners and external organizations in order to institutionalize research programs. Sharing knowledge resources with IPR respect
Decision-making distributed power	Development of wide participation in project management, judicious delegation of power to promote ownership
Coordination with current EU science and research policies	Fitting the project into research policy goals and initiatives. Usage of existing institutional processes to meet the project needs
Promotion and marketing	Market the project's value, target resources and apply agile methods of project management to help the project be flexible, hold out in lean times, and take advantages of unexpected opportunities

Modelling these sustainability dimensions is not simple, as they do not have equal weights in the decision-making and operational processes. Modelling each dimension separately does not properly address sustainable development issues as they are interrelated and any change in one dimension influences the others. Modern virtual collaborative network are constantly emerging. They are autopoietic, not in the sense that they do not receive inputs from the environment, but rather that they are self-steering. They steer the inputs in directions they determine themselves in strategy vision. This autopoiesis is to ensure their sustainability. Agile project management support post-modern development of virtual networks, particularly continuous innovativeness, and iterative approach to project implementation, delivering the project results adaptable to customer requirements and in the reliable way.

5. CONCLUSIONS

High quality food production and distribution, GMOs products risks, allergies, adequate nutrition are problems important for all people, so the FP6 TP5 Food Quality and Safety projects results have a wide spectrum of recipients. FP6 instruments enable financial support to develop closed or open collaborative networks. In presented in paper projects, the virtual collaboration was utilized to generate knowledge (included in knowledge bases and publications) and social capital (through links and partner relationships) and this way to ensure virtual network's sustainability. The sustainability as qualitative feature must be measured multi-dimensionally.

6. REFERENCES

1. Ahmed M.D. Sundaram D. A Framework for Sustainability Decision Making System: A Proposal and an Implementation, ICDSS 2007 Decision Support for Global Enterprises, Kapartji S (ed.) http://www.cba.uni.edu/ICDSS2007/
2. Besanko D., Dranove D., Shanley M., Schaefer S. Economics of Strategy, J.Wiley & Sons. London, 2007
3. Bondy K., Matten D., Moon J. "Codes of conduct as a tool for sustainable governance in MNCs". In Corporate governance and sustainability, Benn S. Dunphy D. (eds.) London, Routledge, 2007
4. Camarinha-Matos L.M., Afsarmanesh H., Ollus M.: ECOLEAD: A holistic approach to creation and management of dynamic virtual organizations. Collaborative Networks and Their Breeding Environments, Camarinha-Matos L.M., Afsarmanesh H., Ortiz A (eds.) Springer, NY. 2005, 3-17.
5. Classification of the FP6 instruments, October, 2004, http://cordis.europa.eu/fp6/instruments.htm
6. Food Quality and Safety in Europe, Project Catalogue, European Commission, Brussels, December 2007, http://ec.europa.eu/research/biosociety/food_quality/download_en.html
7. Horizontal Research Activities Involving SMEs, The FP6 Integrating and Strengthening the European Research Area, Brussels, 2003, http://cordis.europa.eu/fp6/instruments.htm
8. Kjaer M., Governance, Cambridge, Polity Press, 2004
9. Martin A., Benn S., Dunphy D. Towards a model of governance for sustainability. In Corporate governance and sustainability, Benn S., Dunphy D. (eds.) London, Routledge, 2007
10. Rasche A. The Paradoxical Foundation of Strategic Management, Physica-Verlag, A Springer company, Heidelberg, 2008
11. Russell S., Haigh N., Griffiths A. "Understanding corporate sustainability". In Corporate governance and sustainability, Benn S., Dunphy D. (eds.), London, Routledge, 2007
12. Sunden S., Wicander G. ICT in Developing Countries: to Be Sustainable or Not – Is That the Question? ISD'2005 Proceedings of the Fourteenth International Conference on Information Systems Development: Pre-Conference, 14-17 August 2005, Karlstad, Sweden, 103-115.

GOING VIRTUAL IN THE EUROPEAN BIOPHARMACEUTICAL INDUSTRY: CONDUCTORS AND OXPECKERS MAKE IT

10

Valérie Sabatier[1,4], Vincent Mangematin[1,2,3], Tristan Rousselle[4]
[1] Univ. Grenoble 2, UMR 1215 GAEL, F-38000 Grenoble, FRANCE
[2] INRA, UMR 1215 GAEL, F-38000 Grenoble, FRANCE
[3] Grenoble Ecole de Management, F-38000 Grenoble, FRANCE
[4] Protein'eXpert, F-38000 Grenoble, FRANCE
valeriesabatier@proteinexpert.com, vincent@grenoble.inra.f, tristanrousselle@proteinexpert.com

In the sector of biopharmaceuticals, the dominant business model remains the one of big pharmas: the vertical integration. However we currently observe in the European biotechnology industry the emergence of new business models. This article studies in particular the cases of an orchestra firm and a repurposing firm, both virtual all along the value chain of drugs.

It shows that being virtual is possible in the European biopharmaceutical industry. Small virtual firms are able to play the role of hub firms in networks. These organizations, despite their small size and limited funding, manage to build networks with academics and industrials, long-run partnerships, and, icing on the cake: the drug development cost should be much lower than big pharmas'.

1. INTRODUCTION

Biopharmaceuticals are drugs derived from biotech research, in contrast with the pharmaceutical industry which is traditionally based on chemistry development. The dominant design is the vertical integration. It is comparable with the organization of the computer industry from the mid eighties (Magretta 1998).

The biotech industry, born in the eighties, reaches today its teenage years. Original organizations appear with clever business models, alternative to the vertical integration. Business Models are pictures of a company that show the way the firm organizes its business along the value chain in order to create and capture value. A value chain is "the linked set of value creating activities all the way through from basic raw material sources for component suppliers to the ultimate end-use product delivered into the final consumer's hands" (Govindarajan V. and Gupta A.K. 2001). Regarding drugs the value chain involves four main consecutive steps leading to the market: research and drug discovery, preclinical studies (animal tests), phase I and II (early human clinical trials) and phase III trials (large human tests). Along this value chain there are three types of actors: academics, pharmas and biotechs. In a global vision academics are focused on the first link for fundamental research and drug discovery; pharmas are present at every step and especially on the last links (phase III and market); most of biotech firms are positioned on the first links of the chain and manage very well the early phases of drug development (see figure 1).

Please use the following format when citing this chapter:

Sabatier, V., Mangematin, V. and Rousselle, T., 2008, in IFIP International Federation for Information Processing, Volume 283; *Pervasive Collaborative Networks*; Luis M. Camarinha-Matos, Willy Picard; (Boston: Springer), pp. 93–104.

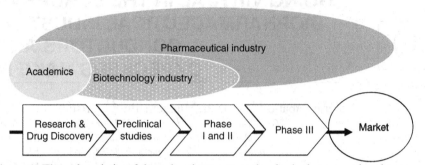

Figure 1: The value chain of drug development: technological steps and main actors.

The value chain of biopharmaceuticals is about 10 years and requires huge investments. The development cost for a new medicine is about US$ 800 million (DiMasi J.A., Hansen R.W. et al. 2003) and US$1.2 billion (DiMasi J. and Grabowski H.G. 2007) for a biopharmaceutical. However these results have to be considered with caution because data come from American large pharmas and four big international biotechs. The business model of all these firms is the full integration: they have internalized all the development steps.

Most of biotech firms born in the eighties were start-ups with a product in their pipeline or a service to sell. There were two main business models: the business model of the product developed in-house for early stage and the business model of the technology platform: a good expertise sold as services.

Focusing on business models we observe that the product model should give rise to several business models which appear since 2000 and by which biotech firms mimic the integrated model. Companies try to cover all the value chain and develop a pipeline of drugs. Despite the fact that fundings are much lower than cash flows available in the pharmaceutical industry to support drug development, some small biotechs have made their way up thanks to reticular organizations: they cover the value chain with a network of partners and suppliers. These firms by themselves do not have real laboratories, manufacturing capabilities or other usual departments of firms; they are virtual. It raises many questions: How do they organize themselves? How do they manage their network? What are the relationships between the actors? How is intellectual property managed? How is value created? How is value captured? Are these virtual firms more efficient than big pharmas? Is the cost of drug development reduced?

To answer these questions two firms that manage pretty well the mimicry of the business model of full integration have been studied: an orchestra firm and a repurposing firm. After a brief presentation of the methodology and the research positioning in the theoretical field, both cases will be detailed. Last part of the article is dedicated to a discussion and a conclusion.

2. METHODOLOGY

This research strategy focuses on understanding the dynamics present within single settings. Therefore the qualitative approach with case studies appears to be the more suitable (Eisenhardt K. 1989). The objective is to detect, characterize and describe new forms of organizations. The aim is not to generalize what is observed and two organizations are chosen precisely because they are very specific: they allow to gain certain insights that other organizations would not be able to provide (Siggelkow N. 2007). In order to determine a choice of sample, an exploratory study is done with opinion leaders in the European biotechnology industry. It includes the scientific director of a French international competitive cluster, the European vice president of one of the biggest international biotech firms and several CEOs of European biotech SMEs specialized in biopharmaceuticals. They give the trends of biotechnology sector and how they anticipate the future business of drugs. This global view is completed with the monitoring of technical and economical issues of the biopharmaceutical industry. A Chief Executing Officer of a biotech firm is involved in the research. He is interested in the problematic and allows access to the firms targeted. He acts as a trust facilitator (Mesquita L.F. 2007). He takes part in the first step of the study: the meetings with the main founders of the chosen firms. At that moment researchers are only lightly informed about the firms. The trust facilitator is there to observe and point out subjects that could have unfortunately been forgotten. Each interview lasts at least for two hours and depicts the global picture of the firms and their business models. A high level of confidentiality is assured to have access to strategic information.

The second phase is dedicated to documents analyses. Internal sources are crossed with documents found on specialized press and websites. Special attention is paid to websites when the company is not public: the repurposing firm is financed by venture capitalists and informs them directly. So the website is principally a showcase. On the opposite, SEC reports and a lot of public information are available for the European orchestra firm since it is quoted on the NASDAQ.

The third phase is the moment of deep interviews. Regarding the orchestra firm the CEO, the CSO (Chief Scientific Officer) and the CFO (Chief Financial Officer) are interviewed and for the repurposing firm it is the CEO, the CFO and the COO (Chief Operating Officer). Each individual interview lasts for one hour and half. Notes are taken during interviews. Then an oral report is recorded at the very end of the visit in order to remind the maximum of information as well as opinions and impressions. Finally longs and rich monographs are written with every detail and information. In conclusion all arguments are directly extracted from raw material.

3. LITERATURE REVIEW

The research question has its origin in the concept of hub firm. Dhanaraj and Parkhe (2006) explain that hub firms orchestrate network activities to ensure creation and extraction of value created among innovation networks. A hub firm is *"one that possesses prominence (Wasserman & Galaskiewicz, 1994) and power (Brass & Burkhardt, 1993) gained through individual attributes and a central position in the network structure, and that uses its prominence and power to perform a leadership role in pulling together the dispersed resources and capabilities of network members"* (Dhanaraj C. and Parkhe A. 2006). They study hub firms in networks that are loosely coupled coalitions (Provan K.G. 1983) as it is the case in biotechnology field. On Dhanaraj and Parkhe assumption a hub firm increases network innovation output if it manages to organize good knowledge mobility and the right innovation appropriation in accordance with the participation of each of actors. This outstanding article gives to the present research subject a strong support: a good framework and an invitation to study the concept in small firms. The hub firm, conceptualized such as they do, is a big firm. The same review can be done for the concepts of flagship firm (Rugman A. and D'Cruz J. 1997) or central firms (Lorenzoni G. and Baden-Fuller C. 1995). The orchestrator of the network is always seen as a big company. So we will look from a practical point of view if a small firm can play the role of the hub firm.

Proposition 1: A small firm can play the role of hub firm.

The perspective of drug development implies that a company masters all the technological steps. For a small firm it appears impossible: it requires a lot of people, laboratories, competences, from early discovery to market production. The only issue is to outsource a maximum to a network of partners, allies or suppliers, in other words, becoming a virtual firm. Thus, being in a network will bring all the competences as well as facilities needed. The term virtual firm is often associated to a firm doing business by internet or utilizing electronic capabilities that make it possible to respond and collaborate in more flexible manners and to organize activities in ways that were not previously possible (Cooper W. and Muench M. 2000), for example e-business development is technology based. Although the firms studied are not e-business firms it is true that electronic capabilities as well as emails and internet tools will help connecting people in the network. Furthermore virtual firms have sometimes been considered in the literature like a permanent network of independent organizations (Weisenfeld U., Reeves J.C. et al. 2001). The term virtual firm will define here a small biotech firm, outsourcing most of its activities to an array of partners (Chesbrough H.W. and Teece D.J. 1996). We will examine if a virtual firm can play the role of hub firm along the value chain of drugs.

Proposition 2: A small virtual firm can be the hub firm of a network.

If a virtual firm manages the development of a drug with a network of partners the firm should get the best of competences in every domain and avoid the cost of learning. A virtual firm should be far superior to the monolithic and pyramid-shaped corporate structure because it takes technologies and skills in core business of each company of the network (Bigras, 2002). Advantages of virtual firms result from the "networked intelligence" they enable among the flexible components that comprise them (Sawhney M. and Parikh D. 2001). In addition, other costs can be saved because there are no heavy investments for laboratories or manufacturing capabilities and few costs of staff. Next, a good orchestration should leads to good link between the phases and time should be shortened. So we state the hypothesis that a virtual firm developing drugs is value creator because of more flexibility, lower fixed costs and better integration of the different phases.

Proposition 3: The cost of a biopharmaceutical developed by a virtual firm orchestrating a network will be lower than the cost of a (bio)-pharmaceutical developed by a big pharma.

These hypotheses are tested using the framework of the business model: structure of the firms (size, age, financing, and governance), links with the other firms of the network (type of relationships, innovation appropriation with intellectual property, information flow, risk sharing, and opportunism), points of value creation (development of the drug, scientific process, management and capitalization of competences) and process of value capture (revenue model, time and cost savings).

4. THE ORCHESTRA FIRM: CASE STUDY OF EMICS

The orchestra firm Emics is product based: it develops a prophylactic vaccine. Emics is a small biotech company based today in Switzerland, made up of three persons: a CEO, a CSO and a CFO. The scientific advisory board is also made up of three scientists and experts in the therapeutic domain. The business model of Emics is the orchestrator model: it develops a drug along the value chain orchestrating a network of partners and suppliers. Emics does not have any laboratory or factory, it is a virtual enterprise.

Emics was founded in France in 1990's. In 2000 it goes through a reverse merger with an American company listed on the NASDAQ. After a series of difficulties a new management team takes over the control in 2003. At that time the firm is already listed on OTCBB[1]. Although it is public there is no liquidity: stocks are not fluid and there is no reserve. From the very beginning, Emics does not have any sales or revenue because it does not sell product or service. The company runs thanks to the contribution of some private investors. The funds are invested in the development of the company's drug pipeline.

The management team is rather experienced. The CEO was an independent business consultant for years. He worked for a firm doing business in the medical field. However he does not have a strong specialization in biotech industry. The CSO worked previously in an academic laboratory within the same therapeutic field where he gains strong recognition. The CFO worked as auditor and consultant in European banks. Since 1991 he evolves professionally in the biotech sector. This "dream team" met when they were all shareholders of Emics. They decided together to save the firm which situation was going from bad to worse. In 2003 they did a kind of putsch and took the control of the company. Emics was already virtual, working with subcontractors to develop drug candidates. The team realigned the scientific project and chose to focus on one prophylactic vaccine, against a worldwide infectious disease.

Since 2003, all efforts are done in order to develop the vaccinal approach. However, Emics had serious financial difficulties. They should have ended up but a providential investor retrieved the situation. In a way, the pathology helped them: it is a worldwide and mortal infectious disease that anyone can catch and no vaccine exists. Investors as well as some of their suppliers were sensitive to the ideological aim.

The vaccine is developed within a network of twelve partners: two strategic industrial partners and two strategic academic partners, plus five industrials and three academics suppliers. A strategic partner is a partner involved in the developed of the vaccine; he exercises a major influence in the project, without him innovation is impossible. The upstream research is done with the academic strategic partners and crucial development steps are done with strategic industrial partners. The others

are service or product suppliers: they are doing the preclinical trials; they produce a
piece of the vaccine, etc. (see figure 2).

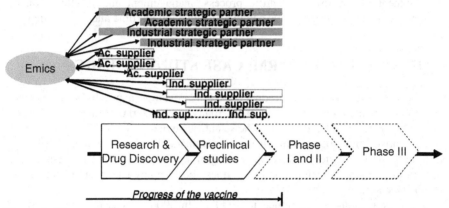

Figure 2: The network managed by Emics and position of actors on the value chain.

Emics interacts with its partners on a long run perspective. But surprisingly relations
are dyadic with every member of the network: there is no contact between the
different firms involved in the process of the drug development. It really looks like
an orchestra: the conductor shapes the process the players do. Each musician plays
his music and although he knows the others are also working, he obeys to the
conductor instructions. He does not need to know exactly what the others do as long
as he follows the conductor. The orchestra firm selects and distributes information.
Emics gives almost all information to the strategic partners but they do not have a
central position: like the others they are only in touch with Emics. The role of the
chief scientific officer is fundamental because he coordinates and controls every
technological step. He is the only in Emics that can follow the vaccine development
and define medical strategies.

Regarding intellectual property Emics owns the patents linked to the vaccine
because it was in the package of the firm when the team took it over. But a vaccine
includes different and specific technologies. When a strategic partner develops a
critical technology for the vaccine, IP is shared with him. The risk is also divided:
when Emics had financial problems its strategic partners accepted to be paid with
stocks and delays. This is even the case with one academic collaborator. This is not
the case with the suppliers like the contract research organization doing the animal
trials: Emics pays in time under the exact terms of the contract.

Value created by Emics comes from many sources. Obviously, the fact that
there is no physical structure leads to weak investments. Next, as the development is
only the CSO's will, decisions are taken quickly. The phases of development are
going one after the other very rapidly. They are doing a lot of savings with the
scientific strategy because reducing time and cost is a very important objective: they
are always on a tight budget. As an example, they watch very carefully at the
scientific results and as soon as one is not concluding they stop it. On the opposite,
big pharmas test simultaneously several strategies and stop it only when the protocol
is over. Next, the ability to choose partners and suppliers is value creator: Emics gets
the best of competences in every domain. Afterwards, another point of value
creation is the way they manage the network: long run relationship, co-development

including risk and IP sharing with strategic partners. These long-run relationships and the sensibility of the academic and biotech SMEs partners for the vocation of the vaccine led to low costs: they sometimes behave like philanthropists. In four years of development Emics spent 7.945 million US$. This is ten times lower than what big pharmas announce from preclinical studies to phase I clinical trial for drugs (see DiMasi et al. 2003). In terms of revenue model Emics forecast a hypothetical exit of the project after phase II. Phase III clinical trials, especially for vaccine development, are huge, longs and expensive. Big pharmas are used to these kinds of trials and this is why there are predominant on the end steps of the value chain. They have competences and cash flows available. Thus Emics hopes for finding a partner or a buyer to lead end clinical trials.

However everything is not so easy for Emics. The management team has difficulties to face the problem of solvability and credibility as an orchestra firm. Because of its size and its limited financial capabilities Emics may have a low bargaining power in front of a supplier but also in the scientific field. The scientific approach of the vaccine is very peculiar and difficult to use to convince new partners. For example they could not convince a big pharma that their approach was good.

Finally, Emics will start first human trials very soon. Their financial situation is in order. Indeed and after a quite long period of hard days, their product recently obtained very good results in preclinical studies on macaques. So investors are more upbeat and support them. Emics keep its way of working. Like a conductor, it indicates to each musician how to play in unison, sending signals to each one of them and being the center of the information flow.

5. THE REPURPOSING FIRM: CASE STUDY OF OPHSMART

OphSmart is a product based firm that develops drugs. It is a small biotech company based in France with an office in USA. OphSmart is made up of thirty persons, including seventeen scientists. The company is governed by a management team, a scientific advisory board and a board of directors. Everybody is located in the offices in France except a person of the management team based in USA.

The business model is twofold: OphSmart pursue some in-house and very upstream research in a long run perspective; and it develops repurposed molecules. The repurposing consists of taking a molecule in development or on the market for another therapeutic domain and positioning it on a new therapeutic domain. In other words a firm takes a molecule outside and intended for example for regenerative medicine and then develops it in another application like Alzheimer disease: the molecule is repurposed. This is what OphSmart did for four products obtained from other companies. This small firm has 4 repurposed drugs in development and 4 molecules in research: it is exceptional for such a small team. OphSmart outsources almost all activities along the drug development chain. The repurposing is the main activity of OphSmart because in-house research requires a small team and most of the company is mobilized in the business of repurposing.

The CEO, founder of OphSmart, has a strong experience in the biotech industry as a scientist, general manager and investor. In 1997 he met an academic, major actor in the therapeutic domain they now both work in. At the end of 2004 they thought that time had come to create OphSmart. They came across another fellow, a well-known business developer. The hardcore of OphSmart was ready and the firm has been founded end of 2005. The business developer is now Chief Operating Officer (COO) and the academic is chairman of the scientific advisory board. The management team is made up of nine persons: the CEO, the COO plus a chief medical officer, a chief financial officer (CFO), a chief business officer, a global project leader, a person in charge of the preclinical development, the administration and finance director and the head of scientific operations. Specifically there is no chief scientific officer. This activity is shared between the chief medical officer, the head of preclinical development and the head of scientific operations.

At the first financial round OphSmart rises more than 20 million Euros. The firm is supported by five investors, venture capitalists. Funds are found quite easily because the business model is very attractive and promises high return on investment on a short run (3 to 5 years) thanks to the repurposing and an in-house research very light in terms of cash burn.

OphSmart's management team is aware of clinical trials in progress in pharmaceutical or biopharmaceutical industry thanks to the large network of contacts they have. This is how they find the molecules to be repurposed.

The network of OphSmart is stable and made of an academic laboratory and many industrial suppliers and partners. The links with the academic partner are very strong. This partner is involved in both processes: repurposing and in-house research. It is the only strategic partner. OphSmart has got a big network of industrials and cultivates redundancy. For example they work regularly with seven firms for the formulation, five for the toxicity of the drug and six for the production of clinical batches. It allows them to have the core competence of each firm but also to go quickly and cheaply through the drug development: they choose the partner in accordance with the competences, the availability at the very moment they need and the price.

The relationships with suppliers are based on the long run. OphSmart manages and regulate the information flow. Like in the previous case relations are dyadic and OphSmart is the central actor of the network (figure 3).

The issue of intellectual property is more subtle because in the repurposing model the molecule is already patented. When a company files a patent application, the company specifies the therapeutic domain. In the repurposing the therapeutic domain is different. So OphSmart patents the same molecule but for another therapeutic domain. Then they negotiate a use-of-patent with the original owner because patents are linked. They pay milestones and royalties to the original owners. Smartly OphSmart convinced the Pharmas to back load most of payments because they were a small biotech. The Pharmas accepted as it was an unexpected outcome for them. They did not forecast a repurposing of their molecule. Among its network of partners, OphSmart shares IP when a critical technological development has to be done but it is rare and OphSmart keeps IP as much as possible.

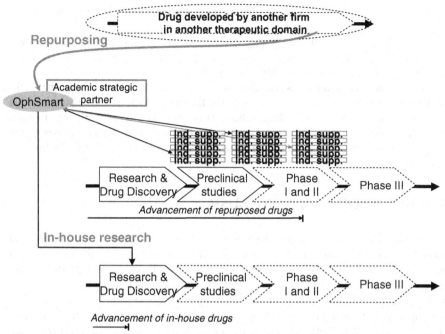

Figure 3: The network managed by OphSmart and position of actors on the value chain.

Most of the risks are supported by OphSmart. This inner management of risk is divided in two parts: a high risk with in-house research, but investments are low; and a low risk with the repurposing, with requires more funds because of the stages of developments. Actually risks of failure of the repurposed molecules are low because it has already shown safety and efficacy in other human applications.

Regarding value there is some similarities with Emics: no laboratories or manufacture capabilities, getting the best of competences in the network, choice of partner and long-run relationships. Over that, value created also comes from their skills in project management as well as a very deep understanding of the process of drug development. They manage a project with 6 persons where the pharmaceutical industry would need up to 150. This performance comes from strong experiences and competences. OphSmart is not a place to start a carrier; it is a place to make the most of an experienced carrier. This is also valuable for the business part of OphSmart: the business model is very attractive for investors and the business developers are highly skilled in negotiation The process of development of repurposed drugs creates a lot of value: risks are low, developments are shortened because steps of toxicity and safety are very easy, and there is no fundamental research to do. As soon as they get the authorization they can start the preclinical phases and the pharmaceutical formulation. . Regarding value of in-house research, which could be perceived as a dead weigh by investors, it is on the contrary a positive signal. It is like a scientific guarantee. Organization is another point of value creation. The management team is very aware of methodology and management tools. As an example there is no reporting for the salaries: as OphSmart is small and informal in the way of management, nobody spends an hour in reporting.

Regarding the cost of repurposed drugs, there is the example of one of their molecule. They spent 15 million Euros in two years from preclinical studies to the end of phase I. The gap with big pharmas one is huge.

Oxpeckers are small birds that feed on insects which they pick from the backs of wild mammals like rhino. That illustrates the case of the repurposing firm that takes innovation from another bigger biotech or pharmaceutical company. It has a positive impact as unexpected revenue goes to the big pharma and an unexpected drug is developed for humankind. Meanwhile, the oxpecker find value for him: he has got bread and butter.

6. DISCUSSION AND CONCLUSION

These two case studies show that being virtual is possible in the European biopharmaceutical industry. The size and the prominence of a firm are not determining criteria to play the role of hub firm. Emics and OphSmart play successfully but differently this role. Regarding the knowledge mobility, enhanced in the concept of hub, information is shunted by the hub firms. It is more a selective sort than a wide delivery of information. The distribution of industrial property rights is different in both cases: Emics shares it with its strategic partners while OphSmart do it only under duress. Thus both firms attend to a right appropriation of innovation in accordance with the participation of each of actors. But networks are different (table 1). Emics lean on four strategic partners. This way the network is more solicited and involved in the vaccine development. On the opposite OphSmart is only backing on to its academic partner. The academic laboratory is one of the best in the world in the therapeutic domain of OphSmart. More than a simple collaboration there is also a strong commitment. The other actors of the network are less involved in the projects.

Actors of the network	Academic strategic partners	Industrial strategic partners	Academic suppliers	Industrial suppliers
Emics' network	2	2	3	5
OphSmart's network	1	0	0	More than 18

Table 1: Type and number of actors involved in the network of each firm

Both firms have a very light structure. Although they are virtual they keep a good control on the technological steps because they have a deep understanding of scientific issues. This is precisely a striking feature: the scientific team is a key for success in the complex environment of drugs. It appears to be easier for OphSmart to manage the value chain than for Emics because the scientific team is stronger and, more than the scientific level, they have experienced the process of drug development. It is in contradiction with Bamfield work for who virtual companies should use consultants and other outside agencies to advise on the various stages of the product development (Bamfield P. 2003). The scientific development is very complex and should be deeply understood by the virtual firm. Thus a virtual firm made of only venture capitalists would not be viable.

But to be virtual implies the problem of credibility. Emics has difficulties to prove its credibility in front of other big pharmas and investors. OphSmart had to prove good skills in negotiation with suppliers: compared to big pharmas the bargaining power of virtual firms is small. When they want a supplier to do their study cheaply, quickly and before a study financed by a big Pharma, Emics and OphSmart showed high talents of negotiator. They do not have the same financial capabilities.

Regarding the repurposing, Chong and Sullivan (Chong C.R. and Sullivan D.J. Jr. 2007) basing their work on DiMasi et al.(DiMasi J.A., Hansen R.W. et al. 2003) corroborate our cost estimations: drug developers can bypass almost 40% of the overall cost of bringing a drug to market because toxicological and pharmacokinetic steps are easier. OphSmart as well as Emics have cost ten times inferior to the one announced by big pharmas. But these results should not be generalized. The issue of revenue model is also raised. Both firms are product based and expect to make profit when they will sell the product. The more a drug moves forward in a pipeline the more the value perceived is high.

Being virtual gave Emics and OphSmart more flexibility and access to the best of competences available. In both cases the management of the network is a success. However the situation is not so simple and developing a drug being virtual is fishing in troubled waters. We have not pointed out the issue of the market entry but we already know that in both case it is going to be very difficult and these companies should not do it by themselves. The destiny of biotech is still uncertain. In the eighties every body thought that it was going to change the face of the world and it did not (Hopkins M. M., Martin P.A. et al. 2007). Maybe this new way of organizing drug development will lead to a new way of doing business and keep biotech's initial promises.

Acknowledgements

We are grateful to management teams of both companies for permitting us to access to their data and for their willingness to give us details and long interviews. For helpful comments and suggestions we thank editors and anonymous reviewers.
Names of the firms have been changed in order to preserve confidentiality.

Bamfield P. (2003). The structural components of an R&D organisation, Research and development management in the chemical and pharmaceutical industry, Wiley-VCH.
Chesbrough H.W. and Teece D.J. (1996). "Organizing for innovation: when is virtual virtuous? ." Harvard business review.
Chong C.R. and Sullivan D.J. Jr. (2007). "New uses for old drugs " Nature **448**(9): 645-646.
Cooper W. and Muench M. (2000). "Virtual organizations: practice and the literature." Journal of organizational computing and electronic commerce **10**(3): 189-208.
Dhanaraj C. and Parkhe A. (2006). "Orchestrating innovation networks." Academy of Management Review **31**(3): 659-669.
DiMasi J. and Grabowski H.G. (2007). "The cost of biopharmaceutical R&D: is biotech different?" Managerial and Decision Economics **28**: 469-479.
DiMasi J.A., Hansen R.W., et al. (2003). "The price of innovation: new estimates of drug development cost,." Journal of Health Economics **22**: 151-185.
Eisenhardt K. (1989). "Building theories from case study research." Academy of Management Review **14**(4): 532-550.
Govindarajan V. and Gupta A.K. (2001). "Strategic innovation: a conceptual Road Map " Business Horizons: 3-12.

Hopkins M. M., Martin P.A., et al. (2007). "The myth of biotech revolution: an assessment of technological, clinical and organisational change." Research policy **36**(4): 566-589.

Lorenzoni G. and Baden-Fuller C. (1995). "Creating a strategic center to manage a web of partners." California Management Review **37**(3): 146-163.

Magretta, J. (1998). "The power of virtual integration: an interview with Dell computer's." Havard business review: 73-84.

Mesquita L.F. (2007). "Starting over when the bickering never ends: rebuilding aggregate trust among clustered firms through trust facilitators " Academy of Management Review **32**(1): 72-91.

Provan K.G. (1983). "The federation as an interorganizational linkage network " Academy of Management Review **8**: 79-89

Rugman A. and D'Cruz J. (1997). "The theory of the flagship firm " European Management Journal **15**(4): 403-412.

Sawhney M. and Parikh D. (2001). "Where values lives in a networked world." Harvard business review: 76-86.

Siggelkow N. (2007). "Persuasion with case studies." Academy of Management Journal **50**(1): 20-24.

Weisenfeld U., Reeves J.C., et al. (2001). "Technology management and collaboration profile: virtual companies and industrial platforms in the high-tech biotechnology industries." R&D Management **31**(1): 91-100.

---

[1] The Over the Counter Bulletin Board (OTCBB) is a quotation medium for subscribing members, not an issuer listing service and should not be confused with the Nasdaq Stock Market Inc.

PART 4

NEGOTIATION IN COLLABORATIVE NETWORKS

11

AGREEMENT NEGOTIATION SUPPORT IN VO CREATION

Ana Inês Oliveira[1], Luis M. Camarinha-Matos[1,2,] Michel Pouly[3]

[1]UNINOVA, PORTUGAL, aio@uninova.pt
[2]New University of Lisbon, PORTUGAL, cam@uninova.pt
[3]MTO Network/Swiss Federal Institute of Technology, SWITZERLAND,
Michel.pouly@epfl.ch

In order to compete in the global market, companies have to restructure and make use of the infrastructures that allow them to become more agile. The possibility of rapidly form virtual organizations to respond to a business or collaboration opportunity gives companies an expression of agility and survival mechanisms in face of the market turbulence. In this paper it is exemplified the usage of a tool that enables time reducing during the negotiation process of a new virtual organization.

1 INTRODUCTION

The quotation business process is a challenging task for every industrial company active in the subcontracting sector as the customers have nowadays access to a very large global market:

- The success rate of a quotation (transformation into an order) lays around 10%. In other words, it means that 9 out of 10 quotations are only lost time and money;
- The profit margins are reduced and the price calculations must be very accurate;
- The quotation must be ready in a very short time as the competitors also reacts quickly

The quotation process is even more difficult in the case Collaborative Networked Organizations (CNOs). The main drawback here is the supplementary delays induced by the participation of many partners and the need to negotiate till an agreement is reached. In this way, there are several proposed solutions to shorten these delays; for instance, using a kind of workflow tool would enable to follow up the state and the progress of the bid preparation business process. If these delays are not too critical within a local small CNO where the members share the same language and business background and could probably solve all problems by using the traditional communication methods like e-mails and phone calls, the situation is completely different for multicultural and geographical widely spread organizations. Consequently, there is a need to improve the effectiveness of the negotiation processes and to dynamically form virtual organizations (VOs). It is also important to develop forms of e-contracting as they can describe the rights and duties of all virtual organization partners (Rocha et al., 2004), as well as penalties to apply to

Please use the following format when citing this chapter:

Oliveira, A.I., Camarinha-Matos, L.M. and Pouly, M., 2008, in IFIP International Federation for Information Processing, Volume 283; *Pervasive Collaborative Networks*; Luis M. Camarinha-Matos, Willy Picard; (Boston: Springer), pp. 107–118.

those that do not satisfy the agreement. Computer assisted negotiation and e-contracting is expected to provide a faster and cheaper solution than standard contracting. Several significant characteristics for the e-contracting process can be found in (Angelov, 2006).

Such procedures for e-contracting and negotiation are also important in relation to the ISO 9000 certification as they can ensure clearly defined and repeatable procedures within the CNO and not only within the companies members of a CNO.

In this context, this paper describes the usage of a negotiation wizard tool developed in the scope of the ECOLEAD project which allows for time-saving during the negotiation process of a VO creation.

2   VO CREATION CONTEXT

In ECOLEAD, the virtual organization (VO) creation process is considered to happen in the context of a VO breeding environment (VBE) (Luis M. Camarinha-Matos & Afsarmanesh, 2003; Luis M. Camarinha-Matos et al., 2005; Rabelo et al., 2000). The VBE is a long term collaborative association that is composed of organizations that prepared themselves in order to be ready to collaborate and thus rapidly respond to a collaboration opportunity (Luis M. Camarinha-Matos & Oliveira, 2006; L. M. Camarinha-Matos et al., 2007). As illustrated in Figure 1, the VO creation process is started by a business opportunity identified during the operation phase of the VBE. Although, the VBE is created as a long term "controlled border" association where its members are recruited from the "open universe" of organizations, the VO is supposed to be a short term organization where its partners are primarily selected from the VBE members. Nevertheless in case there is lack of skills or capacity inside the VBE other organizations can be recruited from outside the VBE boundaries (L. M. Camarinha-Matos et al., 2007).

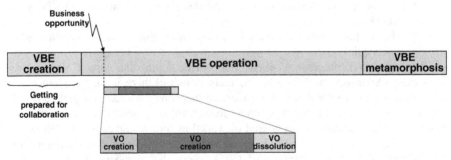

Figure 1 – VO creation in a VBE context

In order to promptly respond to a business / collaboration opportunity, the VO creation process has to be well defined. However, given different market situations, this process has to be set to provide solutions for two distinct cases: (i) when there is already an acquired business opportunity and the objective is to guarantee a consortium to fulfill the opportunity requirements; (ii) before having acquired the business opportunity, it is necessary to go through a quotation process.

Figure 2 shows the simplified process for the VO creation that is supposed to happen when there is already an acquired business / collaboration opportunity. In this case, the process can be split into three distinct phases:

- Preparatory Planning. In this phase the new collaboration opportunity (CO) is identified and characterized. Usually the CO is external (originated by an external client) and identified by a VBE member acting as a broker. After the CO is identified, it is then characterized and the VO roughly planned determining the rough structure of the potential VO, identifying the required competences and capacities as well as the organizational form and corresponding roles of the consortium members.

- Consortium Formation. This is the main phase of the VO creation. It is when the right partners are identified, assessed and selected according to the characterization and rough planning of the previous phase. In order to compose the VO, in this phase it is also necessary to through an iterative process in order to reach agreements and align needs with offers. This iterative process is conducted by a negotiation process.

- VO Launching. Once partners have been selected and agreements reached, it is necessary to better detail the VO plan according to the previous negotiations, as well as to go through a contracting stage, where all partners become committed to the VO, being the conclusion of the entire negotiation process. Finally, it is necessary to put the VO into operation and for that configuring the needed collaboration infrastructures.

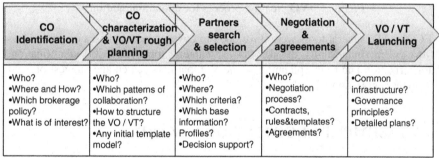

Figure 2 – VO creation process for a given collaboration opportunity

Nevertheless, before starting planning the VO, it might be necessary to go through a quotation / bidding process of a selected CO. This is the case illustrated in Figure 3 that is divided into two distinct phases:

- Quotation / Bidding. If an interesting CO is identified, then a bid / quotation for the potential customer can be prepared. For the preparation of this bid, it is necessary to make a rough plan of the foreseen VO and also to select the core partners. In case the bid is unsuccessful, the core consortium dissolves; otherwise the process continues to the next phase.

- Final VO Creation. In case the bid is successful, the VO's rough plan needs to be revised, based on the specific conditions of the contract with the customer, new additional partners might be necessary, and the VO is finally detailed and launched.

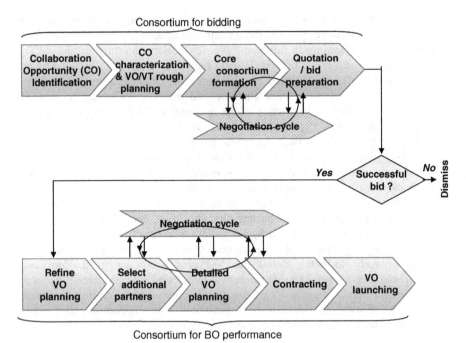

Figure 3 – VO creation process for quotation/bidding

In ECOLEAD, several tools were developed to cover the core phases of the process (L. M. Camarinha-Matos et al., 2007), namely tools for CO identification, characterization and rough planning of the VO, partners search and suggestion, and agreement negotiation wizard.

3   AGREEMENT NEGOTIATION WIZARD

In the previous section, the entire process for the VO creation was briefly described. One important process that runs in parallel with some other steps of the VO creation process is the negotiation and contract establishment. Thus, a tool to support this process was developed. The purpose was not to fully automate the process, but rather to assist the human actors during the negotiation process towards the VO establishment. At this point there are two different situations where negotiation might be required: (i) to select the right partners to compose the VO, and (ii) to reach agreements on the details of the VO. The proposed negotiation wizard (WizAN) is intended to provide facilities for both situations.

Usually contracts / agreements are used to regulate the exchange of values (e.g. money, knowledge), and mainly their provisions are for protection of parties in case that something does not go according to what was planned, and to describe what was agreed in the case that any party forgets it. The main result of WizAN is a contract or agreement summarizing the results of the negotiations / discussions that were performed during the VO creation process. In collaborative business relationships a negotiation might be performed either between two single parties, or among several parties (multi-party negotiation). In the case of the contract / agreement produced by the WizAN tool both negotiation types are supported, depending on what is being negotiated (every issue that is subject of negotiation, it is called *negotiation topic*).

The full negotiation process is guided by a "contract or agreement template" composed of a number of sections. When a negotiation topic is created it is associated to a specific section of the agreement where a link to the topic can be kept (Figure 4). Once all negotiation topics are agreed, the final agreement can be produced representing a kind of "compilation" or integration of the agreements on all these topics.

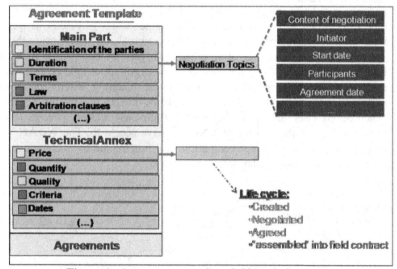

Figure 4 –Agreement template & Negotiation topics

The negotiation processes is quite hard to structure in terms of defined workflows / protocols as several flows depend of the decisions made by the human negotiators and also their individual timing (mostly asynchronous regarding each other). Thus four main modules were developed to assist the human actors in reaching agreements:

- Assisted Contract Elaboration (ACE). This module provides a collection of contract templates and negotiation topic templates to support the VO creation. In the contract construction process it is possible to build or edit the contract skeleton or template.
- Contract Editor (CE). The contract editor in WizAN is the main point of interaction with the user. Here it is possible for the VO planner to initiate, conduct, and monitor the entire negotiation process in the VO creation. For this, the VO planner has some specific functionality available, such as: add partners to the VO; add, read or edit documents that refer to the general part of the VO; create new virtual negotiation rooms (VNRs); and produce the final document that reflects all the agreements established during the negotiation process. If the user is not the planner and is a potential partner of the VO, there some restrictions in terms of functionalities, but there are also

other functionalities available, namely: to accept to participate in the VO; see the general conditions that were specified by the VO planner; know who are the other partners involved; read or add documents to the general part of the VO; have access to the VNRs where he/she was invited to participate; and sign the final agreement. Furthermore, it is important to mention that this editor also keeps a list of all the VNRs that were created along with the discussions carried out and documents exchanged. Here privacy and security are both supported since only allowed potential VO partners can access that information.

- Virtual Negotiation Room (VNR). It is the virtual space where the potential partners of the VO are invited to join in order to discuss the necessary topics that need an agreement. When the VO planner wants to discuss a specific topic with certain members, he/she creates a virtual sub-space inside the VO space, i.e. a new virtual negotiation room (Figure 5). Each VNR is divided into two distinct parts: one for edition of the negotiation topic characteristics and associated documents, and another for enabling discussion among partners involved in the negotiation topic by means of chatting (enabling synchronous communication between participants) and/or specific forums that only the members of a that VNR can have access to. The WizAN VNR concept includes therefore several additional functionalities in comparison to other earlier initiatives (Shelbourn et al., 2005).

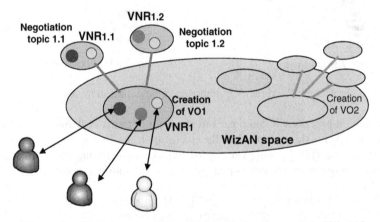

Figure 5 – Virtual spaces (Virtual Negotiation Rooms) in WizAN

- Support for Agreement Establishment (SAE). The e-Notary is a module that allows clients to exchange information with warranty of authenticity and validity as well as providing a safe repository for saving and requesting documentation (through digital signatures and encryption techniques). This module was developed as a web service allowing its clients to use the following facilities: user registry; documents requesting; document signing; document certification; document repository; and document authentication.

In the next section an example of how this tool can be used in a real case scenario is illustrated.

4   ILLUSTRATIVE SCENARIO

The following example scenario is based on the case study of the DecoCHina Swiss-Chinese multicultural CNO. Basically, the DecoCHina CNO consists of two independent networks, the Swiss Microtech regional network (SMT) and a Chinese network located in the Guangdong province, which have their own activities and collaborate on specific orders when it brings a competitive advantage for their customers (Figure 6).

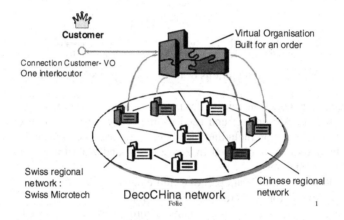

Figure 6 – The DecoCHina CNO

Before starting commercial operations, the following business processes between the two networks have been defined: request for quotation (1), order management (2), and delivery (3).

The *request for quotation process* will be here analyzed in more details to show where a negotiation support tool is required to reduce the delays which are far too long when only traditional communication methods are used (~15 working days to get a quotation).

As shown in Figure 7, the first activity of this business process is the *request for quotation (2.1)* addressed by SMT to the Chinese partner network. This request contains the drawings (dimensions, tolerances, surface quality, and material), the quantities and the corresponding delivery schedules.

The second activity (2.2) is *the selection of the potential partners* within the Chinese network which could participate in a possible order and which must first give their prices and delivery schedules.

The third activity is the *technical clarification* (2.3) of the quotation based mainly on the information included in the drawings of the parts and the preparation of a *quotation* (2.4). The last activity is the *commercial negotiation* (2.5) on prices and schedules.

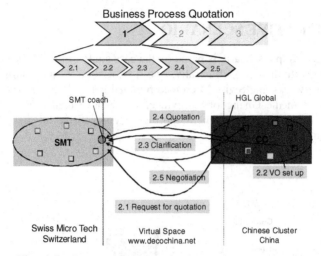

Figure 7 – Interactions of the business process quotation

The agreement negotiation wizard (WizAN) is a tool developed by UNINOVA within the ECOLEAD project and used by the broker or planner in charge of the preparation of a quotation including members of the two networks and allowing him to cover the activities highlighted in 2.2, 2.3, 2.4 and 2.5 with the support of the following functionalities:

- Create and edit the main part of a future agreement;
- Add partners for the agreement preparation;
- Create Virtual Negotiation Rooms according to the requested topics to be discussed and agreed upon and invite all or some partners to enter the corresponding room;
- Keep track of the partner's commitments and agreements (e-signatures);
- Produce the final agreement.

The following steps are required to complete the quotation business process:

Step 1

The SMT broker defines a new possible VO in WizAN (VO characterization - Figure 8) with the corresponding documents (drawings in pdf format with dimensions, tolerances, surface quality, material, the quantities and the corresponding delivery schedules) and invites the Chinese network hub company to join the newly created possible common business.

Step 2
To confirm the reception of the request and in case of interest, the head of the Sales Department accepts the invitation. If not, she must decline it. The SMT broker will call her if no change in the VO partner acceptation status is recorded after max. 1-2 days.

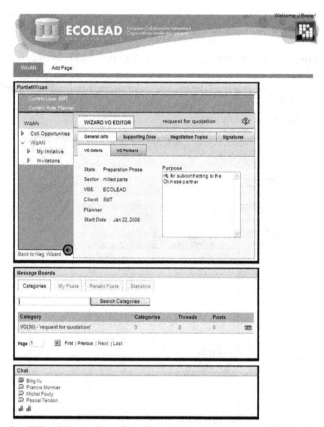

Figure 8 – WizAN user interface for agreement editor – VO characteristics

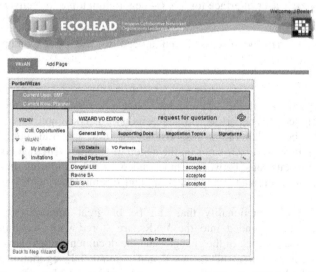

Figure 9 – WizAN user interface for agreement editor – VO invited partners

Step 3

After the acceptation of all partners (Figure 9), the SMT broker creates three negotiation topics:
1. Technical issues (raw material definition, tolerances, applicable norms etc.);
2. Delivery schedules (example in Figure 10);
3. Price and commercial conditions.

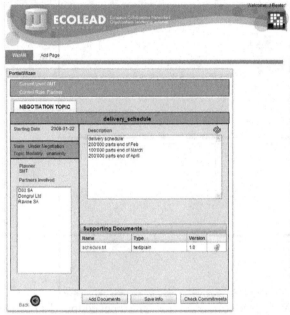

Figure 10 - WizAN user interface for VNR – negotiation topic for delivery schedule

All these topics shall be discussed and agreed by the corresponding partners involved in each topic.

Step 4

The Sales department of the Chinese hub company forwards the request to its Quotation Engineering department for feasibility analysis and cost calculation together with the collaborators responsible for raw material purchasing and subcontracting. Possible discussions on the negotiation topics will then take place.

For the e-discussions between China and Switzerland during the quotation negotiation phase, users can use the chatting and forums functionality provided by the WizAN tool.

A considerable functionality that can be of great importance is that all documents that are uploaded into the VNRs are stored with versioning control allowing users to keep track of the changes that the documents might have suffered.

After the completion of all technical and commercial negotiation topics, the SMT broker will close the negotiation as illustrated in Figure 11.

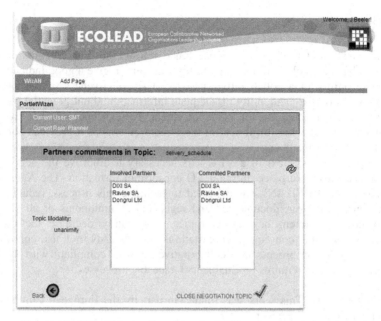

Figure 11 - WizAN user interface for VNR – partners commitment

Step 5

The SMT broker can create the final agreement, which must be signed by all VO partners before completing the VO creation process.

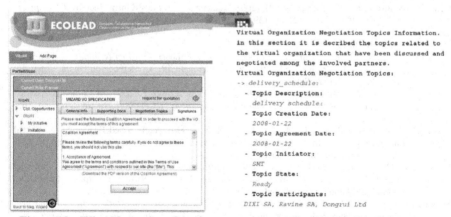

Figure 12 - WizAN user interface for agreement signing / example of agreement document

5   CONCLUSIONS

The time and amount of resources consumed during the VO creation process whenever a business/collaboration opportunity is acquired, give a good indication of the level of agility of a collaborative network. The effectiveness of this process mainly depends on the availability of adequate information about potential partners and their level of preparedness for VO involvement. The existence of a VO breeding environment facilitates the fulfillment of these requirements as it provides common infrastructures to its members.

But even in the context of a VBE it is necessary to improve the negotiation processes that must take place during a VO consortium formation. The Agreement Negotiation wizard (WizAN) was designed to facilitate this process, reducing the required time. Moreover, documented and registered commitments of all partners involved in the different negotiation topics significantly decrease the risk of misunderstandings and consequent contestations. The WizAN tool also contributes to make the quotation process in a collaborative network compliant with the ISO 9000 certification that requires repeatable and traceable processes.

Acknowledgements. This work was funded in part by the European Commission through the ECOLEAD project.

6   REFERENCES

Angelov, S. (2006). *Foundations of B2B Electronic Contracting*. Unpublished PhD, Technische Universiteit Eindhoven, Eindhoven.

Camarinha-Matos, L. M., & Afsarmanesh, H. (2003). Elements of a base VE infrastructure. *J. Computers in Industry, Vol. 51*(Issue 2), pp. 139-163.

Camarinha-Matos, L. M., Afsarmanesh, H., & Ollus, M. (2005). *Virtual Organizations: Systems and Practices*. Boston: Springer.

Camarinha-Matos, L. M., & Oliveira, A. I. (2006, 18-20 September). *Contract Negotiation Wizard for VO Creation*. Paper presented at the 3rd International CIRP Conference on Digital Enterprise Technology - DET'06, Setúbal.

Camarinha-Matos, L. M., Oliveira, A. I., Ratti, R., Baldo, F., & Jarimo, T. (2007). A Computer-Assisted VO Creation Framework. *Establishing the Foundation of Collaborative Networks*, pp. 165-178.

Rabelo, R. J., Camarinha-Matos, L. M., & Vallejos, R. V. (2000). Agent-based Brokerage for Virtual Enterprise Creation in the Moulds Industry, *E-business and Virtual Enterprises* (pp. pp. 281-290): Kluwer Academic Publishers.

Rocha, A. P., Cardoso, H. L., & Oliveira, E. (2004). *Contributions to an electronic Institution supporting Virtual Enterprises' life cycle*. Paper presented at the Virtual Enterprise Integration: Technological and Organizational Perspectives.

Shelbourn, M., Hassan, T., & Carter, C. (2005). Legal and Contractual Framework for the VO. In L. M. Camarinha-Matos & H. Afsarmanesh & M. Ollus (Eds.), *Virtual Organization Systems and Practices*: Springer.

12

USING UML/WS-CDL FOR MODELING NEGOTIATION SCENARIOS

Michał Piotrowski, Henryk Krawczyk

Gdansk University of Technology
Faculty of Electronics, Telecommunications and Informatics, POLAND
bastian@eti.pg.gda.pl, hkrawk@eti.pg.gda.pl

One of the most important aspects of collaboration between people or organizations is effective communication. To support different kinds of human activities (e. g. negotiations), general interaction procedures need to be defined. Scenarios of such activities can be expressed in choreography languages. In the paper WS-CDL language is used to model buy/sell negotiations. The suitable method for generation of scenarios is given and a concrete scenario is analyzed. Moreover, testbed for empirical experiments is presented and some experiment results are discussed.

1. INTRODUCTION

Negotiation is a human activity that occurs between at least two parties (negotiators) and concerns a concrete subject such as selling/buying products, choosing the best solution to a given problem or finding the most suitable services, etc. In the case of distributed computing environments, agents as well as people can be negotiators. Agents are special autonomous and mobile programs which seek either other agents or people to negotiate with them on behalf of their owners. The latter kind of negotiations is called electronic negotiations or briefly e-negotiations.

Let h2h denote human negotiations. Human negotiations can be performed in real and virtual environments. Furthermore, let e2e denote electronic negotiations, where e2e = a2a (a denotes agent or algorithm) or e2e = a2h which denotes humans negotiating with some kind of computer program.

Negotiations can be described by a computational negotiation model. The model proposed in (Krawczyk-Brylka, 2008) is suitable for all types of negotiations. It consists of initial conditions of negotiations, negotiation strategies and negotiation outcomes. Initial conditions describe the subject of negotiation, e. g. purchase of medical equipment, negotiation attributes, e. g. price, delivery date, payment date etc. and an area of expectable negotiation outcomes, e. g. price between minimal and maximal possible values. The model describes the negotiation process as a series of requests (demands) which form the negotiation dance. The demands represent values of negotiation attributes proposed by negotiation partners. The graphical representation of such a sequence is a polygonal curve.

The paper concentrates on a2h negotiations considering experiments in which purchasing of medical equipment was negotiated. First of all we try to design an electronic negotiator which can behave according to the given negotiation scenario.

Please use the following format when citing this chapter:

Piotrowski, M. and Krawczyk, H., 2008, in IFIP International Federation for Information Processing, Volume 283; *Pervasive Collaborative Networks*; Luis M. Camarinha-Matos, Willy Picard; (Boston: Springer), pp. 119–126.

The paper describes the behaviour of the negotiator on two levels. The low level behaviour is described by negotiation dance as sequences of values of negotiation attributes. The high level behaviour corresponds to scenarios described by both modeling and choreography languages, which present sequences of demands/requests messages. In consequence, our e-negotiator is an algorithm which behaves appropriately to the given negotiation task, similarly to a human negotiator. Finally, the paper presents the main principles of the algorithm behaviour, the testbed for a2h negotiation experiments and conclusions.

2. LOW LEVEL DESCRIPTION OF NEGOTIATION SCENARIOS

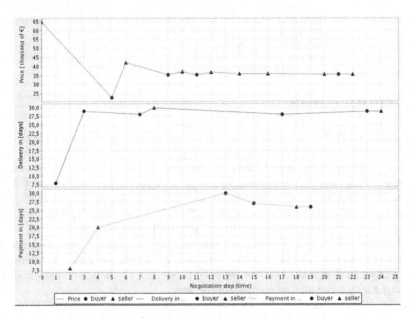

Figure 1 - A sample of h2h negotiation dance

Low level description of negotiation scenarios is related to negotiation dances. Figure 1 presents a negotiation dance obtained in a negotiation experiment. The negotiation dance presents changes of demands in time. In figure 1 one can observe changes in three negotiated attributes. Buyer demands are marked with circle and seller demands are marked with triangle. Price, delivery date and payment date were the attributes considered by negotiators participating in the negotiation experiments. By analyzing negotiation dances it is possible to determine relationships between negotiators' demands.

The proposed negotiating algorithm is based on the model in (Krawczyk B., 2008) and uses parameters obtained from both analyses of the negotiation dances and the obtained negotiation experiments outcomes. The algorithm is constructed to generate suitable requests and responses to a partner in a negotiation. The algorithm takes into account the history of the negotiation in the form of a negotiation dance. The principles of the algorithm are as follows:

1. Its first demand (request) is generated as the best value of a negotiation attribute from its point of view.

2. Its subsequent demands (responses), depend on the history of partner's propositions, specifically the algorithm makes concessions to a similar degree as its partner.

In the process of demands generation, proposed values of attributes are modified by a Gauss distribution with μ equal to the generated attribute value and σ calculated on the basis of statistical data obtained in h2h negotiation experiments. The algorithm is tuned to maximize effectiveness while using cooperative style of negotiations (Fisher, 1991).

The proposed negotiating algorithm is used in a virtual environment as one of the partners in a2h negotiations.

3. HIGH LEVEL DESCRIPTION OF NEGOTIATION SCENARIOS

The negotiating algorithm itself is not sufficient to perform a2h negotiations. Communication procedures and different behaviour patterns should be defined. High level description of negotiation scenarios specifies communication patterns from the global point of view. Choreography languages can be used to describe such interaction scenarios. In general, such languages concentrate on visible aspects of negotiation only, ignoring the logic of parties involved (Peltz, 2003). Recently, languages based on web services architecture have become very popular with the emergence of service oriented architecture (SOA). SOA facilitates integration of different business systems and desktop applications. One of the most important choreography languages associated with SOA is Web Services Choreography Description Language (WS-CDL) (Kavantzas, 2005).

Based on h2h negotiation experiments, a general negotiation scenario has been modeled as a UML sequence diagram (figure 2). In the negotiation experiments two roles were defined: buyer and seller. The goal of the negotiations was to obtain a contract for purchase of medical equipment. The actors in figure 2, buyer (B) and seller (S) negotiate until both of them accept each other's terms (loop box) or when one of the negotiators breaks the negotiation (treated as an exception). The negotiation process consists of exchanges of demands. In each step of the negotiation, one party presents their demands to the other. The order of demands is arbitrary, e. g. more than one set of demands from one of the participants can come in succession or the participants present their demands alternately (alt box). The demands are presented as asynchronous method calls in UML notation, since WS-CDL is based on the concept of web services. "*Demands*", the argument of *propose()* method, represents a set of values of negotiation attributes, e. g. *Demands* = {price = 50000 €, delivery in 14 days}.

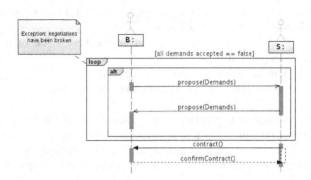

Figure 2 – General high-level scenario of a buy/sell negotiation represented as UML sequence diagram

The next step in the choreography modeling process is the formal notation of the interactions in WS-CDL language. Using a WS-CDL document, the system can manage the negotiation process. Listing 1 presents a section of a WS-CDL document describing interactions modeled in figure 2.

Before interactions can be expressed in WS-CDL language, information types should be defined. Information types represent kinds of information or documents exchanged in all communication processes between parties involved in a negotiation. Parameter *"Demands"* has to be described as an XML Schema type. Afterwards variables containing the exchanged tokens of information have to be defined.

In listing 1 workunit named *PresentingDemands* corresponds to the loop box in the UML diagram, choice corresponds to the alt box in the diagram and interaction named *demandsFromSeller* corresponds to the situation where a seller presents his demands to a buyer.

Listing 1 – Section of WS-CDL document representing modeled scenario

```
<choreography name="Negotiations" root="true">
    ...
  <workunit name="PresentingDemands"
    repeat="not(cdl:getVariable('BuyerAgrees'),'','') or
            not(cdl:getVariable('SellerAgrees','',''))">
    <choice>
      <interaction name="demandsFromSeller"
          channelVariable="tns:SellerToBuyer"
          operation="propose">
        <participate fromRoleTypeRef="tns:SellerRole"
          toRoleTypeRef="tns:BuyerRole"
          relationshipType="tns:SellerAndBuyer" />
        <exchange action="request" name="sendDemandsToBuyer"
            informationType="tns:demndsList">
          <send
              variable="cdl:getVariable('SellerDemands','','')" />
          <receive
              variable="cdl:getVariable('SellerDemands','','')" />
        </exchange>
        <exchange action="respond" name="areDemandsAccepted"
            informationType="tns:boolean">
          <send
```

```
                variable="cdl:getVariable('BuyerAgrees','','')" />
            <receive
                variable="cdl:getVariable('BuyerAgrees','','')" />
        </exchange>
      </interaction>
      <interaction name="demandsFromBuyer"
          channelVariable="tns:BuyerToSeller"
          operation="propose">
          ...
      </interaction>
    </choice>
  </workunit>
  <workunit name="Contract" ...> ... </workunit>
  <exceptionBlock name="HandleExceptions"> ... </exceptionBlock>
</choreography>
```

4. TESTBED FOR A2H NEGOTIATION EXPERIMENTS

The next step is to deploy the choreography in an appropriate environment. Figure 3 presents such an environment. It consists of two main parts: GAJA system and e-negotiator module. The e-negotiator module integrates a WS-CDL scenario with the algorithm simulating a negotiator. A WS-CDL choreography is used to manage the course of negotiations.

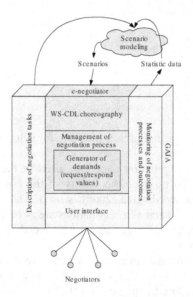

Figure 3 - Architecture of negotiation scenario testbed

The GAJA system provides descriptions of negotiation tasks for the negotiation algorithm and human negotiators. The negotiation algorithm obtains negotiation attributes and initial conditions from the GAJA system as appropriate algorithm parameters. Human negotiator is presented with a precise description of negotiation tasks, including his role in the negotiation experiment, negotiation goals etc.

Moreover, GAJA provides a user interface which acts as a middleware between the e-negotiator and a human negotiator. Figure 4 presents a screenshot of the user interface provided by the GAJA system. In the experiments, the following task was defined: a pair of negotiators had to negotiate the contract for purchase of medical equipment. The contract consisted of the price, delivery and payment dates.

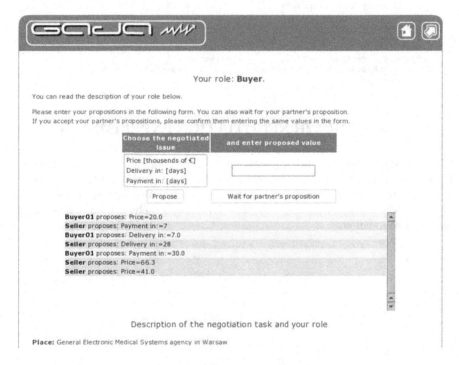

Figure 4 – Screenshot of user interface for a2h negotiations

Parameters observable in negotiation dance are used in the quality evaluation of negotiation experiments. To estimate the quality of the e-negotiator, the modified model proposed in (Krawczyk-Brylka, 2008) is used. The main quality attributes considered for comparing h2h and a2h negotiations are as follows:

● effectiveness – percent of negotiations which ended with a contract which satisfied both negotiators;

● efficiency – based on the time of negotiation measured by the number of steps of the negotiation (number of interactions between negotiators). The lower the number of interactions, the higher the efficiency;

● main negotiation style – negotiation style can be competitive, collaborative or balanced (Fisher, 1991). The collaborative style is assumed to be preferred. The evaluation of the negotiation style is based on the degree of concessions made by negotiators observed in the negotiation dance. In the negotiation dance graph it is possible to observe the change of demands values in each step of the negotiation and compare it to concessions made by a partner in former steps of the negotiation.

Table 1 – Comparison of h2h and a2h negotiation quality

Quality attribute	h2h negotiations	a2h negotiations
effectiveness	broken negotiations - 6.25%	broken negotiations - 27.5%
efficiency	avg. 41 negotiation steps	avg. 28 negotiation steps
negotiation style	73.14% of negotiators used the collaborative style	- 72% of human negotiators used the collaborative style - the computer algorithm always used the collaborative style

50 h2h and 50 a2h experiments were conducted. The participants of a2h experiments had participated in h2h negotiation experiments as well, therefore the results of a2h experiments are directly comparable to the results of h2h negotiations. H2h and a2h negotiation experiments were performed using the GAJA system. In the case of h2h negotiations the communication medium was a chat.

Table 1 summarizes the quality comparison of h2h and a2h negotiations. The results of the experiments were as follows: the efficiency of a2h negotiations is 1/3 higher than h2h negotiations due to the very formal style of communication imposed by the choreography and the user interface. However, the number of broken a2h negotiations was 4 times higher comparing to experiments where both of the negotiators were human. The algorithm assumed that the typical partner will use the cooperative style of negotiations and broke the negotiations if the partner's style deviated from the preferred style of negotiations to a high degree. The preferred negotiation style in both negotiation types was the collaborative style.

A survey was conducted after the a2h negotiation experiments. The main conclusion of the survey was that human negotiators need a broader context of the partner's demands. Human negotiators tend to test the limits of concessions that their partner is willing to make. The algorithm does not warn when it decides that partner's demands are unreasonable and breaks the negotiations immediately. In consequence, human negotiators who wanted to test their partners' limits, accidentally caused the algorithm to make the decision to break the negotiation.

Therefore, interactions representing context information are needed in a2h negotiations. This context information can be a warning for a partner that his demands are unreasonable or that a negotiator is satisfied with the course of negotiations. The algorithm can easily be updated to present this kind of information based on its state and a dictionary of contextual phrases. This improvement can be modeled as a WS-CDL document and integrated into testbed.

5. CONCLUSIONS

Modelling negotiations on a low level is not sufficient. The context of negotiations is a very important factor for successful negotiations. The context can be understood as a business context of the negotiation environment. This knowledge is the basis for proper decisions. Additionally, the context can be understood as a conversational context needed by people to properly understand their partner (Strecker, 2006).

Conversational context can be modeled as WS-CDL documents, which facilitates integration of improvements in e-negotiation systems. WS-CDL can be translated to WS-BPEL notation or a SOA module which can be directly integrated and executed in one of the available SOA middlewares. The initial tests for these procedures were conducted and proved successful (Piotrowski, 2008).

It is possible to automatically translate UML modeled diagrams into executable XML-based languages like WS-BPEL or WS-CDL (Benyoucef, 2005). The next step of development would be to use dedicated modelling environments for orchestration and choreography languages and omit the UML modelling stage. Graphical modelling tools for WS-CDL are in development (e. g. Pi4SOA project). WS-CDL can be used to model negotiations from the global point of view, so it is suitable for integrating models focused on local (negotiator's) point of view. Moreover WS-CDL standard is an information driven language and as such, it facilitates integration of advanced protocols, e. g. states in a social protocol (Picard, 2006) can be directly modelled as WS-CDL variables and any associated logic for such a protocol can be added as a set of web services deployed in a middleware for WS-CDL execution.

In this manner it would be possible to directly modify scenarios in WS-CDL language, deploy a new version of the scenario in a middleware and immediately test the results of changes.

5.1 Acknowledgments

This work was supported under Ministry of Science and Higher Education research project no N516 035 31/3499.

6. REFERENCES

1. Benyoucef M., Rinderle S. A Model-driven Approach for the Rapid Development of E-negotiation Systems. School of Management, University of Ottawa École de gestion, Université d'Ottawa, 2005.
2. Fisher R. and Ury W. and Patton, B. Getting to Yes: Negotiating Agreement Without Giving in. Houghton Mifflin Books, 1991
3. Kavantzas N., Burdett D., Ritzinger G., Fletcher T., Lafon Y., Barreto C., WSCDL: Web Service Choreography Description Language, www.w3c.org, November 2005
4. Krawczyk-Brylka B. Piotrowski M. "Using a computational model to compare objective negotiations in real and virtual environments". In International Journal of Production Research, vol 46; number 5, Taylor & Francis 2008: 1315-1333
5. Peltz C. "Web services orchestration and choreography". In Computer vol. 36, number 10, 2003: 46-52
6. Picard W. "Computer Support for Adaptive Human Collaboration with Negotiable Social Protocols", Proceedings of the 9th int. Conference on Business Information Systems, Klagenfurt, Springer Boston 2006, 353-360
7. Pi4SOA Project homepage, http://www.pi4tech.com
8. Piotrowski M. and Krawczyk-Brylka B. "The Web Based System for Recording and Analysing Different Kinds of Negotiations". In WEBIST 2006, Proceedings of the Second International Conference on Web Information Systems and Technologies: Society, e-Business and e-Government / e-Learning, Setubal, INSTICC Press, Portugal, 2006: 82-87
9. Piotrowski M., "Creating negotiation scenarios using WS-CDL language", to be published in Polish in KASKBook, Gdansk 2008
10. Strecker S., Kersten G., Kim J., Law K. "Electronic Negotiation Systems: The Invite Prototype". In Proceedings of the Collaborative business MKWI'06, Germany 2006

13 | AUTOMATING DECISIONS FOR INTER-ENTERPRISE COLLABORATION MANAGEMENT

Lea Kutvonen, Sini Ruohomaa, Janne Metso
Department of Computer Science, University of Helsinki, FINLAND
Lea.Kutvonen@cs.helsinki.fi

The current trend towards networked business forces enterprises to enter federated, loosely-coupled business networks, since much of the competition takes place between networks and value nets. The Pilarcos B2B interoperability middleware supports trend by providing services such as business service discovery and selection, interoperability management, eContracting, and reputation-based trust management. Although these services automate the interoperability knowledge management and interoperability testing, and may help in routine decisions, an essential element of the architecture involves an expert system that automates or supports decisions on joining collaborations, acting in them, or leaving them. The expert system focuses on a single enterprise needs. This paper focuses on the ways of governing the automation level in the expert system in a way suitable for autonomous enterprises to control their participation in agile collaborations.

1. INTRODUCTION

The collaborative use of software-supported business services has become increasingly important for enterprises, as competition between enterprises is increasingly being replaced by competition between business networks and value nets. Entering the networked business encourages even SMEs (small and medium enterprises) to enter fields that are traditionally dominated by larger companies. The collaborative way of working allows focused fields of expertise to be utilized as elements of large, value-added services.

Enterprises have a strategic need to participate multiple network simultaneously, and for managing changes in these networks. This is reflected as new requirements for the supporting computing facilities [3-5, 10, 12, 13]. The type of joint work and the associated value proposition varies between integration (coordination, communication, channeling) and federated solutions (cooperation, collaboration) [11]. The forms of collaboration vary from loosely-coupled federations of autonomous actors providing services to each [9], to distributed workflow management approaches [1], and the level of automation provided by support facilities varies.

In this area, the Pilarcos architecture provides B2B middleware support for forming and managing loosely-coupled business networks of autonomous actors [7, 9, 19]. Its tasks include partner selection and negotiation, interoperability tests for technical and business aspects of services (such as technical communication

---

Please use the following format when citing this chapter:

Kutvonen, L., Ruohomaa, S. and Metso, J., 2008, in IFIP International Federation for Information Processing, Volume 283; *Pervasive Collaborative Networks*; Luis M. Camarinha-Matos, Willy Picard; (Boston: Springer), pp. 127–134.

interoperability and sufficient match in meeting business processes), collaboration lifecycle management with partner changes, and breach management.

The Pilarcos architecture views the open service market as a breeding environment for different types of value nets; the market is guided by published business network models addressing different motivations for collaboration, coordination, cooperation and communication. The service providers are autonomous: they publish a service offer as an indication of a willingness to provide a given service at given terms and they make independent decisions on whether to join, continue in or leave an eContracted community [7, 9].

In this kind of environment, the nature of decision-making is profoundly different from centrally coordinated collaboration: the trustworthiness of a potential partner cannot be judged based on its service offers alone, a partner may decide to leave the collaboration abruptly or a partner may choose to contradict the contract.

This paper proposes an expert system to support decision-making for participation in inter-enterprise collaborations. The expert system addresses needs for controlling interoperability aspects, for meeting the pressure to balance risks and benefits of collaborating, and for reputation-based trust decisions. Section 2 discusses the information needs of the expert system and negotiation protocols involved. Section 3 discusses the automation potential for the negotiations and decisions, as well as ways of governing the process and making escalation decisions. Section 4 discusses the impact of the system, related work, and future work items.

2. NEGOTIATION SUPPORT FOR JOINING INTER-ENTERPRISE COLLABORATIONS

The expert system role is either a) to make an automated collaboration decision in a routine case or b) to escalate the decision to a human administrator in a new type of situation, together with appropriate information about the proposed collaboration to support the decision.

In the Pilarcos architecture [9], the collaboration establishment process is as follows. First, the initiating partner selects from a public repository a business network model that suits the purposes of the collaboration. The business network model comprises of a set of external business processes between roles, assignment policies determining on what conditions roles in the business processes need to collocate (or are forbidden to collocate) with a partner, and coherence rules for the joint behaviour. The published models are designed by domain experts and can be harmonized to serve the business area. The models are rather abstract to allow technical realizations vary, and model checked to remove deadlocks and other unwanted features; indeed, in future, we even consider privacy-aware analysis for the models. A simplistic business network model may have roles of client, seller, and notary; the interactions denoting offers, counteroffers, contracts, and signatures and archiving actions by the notary.

Second, the populator [7] acts as a secretary for the initiator and seeks suggestions for the missing role players in the business network model through service offer repositories. The populator only acts on the public information and is expected to ensure that the selected offers form an interoperable collaboration community according to the rules of the business network model.

We understand interoperability, or the capability to collaborate, as the effective capability to mutually communicate information in order to exchange proposals, requests, results, and commitments. The term covers technical, semantic and pragmatic interoperability. Technical interoperability is concerned with connectivity between the computational services, allowing messages to be transported from one application to another. Semantic interoperability means that the message content becomes understood in the same way by the senders and the receivers. This concerns both information representation and messaging sequences. Pragmatic interoperability captures the willingness of partners to perform the actions needed for the collaboration. This willingness to participate refers both to the capability of performing a requested action, and to policies dictating whether it is preferable for the enterprise to allow that action to take place.

If no interoperable communities can be found, the initiated activity fails; the involved parties can participate the definition of a new business network model, or push new service offers to be published in order to improve the situation. For minor mismatches, the interoperability criteria can be relaxed, with the condition that there are sufficient translators/interceptors to make the necessary bridges in the technical level, and that the participants trust on those brides suggested.

As the populator returns information of suitable partner sets, the initiator can start the negotiation phase [9]. It informs each of the proposed collaboration partners about the proposed eContract. When all partners have agreed, the eContract is distributed to all, and the committed services are prepared for collaboration activities. The eContract is an active, distributed agent that is used for following the state changes in the collaboration (i.e., progress of work), source of breach detection rule generation, and source of information about identities and properties like location of the partners' service interfaces.

In each enterprise, there is an agent that uses the expert system to provide decisions for accepting the proposal, rejecting it or refining the proposal further. In this phase, information and reasoning used for the decision are private and not exposed to other enterprises, but is embedded in the suggested expert system.

The decisions on joining collaborations are multifaceted. The partners need to determine whether the collaboration is a) interesting, b) acceptable and c) worth taking the risks involved.

Interest in a collaboration depends on business strategic issues, concentrating on whether the collaboration objectives suit the enterprises' own objectives and views on what strategies are plausible to good return of investment or will create a competitive edge on the market. The interest to collaboration may depend on the availability of necessary supporting partners in the business network model, or wish to avoid working for the competitors. In the enterprise, some of the clear strategic decisions can be coded for the expert system to follow. Especially, the interest can be narrowed only to certain kind of business networks, or new partners are less interesting than existing, strategic partners, since these concepts are computationally manageable in the proposed architecture.

Acceptability of a collaboration is here understood as ability to participate the collaboration with the existing facilities within the range of publicly announced policy limits. Technically, this decision can be supported by the selection and interoperability checking process of the populator. An enterprise can limit the amount of suggestions directed to it by advising the populator through the details in the published service offers. For example, an enterprise can publish offers using certain communication technology only. However, acceptability rules like not working with company X are more prone to be left for the negotiation phase for not creating a negative publicity.

Finally, evaluating whether a collaboration is worth taking the risk is a trust decision on two levels: a) is the collaboration as a whole to be trusted with the information feeds, resources, and activity involved, and b) is each of the other partners to be trusted to perform its part sufficiently for the collaboration not to cause major losses.

The Pilarcos architecture relies on reputation-based trust decisions. In the network of autonomous enterprises, a flow of reputation information about the business services is organized: each time a collaboration ends successfully or to a breach situation, positive or negative recommendation can be sent to others. The reputation information can then be used for selecting service offers to new collaborations, and effectively implementing a social regulation system to the overall architecture [7]. The trustworthiness of the reputation information must be taken to account.

We define trust as the extent to which one party is willing to participate in a given action with a given partner in a given situation, considering the risks and incentives involved [16]. Risk we express as the potential benefits and costs of a positive trust decision to a set of assets – namely: money, control of autonomy, and customer satisfaction representing different domains of reasoning – each separately on a scale of expected major or minor loss or gain. Risk tolerance describes a set of thresholds for risk itself and the quality of the reputation information that was used to produce the risk estimate. Multiple threshold sets can be defined; the central two thresholds to set determine obvious positive (allow) and obvious negative (do not allow) decisions: the gray area between the two is left for an actor with higher authorization, a human user, to determine. A threshold set can for example specify that the probability of minor or considerable monetary gain combined be greater than the probability of minor or considerable monetary loss, and that the probability of a minor reputation loss is tolerable. The evaluations of risks and incentives are annotated to the business network models in the design phase, the corresponding thresholds are for business/system administrators to choose/adjust.

To expert system must consider the following information elements and sources:
-    the business network model to describe the shared view of business processes involved; this information is made available in the eContract proposal;
-    the partner's capability to fulfill a role in the collaboration;
-    interceptors needed for communicating with that partner service;
-    the partner's reputation, to base trust decisions on earlier experience;
-    the value proposal of the activity for the enterprise itself;
-    the expected gains in terms of assets such as money, reputation, as well as the possible losses, also in terms of effects to assets; and
-    knowledge of the degree in which interoperability on non-functional aspects can be supported (for example, security and nonrepudiation of the communication between partners, QoS management, etc).

3. GOVERNING AUTOMATION IN DECISION-MAKING

The level of automation in eContracting has to be considered carefully. The risks involved in adopting the Pilarcos style of operation include taking wrong automated decisions, or reacting too quickly or slowly to changed reputation information. Risks may also be introduced by creating vulnerabilities in the middleware layer.

The techniques for avoiding these vulnerabilities include the use of metapolicies for grouping decision situations to routine cases and human-decidable, adjustable thresholds for different types of operational situations for positive and negative routine decisions, and finally building of systemic trust into population and negotiation processes as well as into Pilarcos middleware information repositories. The thresholds were already mentioned in Section 2; systemic trust on Pilarcos middleware level is left to be discussed elsewhere [7]. As the remaining element, we discuss metapolicies.

A metapolicy is a policy about when and how a decision can be made by an automated decision-making system according to its internal rules. We have identified four metapolicy categories:
1. Strategic orientation of the enterprise,
2. Systemic trust on automatically added services,
3. Credibility, correctness and quality of reputation metadata and
4. Privacy policy interfacing.

The strategic orientation metapolicies direct the expert system to use resources only to consider in detail proposals that are interesting in terms of acceptable business network models, acceptable partners, or other crosscutting property known in the expert system but that cannot be published in service offers. This kind of metapolicy effectively guides the expert system to favour collaborations of the already acceptable type; new lines of business need to be introduced to the system by reformulating the policy too. The policy represents the guideline to follow; the guideline itself can be derived from for example managerial or financial reasoning.

Systemic trust on automatically added system level services addresses a new problem created by Pilarcos-like architectures. The Pilarcos middleware allows relaxed matching of service interfaces, and thus, supports automatic configuration of communication channels. The type repository [20] in which interface descriptions and their relationships are stored, also provides references to modifier-interceptors to be placed in the communication channel to for example transform euros to dollars. However, the type repositories may be external to the enterprises, or use externally provided modifier-interceptors; therefore, the trustworthiness of the collaboration can be undermined by that small helping device. These metapolicies should be able to identify which type repositories or which interceptors can be freely used and which should be rejected.

The third category of metapolicies arise from the need of suspecting the quality of information in the Pilarcos middleware repositories and in the reputation information collection process. The reputation information is divided into two types: local reputation, which is gathered from events generated by local monitors and transformed into experiences, and external reputation, which is gathered through agents operating in global reputation networks. Local reputation is reliable and high quality, but expensive to gather, as it requires taking the risk of collaborating with the target actor. On the other hand, external reputation is less expensive to gather but more unreliable, and more likely to contain errors. The relative weights given to local and external reputation in a risk evaluation are determined by the amount, certainty and credibility of each type of reputation information [17]. The weight is increased as the amount of cases seen with a definite outcome increases (uncertain results are noted as a separate category of outcomes), and credibility of reputation information providers is followed as their reputation in their role as seen by their peers. For example, if the reputation system does not support rigorous source credibility evaluation or distorts information passed through it, its credibility is low.

Finally, privacy metapolicy governs privacy-affecting activities in collaborations. From a design point of view, it would be tempting to treat privacy-policies as normal policies governing each service or information element, but the nature of privacy-preservation is to veto otherwise acceptable actions. Therefore, we raise the privacy-policies to the level of metapolicies. For example, it may be the case that the suggested collaboration is interesting, acceptable, and considered at the general level to be trustworthy. However, in the processing it may happen that a service request triggers the need of passing classified documents as part of the service. In this case, it is essential that the privacy classification of information overrides any collaboration agreements, and the individual action of serving a single service request is escalated to human decision-makers. The privacy policies must be attached to all metainformation, in addition to the normal payload data.

4. DISCUSSION

We have outlined a semi-automated negotiation system for establishing inter-enterprise collaborations. The negotiation system takes advantage of multi-agent technology by modeling a single organization as an agent running the negotiations. The agent provides service interfaces towards other such agents in other organizations, and interfaces for local services for accessing collaboration management facilities. The Pilarcos architecture has been partially implemented: the populator general performance behaviour appears to be feasible for its task; a simple negotiation protocol has been implemented to let us try on different ways of decision-making. The reputation-based trust decision system is on its way towards implementation. Thus, the information sources will be there to support a range of negotiation protocols to be evaluated with the expert system.

In the domain of B2B collaboration support systems, the Pilarcos approach can be compared to for example ECOLEAD [14] and many projects with virtual enterprise focus. The main difference between ECOLEAD and Pilarcos approaches is that Pilarcos assumes a truly open service market, and builds a separate trust management system based on reputation information. Other approaches tend to trust on breeding environment of already trusted partners, between whom the business processes are formed around the existing capabilities. In contrast to this, Pilarcos uses the publication of business network models as a tool to direct the service markets. The same difference of approaches appear to some well-known trust management projects, like TrustCom [21], where the pre-existing strategic network of partners also appear. Further comparison between Pilarcos (Tube) concepts with other reputation and trust management systems can be found in our surveys [15,17].

The negotiation protocols supported should flex to different situations – sometimes an auction protocol is suitable, sometimes haggling style. Traditional multi-agent negotiation systems, like Magnet [2], focus on auctions in supply chain integration or marketplaces. Chiu et al. [6] have a meta-modeling based approach where they bring up the notion of log-rolling issues where two negotiators have conflicting interests in bilateral negotiations. In Pilarcos, the same situation may arise, especially where multiple policies need to be agreed on simultaneously. The choice is to be made between abandoning the suggested collaboration, and compromising on favourable policy values. The situation is an extension to the traditional distributed constraint satisfaction problem [8]. Zhang et al. [22] propose a graph-based solution to reason about ordering multi-linked variables. The same kind of model can be used in the Pilarcos negotiations for resolving conflicts.

In comparison to multiagent systems, like OMNI [8], the Pilarcos approach differs by using predefined contract templates, by running multi-party negotiations instead of bilateral, and by supporting privacy of decision-making.

Technical challenges include finding a simple but effective language for expressing various policies; there is no eContracting language, not even an ontology to provide orthogonal vocabulary for structuring the field. Languages such as BCA [18] provide for expressing permissions, obligations and prohibitions for the legal and business logics side of the contracts, but do not cover all the required interoperability levels.

The present pressure towards agile business networks can not be addressed by generative solutions in the long run. The first wave of solutions indeed will rely on jointly designed business processes, agreeing that as an unifying model, and wrapping local business services to meet the expected interfaces. This may work for large scale B2B networks, where the level of agility is reasonable – business strategies and investment directions do not change that often. However, it is clear by now that there is a fast growing market of C2C, and mixed communities that require not only agility support from the platform, but support for truly ad-hoc community management. On this field, only reflective, model-controlled solutions can meet the challenge.

ACKNOWLEDGMENTS

This work has been performed at the Department of Computer Science at the University of Helsinki, where the Collaborative and Interoperable Computing research group builds on work done in various projects funded by the national technology development center TEKES and industrial partners.

REFERENCES

1. CrossFlow WP 5: Deliverable D16: Final report. Tech. rep., CrossFlow consortium (2001). URL http://www.crossflow.org/public/pubdel/D16.pdf
2. Collins, J., Ketter, W., Gini, M., Mobasher, B., A multi-agent negotiation testbed for contracting tasks wih temporal and precedence constraints. International Journal of Electronic Commerce 7,1 (2002).
3. European Commission: EC FP7 ICT Work Programme. Tech. rep., EC (2007). URL http: //cordis.europa.eu/fp7/ict/

4. Fitzgerald, B., et al.: The software and services challenge. Tech. rep., NESSI (2006). URL ftp://ftp.cordis.europa.eu/pub/ist/docs/directorated/st-ds/fp7-report en.pdf
5. Huhns, M.N.: A research agenda for agent-based service-oriented architectures. In: Cooperative Information Agents X, Lecture Notes in Computer Science, vol. 4149, pp. 8?22 (2006). DOI 10.1007/11839354 2. URL http://dx.doi.org/10.1007/11839354 2
6. Chiu, D.K, W., Cheung, S.C., Hung, P. C. K., Chiu, S. Y.Y., and Chung, A. K. K., Developing e-Negotiation support with a meta-modeling approach in a web services environment. Decision support systems 40 (2004), 51-69.
7. Kutvonen, L., Metso, J., Ruohomaa, S.: From trading to eCommunity management: Responding to social and contractual challenges. Information Systems Frontiers (ISF) - Special Issue on Enterprise Services Computing: Evolution and Challenges 9(2-3), 181-194 (2007).
8. Kowalczyk, R., and Bui, V., On constraint-based reasoning in e-negotiation agents. In Agent-Mediated Electronic Commerce III: Current issues in agent based electronic commerce systems (2001), vol LNAI 2003/2001, Springer, 31-46.
9. Kutvonen, L., Ruokolainen, T., Metso, J.: Interoperability middleware for federated business services in web-Pilarcos. International Journal of Enterprise Information Systems, Special issue on Interoperability of Enterprise Systems and Applications 3(1), 1?21 (2007).
10. Li, M.S., Cabral, R., Doumeingts, G., Popplewell, K.: Enterprise interoperability research roadmap, version 4.0. Tech. rep., EC Information Society Technologies (2006). URL http://cordis.europa.eu/ist/ict-ent-net/ei-roadmap en.htm
11. Li, M.S., Grilo, A., van den Berg, R., et al.: Value proposition for enterprise interoperability, version 3. Tech. rep., European Commission (2007)
12. Nachira, F., Dini, P., A.Nicolai, Louarn, M., L?eon, L.: Digital Business Ecosystems. European Commission (2007). URL http://www.digital-ecosystems.org/book/de-book2007.html
13. Papazoglou, M.P., Traverso, P., Dustdar, S., Leymann, F., Kr?amer, B.J.: Service-oriented computing: A research roadmap. In: F. Cubera, B.J. Kramer, M.P. Papazoglou (eds.) Service Oriented Computing (SOC), no. 05462 in Dagstuhl Seminar Proceedings. Internationales Begegnungs- und Forschungszentrum fuer Informatik (IBFI), Germany (2006).
14. Rabelo, R.J., Gusmeroli, S., Arana, C., Nagellen, T.: The ECOLEAD ICT infrastructure for collaborative networked organizations. In: Network-Centric Collaboration and Supporting Frameworks, vol. 224, pp. 451?460. Springer (2006). DOI 10.1007/978-0-387-38269-2 47
15. Ruohomaa, S., Kutvonen, L.: Trust management survey. In: Proceedings of the iTrust 3rd International Conference on Trust Management, 23?26, May, 2005, Rocquencourt, France, Lecture Notes in Computer Science, vol. 3477, pp. 77?92. Springer-Verlag (2005)
16. Ruohomaa, S., Kutvonen, L.: Making multi-dimensional trust decisions on inter-enterprise collaborations. In: Proceedings of ARES 2008. IEEE Computer Society (2008).
17. Ruohomaa, S., Kutvonen, L., Koutrouli, E.: Reputation management survey. In: Proceedings of the 2nd International Conference on Availability, Reliability and Security (ARES 2007), pp. 103?111. IEEE Computer Society, Vienna, Austria (2007)
18. Neal, S., Cole, J., Linington, P., Milosevic, Z., Gibson, S., and Kulkarni, S., Identifying requirements for business contract language: a monitoring perspective. In Proceedings of the 7th international Enterprise Distributed Object Computing Conference 2003, 50-61.
19. Ruokolainen, T., Kutvonen, L.: Addressing Autonomy and Interoperability in Breeding Environments. In: L. Camarinha-Matos, H. Afsarmanesh, M. Ollus (eds.) Network-Centric Collaboration and Supporting Frameworks, IFIP International Federation for Information Processing, vol. 224, pp. 481-488. Springer, Helsinki, Finland (2006)
20. Ruokolainen, T., Kutvonen, L.: Service Typing in Collaborative Systems. In: G. Doumeingts, J. Mller, G. Morel, B. Vallespir (eds.) Enterprise Interoperability: New Challenges and Approaches, pp. 343-354. Springer (2007)
21. Wilson, M., et al.: The TrustCoM approach to enforcing agreements between interoperatingenterprises. In: Interoperability for Enterprise Software and Applications Conference (I-ESA2006). Springer-Verlag, Bordeaux, France (2006).
22. Zhang, X., Lessler, V., Abdallah, S., Efficient ordering and parametrisatio of multi-linked negotiations. In Proc. 2nd Autonomous agents and multiagent systems, 11 (2005), 307-360.

PART 5

CONSTRUCTION OF COLLABORATION STRUCTURES

14

DATA MINING TO DISCOVER ENTERPRISE NETWORKS

Kafil Hajlaoui, Xavier Boucher and Mihaela Mathieu

Ecole Nationale Supérieure des Mines de Saint Etienne, FRANCE, hajlaoui@emse.fr

Within the framework of Virtual Organisations (VO), a decision aid approach was developed to support the identification of collaborative corporate networks. This approach is based on an automated procedure of information extraction to identify key features of potential partners. The added value of this research is to operate in an "open universe" of potential partners, using the company internet sites as the main source of information on firms. The key features extracted concern the activity fields and the competencies of the firms.

1. INTRODUCTION

Data Mining appeared as a new discipline which complements statistics and information technology fields (Friedman, 1997)-.. Data Mining has been described as "*the nontrivial extraction of implicit, previously unknown, and potentially useful information from data*" (Frawley and al., 1992). Data mining has merged with Knowledge Discovery in Databases (KDD) (Hébrail and Lechevallier, 2003). Enterprises amass and refine immense amounts of data routinely: customer profiles, production stock, manufacturing levels, etc. Many data-processing means are implemented nowadays in order to help decision-makers deal with this information overload. Examples abound: data warehouses provide a support for decisional information systems; data mining solutions extract new knowledge from these data warehouses, etc.

The success of Small & Medium-size Enterprises (SME) confronted with the Global marketplace relies more and more on their ability to put into practice business intelligence. The deployment of business intelligence solutions turns out to be essential for many strategic decisions for instance innovation in complex products, or collaboration in or through Virtual Organizations (VO).

In this paper, we present the first results of an approach aimed at facilitating the constitution or set up of Virtual Organizations (VO). The objective is to make a direct use of public information available through company web sites, in order to broadly analyze potential co-operative opportunities. To the best of our knowledge, most previous publications in this field have concerned a semi-closed environment defined by a Virtual organization Breeding Environment (Ermilova & Afsarmanesh, 2007). Such VBEs pre-selects potential partners, who have provided pre-structured information in order to further evaluate collaborative possibilities. The added value of the proposed approach presented, is that there is no need for any pre-treatment phase. Our method is applied within a full and open environment of potential partners. Potential collaborator identification is based on the use of public

Please use the following format when citing this chapter:

Hajlaoui, K., Boucher, X. and Mathieu, M., 2008, in IFIP International Federation for Information Processing, Volume 283; *Pervasive Collaborative Networks*; Luis M. Camarinha-Matos, Willy Picard; (Boston: Springer), pp. 137–144.

information available on the web. This assumption leads to specific information extraction mechanisms.

The rest of the paper is organized as follows. In section 2 we present an overview of the whole approach. In section 3, we focus on information extraction mechanisms to identify correctly activity fields of the company. In section 4, we use these first results for a first level of decision aid based on an enterprise clustering procedure. In conclusion, a brief discussion is presented detailing some of the advantages of the suggested approach and limitations that still need to be overcome.

2. OVERVIEW OF THE APPROACH

Advances in computer networking technology constitute key success factors for the management of Virtual Organizations (Dewey and al., 1996), (Gilman and al., 1997). A typical application is the creation of VO which emerges from the members of a Virtual Breading Environment (Lavrac, 2005), (Camarinha-matos and Afsarmanesh, 2003). Such approaches often use competency analyses to help in identifying potential collaborations among companies. However "complementarities of activity sectors" constitute another partnership criterion already discussed in the literature. It provides one of the main motivations for co-operation, in addition to the traditional motivation of sharing or pooling costs (Géniaux and al., 2003). In the current research we consider both aspects: complementarities on activity sectors and similarity of competencies. As underlined by figure 1, this method works in two steps: first information extraction is employed to identify key characteristics of the company; second a decision aid phase which uses these key characteristics as input to discover potential collaboration alliances.

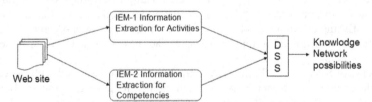

Figure 1- Two extractions mechanisms required

This approach is dedicated to an open environment of potential VO partners. The initial data comes directly from public information available on company internet sites. This is without any restrictions or preconditions imposed by or on potential candidate firms. The extraction mechanisms depicted in figure 1 focus on the 2 main characteristics we have selected to consider collaboration potentials: supplementary activities and competency similarities. We also describe in the paper (section 4) how activity and competency features can be used, in a second step, to generate new knowledge on construction of collaborative networks. Because of space requirements, this paper will only focuses on activity complementarities.

3. DATA MINING FOR ACTIVITY FIELD IDENTIFICATION

The following sections focus on extraction mechanisms applied to the identification of "enterprise sector of activity" (IEM-1 on figure 1). The overall extraction procedure is synthesized by figure 2. This paper briefly details the procedure and concentrates on demonstrating the feasibility by the results described in section 3.1 and 3.2. The main steps are Extraction-lemmatization, Indexation then Similarity matching. The reader can refer to (Hajlaoui et al., 2008) for a complete justification.

The extraction procedure uses an external semantic resource (thesaurus) built from the standardized French NAF code (Nomenclature of French Activity). The NAF is a standard frame used in France to describe the main sector of activity for all French companies. This NAF frame is presented as a hierarchical tree, referencing all potential activity fields into classes and sub-classes. The use of this reference frame facilitates the automation of the indexation algorithms. The aim is to use web site information in order to classify any given company in the NAF tree.

The extraction of information on the activities proceeds statistically, using a controlled indexing approach. As mentioned the NAF code is used as a thesaurus reflecting a semantic and conceptual representation of all potential fields of activity.

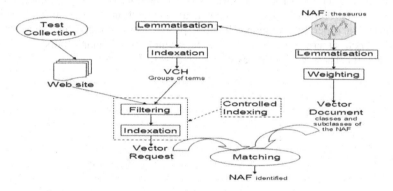

Figure 2-Structure of the information extraction procedure

First this thesaurus is used as a database for the search engine. Second, it constitutes an external semantic resource meant to improve the precision of expression for information needs. Here, an "information request" concerns only one firm's web site. Informally, this request could be expressed by "Which NAF code is correct for a given firm?". This request will be associated to a "request-vector" (figure 2), which is a set of terms extracted from the company web site. The request-vector is built by a controlled indexing with SMART (Salton's Magic Automatic Retrieval Technique)[1]. The controlling vocabulary is provided by the NAF code.

The code NAF is also used as external semantic resource. Each of the classes or subclasses of the NAF code[2] is represented by a specific document. This document is described by a vector called "document-vector". The document-vector contains a set of characteristic terms for each NAF class or subclass. The terms are associated to specific weights according to their relevance in the field.

---

[1] ftp://ftp.cs.cornell.edu/pub/smart/, discussed in (Hajlaoui and al, 2008)

[2] The NAF code has a hierarchical structure of classes and subclasses of activity fields. Example of activity field classes : C28 class- Work of metals, C29 class- Manufacture of machines and equipment, C28.1 subclass - Manufacture of metal elements for construction, etc...

Finally the request-vector is to be matched with the various document-vectors, using a similarity measure. This matching process aims at identifying the most suitable (similar) NAF code to represent the company.

3.1 Results

The experimental phase began with a test-corpus composed of 25 companies with well-known NAF code. The objective is to measure the feasibility and of the reliability of the approach. Thus the objective is to evaluate the results by comparing the code discovered by our approach and the actual NAF code of the company. Initially, the test was conducted with three broad NAF classes in the field of the mechanical industry: classes C28 (metal work), C29 (manufacture of machines and equipments) and C34 (automotive industry). Then the experiment was repeated with more refined subclasses to verify the ability to detect more precise NAF codes.

The similarity comparison of the request and document is done in two stages. First, an attempt to find the most relevant NAF class for the company is effectuated. The highest similarity score is selected. Second, an exploration of the sub-classes is accomplished in order to recompute a more precise NAF code. Three similarity measuring functions are typically used for this comparison: scalar product, cosine, Jaccard (table 1). These 3 alternatives were tested on the corpus.

Measure	*Formulate*
Scalar product	$RSV\ (Q.D_j) = \sum_{i=1}^{N} q_i.d_{ij}$
Cosine	$RSV\ (Q.D_j) = \dfrac{\sum_{i=1}^{N} q_i.d_{ij}}{\left[\sum q_i{}^2\right]^{1/2}\left[\sum d_{ij}{}^2\right]^{1/2}}$
Measure of Jaccard	$RSV\ (Q.D_j) = \dfrac{\sum_{i=1}^{N} q_i.d_{ij}}{\sum_{i=1}^{N} q_i{}^2 + \sum_{i=1}^{N} d_{ij}{}^2 - \sum_{i=1}^{N} q_i.d_{ij}}$

Table 1: Typical similarity measures

Most of the results of this experiment have already been detailed in (Hajlaoui and al, 2008), therefore only a synthesis will be given. The first results of NAF code identification by selecting the highest similarity score are very encouraging. The general performance for this extraction mechanism is 76% (percentage of actual NAF code identified). The robustness of the system was tested by dealing with companies outside the 3 NAF classes considered (C28, C29, C34). The system proved to be accurate, with null similarity measured in such cases. However further testing remains necessary to broadly validate the results. The approach did not seek to be exhaustive since the objective was to test feasibility. Before launching more extensive experimentation which would cover all the classes of the NAF code, the performance of the extraction mechanism requires optimization, based performance indicators as developed below.

3.2 Performance of the information extraction mechanism

In the domain of information research systems, the performance evaluation of tool/method is usually based on two indicators: Recall and Precision. The recall is calculated by the number of common elements among the "relevant-documents" and the "found-documents", divided by the number of relevant-documents. The precision is measured by the number of common elements among the relevant-documents and the found-documents, divided by the number of found-documents. Another performance indicator proposed is the frequency of precisions equal to 0. These situations must be avoided, since a null precision means no relevant-documents.

To measure the performance indicators for each request, 2 sets of relevant-documents and found-documents must be defined. Here, the definition of these sets and then the final performance of the system will depend on two factors which have been further tested:

- The similarity measure. The performance impact of each of the 3 performance measures defined above has been tested: scalar product, cosine, Jaccard. For one request (web site), the similarity provides several scores indicating the similarity of the request-vector to each of the document-vectors.
- The way to determine the "found-documents". This set can be reduced to 1 element with the highest similarity score (scoremax), but it can also gather a set of documents for which the score belongs to an interval [scoremax-α%, scoremax], with different values of α. The values 10, 20 or 33 were tested. The maximum tolerance 33% was determined referring to the possible values for the terms' weights.

Some key results are shown in figure 3. The figure underlines the 3 indicators for different configurations of similarity measures and parameter α. These experiments lead one to conclude that the best performances are obtained with α=33%, and with the function cosine. In that configuration the actual company NAF code is found in 92% of the requests on classes and 76% on subclasses.

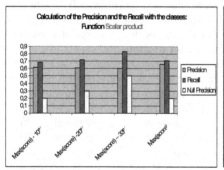 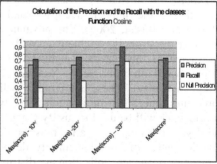

Figure 3 - Performance evaluation of the extraction system.

4. APPLICATION TO NETWORK BUILDING

The final objective of the research is to identify potential collaboration opportunities among companies. In that perspective the complementarities among industrial sectors of activity is a quite common factor when considering collaboration (Milgrom, 1997), (Frayret and al, 2003). The following section refers to the approach defined in (Burlat, Benali, 2007) which was selected in an already published state of the art (Hajlaoui et al., 2008). The authors proposed a decision-making aid based on clustering algorithms which can be applied using the results of the suggested extraction mechanisms as an input.

4.1. Method

To model if the activities are complementary graph theory is exploited to facilitate the mathematic treatment required. A graph is used to represent a set of companies and their complementarities. Each node in the graph corresponds to one company, and the arc between two nodes represents an evaluation of the degree of complementarity. Here we have referred to a definition of complementarity which considers that two sectors of activity are complementary when they can both be used to achieve integrated products/services available on the market. According to this definition, a complementary link between two companies is symmetrical (non-oriented graph). Referring to this definition, some expertise from specialists of the mechanical industrial domain is necessary to formalise an initial generic matrix of complementarity degrees among the various activity fields defined by the NAF code. This matrix is used as a generic data to evaluate complementary links among the companies of the collection.

4.2 Overview on the clustering algorithm

The clustering algorithm proceeds by a progressive elimination of the smallest weighted arcs (i.e., arcs with low degrees of complementarity). First, the weakest arcs are detected and then eliminated. Several steps occur, increasing the elimination threshold each time, thus isolating sub-groups of enterprises which should be more and more complementary. The number of steps for the algorithm will be chosen according to the number of clusters and the degree of complementarity expected (Benali and Burlat, 2004). The advantages of this algorithm are that it does not eliminate the strongly weighted arcs and is rather easy to apply.

The intent of this partition algorithm is to isolate strongly inter-connected sub-graphs based on information loss minimization (loss of arcs, loss of potential complementarity). These sub-graphs will represent set of very complementary companies: later, this information on activity fields clusters (associated with other information) will be used to justify potential collaborations. To apply the algorithm, the degree of complementarity must be determined among all the companies. The generic matrix of complementarity degrees is applied for that purpose. The 25 companies of the test collection are distributed on 8 NAF activity fields. To test the algorithm, one company was chosen to represent each of these 8 sectors. The initial complementarity graph is displayed in the figure 4.

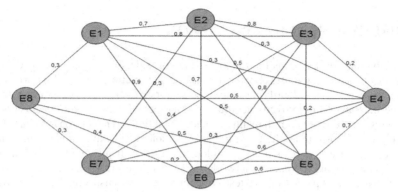

Figure 4: The case study of company graph

With this complementarity graph as a starting data, the algorithm can be applied. The following table presents the results of the various partitioning steps.

Steps	Arc(k)	Removed arc's	I	Sub-groups	Quality
1	0,1	Ø	0	Ø	Weak
2	0,2	{E7, E5}{E5, E3}{E3, E4}	0,05	Ø	
3	0,3	{E1, E4}{E1, E8}{E2, E4}{E2, E7}{E4, E7}{E8, E7}	0,2	Ø	
4	0,4	{E8, E6}{E7, E3}	0,27	{E7}{E1, E2, E3, E4, E5, E6, E8}	Average
5	0,5	{E1, E5}{E5, E2}{E8, E4}{E8, E5}	0,44	{E7}{E8}{E1, E2, E3, E4, E5, E6}	well
6	0,6	{E4, E6}{E5, E6}	0,54	{E7}{E8}{E5, E4}{E1, E2, E3, E6}	
7	0,7	{E1, E2}{E2, E6}{E5, E4}	0,72	{E7}{E8}{E5}{E4}{E1, E2, E3, E6}	
8	0,8	{E1, E3}{E2, E3}{E3, E6}	0,92	{E7}{E8}{E5}{E4}{E1, E6}{E3}{E2}	
9	0,9	{E1, E6}	1	{E7}{E8}{E5}{E4}{E1}{E6}{E3}{E6}{E2}	

Table 4: Partitioning the complementary graph

"I" is an indicator of quality of information contained in the partitioned graph. It evaluates the information lost at each step of the process[3]. At the initial stage the value of *I* is set at zero (all information available). At the end of the partitioning it approaches one. This means that most of the information concerning complementarities has been lost. At the same time, the indicator "Quality" is employed to evaluate the interconnection degree among the enterprises of each sub-graph identified. Based on these indicators, one can choose at which step the procedure should stop. For example after six iterations the following company clusters are obtained with *0,54* for the indicator of information loss and with the level "well" for the quality indicator:

G_1= {E7}; G_2= {E8}; G_3= {E5, E4}; G_4= {E1, E2, E3, E6}.

---

[3] The evaluator is measured by the sum of the removed arcs' weights divided by the total sum of the weight arcs from the initial graph.

5. DISCUSSION AND CONCLUSION

A contribution for the construction of virtual organizations was presented. The approach consists in two stages: the first is an automatic system of information extraction focusing on identifying enterprise sectors of activity from internet sites. Its experimental results proved encouraging. The second stage identifies clusters of companies according to complementary sectors of activity. The approach is based on a partitioning algorithm applied to a graph of complementarities among companies. However this criterion of activity complementarities is insufficient to distinguish correctly operational company networks. For instance, referring only to these criteria, the 25 companies of the test collection are only distributed on 8 distinct activity sectors, limiting diversity. Future research will be oriented on considering additional criteria. The first perspective to consider will be similarity of competencies. This requires a more complex information extraction based on advanced semantic data mining, natural language treatment and ontology. The development of a semantic-oriented analysis, based on a structured model of the "competency" concept should provide significant progress.

6. ACKNOWEDGEMENT

The authors wish to thank Chris Yukna for his help in English

7. REFERENCES

1. Burlat P. and Benali M., A *methodology to characterise co-operation links for networks of firms.* Production Planning and Control Vol.18, No 2, 156-168, 2007.
2. Benali, M. and Burlat, P., *Une démarche d'analyse de la complémentarité des activités dans un réseau d'entreprises,* in 5e Conference Francophone de Modelisation et Simulation, MOSIM'04, Nantes, France, 2004.
3. Camarinha-Matos, LM and Afsarmanesh H., *Elements of a base VE infrastructure Computers in industry,* vol. 51, 139-163, 2003.
4. Dewey and al., *The impact of NIIIP virtual enterprise technology on next generation manufacturing.* In Proceedings of conference on Agile and Intelligent Manufacturing Systems, Troy, NY, October 1-2, 1996.
5. Ermilova E., Afsarmanesh H., *Modeling and management of profiles and competencies in VBEs.* Journal of Intellignet Manufacturing 18, 561-586, 2007.
6. W. Frawley and G. Piatetsky-Shapiro and C. Matheus, "Knowledge Discovery in Databases: An Overview". AI Magazine: pp. 213-228, Fall 1992. ISSN 0738-4602.
7. Frayret J. M., D'Amours F., D'Amours S., *Collaboration et outils collaboratifs pour la PME manufacturière,* séminaire du centre de recherche CEFRIO, Quebec, 2003.
8. Friedman, J.H., *Data Mining and statistics: what's the connection?,* 1997. http://www-stat.stanford.edu/~jhf/ftp/dm-stat.ps
9. Géniaux L., Mira-Bonnardel S., *Le réseau d'entreprises : forme d'organisation aboutie ou transitoire,* Revue Française de Gestion, vol. 29, 129-144, 2003.
10. Gilman C. and al., *Integration of design and manufacturing in a virtual enterprise using enterprise rules, intelligent agents, STEP, and workflow.* In Proceedings of SPIE vol. 3303, 160-171, 1997.
11. Hajlaoui k., Boucher X., Mathieu M., *Information Extraction procedure to support the constitution of Virtual Organisations. Research Challenges in Information Science,* RCIS'2008, Marrakech, 2008.
12. Hébrail, G., Lechevallier, Y.(2003) *Data Mining et Analyse des données in Analyse des données,* G.Govaert éditeur, Hermes, 323-355
13. Milgrom P., Roberts J., (1997) *Economie, organisation et management,* De Boeck Université, Bruxelles, Belgique.
14. Lavrac Nada and al (2005), Automated extraction and structuring of competencies from unstructured company data: Two case studies. International Conference Applied Statistics Ribno (Bled), Slovenia.

LIFE CYCLE OF THE COOPERATION NETWORKS ENVIRONMENT: A CASE STUDY OF A CONSTRUCTION COMPANY'S PROJECT OF AN AUTOMOTIVE MOTOR FIRM

15

Fábio Müller Guerrini, Juliano Borges de Freitas
Escola de Engenharia de São Carlos - Universidade de São Paulo, BRAZIL
guerrini@sc.usp.br; julianobfreitas@yahoo.com.br

A cooperation enterprises network is defined as a group of companies which interact among themselves to exchange competences, therefore, a series of necessities from companies, which would be important in a manufacturing company, and also be in the cooperation network. Through organizational modeling, the manager has a greater view and quicker understanding of the company, which allows the integration among the company's components. An industrial construction project (in this case an automotive motor firm) is characterized by an inter-organizational relationship between companies and an analytical approach based on the life cycle of virtual organization (as a form of cooperation network) is adequate to identify and model functions, once several resources and competences must be guided by an information flow.

1. INTRODUCTION

The organization involved in the productive process is under pressure to adopt new concepts concerning global competition (life cycle reduction of products and mass customization) (Wiendahl and Hobis, 1998).

Among these strategies the company's formation network is a practice, which guarantees the survival and competitiveness of the small and medium size companies (Olave and Amato, 2001).

The model of multidirectional networks is feasible for small and medium size companies and licensing model and production outsourcing is under the control of large companies (Castells, 1999).

The organization, viewed from the process perspective (some crossing-over external limits of the organization) implicates, unavoidably, in an inter-functional and inter-organizational change (Davenport, 1994), leading to organizational designs that are very different from the ones currently known.

There is an unmistakable tendency that shows that the manufacturing process is not executed by a single company but by many companies collaborating in a specific part of the entire process. However, there is a challenge concerning how an

Please use the following format when citing this chapter:

Guerrini, F.M. and Borges de Freitas, J., 2008, in IFIP International Federation for Information Processing, Volume 283; *Pervasive Collaborative Networks*; Luis M. Camarinha-Matos, Willy Picard; (Boston: Springer), pp. 145–156.

industrial manufacturing system will be planned and managed, requiring a Reference Architecture for the flexible cooperation and appropriated protocols and mechanisms. (Camarinha-Matos and Afsarmanesh, 1999b)

This research will define a Reference model to represent the inter-organizational relationship between companies in an automotive motor company construction project; utilizing network companies with an analytical approach in order to understand the problematic situation.

RESEARCH METHOD
The research method is based on an exploratory case study to identify adequate variables to represent the production process in the design of network companies. The research approach was guided by *Soft* methodology (Checkland , 1982).

The *Soft* methodology approach presents the following steps, to create a parallel between the real world and the systemic thought: step 1 (the problematic situation), step 2 (the problematic situation expressed), step 3(key definitions of relevant systems), step 4 (conceptual models), step 5(comparison between conceptual models and expressed problematic situation), step 6(possible desired changes), and step 7(operations to improve the problematic situation) (Checkland , 1982).

According to *Soft* methodology steps, the stages of this research are represented in Figure 1:

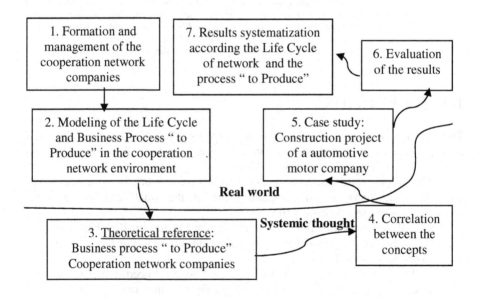

Figure 1: Research steps of this research according Soft methodology

The systematization of inter-organization relationship will be a reference model applying the *Enterprise Knowledge Development* (EKD) (Bubenko et. al., 2001).

The EKD method is composed of conceptual submodels that examine an organization and its requirements in an inter-related perspective. The submodels are: (1) Objective Model, (2) Actors and Resources Model, (3) Business Rules Model,

(4) Concepts and Entities Model, (5) Business Process Model and (6) Requirement and Technical Components Model (Bubenko et. al., 2001).

In order to represent the inter-organizational relationship a Business Process Model will be developed. The EKD methodology allows facilitating organization learning and communication, developing a structured business description to the organization analysts can discuss and determinate clearly the objectives and systems requirements and to produce a document (called knowledge repository). The Business Process Model can be utilized to think about the business, discuss changes and information system requirements.

The analytical object "to Produce" is the Business Process of an automotive motor company construction project. The analysis executed at the end of the construction project provides complete information regarding the Life Cycle project. The information was collected by direct observation in the work site of the construction project.

NETWORKS OF COOPERATION AMONG COMPANIES: MORPHOLOGY, LIFE CYCLE AND BUSINESS PROCESS "TO PRODUCE"

The term *network* can be understood as a representation model and/or hypothesis to collect, structure and coordinate the relationships between companies with their suppliers and competitors (Katzy et al., 1996), focusing on their essential competences, in order to obtain other parts of chain values of strategic partners (Levin, 1998).

The term *network companies* usually falls back on a vast range of inter-organizational relationships (Nassimbeni, 1998). In this manner there are several expressions referring to the same concept or leading to different approaches – Extended Company, Supply Chain Management, Cross Border Enterprise, Agile Manufacture. They cannot be synonymies, but somehow they address similar concepts (Chambers et al., 2000). Other expressions that can be included are: Strategic Alliances and Inter-organizational Networks (Williams, 2002).

The network structures are made up of a Reference Framework that can be applicable towards investigating phenomena characterized by the cooperative relationships density among the agents, which reinforces interdependence among its respective competences and imposes the need for some type of collective coordination of the adopted actions (Britto, 2002).

Although the forms, labels and theoretical contexts of the relationship types of inter-organizational cooperation network differ, three basic characteristics can be identified in the literature (Nassimbeni, 1998):

- The network is made up of two or more companies, at least partly autonomous;
- The legal structure commonly used to administrate is the "estipulated contract";
- Among the parts, dynamic forms of communication and coordination (with more intensity than a person would hope to find in market based changes) are developed as a form to adapt and synchronize the activity of each part (node) to the activities of the whole system.

The inter-organizational cooperation is stimulated by a growing recognition of the fact that any company or organization has all necessary "capacities" (resources and activities) to reach its goals as well as the goals in the market (Gebrtekidan anf Awuah, 2002).

The use of the cooperation network concept can be related to some morphologic elements common to this type of structure. There are four generic morphologic elements defining the network structures: nodes, positions, connections and flows (Britto, 2002).

The nodes constitute the basic units of the network companies, identifying the companies inserted in the network as basic units to be investigated. The positions are related to a certain work division that connects the different agents that are seeking to reach certain objectives, involving the integration of operational capacities and the agents' organizational competences (Britto, 2002).

Gebrekidan and Awuah (2002) discuss the relevance of the position (defined as a direct or indirect relationship with the other specific actors) that each actor (company, organization and individuals), creates for itself. The actor's position is established and developed at every moment, by means of process investments. The actor's position in the network warrants him some power regarding certain network activities. Such power, on the other hand, comes from the direct control that actor has over its activities and from the indirect control over the other activities, through the relationship with the other actors.

Within this context, Williams (2002) states that the location of each organization and its position in the network's structure defines benefit possibilities of the organization.

The links among the constituent nodes may be dispersed (number of connections among points is quite limited) enabling the determination of the network density in the structure.

The flows circulating through the connection channels among the nodes are represented by goods (tangible) and information (intangible) (Britto, 2002).

In the manufacturing ambit, the companies have become organized in effective production system frameworks to satisfy market needs, as the virtual manufacture and agile manufacture (Camarinha-Matos and Afsarmenesh, 1999b).

An effective cooperation requires coordination, since independent actors (members of a network) possess different behaviors, priorities and motivations. The coordination is necessary in order to prevent the companies' inefficiency in obtaining a common goal. (Camarinha-Matos and Lima, 1999)

De Toni and Meneghetti (2000) suggest that the crucial question in network companies is mainly coordination, which is accomplished through production planning, when the focus is production or the business process "to Produce".

The connection and coordination forms should be defined balancing two contrasting needs (Nassimbeni, 1998):

- Coordination mechanisms should not be so rigid so that the nodes become robust, leading to a network structure collapse, once such flexibility guarantees the integrated involvement of independent units.
- The coordination mechanisms must assure that the activities of each node are synchronized to the whole system.

The network life cycle segregates the network existence into phases and processes. Despite all phases and process not being representative to the purpose, it is important to present every cycle in order to have sound understanding of the network dynamics. (Goranson, 1999)

The proposal of Camarinha-Matos and Afsarmenesh (1999 a,b) can be a model to other approaches of cooperation networks among companies. It includes the following phases:

- *Creation/ Configuration*: is based on partner selection, contract negotiation, definition of access rights and sharing levels, definition and configuration of process connection of the parts. The problem of partner selection should be broken down in two groups: essential partners, responsible for the components, critical services and subsidiary partners, who supply components and services of lesser importance.
- *Operation*: is based on the modeling of business process to reach common objectives, requiring functionalities such as: request management, distributed and dynamic planning and scheduling, task management. High level coordination tasks. It is observed that in order to give support at the many interaction levels among members of the Virtual Company, the Production planning and control (PPC) is added by a support layer.
- *Evolution/ Reconfiguration*: is based on exceptional events during the operation phase, as the momentary incapacity of some partner or the need to increase manpower.
- *Dissolution*: based on the end of the business process and the end of inter-organizational relationship.

In a distributed manufacturing environment, the production planning coordinates requests and designates different resources in such cooperative production pertaining to several companies (De Toni and Meneghetti, 2000).

It is recognized that planning and control systems have significant implications for the prosperity of the operations, internally as well as throughout the supply chain. (Kehoe and Boughton, 2001)

There is a growing need for the industrial organizations to explore alternative mechanisms for its operations network management (Kehoe and Boughton, 2001), which can justify the interest in the modeling PPC according to its life cycle network, in order to optimize the productive use of resources, provide production flow, minimize the difficulties and help to keep the efficiency at high levels.

2. THE CONSTRUCTION PROJECT IN A VIRTUAL ORGANIZATION APPROACH

A construction work can be analyzed from a virtual organization approach: it is from a business opportunity exploration (the work itself) that companies are employed for task work, specific services and exercising their competence in a particular phase of the construction project.

During the construction project period, the services of the hired companies are complementary to each other and should be appropriately coordinated to rigorously follow the project scheduling. To analyze the virtual organization characteristics that a construction work possesses and its intervening factors, which are characteristics of the sector.

2.1. Creation/ Configuration

The Automobile Motor Factory was a special order, where the costumer supplied the characteristics of the industrial plant and needs, without needing to directly participate in the project or in the management of the work. Enterprise B was the company that played the "broker" part (searching for partners and management relationships) in the work. The customer met initially with Enterprise B to present project requirements of the factory, and they searched for partner qualifications to form the consortium. It was decided from that meeting that the other three companies, directly contracted by the costumer (Enterprise D, Enterprise A and Enterprise C), would also participate in the business project owing to their specialties.

Therefore, in order to attend such prerogatives, a consortium of four construction companies was formed (Enterprise A, Enterprise B, Enterprise C and Enterprise D), to be responsible for all the stages of the construction project.

At the beginning of the consortium, each company tried to identify individually the competences that the subcontractors would need, also acting as "broker". In the case of the Subcontracted – Sub BCD1 – the company was hired for being the only company in the municipal district, specialized in industrial buildings. The decisive factor for recruiting the company was after a visit to a Compressors factory done by Enterprise B and the client to verify the quality of an oil cooling channel by the Subcontracted Sub BCD1.

For each working contract a competition was performed among the subcontracted companies. The qualifying criterion compared during the judgment was the lowest cost, and the winning criterion of the requests was labor readiness to begin the projects. Each contractor directly hired by the client had autonomy to evaluate proposals for their part in the construction project.

The identification of companies with specific competencies, such as the Subcontracted Sub D2, and all the companies of the industrial assembly were under client responsibility.

The four enterprises (A, B, C and D), in spite of being members of the consortium, were individually hired by the client. This contractual option generated conflicts of interests among the builders because there were no clear distinction of the performance limits and attributions of each company's responsibilities.

2.2. Operation

Enterprise A, at first, was the head of the consortium, responsible for the project, planning and management. The factory design was outsourced to other companies, in agreement with the necessary specialty (foundation design, structural design, and hydraulic facilities design among others).

Enterprise B was responsible for executing construction works (concrete structures, metallic structures, masonry and construction in general). The project to execute this was outsourced to Subcontracted Sub BCD1, Subcontracted Sub B2 and Subcontracted Sub B3 (accomplish work); Subcontracted Sub B4 (steel structure), Subcontracted Sub B5 (floor preparation to install machines). In addition, it possessed its own labor force to work the night shift.

Enterprise C was responsible for the work execution related to road and urban infrastructure of the factory. The implementation was performed by Subcontracted Sub BCD1 (execution work), Subcontracted Sub C2 (network of sewer installation and heliport) and four other subcontracted companies that had a short-term participation in the construction project.

Enterprise D was responsible for implementing work related to sanitation and electric facilities that besides using its own labor in a large part of the construction project, outsourced parts of the work. The execution was performed by Subcontracted Sub D2 (fire prevention), Subcontracted Sub D3 (electric assembly) and Subcontracted Sub D4 (cabinet).

At the second stage of the construction project, other companies were directly contracted by the client for specific outdoor illumination (Subcontracted Sub CL1) and industrial assembly.

2.3. Evolution / Reconfiguration

The responsible company to manage the joined competences, became Enterprise B, caused by a function distortion that initially belonged to Enterprise A. Enterprise B was responsible for managing the work, demanding deadlines from the subcontracted and other participating companies. One such example that can be pointed out was the placement of the floor in a factory section before Enterprise D had finished the water and sewer systems.

This fact occurred due to the individual contractual form of four companies linked directly to the client. If the contract had been signed in terms of a consortium, all the functions and responsibilities would have been pre-defined before beginning the work. This example evidences the lack of effective mechanisms for the establishment of contracts and subcontracts in the construction sector, which ends up giving leeway to informal situations and empiricism.

The Subcontracted Sub BCD1 was hired initially by Enterprise B to build the two oil cooling channels and the site for the machinery oil filtration. With the service delays caused by the rain period, it was necessary to allocate a larger labor contingent so the implantation of the second oil cooling channel could begin before finalizing the first. Since Subcontracted Sub BCD1 already had eighty-eight employees working on this construction project, and without the possibility for new recruiting, Subcontracted Sub B2 won the competition for the other channel.

During the course of the work, in many situations, subcontracted companies also participated in specific stages of the construction project for specific building services. This way, the reconfiguration of the subcontracted in the consortium followed through according to contingency.

2.4. Dissolution

At the end of the construction project, the consortium was dissolved with the withdrawal of Enterprises B and A from the construction site. The two last companies to leave the construction site, which were responsible for the final repairs and works, were Enterprises C and D. That stage extended for 7 months and showed several performance mistakes, mainly related to the inspection boxes pertaining to the sanitary sewer, where the woodwork that served as form was found under the concrete. The Subcontracted Sub BCD1 was the last construction company to end its activities after 7 months of re-work, when all services ended.

3. PROPOSAL OF A BUSINESS PROCESS MODEL AND ITS APPLICATION IN THE CONSTRUCTION PROJECT

Business processes represent the control flow of what happens within the company, they materialize management policies, documentation flows, operational processes, manufacture and administrative processes and regulations. And the inter-managerial integration is the concomitant integration of business process of a company to the businesses processes of another, or even sharing parts of business processes by different managerial cooperations. It is inferred that the modeling and the managerial integration are obtained through the modeling and integration of business processes. (Vernadat, 1996)

3.1. Modelling using EKD methodology

With that combination, , according to the EKD methodology (Figure 2), a model is presented in which the network Life Cycle is approached, aggregating to it the four morphologic elements proposed by Britto (2002) (nodes, positions, connections and flows), drawn by the business process "to Produce". Such business process is responsible for planning and controlling of the necessary resources with which to convert incomes into products, including PPC activities that enable increasing effectiveness and efficiency.

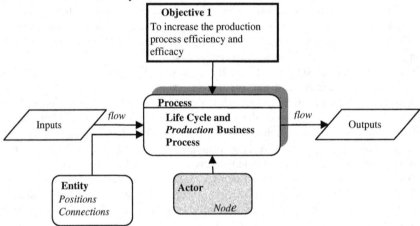

Figure 2: Model proposed according to EKD

3.2. Case study aplication

In this way, the application of EKD Business Process Model (Figure 2) to the construction project in question, the model is broadened in order to obtain an outlook of the construction activities according the life cycle and its morphological elements, converging to the model proposed below (Figure 3). In order to understand the model proposed it is pertinent to define the following notation: Sub B – Subcontracted of Enterprise B; Sub C – Subcontracted of Enterprise C; Sub D - Subcontracted of Enterprise D and; Sub BCD - Subcontracted of Enterprise B, C and D.

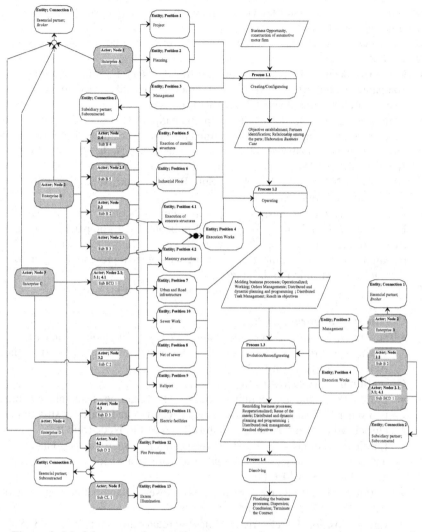

Figure 3: Model proposed according to automotive motor company construction project

The dynamics of the network is linked to the analysis of its life cycle, together with this is the business process "to Produce" throughout the entire network life cycle, according to Camarinha-Matos and Afsarmanesh (1999a, b) (creation/ configuration, operation, evolution/ reconfiguration and dissolution). Thus, the following configuration is given:

- Process 1.1: creation/ configuration
- Process 1.2: operationism
- Process 1.3: evolving/ reconfiguration
- Process 1.4: dissolving

Figure 3 shows essential or subsidized partnership and, acting as a "broker" or subcontracted, forms three different entities and connections (1- essential partnership, broker; 2- subsidized partnership, subcontracted; 3- essential partnership, subcontracted).

The Entities; Connections exposed above are composed of the following Actors;Nodes:

- Entity;Connection 1 (essential partnership; broker) is composed of four companies (Enterprises A, B , C and D) morphologically analyzed like *nodes* (the Actor;Node 1, 2, 3 and 4, respectively);
- Entity;Connection 2 (subsidized partnership;broker) is composed of subcontracted companies: seven companies that subsidize the enterprise, morphologically analyzed like   *nodes* (the Actor;Node 2.2 – Sub B2, Actor;Node 2.3- Sub B3, Actor;Node 2.4 – Sub B4 and Actor;Node 2.5- Sub B5;   Actor;Node 2.1,; 3.1; 4.1- Sub BCD1; Actor;Node 3.2- Sub C2; Actor;Node 4.3- Sub D3);
- Entity;Connection 3 (essential partnership; subcontracted) similar to Entity;Connection 2, it is composed of subcontracted companies: totalling two (Actor;Node 4.2- Sub D2; Actor;Node 5 – Sub CL1). However the proximity of the two companies with the Customer represents a larger role than only subsidization to the enterprise.

The nodes are related to the *positions*, along the phases of the network life cycle, according to the configuration below:

Creating/ Configuration (Process 1.1):
- The Entity; Position 1 (project), Entity; Position 2 (planning) and Entity; Position 3 (project), Entity; Position 3 (management) are related to the Actor; Node 1(Enterprise A).

Operationalism (Process 1.2):
- Entity; Position 4 (execution services), which can be dismembered into two other Entities; Positions (concrete execution and masonry structures) are related to Actor; Node 2.2 (Sub B2) and Actor; Node (Sub B3);
- Entities; Positions 4.2, 7 and 10 (respectively, execution masonry, road and urban infrastructure, and sanitation) are related to the Actor; Node 2.1; 3.1; 4.1 (Sub ABC1);
- Entities; Positions 8 and 9 (respectively, sewer net and heliport) is related to the Actor; Node 3.2 (Sub C2);
- Entity; Position 11 (electric facilities) is related to Actor; Node 4.3 (Sub D3);
- Entity; Position 12 (prevention to fire) is related to Actor; Node 4.2 (Sub D2);

Evolving/ Reconfiguration (Process 1.3):
- Entity; Position 3 (management) begins to relate to   Actor; Node 2 (Enterprise B) and no longer to Actor; Node 1 (Enterprise A);
- After replacement of the company Sub BCD1, due to lack of resources and arrears, Entity; Position 4 (execution of services – related to the oil cooling channels construction and the site to filter the oil machine) begins to relate to Actors; Nodes 2.2; 2.1; 3.1; 4.1 (Sub C2 and Sub BCD1);

In relation to the connections, it can be observed along the life cycle, that the tendency is an approximation to Entities; Positions; once the positions are associated to a certain work division of a construction project , connecting different agents, seeking to reach certain objective and integrating operational capacities.

4. CONCLUSION

The term "network companies" usually recurs to a vast range of inter-organizational relationships, but the "network" type differs in form, labels or theoretical basis. However, they usually refer to similar concepts.

The morphologic elements (nodes, positions, connections and flows) are concepts that attempt to pattern the complex contingent network structure, whose limits are not always well defined and diffused mechanisms. The network life cycle aids in modeling and understanding the inter-organizational relationships. By the business process "to Produce" the managerial politics, operational procedures and manufacture processes are materialized, enabling observation of the activities of PPC, manifesting what the organizational actors do to reach such objectives. It is inferred that the organizational modeling is obtained through modeling of the business process. As synthesis of such reasoning the EKD Business Process Model was proposed in order to represent the construction project of automotive motor company.

In spite of a construction project it is necessary to regulate the mechanisms that supply quantitative and qualitative acting data, thus reducing situations of uncertainty, enabling configuring businesses within a concept of effective virtual organization.

The proposal modeling (Figure 3) supports the specific information of the contractors that the expected results to be accomplished are anticipated, aiding the anticipation of events and the programming of activities, once it enables better understanding of the enterprise.

The modeling facilitates easy visualization of the process "to Produce" in relation to the network life cycle, thus acquiring temporary characteristics.

The model in EKD represent a knowledge base that allows modifications, such as the introduction of new rules in the process or new agents representing the structure, activities, process, information flow and the objective appropriately. The model presented serve to intensify the information exchange among network partners, suggesting the creation of a data base patter, to propitiate consistency of generated data. The presented EKD Business Process Model must be seen as a starting point, since it can be enriched by other models (rules, objective, components and technical requirements), contributing to better visualization and understanding of the approach situation.

5. REFERENCES

1. Britto, J. "Cooperação interindustrial e redes de empresas", in Kupfer, D.; Hasenclever, L. (Org's). Economia Industrial: fundamentos teóricos e práticos no Brasil. Rio de Janeiro: Campus, 2002.
2. Bubenko Jr, J. A.; Stirna, J.; Brash, D. "EKD user guide", Dpt. Of computer and systems sciences. Stockholm". Stockholm: Royal Institute of Technology, 1998.
3. Camarinha-Mattos, L. M.; Afsarmanesh, H. "The virtual enterprise concept". Working Conference on Infrastructure for Virtual Enterprise (PRO-EV'99), 27-28 out. Porto, Portugal 1999a; pp. 3-14.
4. Camarinha-Mattos, L. M.; Afsarmanesh, H. "Tendencies and general requirements for virtual enterprises". Working Conference on Infrastructure for Virtual Enterprise (PRO-EV'99), 27-28 out., Porto, Portugal 1999a; pp. 15-30.
5. Camarinha-Mattos, L. M.; Lima, C. P. "Coordination and configuration requirements in a virtual enterprise". Working Conference on Infrastructure for Virtual Enterprise (PRO-EV'99), 27-28 out., Porto, Portugal 1999; pp. 49-64.

6. Castells, M. A sociedade em rede. São Paulo: Paz e Terra, 1999.
7. Chambers, D. B.; Báguena, F. S.; Fernández, M. G. (2000). "Production planning and control information system for the engineering and make to order environment: a virtual enterprise approach". Working Conference on Infrastructure for Virtual Enterprise (PRO-EV'00), 4-6 dec., Florianópolis, Brazil 2000; p. 333-340.
8. Checkland, P. B. Systems thinking, systems practice. New York: John Wiley & Sons, 1981.
9. Davenport, T. H. Reengenharia de processos: como inovar na empresa através da tecnologia da informação. Rio de Janeiro: Campus, 1994.
10. De Toni, A.; Meneghetti, A. "The production planning process for a network of firms in the textile-apparel industry." International Journal of Production Economics, 65; 2000, pp.17-32.
11. Goranson, H. T. "The agile virtual enterprise: cases, metrics, tools". Westport, USA: Quorum Books, 1999.
12. Katzy,B. R.; Schuh, G.; Millarg, K. "Die Virtuelle Fabrik – Produziere im Netzwerk". Tecnische Rundschau Transfer, 43. Swiss: Universität St. Gallen, 1999.
13. Kavakli, V.; Loucopoulos, P. "Goal-driven business process analysis application in electricity deregulation". Information Systems, v. 24, 3; 1999, pp.187-207.
14. Kehoe, D.; Boughton, N. "Internet based supply chain management: A classification of approaches to manufacturing planning and control". International Journal of Operations & Production Management, 21, 4; 2001, pp. 516-524.
15. Levin, B. M. "Strategic networks: The emerging business organization and its impact on production costs". International Journal of Production Economics, 56-57; 1998, pp. 397-405.
16. Mizruchi, M.S. & Galaskiewicz, J. "Networks of Interorganizational Relations". Sociological Methods & Research. v 22, 11; 1993, pp. 46-70.
17. Nassimbeni, G. "Network structures and co-ordination mechanisms: a taxonomy". International Journal of Operations & Production Management, v 18, 6; 1998, pp. 538-554.
18. Olave, M. E. L.; Amato, J. "Redes de cooperação produtiva: estratégia de competitividade e sobrevivência para pequenas e médias empresas". Gestão & Produção, v8, 3; dez 2001, pp.289-303.
19. Rolland, C.; Nurcan, S.; Grosz, G. "A decision making pattern for guiding the enterprise knowledge development process". Information and Software Technology, 42; 2000, pp.313-331.
20. VERNADAT, F. B. (1996). Enterprise Modeling and Integration: principles and applications. New York: Chapman & Hall, 1996.
21. Vilkamo, T.; Keil, T.. "Strategic technology partnering in high-velocity environments-lessons from a case study". Technovation, 23; 2003, pp. 193-204.
22. Wiendahl, H. P.; Höbig, M. "Balanced production planning and control in production networks". Proceeding of the International Conference of Manufacturing Value-Chain, Troon, Scotland, UK, 1998.
23. Williams, T.. "Cooperation by design: structure and cooperation in interorganizational networks". Journal of Business Research, 5867, p.1-9, Acessível on line 21 nov. 2002.
24. Yin, R. K. Estudo de Caso: planejamento e métodos. Porto Alegre: Bookman Companhia Editorial, 2001.

16

CRITICAL THINKING AND CONCEPT DESIGN GENERATION IN A COLLABORATIVE NETWORK

Antonio P. Volpentesta, Maurizio Muzzupappa, Salvatore Ammirato
Università della Calabria, ITALY
volpentesta@deis.unical.it, muzzupappa@unical.it, ammirato@deis.unical.it

The key focus of this paper is to introduce an approach to collaborative concept design which makes use of critical thinking styles and methods. It consists of four stages aimed to generate concept ideas, in response to identified needs, to explore them, to develop a set of solutions, and to finally choose a solution through critical examination of the solution set. Experimental findings and results obtained from an implementation of this approach in a blended learning classroom are also presented and discussed.

1. INTRODUCTION

Collaborative concept design refers to intensive collaboration among designers, who strive for and create a shared understanding of the product concept (Volpentesta and Muzzupappa, 2006). Mamykina et al., (2002), Rodgers et al., (2001) and Ulrich et al., (1995) define a *product concept* as a description of the form, function, and features of the product which is usually accompanied by a set of specifications, an analysis of competitive products, and an economic justification of the project. They define *concept development* as the first phase in the product development process where the needs of the target market are identified, alternative product concepts are generated and a single concept is selected for further development. They define *concept design* as the work (task clarification, hypothesis formulation, solution searching) done on a product concept by designers in the concept development phase in order to determine a product concept architecture. Concept design is a process that often requires participation of individuals from different disciplines, e.g. electronics, software, mechanical, industrial and management engineering, in sharing knowledge, performing design tasks and organizing resources.

A fundamental part of this process is constituted by collaborative generation of what is called "the seeds of innovation", i.e. ideas for a new product concept (Flynn et al., 2003). Such activity is creative in the sense given in Farid-Foad et al. (1993) and Martins et al. (2003) where creativity is defined as the capacity to produce new and useful ideas, or the combination of existing ideas into new and useful concepts, to satisfy a need in a specified organizational context. The importance of collaborative creativity is readily apparent when one considers that most creative pursuits in industry involve many individuals with various competencies working

Please use the following format when citing this chapter:

Volpentesta, A.P., Muzzupappa, M. and Ammirato, S., 2008, in IFIP International Federation for Information Processing, Volume 283; *Pervasive Collaborative Networks*; Luis M. Camarinha-Matos, Willy Picard; (Boston: Springer), pp. 157–164.

together to develop a product concept that cannot be created by a single individual alone (Mamykina et al., 2002). A collection of differently skilled designers can, in principle, go beyond individual knowledge and reach new concept ideas because design problems are understood from different perspectives (Barlow, 2001; Ivanitskaya et al., 2002; Alves et al., 2006).

Creativity involves critical thinking, i.e. observing laterally the information that has been available to everyone else's observation but that no one else has been able to interpret with a fresh perspective, (De Bono, 1990). In Sofo (2004) critical thinking is said to be "about stopping to reconsider what we take for granted. It means re-evaluating our habits to improve the way we do things. Thinking critically is a journey of exploration. It is about re-discovering something we already know. It will take as back to where we started so that we will understand in a new way. Thinking critically is a shift in perspective, even if it is just a very small shift. It is about increasing our own awareness of how we think, letting go of strongly held beliefs, and creating a new mental model, a new mindset". Moreover, some of the most potent outcomes of critical thinking can occur when groups or teams of people engage in the concept design process together, offering multiple perspectives and providing opportunities for designers to practise different approaches to problem solving.

Recently, critical thinking methods have been used in product concept design by Johnson et al. (2007) who reported a comparative study on the results of a competitive design project undertaken simultaneously by two multidisciplinary new product development teams. They play an important role in the first two phases of the design process, namely: 1) planning and clarifying the task (or idea development) and 2) conceptual design. These two phases are mostly creative and are much less costly than the later stages of the design process (Pahl & Beitz, 1996). It thus makes sense to maximize its output by providing a larger number of ideas/concepts for further exploitation. The basic rationale is "the greater the number of ideas/concepts at the start of the new product development process, the greater the probability of ending up with successful products" (Alves et al., 2006).

In a previous paper, a double-sided approach was proposed to blend the "creativity" of various designers in a Virtual Breeding Environment (Volpentesta et al., 2007). In this paper we present a modified and reduced version of the approach particularly focused on the concept generation (without considering the question of how to configure virtual groups and teams). The approach we introduce here can be applied in a *Collaborative Network of Designers*, (CND), that supports a master company in creating a new product concept to respond to some identified potential opportunities. In such CND, designers, from many dispersed organizational units, should provide the critical mass required for knowledge overflows and synergies that favour creativity in new product concept development. The entire process is performed by a virtual group and a team coordinated by a concept design manager.

A critical thinking method was applied to the work of virtual groups who generated ideas and solutions successively evaluated by a team in a collaborative section. Lastly we present some experimental findings from a project conducted in a blended learning classroom. Our goal is to demonstrate how collaborative creativity may constitute an added value to design activities, above all in the early phases of a new product development life-cycle.

2. COLLABORATIVE GENERATION OF A CONCEPT

The approach we present is aimed to tackle the problem of how a master organization can manage the collaborative creativity of product concept designers working as a virtual group and as a team in a network environment. According to Furst et al. (1999), we define a *group* as a "collection of individuals whose contributions to a product or a process are additive and can be collated and presented by a group manager as the result of group effort. Performance evaluation and accountability for a group will occur at the individual rather than the collective level"; we define a *team* as a "collection of individuals who interact more extensively than group members to produce a deliverable, who are evaluated based on the team outcome and who are accountable as a team (instead of or in addition to individual accountability) for team outcomes". We define a *virtual group* (or *virtual team*) as a group (team) whose members are geographically, temporally, and/or organizationally dispersed and brought together across time and space by way of information and communication technologies to accomplish an organizational task. The following roles are taken into consideration (see Fig. 1):

1. Concept Design Manager (CDM) from the master organization;
2. Creative Designers Group (CDG) formed by some designers in CND;
3. Evaluation Designers Team (EDT) formed by some designers in CND.

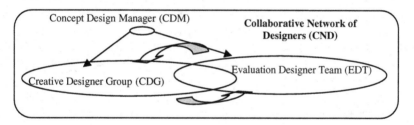

Figure 1- Roles in a CND

Many researchers in the psychology of community have shown that team (also called *real group*) creativity is not as effective as group (also called *nominal group*) creativity (Taylor et al., 1958; Demhis et al., 1993), when problem solving tasks are tackled. Other studies, on the contrary, have shown that the utilization of a team is more successful in the creative process at the ideas/solutions evaluation phases, (War et al., 2005; Ulrich et al., 1995).

In our approach, members of the CDG that may be geographically dispersed are required to work independently on creative problem solving task and their outputs are successively collected by the CND to form a cumulative output. Members of the EDT interact face to face and work together in a collaborative session to evaluate ideas and solutions previously collected.

The approach comprises a cascade of four stage-gates consisting in defining concept visions, functional schema, functional layouts and construction solutions for a digital mock-up of an innovative product (e.g. a device):

1. the first stage generates product concept visions (cs_i) in response to a request forwarded by the CDM to the CDG;
2. the second stage receives as input cs_i and generate functional schema fs_i related to each of them. The purpose of a functional scheme is to define the functional structure of the product, i.e. macro system components and their interactions;
3. the third stage receives as input fs_i and gives out functional layouts (fl_i) each of which specifies the preliminary layout ,i.e. mutual position of each sub-systems and their possible volumes, and principle solutions for each subsystem.
4. the fourth stage generates some constructive solutions (cs_i) with respect to selected fl_i.

A graphical representation of the process is shown in Figure 2.

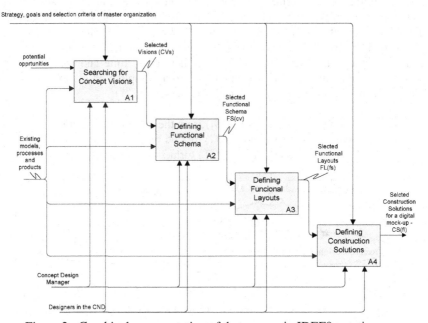

Figure 2 - Graphical representation of the process in IDEF0 notation

Each stage consists of five sequential steps that can be summarized as follows (see Table 1): a request for proposal (ideas or solutions) is transmitted by the CDM to the CDG; responses (coming from the CDG) are collected by the CDM and assessed in a collaborative session by the EDT (using the six thinking hats method); the most suitable ideas or solutions are ranked and selected for successive development by the CDM.

Each evaluation step of any stage consists of a collaboration session performed by the EDT and is based on the De Bono's "six coloured hats" method, (De Bono, 1990). The "six coloured hats" is a critical thinking method of organizing thinking patterns so that a person who is thinking can adopt a specific thinking style at any time, instead of having to try to combine all thinking styles at once. Multicolour printing has been considered the best analogy to explain this method. Each colour is printed in a separate step and in the final step, all the colours are combined.

Table 1- Steps and roles in each stage.

Steps in each stage	Roles
Launching a call for proposal	CDM
Generating ideas/solutions	Designers in CDG
Collecting ideas/solutions	CDM
Evaluating ideas/solutions	Designers in EDT
Ranking and selecting ideas/solutions	CDM

This method has been used already to design product concept by Johnson et al. (2007) who reported a comparative study on the results of a competitive design project undertaken simultaneously by two multidisciplinary new product development teams.

In the application of this method we consider six "coloured" sub-sessions. During each of them all members of the EDT metaphorically wear a hat of the same colour of the sub-session. These hats indicate the type of thinking being used by EDT's members and the type of contribution they are required to give, (see Tab. 2).

Table 2 - A framework for critical thinking in collaborative evaluation sessions.

Colour	Type of thinking	Type of contribution
White	Impartial and objective; neither interpretations nor opinions are taken into account; search for information related to the proposed ideas/solutions.	Use data requests and precise questions in order to obtain new information or supplement incomplete information.
Yellow	Positive and constructive; search for benefits, values, and reasons to be optimistic about the proposed ideas/solutions.	Positive assessments that cover a spectrum ranging from the logical and practical at one end to dreams, visions and hopes at the other end.
Black	As devil's advocate to see why something won't work; search for faults, problems, risk and dangers related to the proposed ideas/solutions.	Negative assessments that point out what is wrong, incorrect or defective and ways in which something is contrary to experience or established knowledge.
Red	Awareness of hunches, premonitions and intuitions about the proposed ideas/solutions. Feeling and emotions are legitimized as essential components of thinking.	Expressions of feelings so that they can be integrated in the thought map and also made part of the evaluation system that selects the route on the map.
Green	Creative, lateral and fertile in order to see beyond the familiar, the obvious and the "good enough".	Creative statements and sowing seeds for alternative ideas or solutions.
Blue	Cool and controlled; thinking about thinking that is necessary for the evaluation of ideas/solutions.	Organization and summarization of outputs of other coloured sub-sessions, Requests of opening another coloured sub-session with the definition of the objects to which thinking is to be applied and the thinking tasks to be performed.

3. AN EXPERIENCE IN EDUCATIONAL ENVIRONMENT

The project consisted of selected activities developed in a blended (virtual and traditional) learning classroom attending the master course in Industrial Design held at University of Calabria in A.Y. 2007/08.

Students and teacher could interact and collaborate using a variety of tools, such as:

- information sources - on line and off line learning materials (books, encyclopedias, teacher's notes, digital libraries,…etc.), software reference guides, students' curricula;
- technological infrastructure – a set of ICT tools for asynchronous and synchronous interaction, search for and access to information sources and virtual services, symbols construction and manipulation;
- sketch and cad tools.

The blended classroom has been regarded as a CND where product concept design has been developed. During a week period, teachers played the role of concept design manager, while 12 students (9 students with Mechanical, Management and Civil Engineering background and 3 students with Architectural background) played the role of concept designers.

Rather than start with the phases of planning and clarifying the task, the experience started from a proposal to generate a concept for "an innovative bookcase for a living room". Due to the requirements of the proposed device, we conducted only 3 stages of the methodology introduced in section 2, namely, the Concept Vision, Functional Layout and Constructive Solution stages.

As showed above, each stage is made up of five sequential steps. The first step consisted in the launch of a *Request for Concept Vision* (RCV) for the considered device; it was submitted by the concept manager to designers. Then all designers were required to generate their concept visions (step2).

After having collected 12 concept visions (step 3), CDM set up 4 EDTs, each of them with 3 students with different backgrounds in order to obtain a multidisciplinary team.

Each EDT was charged with the task of evaluating 3 concept vision ideas according to the "six hats" method (step 4). Within an EDT, each student analyzed the proposed project wearing, in rotation, a different hat. The rationale was to drive the designer's critical thinking in concepts evaluation. At the end of the evaluation process, the teacher gathered the report cards and selected the three most promising concept visions (see Tab. 3).

Table 3 - Concept visions selected by the CDM

Concept	*cv3*	*cv5*	*cv9*
	Bookcase with integrated multimedia tools	Bookcase with door for separating different spaces	Flexible and modular bookcase

Moving from the three selected concept visions, three requests for functional layouts (RFL(*cv*)) were successively submitted to the designers. Four functional layouts (*fl1* … *fl4*) for *cv3*, seven (*fl5* … *fl11*) for *cv5* and one for *cv9* (*fl12*) were generated. They were evaluated by EDTs and three functional layouts were selected by the CDM (see Figure 3).

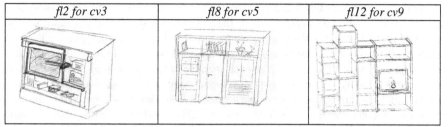

fl2 for cv3	*fl8 for cv5*	*fl12 for cv9*

Figure 3 - Functional layouts selected by the CDM

In the last stage, CDM submitted requests to the designers to define construction solutions for any selected layouts (namely: RCS1 for *fl2*, RCS2 for *fl8* and RCS3 for *fl12*). Responses were collected and the most promising was selected by the CDM (see Figure 4).

cs5 for fl2

Figure 4 - The final concept of an innovative bookcase for living room

The final solution does not identify a definitive product, but it constitutes a useful input for future work on a complete product concept development. This concept is thus the result of a collaborative experience among different designers and it can be seen as the outcome of a creative process involving different individuals (see Fig.5).

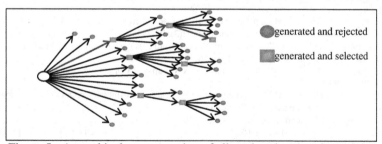

generated and rejected

generated and selected

Figure 5 - A graphical representation of all explored paths of creativity

4. CONCLUSION

This paper has addressed how a master organization can manage the collaborative creativity of product concept designers working in many geographically dispersed organizational units. Our methodology proposes two novel aspects. The first one can be found in the widening of the idea generation activities to the conceptual design phase in product design. In this process, new creative contributions coming from concept designers in a CND are progressively generated and combined disclosing new exploratory directions (Fig.5). On the other hand, the traditional approaches proposed in the literature (Pahl et al., 1996), embrace the funnel metaphor, (Flynn et al., 2003) that consists of a series of "stage-gates" where several initial ideas equally promising go through the funnel, are evaluated, selected and refined and, at the end of the process, only one of them is developed concretely. A second novel aspect consists in a collaboration session performed by the designers, based on the De Bono's "six coloured hats" method. In particular, we have applied the six hats method during the evaluating session and not for generating ideas (Johnson et al.,2007). Lastly, we have described results obtained from a project we conducted in a blended learning classroom. Direct observation and involvement in project development have provided some credible basis for the validation of our approach. The experience has shown how collaborative creativity may constitute an added value to project activities in the early phases of a new product development life-cycle. We intend to conduct more significant experiences studies and develop more interpretative perspectives in our future work.

5. REFERENCES

1. Alves J, Marques MJ, Saur I, Marques P. Building creative ideas for successful new product development. Transformations, eds. M.K. Stasiak; J.Buijs, w Lodzi Publ., 2006; 363-383.
2. Barlow CM. Insight or ideas: Escaping the idea centered "box" defining creativity. Proc. HICSS-34, Los Alamitos (USA), IEEE Computer Soc. 2001; 2877-2885.
3. De Bono E. Six Thinking Hats. England: Penguin, 1990.
4. Demhis AR and Valacich JS. Computer Brainstorms: More Heads Are Better Than One. Journal of Applied Psychology 1993; 78(4): 531- 536.
5. Farid-Foad A, El-Sharkawy R, Austin LK. Managing for creativity and innovation in A/E/C organizations. J. of Manag. in Eng.: American Society of Civil Engineers 1993; 9(4): 399-409.
6. Flynn M, Dooley L, O'Sullivan D, Cormican K. Idea Management for Organisational Innovation. Int. J. of Innovation Management 2003; 7(4): 417-442.
7. Furst S, Blackburn R, Rosen B. Virtual team effectiveness: a proposed research agenda. Information Systems Journal, Blackwell Science 1999; 9: 249-269.
8. Ivanitskaya L, Clark D, Montgomery G, Primeau R. Interdisciplinary Learning: Process and Outcomes. Innovative Higher Education 2002; 27(2): 95-111.
9. Johnson P, Griffiths R and Gill S. The 24 hr product: from concept to interactive model in less than a day. Int. J. Design Engineering 2007; 1(1): 56–70.
10. Mamykina L, Candy L, Edmonds E. Collaborative Creativity. Communication of the ACM, 2002; 45(10): 96-99.
11. Martins EC, Terblanche F. Building organisational culture that stimulates creativity and innovation. Eur.J.of Innovation Management 2003; 6(1): 64-74.
12. Pahl G, Beitz W. Engineering Design. Springer, 1996.
13. Rodgers PA, Calwell NHM, Clarkson PJ, Huxor AP. The Management of Concept Design Knowledge in modern product development organizations. Int. J. of Computer Integrated manufacturing 2001; 14(1): 108-115.
14. Sofo F. Open Your Mind. Allen & Unwin, 2004.
15. Taylor DW, Berry PC and Block CH. Does Group Participation When Using Brainstorming Facilitate or Inhibit Creative Thinking?. Administrative Science Quarterly 1958; 3(1): 23- 47.
16. Ulrich KT, Eppinger SD. Product Design and Development. McGraw-Hill, 1995.
17. Volpentesta AP, Muzzupappa M. "Identifying partners and organizational logical structures for collaborative conceptual design". In Network-Centric Collaboration and Supporting Frameworks, Camarinha-Matos L, Afsarmanesh H, Ollus M, eds. Boston: Springer, 2006; 224: 397-406.
18. Volpentesta AP, Muzzupappa M, Della Gala M. Managing collaborative creativity for product concept design. , in Proc. of 9th Int. Conf. on MITIP of the Industrial Enterprises, Rapaccini M, Visintin F, eds. Florence, Italy 2007; 110-117.
19. War A and O'Neill E. Understanding Design as a Social Creative Process. Proceedings of the 5th conference on Creativity & cognition, London, United Kingdom 2005; 118-127.

PART 6

MANAGEMENT OF COLLABORATIVE NETWORKS

17

A TOC PERSPECTIVE TO IMPROVE THE MANAGEMENT OF COLLABORATIVE NETWORKS

Alexandra Tenera, António Abreu
New University of Lisbon
Quinta da Torre – 2829 Monte Caparica, PORTUGAL
abt@fct.unl.pt, , ajfa@fct.unl.pt,

Collaborative networks are typically assumed to bring clear benefits and competitive advantage to the participating members. On the other hand, since the networks are typically formed by heterogeneous and autonomous enterprises, it is natural that each member has its own culture and set of interest. As result, the development of methodologies to facilitate the management process during the operation phase of a virtual enterprise (VE) is an important element for the wide adoption of this paradigm. Departing from a brief presentation of the Theory of Constraints this paper introduces an approach of these concepts to collaborative networks and discusses its potential application in the context of a (VE). To conclude, experimental results based on data from a collaborative network are presented and discussed.

1. INTRODUCTION

The business environment has changed radically during the last years and new changes will certainly continue (Abreu and Camarinha-Matos, 2006).

According to Penã and Arroyabe (Penã and Arroyabe, 2002) there are three environmental factors that have had the most decisive influence to encourage collaboration among organizations.

The first is economic globalisation. The world economy at the beginning of the twenty-first century is experiencing one of its moments of its greatest dynamism and change. This dynamism is reflected in the growing interdependence of markets for goods, services and production factors.

The second factor is the increase of business uncertainty. The speed in which changes are occurring in the economic world is introducing great uncertainty, especially in business areas where constant transformations, that are often difficult to predict, resulting from reductions in technological and product cycles, from improvements in productive processes and so on, are demanding greater follow-up capacity from enterprises in order to adapt to the new surrounding conditions.

Finally, the third feature is the high level of competitive rivalry. The increased customer requirements and market saturation are constantly obliging the enterprises to dig deeper in their search for competitive advantages in order to improve their position in the market. As a result, there is a tendency for enterprises to concentrate on know-how, or on those aspects of added value chain that they really dominate.

Consequently, the traditional forms of inter-organizational co-work such as outsourcing, spin-off, franchises, joint venture, consortium, etc, are changing for a

Please use the following format when citing this chapter:

Tenera, A. and Abreu, A., 2008, in IFIP International Federation for Information Processing, Volume 283; *Pervasive Collaborative Networks*; Luis M. Camarinha-Matos, Willy Picard; (Boston: Springer), pp. 167–176.

new form of collaborative environments supported by the continuous advances in information and communication technologies. Examples of these later developments are advanced and highly integrated supply chains, virtual enterprises/virtual organizations, virtual (professional) communities and value constellations, etc., where most of these collaborative environments imply some kind of organizational configuration of activities within the environment and its constituents.

On the other hand, in most literature about collaboration there is an assumption that collaboration networks can bring a clear intuitive advantages to its members and can even represent a survival factor in turbulent socio-economic scenarios. On the basis of these expectations are, among others, the following factors among others: sharing of risks and resources, joining of complementary skills and capacities, acquisition of an apparently higher dimension, access to new / wider markets and new knowledge (Camarinha-Matos and Abreu, 2004).

However, in spite of these advantages, it is also frequently mentioned that collaboration also involves additional overheads (e.g. transaction costs) (Williamson, 1985) and several risks and the lack of tools tailed to support management activities is an obstacle for a wider acceptance of this paradigm.

In order to contribute for the development of a tool that supports the management activities in a collaborative context, the suggested approach doesn't want to "re-invent the wheel" but rather to adapt and take into account possible contributions from others disciplines. However it´s necessary to take into account that these approaches and corresponding tools have been developed for different contexts (Camarinha-Matos and Abreu, 2003). Therefore their application to collaborative networks requires assessment, adaptations, and further developments. Furthermore, there are a large number of different perspectives that cannot be covered by a single theory or single modeling approach.

This paper introduces some discussion about the applications of the Theory of Constraints' concepts in collaborative networks and discusses its potential application in the context of virtual enterprises.

2.   THE THEORY OF CONSTRAINTS

The Theory of Constraints (TOC) introduced a new perspective on system management that is distint from the classical approaches. According to this approach the systems should be managed taking into account its main constraint and the improvement of the system requires its improvement or elimination.

The TOC was developed initially for Production Systems (Goldratt and Cox, 1992), and later for Project Management (Goldratt, 1997) and more recently has also been applied to Strategic Planning (Dettmer, 2003).

The TOC can be seen as a prescriptive theory that promotes an increase of the system's performance based on an identification and subsequent improvement of the main constraint of the system (which can be applied to an organization or to a network of organizations) in a systematic, successive and continuous way considering several conceptual principles (Dettmer, 1997), from which the following ones can be pointed out:

- Systems can be viewed as a chain of interrelated elements in which the global performance is constrainted by its weekest link.

- Local optimization does not guarantee global optimization.
- Optimal solutions tend to deteriorate as the system's environement changes.
- System's constraints can be physical or policy, these last ones are more difficult to identify, change or eliminate but when achieved they usually result on a larger degree of system improvement.
- To know what to change in systems requires the understanding of their current reality and goals, as well as the magnitude and direction of the difference between them.
- Many of the undesired effects (UDEs) in systems are manisfestations of core problems, that when solved, eliminate all resulting UDEs, althought the individual eliminations of UDE's does not eliminate the core problem.
- Core problems manifest themselves through UDEs linked by a network of cause-effect and are perpetuated by hidden or underlying conflicts.
- Solution of core problems requires challenging the assumptions underlying each conflict and at least one assumption must be invalidated to solve the conflict.
- Solutions tend to create resistance for further change, that is why inertia shoud be combated.

As result, TOC is being seen as a management philosophy where the system is managed from a global perspective. The continuous improvement is obtained from the management of the system elements' interactions where the individual performance of each member is defined by taking into account the main system constraint also called the weakest link.

TOC includes several elements that can be classified in four domains (Tenera, 2006), as shown in the Figure 1.

Prescriptive Component		Thinking Component	
1. Concepts and Principles		**2. Logical Thinking Tools**	
Strategic Component	- Main Concepts - General Principles (Fundamental questions and focusing steps) - Layers of Resistance to change		- Thinking Tools (CRT, CRD, FRT, NBR, PRT, TT) - Categories of Legitimate Reservation (CLR)
	3. Specfic Solutions		**4. Performance Measurements**
Operational Component	- Drum-Buffer-Rope (DBR) - Critical Chain (CC) - Buffer Management (BM) - V-A-T Analysis		- Throughput, T - Inventory, I - Operating expense, OE

Figure 1 – TOC Schematic Summary

These four domains result from crossing two main variables: the scope of the problem which can be more strategic or more operational and the type of approach used to analyse the system which can have a more prescriptive or thinking nature. As result, the domains can be identified as: 1. Main concepts and general principles, which give the general guidelines of TOC logic in any system, 2. Logical thinking tools to identify core problems and solutions, 3. Solutions for specific environments and finally 4. Evaluation performance measurements to evalute systems performance.

In the domain of the specific solutions (3.), TOC proposed the Drum-Buffer-Rope approach to improve production system results which promotes the introdution of material Buffers to maximize the performance of the constrainted resource (the Drum) and better sincronization of the production flows through alert or information mechanisms (Rope) that will give the information needed to manage the production flow taking into account the buffers consumption (Goldratt and Cox, 1992). Similar approach in Project Management results in the critical chain (CC) as the drum of the project (activities linked by technical and resource dependencies that defined the project duration) and a proposed solution to manage projects best known as Critical Chain Project Management (CCPM) which will be presented in next section.

3. THE CRITICAL CHAIN APPROACH

The Critical Chain (CC) concepts were introduced by Goldratt in 1997 as an alternative approach to classical ones in Project Management (Goldratt, 1997) like PERT (Program Evaluation and Review Technique) or CPM (Critical Path Method). Best known as CCPM, the solution proposed by this approach incorporates technical elements for planning, schedule and control of project networks, and operational elements which include human actions and behaviors like the *roadrunner mentality*.

According to CCPM the network planning and schedule process should be developed in four fundamental phases:

a) Network Building
The network is built in two phases: first the network is created using an inverse logic i.e. from the last to the first activity. During this phase the project management team should identify the deliverable associated to each activity, the prerequisites and assumptions assumed. During the second phase the classical direct logic is used to verify and reformulate if necessary the activities relations identified in the first phase. The output of this approach will be an activity on node (AON) network with preferably *Finish-to-Start* (FS) activities and assumed resource constraints.

b) Activity Durations Estimation
The activity duration is probabilistic (Goldratt, 1997) and at least two estimations have to be made: a target duration (generally median or average duration) and a pessimistic duration.

c) Critical Chain Identification
The Critical Chain (CC) is the set of activities scheduled according to a *As Late as Possible* (ALAP) process that defines the project duration, based on activity durations, technical and resource dependencies.

d) Time Buffers Insertion and Network Scheduling

For each activity, CCPM builds schedules using target duration tight, Finished to Start (FS) dependencies and an *As Late As Possible* (ALAP) logic with buffers. The time buffers are time blocks incorporated on schedule in special points of the network to reduce the impact of duration variability of the activities on network, i.e a safety margin is aggregated at the end of the project, where it acts as a protection of the project due date, called Project Buffer (PB), and also in Feeding Buffers (FB), placed whenever a non-critical activity joins the critical chain, to protect critical activities against variations of the feeding chains.

Figure 2 illustrates a very simplified AON network with six activities (from A1 to A6) where the bar size defines the activity duration.

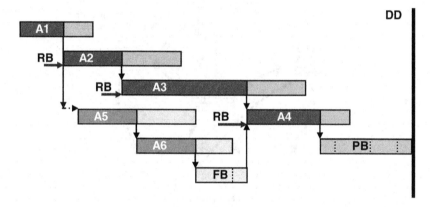

Figure 2 – CCPM Scheduling

In Figure 2 the CC is given by path A1, A2, A3, A4. To protect the project Due Date (DD) against CC duration variability a time buffer designed by Project Buffer (PB) is introduced after the last activity of the project. The PB is set to work as a time pillow or damper against schedule variability of critical chain activities as well as a visual register of the time impact of the randomness occurred in the network activities. This register is used as the control tool of the project execution and is intended to be efficient, focused and global.

To protect the CC from the variability of non critical activities durations (A5 e A6) another time buffer is inserted in arcs that connects non critical activities and critical activities. This type of buffer is designated by Feeding Buffers (FB).

To size the buffers Goldratt suggested a practical and simple cut of 50% in the pessimistic duration and schedule a buffer of 50% of the trimmed duration of the chain with n activities. After Goldratt's proposal of the critical chain principles of scheduling and management for projects (Goldratt, 1997) several other authors (Newbold, 1998; Hoel and Taylor, 1999; Leach, 2000; Shou and Yeo, 2000; Park and Pena-Mora, 2004; Tenera and Cruz-Machado, 2007) have proposed different methods for sizing projects and feeding buffers.

4. POTENTIAL APPLICATION IN CN CONTEXT

The concept of virtual enterprise is considered by a growing number of authors as a temporary network of enterprises, that is formed to explore a business opportunity; a Project is also viewed as "a temporary endeavor undertaken to create a unique product, service or result" (Project Management Institute, 2004) that can be modeled by a network of activities.

Assuming that, a virtual enterprise can be managed through a project network where the activities are replaced by enterprises and the links between activities represent dependences among enterprises, both concepts can be related as illustrated in Figure 3.

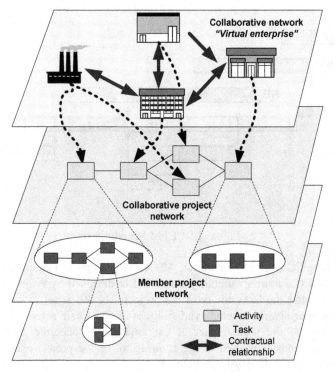

Figure 3 – Relation between project network and virtual enterprise

However, the success of this approach requires the existence of mechanisms that act as incentives for collaboration and punish the infractors. Futhermore, the partners involved in a collaborative network must provide to the VE coordinater, reliable information in useful time during the execution of the project; as well as, when was necessary to participate effectively in the recovery of delays.

5. EXPERIMENTAL RESULTS

The approach described earlier was applied in a major civil construction project, which comprised the construction of two twins towers at the municipality of Lisbon. According to the contract agreement the main goal was to build the towers within the time settled. The contractor was in charge for the planning, scheduling and construction. In order to built the towers the contractor worked with several subcontractors, resulting in a collaborative network with different entities and activities to develop. However, the number of resources involved in the construction of the first tower was greater than in the second tower.

In terms of management tools, the first tower was managed applying classical tools for project management while the second one was managed based on a CCPM collaborative approach.

Based on this approach the process of planning and scheduling the resources was applied at macro level where each member of the collaborative network had a set of tasks and sequences which were not programmed in the baseline of the collaborative project network but at the company project level.

After the identification of the critical chain of the collaborative project network the time buffers, BfS, were introduced. The size of all time buffers was calculated according to SMC method (which stands for *Simulação para a Melhoria da Calendarização*). The underlying logic of the proposed method (Tenera, 2006) is to size buffers addressing the risk using a simulation technique (Monte Carlo) of overrun the scheduled date of last activities of the chains (see Figure 4) considering the project schedule in the ALAP logic, as proposed in CCPM methodology.

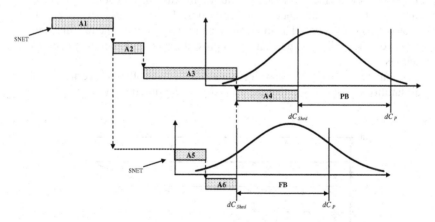

Figure 4 – SMC Logic

Considering, as an example, the very simple project network introduced earlier (Figure 2) with activities, A_i, interrelated with Finish to Start (FS) activities relations, schedule in an As Late As Possible (ALAP) logic assuming target durations for each activity. From Figure 4 it was possible to identify activities A1,

A2, A3 e A4 as the critical activities of the project and activities A5and A6, as non critical activities.

Assuming the ALAP scheduling logic of CCPM, the start of non critical activities, not depending from preceding activities conclusion, should not start before their ALAP schedule start date (with buffers included). Time buffers should be sized using: an assumed risk level for time overrun of the last activity of the critical chain for project buffer (PB) sizing purpose, and; a risk level for time overrun of end schedule dates of non critical activities converging to critical activities in sizing feeding buffers (FB).

To define the risk of overrun schedule activities end time, Monte Carlo Simulation was chosen as the simulation tool; it is a well known tool, and it has been used in project management risk analysis (Law and Kelton, 1991).

The difference between the simulated end date of these activities, associated with a chosen confidence level (dC_p), and the schedule date (dC_{Shed}), will be the time buffer to schedule (1). This buffer is intended to reduce the impact of non critical activities in the critical chain and to protect the project end date against variability. With this in mind, feeding buffers insertion can require the creation of a gap on the critical chain, as the duration variability of non critical chain should not delay the schedule start of critical chain activities (Goldratt, 1997) in order to improve the stability of the critical chain.

$$BfS = dC_p - dC_{Shed} \qquad\qquad (1)$$

During the execution of the project the scheduling update process was done considering not only the conclusion percentage of the undergoing activities but also using estimated and approved activity remaining durations. If needed, to reduce project buffer consumption the target duration was also changed in activities immediately following the undergoing activities. For that each member of the collaborative project network has to evaluate and if required, reschedule his member project network according to the changes approved for the collaborative network, in site reunions.

If we compare the activities baseline durations of the collaborative network and the real durations, one can see that the majority of the durations were not respected (Figure 5).

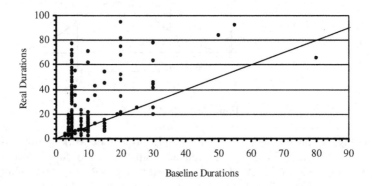

Figure 5 – Real durations *versus* Baseline durations

However, comparing the scheduled durations of the collaborative project network with the real ones, it can be seen that there is a greater linearity relation (Figure 6). These results show a more aligned schedules durations with the real activities durations, as a result of the CCPM management process used.

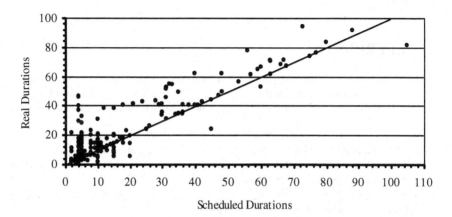

Figure 6 – Real durations *versus* Schedule durations

As illustrated in Figure 7 and in opposition to the First tower, managed according to traditional approaches, the application of the CCPM approach allowed to anticipate the schedule conclusion of the CCPM tower, managed using the proposed approach.

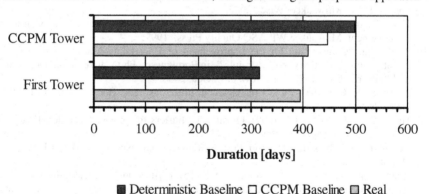

Figure 7 – Final phase durations of First Tower and CCPM Tower

6. CONCLUSIONS

Forms of collaboration have changed over the years and have become increasingly visible and complex. However, the development of models and tools that support management activities in collaborative environments will not only help to better understand the area, but also for a wide adoption of the collaborative networks paradigm in its various manifestation forms.

Some preliminary steps in this direction, inspired in critical chain concepts were presented. Initial results illustrate the applicability of the suggested approach. Further steps are necessary towards the elaboration of a robust tool as well as its validation.

7. REFERENCES

1. A. Abreu and L. M. Camarinha-Matos, "On the role of value systems and reciprocity in collaborative environments" in IFIP International Federation for Information Processing vol 224, L. M. Camarinha-Matos, H. Afsarmanesh, and M. Ollus, Eds. Boston: Springer, 2006, pp. 273-284.
2. N.A Penã, and J.C.F.Arroyabe, Business Cooperation, Palgrave:Macmillan, 2002.
3. L. M. Camarinha-Matos and A. Abreu, A contribution to understand collaboration benefits, in *Emerging Solutions for Future Manufacturing Systems*, L. M. Camarinha-Matos, Ed.: Springer, 2004.
4. Williamson, O. E. (1985). The Economic Institutions of Capitalism: Firms, Markets, Relational Contracting, New York: Free Press.
5. L.M. Camarinha-Matos and A. Abreu,"Towards a Foundation for Virtual Organizations," in Proc. of Business Excellence I: Performance Measures, Benchmarking and Best Practices in New Economy. Braga, 2003, pp. 647-652.
6. E.M. Goldratt, and J. Cox, The Goal: An Ongoing Improvement Process (2ª ed.), North River Press, Great Barrington, Mass., 1992.
7. Goldratt, E. M. (1997). Critical Chain. Great Barrington, MA, EUA: North River Press.
8. H.W. Dettmer, Strategic Navigation: A Systems Approach to Business Strategy, ASQ Quality Press, Milwaukee, Wisc., 2003.
9. H.W. Dettmer, Goldratt's Theory of Constraints: A System Approach to Continuous Improvement, Milwaukee WI: ASQ Quality Press,. 1997.
10. A. Tenera, "Contribution for the Improvement of Uncertainty Management in Project Duration through Theory of Constraints," (in Portuguese), Ph.D. dissertation, Dept. Mech. and Industrial Eng., University Nova of Lisboa, 2006.
11. Newbold, R. C. (1998). Project management in the fast lane. Boca Raton, FL, EUA: St. Lucie Press.
12. Hoel, K., & Taylor, S. G. (1999). Quantifying buffers for project schedules. Production and Inventory Management Journal, 40, 43-47.
13. Leach, L. (2000). Critical Chain Project Management. Norwood, MA, EUA: Artech House.
14. Shou, Y., & Yeo, K. T. (2000, November 12-15). Estimation of project buffers in critical chain project management. IEEE International Conference on Management of Innovation and Technology, Singapore.
15. Park, M., & Pena-Mora, F. (2004). Reliability buffering for construction projects. Journal of Construction Engineering and Management, 130, 626-637.
16. Tenera, A., & Cruz-Machado, V. (2007). Critical chain project management: A new approach for time buffer sizing. in Proc. of the Institute of Industrial Engineering Annual Conference, Nashville.
17. Project Management Institute [PMI]. PMBOK® Guide. ANSI/PMI Standard 99-001-2004, 2004, p.5.
18. Law, A. M., & Kelton, D. (1991). Simulation Modeling and Analysis (2ª ed.). Singapure: McGraw-Hill.

<table>
<tr><td>18</td><td></td></tr>
</table>

18   THE APPLICATION OF THE CLOSED-LOOP LIFECYCLE MANAGEMENT IN VIRTUAL ORGANIZATION

Rosanna Fornasiero
r.fornasiero@itia.cnr.it
ITIA - CNR,
Milan-ITALY

Daniele Panarese
d.panarese@fidia.it
Fidia s.p.a.
Torino-ITALY

In this paper we propose the implementation of a distributed architecture for product lifecycle management in Virtual Organization created to manage the Middle-of-Life phase. After a short introduction of the innovative Promise-PLM system which support decision making process based on dynamic creation of knowledge, the application of the system to a case study for maintenance management demonstrates how the system can be customized to change process organization guarantying better integration between the actors. The system is studied to be easily accessible and usable by different kind of companies in different industrial sectors.

1. INTRODUCTION

Manufacturing industry is shifting production from pure physical products towards knowledge intensive and service oriented solutions to answer to new market requests. This goes in the direction of lifecycle management view to offer solutions which are reliable and controllable in any phase of their life, solutions which have innovative approach to solve and prevent customer's problems. Smart tags, tracking systems, RFID devices are some of the available systems in the market which can be embedded in the product in order to collect information and data useful in different lifecycle phases.

The development of an integrated solution where it is possible to retrieve, use, manage data and information to obtain knowledge useful for supporting and taking decisions along the product lifecycle is one important issue which is held in many different research projects. Such integrated systems for Product Lifecycle Management (PLM) have a strong impact in the improvement of the Virtual Organizations management since they permit to easily merge and share information and knowledge necessary for many different actors.

In particular the breakthrough contribution of PROMISE project (EU, IST-507100) allows information flow management to go beyond organizational barriers effectively closing the product lifecycle information loop using the latest ICT, and seamlessly transforming that information into knowledge (Kiritsis et al., 2003).

In the present work we describe how the implementation and integration of these

Please use the following format when citing this chapter:

Fornasiero, R. and Panarese, D., 2008, in IFIP International Federation for Information Processing, Volume 283; *Pervasive Collaborative Networks*; Luis M. Camarinha-Matos, Willy Picard; (Boston: Springer), pp. 177–184.

technologies have been applied to the case of a company producing milling machine. After a short description of the Promise-PLM technologies we will show the advantages of implementing such a system in a company producing durable equipment and in particular we will show how the implementation of 2 components have been carried on customizing their generic structure for the specific application scenario. Virtual Organization here is intended as the temporary relationship which is established between the customer and the service provider in order to manage maintenance in an innovative way according to data collected along the whole lifecycle. Also other actors like designers of the milling machine can be part of the Virtual Organization and have benefits from sharing information of the product status and usage.

2. THE APPLICATION OF PROMISE-PLM SYSTEM IN THE VIRTUAL ORGANIZATION

The Promise-PLM system is based on many different modules interacting each other to improve the capability of the companies to manage product along its lifecycle. In particular the system is composed of:

- PEID (Product Embedded Information Device), a data storage device to identify the unique product and which can be read or written to (mainly active and passive RFID tags). On board devices capture lifecycle events or specific conditions that can impact the product performance.
- Middleware: Promise-PLM middleware enables both device management and communication between one or more PEIDs and existing enterprise backend software. Middleware also acts as the networking layer of the Promise-PLM systems, enabling different players in the Virtual Organizations to have controlled and secure access to relevant information.
- PDKM (Product Data Knowledge Manageme) integrates and manages information from all lifecycle phases of the product.
- DSS (Decision Support System) provides algorithms for decision management in different industrial applications for predictive maintenance, diagnosis and analysis of use patterns.

The innovation of PROMISE-PLM system is in its capability to manage and optimize knowledge on product lifecycle thanks to up-to-date and accurate collection and retrieval of related information which can have significant influence on residual life decisions regarding individual sub-assemblies or components and positively impact the usage, the environment, the production through improved and more efficient decisions (Cao et al., 2007).

The Promise-PLM system has been developed to provide integrated and innovative technologies to help companies to manage the Beginning-, the Middle- and the End-of-Life phases (respectively BOL, MOL, EOL) allowing many actors to create and manage Virtual Organizations integrating the product's lifecycle where they are involved (managers, designers, service and maintenance operators, recyclers, etc.) to track, manage and control product information at any phase of the product and process lifecycle.

During the project the Promise-PLM system has been applied to many different applications which have adapted and used some of the components according to the specific needs.

The virtual enterprise is a relatively consolidated approach in modern company organizations. It means that there is a stable and continuous link between a company and, from one side its customers and from the other side its providers. This allows a seamless production flow along the whole process chain. This model is guided by the effort of reaching a greater efficiency in a extremely competitive market characterized by globalization, technological development and differentiation of client requires.

Virtual enterprises are based on reliance between the companies involved. From such a flexible, but coordinated, organization several advantages can be retrieved. Time and costs reduction in service, manufacturing, supplying processes for instance.

In this large context the closed loop lifecycle management of an industrial product has its important part. In fact an integrated solution (hardware architecture and information flows) where it is possible to retrieve, use, manage data and information to obtain knowledge useful for supporting and taking decisions along the product lifecycle is an one important issue that makes things from virtual (that means it exists as potentiality, but not yet in things/acts) to real.

In particular the company under study represents one of the MOL cases on predictive maintenance for milling machines. The company expects the benefits of exploiting PLM functionalities enriched with Promise-PLM technology implementing a closer integration both in terms of information and material flows between maintenance staff and machine owners: the system will allow organization of maintenance activities mainly between these two actors optimising the number and the typology of intervention. Moreover the system will allow an enriched information feedback loop from MOL on certain parameters selected for BOL phase in order to improve the performance of the design phase.

3. THE IMPLEMENTATION OF THE PDKM

The PDKM (Product Data and Knowledge Management) module is responsible for the integration and management of both product data and knowledge from all lifecycle phases from different sources and to the creation, update and management of knowledge, in order to improve future generations of products, starting from data on the current products collected directly from the field.

Starting from the semantic object model of the PDKM developed within the project (Cassina et al., 2006) the Product Data Structure for this application scenario was formalized according to pre-defined categories for each product instance and related characteristics of each product lifecycle phase. The product structure of milling machine has been analysed and studied together with the company in order to create the related class diagram. The information collected from the company have been used to create the objects and the structure and then have been inputted in the PDKM. An example of the structure of one component is here given (Fig. 1).

Milling machine is a complex product with many different components. For each component measuring points have been foreseen in order to collect field data on the performance of the components themselves during MOL phase and are used by the DSS module to plan maintenance actions.

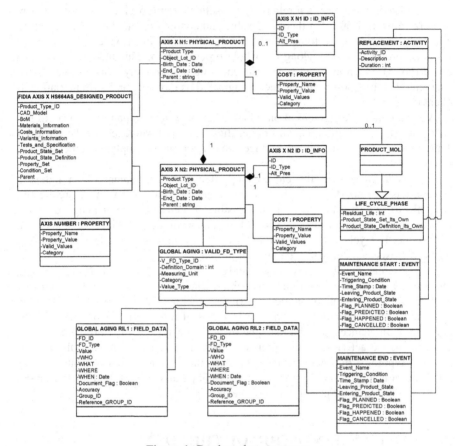

Figure 1: Product data structure

4. THE IMPLEMENTATION OF THE DSS

The DSS of the Promise-PLM system offers a set of functions which are important for a variety of actors in the Virtual Organization.

The Promise-PLM DSS is based on a set of strategies defined in the project which are thought to support companies in strategic and operational tasks and which can be used for a variety of different optimization problems according to the specific lifecycle phase under analysis and to the actions the company wants to undertake. In the Promise-PLM DSS some of the most important strategies considered are linked to data mining and pattern search based on field-, diagnosis- and environmental data, evaluation and measurement of the efficiency of a set of products compared to their design target values, predictive-maintenance management to evaluate the status of deterioration or upcoming breakdowns, etc

Each of these strategies has been designed with lifecycle perspective and has been applied to some application scenarios for test and validation.

The integrated Decision Support System developed for the milling machines producer goes in the direction of predictive maintenance strategy as suggested in many approaches proposed in literature (Swanson, 2001; Pinjalaa et al. 2006; Takta et al., 2004; Yam et al.2001) and is the results of the merging of 3 different modules of the overall Promise DSS interacting each other in order to reduce the number of unexpected stops for maintenance and to minimize the overall lifecycle costs of the product avoiding component breakdowns (Fornasiero et al.,2007).

In the figure below the Use Case for the MOL phase shows the sequence of events when participants to the Virtual Organization at any lifecycle phase wishes to interrogate the machine status. The creation of a new collaborative environment is based on technological development and improvement which have been carried out both at customer and service provider site. Sensors measures the relevant parameters related to the components and to their usage and send this information to the onboard computer where a first module of the DSS has been installed to filter, analyse and store data. The customer (machine user) can activate the modules of the DSS (diagnostic and ageing module) on the on-board computer of the milling machine in order to evaluate the status of the parameters and to calculate the residual life of the components. With the companies it was defined which are the most critical parameters to be sent to the central server of maintenance Service. Data are stored in the PDKM and can be used to monitor the status of the machines around the world. This data is used to activate another module of the DSS which has been developed for maintenance cost management with which the service staff can plan the maintenance interventions around the world.

The DSS evaluates maintenance costs with an iterative process on each machine for components exceeding a given threshold value of "criticality". Once the machine user has verified the status of the components with the testing module, an alarm on aging is sent to the Maintenance Service which collects the alarms from all the machine tools under maintenance and calculate the economic value of different maintenance actions according to residual life costs estimation. Risk of failure are evaluated and are used to weight the costs.

The system is meant to provide a list of suggested interventions that can be performed on the machine when the monitored mechanical components are expected to fail according to alarms from the aging module which gives in input the residual lifespan of the machine and components through the PDKM where these information are stored.

Data are collected from all the machines and LCRC (Life Cycle Residual Cost) for each maintenance action is computed (see fig.3). The system minimizes the LCRC according the residual life of the machine and of the components taking into consideration a long term view on the impact of maintenance. Forecasting future intervention and probability of failure are based on historical data collected along the life of the machine.

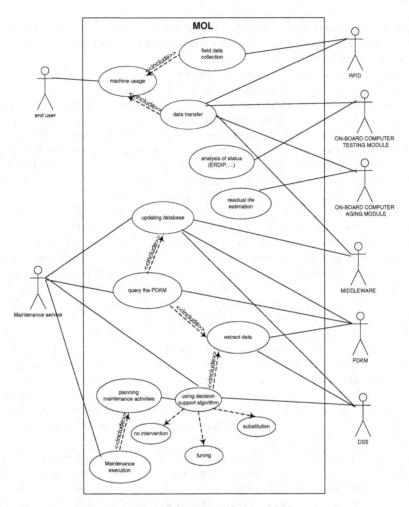

Figure 2: Use case for the MOL

5. IMPACT ON THE COLLABORATIVE ENVIRONMENT OF THE COMPANY

The implementation of the Promise-PLM solution in the specific case under consideration has been critically evaluated according to assessment criteria defined within the project and shared with the other partners. The integration between the various components of the Promise-PLM system have been tested so that the sensors on the machine, the PDKM and the DSS communicate via middleware system. The system can manage a multiple number of machines according to security and reliability criteria. The most important functionalities which have been tested are:

- the link to active PDKM (real data filled-in database), to retrieve cost elements, residual life, historical data, etc.

- import/export functionalities with the Computerized Numerical Control
- adequacy of the models by refinement of algorithms implemented
- DSS capability to manage to variable multiple-axis machines

The overall implemented system covers most of the functionalities required by the company like assessment of the residual life of machine components, classification of maintenance actions, evaluation of costs associated to maintenance actions, evaluation of the life cycle residual costs.

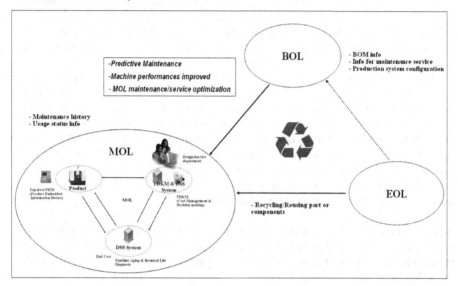

The business model for the company is based on reliable relationship established with the customer in order to provide an after-sale service which is based on updated and shared data. The milling machine builder strictly collaborates with the milling machine user. The PDKM can be used both in the BOL and EOL phase according to data needed by the specific phase.

The advantage of implementing such a system overcome the problem met by the company of collecting data based on the experience and sensibility of technicians that set the thresholds and analyse great quantity of historical data to be affordable. Therefore model based algorithm requires a start-up period in which continuous refinements could be done during first years due to the interpretation of data coming from the field. On one hand the application of fuzzy logic algorithms for the DSS are more flexible and can be programmed so that self-improvements are possible in the future when enough field data will be available, gathered through the maintenance crews, or the centralized data management infrastructure (PDKM). On the other hand the application of maintenance cost minimization is based on evaluation of actions postponement and of the cost all along the residual lifecycle is taken into consideration.

6. CONCLUSIONS

The MOL phase of a product expands the value-added processes after the delivery of the product to the customer; indeed, this phase of the lifecycle is experiencing rapid growth. After-sales market sizes is increasing because service provision and high quality performance of product is essential to keep customers.

In the implementation of Promise-PLM system, the overall structure has been matched with the industrial requirements derived from the company analysis and have been customized using the modules of the system necessary for the specific case. The PDKM gives the company the possibility to manage and formalize data on the product and its components updating them according to periodically collected field data. The DSS gives the company the possibility to optimise and manage maintenance delegating to the machine user the capability to easily control and monitor some parameters and to the maintenance provider to plan the intervention all over the world.

Rules of behaviour and process flow have been defined at different level of detail to use the Promise-PLM system in different steps of the product lifecycle for the establishment of a collaborative environment based on Virtual Organization principles between machine user and maintenance provider to optimise the performance of the machine and the cost of maintenance. The overall decision support system can have a double impact on maintenance management. In fact it may support the machine user who can monitor machine performance and ageing of the components and the maintenance service provider who can plan and forecast interventions needed and optimise maintenance costs.

Acknowledgment. The work described in this paper has been conducted as part of the IP project (FP6-IP-507100) PROMISE (PROduct lifecycle Management and Information tracking using Smart Embedded systems), funded by the EC under the IST-NMP program.

REFERENCES

Cao H., Folan P.; Mascolo J.; Browne J.: RFID in product lifecycle management: a case in the automotive industry in International Journal of Computer Integrated Manufacturing, First published on 19 October 2007

Cassina J., Tomasella M., Marquard M., Metin A., Matta A., Taisch M.: Development of the semantic object model for a PDKM system in proceedings of the International Conference of Concurrent Engineering, 2006.

Fornasiero R., Zangiacomi A., Panarese D., Cassina J., Taisch M.: An integrated approach to decision support for maintenance management: a case study for machine tools . In the proceedings of PLM, International conference on Product Lifecycle Management, 2007, pp.791-798.

Kiritsis, D., A. Bufardi and P. Xirouchakis (2003). Research issues on product lifecycle management and information tracking using smart embedded systems. In Advanced Engineering Informatics, 17, 189-202

Pinjalaa S.K., Pintelona L., Vereeckeb A.: An empirical investigation on the relationship between business and maintenance strategies International Journal of Production Economics Vol. 104-1, (2006), 214-229

Swanson L. (2001). Linking maintenance strategies to performance. International Journal of Production Economics, 70, 237-244

Takta S., Kimura F., Van Houten F.J.A.M., Westkamper E., Shpitalni M., Ceglarek D., Lee J. "Maintenance: changing role in life cycle management", Annals of the CIRP, 53/2, 2004

Yam, R. C. M., P. W. Tse, L. Li and P. Tu (2001) Intelligent Predictive Decision Support System for Condition-Based Maintenance. International Journal of Advanced Manufacturing Technology. 17:383–391.

Iris Karvonen, Martin Ollus, Mikko Uoti
VTT Industrial Systems, FINLAND
Iris.Karvonen@vtt.fi
Martin.Ollus@vtt.fi
Mikko.Uoti@vtt.fi

The paper aims to contribute to the development of pro-active Virtual Organization (VO) management. A method called "VO qualitative monitoring" is proposed based on the analysis and monitoring of VO success factors. The approach is applicable especially for VOs which have abstract objectives (difficult to measure quantitatively) and require personal and organizational commitment. Also the first implementation of the method is described.

1. INTRODUCTION

Virtual Organizations (VO) are created to fulfill a specific task, for example a delivery of a product or service to a customer. The task of VO management is to support the achievement of the VO objectives, mainly the customer requirements in the defined time, cost and quality frame [Karvonen et al 2005]. To do this, the status of the VO should be identified and actions to correct or avoid deviations should be implemented. Decision about actions is usually based on the comparison of actual achieved behavior compared to the wanted behavior. Methods like task monitoring and VO performance measurement [Westphal 2007] and simulation [Hodik et al 2007] are developed to support this. The actions are supposed to be proactive in order to avoid also emerging deviations from the expected outcome. However, it is difficult to act proactively and to identify hidden problems which would cause deviations later.

There are different types of VOs and they require different approaches for the VO management. One of the main determining factors is the type of the VO objective [Karvonen et al 2005]. This paper proposes a method called "VO qualitative monitoring" tracing factors affecting to the VO performance but not visible in quantitative measurements. The approach is applicable especially for VOs which have abstract objectives, which are difficult to measure quantitatively and require personal and organizational commitment (chapter 2). The method is based on a qualitative VO partner success model presented in chapter 3. The paper also presents the first implementation of the methodology as a tool in chapter 4. Suggestions for further advancement of the methodology are presented in chapter 5.

Please use the following format when citing this chapter:

Karvonen, I., Ollus, M. and Uoti, M., 2008, in IFIP International Federation for Information Processing, Volume 283; *Pervasive Collaborative Networks*; Luis M. Camarinha-Matos, Willy Picard; (Boston: Springer), pp. 185–192.

2. DEVELOPMENT OF VO QUALITATIVE MONITORING

2.1 Definition & objectives

"VO qualitative monitoring" (VOQM) is defined here as the collection and analysis of qualitative aspects which affect the success or non-success of a VO. They do not typically have an immediate influence on the VO performance; the effects develop gradually and can be seen in the quantitative performance measurements in delay. The objective of VO qualitative monitoring is to support VO management by the identification of the VO status in a proactive manner. It may thus complement VO performance measurement. The qualitative factors include items like VO partner satisfaction, commitment and motivation which partly also describe "VO feelings" or "VO atmosphere". Periodical follow-up can support the identification of changes in the hidden factors or the "VO feelings".

2.2 VO management approaches and VOQM

Different VOs have different types of objectives, challenges and the operating environment. The main objective of a VO is to create value to the customer but most often constraints of time and costs exist. A VO, which has been able to create a high quality customer solution, but has exceeded the allowed costs or time, is usually not considered a success.

There are also differences with respect to the goal specificity, clarity and stability. Typically the customer requirements set up the expected outcome (product or service), but not all its details. In product development or innovation VOs the goal is necessarily not quite clear. Often the VO objective may change during its operation.

The objectives considered most important and most difficult affect the focus of the management. In case of a dynamic goal it is important to be able to guide the VO to understand and pursue the up-to-date goal. In some cases the main problem may be the technical integrability of the partners' results or contributions, whereas in some other cases most problems are encountered in keeping to the schedule and/or cost limit. If there is a shortage of resources their management within a specified frame of time and costs may become the main issue in a VO.

By definition a VO always has a common goal. The need for collaboration and mutual dependences between the partners may vary. The degree of dependency has effect on the intense of VO management. Though in typical business cases the role of VO management is very important, there may be some specific cases, where this role may, at least partly, be replaced by well defined rules and practices.

The objectives of a VO are necessarily not fully in line with the objectives of the VO participants. Partners are independent organizations and may participate in several VOs at the same time. The contribution and behavior of each partner in a VO is affected by its objectives. The objectives of the different coexistent VOs and the different organizations may cause conflicts, especially if there is a shortage of resources. Thus it is useful to consider the objectives and motivating factors of the participants. These are qualitative, often hidden factors.

In the short term the companies want to achieve the customer satisfaction and make profit in their current VOs. For the long term, while working in a VO, they want to gain future potential (references, customers), learn & increase their knowledge and / or test and improve the processes & tools.

In [Karvonen et al. 2005] the VO descriptive parameters [Pedersen 1999] were analysed to identify needs for different VO management approaches. The main factors affecting the VO management approach were identified to be the type of VO objective, the importance of dependencies and risks (probability and consequences). The following (partly overlapping) management approaches were identified:
- Multi-organizational (collaborative) project management
- Encouragement approach
- Self-organizing approach
- Automatic control VOs
- Supply chain management approach.

VO qualitative monitoring is applicable especially for VOs which have abstract objectives (difficult to measure quantitatively) and require personal and organisational commitment, that is for the "Encouragement approach", most often also for Collaborative project management and potentially for the self-organizing approach.

VO qualitative monitoring aims to support the VO management. Thus it takes mostly the viewpoint of VO manager. It is planned to operate as a tool of VO manager or VO management team to monitor the qualitative status of the VO and thus to support the identification of potential deviations.

2.3 Methodology for VOQM development

As a basis to develop VOQM, a qualitative success model of factors affecting to VO partner performance has been used. The model has been presented as a success tree presenting the different factors required for the VO success. The tree format is able to present the logic (obligatory or alternative factors; and/or-gates) and enables the break down of the factors to lower level elements and factors. As an alternative, opposite logic, VO fault tree could be used.

For the VOQM, the success factors have been turned into a questionnaire. The same qualitative model has been used both for the "VO feelings" questionnaire where the VO partners assess the VO as a whole from their own viewpoint and for the "VO partner assessment" tool where the VO management team is planned to assess the VO partners. Each branch in the tree has been broken up to more detailed "leaves" and turned to questions. The questionnaire is presented in the form of statements. The idea is that the query participants assess the degree how far they agree or do not agree about the given statements.

Partly the statements deal with partner specific issues, partly they concern factors common to the whole project. In this way it is possible to collect views and opinions about the status of the whole VO, as reviewed from the VO partner. The collected information is aggregated together. The initial idea has not been that the VO manager is allowed to identify the single answers, even if this in some cases could be a workable method.

Even if the respondents are not identified, the information received with such a query cannot be considered completely reliable. The respondent may be willing to answer "as expected" or to hide some problems. The self-assessment may thus be partially distorted or even false. The higher the common trust in the network, the more reliable information can be expected.

3. VO QUALITATIVE MONITORING CONTENTS

3.1 VO success model

To build the needed base model the conditions of success were analysed: what is needed to achieve the VO success. The VO success is dependent on the performance of the VO partners and some common and external factors, like VO management actions and customer behavior. Figure 1 presents a high-level success tree presentation of VO partner performance. Here the external and common factors are also included in the VO partner model because they may prevent the partner to succeed in the VO; even if the partner itself may not be "guilty" to these deviations. In the success tree two kinds of "gates" are used:

-      &-gate (AND) means that the output (on the left side in this figure) is true only if all the inputs to the gate (on the right hand side) are true.

-      V-gate (OR) means that the output is true if at least one of the inputs is true.

Thus the interpretation is that to perform as needed in a VO the partner must have (AND-gate) first the four elements:

-      motivation (reason why to perform as required for the VO; especially in case of other concurrent and conflicting interests). The best alternative is that both the organization and the persons involved are motivated, in minimum not one of them prevents the other one from the work.

-      knowledge/capability (professional skill)

-      the possibility/ availability of resources (free resources / time).

-      no failures or deviations occur

If one of these elements is missing the partner performance may fail. If motivation is not high enough, good results may not be achieved even if there is knowledge and time to perform the task. As well if the professional skill is not high enough, the results are not of high quality. If there is motivation and knowledge, but no time (free resources) to perform the task, it cannot be performed. Furthermore, even if all the other elements are in place, occasional failures may destroy the success.

Collaboration and mutual dependencies create additional challenges, which are here turned to requirements about understanding the VO goal, quality of VO management and collaboration.

Furthermore, each component can be analysed more in detail. For example, as described in figure 1, motivation may come from different sources (OR-gate):

-      expected benefit; in short or long term and potentially compared with competing benefits. A short-term benefit may be a good price received from the performance.   Long-term benefits may be linked to the expectation of future contracts, development of customer relationships, increase of knowledge or support to the strategic objectives of the partner.

-      penalties or other threats in case of non-performance or

- issues linked to human interaction, like values, will, duty, friendship, pleasure etc. These may be important if the motivation of a person/persons involved is important. This is especially the case in the areas where innovation is more important than routines. At the same time it must be noted, that the motivation of a person does not always lead to the motivation of the organization.

Similarly the other factors can be opened more to define in more detail, for example, what kind of knowledge and capabilities are needed, what are the prerequisites for sufficient resources etc.

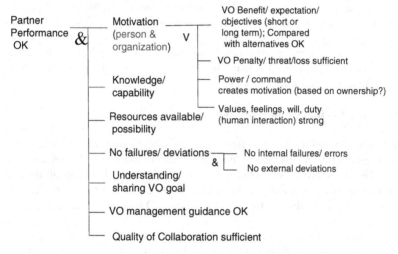

Figure 1. High level success tree for VO partner performance

3.2 VO qualitative monitoring contents

The success model presented above has been used as the base for developing the questionnaires for VO qualitative monitoring. The current version of VO qualitative monitoring tool and methodology includes two parts:
- identification of the VO qualitative status ("VO feelings" or "VO climate"), based on the views of all VO partners about their own status and the VO status as a whole
- qualitative assessment of (selected or all) VO partners, planned to be based on the views of VO management team.

The current version of the partner questionnaire includes the following main topics, providing input to the mentioned issues:
- VO objectives & results -> Is there a need to clarify the expected result?
- VO importance -> Measure of motivation of the person & organization
- Knowledge& resources -> Identify lack of knowledge/resources
- Collaboration -> Identify the status of collaboration
- VO/task performance-> identify problems
- VO management -> identify weaknesses in VO management
- Risk assessment- > Free text on comments and proposals

If the query is performed repeatedly during the VO it can be able to reflect potential changes in the mentioned factors, like understanding, motivation and commitment.

The above assessment is planned to be performed as a self-assessment: each partner or even each person participating the VO evaluates the presented factors. This assessment can be complemented with an assessment of VO partners performed by the VO manager or VO management team. The idea is that this partner assessment could be performed proactively already in the beginning of the VO to be able to foresee potential future problems, and then repeated during the VO operation as there is some experience about the running VO.

The assessment of partners uses the experience and opinions of VO manager and the management team. In principle it could collect views of all partners about all partners but this would in practise most often be too heavy. This assessment includes the criticality of the partner (defining how important the questions of the next topics are), commitment, performance and collaboration and comments. If the VO has a high number of partners it may not be useful to assess them all but select only the most critical ones for the analysis.

3.3 Utilization for VO inheritance/ lessons learned

VO inheritance is defined as "the practice of storing and passing on the experience and other non-proprietary assets created through collaboration in a VO. " [Karvonen et al. 2007]. The objective of VO inheritance is to enrich the VBE "bag of assets" [Afsarmanesh et al. 2008], thus improving the preparedness of the VBE for business opportunities. The added value, or the contents of the VO inheritance, is called "VO heritage".

The history of the "run-time" analysis of a VO could be saved and used as part of VO heritage. Even more benefit could be gained by comparing the received results later with the realized performance. This would require the comparison of the qualitative and quantitative results which is not necessarily straightforward.

Another way to support the inheritance is to create specific questionnaires performed at the VO dissolution phase. This analysis could be modified from the current questionnaires to collect views of the VO final success and experience.

4. FIRST IMPLEMENTATION OF VOQM TOOL (VOF)

VO qualitative monitoring is currently implemented as a web query to VO partners and VO management ("VOF"-tool). It allows an easy way of sharing and answering the questions by selecting the degree of agreeing/disagreeing of each statement. The results are aggregated without the identification of a single answer.

In the current version the number of statements is 41 for VO partner questionnaire (in 7 groups) and 13 (4 groups) for the VO management (for each partner). Additionally there are 6 free text questions for the partners and one free text comment for the VO management (for each partner).

The current "VOF" tool is implemented using a generic commercial web query tool [Digium 2008]. Respondents can be called to the query by e-mail offering a link to the query web site. The tool offers a selection of different summary alternatives, based on numbering the level of agreement (agree = 4; somewhat agree =3; somewhat disagree = 2, disagree = 1). The statements have been formulated so that in each case disagreeing refers to a weakness. This enables the calculation of mean values for each question and further for each question group. Visualization and comparison of the mean values can support the identification of VO weaknesses.

The VO partners' assessment results may be aggregated and presented equally. Here the first question group assessing the criticality of the partner is different from those assessing their performance. It could be used to order the partners according to criticality. The creation of summaries is not as straightforward as different partners may get different number of assessments.

Sharing the analysis results is dependent on the network and the VO rules and practices. Typically the concluded results, not revealing the answers of any single organization or person, are accepted to be open within the VO. The results of the VO partner assessment, performed by the VO management, are necessarily not open outside the VO management.

The VOF tool has not been tested in industrial cases yet, but it has had a small experimentation in a special VO, ECOLEAD project. The invitation to the query was sent to all people working in the project. The results were partly used for the periodic reporting.

5. CONCLUSIONS AND FURTHER DEVELOPMENT

5.1 Conclusions

The paper presents an approach for the qualitative monitoring of a VO status, to enable the pro-active identification of potential emerging problems. The method with the first query has been implemented and preliminarily tested as a one-off analysis in one specific VO using a web query tool. The tool proved to be easy to take into use, it provided automatic summaries of the results and it was easy and light to use for the VO participants.

The first experimentation showed that the method can give interesting information about the VO status and the "feelings" of the VO partners which have an effect on the VO performance. The results obtained in the test looked reasonable. Even if it can be argued that the given information is not totally reliable, it can give impression about the attitude of the partners.

The experimentation also revealed needs and potential for further development of the methodology. One of the development possibilities lies in the area of adding dynamics in the methodology: Instead of one-off analysis it could be repeated regularly during the VO. This may require the creation of separate queries for the start, operation and dissolution phases. Further, the questionnaire base could be managed in the VBE or network and it could be developed as a learning tool, adding questions about new types of problem or disturbance sources, based on experience. It could also be possible to learn about the reliability of the assessments of the companies after deviations occurred – was this visible somehow in the qualitative assessment before the problem occurrence? Additional benefit can be expected by integrating the qualitative and quantitative (performance measurement) approaches and linking to VO model.

Finally, even if the current tool offers several options for the presentation of the results, new approaches for the visualization could be developed. These could include the visualization on the "VO dashboard" [Negretto et al. 2008] together with the quantitative measures or visualization as a success tree presenting the tree status with early alarms.

5.2 Acknowledgments

The paper is mainly based on work performed in the Integrated project ECOLEAD funded by the European Community under the Framework programme 6 (IP 506958).

6. REFERENCES

1. Afsarmanesh, H., Msanjila S., Ermilova, E. , Wiesner, S., Woelfel, W., Seifert, M. (2008). VBE Management System. In Camarinha-Matos L.M., Afsarmanesh H., Ollus M. (eds.) Methods and Tools for Collaborative Networked Organizations, Springer (to appear).

2. DIGIUM (2008). http://www.digium.fi/en/page313.html, April 2008.

2. Karvonen, I.; Salkari, I.; Ollus, M. (2005). Characterizing Virtual Organization and Their Management. In Camarinha-Matos, L., Afsarmanesh, H. & Ortiz, A. (Ed.), Collaborative Networks and Their Breeding Environment (pp 193- 204). Springer.

3. Karvonen, I.,Salkari. I., Ollus, M. (2007) Identification of forms and components of VO inheritance. In Camarinha-Matos, L., Afrmanesh, H. , Novais, P. & Analide, C., Establishing the Foundation of Collaborative Networks, Proc. 8th IFIP Working Conference on Virtual Enterprises, (pp. 253-262). Springer.

4. Negretto U, Hodík J, Král L, Mulder W, Ollus M, Pondrelli L, Westphal I. (2008). VO MANAGEMENT SOLUTIONS - VO Management e-Services. In: Camarinha-Matos L.M., Afsarmanesh H., Ollus M. (ecs.) Methods and Tools for Collaborative Networked Organizations, Springer (to appear).

5. Pedersen, J.D., Tolle, M. Vesterager, J. Final report on Models. Deliverable 1.3 of Esprit 26509 Globeman 21 project. 1999.

6. Westphal, I., Thoben,K. Seifert, M. (2007). Measuring Collaboration Performance in Virtual Organisations. In Camarinha-Matos, L., Afsarmanesh, H. , Novais, P. & Analide, C., Establishing the Foundation of Collaborative Networks. Proc. 8th IFIP Working Conference on Virtual Enterprises (pp. 33-42). Springer.

7. Hodík, J., Mulder, W., Pondrelli, L., Westphal I. (2007) ICT services supporting virtual organization management. Proceedings of the 3rd I*PROMS Virtual International Conference, July 2-13, 2007. ISBN 978-1904445-52-4.

20

COORDINATION OF SUPPLY CHAIN ACTIVITIES: A COALITION-BASED APPROACH

Dhouha Anane* — Samir Aknine** — Suzanne Pinson *

*Université Paris-Dauphine CNRS/LAMSADE UMR 7042
75775 Paris cedex 16, FRANCE
dhouhaanane@yahoo.fr, suzanne.pinson@.dauphine.fr
** Université Paris 6 Lip6 104 Avenue du Président Kennedy
75016, Paris, FRANCE
Samir.aknine@lip6.fr

Companies operate in an environment increasingly demanding in terms of flexibility and reactivity. The introduction of the entities resulting from Distributed Artificial Intelligence (DAI) and Multi-Agent Systems (MAS) in the management of enterprises prove to be an interesting technology to simulate and reproduce the collaborative and adaptive behaviors of enterprises. This article models the coordination of the various collaborative parties both inside and outside a supply chain using coordination methods of MAS mainly coalition formation mechanisms. In this paper, we present our agent modeling of supply chains, and then we detail the coalition formation algorithm. Lastly, we illustrate our approach with an example chosen in the industrial domain.

1. INTRODUCTION

A Supply Chain (SC) is a set of autonomous entities, internal or external to a company, interacting with each others in order to maximize a global wellbeing and this by searching a compromise regarding their own constraints and goals. This compromise is difficult to reach given the constantly dynamic environment in which these companies evolve. The characteristics of such systems, namely complexity, changing environment and autonomy of each entity implied in the *SC*, motivate researchers to use multi-agent techniques for modeling and studying their behaviors.

The aim of this paper is to propose a coordination method using a coalition formation mechanism for supply chain management. According to (Shehory and Kraus, 1998), a *coalition* is defined as a group of agents which have decided to cooperate in order to reach a common goal. A shared utility is expected from the achievement to this goal. The aim is to model the possible partnerships that could be established between entities. In our approach we make a distinction between two abstract levels of coalitions:

- Internal coalitions: are the coalitions formed of the entities in the same company, i.e. a sort of alliances between plants of the same company in order to face huge orders.

- External coalitions: are the partnerships which could be established between internal and external entities in order to acquire missing resources and competences.

Please use the following format when citing this chapter:

Anane, D., Aknine, S. and Pinson, S., 2008, in IFIP International Federation for Information Processing, Volume 283; *Pervasive Collaborative Networks*; Luis M. Camarinha-Matos, Willy Picard; (Boston: Springer), pp. 193–202.

This paper is organized as follows: section 2 presents a review of existing approaches. Section 3 describes the coordination problem with an example and formalizes it. Section 4 proposes a coalition formation method adapted to this problem of supply chain management, and then we present our algorithm. Finally we conclude on this work.

2. RELATED WORK

Modeling of Supply Chains (SC) is one of the main topics in Operations research (OR) (Kok *and al.*, 2003), (Beamon, 1998), (Giard *and al.*, 2007), factories' localization, production planning, stock management, transport and distribution. Most of these works propose centralized approaches based on analytical models. Since the emergence of distributed techniques and multi-agent systems, several approaches studied the collaborative behaviors between supply chain entities using agent mechanisms (Dodd *and al.*, 2001). The advantage of these approaches consists in the possibility to explicitly model the behaviors of these entities as well as their interactions and their organization (Parunak *and al.*, 1998). (Swaminathan *and al.*, 1998) model supply chain dynamics using a multi-agent approach. The contribution of their work is the combination of both analytical and simulation methods in order to respectively model the static and dynamic aspects of supply chains. Other works studied the dynamics in supply chain using more specific techniques to multi-agent systems such as interaction languages and protocols. For example, (Fox *and al.*, 2000) have defined a coordination system using conversation structures while introducing a communication language (COOL) which is based on KQML[i] language and finite states automats. Other works have modeled only part of the supply chain (Hahndel *and al.*, 1994) which uses a negotiation protocol to coordinate activities of the production planning. To date, few works focus on the use of coalition formation techniques to model coordination in supply chains.

3. MULTI-AGENT MODELING APPROACH

We consider a company which manufactures and markets planes. We chose this industrial field because of the complexity of its supply chain which mainly manages the outsourcing of several parts and the multitude of entities that contribute to it. This company is localized mainly in France but it has several production sites (plants) on several continents. It has also various distribution centers in Europe which deliver various markets (Europe, Middle-East...). In addition, its suppliers are physically dispersed.

Inside of each plant (cf. figure 1), we can identify several other units which cooperate with each others. Such situation could be complicated due to relationships that might exist between these entities and the entities of other supply chains. Consequently a delay or dysfunction at a point of the chain could be propagated to all its connected points.

3.1. Agent identification

In our agent approach, we propose to model each entity in the supply chain by an agent (Barbuceanu *and al.*, 1996). We distinguish two abstraction levels for these agents: *internal* and *external agents*:

- ***Internal agents:*** are those located inside the company. In this category, we also distinguish two levels of agents: company agents and plant agents.

  - *Plant agents:*

    - **'Plann'** agents: they deal with the production planning based on received demands and on communications with other agents of the plant.

    - **'Produc'** agents: they manage the production and stocks of the intermediate products. These agents have a perfect knowledge of the plant conditions in term of resources, machines and their sites

    - **'Exped'** agents: they handle the finished products of each plant and their expedition.

    - **'Mat'** agents: they supervise stocks of raw materials (RMS) and treat all information related to orders and raw material reception.

    - **'Info'** agents: they process all information related to the correct processing of the plant (capacities and breakdowns of the machines, information on stocks *RMS*, *IPS* and *FPS*).

  - *Company Agents:*

    - **'Purchases'** agent: it represents the purchase function of the company including the selection and communication with suppliers.

    - **'Sales'** agent: this agent gathers the functions of marketing and sales. It ensures the forecasts of the demand by establishing communications with the customers.

    - **'Transport'** agent: this agent ensures products moving among plants and distribution centers.

    - **'Distribution Centers'** agents: they represent the different distribution centers of the company.

    - **'Logistic'** agents: they supervise the effective communication between the various agents (*purchase, sale, exped, plann* and *prod*).They also manage the events which may occur in the system such as an order modification by a customer, the out-of-stock event of some product, the change of a supplier...

- – ***External agents:*** they represent the agents located outside the company.

  - **'Customers'** agents: these agents correspond to the customers of the company. In our example we have identified two agents: the European market, the Asian and Middle-East Market.

  - **'Supplier'** agents: each supplier is represented by an agent.

  - **'Econ-Part'** agents: they represent any other entity in the environment likely to have a relationship with the company (competitors, partners of transport...).

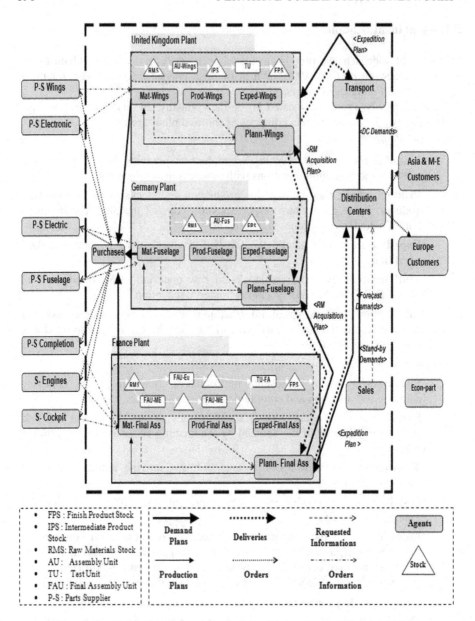

Figure 1 – Example of a supply chain and interactions among entities

4. COORDINATION OF SUPPLY CHAIN ACTIVITIES: COALITION FORMATION APPROACH

4.1. Definitions

We represent a chain of tasks by an acyclic directed graph $<TC, E>$, such that $TC = \{t_1 \cdots t_m\}$ represents the set of complex tasks for which an agent needs to initiate a coalition formation process to perform them. $E = \{(t_i, t_j)\}$ is the set of edges connecting the task t_i which precedes the task t_j with $(\emptyset, t_1) \in E$ as a beginning task, and $(t_m, \emptyset) \in E$ as an ending task. We define also the following concepts:

- Given $A = \{a_1 \cdots a_n\}$ the set of the agents in the system. This set is the union of two subsets $A = A^I \cup A^E$ including respectively the internal agents $A^I = \{a_1 \cdots a_k\}$ and the external agents $A^E = \{a_{k+1} \cdots a_n\}$.

- Given $T = \{t_1 \cdots t_c\}$ the set of tasks composing the chain such that $TC \subseteq T$.

- For the coalition formation, an agent determines, according to a preference model, a set of potential agents noted AP including itself.

- After coalitions are formed, we denote AR the set of agents do not participate to coalitions but contribute to one of chain tasks.

- Each agent a_i has a vector of capabilities $Q^i = \langle q_1^i \cdots q_p^i \rangle$.

- Each activity or complex task t_s has an execution cost denoted C_{t_s} which is the aggregation of several costs of all agents contributing to its execution. This cost represents the utility function of the agent. We suppose that this function could be defined by a linear function.

- We define also, $cp_{a_i, a_j}^{t_s}$, a cost of the output of an activity t_s from agent a_i to agent a_j, this parameter will be used in the total chain cost optimization.

The aim of each agent is to minimize its individual cost and consequently to minimize the cost of the whole chain. In the case of a coalition of several agents and in order to determine an activity cost, a binary variable is used:

$$Z_{t_s}^{a_i} = \begin{cases} 1 & \textit{if agent } a_i \textit{ is chosen to contribute to task } t_s \\ 0 & \textit{else} \end{cases} \quad \text{with } a_i \in AP \text{ and } t_s \in TC$$

The objective is to minimize the total cost $T.C$ by solving the following problem:

$$\text{Min.} T.C = \sum_{a_i \in AP} \sum_{t_s \in TC} z_{t_s}^{a_i} c_{t_s}^{a_i} + \sum_{(t_s, t_l) \in E} \sum_{a_i, a_j \in AP} z_{t_s}^{a_i} z_{t_l}^{a_j} cp_{a_i a_j}^{t_s} + \sum_{a_i \in AR} \sum_{t_s \in T} c_{t_s}^{a_i} \qquad [1]$$

$$\forall t_m, t_l \in TC, (t_m, t_l) \in E \qquad (a)$$

$$\sum_{t_s \in T} q_{t_s}^{a_i} z_{t_s}^{a_i} \leq Q^i \qquad (b)$$

(a) To satisfy the constraint of tasks' order

(b) The sum of agent capacities invested in all tasks cannot exceed its total capacity.

The first two parts of [1] represent the cost of the activities for which the coalitions are formed. The third part describes the cost of the other activities of the chain. We define the preference of an agent to another by the following matrix of preferences:

$$\prod_{a_i} = \begin{pmatrix} y_{i1}^1 & y_{i2}^1 & \cdots & y_{in}^1 \\ y_{i1}^2 & y_{i2}^2 & \cdots & y_{in}^2 \\ y_{i1}^p & y_{i2}^p & \cdots & y_{in}^p \end{pmatrix} \text{ with } \begin{cases} i \text{ index of agents} \in N \\ p \text{ index of criterea} \end{cases}$$

Each element y_{ij}^k of the matrix represents the preference of an agent a_i for the agent a_j according to criterion k. To obtain the multi-criteria preference of an agent for another, this matrix is reduced to a vector using an aggregation operator which can be *the balanced sum* or *the integral of Choquet* (Grabisch, 1996).We chose to use the second operator which has the advantage, contrary to the balanced sum, not to distort the result of aggregation when the criteria are not independent. It is based on the following principle: the agent a_i ranges by descending order the column of its preferences for an agent a_j according to specific criteria y_{ij}^k, according to given *individual* and *collective* weights of various criteria k noted $\mu(E_k)$ predefined by the system designer (with E_k a set including rather only one or several criteria).It calculates then its preferences' vector $\prod_{a_i} = (x_{ij})$ as follows:

$$x_{ij} = \sum_{0 \le k \le p} (y_{ij}^k - y_{ij}^{k+1})\mu(E_k) \text{ with } y_{ij}^{p+1} = 0 \text{ and } y_{ii}^k = 0 \qquad [2]$$

We define another concept: **attraction indices** which can be **unilateral (U-Att)** or **bilateral (B-Att)**:

- **Unilateral attraction** represents the force measurement of an agent to convince the other agents, not yet members, to join the coalition. To be able to determine it, the agent classifies the various values of the vector $\prod_{a_i} = (x_{ij})$ according to a descending order. This value is defined as follows:

$$\textbf{U-Att}(a_i) = \sum_{j=1}^n (x_{i,j} - x_{i,j+1})\mu(A_j) \text{ with } i \ne j \qquad [3]$$

In [3], $\mu(A_j)$ is a predetermined weight for the agent a_i or for the set of agents $A_j \in A = \{a_1 ... a_n\}$

- ***Bilateral attraction*** represents at the same time the desire of an agent to join a coalition and the desire of this coalition to integrate this agent. It is defined as follows:

$$\textbf{B-Att}\ (a_i, C_k) = \prod_{ki} \times \Re\ (a_i, C_k) \tag{4}$$

In [4], $\Re\ (a_i, C_k)$ represents the preference of an agent a_i to the coalition C_k and $\prod_{ki}$ represents the preference model of the coalition C_k for the agent a_i.

4.2. Coordination mechanism steps

An agent a_i receives a new message from its environment; it analyzes using its *detection function* which transmits it to the decision function. Then the *decision function*, having the agent's objectives, its current state and knowledge, chooses which action to undertake. *The action function* is then activated to launch the coordination process by sending messages to other agents; after that it updates the state and knowledge of the agent. If it is question of a coalition formation process for carrying out a complex task, the agent a_i take the role *of initiator* and enters in communication with the other agents according to the following algorithm whose two principal steps are:

- *Step 1.*

The agent, after having built its preference model, it contacts the internal and external agents which it prefers i.e. having the maximum values in its preference model (cf. Figure 2). Note that each agent a_i builds its preference for an agent a_j according to various criteria such as time, distance, quality...these criteria are predetermined by the system designer.

- *Step 2.*

Each solicited agent a_j checks its capabilities in order to determine it can contribute to this activity and also checks its planned activities, then it answers the initiator agent by a temporary acceptance or refusal. If the initiator agent receives only a refusal, it has to decide if it continues or cancels the process. In the first case, it sends a message to the solicited agents so that they confirm their participation and thus if they accept definitively, the initiator agent adds them on the list of confirmed coalitions and determines the total cost of the coalitions.

Step 1: Agent identification by calculation of the preference model:
Each agent a_i in need to launch a coalition formation (CF) process has to:
- Identify, according to its knowledge on environment, the potential agents simultaneously internal $\forall a_j \in A^I$ and external $\exists a_j \in A^E$ and then add them to the set AP

- Build its preference $\prod\limits_{a_i}^{p}$ according to predetermined criteria $(1...p)$

- Build its aggregated preference vector $\prod\limits_{a_i} = (x_{i1},...x_{ii},..., x_{i|AP|})$ with $x_{ii}=0$.

- Send its model to other agents and wait in return their models. At the same time it adds these proposals to its list 'proposed coalitions'.

- When received other models : Calculate unilateral attraction indices

$$\text{U-Att }(a_i) = \sum_{j=1}^{|AP|} (x_{i,j} - x_{i,j+1}) \mu(A_j) \text{ such that } \begin{cases} i \neq j \\ A_j \in AP \end{cases}$$

- **If** the U-Att $(a_i=$ initiator) is the highest
     (*) Block the CF process   //one CF process at time.
           Calculate bilateral attraction indices **B-Att** $(a_i, C_k) = \prod\limits_{ki} \times \Re(a_i, C_k)$

  Else The agent having the highest **U-Att** becomes the initiator and back to (*)
           $AP = AP\backslash \{a_i\}$ \\ in the case of a task outsourcing
  End If

Step 2: The coalition formation and calculation of the total cost
While the coalition objective not yet reached **and** $\{AP\} \neq empty$ **do**
- (**) Contact in the order the agent a_j having the highest **B-Att**

  For all t_l such that $(t_l, t_s) \in E$ **do**

  If $\sum\limits_{t_s \in T} q_{t_s}^j < Q^j$ **then**

                 // The accomplishment cost of a task is the sum of the preceding
                 tasks costs.

                 ▪ $c_{t_s} = \sum\limits_{(t_l,t_s)\in E} c_{t_l}$

                 // The agent capacity is the sum of the actual capacity and the all
                 capacities invested in preceding tasks.

                 ▪ $q_{t_s}^j = \sum\limits_{(t_l,t_s)\in E} q_{t_l}^j$

                 ▪ Remove (t_l, t_s) *from* E

                 ▪ $Z_{t_s}^{a_j} = 1$ // The agent wishes participate to the coalition

                 ▪ $C_k = C_k \cup \{a_j\}$

  Else $Z_{t_s}^{a_j} = 0$ // The agent cannot participate to the coalition
           Back to (**)
  End If
  End For
- Send a message to the agent concerned by the coalition.
- Receive the answer (confirmation or refusal).
End While

Calculate the total cost of the chain:

$$\text{Min } T.C = \sum_{a_i \in AP} \sum_{t_s \in TC} z_{t_s}^{a_i} c_{t_s}^{a_i} + \sum_{(t_s,t_l)\in E} \sum_{a_i,a_j \in AP} z_{t_s}^{a_i} z_{t_l}^{a_j} cp_{a_i a_j}^{t_s} + \sum_{a_i \in AR} \sum_{t_s \in T} c_{t_s}^{a_i}$$

Figure 2- Algorithm of the coalition formation process

5. CONCLUSION

In this article, we showed that the multi-agent approach is well adapted to model the supply chain management. With the aim of improving and optimizing the management of the logistic chain, the agents resort on coordination mechanisms in order to achieve their common tasks. We have proposed a distributed coordination method: the coalition formation mainly used in multi-agent systems. Given that, in supply chains, the entities appear and disappear dynamically, multi-agent approach makes it possible to simulate open systems what guarantees flexibility, effectiveness and evolution of such systems. We have, in a second time, presented an algorithm of coalition formation. We illustrated our proposals with an example of a supply chain taken in the industrial field. A prototype implementing our algorithm of coordination and the protocol of agents' interactions is under development and tests.

As research perspectives, several assumptions made in our modeling could be improved: 1) once the coalition formation is chosen as a coordination method, *the choice and the definition of the corresponding protocol remains problematic*. This choice is actually very depend on the type of problem studied i.e. parameters to be taken into account such as the fact that *the agents have or not the same objective* even the same utility function, or *the fact that they trust each other or not,* or their ability to exchange their knowledge... all these parameters can generate totally different protocols which must be tested, 2) the suggested protocol is based on several principles which cannot usually be adapted to industrial reality in particular in the case of a competitive partners of a supply chain. They can also have radically opposed objectives as in the relation supplier-producer; all will then depend on the negotiation which should also to be modeled.

6. REFERENCES

1. Aknine S., Pinson S. and Shakun M. (2004), "A Multi-Agent Coalition Formation Based on Preference Models", International Journal Group and Decision and Negotiation, Kluwer. Vol 13 N° 6, p 513-538.

2. Barbuceanu M., Fox M. S. (1996), "The Architecture of an Agent Building Shell", in Intelligent Agents II , Wooldridge M., Muller J. P. and Tambe M.(Eds.) Lecture Notes in Artificial Intelligence, Springer-Verlag, Berlin, Vol 1037 p 235-250

3. Beamon B. M. (1998), "Supply Chain design and analysis: Models and Methods", The International Journal of Production Economics, N ° 55 p 281- 294.

4. Dodd C. and Kumara S.R.T. (2001). "A distributed multi-agent model for value nets". IEA/AIE 2001, 718-727.

5. Fox M. S., Barbuceanu M. and Teigen, R. (2000), "Agent-Oriented Supply-Chain Management", The International Journal of Flexible Manufacturing Systems, 12 p 165- 188.

6. Giard V., Balin, S. (2007) Problèmes méthodologiques posés par la simulation de processus de production de services, Journal Européen des Systèmes Automatisés (APII-JESA) 41(9-10), 2007.

7. Grabisch, M. (1996) "The Application of Fuzzy Integrals in Multi-criteria Decision Making". European Journal of Operational Research, Vol. 89.

8. Hahndel S., Fuchs F. and Levi P. (1994) "Distributed Negotiation-Based Task Planning for a Flexible Manufacturing Environment". In Proceedings of the 6th European Workshop on Modeling Autonomous Agents in Multi-Agent World, p 147- 158. Odense, Denmark.

9. Kok, A. G. and Graves, S. C. (2003), "Supply Chain Management: Design, Coordination and Operation", Handbooks in Operation Research and Management Science, Elsevier Vol. 11 p 1- 16.

10. Parunak H.V.D. and VanderBok R. (1998),"Modeling the extended Supply Networks", In ISA-Tech'98 (Houston), Industrial Technology Institute.

11. Shehory O. and Kraus S. (1998), "Methods for Task Allocation via Agent Coalition Formation"; Artificial Intelligence Journal, Elsevier Science Vol. 101 (1-2) p 165-200.

12. Swaminathan J.M, Smith S.F and Sadeh N.M (1998), "Modeling Supply Chain Dynamics: A Multi Agent Approach"; Decision Sciences Journal, Vol. 29, N° 2 p 607-632.

---

[i] KQML : Knowledge Query and Manipulation Language

PART 7

PROCESS DEFINITION AND MODELING

21

COLLABORATIVE PROCESS DEFINITION USING AN ONTOLOGY-BASED APPROACH

Vatcharaphun Rajsiri, Jean-Pierre Lorré
EBM WebSourcing
netty.rajsiri, jean-pierre.lorre@ebmwebsourcing.com
Fréderick Bénaben, Hervé Pingaud
Ecole des Mines d'Albi-Carmaux, Centre de Génie Industriel
benaben, pingaud@enstimac.fr
FRANCE

This paper presents an ontology-based approach dedicated to automate the specification of collaborative processes for virtual organization networks. Our approach takes as input the knowledge coming from the characterization of network and produces as output a BPMN (Business Process Modeling Notation) compliant process. The collaborative network ontology (CNO) including deduction rules has been defined in order to accomplish this approach under two keys (i) some specific attributes of the considered collaboration included network and participant (ii) collaborative processes inspired from the enterprise Process Handbook (MIT). This CNO coupled with a reasoning engine will be used with an editor, provided by EBM WebSourcing, to model the network and build the collaborative process of a given collaboration. A model transformation will be applied after that to convert a collaborative process of the editor to a BPMN relevant one.

1. INTRODUCTION

Nowadays companies tend to open themselves to their partners and enter in one or more networks in order to have access to a broader range of market opportunities. The heterogeneities of partners, the long-term relationships and establishing mutual trust between its partners are the ideal context for the creation of collaborative networks. The interoperability is a possible way toward the facilitation of integrating networks (Konstantas et al., 2005) (Vernadat, 2006).

General collaboration issue of every company is to establish connections with their partners. Partners collaborate principally through their information system. The concept of collaborative information system (CIS) has been evolved to deal with the interoperability issues. According to (Touzi et al., 2006), this concept focuses on combining the information systems of different partners into a unique system.

Developing such a CIS concerns the transformation of a BPMN (Business Process Modeling Notation) collaborative process model into a SOA (Service Oriented Architecture) model of the CIS. This is based on the Model Driven Architecture (MDA) approach (Millet et al., 2003), as discussed in (Touzi et al., 2007). The BPMN supports the Computation Independent Model (CIM) of the MDA, while the SOA-based CIS supports the Platform Independent Model (PIM).

Please use the following format when citing this chapter:

Rajsiri, V., Lorré, J.-P., Bénaben, F. and Pingaud, H., 2008, in IFIP International Federation for Information Processing, Volume 283; *Pervasive Collaborative Networks*; Luis M. Camarinha-Matos, Willy Picard; (Boston: Springer), pp. 205–212.

Hence, our research focuses on the CIM model. We assume that partners are able to express informally and partially their collaboration requirements. However, how to make these requirements more formalized and completed? The schema below shows the approach of how we answer this question:

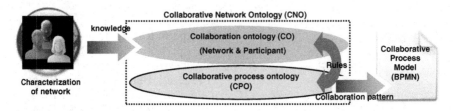

Figure 1 - Our approach for defining a BPMN

The approach has been developed on a basis of ontology and deduction. The main idea is to use ontology and deduction rules to automate the specification of collaborative processes. Thus, defining the collaborative network ontology (CNO) including the deduction rules is essential. The CNO itself consists of the collaboration ontology (CO), collaborative process ontology (CPO), and the deduction rules. The deduction rules establish the interactions between the two ontologies inside the CNO. The corresponding between the role and service concepts defined in the CO and the CPO respectively makes the deduction possible, according to (Malone et al., 2003) and (Sobah Abbas Petersen, 2005).

The approach starts at receiving the knowledge from the characterization of network, expressed by partners. The knowledge will be imported into the CO. Then the rules will be executed in order to derive new knowledge in the CPO or complete missing knowledge in the CO. Finally, the collaboration pattern matching the network will be extracted and will be transformed later into BPMN relevant process.

The paper is focused firstly on introducing the CNO and the deduction rules. Secondly, the supporting tools and a scenario will be presented. At the end, the on-going works will be discussed.

2. CNO AND DEDUCTION RULES

As we have described previously about the ontology-based approach shown in the figure 1, this section aims at introducing the main part of the approach regarding the CNO and the deduction rules.

2.1 Collaborative network ontology (CNO)

The domain of interest for developing the CNO relies on the collaborative network domain especially for designing collaborative process (Rajsiri et al., 2008).

The CNO, as shown in the figure 2, is composed of two ontologies which are (i) the collaboration ontology (CO) including network, and participant, and (ii) the collaborative process ontology (CPO). Each ontology defines the concepts, relations between concepts and properties. A knowledge base built under this ontology covers these two ontologies.

The following paragraphs will describe these two ontologies:

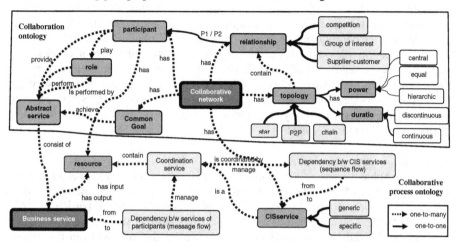

Figure 2 - CNO composing of Collaboration and Collaborative process ontologies

Collaboration ontology (CO)

The CO, as shown in the figure 2, concerns the characterization of collaborative network (e.g. common goal, relationship, topology) (Rajsiri et al., 2007) and the participant's details (e.g. role, abstract service).

A collaborative network ha1s common goals (e.g., group same products to buy together) and participants. Common goal achieves abstract services. Participants play roles (e.g., seller, buyer, producer) and provide abstract services (e.g., marketing and sale, procurement) corresponding to the roles they play. A network can have also several topologies which have duration and decision-making power characteristics and contain relationship.

Collaborative process ontology (CPO)

The CPO, as shown in the figure 2, is an extension of the concepts developed by the MIT Process Handbook project (Malone et al., 2003) and integrates the collaborative process meta-model (Touzi et al., 2007).

Business service concept explains task at functional level (e.g., obtain order, deliver products, pay against invoice). Each of them has input and output resources (e.g., machine, container, technology). Two business services will be dependent to each other when they have a common resource according to (Malone et al., 2003). Each dependency will be associated to a coordination service (e.g., manages flow of materials, manage sharing of resources). The concepts of dependency and coordination are related because coordination is seen as a response to problems caused by dependencies. This means a coordination service manages a dependency.

CIS service is considered as a coordination service as discussed in (Touzi et al., 2006) since CIS is defined as a mediation system managing the collaboration, dealing with the data and applications of participants.

2.2 Deduction Rules

The interactions between these two ontologies can be established via the deduction rule. Rule is written as antecedent-consequent pairs. The antecedent is referred to the rule body and the consequent is referred to the head (O'Connor et al., 2005).

The deduction rules should cover the organization of collaborative networks (e.g. goal, service, topology) and management of resources (coordination service, dependency). Five groups of rules have been defined: (i) role and abstract service, (ii) business service, (iii) dependency, coordination service and CIS service, (iv) common goal, and (v) topology. The following paragraphs provide some examples of rules of the first three groups:

Rule1: role → abstract service
(Sobah Abbas Petersen, 2005) affirms the existing of relation between role and activity. The aim of this rule is to derive abstract services when a role is provided which is in the first group. This rule can be explained for instance: if participant "A" plays role "seller" then the participant "A" provides abstract services "sell service", "sell product", "sell items from stock", etc. However, this rule will run fine when each role in the knowledge base has already been predefined its corresponding abstract service.

Rule2: abstract service → business service
This rule is in the second group, interesting in the deduction of business services when an abstract service is provided. For instance, if participant "A" provides abstract services "sell product" then the participant "A" provides also the business services "obtain order", "prepare products to deliver", "transfer invoice", etc. However, this rule will run fine when each abstract service in the knowledge base has already been predefined its corresponding business services. The idea of separating two levels of services into abstract services and their related business services comes from the MIT Process Handbook (Malone et al., 2003).

Rule3: resource → dependency → coordination → CIS services
Regarding the third group of rules, the aim of this rule is to derive dependencies when two business services have a common resource as discussed in (Malone et al., 2003). For instance, if the "place order" service of a buyer produces a purchase order as output and the "obtain order" service of a seller uses a purchase order as input then a dependency of purchase order between these two services will be established.

Once the dependencies have been established, we will deduce coordination and CIS services from dependencies. The relation between dependency and coordination is discussed in (Crowston, 1994), while the coordination service comparable with the CIS service is talked in (Touzi et al., 2006). For instance, if the dependency contains resource "purchase order" then the coordination service which is managed the resource "purchase order" is "manage flow of document" and then these coordination service is also the CIS service.

3. SUPPORTING TOOLS AND APPLICATION SCENARIO

Previously we have discussed about the ontology and the deduction rules. In this section, we will focus on the development of tools supporting the approach including the ontology, and the rules.

The figure 3 shows that the approach is composed of four parts: (i) knowledge gathering, (ii) knowledge base and deduction of collaboration pattern, (iii) extraction of collaborative process related to given collaboration cases, and (iv) BPMN relevant process.

A simple scenario will be experimented in order to illustrate the principles of the approach. The application covers the first three parts except the complements in the third part. The schema below shows the four parts of the ontology-based approach with tools using at each part:

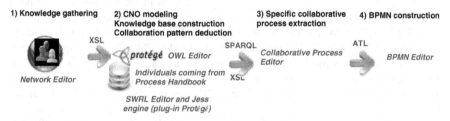

Figure 3 - Four parts of the ontology-based approach and the supporting tools

Part 1: Knowledge gathering

The knowledge to be gathered is composed of: (i) characteristics of network which concern the relationship between each pair of participants and common goal, and (ii) participants' details concerning their roles and services in the collaboration context.

Role and service are mandatory to have at least one of them since they can be completed by each other by deduction.

To gather the knowledge, we have developed a tool called "Network editor (NE)". It will be used to facilitate the consultants of EBM WebSourcing to define, and characterize manually the collaborative network of their clients.

Result of the scenario: the network scenario has three participants: A, B, and C which play role buyer, seller, and distributor respectively. The supplier-customer relationships are continuous, and hierarchic, established between A-B and A-C. The common goal of the network is to distribute goods. The figure below shows the characterization of the studied network:

Figure 4 - Characterization of the network

Once the collaborative network model has been defined, and all involved participants have agreed on it, we will enter now to the second phase of the part 2.

Part 2: CNO modelling, knowledge base construction and collaboration pattern deduction

The part 2 can be separated into two phases: (i) knowledge base preparation and (ii) collaboration pattern deduction. The first phase concerns the preparation of the knowledge base and its fundamental components which can be applied in any cases. The second phase will be performed after importing new individuals to the knowledge base.

In the first phase, the knowledge base will be created, and populated by some individuals. The knowledge base will contain only standard individuals (e.g. business services, roles, coordination services…). Constructing a knowledge base requires an ontology which is the CNO in this case.

The CNO has been informally defined as discussed in the section 2.1. We need to formalize it with a rigorous syntax and semantic language. According to (Young et al., 2007), OWL (Web Ontology Language) is good at representing the semantic objects but weak in process definition. Similarly the PSL (Process Specification Language) has a strong process representation capability but is weak in representation of objects. Hence, in this work the formalization of the CNO in order to construct a knowledge base is written in OWL using the Protégé (Rajsiri et al., 2008).

The deduction rules, discussed in the section 2.2, will be written in SWRL (Semantic Web Rule Language). They will be saved as a part of the ontology (O'Connor et al., 2005). This is an example of the Rule1 (role → abstract service), discussed in the section 2.2, written in SWRL: Participant(?x)^playRole(?x, ?y) ^ performAbstractService(?y, ?z) → provideAbstractService(?x, ?z).

The individuals coming from the dataset which is an OWLized[i] version of the MIT Process Handbook will be stored in the knowledge base in their corresponding classes and properties.

The second phase starts once the collaborative network from the NE has been characterized and imported to the knowledge base as a new individual.

To be able to import, a transformation of the collaborative network model to the OWL model supporting the knowledge base is required. We do the transformation at this phase using the XSL (eXtensible Stylesheet Language).

After importing, the deduction can be performed by executing the SWRL rules with the Jess engine (O'Connor et al., 2005). The Jess is in charge of creating new OWL concepts and then inserting them into the knowledge base.

Result of the scenario: after performing the deduction, new individuals and properties are created and inserted in the knowledge base. For instance, the participant "C" as distributor performs "deliver" service, "A" as buyer performs "place order", "pay" services. Once the rules have been executed without any errors, we can start the next part.

Part 3: Specific collaborative process extraction

In this part, we try to extract and illustrate collaborative process. The queries, written in SPARQL, are required here to execute in order to extract from the knowledge base only the collaboration pattern that matches to the input network.

Then the collaboration pattern obtained will be restructured and transformed into a corresponding collaborative process using the XSL. The collaborative process will be illustrated on the "Collaborative process editor (CPE)".

The users of the CPE are the consultants of EBM WebSourcing. Once the collaborative process has been produced, the users are in charge of completing and validating the collaborative process by adding some missing elements (e.g. type of gateways, events).

Result of the scenario: after querying, the obtained pattern will be transformed into a relevant collaborative process respecting to the CPE model. However, the collaborative process obtained is just a solution for the given use case and based on the CNO shown in the figure 2. It is possible to have other solutions corresponding more or less than the proposed one. The process shown in the figure 5 was already simplified for the readability reason of the figure. Normally the obtained collaborative process is more complicated.

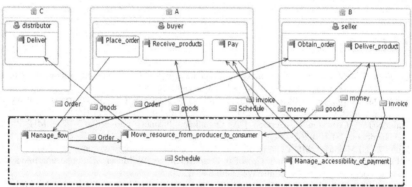

Figure 5 - Collaborative process

Part 4: BPMN collaborative process construction

What we are waiting for at the end is not the collaborative process which is compatible with the CPE but with the BPMN. Thus, a transformation of collaborative process from the CPE to the BPMN model is needed.

The transformation language we use here is the Atlas Transformation Language (ATL). ATL is QVT (Query, View and Transformation) compatible which is a specialized language that has been developed under the Object Management Group (OMG). The main purpose of this language is to allow the transformation between models (Touzi et al., 2007).

Result of the scenario: not provided.

4. PERSPECTIVES

The ontology-based approach aims at automating the specification of BPMN collaborative processes by taking as input the informal knowledge coming from the characterization of network. The approach uses the ontology (CNO) and the deduction rules to accomplish the aim.

Since, during the conceptualization of the CNO, we have integrated the meta-model of collaborative process. Thus, this can guarantee the conformity of the result obtained from the part 3 (Figure 5) of the approach to the BPMN model. We can see that the actual collaborative process is really near the BPMN but still not complete. There are some missing elements such as gateways and events. These elements are needed to be implemented before transforming to the BPMN compliant process because they can make process more dynamic. Other complements that should also be done in the part 3 are validating process and removing worthless elements or dependencies.

Our current work is focused on adding the dynamic aspect by completing the actual result of the part 3 by taking into account with gateway and event elements as well as validation. After that, we will handle the transformation into BPMN collaborative processes.

5. REFERENCES

1. Crowston, K. A Taxonomy of Organizational Dependencies and Coordination Mechanisms (Working paper No. 3718-94): MIT, Sloan School of Management, 1994.
2. Konstantas D, Bourrières JP, Léonard M, Boudjlida N. Interoperability of enterprise software and applications, INTEROP-ESA'05, Geneva Switzerland, Springer-Verlag, 2005
3. Malone TW, Crowston K, Herman GA. Organizing business knowledge – The MIT Process Handbook, ISBN 0-262-13429-2, Chapters 1 and 3, 2003.
4. Millet J. and Mukerji J. MDA Guide Version 1.0.1, available on http://www.omg.org, 2003
5. O'Conner M, Knublauch H, Tu S, Grosof B, Dean M, Grosso W, Musen M. Supporting rule system interoperability on the Semantic Web with SWRL, 2005.
6. Petersen SA. The role of enterprise modelling in virtual enterprises, Collaborative Networks and Their Breeding Environments, Springer, 2005.
7. Rajsiri V, Lorré JP, Bénaben F and Pingaud H. (2007). Cartography based methodology for collaborative process definition, Establishing the Foundation of Collaborative Networks, 2007.
8. Rajsiri V, Lorré JP, Bénaben F and Pingaud H. (2008). Contribution to the knowledge-based methodology for collaborative process definition: Knowledge extraction from 6napse platform, accepted paper for I-ESA 2008, March 2008, Berlin, Germany.
9. Touzi J, Lorré JP, Bénaben F and Pingaud H. (2006). Interoperability through model based generation: the case of the Collaborative IS. Enterprise Interoperability.
10. Touzi J, Bénaben F, Lorré JP and Pingaud H. (2007). A Service Oriented Architecture approach for collaborative information system design, IESM'07, Beijing China.
11. Vernadat FB. (2006). Interoperable enterprise systems: architectures and methods, INCOM'06 Conference, St-Etienne, France.
12. Young RIM, Gunendran AG, Cutting-Decelle AF, Gruninger M (2007). Manufacturing knowledge sharing in PLM: a progression towards the use of heavyweight ontologies. International Journal of Production Research Vol 45 No7, ISSN 0020-7543.

---

[i] http://www.ifi.unizh.ch/ddis/ph-owl.html

BUSINESS PROCESS MODELLING FOR ACADEMIC VIRTUAL ORGANIZATIONS

22

Paul Cotofrei[1], Kilian Stoffel[2]

[1]Information Management Institute, University of Neuchâtel, paul.cotofrei@unine.ch
[2]Information Management Institute, University of Neuchâtel, kilian.stoffel@unine.ch
SWITZERLAND

The increasing mobility due to Bologna process forces the academic partners to increase the inter-operability of their administrative processes, by interacting through a collaborative networks and therefore acting as an academic virtual organization. To facilitate the communication and the comprehension of the administrative processes between the components of the CN, the Business Process Modeling Notation (BPMN) is proposed in this paper as a standard graphical model for administrative processes and transactions. The adaptability of this standard for academic processes and the difficulties of "translating" the actual administrative models (legal texts) in BPMN diagrams are analyzed.

1. INTRODUCTION

One of the goals of the Bologna process [1] - an intergovernmental initiative which aims to create the European higher education area by making academic degree standards and quality assurance standards more comparable and compatible throughout Europe – is the increasing of student's and teacher's mobility (inside a country and across countries). Consequently, the institutions of the educational area (universities, engineering colleges, high schools of applied science,...) must respond by an increasing inter-operability of their administrative processes, acting as a single higher educational virtual organization. Those institutions (academic partners) often interact through collaborative networks.

These virtual organizations must offer services to its "customers": course subscription, exam registration, library application, etc. (for students), curriculum recognition, session exam results management, etc. (for the administrative staff), educational program implementation, pre-requisite course preparation, etc. (for the teaching staff). And each partner of the academic virtual organization (AVO) often still has the tendency to protect its autonomy by implementing its own workflows for these services. The realization of collaborative administrative processes and of their support systems in this "multi-enterprises" context becomes so an important issue. Consequently, academic partners must "re-think" their administrative process organisation to find the suitable implementation of these services. A first important step in this direction can be attainted by modelling and decomposing recursively these processes, which are turned into appropriate services either by adding a convenient interface directly, or by associating them to composed services.

Please use the following format when citing this chapter:

Cotofrei, P. and Stoffel, K., 2008, in IFIP International Federation for Information Processing, Volume 283; *Pervasive Collaborative Networks*; Luis M. Camarinha-Matos, Willy Picard; (Boston: Springer), pp. 213–220.

Even if today the universities are forced to operate in a globalising market with powerful new competitors (e.g. open universities), and are pushed by financial necessities to become "hybrid" institutions (semi-public and semi-private), their management is in our regions still not identical to an enterprise management (at least at the strategic level) [2]. Usually, the model of an administrative process (the process which, into a classical enterprise context, would be identified as an "operational business process"), is in written form, mostly plain text, with semantic constraints - laws, faculty regulations, department regulations, education office directives, dean directives, secretary rules, etc.(see Section 2). This form is far-a-way to be easily comprehensible, even for in-house students or administrative staff, and do not facilitate the collaboration inside AVO.

Different studies were conducted concerning the management of business processes in collaborative networks, which propose a number of frameworks for process modelling to facilitate the partnerships across units that have been traditionally autonomous to large extent [3-4]. But in many cases, these studies concentrated on the technological aspects (WSDL [5], WSDL-S [6] for describing services; SOAP [7], REST [8] for communicating) of the interoperability among heterogeneous tools and platforms [9-10].

Based on the studies of collaborative processes for virtual enterprises [11-12] and on the intuitive equivalences: "university ≈ enterprise" and "administrative process ≈ business process", we investigate in this paper the suitability of the Business Process Modelling Notation to represent administrative processes inside an AVO. BPMN is a standardized graphical notation that depicts the steps in a business process and facilitates the understanding of high-performance collaborations and administrative transactions between the organizations. By applying a "translating" procedure (in this incipient phase, demanding a strong implication of the user, but intended to become, in the future, an almost automatic procedure), we obtained BPMN diagrams for some of most useful (and used) services (see Section 3). These diagrams were then used in a survey study, designed to establish the degree of comprehension (measured as the rate of correct answers) of the textual model (the regulation), respectively of the corresponding graphical model (see results in Section 4). The encouraging results of our study proved the feasibility of the proposed approach and permitted the opening of the second phase of our project, the creation of a knowledge base of BPMN diagrams for all services supplied by academic partners in a AVO, by using a formal, ontology based, "translation" procedure of the textual models (see Section 5 for a detailed discussion).

2. MOTIVATING EXAMPLE

The University of Neuchâtel participates in different exchange programs, either at a national level (BeNeFri and "Triangle d'azur" programs with the universities of Lausanne, Geneva, Fribourg and Bern) or at an international level (Erasmus Program, with universities inside the EU, and specific programs, with universities from the USA and Canada). We propose as illustration the following situation: suppose that a student enrolled in a mobility program wants to attend a course of the program "Master of Science in Information Systems" of the Faculty of Economics, University of Neuchâtel.

The academic procedures he must follow in order to obtain his ECTS credits are specified in different legal texts - regulations, rules and instructions – that the student has to understand in order to follow the correct administrative procedure. In any academic unit the models of the administrative processes are represented in written forms with semantic constraints (the terms used in these texts have precise meaning and can not be interpreted outside a specific ontology). Usually we can differentiate three levels of the model specification: a "strategic"[1] level (the process is formulated in a general manner, or even only named), a "tactic" level (the process is described more precise and the agents (rolls) are enumerated), and an operational level (containing the detailed description of the tasks, decisions, agents implied in the process and eventually the connection with other processes).

We will now illustrate the steps a student has to follow and, at the same time, will present the texts "describing" these steps. The first procedure the student must execute is the registration for the chosen course. The legal text containing the specification of the process model at strategic level is the "Regulation of Studies for the Master of Science in Information Systems" [13]:

*"Students must **register** for the examination session..."* (art. 9, par. 3).

There is no mention about the registration for a course, the dependence between the two kinds of registration procedures being made clear only at the tactic level of the process model, in the "Rules for attendance and examination of the Bachelor's degree in economic sciences" [14]:

*"Students must **register** for each **course** they want to attend, within the time prescribed by the academic calendar..."* (art. 10, par. 1)

"Registration for a course gives the right to register to the corresponding assessment." (art. 10, par. 2)

How the student may register in practice is described at the operational level of the process model, in the document "Instructions concerning registration for courses and examinations" [15]:

*"...It is not allowed to register for an exam without having pre-register for the course ... Joint registration courses/exams is not technically possible, you must register twice.... Please **go to page** http://www2.unine.ch/ /academia and **log you in** with your user name and password. You can **find instructions** for general use..."* (art. 2, par. 1)

*"Remember to **save your registration** before leaving the page. **Print your registration** to keep a written record"* (art. 2, par. 4)

According to the detailed instructions, the registration for a course is performed using a web service (IS-Academia), which demands firstly an authentication phase. A student enrolled at e.g. the University of Lausanne for the Master in Information Systems (which is a collaborative program between the universities of Neuchâtel and Lausanne) has no user name and password for IS-Academia. He must firstly find and then follow the supplementary instructions for this specific case [16]:

---

1   We use these terms in order to make allusion to the corresponding businesses process levels.

"Complete the form Enrolment Application - Courses at UniNE and return it to the Secretariat of the Faculty of Economics, with a registration certificate of your university. You will receive a letter giving you a username and password in order to access the university's email system.."

This is only an example of the difficulties a student participating in an exchange program may face trying to achieve all the administrative procedures demanded by the host institution. Furthermore, the details of some academic processes remain obscured even for the teaching or the administrative staff. This is true especially for those processes with a large number of tasks and roles: the creation of a master program, for example, implies the institute which propose the master, the expert group which elaborate the proposal, the council of the faculty which vote the proposal, the dean's office which elaborate the final proposal and the university council which analyse and approve the program.

3. IMPLEMENTING ACADEMIC PROCESSES

Academic processes modeled as legal texts do not facilitate the collaboration between the academic partners of a virtual organization. A better approach, in our opinion, is the use of a standard graphical notation for academic processes, readily understandable by all the implied actors: students, professors, secretaries, etc. The standard we chose was designed for business process and is called Business Process Modeling Notation [17]. BPMN provide businesses with the capability of understanding their internal business procedures in a graphical notation and give organizations the ability to communicate these procedures in a standard manner. Furthermore, the graphical notation facilitates the understanding of high-performance collaborations and business transactions between the organizations.

The modeling in BPMN is made by simple diagrams with a small set of graphical elements. The four basic categories of elements are the following:

Table 1 – Elements of BPMN

Categories	Elements	Some examples (graphical notations)
Flow objects	Events	Start Intermediate End
	Activities	Task Sub-Process (Collapsed)
	Gateways	Exclusive Decision Merge Inclusive Decision Merge Parallel Fork/Join
Connecting objects	Sequence Flow	
	Message Flow	
	Associations	
Swimlanes	Pool	Pool / Lane
	Lane	Lane
Artifacts	Data Object	Data Text Annotation Group
	Group	
	Annotation	

By using these elements, we were able to represent the academic process "Course registration", as is shown in Figure 1.

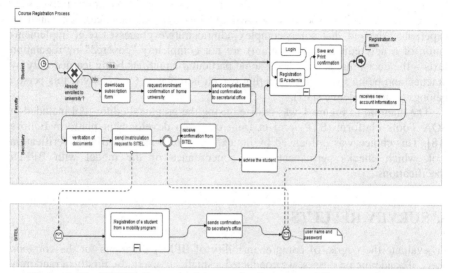

Figure 1. The BPMN diagram of the academic process "Course registration"

Almost all the graphical elements enumerated in Table 1 have been used in this diagram: pools[2] ("Faculty", with two lanes (or roles) – "student" and "secretary" – and "SITEL"), Start Events (of type "Timer" (see Figure 2) – the process is trigged by a specific date from the academic calendar – and of type "Message" – the process is trigged by a received message), End Events (of type "Link" – the process' end will trigger another future process – and of type "Message" – a message is send to a participant), Tasks (e.g. "downloads subscription form"), Sub-processes (e.g. "registration of a student from a mobility program"), Gateway (of type "Exclusive decision/merge", e.g. "Already enrolled to university?"), Sequence Flows, Message Flows, Data and Annotations.

Figure 2. Graphical notation for some specific events

As mentioned in its specifications, BPMN is constrained to support only the concepts of modeling that are applicable to business processes. Academic institutions are organizations with non-business purposes, but the type of services they offers are still equivalent to the services implemented by any common business-oriented organization for its customers. Consequently, the expressiveness of BPMN is sufficient to allow the modeling of any of the academic processes.

---

2   A pool represents a participant in the process

From a methodologically point of view, modeling an academic process using BPMN starts by a deeper analyse and comprehension of the process workflow. This task is realized by a person knowing well the semantics of BPMN diagrams, either by analyzing the relevant legal texts or by interrogating administrative staff (especially when the process is known only as a usual practice). The authors' experience showed that some complex administrative processes (e.g. implement-tation of a new educational program) are not completely "covered" by regulation texts – the decisional approach for some particular situations being learned only by practice and being lost if the executing person is replaced (especially if this person belongs to the academic staff).

The diagram in Figure 1 was realized using the graphical editor tool included in SOA Tools Platform (STP) project from the open development platform Eclipse [18]. This choice was influenced by the existence of a build-in BPMN verification tool, which checks permanently the concordance of the model with BPMN specifications.

4. SURVEY RESULTS

To evaluate the degree of comprehensibility of BPMN diagrams for the common users of academic processes, we conducted a small survey study. Firstly, a randomly sample of 57 students[3] (including also persons participating in mobility programs) was divided randomly in two groups. One of the groups received the text of the regulations' articles concerning the registration process; the other group received the BPMN diagrams of the same process (the diagram represented in Figure 1 and another, not represented here, for the exam registration process). All the students received also an identical questionnaire, with questions about specific details of the registration process and questions concerning the general appreciation – a note between 1 and 5 - of the process model (text or diagram). At the end, all students received both models and were asked to indicate their preference. A similar study, but less structured and at a very small scale, was conducted for the administrative staff (the secretaries of the Faculty of Economics and the members of the dean's office of the same faculty). In this last study the questions concerned the academic process of the creation, implementation and maintenance of an educational program.

The analysis of the questionnaires (Table 2) showed a rate of preference for BPMN diagrams twice greater than those of regulation texts, even if there are not great differences between the rates of correct answers (or general appreciation) for the two models. Furthermore, the diagrams submitted to administrative staff allowed to bring out some aspects of the academic process, not enough detailed in legal texts.

Table 2. Some results of the survey concerning the BPMN diagrams

	BPMN diagrams	Regulation texts
Rate of accurate answers	87%	71%
Positive appreciation (per group)	3.4	3.7
Global preference (per sample)	48%	22%

[3] Enrolled in the first year of a master programs, only 30% graduated in Neuchâtel

5. DISCUSSIONS AND FUTURE WORK

The advantages of BPMN as a standard modeling language for administrative processes in an academic virtual organization are obvious: easily understandable by users without business background (students, administrative staff, teaching staff), high expressiveness (sufficiently to model any kind of administrative process), user-friendly graphical tools for diagram creation. Furthermore, the possibility of mapping a BPMN diagram into a BPEL processes facilitates the implementation of collaborative processes between academic partners based on Web Service interfaces.

The procedure applied to extract a graphical model (BPMN diagram) from unstructured legal texts originating from different repositories, demands certains abilities from the user (knowledge about the administrative structure of an academic institution and of the relationships between the members of the academic hierarchy, juridical capabilities, and BPMN specifications). So this procedure is only conceivable when applied to construct a small number of models.

For a large number of administrative models (hundreds for the University of Neuchâtel) we suggest another approach (which is briefly outlined here and is part of our planed future work). In a first phase, an ontology of the legal texts defining the structure and the activities of an academic institution is created (usually, these texts employ terms with non-ambiguous meaning). Two distinct categories must be emphasized in this ontology: the hierarchy of the actors (roles) inside the institution, and the activities (tasks) each actor has the competence to execute. In a second phase, a user-driven procedure identifies possible processes by exploring the relationships defined in the ontology (applying either a top-down approach – starting with very general processes and checking if the executed tasks can be expanded into sub-processes – or a bottom-up approach – starting with atomic processes, collapsing them and checking if more general processes can be identified) and transforms them to an "intermediate" model. We believe that the concept of social networks [19-20] could represent a satisfactory solution for this intermediate model. It can be represented in a graphical form (as a finite state machine), captures the behavior of the process (the roles and their actions) and can model the same process at different levels of details, using building blocks [21]. Finally, during the third and last step, an automatic procedure transforms the social networks in BPMN diagrams, using a dedicated knowledge base of equivalences (an example is presented in Figure 3, where at the left we have a social network model and at right the corresponding BPMN diagram).

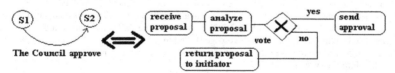

Figure 3. Two equivalent models (at left, a social network and at right, a BPMN diagram, for the administrative process "Approval by the Council")

6. CONCLUSIONS

The collaboration process inside a virtual organization, between non-business institutions for which the models of administrative processes are represented by legal texts, may be facilitate, in our opinion, by adopting BPMN as standard process modeling notation. Our analyze proved the adaptability of this approach for academic processes and proposed to study, while stressing the inherent difficulties, a user-driven, ontology based procedure for "translating" textual models into BPMN diagrams.

7. REFERENCES

1. Confederation of EU Rectors' Conferences. "The Bologna Declaration on the European space for higher education". http://ec.europa.eu/education/policies/educ/bologna/bologna.pdf
2. Shattock, Michael. "Strategic Management in European Universities in an Age of Increasing Institutional Self Reliance". In Tertiary Educational and Management, vol.2, no. 6, 2000, 93-104
3. Krogstie, John; Dalberg, Vibeke; Jensen, Siri Moe. "Harmonising Business Processes of Collaborative Networked Organisations Using Process Modelling". In Proceedings of PRO-VE 2004, Toulouse, 81-88
4. Biennier, Frédérique; Favrel, Joël. "Integration of a Contract Framework in BP Models". In Proceedings of PRO-VE 2004, Toulouse 2004, 97-104
5. WSDL link. http://www.w3.org/TR/wsdl
6. WSDL-S http://www.w3.org/Submission/WSDL-S/
7. SOAP link http://www.w3.org/TR/soap/
8. Fielding, R. T. "Architectural Styles and the Design of Networked-based Software Architectures". Doctoral dissertation, Chapter 5, University of California, 2000
9. Carreras, M. A.; Skarmeta, M.; Gomez, A. F. "Towards Interoperability in Collaborative Environments". In Proceeding of "Collaborative Computing: Networking, Applications and Worksharing", 2006, 1-5
10. Franco, Rubén Darío; Bas, Ángel Ortiz; Anaya, Víctor; Esteban, Francisco-Cruz Lario. "IDR: A Proposal for Managing Inter-Organizational Business Processes by Using Web-Services Oriented Architectures". In Proceedings of PRO-VE 2004, Toulouse 2004, 89-96
11. Westphal, Ingo; Thoben, Klaus-Dieter; Seifert, Marcus. "Measuring Collaboration Performance In Virtual Organizations". In Proceedings of PRO-VE 2007, Guimaraes, 33-42
12. Robinson, P.; Karabulut, Y.; Haller, J. "Dynamic virtual organization management for service oriented enterprise applications". In Proceedings of International Conference on Collaborative Computing, 2005.
13. "Master of Science in Information Systems – Règlement d'études". http://www2.unine.ch/webdav/site/mscis/shared/documents/reglement-final-MScIS.pdf
14. "Règlement d'études et d'examens du baccalauréat universitaire en sciences économiques". http://rsn.ne.ch/ajour/default.html?4163301.htm
15. "Inscriptions aux cours et aux examens : Bachelor en sciences économiques 2007-2008". http://www2.unine.ch/webdav/site/seco/shared/documents/PROCEDURE_Exa_etudiants0708.pdf
16. "For students registered at UNIL and UNIGE (Triangle Azur) and following courses at the University of Neuchâtel". http://www2.unine.ch/seco/page21606.html
17. "Business Process Modeling Notation Specification". http://www.bpmn.org
18. Eclipse link http://www.eclipse.org
19. Picard, Willy. "Computer Support for Adaptive Human Collaboration with Negotiable Social Protocols". In Proceeding of BIS 2006, 90-101
20. Picard, Willy. "Continuous Management Of Professional Virtual Community Inheritance Based On The Adaptation Of Social Protocols". In Proceeding of PRO-VE 2007, 381-388
21. Simon, E.; Künzi, C; Stoffel, K. "Scalable Social Protocols to Formalize Systems Development Life Cycles", In Proceedings of IADIS International Conference e-Society 2007, 177-184.

USING BPEL FOR BEHAVIOURAL CONCEPTS IN ODP ENTERPRISE LANGUAGE

23

Youssef Balouki, Mohamed Bouhdadi

A Department of Mathematics & Computer Science,
University Mohammed V Morocco, MOROCCO
email: balouki@cmr.gov.ma
bouhdadi@ fsr.ac.ma

This paper studies the specification and the execution of behavioral concepts for Open Distributed Processing (ODP) Enterprise Language. The behavior of an ODP system is determined by the collection of all possible actions in which the system (acting as an object), or any of its constituent objects, might take part, together with a set of constraints on when these actions can occur. In order to specify the executable behavior of a system and to make the processes of the enterprise executable and controllable, the Reference Model for ODP RM-ODP can be used as a meta-model for behavioral specifications. In the enterprise language the behavior is specified in terms of roles, processes, policies, and the relationships between these concepts. Firstly, we give the description and specification of the behavior by the activity diagrams. Secondly, we define the mapping from the concepts of behavior enterprise language to BPEL concepts and we present the syntax and the structure of a BPEL Behavior process. Then we generate the corresponding BPEL and computational files to implement the specified process.

1. INTRODUCTION

The rapid growth of distributed processing has led to a need for coordinating framework for the standardization of Open Distributed Processing (ODP). The Reference Model for Open Distributed Processing (RM-ODP) [1-4] provides a framework within which support of distribution, networking and portability can be integrated. The foundations part [2] contains the definition of the concepts and analytical framework for normalized description of (arbitrary) distributed processing systems. These concepts are grouped in several categories. The architecture part [3] contains the specifications of the required characteristics that qualify distributed processing to be open. It defines a framework comprising five viewpoints, viewpoint language, ODP functions and ODP transparencies. The five viewpoints, called enterprise, information, computational, engineering and technology provide a basis for the specification of ODP systems.

Each viewpoint language defines concepts and rules for specifying ODP systems from the corresponding viewpoint. The ODP functions are required to support ODP systems.

The transparency prescriptions show how to use the ODP functions to achieve distribution transparency. The first three viewpoints do not take into account the

Please use the following format when citing this chapter:

Balouki, Y. and Bouhdadi, M., 2008, in IFIP International Federation for Information Processing, Volume 283; *Pervasive Collaborative Networks*; Luis M. Camarinha-Matos, Willy Picard; (Boston: Springer), pp. 221–232.

distribution and heterogeneity inherent problems. This corresponds closely to the concepts of PIM (Platform Independent Model) and PSM (Platform Specific Model) models in the OMG MDA architecture.

However, RM-ODP can not be directly applicable [5]. In fact, RM-ODP only provides a framework for the definition of new ODP standards. which include standards for ODP functions [6-7]; standards for modeling and specifying ODP systems; standards for programming, implementing, and testing ODP systems.

We treated the need of formal notation for behavioral concepts in the enterprise language [8]. Indeed, the viewpoint languages are abstract in the sense that they define what concepts should be supported, not how these concepts should be represented. It is important to note that, RM-ODP uses the term language in its broadest sense: "a set of terms and rules for the construction of statements from the terms". It does not propose any notation to support the viewpoint languages. Using the Unified Modeling Language (UML)/OCL (Object Constraints Language) [9, 10] we defined a formal semantic for a fragment of ODP behavior concepts defined in the RM-ODP foundations part and in the enterprise language [11]. These concepts (time, action, behavior constraints and policies) are suitable for describing and constraining the behavior of ODP enterprise viewpoint specifications.

A part of UML meta-model itself has a precise semantic [12, 13] defined using denotational meta-modeling approach. A denotational approach [14] is realized by a definition of the form of an instance of every language element and a set of rules which determine which instances are denoted or not by a particular language element.

For testing ODP systems [2-3], the current testing techniques [15] [16] are not widely accepted. A new approach for testing, named agile programming [17] or test first approach [19], is being increasingly adopted. The principle is the integration of the system model and the testing model using UML meta-modeling approach [20] [21]. This approach is based on the executable UML [22].

In this context, OCL is used to specify the properties to be tested. The UML meta-models provide a precise core of any ODP tester.

In this context we use in this paper the BPEL (Business Process Execution Language for Web Services) (BPEL4WS or BPEL for short) to specify process behavior based on actions and policies in the context of ODP systems. The BPEL is an XML-based standard for defining how you can combine Web services to implement business processes. It builds upon the Web Services Definition Language (WSDL) and XML Schema Definition (XSD). This article specifies the behavior processes by the activity diagrams, and generates the corresponding BPEL and computational files to implement that process. This capability is used to highlight some benefits of the Object Management Groups (OMG) Model Driven Architecture (MDA) initiative: raising the level of abstraction at which development occurs; which, in turn, will deliver greater productivity, better quality, and insulation from underlying changes in technology.

The paper is organized as follows. Section 2 introduces, both BPEL and the core behavior concepts (time, action, behavior, role and process). Section 3 describes and specifies the behavior by the activity diagrams. In Section 4, we define the mapping from the concepts of behavior enterprise language to BPEL concepts and we present the syntax and the structure of a BPEL Behavior process. We focus on behavioral policies. A conclusion ends the paper.

2. PRELIMINARIES

2.1 BPEL

BPEL, also known as BPEL4WS, build on IBM's WSFL (Web Services Flow Language) and Microsoft's XLANG (Web Services for Business Process Design). It combines the features of a block structured process language (XLANG) with those of a graph-based process language (WSFL). BPEL is intended to describe a business process in two different ways: executable and abstract processes. An abstract process is a business protocol specifying the message exchange behavior between different parties without revealing the internal behavior of any of them. An executable process specifies the execution order between a number of constituent activities, the partners involved, the message exchanged between these partners and the fault and exception handling mechanisms.

A composite service in BPEL is described in terms of a process. Each element in the process is called an activity. BPEL provides two kinds of activities: primitive activities and structured activities. Primitive activities perform simple operations such as receive (waiting for a message from an external partner), reply (reply a message to a partner), invoke (invoke a partner), assign (copying a value from one place to another), throw (generating a fault), terminate (stopping the entire process instance), wait (wait for a certain time) and empty (do nothing).

To enable the representation of complex structures, a structured activity is used to define the order on the primitive activities. It can be nested with other structured activities. The set of structured activities includes: sequence (collection of activities to be performed sequentially), flow (specifying one or more activities to be performed concurrently), while (while loop), switch (selects one control path from a set of choices), pick (blocking and waiting for a suitable message). The most important structured activity is a scope. A scope is a means of explicitly activities packaged together such that they can share common fault handling and compensation routines. It is composed of a set of optional fault handlers (exceptions can be handled during the execution of its enclosing scope), a single optional compensation handler (inverse some effects which happened during the execution of activities), and the primary activity of the scope which defines its behavior.

The sequence, flow, switch, pick and while constructs provide a means of expressing structured flow dependencies. In addition to these constructs, BPEL provides another construct known as control links which, together with the associated notions of join condition and transition condition, support the definition of precedence, synchronization and conditional dependencies on top of those captured by the structured activity constructs. A control link between activities A and B indicates that B cannot start before A has either completed or has been skipped. Moreover, B can only be executed if its associated join condition evaluates to true, otherwise B is skipped. An activity X propagates a positive value along an outgoing link L if and only if X was executed (as opposed to being skipped) and the transition condition associated to L evaluates to true. Transition conditions are Boolean expressions over the process variables. The process by which positive and negative values are propagated along control links, causing activities to be executed or skipped, is called dead path elimination.

Figure 1 defines the BPEL core concepts [23]

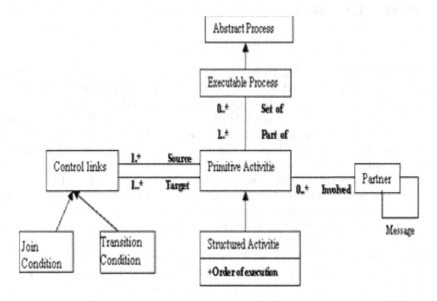

Figure 1 – Model of BPEL Core Concepts

2.2 The Core behavioral Concepts in RM-ODP Foundations Part

We consider the minimum set of modeling concepts necessary for behavior specification. There are a number of approaches to specify the behavior of distributed systems proposed by searchers with different background and considering different aspects of behavior. We use the formalism of the RM-ODP model, written in UML/OCL. We mainly use concepts taken from the clause 6 "Enterprise Language" of the RM-ODP. The behavior of a community is a collective behavior composed of the actions in which the objects of the community participate in fulfilling the roles of the community, together with a set of constraints on when these actions may occur, It may be interesting to specify which actor (enterprise object) initiates that action.

There are many specification styles for expressing when actions may occur (e.g. sequencing, pre-conditions, partial ordering, etc.). The actions and their ordering can be defined in terms of processes.

A process identifies an abstraction of the community behavior that includes only those actions that are related to achieving some particular sub-objective within the community. Each abstraction is labeled with a process name. The emphasis is on what the behavior achieves. Processes decompose the behavior of the community into steps. Its specification shall include specification of how it is initiated and how it terminates.

We represent a concurrent system as a triple consisting of a set of behavior, a set of process and a set of action. Each behavior is modeled as a finite or infinite sequence of interchangeable behavior and actions. To describe this sequence, there are mainly two approaches [24].

1. "Modeling systems by describing their set of actions and their behaviors".
2. "Modeling systems by describing their action spaces and their possible sequences of action changes".

These views are dual in the sense that a behavior can be understood to define action changes, and action occurring in action sequences can be understood as abstract representations of process. We consider both of these approaches as abstraction of the most general approach based on RM-ODP. We provide the formal definition of this approach that expresses the business process models.

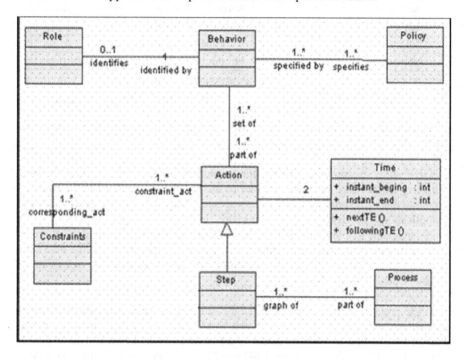

Figure 2 – Core Behavior Concepts

3. UML PROFILE FOR AUTOMATED BEHAVIOR PROCESSES

The ability to extend or customize UML is essential to MDA; UML can be customized to support the modeling of systems behavior. The scope of this article is mainly centered on stereotypes. Stereotypes are a way of categorizing elements of a model. We can combine a set of these stereotypes in a Profile. A UML Profile is used to define a specific set of extensions to the base UML in order to represent a particular domain of interest. For instance there are Profiles defined for CORBA and Data Modeling. A profile defines what elements of UML are to be used, how they may be extended, and any well-formedness rules to constrain the assembly of the elements.

This section introduces a UML Profile which supports modeling with a set of semantic constructs that correspond to those in the Business Process Execution Language for behavior in enterprise language (see table 1).

Table 1 – Sample table

Behavior Concepts	Profile Construct
Process_El	<< process>> class
Action	Activity graph on a <<process>> class
Actor	<<partner>> class
Policy	<<process>> class attributes
Objective	Hierarchical structure and control flow
<<receive>>, <<reply>>, <<invoke>> actions	<<receive>>, <<reply>>, <<invoke>> activities

We represent a subset of the UML profile through ODP trader [25] that defines a simple behavior process. It may be summarized as follows:

"ODP aims to provide distribution-transparent utilisation of services over heterogeneous environments. In order to use services, users need to be aware of potential service providers and to be capable of accessing them. Since sites and applications in distributed systems are likely to change frequently, it is advantageous to allow late binding between service users and providers. If this is to be supported, a component must be able to find appropriate service providers dynamically. The ODP trading function provides this dynamic selection of service providers at run time."

BPEL processes are stateful and have instances, so in BPEL this scenario is implemented as a behavior process which would have an instance for each actual behavior application being processed. Each instance has its own state which is captured in BPEL variables. In the UML profile, a process is represented as a class with the stereotype <<Process>>. The attributes of the class correspond to the state of the process (variables in BPEL 1.1). The UML class representing the behaviorl process is shown in Figure 3.

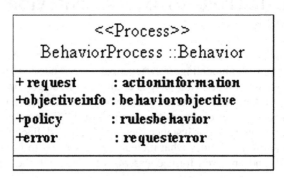

Figure 3 – A UML class used to model a Behavior BPEL Process

The behavior of the class is described using an activity graph. The activity graph for the behavior process is shown in figure 4. The activities, such as invoke, are shown as the rectangles with rounded corners. The actions to be performed are shown as Entry conditions to the activity. For example, action constraint (a variable) is set to the result of the check service. The partners with which the process communicates are represented by the UML partitions (also known as swimlanes):Trader, Client and Server. The activities that involve a message send or receive operation to an partner appear in the corresponding partition. The arrows indicate the order in which the process performs the activities. Note that the assignment activity is not in a swimlane; it depicts an action that takes place within the process itself.

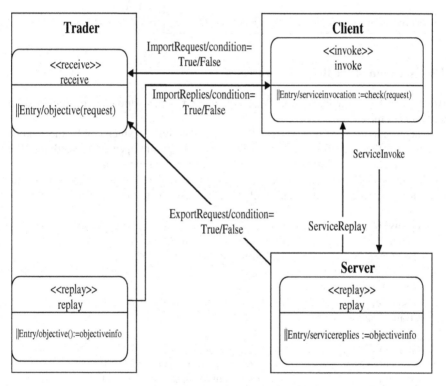

Figure 4 – An Activity Diagram for the Behavior Process

The reply activity returns a response back to the client, completing the execution of the process. Each activity has a descriptive name and an entry action detailing the work performed by the activity.

4. MAPPING TO BPEL

4.1 From UML to BPEL

The UML profile for automated behavior processes expresses that complete executable BPEL artifacts can be generated from UML models. Table 2 shows an overview of mapping from the profile to BPEL covering the subset of the profile introduced in this article.

Table 2 – UML to BPEL mapping overview

Profile Construct	BPEL Concept
<< process>> class	BPEL process definition
Activity graph on a <<process>> class	BPEL activity hierarchy
<<process>> class attributes	BPEL variables
Hierarchical structure and control flow	BPEL sequence and flow activities
<<receive>>, <<reply>>, <<invoke>>activities	BPEL activities

4.2 Execution of the Behavior processes

BPEL is an XML representation of an executable process which can be deployed on any process motor.

The atomic element of a process BPEL is an "activity", which can be the send of a message, the reception of a message, the call of an operation (sending of a message, makes an attempt of an answer), or a transformation of data.

A process BPEL defines, in XML, the activities realized by the framework of the behavior process execution. In the following we describe its structure and syntax.

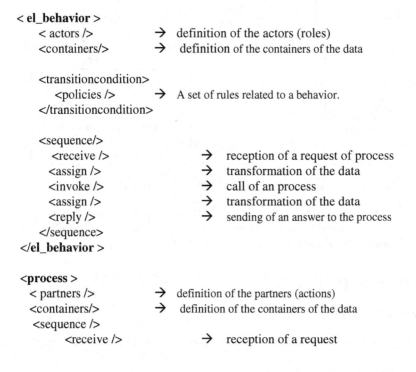

```
< el_behavior >
      < actors />            →   definition of the actors (roles)
      <containers/>          →    definition of the containers of the data

      <transitioncondition>
            <policies />     →   A set of rules related to a behavior.
      </transitioncondition>

      <sequence/>
        <receive />          →    reception of a request of process
        <assign />           →    transformation of the data
        <invoke />           →    call of an process
        <assign />           →    transformation of the data
        <reply />            →    sending of an answer to the process
      </sequence>
</el_behavior >

<process >
   < partners />             →   definition of the partners (actions)
   <containers/>             →    definition of the containers of the data
    <sequence />
        <receive />              →    reception of a request
```

```
        <assign />        →    transformation of the data
        <invoke />        →    call of an action
        <assign />        →    transformation of the data
        <reply />         →    sending of an answer
        </sequence>
</process>

<policies>  name = "namepolicy"
      <process name ="process"/>
      < actors  name =  "actor"/>
       <choice >
          <policy type ="obligations"/>
          <policy type ="permissions"/>
          <policy type ="prohibitions"/>
          <policy type ="authorizations"/>
       </choice >
</policies>
```

A cutdown version of the BPEL document that would be generated from the behavior process example is shown in Listing 1 (much of the detail is omitted here due to space constraints).

Listing 1. Excerpt of the BPEL listing

```
<process name="behaviorProcess" ...>
 <variables>
  <variable name="request"
messageType="objectivedef:actionInformationMessage"/>
  <variable name="action_constraint"      messageType="asns:
action_constraintMessage"/>
  ...
 </variables>
 ...
 <flow>
    <receive name="receive" partner="trader"
        portType="apns:behaviorprocessPT"
        operation="objective" variable="request"
        createInstance="yes">
      <source linkName="receive-to-client"
       transitionCondition=
       "bpws:getVariableData('request', 'condition') = true"/>
      <source linkName="receive-to-server"
       transitionCondition=
       "bpws:getVariableData('request', 'condition)=false"/>
    </receive>
    <invoke name="invokeservice" partner="client"
          portType="asns:actionconstraint"
          operation="check"
          inputVariable="request"
```

```
             outputVariable="action_constraint">
      <target linkName="receive-to-server"/>
      <source linkName="action3-to-setMessage"
         transitionCondition=
           "bpws:getVariableData('action_constraint ', 'check')='true'"/>
      <source linkName="reply-to-invoke"
         transitionCondition=
           "bpws:getVariableData('action_constraint ', 'check')!='true'"/>
    </invoke>

  <assign name="assign">
   <target linkName="invoke-to-setMessage"/>
   <source linkName="setMessage-to-reply"/>
   <copy>
    <from expression="'yes'"/>
    <to variable="objectiveInfo" part="accept"/>
   </copy>
  </assign>
  ...
  <reply name="reply" partner="actor1" portType="apns:behaviorprocessPT"
       operation="approve" variable="objectiveInfo">
   <target linkName="setMessage-to-reply"/>
   <target linkName="objective-to-reply"/>
  </reply>
 </flow>
</process>
```

4.3 The UML to BPEL Mapping Transformation

The approach comes with a set of sample files for different scenarios [26]. The sample files are of two main types: UML model files which can be opened and modified with tools, and XML files containing the XMI version of the UML models and which are exported by theme. In figure 5, we can see that this corresponds to the UML models, or the XMI output of these tools.

Figure 5 uses a UML Activity Diagram to show the overall process of transforming the files; isn't UML useful? The boxes represent artifacts (usually files) while the ellipses represent an action or activity. The main stages are:

- Building and exporting the UML model to XMI (tools)
- Generating the BPEL, Actions, and behavior files
- Deploying these on the BPEL motor.

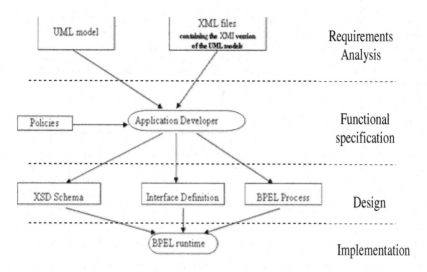

Figure 5 – Developing a process

5. CONCLUSION

This article has introduced a UML profile for automated behavior processes with a UML to BPEL translator. The profile allows developers to use normal UML skills and tools to develop behavior processes using BPEL. This approach enables service-oriented BPEL components to be incorporated into an overall system design utilizing existing software engineering practices. Additionally, the mapping from UML to BPEL a model-driven development approach in which BPEL executable processes can be automatically generated from UML models.

Although we have only shown our method for the Trader behavior from the Enterprise Viewpoint, the method is generic enough to be applied in other viewpoints, such as trader from the Information Viewpoint.

6. REFERENCES

1. ISO/IEC, "Basic RM-ODP-Part1: Overview and Guide to Use, "ISO/IEC CD 10746-1, 1994
2. ISO/IEC, "RM-ODP-Part2: Descriptive Model, " ISO/IEC DIS 10746-2, 1994.
3. ISO/IEC, "RM-ODP-Part3: Prescriptive Model, " ISO/IEC DIS 10746-3, 1994.
4. ISO/IEC, "RM-ODP-Part4: Architectural Semantics, " ISO/IEC DIS 10746-4, July 1994.
5. M. Bouhdadi, et al. " An UML-based Meta-language for the QoS-aware Enterprise Specification of Open Distributed Systems, " Collaborative Business Ecosystems & Virtual Enterprises, IFIP Series, Vol. 85, Springer Boston, pp.255-264, 2002.
6. ISO/IEC, "ODP Type Repository Function, " ISO/IEC JTC1/SC7 N2057, 1999.
7. ISO/IEC, The ODP Trading Function, ISO/IEC JTC1/SC21 1995.
8. ISO/IEC, "RM-ODP Enterprise Langauge," ISO/IEC 15414, July 2006.
9. J. Rumbaugh, G. Booch, J. E. Jacobson, The Unified Modeling Language, Addison Wesley, 1999.
10. J. Warner and A. Kleppe, The Object Constraint Language: Precise Modeling with UML, Addison Wesley, 1998.
11. M. Bouhdadi, Y. Balouki, "Meta-modelling Semantics of Behavioral Concepts for Open Virtual Enterprises," ECC 2007, Athens 25-27 Sep, Springer Verlag (to appear

12. S. Kent, S. Gaito, N. Ross, "A meta-model semantics for structural constraints in UML, ', In H. Kilov, B. Rumpe, and I. Simmonds, editors, Behavioral specifications for businesses and systems, Kluwer Academic Publishers, Norwell, MA, September 1999. chapter 9.

13. E. Evans, R. France, K. lano, B. Rumpe, "Meta-Modeling Semantics of UML, " In H. Kilov, B. Rumpe, and I. Simmonds, editors, Behavioral specifications for businesses and systems, Kluwer Academic Publishers, Norwell, MA, September 1999. chapter 4

14. D.A. Schmidt, "Denotational semantics: A Methodology for Language Development, " Allyn and Bacon, Massachusetts, 1986.

15. G. Myers, "The art of Software Testing, ", John Wiley &Sons, 1979

16. R. Binder, " Testing Object Oriented Systems. Models. Patterns, and Tools, " Addison-Wesley, 1999

17. A. Cockburn, "Agile Software Development. "Addison-Wesley, 2002.

18] B. Rumpe, " Agile Modeling with UML, " LNCS vol. 2941, Springer, 2004, pp. 297-309.

19. K. Beck. Column on Test-First Approach. IEEE Software, vol. 18, no. 5, pp.87-89, 2001

20. L. Briand , "A UML-based Approach to System testing, " LNCS vol. 2185. Springer, 2001, pp. 194-208,

21. B. Rumpe, " Model-Based Testing of Object-Oriented Systems; " LNCS vol.. 2852, Springer; 2003; pp. 380-402.

22. B. Rumpe, Executable Modeling UML. A Vision or a Nightmare?, In: Issues and Trends of Information technology management in Contemporary Associations, Seattle, Idea Group, London, pp. 697-701.

23. Dimitris Karagiannis et al. Business-oriented IT management developing e-business applications with E-BPMS," ICEC 2007, 97-100

24. M. Broy, "Formal treatment of concurrency and time," Software Engineers's Reference Book, Oxford Butterworth-Henenmann (1991).

25. ISO/IEC. Information Technology - Open Distributed Processing - ODP Trading Function, ISO/IEC JTC1/SC21/N9122, August 1994.

26. keith_mantell," From UML to BPEL Model Driven Architecture in a Web services world" ,Report IT Architect, IBM 2003

24

RISK TREATMENT TEMPLATES FOR CONFIGURABLE REFERENCE MODELING IN THE CONSTRUCTION INDUSTRY

Wael Sharmak, Sven-Eric Schapke, Raimar J. Scherer

Institute of Construction Informatics, Dresden University of Technology, GERMANY
{Wael.Sharmak@mailbox.tu-dresden.de; Sven.Schapke; Raimar.Scherer@tu-dresden.de}

Numerous risks impact construction projects and cause changes in their management plans. Unfortunately, not all of them can be identified in advance. Hence, risk management in construction requires proactive as well as reactive treatment. Among the other risk management tasks, risk treatment requires a sound methodology to rapidly develop concrete change actions and alter the corresponding project management plans. In this paper, process modeling techniques are used to develop configurable treatment templates, which describe how treatment can change the schedule plan. Such templates can contribute in structuring configurable reference models which in turn can be tailored and assembled to form up-to-date project schedules. Risk data as a part of reference repository may serve as means of knowledge management by providing all available risk-related information as response to critical events.

1. INTRODUCTION

The construction industry is project-based. Each project is a one-off unique venture that is characterized by a user-driven initiation, a multitude of project stakeholders and disciplines as well as integral contracts for works and services. As such, construction projects have always been executed by *construction networks*, i.e. temporal collaborative networked organizations that bring together the required expertise and resources and share the respective project risks.

For the management of construction activities, traditional project management techniques are used that break down the project into manageable, self-containing subtasks with specific goals. Based on a system engineering approach various separate models of the delivered goods and services are used to support planning, coordination and control of the design and production processes. However, no project ever goes totally as planned. Construction projects are exposed to numerous uncertainties and unforeseeable risks that may result in changes to the initial financial, temporal and functional goals as well as the respective design and construction management plans

Particularly, *construction-driven risks* such as unexpected weather, soil and groundwater conditions, possible accidents as well as changing public regulations and policies are difficult to assess. Most often they require instant decisions on what

Please use the following format when citing this chapter:

Sharmak, W., Schapke, S.-E. and Scherer, R.J., 2008, in IFIP International Federation for Information Processing, Volume 283; *Pervasive Collaborative Networks*; Luis M. Camarinha-Matos, Willy Picard; (Boston: Springer), pp. 233–240.

treatment measures have to be taken as well as on the required adjustments of the current designs and the respective project management plans.

Moreover, there are also sever *design-driven risks* that result from conflicting interests of the project stakeholders and changing owner requirements as well as design errors and omissions induced by short design times and the uniqueness and complexity of products. Design-driven errors are often recognized at a later stage of the project and often require considerable redesign and rework.

The paper introduces a novel, process-centered view on risk management that focuses on the risk treatment plans in foresight of possible as well as in reaction to already occurred risks. To allow for a more rapid development of the risk treatment plans the research pursues the use of reference processes for risk treatment as described in chapter 2.3. To support the approach risk treatment templates have been developed that constitute the structural foundation for altering the current project schedule in accordance to the required risk treatment tasks as shown in chapter 3.

2. PROCESS MODELING FOR RISK TREATMENT IN AEC

Although risks in architecture, engineering and construction (AEC) usually affect several aspects of a structure's design and the construction plans, risk management is (if at all) limited to a few separated project management plans. While cost management and scheduling make projections of the anticipated time and money consumption, there are only insufficient management systems to handle threats from external events and later discovered errors and omissions. Most often ad hoc decisions are made that later result in unintentional changes to the project plans. Hence, there is a need for an extension to risk treatment methodologies that allows for handling commonly emerging and unforeseen risks as well as for projecting the risk treatments effects on the overall project plans.

In our research we pursue a process-centered approach to risk treatment planning in which extended business process models provide for (a) the positioning of the risk within the project process, (b) the identification of interdependent elements in related engineering and management systems as well as (c) the analysis and simulation of risk treatment measures. Moreover, to allow for a rapid development of risk treatment plans reference process models that can be adapted to the current project situation are predefined for all-known project risks.

2.1 Risk Management

In corporate and project management literature risk management is usually considered a supporting function. Risks are treated in proactive way by monitoring external threats and internal operations in regard to previously identified and classified risks of high probability and/or high impact. According to the established standards [1, 9] such risk management typically involves a series of management tasks such as: the (a) identification, (b) assessment, (c) treatment planning, (d) treatment, (e) monitoring, and (f) documentation of the risks.

However, due to the uniqueness of construction products and the multitude of external influences it is hardly possible to identify all construction risks in early project stages. Moreover, even if a risk is identified, it can be underestimated and thus excluded from the proactive risk treatment group. In addition, there is a tendency in the construction industry to leave probable risks and react to them when they have occurred, rather than dealing with them in advance [7]. Therefore, an extension to traditional risk management for *reactive risk treatment* is suggested to more accurately handle problems that are detected during project execution. Figure 1 depicts the two interdependent risk management cycles of proactive and reactive risk treatment.

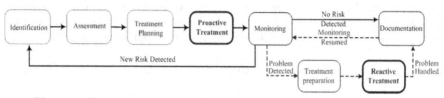

Figure 1 – Proactive and Reactive Treatment Cycles within RM Process.

2.2 Reference Process Modeling in Construction

A reference model is a generic conceptual model that formalizes recommended practices for a certain domain. It constitutes a best-practice yet universal description of a class of application domains that can be reused for information systems development in related projects and enterprises [3].

Reference modeling constitutes all activities for constructing and applying reference models. Differences between the existing reference modeling approaches mainly result from the applied technologies for the reuse of the reference models. In respect to the decomposition of the model and the degree of adaptability various forms of reuse from static enterprise-wide recommendations to configurable model modules can be distinguished. In line with several authors in [2] and [3] we distinguish four approaches to reusing reference models:

- *Analogical Reuse* that imposes no restrictions on the use of reference models.
- *Rule-based Configuration* in which the reference models comprise explicit rules for their adaptation.
- *Generic Configuration* in which the possible adaptations of reference models, such as their specialization and instantiation are defined by the methodology.
- *Composition* that combines multiple reference models in a superordinate one.

A prerequisite for the effective reuse a reference process models is a comprehensive description of its application context. However, despite the importance of process management, integrated process and enterprise models are rarely used in AEC due to the heterogeneity and dynamics of the construction networks. One suitable methodology for modeling collaboration networks from project initiation to workflow definition was proposed in the ArKoS project [6]. Conceptually the modeling architecture comprises three model components:

- *Construction Network Model* that captures the contextual information of the organizational structures and infrastructures of construction networks,
- *Inter-organizational Process Module Chains* that represent the goods and service delivery processes on the inter-organizational level.
- *Event-driven Process Chains and Workflow Models* that detail and finally formalize the processes of the process modules on the task level.

Based on the three modeling components some general solutions to reference process modeling in AEC can be illustrated. Firstly, the construction network model provides general context information for the adaptation of reference processes to the current project situation. Secondly, process modeling on the inter-organizational level mainly requires the composition of corporate deliveries in regard to the technical and organizational interfaces of the modules and their pre- and post-conditions. Thirdly, the development of the process task models is ideally supported by a comprehensive contextual framework of a construction network and a process module chain. Thus, an effective reuse of reference processes here first of all requires the configuration of process templates to execute the predefined tasks under the given conditions as well as the instantiation of the template parameters.

2.3 Risk Treatment Planning in Construction

Central point of reference for the proposed process-centered risk management is the task level representing the detailed design and execution plans. While financial risks can be managed based on subcontractor records, the occurrence of critical events, errors and omissions requires the instant identification of all affected tasks.

The overall goal of the approach is to support the alternation and complementation of the current project plans with predefined reference models for risk treatment called *reference risk treatment processes* (RTP). Prerequisite for the efficient development of risk treatment plans is a detail model of the current processes. It is assumed that the project processes have been modeled by extended event-driven process chains (eEPCs) [5] to:
- *Support Process Planning and Workflow Management:* While the eEPC is mainly indented for the integrated modeling of the business processes it also supports construction-specific schedule and resource planning approaches as well as the automatic generation of corresponding workflows [6].
- *Support Reuse of Risk Treatment Processes:* The eEPC do not only model the technical and organizational context of a task but also allow for representing occurred risks and treatment plans as deviation events and treatment functions. Moreover, it provides for modeling process templates in Configurable EPC (C-EPCs) that extend regular EPCs and allow for defining configuration connectors and configuration functions in reference processes [8].

Figure 2 depicts the overall modeling process of the approach. Overall it comprises a risk effect analysis as well as the selection, configuration and integration of RTPs:

Risk effect analysis: The elicitor of risk treatment planning is the detection of a particular past or future risk. Project management needs to analyze the risks' effects consulting expert knowledge as well as the project schedules identifying all the tasks that can be affected. Moreover, interim goals for the treatment plans shall be defined that must be met under all circumstances.

Selection of Reference Risk Treatment Processes: The RTPs are provided via a reference process catalogue that can be filtered based on the contextual information of the eEPC as well as the risk information and interim goals. The reference catalogue will be developed based on the Process Matrix that already constitutes a collection of over 300 reference processes for AEC in a facet classification [4]. For the management of the RTPs the facets of the process matrix classification will be aligned with eEPCs and extended by risk and performance parameters. Moreover, the reference risk treatment processes will be liked to configurable process structures, such as the risk treatment templates (RTTs) described in chapter 3.

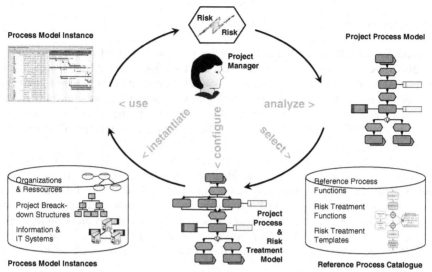

Figure 2 – Process of risk treatment planning.

Configuration of Reference Risk Treatment Processes: The configuration of the RTPs is first of all limited to the configuration functions provided by C-EPCs and formalized in the RTTs. For now it can be assumed that the reference process catalogue contains a RTP for all the affected functions as the original project processes are developed based on the same catalogue. Hence, the biggest challenge of the configuration tasks is to achieve structurally correct processes as demonstrated in chapter 3. However, future research will also have to provide guidance and support for the adaptation of the RTPs to the technological and organizational context of the overall eEPC.

Integration, Instantiation and Usage of Reference Risk Treatment Processes: The integration of the RTPs with the former process plans first of all requires the combination of the affected tasks with the newly developed risk treatment processes. Moreover, until now risk treatment modeling was carried out configuring general process models. For applying the develop process models in project management they have to be transformed to actual project schedules or workflows. This also requires the instantiation of all attributes left unspecified, e.g. assigning values for the names and addresses of responsible persons from the construction network model or start and end times from the overall project process.

3. TEMPLATES FOR RISK TREATMENT MODELING

Based on an analysis of possible activity sequences, six risk treatment templates have been developed that represent general types of process changes caused by risks. The risk treatment template can be considered a case-oriented configurable process model that describes a set of possible risk-related sequence change scenarios. After the configuration of the template only one of these scenarios will be used to represent an "actual or virtual" schedule change caused by a specific risk event.

3.1 Suggested Risk Treatment Templates

In accordance to the risk management cycles presented in chapter 2, risk treatment templates are classified into proactive and reactive risk treatment templates. In all templates, the expressions "Risk=ON, Risk=OFF" are used in the *if-then* statements to indicate the current status of a risk. *Risk ON* in proactive treatment means that the mentioned risk has approved probability/impact exceeds the agreed threshold. In reactive treatment it means that the risk has evolved to a real problem and the required changes have been approved. *Risk OFF* indicates the opposite.

In the templates the actual treatment of each risk is defined by a function named "treatment". This function as hierarchical one can be refined into another EPC, which shows the details of the needed actions to handle one specific risk-activity case. Moreover, according to task dependencies, risk treatment can cause cascade action, which means that a treatment in one activity may create problems in logically related activities. Therefore, other actions may be needed to be done to some interrelated activities, e.g. durations and dates adjusting or resources leveling, which is not included in our work.

3.2 Proactive Risk Treatment Templates

Insertion Case: In this template, see Figure (3-1), the treatment is done before the risk evolves to a real problem. When it will be found that the risk event has a considerable probability/impact on the targeted activities according to the agreed tolerance thresholds, then treatment function will be included in the schedule plan. The needed resources will be allocated and the needed cost and time will be considered in the project management plans.

Substitution Case: As a countermeasure to the coming danger, certain activities may need to be substituted with other activities which are more suited to the probable new case. In the template shown in Figure (3-2), function (n) is substituted with function (m) to react/avoid/mitigate the highly expected high risk impact. This alternative function, function (m), was not preferred in normal cases because of, e.g. its higher cost, its longer duration, or its complex execution technology etc.

Function Cancelation Case: This template, Figure (3-3) can be used for example in the case when a threat becomes highly expected, so some changes must be done as a response to the coming danger by canceling some planned tasks and adding other new tasks somewhere else in the project schedule.

Parallelism Case: The treatment will be done in parallel with some planned tasks, Figure (3-4). The configurable OR is used and a requirement will limit its configured scenarios to two models only; (1) AND when Risk=ON, (2) normal sequence when Risk= off.

3.3 Reactive Risk Treatment Templates

In reactive templates, risk event will interrupt and stop temporarily the execution of a function, and four important elements will appear between the interrupted function and its following event: risk event, Treatment preparation and Treatment functions, and Resuming function. The developed interruptive treatment models are:

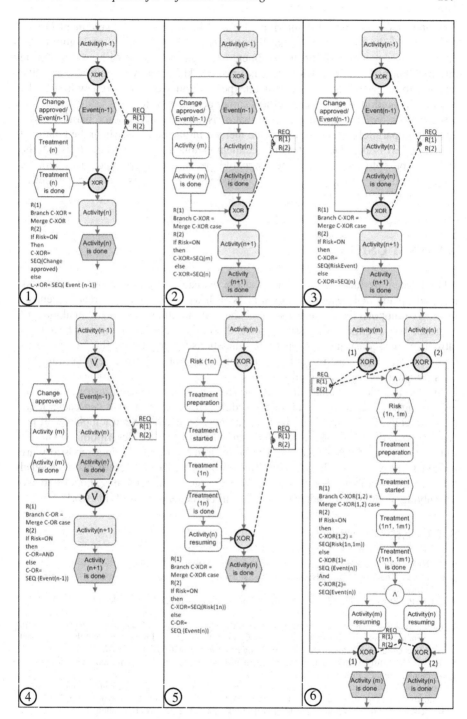

Figure 3 – Proactive and Reactive Risk Treatment Templates

Treatment Case: Risk (1n) interrupted Function (n), therefore Treatment (1n) is needed to handle the risk, after that Function (n) can be resumed, see Figure (3-5). Stop case is a special case of the treatment one. The risk event will cause a stop in this function until the risk bad effect is finished. This case represents the negative reaction to the risk, e.g. the case of unexpected bad weather which will stop the work in the outdoor activities until the weather becomes better.

Parallel Activities Case: In the case that a risk will interrupt some parallel tasks, all affected parallel paths will need to be merged in one path, on which the treatment of this risk will take place. After the treatment is done/the risk effect is finished, the path can be splitted again to the same old paths, the interrupted tasks will be resumed and after that the successor planned tasks will be executed in parallel as planned, see Figure (3-6).

4. CONCLUSION

The paper introduces a novel view on risk management that focuses on the risk treatment plans in foresight of possible as well as in reaction to already occurred risks. To support the development of the risk treatment plans a catalogue of reference risk treatment processes is pursued. Six risk treatment templates have been introduced that constitute the structural foundations for developing the reference risk treatment processes. Each template is a configurable branch which can be linked to the schedule network using configurable connectors. Configurable connectors can be adapted to include or exclude the exceptional path. Each template illustrates one way of risk-caused change in the project schedule. However each risk can cause more than one change so more than one template may be needed. Such template will not provide how to treat a risk, as it is only an *activity-sequence* description which can suit many kinds of risk situations. Therefore, joins to reference data repository are needed to provide all related *Risk-Task* information. The structure of the needed database, the ontology description of the suggested task reference model and the assembling method of the adapted models will be the next steps of this work.

5. REFERENCES

1. AS/NZS 4360: *Risk Management Standards*, Australia, 1999.
2. Becker J., Knackstedt R. (Eds.) Referenzmodellierung 2002. Methoden - Modelle - Erfahrungen. Münster 2002.
3. Fettke P, Loos P, (Eds). Reference Modeling for Business Systems Analysis. Idea Group Publishing, 2007.
4. Katranuschkov P., Gehre A., Scherer R.J., Wix J. & Liebich T. (2004): User Requirements Capture in Distributed Project Environments: A Process-Centred Approach. In: Proceedings of Xth International Conference on Computng in Civil and Building Engineering (ICCCBE), Weimar, Germany, 2004.
5. Keller G, Nüttgens M, Scheer A-W. Semantische Prozessmodellierung auf der Grundlage„ Ereignisgesteuerte Prozessketten (EPK)", *1991.*
6. Loos P., Vanderhaeghen D. (Eds.) Kollaboratives Prozessmanagement: Unterstützung kooperations- und koordinationsintensiver Geschäftsprozesse am Beispiel des Bauwesens, Logos Berlin, 2007.
7. Loosemore, Martin. Risk Management in Projects. Taylor & Francis Group, London, 2005.
8. Mendling J, Recker J, Rosemann M, van der Aalst W. Generating Correct EPCs from Configured C-EPCs. In: Proceedings of the 21st Annual ACM Symposium on Applied Computing. France, 2006.
9. PMBOK Guide. A Guide to the Project Management Body of Knowledge, Project Management Institute, Pennsylvania, USA, 2004.

PART **8**

KNOWLEDGE MANAGEMENT AND ONTOLOGIES

25

A RULE-BASED APPROACH FOR CUSTOMIZING KNOWLEDGE SEARCH IN CNOS

Rui J. Tramontin Jr. [1], Chihab Hanachi [2], Ricardo J. Rabelo [1]

[1] *Federal University of Santa Catarina, Department of Automation and Systems GSIGMA – Intelligent Manufacturing Systems Group, Florianópolis (SC), BRAZIL*
tramontin@gsigma.ufsc.br
rabelo@das.ufsc.br

[2] *Institut de Recherche en Informatique de Toulouse IRIT, UMR 5505, Université Toulouse1, 2 rue du Doyen-Gabriel-Marty, 31042 Toulouse Cedex 9., FRANCE*
hanachi@univ-tlse1.fr

Searching for knowledge in Collaborative Networked Organizations (CNOs) is an important issue as partners must share and use the knowledge spread over the network. Besides that, partners of such networks work in several contexts (roles, activities, processes) and have individual interests. Based on these observations, the aim of this work is to provide and combine concepts such as topics, profiles and context in a model for customizing knowledge search in CNOs. The basic assumption is that the relevance of the search results in the CNO domain is not only defined by the terms of the query but also by the context and the profile of the user performing the search. Besides the model, a set of rules for query customization is presented and all these elements are framed in an existing framework for knowledge search.

1. INTRODUCTION

Due to new characteristics of the global economy and society, new forms of inter-organizational interactions are emerging and have been classified into the general concept of Collaborative Networked Organization (CNO). A CNO can be defined as group of distributed, heterogeneous and autonomous entities (organizations or people) that formally collaborate in response to business opportunities and their interactions are supported by computer networks (Camarinha-Matos, 2005).

As collaboration among CNO partners is of paramount importance, the quality of the information / knowledge exchanged and searched may have a relevant impact on the performance of the network. In particular, the search for CNO knowledge is essential for supporting the different activities during the CNO life cycle like partners selection, performance indicators selection, *CNO management* and *inheritance*.

Knowledge search rises up as an alternative in order to support these and other activities that are performed by partners playing some role in the CNO, like managers, brokers, planners, or even simple members. Knowledge search in CNOs can be represented by the abstract architecture shown in Figure 1. In the top layer, there are *knowledge consumers*, which are the actors that perform knowledge search: CNO applications in general and CSCW tools. The second layer presents a

Please use the following format when citing this chapter:

Tramontin Jr, R.J., Hanachi, C. and Rabelo, R.J., 2008, in IFIP International Federation for Information Processing, Volume 283; *Pervasive Collaborative Networks*; Luis M. Camarinha-Matos, Willy Picard; (Boston: Springer), pp. 243–252.

knowledge search system, which is abstracted by a search engine and its index repository. The CNO knowledge is located in the third layer, and it is defined as the combination of concrete information and the CNO ontology (linked by means of semantic annotations). Concrete information is stored in documents and databases such as: a common CNO repository, (contracts, business process specifications, templates), legacy databases, forums, wikis, weblogs, etc (resulting from interactions among partners). CNO knowledge is also composed of additional general-purpose metadata (authors, title, date, etc.) and comments from CNO partners (different views / opinions). Finally, the bottom layer is composed by *knowledge providers*, which are the applications that make CNO knowledge available. It is important to highlight that in some cases applications are simultaneously knowledge providers and consumers.

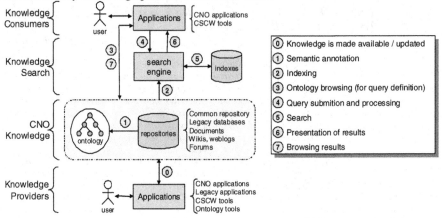

Figure 1 – Knowledge Search in CNOs.

This picture also shows the main supporting functionalities for knowledge search. Each supporting functionality can be seen as a sub-problem: 1) *semantic annotations* can be defined according to several techniques related to information extraction and natural language processing (Uren, 2006); 2) *indexing* of the knowledge (it means, semantically annotated information) should take into account that such knowledge is distributed over the CNO, so a strategy for locating it should be defined (for instance, using a *crawler*); 3) *ontology browsing* requires easy-to-use interfaces (usability problem); *query definition* assumes the existence of a language for representing queries; 4) *query processing* involves the expansion and / or customization of the query (Bhogal, 2007); 5) *search* involves how to define a relevance order for the results according to the query; 6/7) *presenting and browsing results* are also related to usability.

This paper focuses on the functionality for query processing, particularly in *query customization*. Under this perspective, *customization* means to take the *context* into account in order to adapt information and services in a specific way to match the unique and specific needs of an individual user or a community of users (Renda, 2005). This subject is a well-explored theme in the literature, being also referred as *personalization* or *adaptation*. It is used in a wide range of application domains such as digital libraries (Renda, 2005), information gathering (Bouslimi, 2008), and scheduling in CNOs (Almeida, 2007).

The customization of the knowledge search in the scope of a CNO is a very relevant problem as the user's context has an impact on the knowledge search and access. Such context is defined by the CNO where each user is taking part, his/her role (or the role of the organization he/she works for), the activity and process he/she is involved in, the life cycle stage. Another aspect to be considered is the individual interests of the user, that is, the profile. The basic assumption is that the relevance of the search results in the CNO domain is not only defined by the terms of the query but also by the context and the profile of the user performing the search. In this sense, the same query provided by users (or the same user) in different contexts will provide different (customized) results. The benefit of a personalized search is decreasing the time it takes people to find information (Pitkow, 2002).

In order to do customization, four main issues should be addressed: (i) How to represent the context and the user interests (models)? (ii) How to build and maintain the user's profile (search history / collaborative filtering)? (iii) How to capture the context (it may vary according to the nature of the context)? (iv) How to perform the personalization (query expansion / recommendation systems)?

This paper focuses on issues (i) and (iv) and proposes both a model and rules for customizing queries using the notion of *context* (dynamic situation), *user profile* (individual interests of the user) and the use of *topics* for structuring both the CNO ontology and the profiles. The work described in this paper is an extension of the architecture for *knowledge search services* proposed by Tramontin Jr. (2007).

The paper is organized as follows. Section 2 describes a model that supports the customization process. Section 3 shows the query customization process through rules. An architecture for extending the current knowledge search services is presented in section 4. Section 5 discusses the related work. Final remarks and next steps of this work are presented in section 6.

2. MODEL FOR CUSTOMIZING QUERIES

In order to allow a system to capture the user's context and use it for customizing queries, such context should be modeled. Besides that, the user's interests (profile) should also be represented. Figure 2 shows an ontology that models these and other correlated elements of a knowledge search system: user, query and the CNO ontology.

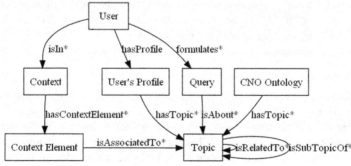

Figure 2 – Ontology for supporting the customization of K. search (with Protégé).

According to this ontology, a *user* has a *profile*, is in a certain *context*, and can formulate *queries*. A *context* is composed by *context elements*, which represent particular aspects of the context, such as the role of the user, the activity and process he/she is involved in, and so forth. *Topics* extend the expressiveness of ontologies (in particular the CNO ontology) by grouping classes and attributes that belong to the same semantic subject. Topics are used both by *profiles* (representing the interests of the user) and by *queries* (referring to the topics the user wants to search).

2.1 User's Profile

As previously mentioned, the *user's profile* is composed by a set of topics to which the user is interested in. It is used to either restrict or provide additional results (not explicitly mentioned in the query) to the user according to his/her topics of interest, and hence providing a customized search.

A *topic* (Bouslimi, 2008) is a view on an ontology and corresponds to a set of classes, attributes and links between them, all being related to the same semantic subject. So, similar to a view in a database, it can filter a set of classes and the attributes of each class belonging to this topic. Nevertheless, unlike a database view, a topic can have subtopics and be related to other topics, allowing the navigation through correlated topics, allowing the user to control the dimension of the *knowledge search space*. Topics provide means to structure the universe of discourse in manageable conceptual units that have a concrete meaning for the user providing a good trade-off between querying at a very low level (attributes) and vague querying at the ontology level.

Examples of topics in a CNO ontology can be: the *organizational* aspect of CNOs (partners, roles, relationships, competencies); the CNO *resources* (hardware, software, people); *management* aspects (control, supervision); *operational* or *functional* issues (tasks, processes), among others. Since a CNO ontology will provide the structure for queries, topics can help on two aspects: facilitating the query definition process and providing additional results.

Topics facilitate the query building process in the sense that the user does not need to define a very detailed query (that would oblige him/her to be aware of the whole ontology schema), but rather to select one or more topics of interest. For instance, instead of defining a query for searching all purchasing orders from a given partner, the user could simply search for the topic "purchasing". Following the same example, the system could suggest additional results concerning the topic "delivery", as it is somehow related to "purchasing".

2.2 Context

Like profile, the *context* is another element that supports query customization. According to Dey (2001), a context is *"any information that can be used to characterize the situation of an entity that is considered relevant to the interaction between a user and an application"*. Taking this definition into account, the profile could be considered as part of the context. However, we decided to include in the context only the dynamic aspects (mainly CNO-related issues) and to include the individual interests of users in the profile (although it can evolve over time, it is more static than the information contained in the context).

The context is composed by *context elements*, which in turn can be specialized in *physical* (regarding the geographical location of the user, application and device he is using) and CNO-related (the CNO the user is involved in, roles, the activities and processes he is working on, the stage of the CNO life cycle). All these concepts are presented in the fragment of the customization ontology shown in Figure 3.

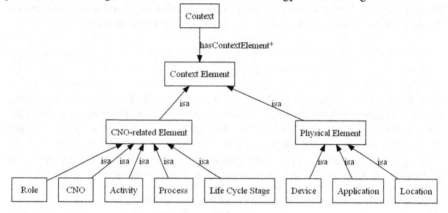

Figure 3 – Elements that compose a context (with Protégé). [Adapted from Kirsch-Pinheiro (2004)]

3. RULES FOR QUERY CUSTOMIZATION

This section illustrates how the model presented in the previous section is used to customize queries. In order to show how this process works, the elements of this model and their relationships will be represented as predicates, and then rules for customization will be presented. Table 1 below shows such predicates.

Table 1 – Customization Model defined as predicates.

	Predicates	Description
user & query	`hasProfile(U,UP)`	User U has profile UP.
	`formulatesQuery(U,Q)`	User U formulates query Q.
	`isAbout(Q,T)`	Query Q is about topic T.
	`isIn(U,C)`	User U is in context C.
topics & profile	`isSubTopicOf(T₁,T₂)`	Topic T_1 is subtopic of topic T_2.
	`isRelatedTo(T₁,T₂)`	Topic T_1 is related to T_2. (symmetric)
	`containsTopic(UP,T)`	User profile UP contains topic T.
context	`hasContextElement(C,E)`	Context C has context element E.
	`isAssociatedTo(E,T)`	Context element E is associated to topic T.

The first three predicates show the relationships between users, profiles and queries. Moreover, there are some predicates for topics: one representing the notion of subtopics (inheritance) and the other one representing the idea of correlated topics (meaning that they have some semantic connections between them). It is important to notice that the *isRelatedTo* predicate is symmetric, which means that if T_1 is related to topic T_2 then T_2 is related to topic T_1. There is another predicate that specifies a profile containing topics. Finally, there are predicates representing relationships between contexts and context elements and between contexts elements and topics.

3.1 The Customization Process

The query customization process is defined by five rules (declared in Prolog syntax). The first rule adds correlated topics to the ones referred in the query:

```
isAboutRelatedTopic(Q,T1)  :- isAbout(Q,T2),
                               isRelatedTo(T1,T2),                    (1)
                               not(isAbout(Q,T1)).
```

Rule 1 says that a query Q *is about a related topic* T_1 if Q refers to a certain topic T_2 which in turn is related to T_1, and T_1 is not referred by Q. The purpose of this rule is to add topics that are correlated to the ones mentioned in a query, but not considering either the profile or the context.

In order to extend a query with topics contained in the user's profile, it is necessary to deduce the profile which is associated to this query:

```
isAssociatedToProfile(Q,UP)  :- formulatesQuery(U,Q),
                                 hasProfile(U,UP).                    (2)
```

Based on rule 2, a query Q *is associated to a profile* UP if user U formulates the query Q and U has UP as profile. Now, having rules 1 and 2, it is possible to customize the query by taking into account the correlated topics contained in the user's profile:

```
isAboutTopicInProfile(Q,T1)  :- isAboutRelatedTopic(Q,T1),    (1)
                                 isAssociatedToProfile(Q,UP),  (2)    (3)
                                 containsTopic(UP,T1).
```

Rule 3 says that a query Q *is about a topic* T_1 *in profile* if T_1 is related to a topic T_2 (based on rule 1), Q is associated with profile UP (rule 2) and the profile UP contains T_1. Rule 3 is a more restrict case of rule 1 in the sense that it selects only correlated topics that are also in the user's profile.

Rule 4 deduces the context in which the query was formulated, by taking the context of the user who formulated the query:

```
isFormulatedIn(Q,C)  :- formulatesQuery(U,Q),
                         isIn(U,C).                                   (4)
```

Finally, rule 5 uses rule 4 to select topics associated to the context:

```
isAboutTopicAssociatedToContext(Q,T1)  :- isFormulatedIn(Q,C),   (4)
                                           hasContextElement(C,E),
                                           isAssociatedTo(E,T1),     (5)
                                           not(isAbout(Q,T1)).
```

Based on rule 5, a query Q *is about a topic* T_1 *associated to the context* if the context C in which Q was formulated contains a context element E associated to T_1 and T_1 is not referred by Q.

It is important to mention that the customization is performed by rules 1 (correlated topics), 3 (topics in profile) and 5 (topics associated to the context).

Rules 2 and 4 are supporting rules for the others, responsible for deducing respectively the user's profile and context.

The use of these rules should be configurable and it is also desirable to allow the user to have control over the customization, by accepting or changing the effects of them. Therefore, once the customized query is defined and accepted by the user, it is submitted to the search engine, which in turn should be able to distinguish the original topics (mentioned in the original query) and the topics deduced in the customization. The purpose of this approach is to allow the system to make a distinction between "normal" results and the "customized" results. It means that although the customization is made in the query, it has impact in the other parts of the knowledge search process (search and presentation of results).

3.2 Example

An example of the customization rules is presented in Figure 4. It is about a VBE[1] scenario, where a user (playing the role of *VO Broker*) submits a query associated to topics of the VBE ontology. The left part of the figure shows an instance of the model containing a user (John) who has a profile (this profile is associated to the topics *Resources*, *Products* and *VO Planning*). The user is taking part of a context (relation "is in") Context_VO1, as a VO broker. The right side of the figure shows the results of the five rules. In order to facilitate the understanding, this example shows only one context. However, users can be associated to several contexts, and one of them will be captured at runtime in order to support the customization. For instance, this user can be the VBE manager in a different context.

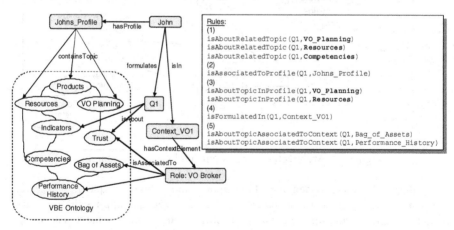

Figure 4 – Example of customization.

According to this example, John formulates a query (Q1) about topics *Indicators* and *Trust*. Rule 1 adds the topics correlated to the ones referred by the query: *Resources*, *VO Planning* and *Competencies*. Rule 3 is more restrictive than 1 as it adds only the correlated topics that are also in the user's profile (*Resources* and *VO Planning*). Rule 5 adds topics according to the elements of the context. In this case,

---

[1] Virtual Organization Breeding Environment: this kind of CNO provides support for the formation of dynamic Virtual Organizations (VOs).

topics *Bag of Assets* and *Performance History* are added as they are associated to the user's role (VO Broker). Therefore, considering that the user can accept or not the new topics, Q1 can be extended by adding any subset of {*Resources, VO Planning, Competencies, Bag of Assets, Performance History*}. As mentioned, rules 2 and 4 are just supporting rules, responsible to associate the query respectively to the profile (used by rule 3) and to the context (rule 5).

This example considers only the role as contextual element having impact on the customization, but it is not difficult to think on similar scenarios related to users working in a given activity / process, or a combination of role and activity.

4. SYSTEM ARCHITECTURE

This work is an extension of an existing framework for knowledge search in CNOs called *Knowledge Search Services* (Tramontin Jr., 2007). Such framework provides functionalities for ontology management, automatic semantic annotation of documents and ontology-based search. The objective is to add new elements for implementing the model and rules presented in this work as well as to extend the ontology used by this framework with the notion of topics.

From the architectural point of view, the customization is performed by a new component called *query customizer*. The architecture for customized knowledge search can be seen in Figure 5. The new component as well as the repositories for contexts, profiles and rules are highlighted by a dashed rectangle.

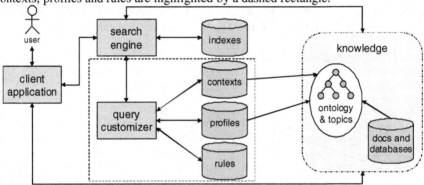

Figure 5 – Architecture for customized knowledge search.

In this architecture, when the client application submits a query, the search engine sends it to the query customizer. The customizer then applies the rules and extends the query according to the user's profile and the current context. The search engine gets the customized query and sends it back to the user. The new query is accepted or changed by the user and it is submitted again to the search engine, which finally performs the search.

5. RELATED WORK

This work shares similar ideas from some correlated areas, namely: context-aware systems, rule-based personalization and query expansion.

Firstly, this work is related to *context-aware systems* as it defines a model for representing the context as well as the user's profile. Specifically, an ontology-based model is proposed, which was adapted from the object-oriented model for context defined by Kirsch-Pinheiro (2004). Other works in this area include Baldauf (2007), who evaluated the existing context-aware systems and models, and Gensel (2008), who presents an approach for adapting information systems in the Web.

Another correlated subject concerns rule-based personalization. *Rules* are used as specific knowledge extracted from historical information (data mining), like done by Mobasher (2001). Such approach of gathering the user's search history is related to *recommendation systems* (Balabanovic, 1997; Renda, 2005) and *information filtering* (Belkin, 1992), and can be seen as a complementary aspect to the focus of this paper. Rules are used in this paper as a more generic and formal way to add correlated topics to queries based on the user's profile and context.

Concerning *query expansion*, the approach used in this paper borrows the same idea, but with a different motivation. Query expansion is the process of adding new terms to the query in order to reduce its ambiguity (Bhogal, 2007), and hence to improve the search efficiency. In this paper, the query is expanded, but the new terms (in this paper, *topics*) are related to the context and profile of the user. In a similar way as the usage of rules, query expansion based on ambiguity can also be seen also as a complementary aspect to the expansion based on the context and profile. Nevertheless, it is important to define ways to compare the performance between these two approaches, and we intend to define measures for doing so in the future.

It is also important to mention that the principle of using both profile and context for query expansion is shared by Pitkow (2002). The difference is that their focus is on Web search, while this paper focuses on customizing knowledge search in the CNO domain.

6. FINAL REMARKS

This paper presented an ontology and rules for customizing knowledge search in CNOs. The objective is to improve the relevance of searches by considering the user's *context* (specially the CNO context: role, activity, life cycle, etc.) and *profile* (individual topics of interest). The approach also used the concept of *topics* (Bouslimi, 2008), which extend the expressiveness of ontologies and thus facilitates the query definition.

An aspect not covered in this paper is how the context is captured. Nevertheless, assuming the existence of a security framework (like the one developed by Sowa (2007)), part of the context (CNO and role) can be obtained when the user logs in the system (authentication).

Next steps involve extending the current implementation of the knowledge search services by adding a new service for query customization as well as the validation of this implementation. The rules will be first tested in Protégé[2] and then they will be added to the concrete implementation of the customizer. Finally one issue that will be faced is that the notion of topics, though it already exists, it is not implemented by the current ontology languages (for instance, OWL). So, in order to

---

[2] http://protege.stanford.edu/index.html

be used in practice, such languages must be extended as well as the corresponding implementations.

6.1 Acknowledgments

This work has been partially supported by the Brazilian council of research and scientific development – CNPq. It has been developed in the scope of the Brazilian IFM project (www.ifm.org.br) and the European IST FP-6 IP ECOLEAD project (www.ecolead.org). Special thanks also to Mr. Wassim Bouaziz for his help on the model and rules definition, and Mr. Leandro Loss and Mr. Fabiano Baldo for their valuable comments.

7. REFERENCES

1. Abdelali, A.; Cowie, J.; Soliman, H. S. Improving query precision using semantic expansion. Information Processing and Management 43, pp. 705–716, 2007.
2. Almeida, A; Marreiros, G.; Martins, C. Collaboration and Adaptation in Scheduling. In: Proceedings of PRO-VE'2007 – 8th IFIP Working Conference on Virtual Enterprises, 2007.
3. Balabanovic, M.; Shoham, Y. Fab: content-based, collaborative recommendation. Communications of the ACM CACM 40 (3), pp. 66-72, 1997.
4. Belkin, N. J.; Croft, W. B. Information filtering and information retrieval: two sides of the same coin? Communications of the ACM 35 (12), pp. 29-38, 1992.
5. Baldauf, M.; Dustdar, S.; Rosenberg, F. A survey on context-aware systems. Int. J. Ad Hoc and Ubiquitous Computing, Vol. 2, No. 4, 2007.
6. Bhogal, J., Macfarlane, A.; Smith, P. A review of ontology based query expansion. Information Processing and Management 43, pp. 866–886, 2007.
7. Bouslimi, I.; Hanachi, C.; Tout, H.; Ghedira K. "Coordination Framework for Cooperative Information Gathering", International Journal of Advanced Intelligence Paradigms, Inderscience, to be published 2008.
8. Camarinha-Matos, L. M.; Afsarmanesh; H.; Ollus, M.. ECOLEAD: A Holistic Approach to Creation and Management of Dynamic Virtual Organizations. In: Proceedings of the Sixth IFIP Working Conference on Virtual Enterprises (PRO-VE'05). pp. 3-16, 2005.
9. Dey, A. K. Understanding and using context. Personal and Ubiquitous Computing, Vol. 5, No. 1, pp 4-7, 2001.
10. Gensel, J.; Villanova-Oliver, M.; Kirsch-Pinheiro, M. Modèles de contexte pour l'adaptation à l'utilisateur dans des Systèmes d'Information Web collaboratifs. In: Workshop from "8èmes journées francophones". Sophia-Antipolis, France. pp. 5-16, 2008.
11. Kirsch-Pinheiro, M.; Gensel, J.; Martin, H. Representing Context for an Adaptative Awareness Mechanism. CRIWG 2004: 339-348, 2004.
12. Mobasher, B.; Dai, H.; Luo, T.; Nakagawa, M. Effective Personalization Based on Association Rule Discovery from Web Usage Data. Proceedings of the ACM Workshop on Web Information and Data Management (WIDM01). Held at CIKM 2001, Atlanta, Georgia, November 2001.
13. Pitkow, J. E.; Schütze, H.; Cass, T. A.; Cooley, R.; Turnbull, D.; Edmonds, A.; Adar, E.; Breuel, T. M.. Personalized search. Commun. ACM 45(9): pp. 50-55, 2002.
14. Renda, M. A.; Straccia, U. A personalized collaborative Digital Library environment: a model and an application. Information Processing and Management 41 (2005) 5-21, 2005.
15. Sowa, G.; Śnieżyński, T.; 2007. Technical Report (Deliverable) D61.4b - Security framework and architecture.
16. Tramontin Jr., R. J.; Rabelo, R. J. A Knowledge Search Framework for Collaborative Networks. In: Proceedings of PRO-VE'2007 – 8th IFIP Working Conference on Virtual Enterprises, 2007.
17. Uren, V.; Cimiano, P.; Iria, J.; Handschuh, S.; Vargas-Vera, M.; Motta, E.; Ciravegna, F. Semantic annotation for knowledge management: Requirements and a survey of the state of the art. In: Journal of Web Semantics. 4(1): 14-28, 2006.

EXPLORING ONTOLOGY ADOPTION AND DIFFUSION IN THE CONSTRUCTION VIRTUAL ENTERPRISE

26

Yacine Rezgui

Informatics Research Institute, University of Salford, Salford, UK.
y.rezgui@salford.ac.uk

The construction sector has adopted for decades the modus operandi of the virtual enterprise. In this context, a large number of semantic resources have been developed to support seamless collaboration between individuals and teams on projects. However, these tend to be (a) discipline oriented and geared towards servicing specific user community needs or applications; and (b) incomplete in terms of concept, and relationships between concepts covered and conveyed. Therefore, none of these (a) enable effective knowledge management across projects and organizations, (b) are accepted across disciplines, and (c) provide a true conceptualization of the construction domain. The paper argues the case for the development of knowledge-rich ontologies, and explores the factors that may hinder or promote their wide adoption and diffusion.

1. INTRODUCTION

Construction is a knowledge intensive industry characterized by its unique work settings and virtual enterprise like modus operandi [1]. Buildings have long been designed and constructed by non co-located teams of separate firms, with various levels of IT maturity and capability, which come together for a specific project and may never work together again. Moreover, the Construction sector is fragmented and the major consequence is the difficulty to communicate effectively and efficiently among partners during a building project or between clients and suppliers of construction products. Several initiatives led by standardization and / or industry consortia have developed data / product models aimed at facilitating data and information exchange between software applications. These efforts include STEP [2] and the Industry Foundation Classes (IFCs). Several other initiatives at a national and European level have developed dictionaries, thesauri, and several linguistic resources focused on Construction terms to facilitate communication and improve understanding between the various stakeholders operating on a project or across the product supply chain. However, these initiatives tend to be country specific and not adapted to the multi-national nature of the sector. Also, given the vast scope of Construction, these semantic resources tend to be specialized for dedicated applications or engineering functions, e.g. product libraries and HVAC (Heating, Ventilation and Air Conditioning), respectively. Some recent research has started highlighting the need for an ontology in the sector [3], while others have already started referring to the IFCs as being an ontology or suggesting that they be extended to become an ontology [4].

Please use the following format when citing this chapter:

Rezgui, Y., 2008, in IFIP International Federation for Information Processing, Volume 283; *Pervasive Collaborative Networks*; Luis M. Camarinha-Matos, Willy Picard; (Boston: Springer), pp. 253–262.

The aim of the paper is to explore adoption and diffusion factors of a domain ontology. As such, the core research question is: *What are the factors that may promote or hinder the adoption of a construction ontology?* First, a critical discussion on product data technology is provided arguing the case for knowledge-rich ontology. The requirements for such ontology are then provided supported by an illustration of the eCognos ontology [3]. The paper then discusses the validation process of the eCognos ontology, and answers the main research question. Finally the paper provides concluding remarks and future directions for research.

2. THE NEED FOR RICHER CONCEPTUALISATIONS THROUGH ONTOLOGY

The progress made so far in arriving at the Building Information Model (BIM) concept and its associated tools is undoubtedly a sizeable step forward in the management, communication and leveraging of construction project information. Both the BIM models used by the commercial vendors and the international standards developed for construction such as STEP, IFC and CIS/2 do however still exhibit a number of shortcomings identified in [1; 5; 6] related to the degree of expressiveness, lifecycle support, and comprehensiveness of these product models. Other problems that render data level integration in the STEP or IFC mould less effective than might otherwise be the case. To understand this position it is necessary to consider the way in which data integration mandates a considerable degree of work up-front. This is required in order to agree upon standards, construct a schema for integration, adapt applications to the standards etc. all before any benefits are realized. These issues become more onerous the larger the scope of agreement one is trying to achieve (inter-organizational, national, international etc.). Finally, for large international standards efforts, agility is something of a problem. Once the standard is agreed, changing it can take a considerable amount of time, which in an age of rapidly evolving business needs can turn a formerly helpful system into a hindrance.

This is where an ontology can leverage many of the above problems. Various definitions of what forms an ontology have been formulated and have evolved over time. A good description of these can be found in [7]. From the author's perspective, the best definition that capture's the essence of an ontology is the one given by Gruber [8]: "an ontology is a formal, explicit specification of a shared conceptualization". As elaborated in [9]: "Conceptualization refers to an abstract model of some phenomenon in the world which identifies the relevant concepts of that phenomenon. Explicit means that the types of concepts used and the constraints on their use are explicitly defined. Formal refers to the fact that the ontology should be machine processable".

The use of an ontology or multiple ontologies of the construction domain could act as a semantic abstraction layer above current standards and models, which would help to resolve some of the issues outlined above and further integrate project data in a more intelligent fashion. For example, an ontology with appropriate mappings into the underlying data models could be used to provide a more intuitive view of project data for any given actor based on their particular disciplinary concepts and terminology. That same ontology could also provide the view for an actor from a different discipline, based on the relationships explicated within the ontology itself providing links to the appropriate terminology for the same data items. This type of 'translation' function becomes more compelling when used to view initial project briefs or client constraints and later when viewing the rationale for changes as it helps all actors to understand the reasoning involved in a language they can comprehend easily. With respect to unstructured project information, the use of ontologies in tandem with other techniques drawn from information retrieval/extraction could be used to automatically infer links between the structured and unstructured information and indeed between items of unstructured information, based on the links defined in the ontology. These links lend a greater degree of context to each item relative to the project as a whole. Benefits may also be derived from uncovering previously unseen linkages between various elements of project data using such analysis methods. The e-Cognos project for example, developed and used a construction oriented ontology to augment the services that it offered as part of the collaborative knowledge management environment also developed on the project [1,4]. In the following section, we introduce the requirements of such ontology and provide an illustration of a potential ontology for the sector.

3. REQUIREMENTS FOR ONTOLOGY DEVELOPMENT IN CONSTRUCTION

A critical analysis of the structure and overall practices in the industry [1] as well as available semantic resources, ranging from taxonomies to thesauri, have helped formulate a set of requirements that ought to be addressed in order to maximize the chances of a wide adoption of any ontology project in the construction sector. These requirements are listed below:

- The ontology should not be developed from scratch but should make as much use as possible of established and recognized semantic resources in the domain.
- The ontology should be built collaboratively in a multi-user environment: the construction sector involves several disciplines and communities of practice that use their own jargon and have specialized information needs.
- There is a need to ensure total lifecycle support, as the information produced by one actor within one discipline should be able to be used by others working in related disciplines.
- The ontology must be developed incrementally involving the end-users. This is important given the multi-disciplinary and multi-project nature of the industry, and the fact that each project is a one-off prototype.
- The ontology should be flexible and comprehensive enough to accommodate different business scenarios used across projects and disciplines.
- The ontology should be user friendly, i.e., easy to use and providing a conceptualization of the discipline / domain being represented that embeds the technical jargon used in the sector.
- The ontology should be a living system and should allow for future expansion.

Given the following factors [1]: (a) the fragmented and discipline-oriented nature of the construction sector; (b) the various interpretations that exist of common concepts by different communities of practice (disciplines); (c) the plethora of semantic resources that exist within each discipline (none of which have reached a consensual agreement); (d) the lifecycle dimension of a construction project with information being produced and updated at different stages of the design and build process with a strong information sharing requirement across organizations and lifecycle stages; a suitable ontology development methodology should accommodate the fact that the ontology should be specific enough to be accepted by practitioners within their own discipline, while providing a generic dimension that would promote communication and knowledge sharing amongst these communities.

4. THE ECOGNOS ONTOLOGY

Given the above requirements, an ontology is developed, referred to as eCognos [3]. The eCognos ontology is structured into a set of discrete, core and discipline-oriented, sub-ontologies. Each sub-ontology features a high cohesion between its internal concepts while ensuring a high degree of interoperability between them. These are organized into a layered architecture (three layers) with, at a high level of abstraction, the core ontology that holds a common conceptualization of the whole construction domain enabled by a set of inter-related generic core concepts forming the seeds of the ontology. These generic concepts enable interoperability between specialized discipline-oriented modules defined at a lower level of abstraction. This middle layer of the architecture provides discipline-oriented conceptualizations of the construction domain. Concepts from these sub-ontologies are linked with the core concepts by generalization / specialization (commonly known as IS-A) relationships. The third and lowest level of the architecture represents all semantic resources currently available, which constitute potential candidates for inclusion into eCognos either at the core or discipline level.

There are a large variety of available semantic resources that can form the basis for building the eCognos core ontology. These range from classification systems to taxonomies. The latter do deserve particular attention as argued in [10]. One of the principal roles of taxonomies is to facilitate human understanding, impart structure on an ontology, and promote tenable integration. Furthermore, properly structured taxonomies: (a) help bring substantial order to elements of a model; (b) are particularly useful in presenting limited views of a model for human interpretation; and, (c) play a critical role in reuse and integration tasks. Improperly structured taxonomies have the opposite effect, making models confusing and difficult to reuse or reintegrate [10]. IFCs, being more recent and also the closest taxonomy currently in use in the sector, are therefore the preferred candidate semantic resource that can provide the skeleton on which such a core ontology can be built.

A particular approach is adopted for building and / or expanding the discipline-oriented sub-ontologies. This involves selecting and making use of a large documentary corpus used in the discipline and ideally produced by the end-users. The sub-ontologies are then expanded and built from index terms extracted from commonly used documents using information retrieval techniques [3].

5. TECHNICAL EVALUATION OF THE ONTOLOGY

Two main metrics are used to evaluate the eCognos ontology:

(a)   performance evaluation in terms of response time delivered by the use of the ontology; and,

(b)   the retrieval performance in terms of relevance of the retrieved document set through the use of ontology.

A sample document set comprising about 12,000 documents is used. This was gathered from several recently completed projects. 15 queries have been formulated by discipline experts involved in the research. These were based on their own information needs experiences on projects, traditionally performed manually or using ad-hoc search facilities.

The experts were asked to identify manually the document set matching each formulated query. While the identification process was achieved in a matter of days, this did reflect (timescale wise) the current information and document search practices in the construction industry. These identified relevant document sets have then been used as a basis to compute the average Recall (the fraction of the retrieved relevant documents) and Precision measures (the fraction of the retrieved documents which is relevant). These have been quantified in two scenarios: (a) through the simple use of index terms; and, (b) through the use of the eCognos ontology.

In the first scenario, a full-text summarization of the documents and queries was preformed, while in the second scenario the summarization relied exclusively on concepts of the ontology. The discipline experts that generated the queries in the first place and identified the relevant document sets have been involved in the relevance assessment work.

In terms of response time, the difference between the two approaches (with and without the use of ontology) was comparable. The difference was in the retrieval performance provided by the ontology. For further details please see (Rezgui 2007). The main results of the evaluation are summarized below.

Despite reporting missing concepts, the search functionality with ontology outperformed the traditional full-text search approach as more relevant document subsets have been retrieved. The knowledge representation technique, based on ontology, provides a more accurate user and machine interpretable summarization of documents, as illustrated by the field trial results with significant improvements in the Precision and recall factors.

The use of integrated services articulated around a common in-house ontology promotes the wide adoption of common standards and the sharing of a common understanding of terms and concepts. However, subtle variations of the semantics of certain terms may exist across companies. This suggests that discipline ontologies in the construction sector may need further refinement to be adapted to the norms and values of an organization. Some business processes involve the use of concepts from more than one discipline ontology. While this is supported by the eCognos methodology through the generic core ontology, it triggers another issue in relation to supporting dynamic views or perspectives that involve concepts drawn from more than one discipline ontology.

6. ECOGNOS ONTOLOGY ADOPTION AND DIFFUSION

A number of studies have been reported in the literature describing various theories and models related to information technology adoption, diffusion, and innovation into the workplace, as reported in [11]. Some of these theories describe transition processes and mechanisms, including Rogers's stage model of innovations in organizations [12]; whereas others define causality among factors to predict successful transition of a technology, including Davis's Technology Adoption Model (TAM), [13]. TAM argues that end-user acceptance and use of information systems innovations is influenced by their beliefs regarding the technology. In particular, it proposes that perceived usefulness and perceived ease of use influence the use of information systems innovations and that this effect is mediated through behavioural intentions to use (Davis, 1989). The model highlights the critical role of extrinsic motivation and, in particular, expectations of task-related performance gains in end-users' adoption and use of Information Systems innovations (Davis, 1989). TAM is used to discuss the adoption and diffusion of the eCognos ontology. It has been applied in the context of the validation process described in the previous section, whereby a set of KM services articulated around the eCognos ontology have been developed, using the Web services model, tested and validated in a real organizational setting [14].

6.1. The Case Study

The eCognos ontology and overall solution has been introduced within OTH, a French construction engineering company, as an enhanced service of the documentation department. The latter is, by nature, a knowledge centre for the whole organization. Its mission is to collect, organize, classify and disseminate knowledge throughout the group on regulatory, standardisation, technical and commercial issues. Its manager has specific skills in information indexing, searching and retrieval and more generally knowledge management. She has been assigned the role of eCognos manager. The field trial is used to evaluate the integration capacity of the system and the benefits that can be derived from integrating within it various knowledge sources already available and used throughout OTH. In the context of the field trials, deployment of the system has been limited to a consistent and knowledge-friendly group of users drawn from 3 OTH subsidiaries. Five users per subsidiary have been retained supported by the manager of the documentation department. It was decided to base the trial on the "electrical design" domain. An OTH-specific ontology has been developed. It contains general concepts relevant to OTH at a high level, and more detailed concepts in the field of electrical design at lower levels. It includes over 830 ontological concepts. The 3 subsidiaries have been granted access to the deployed eCognos system through an existing Virtual Private Network (VPN).

Three scenarios have been developed simulating (a) the process of setting-up a specialised corporate memory, (b) locating a knowledge asset, and (c) creating value by exploiting available knowledge.

6.2. Perceived Usefulness of the eCognos Ontology

Overall, the trials confirmed the positive role that the use of an ontology can have in addressing the knowledge management needs of employees. Also, it was found that developing and using an in-house ontology gave the users a strong feeling of acceptance of the system. In particular, the use of the knowledge extractor service [14] was highly valued as the mapping of index terms with ontological concepts enables intelligent, automatic indexing (the documentation department no longer need to index manually their documents). The search service was enhanced through the use of the Ontology and provided substantial improvements to the existing system. These have in particular highlighted the advantages that can be gained from an organizational as well as a technical level by providing an integrated and unique access point to all OTH applications. Moreover, by integrating legacy systems within eCognos as well as having access to more advanced functionality, users felt that they could continue using their accustomed tools to manage their projects and at the same time share their knowledge with colleagues in a transparent, integrated and effective way. KM becomes part of the day-to-day work and takes place in the background without intrusion to the practice. Application integration through the system did highlight interesting potentials for improved process integration. The perceived usefulness of the eCognos ontology has been reported on several fronts:

- Organizational support: eCognos is perceived as having the potential to leverage intellectual capital both inside as well as outside the organization. It also contributes to lowering project costs through the use of an integrated mechanism for managing centralised or distributed services. Also, the semantics of Construction terms and concepts hold different meaning for different users depending on their work discipline as well as their education background. The use of integrated services articulated around a common in-house ontology promotes the wide adoption of common standards and sharing of common understanding of terms and concepts.

- Team support: collaboration is perceived now as possible across distance and time zones as users can now easily publish documents within and across the organization while gaining access to others' experiences. Physical location of people and knowledge sources become irrelevant. Teams on projects have now the potential to better combine distributed competences via eCognos.

- User support: ICT systems are generally perceived by users to be invasive and individuals need constantly to adapt to continuous introduction of new emerging technologies in the workplace. The integration of new functionality through the ontology-based web services model becomes transparent to users who do no longer have to use multiple windows, requiring each its own authentication, to conduct a specific task. Activities and business processes encapsulate relevant knowledge sources accessible through a role / right-based approach across the organization and projects. Access to useful and timely information becomes possible regardless of its location, native format or system. The search facility is perceived as a strong advantage, and the information that is pushed to users is filtered and personalised thus avoiding information overload.

6.3. Ease of Use of the eCognos Ontology

In terms of ease of use of the eCognos ontology, it is worth noting that users were not exposed directly to the ontology as they were interacting with it transparently through the invocation of services that relied on the ontology. But still, the trials provided means to assess the level of familiarity and comprehension of the ontological concepts. In that respect the end-users highlighted two important aspects of the ontology:

- The modular structure of the ontology: The ontology takes into account the fragmented nature of the construction sector and its organization into established disciplines. It, therefore, mirrors the discipline-oriented nature of the industry.
- The support for the multiple interpretations of concepts across disciplines: the construction disciplines have their own norms and values, reflected in the development of dedicated semantic resources. The proposed ontology architecture is modular, with sub-ontologies dedicated to each established discipline, federated by a core ontology defined at a higher level comprising generic concepts applicable across sectors and enabling reconciliation of different terminologies used across disciplines.

Also, it is worth noting that the Ontology has been developed with the objective of facilitating its comprehension and use by end-users. In that respect, the following is worth highlighting:

- The collaborative nature of the ontology development process: It supports parallel development of the various ontology modules while promoting their integration through the core ontology.
- The iterative nature of the ontology development process: given the large-scale dimension of the construction industry and its project-oriented nature, an iterative process that proceeds by refining and extending the ontology over time helps converge towards a complete and true conceptualization of the domain.
- The ontology development approach: this is semi-automated and relies on discipline-oriented documentary corpuses to identify concepts and relationships using tf-idf and metric clusters techniques [3], which are then validated by human experts.

7. CONCLUSION

The paper presented an ontology initiative to support the knowledge management needs of practitioners in the construction sector, including support for seamless collaboration. The ontology developed to date is far from being complete, and will probably never be, as an ontology should be viewed as a living system. Similar efforts, such as the ISO STEP project and its application to various industry sectors (including manufacturing), have taken almost a decade or longer to come to fruition. The eCognos ontology is by no means different. The issue of the existence of a unique ontology for an entire sector remains open.   This suggests that while the eCognos Core Ontology forms a robust basis for interoperability across the discipline-oriented ontologies, the latter will need adaptation and refining when deployed into an organization and used on projects. Another issue that was raised is that related to the adoption of user specific views or perspectives on the global ontology. In fact, in many instances, some actors might be required as part of their job to deal with more than one discipline ontology to conduct a task. This necessitates some flexible mechanisms that can enable the rapid combination of two or more discipline ontologies into a single view / perspective. This constitutes one of the author's future research objectives.

Also, TAM, the model used to assess the adoption and diffusion of the ontology – with its original emphasis on the design of system characteristics – does not account for social influence in the adoption and utilization of new information systems [13]. Furthermore, It has been reported that when TAM is applied to collaborative systems, it is often observed that the belief structures (perceived ease of-use and perceived usefulness) are not stable, and that the influence of these belief structures act in combination with the effect of social influences to determine the use of the system [15, 16, 17]. The author encourages researchers to explore further models to investigate the adoption and diffusion factors of any ontology project.

8. REFERENCES

[1] Rezgui, Y. and Zarli, A. (2006) Paving the way to digital construction: a strategic roadmap, Journal of Construction Engineering and Management (Journal of the American Society of Civil Engineers), Volume 132, Issue 12, pp. 767-776.

[2] ISO 10303-1:1994. Industrial automation systems and integration – product data representation and exchange – Part 1: Overview and fundamental principles. International Standards Organization. TC 184/SC 4, 1994. http://www.iso.ch/cate/d20579.html.

[3] Rezgui, Y. (2007) Text Based Domain Ontology Building Using tf-idf and Metric Clusters techniques, Knowledge Engineering Review (Cambridge Press), Volume 22, Issue 4, pp. 379-403.

[4] Lima C, Al Diraby T, Fies B, Zarli A, Ferneley E. The E-COGNOS Project: current status and future directions of an ontology-enabled IT solution infrastructure supporting knowledge management in construction. In: Molenaar Keith R, Chinowsky Paul S, editors. Winds of change: integration and innovation of construction. Construction research congress 2003, Honolulu, Hawaii, USA, 19– 21 March 2003, 2004.

[5] Eastman CM, Sacks R, Lee G. Strategies for realizing the benefits of 3D integrated modeling of buildings for the AEC industry. In: Proceedings of ISARC-19th international symposium on automation and robotics in construction, Washington, DC, 2002. p. 9–14.

[6] Boddy, S, Rezgui, Y., Cooper, G., Wetherill, M, (2007), Computer Integrated Construction: A review and Proposals for Future Directions, Advances in Engineering Software (Elsevier), Volume 38, Issue 10.

[7] Corcho, O, Fernando-Lopez, M, Gomez-Perez, A, 2003. "Methodologies, tools and languages for building ontologies. Where is their meeting point?" Data and Knowledge Engineering, 46 pp 41-64.

[8] Gruber, T., 1994. "Towards principles for the design of ontologies used for knowledge sharing" International Journal of Human Computer Studies 43(5/6) pp 907-928.

[9] Studer, R., Benjamins, V., and Fensel, D, 1998. "Knowledge engineering: Principles and methods" IEEE Transactions on Data and Knowledge Engineering 25 pp.161-197.

[10] Welty, C, and Guarino, N, 2001. "Supporting ontological analysis of taxonomic relationships" Data and Knowledge Engineering 39 (1) pp. 51–74.

[11] Zmud, R.W., 2000. Framing the Domains of IT Management: Projecting the Future Through the Past. Pinnaflex, Cincinnati.

[12] Rogers, E.M., 1995. Diffusion of Innovations, fourth ed. Free Press, New York.

[13] Davis, F.D., 1993. User acceptance of information technology: system characteristics, user perceptions and behavioural impacts. International Journal of Man–Machine Studies 18 (3), 475–487.

[14] Rezgui, Y. (2006) Ontology Driven Knowledge Management Using Information Retrieval Techniques, Computing in Civil Engineering (Journal of the American Society of Civil Engineers), Volume 20, Issue 3, pp. 261-270.

[15] Easley, R.F., Devaraj, S., Crant, J.M., 2003. Relating collaborative technology use to teamwork quality and performance: an empirical analysis. Journal of Management of Information Systems 19 (4), 247–268.

[16] Rezgui, Y. Role-Based Service-Oriented Implementation of a Virtual Enterprise: A Case Study in the Construction Sector, Computers in Industry (Elsevier), 58(1), pp 74-86, 2007.

[17] Rezgui, Y. Exploring Virtual Team-Working Effectiveness in the Construction Sector, Interacting with Computers (Elsevier), 19(2), pp 96-112 , 2007.

27

UNDERSTANDING OF KNOWLEDGE FROM TWO MUTUALLY RELATED ASPECTS

Kešeljević Aleksandar

Teaching assistant, Faculty of Economics, SLOVENIA
saso.keseljevic@ef.uni-lj.si

The challenges of the new millennium and specific properties of knowledge require a new understanding of knowledge. Author's approach to knowledge is based on three mutually related aspects. From the aspect of substance, the author understands knowledge as a set of experiences where information, based on rational combination is classified into patterns of thought through cognitive processes. The subject (individual, organization) to whom the capacity of cognition is ascribed and in which knowledge is to a certain extent institutionalized may use and exchange knowledge, through the system of property rights, for other rights in the market. Characterizing knowledge as capital brings economic effects to its owners, as it is ascribed certain economic market value. From a subjective-market aspect knowledge is defined in the relation to the individual, organization and market.

1. IN PLACE OF AN INTRODUCTION

Knowledge appears as the subject of research of many scientific disciplines. We can hardly find a scientific discipline where knowledge or terms closely related to it are not mentioned. However, the history of science witnesses that these authors mainly define knowledge from the aspect of scientific communities to which they belong.

Psychology deals predominantly with the cognitive process, since authors hold that the capacity of the human mind is relatively small compared to the scale of problems that individuals face (e.g. Simon, 1979, 1955, 1957). Sociology studies the effect of relations and networks on the transfer of knowledge, which is thus becoming increasingly sociologically contingent (e.g. Granovetter, 1985; Etzioni, 1990). Economic theory equates knowledge mainly with information (e.g. Stigler, 1961; Hirshleifer, 1973), human capital (Schultz, 1961; Becker, 1964; Mincer, 1958) and technological progress (e.g. Solow, 1956; Romer, 1990, 1994). Such understanding of knowledge within the economic scientific community is also supported by the Machlup trilogy (1980, 1982, 1984) which is one of the most complete classifications of knowledge. Managerial theory foregrounded the categorization of various types of knowledge in order to generate sound business performance. Knowledge has been usually defined through particular pairs that express the opposite poles of the methods of acquiring, creating, and transferring knowledge (e.g. explicit/tacit, individual/social). Subsequently, attention was drawn to the problem of efficient knowledge management and evaluation of knowledge within intellectual capital theory (e.g. Roos 1997; Edvinsson and Malone, 1997).

Please use the following format when citing this chapter:

Aleksandar, K., 2008, in IFIP International Federation for Information Processing, Volume 283; *Pervasive Collaborative Networks*; Luis M. Camarinha-Matos, Willy Picard; (Boston: Springer), pp. 263–274.

In the paper, I wish to: 1. Show, that a profound understanding of knowledge requires a considerable scope, or breadth, in the analysis and selected literature; 2. Define knowledge from the aspect of its content (substance view) and in relation to all major agents of knowledge (subjective-market view); 3. Show how these two aspects are mutually related; 4. Show how important is the concept of networks for the correct understanding of knowledge. Our analysis will identify three elements (e.g. social capital in organization, cooperation in the scientific community, market mechanism of social learning), in order to show the importance of networks for the understanding of knowledge.

2. KNOWLEDGE FROM THE ASPECT OF SUBSTANCE

Knowledge is a whole comprising experience where information, based on combination of data, is sorted through cognitive process into patterns of thought. Understanding knowledge as capital means that knowledge is ascribed a certain economic value that is defined in accordance with supply and demand for it on the market. From the aspect of substance, I shall consequently understand knowledge as information, cognitive process, and capital.

2.1. Knowledge as information

Knowledge can be understood as information based on rational combination and relation of data acquired by observation. Information is produced by combination and classification of data. Understating of information is of key importance for definition of knowledge, because information is important in decision-making of individuals or entities (Schwalbe, 1999) and in establishing their equilibria (Machlup, 1984). Regardless of the type of equilibrium (partial/general, static/dynamic), market is in the center of this type of analysis, as the occurrence of equilibria is ensured by its allocative efficiency which hence becomes a synonym of information efficiency. Rationality and utility maximization lead, through price mechanism, to a partial of general equilibrium.

However, information function of the market and equilibrium cannot provide a satisfactory insight into the understanding of. Knowledge should not be equated with information, because it is a set of experiences where information is classified into patterns of thought through cognitive processes. It means that knowledge, through cognitive processes, involves also capacity to solve problems (Dosi, 1998). The following section is dedicated to the cognitive processes.

2.2. Knowledge as cognitive process

Three aspects of cognitive process are perception, learning and thinking (Pečjak, 1975). Simon (1955, 1959) links the aspect of learning and thinking with the question of 'what is rational'. Blaug (1992) defines rationality as an approach where individual economic agents maximize their utility, subject to given constraints, by choosing among alternatives in accordance with their preferences; furthermore, complete and free information is available to all agents. The desire for rationality is understandable, as it employs deduction to lead to elegant models.

Economic theory has performed a reduction of the entire cognitive process to rationality and mechanics of processes where one's conduct is subject to objectively calculated laws. Due to perfect information and unlimited cognitive capacity, individuals have no problems comparing and choosing among the alternatives (unbounded rationality). Socio-cultural considerations do not influence the choice (universal rationality), and subjective knowledge is – due to perfect information – not relevant in decision-making (objective rationality). However, completely rational and quantitatively utilitarian 'homo oeconomicus' does not have any psychological cognitive characteristics:

- Unbounded rationality requires mutual comparison and selection of the best possibility; however, the complexity of this task precludes human mind from accomplishing this in a rational manner, because its cognitive capacity is bounded (Simon, 1979). Simon (1955) proposes the substitution of rationality with 'satisficing behavior', as it better describes human conduct.
- Sociologization of economics proves that an individual is not merely 'homo oeconomicus', but most of all a social and cultural being; hence, we may only speak of socially contingent rationality. Cyert, March (1963), Sen (1977), and Fukuyama (1995) call attention to the fact that inclusion of an individual into the society has an impact on the cognitive processes. Mill (1956) holds that due to the integration into society, cognitive processes can never be entirely individual.
- Rationality of 'homo oeconomicus' is in relation to an external observer who evaluates the conduct of the subjects studied. According to the assumption of the neoclassical theory, future changes are known to economic agents with certainty; hence, it is also called the 'single outcome theory', as it only offers one à priori solution. However, subjects under study act based on their own knowledge and not according to the knowledge of an external observer. Penrose (1980) believe that rationality is subjective because it depends on individual's perception.

The contributions cited above point to the fact that human cognitive capacity is bounded, due to imperfect information and the limits of the mind. Knowledge as a cognitive process is basically related with the individual, since only subjective knowledge can provide the basis of decision-making. With individual's inclusion into the society, cognitive processes are becoming socially contingent. Nevertheless, the subject to whom the capacity of cognition is ascribed may use and exchange knowledge, through the system of property rights, for other rights in the market. Market becomes a process of value through which knowledge is becoming capital.

2.3. Knowledge as capital

Characterizing knowledge as capital brings economic effects to its owners, as it is ascribed certain economic market value. I believe that cohabitation of human, social, and intellectual capital enables understanding knowledge as capital in its full meaning. The value of knowledge was defined for the first time through the neoclassical theory of human capital (e.g. Mincer, 1958; Becker, 1964; Schultz, 1961). Knowledge represents an investment into an individual who is giving up a part of his or her income during education, trading it for higher income in the future. However, the failure to adequately comprehend relations prevents the human capital theory from accounting problems related to the transfer of knowledge and returns:

- Coleman (2000) for example argues that the quality of knowledge transmission from parents to children depends on the education of parents, and the time devoted to their children. Lack of human capital can motivate parents to spend on much more time with their children, thus generating a higher level of social capital between them, and consequently in lesser percentage of school dropouts.
- Sawyer (1978) finds that falling returns of human capital are a result of the separation of an individual from the environment as the individual is bounded in the capacity to employ his or her knowledge efficiently. However, knowledge is not a conventional commodity, as it is never lost upon sale of purchase; each transaction only increases it, leading to increasing returns.

To properly understand the increasing returns of knowledge and the transfer of knowledge, the broader social inclusion of an individual should be grasped; it is only through relations that one can fully employ the knowledge acquired primarily for oneself. Human capital theory does not account for sociological factors, mostly because they are strongly subjective and because the theory does not wish to threaten the position of the individual as the fundamental unit of analysis; hence, society is understood as a group of atomized individuals (Sawyer, 1978).

Considering these shortcomings, the only sensible appraisal of the theory is one made from the viewpoint of an alternative one. Since human capital theory has simply no competition of a comparable scope in the field of economics, while the new theories (e.g. segmented markets theory, signal theory) mostly supplement it, it may be sensible to look for solutions in deeper cooperation with other disciplines.

Upgrading the concept of human capital with that of social capital requires an interdisciplinary approach which is reflected in the tradition of economic sociology. Economics and sociology are connected through the treatment of knowledge as capital which appears in the form of human capital in economics, and in form of social capital and its impact on knowledge in sociology. The emphasis on the word 'capital' indicates that the value component of relations is expressed, and that this component may become a source of competitive advantage (Nahapiet, Ghoshal, 2000; Adler, Kwon, 2002). Human capital theory underlines that knowledge is basically a personalized process. On the other hand, through learning, values, and communication, knowledge is becoming more sociologically contingent; hence, the failure to grasp properly the notion of social capital will prevent any adequate understanding of knowledge as a factor of production. I believe that the success of an organization depends on the ability to manage relations within organizations (organizational level), among them (inter-organizational level) and on relations between organizations and its environment (institutional level).

The key inadequacies of such a socio-economic approach are manifested from the aspect of measuring external effects of knowledge. Without measurement, there can be no efficient knowledge management. Measuring human capital is not simple because its effect are not easily measurable (Machlup, 1984; Adler, Kwon, 2002). There is also no consent on the method of measuring social capital; thus authors arrive at opposing conclusions (e.g. Putnam, 1995 vs. Paxton, 1999). Hence, solution is sought in a more profound cooperation with the managerial theory that stresses measurement and management of knowledge. Knowledge management is becoming a tool for boosting intellectual capital. Wiig (1997) and Edvinsson (1997) understand intellectual capital as a broader term; knowledge management is focused on the processes related to knowledge (e.g. Roos et al., 1997; Edvinsson, 1997; Jones, Jordan, 1997; Edvinsson, Malone, 1997).

Knowledge is becoming today the center of the new managerial paradigm and a new way of managing business changes. This involves the use of management methods at a new intellectual level, establishing a new culture of business change, and the corresponding (re)forming of the organizational structure. Management of knowledge must ensure that knowledge is translated into action, with the maximum permanent effect. The ability to measure the externalities of knowledge is gaining relevance, since only what is measurable can be efficiently managed. New approaches to measurement are devised at the cross-section between the traditional approach that relies on recognition and management of knowledge and accounting techniques. Kaplan and Norton (2000) build a 'balanced scorecard', system which highlights the non-financial indicators that are related to knowledge.

The soundness of seeking solution in deeper cooperation with managerial theory and upgrading the understanding of knowledge in terms of human and social capital with intellectual capital is further corroborated by the fact that most definitions of intellectual capital emphasize the importance of human and social capital:

- Edvinsson (1997) divides intellectual capital into human and structural capital. Structural is divided into partnership and organizational capital, where the former is related to company's external environment and the second to internal.
- Roos, Roos (1997) divide intellectual capital into human, organizational, and relational-consumer capital.
- Sveiby (1997) divides intellectual capital into the capacity or capabilities of the employees, external relations, and internal relations.

The authors foreground human capital either directly (e.g. Edvinsson, Ross, Ross) or indirectly through the understanding of the capabilities (e.g. Sveiby). Highlighting relational capital (e.g. Roos), structural capital (e.g. Onge), and external or internal relations (e.g. Sveiby) certainly points to an understanding of social capital.

The theory of human capital emphasizes that knowledge is related to the individual. Through the processes of socialization, knowledge is becoming increasingly socially contingent; hence, adequate grasp of transfer of knowledge and increasing returns on knowledge requires that more attention be paid to social capital. The major deficiency of the socio-economic approach is the immeasurability of the externalities of knowledge. Therefore, understanding of knowledge within the human and social capital theory should be upgraded through the theory of intellectual capital. Without measuring and market evaluation of knowledge there can be no economic decision-making and rational management of knowledge. Such definition of intellectual capital represents a conception of knowledge as capital in the full meaning of the word.

3. KNOWLEDGE FROM SUBJECTIVE MARKET VIEW

Knowledge requires its carrier (e.g. individual, organization) in which it is to a certain extent institutionalized, and by which this knowledge is used in the market and exchanged for other entitlements. Therefore, from a subjective-market aspect I understand knowledge in relation to the individual, organization, and to the market.

3.1. Individual as carrier of knowledge

Individuals are one of the main carriers of knowledge, since cognitive processes are basically related to the individual. Acquiring knowledge is an individual process and therefore the individual can acquire knowledge only through individual education. Nonaka (1994) and Grant (1997) emphasize that individual knowledge is stored in physical skills and in the brain, and can therefore only be transferred with the person that possesses it. Consequently, an organization can only learn by learning of its members or by accepting new ones (Senge, 1990). Contemporary business literature lists knowledge managers, knowledge engineers, and knowledge producers as the main agents of knowledge (Nonaka, Takeuchi, 1995; Davenport, 1997; Jones, 1999). Consistently, opening new posts has become a quite common practice in many organizations. Apostolou and Mentzas (1999) warn of the danger of 'knowledge bureaucracy' which can occur as a result of excessive zeal for establishing new functions. Hansen et al. (1999) find that knowledge-related processes should not become and end to themselves. Lank (1997) argues that agents of knowledge should only be focused on as long as the importance of knowledge management is not strongly 'anchored' in the organization.

Viewing individuals as the sole agents of knowledge is in part appropriate, since cognitive processes are primarily related to the individual. With individual learning, individuals upgrade their experience into individual knowledge. However, knowledge is transferred through relations, and it is often materialized in machinery, teamwork, and in production-organizational process; as a result, organization can be also an important agent of knowledge, besides the individual.

3.2. Organization as carrier of knowledge

Organization should be viewed as a lot more than a group of individuals. Numerous authors acknowledge the organization's capacity to create, learn and store knowledge:

- Nelson and Winter (1973, 1982) stress that organization creates through its operations, learning, and experience its own organizational knowledge.
- Penrose (1980) and Nelson, Winter (1982) relate rational capacities with the individuals, and 'organizational routine' with the organization. Routine as a form of organizational memory, and the way the organizational knowledge is stored.
- Ule (1996) uses a metaphor of 'collective brains' which should point out that an organization by itself can 'know', independently of the individuals.
- Holzner and Marx (1979) assert that organization as a 'collective agent of knowledge' has the capacity to learn.
- Nonaka (1994) and Jones (1999) highlight that due to increased scale and complexity of interconnectedness, organization as the agent of knowledge is gaining significance.

From a subjective view, we are dealing with individual knowledge possessed by the individual, and socially contingent knowledge held by the organization. An individual can never appropriate the entire knowledge because some knowledge is necessarily dispersed and not given completely to anyone. Organizational learning, organizational routines, and collective brains are notions that point to a conception of the organization as an agent of knowledge. Thus, for instance, Senge (1990) speaks of a 'learning organization', Quinn (1992) of 'intelligent organization, and Nonaka and Takeuchi (1995) on 'knowledge enterprise'. The process of acquiring knowledge which is fundamentally related to the individual apparently generates externalities that are manifest at the organizational level. Accordingly, contemporary organizations are realizing that organizational knowledge is an important factor of business performance, and consequently devote more attention to its management.

3.3. Market mechanism and understanding of knowledge

Like any other commodity in the market, knowledge requires a carrier, an agent, who understands it as a property right. However, there are certain types of knowledge that can never be owned by an individual subject (e.g. individual, organization); hence, knowledge can never be appreciated entirely through individual subjects, but only through a more profound understanding of the market mechanism. Various school of economics developed different ideas of the market, consistently with the changes in the way economic theory viewed the importance and role of the market throughout the history and its evolution. I strongly believe that these changes also affected the capacity of economic theory to understand knowledge itself. From the aspect of knowledge, it makes sense to remain confined to three periods of development of economic thought that contributed by their differing views on the operation and the role of market mechanism to better apprehension of knowledge itself: 1) the (neo)classical school, 2) the Marxist school, and 3) the Austrian school.

In the classical political economy, Smith's invisible hand pointed to the attainment of broader social interests through maximization of individual benefit, to the importance of freedom of choice, to the division of labor, and to the competitive mechanism of market prices. Marginalists upgraded the ideas of the classical economists with methodological individualism, rationality, maximization of benefit, and the price mechanism that leads to market equilibria. In this period, market became an abstract notion and the main mechanism of allocation which employs the informational mechanism of price to provide for efficient allocation of factors of production, and brings social needs and preferences in line with the productive capacity. Kaldor (1972) and Swedberg (1994) maintain that such a narrow understanding of market mechanism 'only' underscores the allocative function of the market. It soon became clear that (neo)classical theory will not be able to present a satisfactory grasp of knowledge only by focusing on allocation, human capital, and interpreting knowledge as information.

Marxist school developed somewhat different approaches to understanding of market mechanism. With its theory of 'commodity fetishism', it pointed out that the market commodity relations actually hide the background of broader social relations (Swedberg, 1994). Knowledge is a commodity with both, use and exchange value. Knowledge is basically a private commodity because its acquisition pertains to individual who appropriate the majority of the benefit derived from the investment into knowledge. Since individual knowledge cannot be appropriated, only contractual relations are possible between employer and employee. However, such relations also generate externalities, as knowledge is increasingly spilling over to other users, and thus it is becoming a public commodity (World Report, 1999). Thus, social relations appear in the background of knowledge as a commodity; therefore, knowledge is not only embodied in individuals, but also resides in the relations between them.

Unlike (neo)classical and Marxist school, Austrian school was considerably more successful in understanding the relation between knowledge and the market. By viewing market as an economic system of knowledge, Austrian school spotlighted two aspects:

- Hayek (1945) underlines that market represents a means of conveying knowledge among various subjects in the market. Though the information function of prices individuals are learning from each other; hence, learning is not based merely on own experience, but also takes place through the market. It is in the rational interest of an individual to take into account others, which is how market becomes a way of social learning that emphasizes relations between individuals.
- Schumpeter's business cycle theory calls attention to the meaning of knowledge at the entrepreneurial level. Innovations implemented by the most daring entrepreneurs generate dynamic disequilibria and development.

Views of various schools of economics have clearly shown that concentrating merely on the allocative function of the market does not enable satisfactory understanding of knowledge. It is obvious that (neo)classical understanding of the market is too narrow, and that the contributions of Marxist and especially Austrian school provide a deeper notion of knowledge. Highlighting the importance of entrepreneurial innovation and understanding of the market as a result of spontaneous action of the subjects who possess partial knowledge is an important contribution of the Austrian school. Market mechanism of social learning leads to transfer of knowledge between individuals in the market; hence, viewing market as 'only' providing efficient allocation of factors of production does not suffice if we are to understand knowledge inscribed in the relations between individual subjects in the market. This means that knowledge only 'fully comes to life' with Austrian school and its understanding of the market mechanism.

4. INSTEAD OF THE CONCLUSION

By defining an own theoretical model we managed to define knowledge from the aspect of substance and from subjective-market aspect. From the aspect of substance, or content, knowledge should be understood as information, cognitive process, and capital. From a subjective-market aspect knowledge is defined in the relation to the individual, organization and market. These two aspects are related.

Knowledge is from the aspect of substance a whole comprising experience where information, based on rational combination of data, is sorted through cognitive process into patterns of thought. Human cognitive capacity is bounded, due to imperfect information and the limits of the human mind. Knowledge as a cognitive process and the conception of knowledge as human capital highlight the fact that knowledge is a process related mainly to the individual. Acquiring knowledge is in essence a process that pertains chiefly to the individual, since new knowledge is generated primarily through processes of individual education.

Knowledge is becoming with individual's inclusion into the organization and through the processes of socialization increasingly socially contingent; hence, adequate grasp of transfer of knowledge and increasing returns on knowledge requires that more attention be paid to social capital on organizational, inter-organizational and institutional level. From the aspect of subject it is possible to explain that some forms of knowledge are socially contingent since they can be possessed by an organization. Knowledge is namely materialized in machinery, teamwork and production process.

However, there are also some forms of knowledge that cannot be appropriated by individual subjects (individual, organization), because they are inscribed in the relations between these individual subjects in the market, and as such they are dispersed and not appropriable by any single entity. Hence, knowledge cannot be entirely understood through the prism of an individual or an organization, but only through a more profound insight into the market mechanism Knowledge enters the market through the system of property rights, where knowledge can be exchanged for other entitlements. Through market knowledge becomes a capital, since knowledge is ascribed a certain economic value that is defined in accordance with supply and demand for it on the market. I believe that cohabitation of human, social, and intellectual capital enables understanding knowledge as capital in its full meaning. Market mechanism is, becoming through Hayek's conception of social learning, also an important way of transmitting knowledge as a specific type of commodity with increasing returns between individual subjects in the market. In the background, social capital keeps emerging through market as a process of social learning. Through these relations and through the materialization of knowledge, knowledge is increasingly becoming a public one. Knowledge ceases to become a private commodity, where individual subject appropriate the majority of the benefit derived from the investment into it, since knowledge is increasingly spilling over through the market to other users, and thus it is becoming a public commodity.

5. LITERATURE

1. Adler Paul, Kwon Woo Seok. Social capital: Prospects for a New Concept". Academy of Management Review, 2002; 27: 17-40.
2. Apostolou Dimitris, Mentzas Gregory. Managing corporate knowledge: A Comparative Analysis of Experiences in Consulting Firms. Knowledge and Process Management, 1999; 6: 129-138.
3. Becker S. G. Human Capital: A Theoretical and Empirical Analysis with Special Reference to Education. NY : National Bureau of Economic Research, 1964.
4. Blaug Mark. The Methodology of Economics. Cambridge : Cambridge University Press, 1992.
5. Coleman S. J. "Social Capital in the Creation of Human Capital". In Lesser Eric, ed., Knowledge and Social Capital, Boston : Butterworth, 2000.
6. Cyert M. Richard, March G. James. A Behavioral Theory of the Firm. New Jersey : Prentice Hall Inc, 1963.
7. Davenport Thomas. Ten Principles of Knowledge Management and Four Case Studies. Knowledge and Process Management, 1979; 4: 187-208.
8. Dosi Givanni. "The Contribution of Economic Theory to the Understanding of a Knowledge Based Economy". In Neef Dale, ed., The Economic Impact of Knowledge, Boston : Buttenworth Heinemann, 1998.
9. Edvinsson Leif. Developing Intellectual Capital at SKANDIA. Longe Range Planning, 1997; 30: 366-373.
10. Edvinsson L., Malone M. Intellectual capital. NY : HarperBusiness, 1997.
11. Etzioni Atzioni. The Moral Dimension. NY : The Free press, 1990.
12. Fukuyama Francis. Trust. New York : Simon&Schuster, 1995.
13. Granovetter Mark. Economic Action and Social Structure: The Problem of Embeddedness. American Journal of Sociology, 1958; 91: 481-510.
14. Grant M. Robert. The Knowledge Based View of the Firm: Implications for Management Practise. Long Range Planning, 1997; 30: 450-454.
15. Hansen M., Nohria N., Tierney T. What is Your Strategy for Managing Knowledge. Harvard Business Review, 1999; March April: 106-116.
16. Hayek F.A. The Use of Knowledge in Society. The American Economic Review, 1945; 35: 519-530.
17. Hirshleifer J. Where are We in the Theory of Information. The American Economic Review, 1973; 63: 1-39.
18. Holzner Burkart, Marx John. Knowledge Application: The Knowledge System in Society. Boston : Allyn&Bacon, 1979.
19. Jones Penelope, Jordan. Assesing Your Companys Knowledge Management Style. Longe Range Planning, 1997; 30: 392-398.
20. Jones Alan B. Knowledge Capitalism. Oxford : Oxford University Press, 1999.
21. Kaldor Nicholas. The Irrelevance of Equilibrium Economics. The Economic Journal, 1972; 82: 1237-1255.
22. Kaplan R., Norton D. Uravnotežen sistem kazalnikov, Ljubljana : GV, 2000.
23. Lank Elisabeth. Leveraging Invisible Assets: The Human Factor. Longe Range Planning, 1997; 30: 406-412.

24. Machlup Fritz. Marginal Analysis and Empirical Research. The American Economic Review, 1946; 36: 519-554.
25. Machlup Fritz. Knowledge: Its Creation, Distribution and Economic significance, Volume I. Princeton : Princeton University Press, 1997.
26. Machlup Fritz. Knowledge: Its Creation, Distribution and Economic Significance: The Economics of Information and Human Capital, Volume III. Princeton : Princeton University Press, 1984.
27. Mill John Stuart. On Liberty, NY : Macmillan Publishing Company, 1956.
28. Mincer Jacob. Investment in Human Capital and Personal Income Distribution. The Journal of Political Economy, 1958; 66: 281-302.
29. Nahapiet J., Ghoshal S."Social Capital, Intellectual Capital and the Organizational Advantage". In Lesser, ed., Knowledge and Social Capital, Boston : Butterworth, 2000.
30. Nelson R. Richard, Winter G. Sidney. Toward Evolutionary Theory of Economic Capabilities. The American Economic Review, 1973, 63: 440-449.
31. Nelson R. Richard, Winter Sidney. An Evolutionary Theory of Economic Change. Cambridge : Belknap Press, 1982.
32. Nonaka Ikujiro. A Dynamic Theory of Organizational Knowledge Creation. Organization Science, 1994, 5: 14-37.
33. Nonaka Ikujiro, Takeuchi. The Knowledge Creating Company, New York : Oxford University Press, 1995.
34. Onge H. Saint. Tacit Knowledge, the Key to the Strategic Alignment of Intellectual Capital. Strategy review, 1996; March-April: 10-14.
35. Paxton Pamela. Is Social Capital Declining in the USA?. American Journal of Sociology, 1999; 105: 88-127.
36. Pečjak Vid. Psihologija spoznavanja, Ljubljana : Državna založba, 1975.
37. Penrose Edith. The Growth of the Firm, New York : M.E. Sharpe, 1980.
38. Putnam Robert. Bowling alone: America's Declining Social Capital. Journal of Democracy, 1995; 6: 65-78.
39. Quinn James. Intelligent Enterprise, New York : The Free Press, 1992.
40. Romer Paul. Endogenous Technological Change. Journal of Political Economy, 1990; 98: 71-102.
41. Romer Paul. The Origins of Endogenus Growth. Journal of Economic Perspectives, 1994; 8: 3-22.
42. Roos Johan, Ross Goran, Dragonetti Nicola Carlo, Edvinsson Leif. Intellectual Capital, London : MacMillan Press, 1997.
43. Sawyer Darwin. Social Roles and Economic Firms: The Sociology of Human Capital. American Journal of Sociology, 1978; 83: 1259-1270.
44. Schultz W. T. Investment in Human Capital. The American Economic Review, 1961; 51: 1-17.
45. Schwalbe Ulrich. The Core of Economicies with Asimetric Information. Berlin : Springer, 1999.
46. Sen Amartya. Rational Fools: A Critique of the Behavioral Foundations of Economic Theory. Philosophy and Public Affairs, 1977; 6: 317-344.
47. Senge Peter. The Fifth Discipline. London : Century Business, 1990.
48. Simon A. Herbert. A Behavioral Model of Rational Choice. Quaterly Journal of Economics, 1955; 69: 99-118.
49. Simon A. Herbert. Models of Man. London : John Wiley&Sons, 1957.
50. Simon A. Herbert. Rational Decision Making in Business Organizations. The American Economic Review, 1979; 69: 493-513.
51. Solow M. Robert. A Contribution to the Theory of the Economic Growth. Quarterly Journal of Economics, 1956; 70: 65-94.
52. Stigler G. The Economics of Information. Journal of Political Economy, 1961; 69: 213-225.
53. Sveiby Karl Erik. The New Organizational Wealth. San Francisco : Berret-Koehler Publishers, 1997.
54. Swedberg Richard, Smelser J. Neil. The Hanbook of Economic Sociology. Princeton : Princeton University Press, 1994.
55. Ule Andrej. Znanje, znanost in stvarnost. Ljubljana : Znanstveno in publicistično središče, 1994.

56. Wiig M. Karl. Integrating Intellectual Capital and Knowledge Management. Longe Range Planning, 1997; 30: 399-405.
57. World Development Report. Knowledge for Development. Washington : World Bank, 1999.

PART 9

COLLABORATIVE DECISION MAKING

28 DECENTRALISED DECISION MAKING IN NON-HIERARCHICAL NETWORKS

Egon Müller[1]; Sebastian Horbach[1]; Jörg Ackermann[1]

Institute of Industrial Science and Factory Systems,
Chemnitz University of Technology, GERMANY
egon.mueller@mb.tu-chemnitz.de
sebastian.horbach@mb.tu-chemnitz.de
joerg.ackermann@mb.tu-chemnitz.de

Autonomous, elementary units of production, co-operating in temporary networks, are considered as the organisational form of enterprises in the 21st century. A scientific approach is provided by networks based on customer-oriented, directly linked, smallest autonomous business units called Competence Cells.

Simultaneously this concept points out perspectives for present-day small and medium-sized enterprises (SME) to face ever-changing economic conditions. One objective is to make SMEs fit for global supply chain integration as well as collaborative management of complex manufacturing and logistics tasks in several production networks at the same time.

For a decentralised decision making based on the non-hierarchical business model special business logics, algorithms and methods for supply chain integration and management need to be provided and implemented in services and applications.

A first core logic is focused on the matching of partners for composition and operation of temporary production networks. Contrary to existing web portals the basic idea is to make the linking interactive and more flexible by using of different description constructs regarding to satisfy the customer, but also network goals. A second core logic addresses the cascading selection of the partners for a customer order driven supply chain. Firstly the "nodes" (manufacturing, assembly, testing) have to be chosen, secondly the "relations" (logistics). A third core logic deals with these "relations". The idea is to establish an automated determination of the logistic processes and candidates.

1. INTRODUCTION

The economical impact of small and medium-sized enterprises (SME) is undisputed (European Commission, 2007; Verheugen, 2008). In Europe-27 there are 23 million SMEs (99.7% of all European enterprises), which provide work for about 75 million people (up to 80% of the employees in some industrial sectors). European manufacturing industry is embracing the following characteristic transitions and changes (Gregory, 2007): 1. Local to global, 2. Factories to networks, 3. Commoditise to innovate, 4. Volume to flexibility, 5. Hierarchies to teams, 6. Craft to knowledge-based.

Most of today's SME networks are working in a regional environment (Havnes, 2004). Supra-regional global engagements are observed less, but in the future SMEs will have to operate more globally in an agile manner. The management of the

Please use the following format when citing this chapter:

Müller, E., Horbach, S. and Ackermann, J., 2008, in IFIP International Federation for Information Processing, Volume 283; *Pervasive Collaborative Networks*; Luis M. Camarinha-Matos, Willy Picard; (Boston: Springer), pp. 277–284.

participation in several networks at the same time is a complex problem. SMEs struggle to handle this due to a lack of methodological skills and human resources. In result the decision making is chaotic. SME are not able to build and operate complete supply chains e.g. to find the right partners and to keep the costs low.

There is a need to make SMEs fit for global supply chain integration as well as collaborative management of complex manufacturing and logistics tasks in several production networks at the same time. Therefore, a scientific approach and the associated systematic robust implementation methodology is essential and much needed for supporting European manufacturing industry, SMEs in particular, to competitively engage in the dynamic global manufacturing and supply chains.

An approach is requested to point out perspectives for present-day SMEs to face ever-changing economic conditions. Such a scientific approach is provided by networks based on customer-oriented, directly linked, smallest autonomous business units called Competence Cells (Mueller, 2006; Mueller, 2007).

This approach is justified by studies, that autonomous, elementary business units co-operating in temporary networks are considered as one of the most sustainable organisational forms of enterprises in the 21st century (see MIT- and OECD-studies (Laubacher et al., 1997; OECD, 2001)).

2. NON-HIERARCHICAL NETWORKS

The scientific approach and its systematic robust implementation has been ex-clusively researched at Chemnitz University of Technology in the research projects "Non-hierarchical Regional Production Networks" (Collaborative Research Centre 457, duration 2000-2006, see (Mueller, 2007)) and "Competence Cell based Produc-tion Networks" (Project Cluster 196, duration 2007-2009, see (Mueller, 2006)).

The research on competence cells-based non-hierarchical production networks is unique. Usually, strategic, hierarchical corporate networks are the object of research. In the European scientific landscape, there has been an increased concentration on "Virtual Organisations" (starting with Mowshowitz, 1994) and "Collaborative Business Networks" (e.g. Camarinha-Matos et al., 2006) for several years now. In most cases, analogue basic assumptions are made compared to the vision of non-hierarchical networks, which confirms the approach. All of the research projects share the ambition to find new organisational forms. But the characteristics of the analysed competence cell-based networking approach are not considered explicitly.

2.1 Vision

The vision of the competence cell-based networking approach (Figure 1) is the following:

Elementary business units – called Competence Cells – are co-operating in Non-hierarchical Regional Production Networks in a customer-oriented manner and thus are capable of facing global competition.

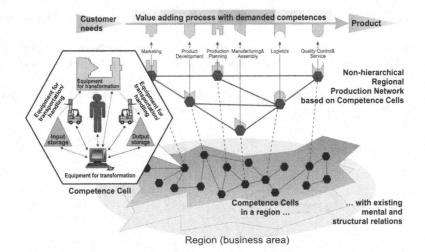

Figure 1 – Conception of Non-hierarchical Regional Production Networks
(Mueller, 2007)

2.2 Models and Methods for non-hierarchical environments

In order to substantiate the vision of competence cell-based networking a model for
the Competence Cell (Figure 3) and a procedure model for the networking (Figure
2) as well as an operationalised concept of organisation (Figure 2) were developed.

Model of the Competence Cell
A Competence Cell (see Figures 1 and Figure 3 left) is considered as the smallest
autonomous indivisible business unit of value adding, able to exist independently.
   The model of the Competence Cell consists of:
-   the human with his competences, arranged according to professional,
    methodical, social and personnel competences (Erpenbeck, 1998)
-   available resources as well as
-   the fulfilled task or executed function.
With this function a business entity can be transformed and a certain
performance can be achieved. The aspects of dimension and structure were
supplemented to obtain a complete technical description.

Procedure Model for networking
The procedure model (Figure 2, left) comprises three levels and seven phases.
   From loose infrastructural and mental relations present in a regional network
(Level I) there initially emerges an institutionalised Competence Network, based on
Competence Cells (Level II, phase Competence Network Composition).
Institutionalisation takes place via the coordination of behaviour (e.g. agreements on
offer generation, agreements on cost allocation) and via the pooling of capacity (e.g.
common servers and data bases). These facilitate an efficient acting towards the
customer and avoid internal discrepancies. Institutionalisation thereby creates the
basis on which autonomous Competence Cells join to find to a collective creation of

value. In order to hold fixed expenses down, the institutionalisation is to be limited to the necessary amount.

The actual creation of value takes place in a Production Network (Level III, phase Production Network composition), i.e. a temporary linking of selected Competence Cells, initiated by a customer's request. In order to select and cross-link Competence Cells and to operate the network, co-ordinated ways of behaviour and pre-installed structures are available in the Competence Network.

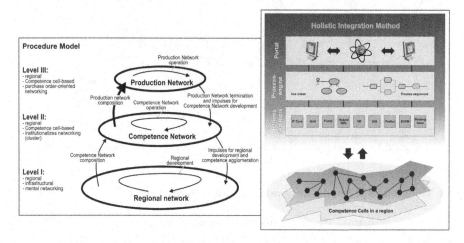

Figure 2 – Procedure model of competence cell-based networking and holistic integration method (Mueller, 2007)

Holistic Integration Method
For running the innovative type of cooperation "Non-hierarchical Regional Production Networks" an operationalised concept of organisation is needed. Such a concept was developed with the "holistic integration method" (HIM). HIM marks a comprehensive instruction as a kind of organisational manual for the Competence Cells. It is based on the levels and phases of the Procedure Model. The general architecture of HIM consists of the levels "Portal", "Process Engine" and "Methods&Tools".

The Competence Cells as users access the functions of HIM through a web-based portal. The portal is linked to the Process Engine. On the highest level of the Process Engine typical cooperative use cases respectively procedures inside the levels and phases of the Procedure Model are defined. In the lowest level the different methods are described in an application-driven form and, if applicable, linked to supporting software tools.

3. DECENTRALISED DECISION MAKING

For a decentralised decision making based on the non-hierarchical business model special business logics, algorithms and methods for supply chain integration and management need to be provided and implemented into services and applications. Three essential core logics are explained in detail.

3.1 Matching

A first core logic is focused on the matching of partners for composition and operation of temporary production networks. Contrary to existing web portals (see eMarketDirectory, 2008) the basic idea is to make the linking interactive and more flexible by using different description constructs (performance, function, competence, resource) in order to satisfy the customer, but also network goals.

The matching of the Competence Cells to a value adding process can be realised in a cascading manner using different description categories depending on the objectives of the customer, the network and the different Competence Cells (Figure 3).

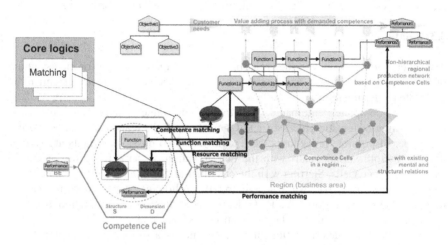

Figure 3 – Matching of Competence Cells to value added processes using different description categories

The matching can be performed using the requested and offered performances, which can also be divided into sub-performances. In case of an entire or a partial failure, the performances can be transformed into functions necessary for their realisation. Then, a matching can be performed using the requested and offered functions, which can also be divided into sub-functions. In case of an entire or a partial failure, the carriers of the functions in terms of competences and resources can be assigned to the functions. Then, a matching can be performed using the requested and offered competences or resources.

3.2 Selection

A second core logic addresses the cascading selection and assigning of the partners to a customer order driven supply chain in two steps. First, the non-logistic candidates (manufacturing, assembly, testing) as the "nodes" are assigned. Then, the logistic candidates (storage, transport) as the "relations" are assigned.

One basic idea is the automation of the configuration procedures. Only if the automated configuration of the production networks fails a complementing planning procedure is deployed (Mueller, 2007). Existing models, concepts and methods for networks are only partially suitable for this (e.g. Herzog, 2008; Kuhn, 2008).

The concepts Extended Value Chain Management (EVCM) and IT core were developed for the automated configuration and operation of Non-hierarchical Regional Production Networks (see Goerlitz et al., 2002). They support the self-organisation (see Herzog, 2008) which is inherent in such networks.

The IT core serves the administration of the data on Competence Cells and variants for production networks. EVCM comprises the necessary business logic with algorithms for the recursive mechanism of creating queries/offers of Competence Cells (Roll-out/Roll-in). It organises the selection of Competence Cells, the administration of the offer data and the determination of the optimal production network configuration. During the operation of the production network EVCM realises the coordination and controlling of the project and order processing.

3.3 Relations

A third core logic deals with the "relations". Several methods exist for the assigning of the logistic processes and candidates. One special idea is to establish an automated determination.

For a complete automated generating of value chains an automated determination of logistic processes and Competence Cells (candidates) is necessary. A number of possible procedures were reviewed. Two possible variants are shortly described. Both variants start with the determination of the non-logistic processes and Competence Cells. Starting with the customer and continued for the whole value adding process in a backward scheduling the following steps are completed in interplay between IT core and EVCM: 1. Determination of destination node, 2. Determination of edge time, 3. Determination of source node.

In result of the determination of potential nodes a process variant plan (Sub-processes for manufacturing, assembly, quality assurance) and a respective candi-date graph are available. These provide the necessary logistical input (e.g. load unit, time window, source/destination location) for the determination of the edges (determination of logistic processes and Competence Cells). From those offers are requested simultaneously. Potential – usually transport – Competence Cells for covering the edges are found by the IT core and enquired by EVCM.

In a first variant transport Competence Cells place an offer for the complete edge. The offer is stored in the offer graph. If they are not able to cover an edge completely themselves they will generate a sub-query for additional transport and storage Competence Cells.

A second variant allows transport Competence Cells to place only partial offers for the edges. If due to a large time window storage is necessary the transport Competence Cells only place offers for the two respective transports of the edge. In the offers additional conditions for storage (time window, distances to storage places) are stated. Then storage Competence Cells can be enquired.

If all value adding processes and candidate Competence Cells are assigned an optimal alternative for the production network can be found according to the preferred objective function of the customer. The resulting production network will start operation then.

4. IMPLEMENTATION

A first prototypical implementation of the matching logic (Figure 3) for demonstration has been realised as a web-based portal (Figure 4).

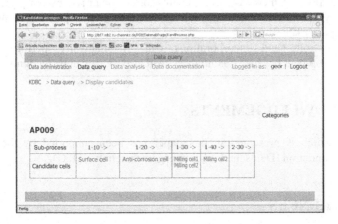

Figure 4 – Web-based portal for matching with an example

Candidates can be searched by the description constructs performances, processes, resources, and competences. Performances are decomposed in sub-performances while processes are decomposed in sub-processes i.e. functions if they are elementary. On the one hand performances, processes, and resources can be selected from existing data. On the other hand complex performances and processes can be composed from existing elementary performances and processes.

If a resource or a competence was selected candidates which own the resource or competence are displayed. In case of the selection of performances or processes candidates are displayed for each elementary sub-performance or sub-process. Usually there is more than one candidate for an item. It is however also possible that no candidate can be found, thus suggesting a deficit in the profile of the network.

Figure 4 illustrates the finding of candidates for a whole work process (AP009). The user picked an already existing process and is provided with a list of Competence Cells which can realise the different sub-processes. There is no candidate for the last sub-process. This means that the Competence Network is lacking competence in a certain field. That way, deficits can be easily identified.

5. SUMMARY

The models and methods of the competence-cell based networking approach – especially the core logics – are expected to contribute to the creation of agile globally operating non-hierarchical supply chains in a systematic way. Thus they will manage the density of information along the supply chain, overcome the complexity of working in several supply chains, ensure flexibility and transparency, and reduce the costs (expenses). The methods and implementing tools will help SME to do the step from currently regional to supra-regional networking.

The methods/services and resulting applications are expected to address many stakeholders:

- Customers can create process chains for both concrete and fictive orders in order to "see" potential partners.
- Enterprises can create process chains for customer requests or product ideas. They have the chance to exploit new markets and to position themselves at these markets.
- Institutions and incorporations can systematically perform regional development because potentials as well as deficits can be recognised.

6. ACKNOWLEDGEMENTS

The work which is presented in this paper has been supported by the German Research Foundation (Deutsche Forschungsgemeinschaft – DFG).

7. REFERENCES

1. Camarinha-Matos LM, Afsarmanesh H, Ollus M (eds.). Networks-Centric Collaboration and Supporting Frameworks. IFIP TC5 WG 5.5 Seventh Working Conference on Virtual Enterprises. Helsinki, Finland, 25-27 September 2006, New York: Springer, 2006.
2. eMarketServices. Do more business with Electronic marketplaces: eMarketDirectory, 2008, http://www.emarketservices.com/start/eMarket-Directory/index.html (accessed 2008-03-04).
3. Erpenbeck J. Kompetenzentwicklung als Forschungsaufgabe. QUEM Bulletin 2/3, 1998.
4. European Commission. Survey of the Observatory of European SMEs. Observatory of European SMEs, Flash EB Series #196. Luxembourg: Office for Official Publications of the European Communities, 2007.
5. Goerlitz O, Neubert R, Teich T, Benn W. "Extended Value Chain Management on electronic marketplaces". In International Journal of E-Business Strategy Management. Vol. III No. 3/2002, London: Winthrop Publications Limited, 2002.
6. Gregory M. Understanding and Interpreting the Future. Report, Cambridge: University, Institute for Manufacturing, 2007.
7. Havnes PA. SMEs and Cooperation. Observatory of European SMEs. Report 2003/5. Luxembourg: Office for Official Publications of the European Communities, 2004.
8. Herzog O (ed.). Collaborative Research Centre (CRC) 637: Autonomous Cooperating Logistics Processes. A Paradigm Shift and its Limitations. Bremen: University, 2008, http://www.sfb637.uni-bremen.de/?&L=2 (accessed 2008-02-28).
9. Kuhn A (ed.): Collaborative Research Center (CRC) 559: Modelling of Large Logistics Networks. Dortmund: University of Technology, 2008. http://www.sfb559.uni-dortmund.de/intro_en.php?sprache=en (accessed 2008-02-28).
10. Laubacher RJ, Malone TW, MIT Scenario Working Group. Two Scenarios for 21st Century Organizations – Shifting Networks of Small Firms or All-Encompassing 'Virtual Countries'? MIT Initiative on Inventing the Organizations of the 21st Century, Working Paper 21C WP #001, 1997.
11. Mowshowitz A. Virtual Organization: A Vision of Management in the Information Age. The information society 1994; 10(4): 267-288.
12. Mueller E (ed.). Collaborative Research Centre (CRC) 457: Non-hierarchical Regional Production Networks. Final Report, Chemnitz: University of Technology. 2007.
13. Mueller E (ed.). Project Cluster (PAK) 196: Competence Cell based Production Networks. Proposal, Chemnitz: University of Technology, 2006, http://www.tu-chemnitz.de/PAK196/en/ (accessed 2008-03-04).
14. OECD. World Congress on Local Clusters: Local Networks of Enterprises in the World Economy. OECD Issues paper, Paris, 23-24 January 2001.
15. Verheugen G. Small business act for Europe. Speech of the Vice-President of the European Commission responsible for Enterprise and Industry, Commission hearing, Brussels, 6 February 2008.

29

A REFERENCE MODEL FOR DISTRIBUTED DECISION MAKING THROUGH A MULTI-AGENT APPROACH

Ilaria Baffo[1,2], Giuseppe Confessore[1],
Giacomo Liotta[1], Giuseppe Stecca[1]

[1] *Istituto di Tecnologia Industriali e Automazione*
Consiglio Nazionale delle Ricerche
[2] *Dipartimento di Ingegneria dell'Impresa*
Università di Roma "Tor Vergata", ITALY
{*ilaria.baffo, g.confessore, g.liotta, g.stecca*}*@itia.cnr.it*

Multi-agent modeling is widely used in collaborative networks for the ability to represent complexity derived from interrelationship. Nevertheless we noticed in the literature a lack of guidelines in formal modeling. In this paper we analyze a reference model to develop multi – agent models able to be applied to a variety of fields. The presented method brings together operations research techniques and UML notation. The reference model is validated in different application fields, in particular in this paper an application to a shoe manufacturing plant is presented.

1. INTRODUCTION

During last years, a lot of studies done in field of complex system management have shown how modeling is one of the key activities in understanding, designing, implementing, and operating systems (Camarinha-Matos *et all*, 2006). A model lets to predict system behavior, evaluate different system problem solutions, test different alternatives and analyze their effect without modifying the real system. The huge potentials offered by models can be exploited particularly in the representation of complex systems such as collaborative networks. Camarinha-Matos and Afsarmanesh, in (Camarinha-Matos *et al*, 2005), defined a collaborative network as a network consisting of autonomous, distributed, heterogeneous entities that collaborate to better achieve common or compatible goals. Following this definition, the application to Multi Agent System (MAS) to collaborative networks modeling results natural. The MAS are widely studied in literature as a method able to represent dynamic and distributed system with several decision makers having different information domains. We can often observe some lacks in investigation of *the problem solving ability of intelligent agents in a multi-agent setting* and a variety of representation methods. In this paper we present a reference model that integrates two types of approach for the models creation in the MAS field. The main purpose is

Please use the following format when citing this chapter:

Baffo, I., Confessore, G., Liotta, G. and Stecca, G., 2008, in IFIP International Federation for Information Processing, Volume 283; *Pervasive Collaborative Networks*; Luis M. Camarinha-Matos, Willy Picard; (Boston: Springer), pp. 285–292.

to provide a set of directives able to support the designer in the system modeling phase of MAS development while indicating in which scenario is more convenient to adopt an approach over another one. The remainder of this paper is structured as follows. Section 2 presents a reference model with a short discussion about model presented in the literature for MAS building. In section 3 an application to flexible manufacturing is used to show like using the guideline offered by the Reference Model for MAS creation. In section 4 two more applications are briefly presented in order to validate the reference model proposed. Finally, conclusions and future works are discussed in section 5.

2. REFERENCE MODEL

2.1 Methods for multi - agent model development

The concept of Multi-Agent System is widely studied in computer science field (Jennings *et al*, 1995). Ever since several researchers studied the MAS theory, offering a lot of agent definitions and application fields of this theory. The different models presented in the literature can be classified into two research traditions: (*i*) the first one IT-oriented and close to MAS origin, (*ii*) the second one closer to the view of actor's system, relationship and functions. The former research field, hereby represented by works of Park and Sugumaran (Park *et al*, 2005) and Trabelsi, Ezzedine, Kolski (Trabelsi *et al*, 2004), is often software system oriented; for this reason the models derived from these studies are usually focused on relationship among agents, rather than on the role they assume. The latter approach is characterized by an higher abstraction level. The system's architecture and the agents role assume in this case more importance, as highlighted in the meta-model for MAS building presented in (Gomez *et al*, 2002). In both cases the ability of agents to solve problems is not considered an important characteristic. A methodology that brings in evidence the agent role assume a key importance in system design and it is a distinguishing point of agent oriented modeling over object oriented modelling; (Zambonelli *et al*, 2003) state that for complex systems, a clear distinction between the active actors of the systems and the passive resources may provide a simplified modelling of the problem. Moreover, delegating control to autonomous components can be considered as an additional dimension of modularity encapsulation

Our proposal for the development of models for MAS building emphasizes this characteristic by focusing on the Operations Research (OR) techniques in order to solve the local or global agent's problem. In the literature, there are several definitions for OR, sometimes dependent of application field. Hereby it is defined as a science that deploys scientific methods like mathematical modeling, statistics, and algorithms in order to make decisions in complex real-world problems. In this paper we propose two possible integrated approaches that can be used for create a MAS model: (*i*) the OR-based one uses algorithms to obtain optimal and shared solutions among agents while (*ii*) the second one is based on MAS traditional approach, more focused on architecture and relationship among system components. For the latter approach we suggest the Unified Modeling Language (UML) which is able to represent the complex system with an object (agent) - oriented view: (Bauer et al, 2005).

2.2 The Reference Model

The reference model described in the Figure 1 consists of six steps: problem analysis, static architecture definition, multi-agent society definition, toolkit selection, model implementation and test & validation. The second and third steps have two different integrated implementations in order to put into evidence the importance of the agent's intelligence properties. The development of a multi-agent model is composed not only of the role and relationship's definition (left branch in Figure 1) but also of the investigation of the agent's ability to solve local problems using OR methods (right branch). Before to select the simulation's tool able to recreate the dynamics of real system, a model check is needed. At the end, the simulation step allows the verification of the impact that agent's decisions have on the achievement of the global objective.

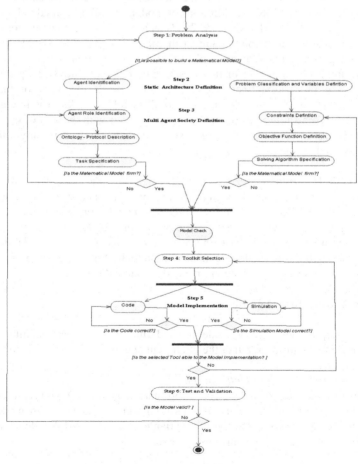

Figure 1 – The Reference Model

3. REFERENCE MODEL: AN APPLICATION TO FMS

In this section we describe how to realize a multi-agent model, with the aims of describing an application of the reference model presented in the previous section and validating it. In particular, the capabilities offered by an application to shoe flexible manufacturing system is investigated.

3.1 Problem Analysis

The concept of Flexible Manufacturing System (FMS) was introduced in response to the following need: to improve the responsiveness to changes in products, production technology and markets. This issue has been discussed deeply in the literature (El Maraghy H.A., 2006). FMSs have high degree of complexity and often are underused mostly due to lack in software systems and communication technologies. Recently, new advances in wireless communication technologies and embedded systems boosted the possibility to implement organization, production planning and scheduling techniques and software tools able to exploit all the opportunities given by FMS. The Multi-agent models are often applied in FMS field (Adacher L. *et al*, 2000) (Hao Q. *et al*, 2003) as a promising technology for dealing with cooperation and decision-making in distributed application. In this work we consider an agile shoe manufacturing plant with innovative transportation lines. The innovative molecular structure of the transportation system allows the products to overtake along production lines, increasing the overall flexibility of the plant (Martinez Lastra J.L *et al*, 2006). In order to allow job overtake, it is important to analyze the job scheduling problem that is usual solved with the aim of optimizing different objectives, such as the makespan, the total cost, or penalty functions compliant with due dates.

3.1.1. Domain Description

The domain can be described through the following components: *(i)* one Information System of the Plant that receives the orders demand from the market; *(ii)* six Manufacturing Cells (IA) processing customer orders. IA are linked by a flexible transportation line; *(iii)* a set consisting of three *customers* C_k ($k = 1,..,3$), in which each customer will issue one order demand with a total of three orders D_k ($k = 1,..,3$). Every order has a specific production time and a related due date.

3.2 Static Architecture Definition

The second step of the reference model is the definition of the static architecture for describing the real entities or rather the intelligent agents operating in the system.

3.2.1. Agents and variables identification.

Two types of agents are modeled. The Coordinator Agent (CA) who represents the Information System and the Island Agents (IA) who represent the manufacturing cells of the plant. Among the system variables we notice order due date and completion time for production and customer service level.

3.2.2 Characterization of the problem.

In order to respect or optimize the lead time for the customer, the agents must decide in which sequence to process the demand orders. In particular: *(i)* IAs decides the sequence of orders to be processed based on the related due date, *(ii)* CA,decides whether making changes to the released production plan.

3.3 Multi Agent Society Definition

An important feature of intelligent agents is their ability to communicate with other agents by sending messages and signals. In several works related to MAS theory the negotiation among competitive agents is often considered. Hereby the agents are cooperative actors that share local information to estimate the goodness of different solutions.

3.3.1 Role identification

CA plays a coordinator and strategic decision maker role, since it is the only agent able to communicate with all other agents and with external market. CA knows the latest information about the change of order's due date, or about the saturation degree of production plant capacity. The IAs have a functional role since they solve a local decision problem and carry out the decision made. They can communicate only with neighbor agents.

3.3.2 Protocol description

The information flow among various agents is regulated by the Overtake Coordination Protocol (OCP) that consists of the following steps:
1. The CA receives orders from the market and communicate to the first IA the release date and due date of orders.
2. The first IA solves a local scheduling problem and communicate to the next IA when it can start to process the orders.
3. If the due date of an order changes during production or distribution process, then the CA communicate the new due date to the IA following the IA who is working the changed order.
4. The IA finds the best schedule and sends to CA this schedule with ending times for every order.
5. The CA calculates the convenience of changing schedule and, if overtaking is convenient, sends the order of overtaking to the IA.

3.3.3 Tasks specification

Each IA solves a *scheduling problem* by determining the best sequence of order processing based on the related due date. The global shared goal is that the system must minimize the order delays for maximizing the customer service level. At more high level, CA decides whether allowing to overtake the order minimizes the following decisional function introduced in (Baffo I. *et al, 2007*):

$$f = \alpha * \Delta T + \beta * \Delta Cmax \qquad (1)$$

where α is a parameter that depends on order priority and β is a parameter depending on how many order must be processed again; ΔT is the change in delay of the order while $\Delta Cmax$ is the change in all orders completion time after that the order schedule is changed.

3.3.4 Constraints definition

In the problem solving process, the following constraints must be respected: *(i)* all orders must be processed; *(ii)* every order must respect the precedence constraints.

3.3.5 Objective function definition

For scheduling problem of the IAs, the objective function is to minimize the lateness like difference between the ending time of every order and their due dates. The problem is known in literature like 1|r|Lmax, where the letter r represents the possibility to consider the preemptive solution. The CA goal is to maximize the service level (SL), the decision is made using function (1).

3.3.6 Solution Algorithm Definition

The IA's scheduling problem is solved through a branch and bound based algorithm.

3.3.7 Model Check

The check of the model is made verifying the correctness of logic relationship among the most important parameters of the problem. Changing the value of some parameters, the output of the model correspond to the output of the real system, with a approximation due to the impossibility to consider all variables of the problem.

3.4 Toolkit Selection

The selection of the toolkit depends on factors such as the problem size, the quality of solution, the number of solutions that can be evaluated, the available time for solving the problem. For the test case presented in this section the Java programming language is used to build the model for the manufacturing and distribution network.

3.5 Test and Validation

Test and validation have been performed in order to show how the model can affect the flexibility performance. We present two exemplificative scenarios of change in order due date while the production and distribution plan is released. In the first scenario the due date of order 1 changes after the first IA. In the second one the due date of order 3 changes after the third IA. In the first case, if we assume that α is the same of β, then the CA is willing to change the schedule because the worsening of the *Cmax* is smaller than the advantages of reducing the tardiness of order 1. In this case the external flexibility in term of *customer service level,* meant as the ability to respond quickly to market change, is more important than the completion of all the orders. In the second scenario, if we assume that α is the same of β, the CA is willing not to change the schedule, because the advantage of reducing the tardiness of order 3 is smaller than the worsening of the *Cmax*. In this case, the *internal flexibility*, meant as the ability to manage in efficient way the plant, is more important than responding quickly to market requests. In both cases the values of α and β determine the decision of CA.

4. REFERENCE MODEL VALIDATION

The reference model validation is reported in terms of applications to several problem to different fields. In particular we report two applications: (*i*) one related to a *Vehicle Routing Problem with Time Window* (VRPTW) in a distribution process faced in (Bianco *et al*, 2005); (*ii*) one related to a *Collaborative Network* in an industrial local system (Baffo I. *et al, 2007*). In the first problem, we identify three types of agents: (*i*) a Logistic Operator (LO), involved in the delivery of goods from a single depot to customers while meeting customer service level requirements; (*ii*) the Truck Operator (TO), responsible for the delivery of goods by means of own vehicles and with the aim of minimizing the total traveled distance; (*iii*) the Customer (C) that has to receive goods within the requested delivery time. The building of a MAS through the presented reference model allowed to obtain a good solution as trade-off between the penalty cost linked to delivery out of time windows and the route distance covered by TO. Moreover the solution proposed can be considered as an output of a negotiation process between the LO and TO. C in this case is an information possessor because the time windows supplied by C cannot be changed by the system dynamics. In the second application proposed, the problem is related to the allocation of project's activities to industrial agent operating in a geographic area. To every activity corresponds a profit and the scope of local enterprises is to maximize the total profit obtaining a great number of activities. The system's agents are: (*i*) *one* coordinator agent (CA) that decides in which way to allocate the project resources on based of enterprise's competence. (*ii*) *n* industrial agents that declare their competence level and during the time invest to increase this level. The solutions of these problems have allowed to measure the results in terms of efficient allocation of the available resources and in terms of system evolution towards growing level of global competence on the territory.

5. CONCLUSION

In this paper we presented a reference model able to support a designer in building multi-agent models for representing complex systems. In particular we provided guidelines in order to create a model in which: (*i*) the intelligent agents solve local problems with OR techniques; (*ii*) a shared solution of the problem at global level is obtained through the communications and collaboration among different plant agents. The applications performed in supply chain and industrial district fields, proved the validity and ability of the study as innovative decision support system that can be designed under a multi-agent point of view. The test cases proved as a well designed model can be applied with a few changes to different environments. Furthermore, the experiments validated the robustness of the reference model with respect to the field of application, type of problem and solution methods.

6. REFERENCES

1. Adacher L., Agnetis A., Meloni C., 2000, Autonomous agents architectures and algorithms in flexible manufacturing systems, IIE Transactions Vol32, 941-951.
2. Baffo I., Confessore G., Rismondo S., Uno strumento di modellazione e simulazione della dinamica di una rete di attori operanti in un territorio, in proceedings of XXVIII Italian Conference of Regional Science, Bolzano, 2007.
3. Bauer B, Odell J. UML 2.0 and agents: how to build agent based systems with the new UML standard. Engineering Application of Artificial Intelligence, 2005; 18: 141-157.
4. Bianco L, Confessore G, Stecca G, A multi-agent model for distribution problems in logistics systems. In Proceedings of 18th International Conference on Production Research ICPR-18: The networked enterprise: a challenge for a sustainable development, 2005; CD-ROM.
5. Camarinha-Matos LM, Afsarmanesh H. A modeling framework for collaborative networked organizations, in IFIP International Federation for Information Processing, volume 224, Network-Centric Collaboration and Supporting Fireworks, eds. Camarinha –Matos, L., Afsarmanesh, H., Ollus, M., (Boston: Springer), 2006; 3-14.
6. Camarinha-Matos LM, Afsarmanesh H. Collaborative networks: A new scientific discipline. Journal on Intelligent Manufacturing, 2005; 16: 439-452.
7. El Maraghy H.A., 2006, Flexible and reconfigurable manufacturing systems paradigms, International Journal of Flexible Manufacturing Systems, Vol17, 261–276.
8. Gomez-Sanz, JJ, Pavon, J, Garijo F. Metamodels for building multi-agent systems, in Proceedings of the 2002 ACM symposium on Applied computing. ACM Press, 2002; 37–41.
9. Hao Q., Shen W., Stecca G., Wang L., 2003, Towards an internet enabled cooperative manufacturing management framework, Processes and Foundations for Virtual Organizations, L.M. Camarinha-Matos and H. Afsarmanesh (eds.), 191-200.
10. Jennings NR, Wooldridge M. Applying agent technology. Applied Artificial Intelligence, 1995; 9: 357-369.
11. Martinez Lastra J.L., Colombo A.W., 2006, Engineering framework for agent-based manufacturing control, Engineering Applications of Artificial Intelligence, Vol19, 625–640.
12. Park S, Sugumaran V. Designing multi-agent systems: a framework and application. Expert Systems with Applications, 2005; 28: 259-271.
13. Trabelsi A, Ezzedine H, Kolski C. Architecture modelling and evaluation of agent.based interactive system. IEEE Internationl Conference on Systems, Man and Cybernetics, 2004
14. Zambonelli F, Jennings NR, Wooldridge M. Developing Multiagent Systems: The Gaia Methodology. ACM Transaction on Software Engineering and Methodology. Vol 12, No. 3. July 2003, Pages 317-370.

Virtual ECare:
GROUP DECISION SUPPORTED BY IDEA GENERATION AND ARGUMENTATION

30

Ricardo Costa[1], Paulo Novais[2], João Neves[3], Goreti Marreiros[4],
Carlos Ramos[4], and José Neves[2]

[1]College of Management and Technology - Polytechnic of Porto, Felgueiras, PORTUGAL
rcosta@estgf.ipp.pt,
[2]DI-CCTC, Universidade do Minho, PORTUGAL
{pjon, jneves }@di.uminho.pt,
[3]Centro Hospitalar de Vila Nova de
Gaia/Espinho-EPE,PORTUGAL
j_neves@hotmail.com
[4]GECAD, Institute of Engineering – Polytechnic of Porto, PORTUGAL
{goreti, csr}@dei.isep.ipp.pt

It is understood that Collaborative Work plays an important role in today's organizations life cycle. On the other hand, any decision that may involve a set of decision makers is, by itself, quite complex. It is under this umbrella that it will be presented the VirtualECare project, that contemplates an intelligent multi-agent system able to monitor, interact and serve its customers in need of (health)care services. We will center our attention on the system group decision and argumentation modules, which use idea generation techniques and resort to argumentation to exchange and justify belief and choice. At the end, a prototype will be presented.

1. INTRODUCTION

In the last years there has been a considerable increase in the number of people in need of intensive care, especially among the elderly, a phenomenon that is related to population ageing (Brown 2003). However, this is not exclusive of the elderly, as diseases as obesity, diabetes, and blood pressure have been increasing among young adults (Ford and Capewell 2007). As a new fact, it has to be dealt with by the healthcare sector, and particularly by the public one. Thus, the importance of finding new and cost effective ways for healthcare delivery are of particular importance, especially when the patients are not to be detached from their environments (WHO 2004). Following this line of thinking, a VirtualECare Multiagent System is presented in section 2, being our efforts centered on its Group Decision modules (Costa, Neves et al. 2007) (Camarinha-Matos and Afsarmanesh 2001).

Please use the following format when citing this chapter:

Costa, R., Novais, P., Neves, J., Marreiros, G., Ramos, C. and Neves, J., 2008, in IFIP International Federation for Information Processing, Volume 283; *Pervasive Collaborative Networks*; Luis M. Camarinha-Matos, Willy Picard; (Boston: Springer), pp. 293–300.

On the other hand, there has been a growing interest in combining the technological advances in the information society - computing, telecommunications and knowledge – in order to create new methodologies for problem solving, namely those that convey on Group Decision Support Systems (GDSS), based on agent perception. Indeed, the new economy, along with increased competition in today's complex business environments, takes the companies to seek complementarities, in order to increase competitiveness and reduce risks. Under these scenarios, planning takes a major role in a company life cycle. However, effective planning depends on the generation and analysis of ideas (innovative or not) and, as a result, the idea generation and management processes are crucial. Our objective is to apply the GDSS referred to above to a new area. We believe that the use of GDSS in the healthcare arena will allow professionals to achieve better results in the analysis of one's Electronically Clinical Profile (ECP). This attainment is vital, regarding the incoming to the market of new drugs and medical practices, which compete in the use of limited resources.

2. THE VirtualECare PROJECT

The VirtualECare project main objective is to present an intelligent multi-agent system able to monitor, interact and provide its customers with healthcare services of the utmost quality, at reasonable costs. It will be mandatory not only to interconnect different healthcare institutions, but also leisure centers, training facilities, shops and patient relatives, just to name a few. The VirtualECare Architecture is a distributed one, with their different subsystems interconnected through a network (e.g., LAN, MAN, WAN), each one with a different role (Figure 1). A top level description of the architecture machinery is given below:

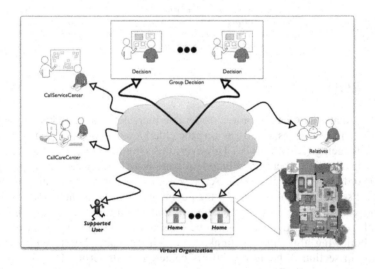

Figure 1 - The VirtualECare Architecture

SupportedUser – elderly people with special health care needs, whose clinical data is sent to the ***CallCareCenter*** and redirected to the ***Group Decision Support System***;

Home – the elderly natural environment, object of a continuous monitoring, where the elderly clinical data is sent to the ***Group Decision Support System*** through the ***CallCareCenter***, being the remaining one redirected to the ***CallServiceCenter***;

Group Decision – it is in charge of all the decisions taken at the VirtualECare platform. Our work will be centered on this key module;

CallServiceCenter – Entity with all the necessary computational and qualified personal resources, capable of receiving and analyze the diverse data and take the necessary actions according to it;

CallCareCenter – Entity in charge of computational and qualified personal resources (i.e., healthcare professionals and auxiliary), capable of receiving and analyze the clinical data, and take the necessary actions according to it;

Relatives – individuals that may have an active role in the supervising task of their love ones, being able to give precious complementary information about them and being able to intervene, in a complementary way, in specific crises (e.g., lowliness).

In order to have the ***Group Decision Support System*** at work, one has to have access not only to the belief of specialize staff (e.g., nurses, pediatrics, cardiologists), but also to the profile of the ***SupportedUser***, leading to a better understanding of his/her special needs. The relevant information may range from the patient Electronic Clinic Record to their own personal preferences (e.g., musical, gastronomic) and/or personal experiences.

This solution will help healthcare providers to integrate, analyze and manage complex and unrelated clinical, explored and/or administrative data. It will provide tools and methodologies for creating an information-on-demand environment that can improve quality-of-living, safety, and quality of patient care.

3. GROUP SUPPORT IN COLLABORATIVE NETWORKS ORGANIZATIONS

3.1 Group Support Systems

By definition, any Collaborative Network Organization (CNO) takes for granted the existence of a group of people, aiming at the completion of a specific task (Camarinha-Matos 2003). The number of elements involved may be variable, as well as the persistency of the group. The group members may be at different places, be asynchronous on their interactions, and/or belong to different organizations. Collaborative work has not only inherent advantages (e.g., better knowledge, different world perspectives, increased acceptance), but it presents, also, some drawbacks (e.g., social pressure, domination, goal displacement, group thinking) (Marreiros, Santos et al. 2007).

3.2 Meeting phases

In this work we will call *meeting* to all the phases necessary to the completion of a specific task, i.e., a meeting results from the interaction between two or more individuals (Bostrom, Anson et al. 2003). Physically, a meeting can be realized in one of the four scenarios: same time / same place, same time / different places, different times / same place and different times / different places. Each one of these scenarios will require from the GDSS a different kind of action.

Until now we have been talking about collaborative work and present group members as the unique people involved in the process; however, it is very common to see a third element taking part in the course of action, the facilitator. The meeting facilitator is a person welcomed in the group, nonaligned, which arbitrate all the meeting phases (Marreiros et al, 2007).

According to Dubs and Hayne (1992), a meeting has three distinct phases, as it is depicted in Figure 2.

Figure 2 - Meeting Phases

In the Pre-Meeting phase the facilitator prepares the meeting, i.e., establishes the meeting goals, proceeds with the group formation (making sure that all the participants have the necessary background), selects the best tools, informs the meeting members about the goals, and distributes among them the meeting materials.

In the In-Meeting phase the participants will be working in order to accomplish the meeting goals, and the facilitator has the task of monitor the elapsing of the meeting (e.g., to observe the relationship between the group members), and to mediate if necessary.

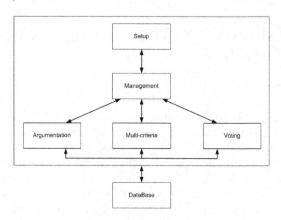

Figure 3 – VirtualECare Group Decision Architecture

In the Post-Meeting phase it is important to evaluate the results achieved by the group, as well as how much each group member is acquit with the achieved results (satisfied/unsatisfied). Still, in this phase it is very important to identify and store information that can be helpful in future meetings (e.g., how to actualize the participant's profile for future selection). The VirtualECare Group Decision Support System Architecture is built on several modules, as it is depicted in Figure 3.

Setup module – it will be operated by a *facilitator* during the pre-meeting phase, in charge of configuration and parameterization activities;

Multi-criteria module – it will be operated by a *facilitator* during the pre-meeting phase, being in charge of the definition of the evaluation criteria and scaling of all the sub-systems;

Argumentation module - This module is based on the IBIS (Issue Based Information System) argumentation model, developed by Rittel and his colleagues in the early 70's, where an argument is a statement or a belief, which may support or pointed out to one or more thoughts (Figure 4).

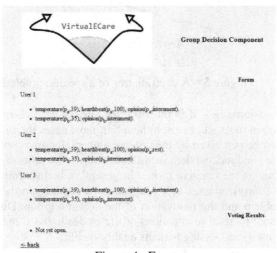

Figure 4 –Forum

Voting module - This module is responsible for allowing each intervenient of the decision group component to "vote" for his preferred choice, normally the one most similar to his "opinion" (Figure 4).

4. IDEA GENERATION

The *Group Decision* module is a major module in our system, a fact that is associated with the significance of decision-making in today business activity, and the celerity required in obtaining a solution to a problem under evaluation. Therefore, the flow of new ideas is central in an environment as the one presented above. Indeed, several idea generation techniques were popularized during the early 1950's in order to assist organizations to be fully innovative. These techniques, although primarily born and used in the advertising world, can be applied to an infinite number of up-and-coming areas. Many idea techniques emerged at that time and continue nowadays, such as Brainstorming, Nominal Group Technique (NGT), Mind-mapping, SCAMPLER, among others.

In order to face the real challenges with which we have to deal with, we selected two idea generation techniques, which will be applied in two different situations:

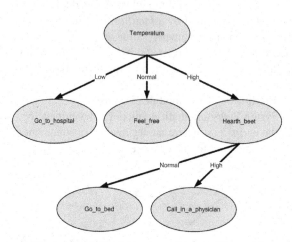

Figure 5 – A decision tree of a specific problem

- Brainstorming – it is probably the best-known creative tool. It can be used in most situations, although in most cases the rules that oversee it must be perceived by the group members. It comes with all its potential when and independent facilitator manages the process (so the group can focus on the creative tasks). In general, a brainstorming takes between 30 (thirty) minutes to 1 (one) hour, depending on the difficulty of the problem and the motivation of the decision group. Due to this detail it cannot be used in situations of life or death, but it may and is going to be used in assessing patients quality-of-life;
- Mind-mapping – it is best used when one needs to explore and/or develop ideas to help in getting a solution to a specific problem, or when we need to take notes and/or summarize meetings. It may be used to obtain instant answers in critical situations.

In Mind-mapping the specific problem is presented in the form of a decision tree, being the vital data obtained, for instance, from the sensors attached to the **supported user** (Figure 5).

5. ARGUMENTATION MODULE

Once some ideas have been put forward (e.g., through the tools referred to above, or simply by intuition) the participants are expected to "defend" those ideas, in order to reach consensus or majority. Each participant will, therefore, argue for the most interesting alternatives or against the worst ones, according to his/her preferences and/or skills. By expressing their arguments, participants expect to influence the others belief and make them change their own (Brito, Novais et al. 2003).

This module is based on the IBIS (Issue Based Information System) argumentation model developed by Rittel and his colleagues in the early 70's (Conklin). The core of this methodology is based on a matrix of questions, ideas and arguments that, being combined, make a dialogue. According to this model, an argument is a statement or an belief which may support or pointed out one or more ideas. Among the elements of the IBIS model, there exists nine possible links, as it is depicted in Figure 6.

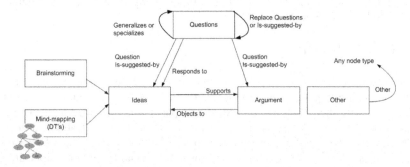

Figure 6 – IBIS model adapted from Conklin and Begeman

In the implementation process of the Group Decision apparatus, and the respective software, some modifications to the model have been made, namely:

- The **question** in the IBIS model maps, in the Group Decision apparatus, on the **goal** of the meeting;
- **Ideas** are the alternatives of the multi-criteria decision problem, and arise from the idea generation tool throughout brainstorming or through mind mapping;
- **Arguments** in IBIS can be pros or cons vis-à-vis a given idea. In the Group Decision module they are based in two types of information: Patient Electronic Clinical Profile and a set of Decision Trees. Additionally, the possibility for one participant to argue using an argument borrowed from another member, is real.

Figure 7 – A **Group Decision** assessment reported on a person mobile phone.

This module is paramount on the in-meeting phase. It is not only used by the participants to defend their points of view, but also in the post-meeting phase, by the facilitator (e.g., if the group does not reach a solution, the facilitator may use this module to check for the most consensual alternative). The IBIS model has been used over and over again in the development of GDSSs, the first realization being gIBIS (Conklin and Begeman 1988). By adopting this representation, the Group Decision module will accommodate a better organization of the arguments exchanged by the participants. This may facilitate belief convergence, and reduce the meetings "noise". Once a decision has been made, it is (automatically) sent to the person under monitorization (the supported user in Figure 1) by a mobile device (Figure 7), in order to keep him/her informed.

6. CONCLUSION

In the healthcare arena one aims at a distinguished deliverance of healthcare services to the population in general, and to the elderly in particular, without delocalizing or messing up with their routines. Indeed, in this paper it is described a VirtualECare multi-agent system, being studied in special its Group Decision features, aiming at multi-criteria decision problems, in order to answer to requests posted by its users (e.g., to sustain his/her ideas, each participant should argue for the most appealing or against the worst ones, according to his/her preferences and/or skills, expecting to influence the others' views).

In future work the argumentation module will be re-adjusted in order to provide not only a simple way of belief revision, but also a dialogue component to convey one beliefs, i.e., one may go from pre-argument reasoning to argument-based negotiation, influencing others through the confrontation of mental conceptions or ideas.

7. REFERENCES

1. Bostrom, R., R. Anson, and V. Clawson, Eds. (2003). Group facilitation and group support systems. Group Support Systems: New Perspectives, Macmillan.
2. Brito, L., P. Novais, and J. Neves (2003). The logic behind negotiation: from pre-argument reasoning to argument-based negotiaion. Intelligent Agent Software Engineering. V. Plekhanova, Idea Group Piblishing: 137-159.
3. Brown, S. J. (2003). "Next generation telecare and its roles in primary and community care." Health and social care in the community 11(6): 459-462.
4. Camarinha-Matos, L. (2003). New collaborative organizations and their research needs. PRO-VE'03, Kluwer Academic Publishers.
5. Camarinha-Matos, L. M. and H. Afsarmanesh, Eds. (2001). Virtual Communities and Elderly Support. Advances in Automation, Multimedia and Video Systems, and Modern Computer Science, WSES.
6. Conklin, J. The IBIS Manual: A short course in IBIS methodology, GDSS Inc.
7. Conklin, J. and M. Begeman (1988). gIBIS: A Hypertext tool for exploratory policy discussion.
8. Costa, R., J. Neves, P. Novais, J. Machado, L. Lima and C. Alberto, (2007). Intelligent Mixed Reality for the Creation of Ambient Assisted Living. Progress in Artificial Intelligence, Lecture Notes in Artificial Intelligence 4874, Springer, ISBN 978-3-540-77000-8.
9. S. Dubs, and S. C. Hayne (1992), "Distributed facilitation: a concept whose time has come?," in Computer Supported Cooperative Work, pp. 314-321.
10. Ford, E. S. and S. Capewell (2007). "Coronary Heart Disease Mortality Among Young Adults in the U.S. From 1980 Through 2002: Concealed Leveling of Mortality Rates." JACC(50): 2128-2132.
11. Marreiros, G., R. Santos, C. Ramos, J. Neves, P. Novais, J. Machado and J. Bulas-Cruz (2007). Ambient Intelligence in Emotion Based Ubiquitous Decision Making. Proceedings of the International Joint Conference on Artificial Intelligence (IJCAI 2007) - 2nd Workshop on Artificial Intelligence Techniques for Ambient Intelligence (AITAmI'07).
12. WHO (2004). Active ageing: towards age-friendly primary health care, World Health Organization.

31   COMMUNICATION PROTOCOLS FOR COLLABORATIVE FORECASTING

Chin-Yin Huang
Department of Industrial Engineering and Enterprise Information
Tunghai University, Taichung, TAIWAN, huangcy@thu.edu.tw

Wu-Lin Chen
Department of Computer Science and Information Management,
Providence University, Taichung, TAIWAN, wlchen@pu.edu.tw

Jhih-Ming Chen
Department of Industrial Engineering and Enterprise Information
Tunghai University, Taichung, TAIWAN, farmer1003@hotmail.com

In this research, protocols for activities of collaborative forecasting among the partnered companies are developed in accordance of twelve scenarios derived by market types (excess supply or excess demand), types of focal company (retailer, manufacturer, or material supplier), and type of integration (integrated or disintegrated). Each of the twelve scenarios has its specific protocol in modified sequence diagram. Additionally, eleven protocol modules are developed for constructing the twelve protocols. With the protocol modules, the protocols are presented in a more structural format and are more readable. A prototype system in Java program is also developed to illustrate the applicability of the protocols. By deploying the system over internet, the twelve protocols are realized and can regulate the communications of collaborative forecasting.

1. INTRODUCTION

Shorter product life cycle and uncertain market demands have forced today's companies not to choose a strategy of vertical integration, but to collaborate with other companies. The collaborative companies can flexibly and adaptively grasp transient opportunities by sharing the investments in human, machine, and facility resources (Abreu and Camarinha-Matos, 2008). However, as the size of a collaborative manufacturing network becomes large, bullwhip effect will significantly reduce the advantages of the network because the participating members are unable to economically meet the demand orders due to excessive or inadequate inventories. Fortunately, Lee and Whang (Lee and Whang, 2000) point out that though bullwhip effect is inevitable, collaborative forecasting could eliminate the disadvantageous effect.

Although some of systems have been defined to provide a platform for collaborative forecasting, e.g., VMI, CPFR, and Rosettanet, little research points out

Please use the following format when citing this chapter:

Huang, C.-Y., Chen, W.-L. and Chen, J.-M., 2008, in IFIP International Federation for Information Processing, Volume 283; *Pervasive Collaborative Networks*; Luis M. Camarinha-Matos, Willy Picard; (Boston: Springer), pp. 301–312.

two critical concerns. First, companies in a collaborative manufacturing network are independent and autonomous. Although the focal company in a supply network is influential in a supply network, participating companies can still have their own freedom to cooperate with companies that does not belong to the same network. Second, because participating companies may not want to share completed information for collaboration, they may partially interchange erroneous or inflated information with each other (Cachon and Lariviere, 2001). As such, it results in a failure in the collaboration.

Applying simple protocols to coordinate the message interchanges among collaborative companies have been suggested as an effective approach for collaborative manufacturing (Chen, et al., 2008, Huang, et al., 2008a, Huang, et al., 2008b). However, the applications have been limited in production planning. Demand forecasting, as a key element that drives the collaborative manufacturing activities, is rarely investigated because of at least two reasons. First, usually demand forecasting is performed by the focal company in a supply network. Second, diverse market characteristics increase a difficulty to develop standardized protocols for companies.

This research intends to develop communication protocols for collaborative forecasting. The protocols define canonical interactive behaviors among companies, so efficient collaboration can be achieved. Additionally, the protocols are developed based on a peer-to-peer perspective. Therefore, the forecasting activities are not dominated by the focal company. Because only limited information that is defined in the protocols is shared in the activities of collaborative forecasting, participating companies can still hold their autonomy and privacy.

2. LITERATURE REVIEW

2.1 Information sharing in supply chain

Information sharing is a critical issue in supply chain. Due to complicated structures and constraints of supply chains, benefits of information sharing can only be limited in given conditions. It still lakes a comprehensive model for optimizing the design of information sharing in supply chain (Huang, et al., 2003). Xu et al. (Xu, et al., 2001) point out that one-forecast policy is a key to success of supply chain collaboration. According to their idea the one-forecast policy is made by either the retailer or the manufacturer. Actually communication protocols would provide a synthesizing mechanism for integrating multiple forecasts made by the participating companies (or supply chain entities). More specifically, not every participating company can receive benefit from information sharing. Zhao and Xie (Zhao and Xie, 2002) use simulation to explain that despite the retailers share forecast information (e.g., projected net requirement), their costs, including order processing costs, transportation costs, and inventory carrying costs, actually increase. Only the manufacturers receive substantial large cost savings. Additionally, the demand pattern significantly affects how forecasting errors influence the value of information sharing (Zhao and Xie, 2002). Literature indicates that the design of production information sharing is actually under a lot of design considerations of supply chain. How to share information so the participating companies can receive benefits and hold their autonomy is still a research issue.

2.2 Design concerns of collaborative forecasting

Sauer (Sauer, 2006) points out that performing production planning with distributed processes has the following concerns:

1. Interdependencies between companies
2. Integration of local companies' production plans
3. Necessity to co-ordinate with other companies' production plans
4. Uncertainties happening in each local company.

Similar concerns could also occur in collaborative forecasting. By revising the above concerns, design concerns of collaborative forecasting are as follows:

1. Interdependent forecast on demands and supplies between participating companies.
2. Integration of multiple interdependent forecasts
3. Necessity to coordinate with other companies' forecasts
4. Uncertainties happening in each participating company.

2.3 Communication protocols for information sharing

Huang et al. (Huang, et al., 2008a) propose the concept to apply communication protocols for interchanging order information. Their approach reduces the costs and risks of full sharing information among the participating companies. Applying rules of communication (protocols) for integrating collaborative activities has been proposed in various articles as a feasible and important direction in collaborative manufacturing (Hammami, et al., 2003, Neubert, et al., 2004, Nof, et al., 2006). Chen et al. (Chen, et al., 2008) applied communication protocols for multi-tier and multi-site production planning of TFT-LCD manufacturing. However, to the authors' best knowledge, there is still no research investigating how to integrate demand forecast activities across collaborative manufacturing companies.

2.4 Supply and demand in the market

Many unexpected costs (e.g., late shipments, unhappy customers, too much inventory, lengthy lead time, and excess manufacturing costs) could occur when demand and supply are not balanced at the volume and the mix levels (Wallace and Stahl, 2002). In a supply network, the demand information is forecasted by the downstream company, whereas the supply information is forecasted by the upstream company. It becomes more complex when the forecasting activities are performed by companies along multiple tiers of a supply chain. Excess demand or excess supply in the market largely affects the activities of collaborative forecasting. Hence, both market types (excess demand and excess supply) will be a classifier when we design the scenarios of collaborative forecasting.

3. COLLABORATIVE FORECASTING FRAMEWORK

3.1 Scenarios of collaborative forecasting

Variation of forecasting is associated with three factors: market type, type of focal company, and type of integration. Market type is about the balance of demand and supply of the product. There are three kinds of market types: balanced, excess demand, and excess supply. This research focuses only on excess demand and excess supply. Lambert and Cooper (Lambert and Cooper, 2000) specify the existence of a focal company in a supply chain (network). A focal company is the most influential company in a collaborative network. It is of three types (a retailer, a manufacturer, or a supplier). However, an influential focal company may not be powerful enough to obtain detailed forecasting information from the other participating companies, unless the focal company can control the other participating companies by acquisition or some other marketing strategies. The third factor, type of integration, is to explain such a condition. If the other companies are controllable, the type of integration is integrated. Otherwise, it is disintegrated.

Based on the three factors, twelve scenarios can be developed, as shown in Figure 1.

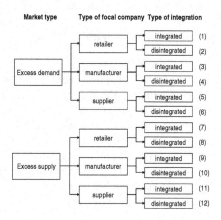

Figure 1 – Twelve scenarios of collaborative forecasting

3.2 Protocol modules

In order to correspond with the twelve scenarios, forecast-related production information is further classified into three types: general, expanded, and advanced. General type of production information is applied when only limited information is required for decision. For example, in a market of excess demand each company will only require sending an overall demand to its upstream companies. Expanded type of production information is applied when additional information is required. For example, in a market of excess supply an upstream company will require specific information regarding each product (e.g., due date, specifications, quantity, etc.), so inventory can be minimized. Advanced type of production information is applied when further sales and shipping plan are required for decision. This kind of production information is required when the companies are under high pressure of cost control in the operation. Table 1 shows the protocol modules that have been defined in this research in four categories. Each protocol module is defined by an icon for better visualization and a set of messages that will be applied in protocols.

Table 1– Protocol modules for protocols of collaborative forecasting

Category	Protocol module	Icon	Message	Direction
Order	General order forecast	G	customer/order ID/ product/overall demand /inventory/due date	Upwards (from retailer to manufacturer or from manufacturer to Supplier)
	Expanded order forecast	E	customer/order ID/ product/individual demand/inventory/due date	
	Advanced order forecast	A	customer/order ID/ product/sales plan/ individual demand/ inventory/due date	
Market	General market information	G	customer/order ID/ product/overall demand/ new market information/ inventory/due date	Upwards (from retailer to manufacturer or from manufacturer to Supplier)
	Expanded market information	E	customer/order ID/product/individual demand/new market information/inventory/due date	
	Advanced market information	A	customer/order ID/product/individual demand/new market information/sales plan/ individual demand/new market information/ inventory/due date/	
Reply	General order acceptable	G	replier/order ID/product/date	Downwards (from manufacturer to retailer or from supplier to manufacturer)
	Advanced order acceptable	A	replier/order ID/product/ date/inventory/delivery plan	
	General partial order acceptable	GP	replier/order ID/product/ date/promised quantity	
	Advanced partial order acceptable	AP	replier/order ID/product/ date/inventory/promised quantity/delivery plan/	
Other	invitation		sender/ *"request for a forecast"*	Sender to invitee

Each protocol module is specified by detailed message passing. Through the modified sequence diagram (Odell, et al., 2000), each protocol module is defined as the example in Figure 2. Figure 2 shows protocol module of general order forecast.

It is a simple protocol that sending general order forecast from the retailer to the manufacturer. After receiving the information, the manufacturer simply store the information and then feedback a success or failure message about receiving the forecast information back to the retailer. Due to space limit, the other ten protocol modules are not shown.

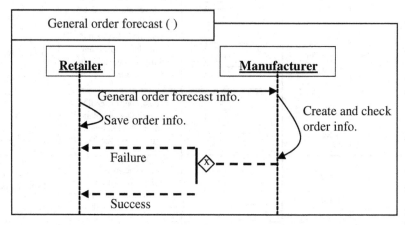

Figure 2 – Protocol module of general order forecast

3.3 Protocols

Due to the space limit of the article, only three scenarios (Nos. 1, 12, and 3 in Figure 1) and their corresponding protocols are introduced.

Scenario No. 1
Figure 3 shows a protocol that is applied for the following scenario. The scenario is separated into two phases: (1) regular forecast and (2) forecast update.

In the beginning of Phase (1), the retailer (focal company) sends a demand forecast to the manufacturers. Since the market type is excess demand, only simple information (products and overall demands) are required in the message transmission. When a manufacturer receives the forecast, it makes a plan for materials and capacity, so further inventory replenishment plan can be made. Based on the inventory replenishment plan, each manufacturer can send a demand forecast for the materials (including the forecast from the retailer) to the suppliers. When a supplier receives the forecasts from the downstream companies, it sends an acceptance message back. Due to the characteristics of excess demand, the supplier basically will try to meet the demand and apply the protocol module of *general acceptable order* to send back the acceptance information to the manufacturer. When a manufacturer receives the information from the supplier, it actives the *advanced partial-acceptable order* to give information to the retailer about the quantity of the products it can deliver. The retailer may inform some other associated manufacturers about its forecast. Therefore, further information is transmitted to the manufacturers accordingly.

However, market demand is fluctuating. Therefore, forecast should be updated. Phase (2) is applied to perform the update throughout the collaborative network. The major objective of Phase (2) is to provide a consistent forecast for the participating companies. Phase (2) starts when the retailer (focal company) creates an update on the forecast. The update affects the upstream companies. Hence, it has to be transmitted upwards for updating each participant's forecast. Further acknowledgements by protocol module *general acceptable module* are sent back to the retailer accordingly.

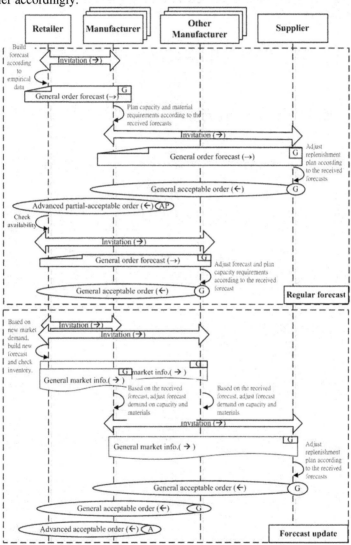

Figure 3 – Protocol for Scenario No. 1

Scenario No. 12

An opposite scenario (Scenario No. 12) to Scenario No. 1 is shown in Figure 4. In Phase (1) of the protocol, the supplier invites the downstream companies to participate in the forecasting. Then, the retailer gives the *general order forecast* to its neighboring upstream partner. Since the supplier is unable to integrate the downstream partners, the upstream partners (including the retailer) only need to apply *general order forecast* protocol module. Similarly, each participant sends *general order forecast* upwards. When the supplier receives the forecasts, it decides the replenishment plan and actuates *general order accept* protocol module to sends an agreement downwards to the participants. Phase (2) is similar to Phase (1) except that this portion of the protocol is activated by the retailer to adjust the forecast made in Phase (1).

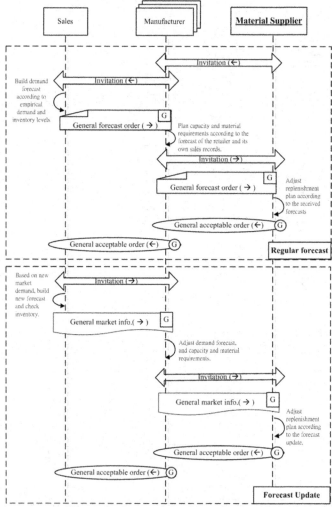

Figure 4 – Protocol for Scenario No. 12

Scenario No. 3

The third scenario (Scenario No. 3) in Figure 5 is about an excess demand market, within which the manufacturer is the focal company. The manufacturer is able to integrate the upstream and downstream partners. In this scenario, because the manufacturer can control other companies, the retailer activates an *expanded order forecast* protocol model in the beginning to deliver more detailed forecast information to the manufacturer. After receiving the forecast from the retailer, the manufacturer may proceed its forecasts based on its available capacity and materials in the inventories. Then, the forecasts are sent to its outsourcers (some other manufacturers) and suppliers. The outsourcers and suppliers can make their forecast accordingly and feedback their forecasts. It should be noted that the supplier should applied the *advanced acceptable order* protocol module to feedback detailed forecast, because the manufacturer is the integrated company. Similar interactions in Phase (2) will be proceeded when the retailer updates the forecasts according to the condition changes of the market.

4. SYSTEM DEPLOYMENT

This research deploys the protocols into a collaborative manufacturing network through internet, as shown in Figure 6. The collaborative manufacturing network consists of four participating companies: a retailer, two manufacturers, and a supplier. Each participant has two interfaces (developed by Java language), one for sending messages and one for receiving messages. Figure 7 shows an example of how a manufacturer interacts with its supplier. The left panel shows the manufacturer is expecting a demand of 200 units in day 23. It has 100 units in the inventory. By applying the *general order forecast* protocol module, it sends the forecast to the supplier. When the supplier receives the information, it agrees with the demand of 200 units. Then, it freezes the demand until day 20. It also has 100 units in the inventory. The information is entered into the right panel in Figure 7 and sends to the manufacturer by the protocol module of *general acceptable module*.

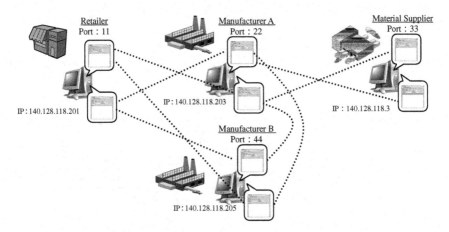

Figure 6 – Protocol deployment for four companies

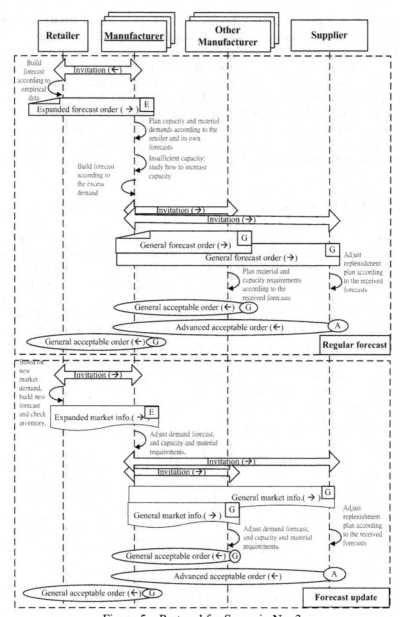

Figure 5 – Protocol for Scenario No. 3

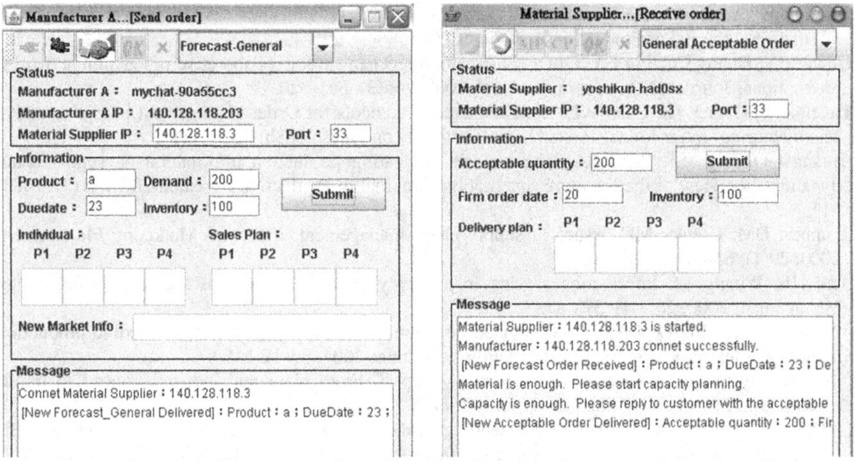

Figure 7 – Two illustrative interfaces (left: manufacturer; right: supplier)

5. CONCLUSIONS AND FUTURE RESEARCH

Information sharing among collaborative manufacturing companies is beneficial. However, to share forecast information is not easy for many reasons (autonomy and privacy of local companies, etc.). This research intends to provide communication protocols for collaborative forecasting. Only limited information is required to be shared with other partners for the collaboration. Hence, autonomy and willingness of collaboration for the participating companies will increase for collaborative forecasting. Twelve protocols are developed in accordance with the market type, type of focal company, and type of integration. An information system is also developed to deploy the protocols.

The future research based on this research could be (1) to realize the protocols in the real world applications and (2) to develop an evaluation model to justify the value of the protocols.

6. ACKNOWLEDGEENTS

The authors would like to thank the financial support from the research project NSC 95-2221-E-029-031, National Science Council, Taiwan.

7. REFERENCES

1. Abreu A, Camarinha-Matos LM. On the role of value systems to promote the sustainability of collaborative environments. International Journal of Production Research 2008; 46(5): 1207-29.
2. Cachon GP, Lariviere MA. Contracting to assure supply: How to share demand forecasts in a supply chain. Management Science 2001; 47(5): 629-46.
3. Chen WL, Huang CY, Lai YC. Multi-tier and multi-site collaborative production: Illustrated by a case example of TFT-LCD manufacturing. Computers & Industrial Engineering 2008; To appear.

4. Hammami A, Burlat P, Campagne JP. Evaluating orders allocation within networks of firms. International Journal of Production Economics 2003; 86(3): 233-49.
5. Huang CY, Huang CC, Liu CY. Order confirmation mechanism for collaborative production networks. International Journal of Production Research 2008a; 46(3): 595-620.
6. Huang CY, Huang TS, Chen WL. Communication Protocols for Order Management in Collaborative Manufacturing. International Journal of Production Economics 2008b; To appear.
7. Huang GQ, Lau JSK, Mak KL. The impacts of sharing production information on supply chain dynamics: a review of the literature. International Journal of Production Research 2003; 41(7): 1483-517.
8. Lambert DM, Cooper MC. Issues in supply chain management. Industrial Marketing Management 2000; 29(1): 65-83.
9. Lee HL, Whang SJ. Information sharing in a supply chain. International Journal of Technology Management 2000; 20(3-4): 373-87.
10. Neubert R, Gorlitz O, Teich T. Automated negotiations of supply contracts for flexible production networks. International Journal of Production Economics 2004; 89(2): 175-87.
11. Nof SY, Morel G, Monostori L, Molina A, Filip F. From plant and logistics control to multi-enterprise collaboration. Annual Reviews in Control 2006; 30(1): 55-68.
12. Odell J, Parunak HVD, Bauer B. Extending UML for agents Proceedings of the 2nd Int. Bi-Conference Workshop on Agent-Oriented Information Systems, AOIS'00 Austin (USA), 2000:3-17.
13. Sauer J. Modeling and solving multi-site scheduling problems. In: W. van Wezel, R.J. Jorna, Meystel AM, eds. Planning in Intelligent Systems: Aspects, Motivations and Methods Hoboken, NJ: John Wiley & Sons, 2006:281-99.
14. Wallace TF, Stahl RA. Sales forecasting : a new approach : why and how to emphasize teamwork, not formulas, forecast less, not more, focus on process improvement, not forecast accuracy. Cincinnati, Ohio: T.F. Wallace & Co., 2002.
15. Xu KF, Dong Y, Evers PT. Towards better coordination of the supply chain. Transportation Research Part E-Logistics and Transportation Review 2001; 37(1): 35-54.
16. Zhao XD, Xie JX. Forecasting errors and the value of information sharing in a supply chain. International Journal of Production Research 2002; 40(2): 311-35.

PART 10

AFFECTIVE COMPUTING AND CULTURAL ISSUES

AFFECTIVE COMPUTING AND COLLABORATIVE NETWORKS: TOWARDS EMOTION-AWARE INTERACTION

32

Andrej Luneski
South-East European Research Centre, Thessaloniki, GREECE, anluneski@seerc.org
Roger K. Moore
The University of Sheffield, UK, r.k.moore@dcs.shef.ac.uk

Affective computing is a young field of research that interconnects many different domains and has a range of important applications. However, little attention has been given to the employment of affective computing in collaborative networks. This paper examines the possible challenges for 'injecting' emotion-awareness into collaborative networks with a view to improving the effectiveness, motivation and naturalness in the communication between their members. Moreover, by observing the state of the art in affective computing, we present certain needs and benefits (why) as well as possible approaches (how) to the application of affective computing technologies in collaborative networks, with the focus on affective interaction.

1. INTRODUCTION

The constant and rapid evolution of information and communication technologies has enabled efficient and effective collaboration among geographically dispersed networks of people. In particular, recent years have witnessed the appearance of a range of virtual communities, virtual organizations, virtual enterprises and other types of 'collaborative networks' (CNs) (Camarinha-Matos, 2005). Since its introduction as a new scientific discipline, CN is facing many challenges primarily focused on the improvement of the collaboration process. Apart from efficiency, both the business and the scientific communities desire naturalness in their communications.

Nowadays, intelligent, natural and effective interaction is considered to be one that incorporates the recognition and expression of emotion, i.e. affective interaction (Salovey, 1990). However, emotions were formerly considered as an exceptional human ability that gets in the way of effective and intelligent human communication and is undesirable for rational behaviour (Goleman, 1995). As a result, emotions have only recently entered into the spectrum of attractive and significant research topics. A principal reason for this is a growing appreciation of the strong interconnection between human emotions and intelligence (Salovey, 1990, Goleman, 1995). Indeed, the realisation of the significance of emotions in the expression of intelligence gave birth to the term 'emotional intelligence', defined as "the capacity to understand emotional information and to reason with emotions" (Salovey, 1990).

Affective computing (AC) is the scientific discipline that is concerned with emotional interactions performed with and through computers (Picard, 1997). Picard

Please use the following format when citing this chapter:

Luneski, A. and Moore, R.K., 2008, in IFIP International Federation for Information Processing, Volume 283; *Pervasive Collaborative Networks*; Luis M. Camarinha-Matos, Willy Picard; (Boston: Springer), pp. 315–322.

(1997) defines AC as "computing that relates to, arises from, or deliberately influences emotions". In fact, AC is an interdisciplinary field that introduces new domains and applications mostly, but not exclusively, related to advanced human-computer interaction (HCI). Affective HCI assumes that the computer is emotion-aware, i.e. it is both able to recognise emotions and to intelligently or appropriately express them. In the investigation of possible application areas of AC, researchers have recently been interested in virtual environments, communities and networks, among others (ref), although not much has been achieved so far.

This paper discusses the main challenges arising from the application of AC technologies in the sphere of collaborative networks. By presenting the key aspects and the state-of-the-art in AC, we examine possible future directions and fields where emotion-aware and emotionally-intelligent technologies might provide particular gains. Moreover, the paper investigates the need (why) of affective interaction in CN, the benefits arising from 'injecting' emotions into the communication channels and the possible approaches (how) towards the application of affective computing technologies in collaborative networks, with focus on affective interaction.

2. NEED FOR AFFECTIVE INTERACTION IN CN

Emoticons have been used as a tool for the 'graphical' representation of the emotion hidden behind a textual message, and their extensive usage (whether in a form of a simple smile or a 3D cartoon avatar) provides clear evidence that people feel the need to convey their emotions to the other party in their communications. Therefore, it is argued that the nature of human expression requires an 'injection' of emotions into the communication in CN platforms.

In order to understand what CN might gain from affective interaction[1], we first have to examine the impact of emotions on some key aspects of human forms of communication and collaboration. In particular, emotions directly influence human physical and especially mental states and this in turn has an impact on the performance in CN. The very principal underlying any type of CN is the improvement of communication within networks where people with mutual goals are striving to come up with the best output collaboratively. The quality of the collaboration and the output might directly depend on the creativity of the members of a CN. According to the 'broaden-and-build model' (Fredrickson, 2003), positive emotions play a key role in increasing an individual's creativity. Moreover, emotions can control the motivation for achieving goals (Cooper et al, 2000; Parkinson 1995; Brewer, 2004) as well as improving a person's problem solving ability (Damasio, 1994). A person in a happy state is most likely to accomplish their pre-set goals, and will perform better than if they were in a negative emotional state such as anger or depression. Affective interaction could be used as a positive instrument to create emotional-awareness between the members of a CN.

---

[1] The term 'affective interaction' often refers to human-human interaction. When discussing CN, affective interaction includes any computer-related interaction i.e. computer-mediated human-human, computer-generated or computer-interpreted interaction.

Additionally, it can help in the discovery of methods for increasing the level of performance, creativity and motivation inside a CN.

Many researchers consider empathy to be a strong mechanism for reducing frustration and generally improving the emotional state and mood (Hone, 2006; Klein et al., 2002). We argue here that empathy is one of the missing aspects that differentiate communication in CNs from direct physical human-human interaction. With affective interaction, users are capable of expressing their empathy towards other CN participants (empathic interaction), thereby increasing the closeness and the levels of trust between CN members.

The naturalness of the affective communication process brings about increased interactiveness and, by focusing on the CN participant's involvement, it sets the base for the sense of "social presence". Social presence was introduced by Shoer et al and is defined as "the salience of the other in a mediated communication and the consequent salience of their interpersonal interactions" (Shoer et al, 1976). The expression of emotion, feelings, and mood in a mediated interaction has been considered as a defining characteristic of social presence (Garrison et al., 2000). The notion of social presence in CNs can be realised with ubiquitous computing where the computer still acts as a mediator in the communication but it is demilitarised as a single entity i.e. the participants do not 'notice' the computer-mediation process. This issue is further discussed later in the paper.

Furthermore, a CN is described as a network of entities that are "geographically dispersed and "heterogeneous in terms of their...culture..." (Camarinha-Matos, 2006). There are many theories that support the notion of universal emotions, according to which emotions are expressed in the same manner, regardless of the cultural diversities (Ekman, 1972, Mesquita,1992, Plutchik, 2001). If these theories are adopted in the domain of CN, emotional expression and interaction might bridge the potential cultural or even the social gap between the diverse entities in a CN.

In summary, affective interaction, as a new and more advanced type of interaction, can bring about a certain level of excitement to CN participants, as well as, change the whole perception between them.

3. EMOTION AWARENESS AND INTELLIGENT EMOTIONAL EXPRESSIVNESS IN A CN

In affective communication there is a need for emotion-awareness and emotionally intelligent expressiveness. Awareness is known to play a crucial role in a collaborative environment i.e. people need to be 'aware' of each other in such an environment in terms of their intentions, general feelings, influence on the shared workspace etc. (Garcia et al, 1999). Since we are concerned with computer-mediated affective interaction, the computer[2] has to posses the ability of emotion-awareness and through emotion expressiveness to enable users to be aware of the emotional state of others. In other words, it has to be aware of the emotional state of the user

---

[2] By computer we mean the communication mediator (it does not necessarily refer to the notion of a desktop computer)

on one side of the communication (input), interpret, transmit and, on the other side, express it in an emotionally intelligent and effective manner.

Emotional input can be comprised of one, or preferably a combination of all, channels and from the different input forms a clear interpretation/specification of emotional state has to be obtained. Additionally, that emotion specification is expressed in one or a combination of emotional output channels. Therefore, when referring to emotion-awareness and emotional intelligence in CNs we are focusing on the computer means for exhibiting these capabilities. In order to do so, the computer has to be equipped with AC mechanisms and technologies.

3.1. Emotion awareness

The complexity of the emotion has been studied for a long time and researchers still debate on the theory(s) that most appropriately describes this 'human ability'. One group of researchers state that there exists a set of basic emotions or emotion categories, such as anger, fear, joy, sadness, disgust etc. (Plutchik, 1990; Ekman, 1971). Others use the 'dimensional approach' for describing affective space emotions, where emotions are represented through values in an n-dimensional space (Scholesberg, 1954; Lang et al, 1997). The affective space typically consists of two dimensions: arousal (calm/excited) and valence (negative/positive). Furthermore, there have been many studies and debates on the affective states that a person can experience and the channels through which those states are expressed to the outer world. For an affective communication in CN we are interested in the most proper communicative channels of emotion, through which the user can portray to the computer and through which the computer can identify the emotional state of the user. This is not exclusive to the output/expressive channels (since the internal physiological reactions to emotions are not necessarily visible by others). Mainly, emotions are communicated/expressed vocally, through facial expressions and through gestures (Clynes 1977; Planalp, 1999). Additionally, through specific sensors the computer can identify the emotions form physiological signals (Bauer, 1998).

Vocal Emotion Communication. Human speech caries emotional information in the semantics and in the speech prosody. While semantics (what has been said) is a more obvious expression of emotion, prosody holds more detailed emotional information. Prosody combines nonsemantic cues in spoken language, such as: fundamental frequency (pitch), loudness, rhythm, formant structure of speech sounds, intonation etc. An extensive research has been done on affect encoding and decoding in vocal communication (Banse, 1996; Cowie and Douglas-Cowie, 1996; Bachorowski 1999). See (Scherer, 2003) for more comprehensive review. Generally studies have been oriented in recognition of six basic emotions (anger, joy sadness, fear, disgust and surprise) from speech and significant results have been reached (Yu et al, 2001; Dealert et al, 1996; Nogueiras et al, 2001). The average success rate in the recognition process is between 70% and 80%, which is higher that the human recognition rate of around 60%.

Affective facial expressions and gestures

Facial expression are mostly used by humans in identifying certain emotional categories due to the distinct facial expressions for the "universal" human emotions such as happiness, anger, sadness, surprise, fear and disgust (Ekman, 1972).

Body gestures play a vital role in conveying human emotional states, and due to the high variability of the emotional body posture and gesture facial expression are strongly influenced by the concurrently presented body language (Ambady, 1992; Meeren, 2005).

Affective psychophysiology. Most of the disturbance caused by a certain emotion influences the internal physiology of the human body (alteration of brain states, increase of the heart-beat rate, hands sweating, (face) muscle movements, increase of the respiration rate etc). Monitoring these types of emotional expressions requires employment of specific sensors and recordings of their output such as Electroencephalogram (EEG), Electrocardiogram (ECG), Skin Conductnce or Electrodermal Activity (EDA), Electromyogram (EMG) etc. The usage of physiological signals in identifying a user's emotional state has became popular in recent years due to the advanced development and availability of unobtrusive sensors that can provide constant and reliable monitoring of a user's internal emotional reaction (Picard, 1997). Physiological sensors have been integrated into clothing and jewellery; skin conductivity sensor in shoes, blood volume pressure sensor in earrings, respiration sensor in a sports bra and numerous others (Picard, 2001). Bamidis et al have proposed a multi-channel framework for experimenting with physiological sensing of human emotion (Bamidis et al, 2007).

3.2 Emotionally expressiveness

Human-like and emotional intelligence is the key factor that is required in the computer for the user to feel that is engaged into a natural, intelligent and realistic communication. In a CN, the computer acts as a representation of the person on the other side of the communication. As such, not only it has to provide the best possible interpretation of the other person, but it should provide additional information that may assist the user in connecting better with that representation as if it were the other person. Going along with this requirement is the belief of philosophers and psychologists that "what matters in human-human interaction is the individual's subjective belief about each other, not the objective truth of the interaction" (Bailenson et al, 2000). Computer appearance is one of the principal design issues for emotional expression; it has to provide the user with an interface similar to a face-to-face interaction (Picard, 1997).

Avatars have been used as a visual representation of human characters for more natural human-computer interaction. They are seen as "the physical representation of the self in virtual reality" (Castronova, 2003). Moreover, emotional interaction through avatars has already been seen in collaborative virtual environments and other types of collaborative systems (Fabri, 2005; Garcia, 1999; Selvarajah, 2005). Studies have shown that users interact with avatars as with other human beings (Bailenson, 2005). Since the intention of the avatar is to visually represent a human character, emotional expressiveness would require adoption of all the principles behind the human visual emotional expressiveness. More specifically, the relation between emotions and facial expressions, as well as, body gestures, as described in the previous section. Apart from the visual, emotions can be expressed through affective synthetic speech.

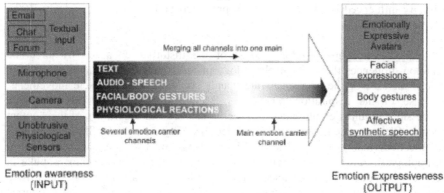

Figure 1 - Affective Interaction in CN

4. DISCUSSION

The main aim of this paper was to review the needs and significance of emotions in human interaction, and the key aspects of affective interaction in CN, based on the facts in the existing literature. We have discussed the impact of emotions on human rational behaviour in CN, as environments with computer-mediated interaction human-human interaction. By presenting the key aspects of affective computing in relation to affective interaction we merely described possible application mechanism of affective computing in CN. CN as an interdisciplinary topic includes many domains that can benefit from affective interaction and emotion-awareness among the participants. Imagine a scenario where tasks or projects have to be appointed to team/group members. If the delegator knows which team member is mostly excited or motivated for a specific task, a most effective delegation would be achieved and the team could have greater success. Moreover, decision support and group conflict mechanism can be constructed, based on emotional interaction, which could be used in electronic meetings inside CN (Garcia, 1999).

Collaborative Innovation Network (CoIN) is a type of CN defined as "a cyberteam of self-motivated people with a collective vision, enabled by the Web to collaborate in achieving a common goal by sharing ideas, information, and work" (Gloor, 2005). Affective interaction is specifically important for CoIN since it is a non-hierarchical CN with principles based on honesty, trust, innovation, creativity motivation, transparency and closeness.

5. REFERENCES

Ambady N, Rosenthal, R. "Thin slices of expressive behaviour as predictors of interpersonal consequences: A meta-analysis". Psychological Bulletin, 1992; 111(2). Pp 256–274.

Bachorowski JA. "Vocal expression and perception of emotion". Current direct. Psychol. Sci., 1999; 8 (2), pp 53-57.

Bailenson J, Beall A, Blascovich J, Raimundo M, Weishbush M. "Intelligent agents who wear your face: User's reactions to the virtual self". Technical Report. Center for the Virtual Environment and Behaviors, Department of Psychology, University of California, Santa Barbara, 2000.

Bamidis PD, Luneski A, Vivas A, Papadelis C, Maglaveras N, Pappas C. "Multi-channel physiological sensing of human emotion: insights into Emotion-Aware Computing using Affective Protocols, Avatars and Emotion Specifications". In Proceedings of Medinfo 2007. Brisbane, Australia. pp 1068-72.

Banse R, Scherer KR. "Acoustic profiles in vocal emotion expression". J. Pers. Soc. Psychol, 1996; 70 (3). Pp 614-636.

Burgoon JK et al. "Augmenting human identification of emotional states in video. In *International Conference on Intelligent Data Analysis*, 2005.

Bauer RM. "Physiologic Measures of Emotion". Journal of Clinical Neurophysiology: 15(5), 1998. pp 388-396.

Brewer MB, Hewstone M, Emotion and Motivation: Perspectives on Social Psychology, Blackwell Publishing, 2004.

Camarinha-Matos LM, Afsarmanesh H. "Collaborative Networks: A New Scientific Disipline", Journal of Intelligent Manufacturing: 16 (4-5),2005. pp 439-452, 2005.

Camarinha-Matos L, Afsarmanesh H, "Collaborative networks: Value creation in a knowledge society", In: PROLAMAT 2006, IFIP Int. Conf. On Knowledge Enterprise – New Challenges, Shanghai (CH), 2006.

Castronova E. "Theory of the Avatar". CESifo Working Paper Series No. 863, Fevruaty 2003.

Clynes M., "The Touch of Emotions",.Anchor Press/Double Day, 1977.

Cooper B, Brna P, Martins A. "Effective Affective in Intelligent Systems – Building on Evidence of Empathy in Teaching and Learning". in Ana Paiva (Ed.) Affective Interactions: Towards a New Generation of Computer Interfaces. Springer Verlag, 2000. pp 21-34.

Cowie R, Douglas-Cowie E. "Automatic statistical analysis of the signal and prosodic signs of emotion in speech", In: Proc. ICSLP_96, Philadelphia, 1996. pp. 1989-1992.

Damasio A. Descarte's Error: Emotion, Reason and the Human Brain. Avon, New York, 1994.

Dellaert F, Polzin TS, Waibel A. "Recognizing emotion in speech". *Int. Conf. on Spoken Language Processing (ICSLP)*, Pittsburgh, 1996.

Ekman, P. "Universals and cultural differences in facial expressions of emotion". In J. Cole (Ed.), Nebraska Symposium on Motivation 1971; 19. Lincoln, NE: University of Nebraska Press, 1972. pp 207-283.

Fabri M, Moore DJ. "The use of emotionally expressive avatars in Collaborative Virtual Environments". in Proceedings of the AISB Symposium on Virtual Social Agents. University of Hertfordshire, UK. April 2005. pp 88-95.

Fredrickson BL. The value of positive emotions. American Scientist. 2003: 91. pp 330-335.

Garcia O, Favela J, Machorro R. "Emotional Awareness in Collaborative Systems," *spire*, p. 296, String Processing and Information Retrieval Symposium & International Workshop on Groupware, 1999.

Gloor P. Swarm Creativity: Competitive Advantage Through Collaborative Innovation Networks, 2005.

Garrison R, Anderson T, Archer W. Critical inquiry in a text-based environment: Computer conferencing in higher education, Unpublished manuscript, 2000.

Goleman D, Emotonal Intelligence, Bantham Books, New York, NY, 1995.

Hone K. "Empathic Agents to Reduce User Frustration: The Effects of Varying Agent Characteristics", Interacting with Computers, 2006; 18 (2), pp 227-245.

Kapoor A, Picard RW. "Multimodal affect recognition in learning environments". In *ACM International Conference on Multimedia*, 2005.

Klein J, Moon Y, Picard RW. "This computer responds to user frustration: theory, design and results". Interacting with Computers, vol. 14, issue 2, pp. 119-140, 2002

Lang, PJ, Bradley MM, Cuthbert BN. 1997). "Motivated attention: affect, activation and action". In Attention and orienting: sensory and motivational processes, P. J. Lang, R. F. Balaban ed. Hillsdale, NJ: Lawrence Erlbaum Associates, Inc, 1997. pp 97-134.

Mesquita B, Frijda, NH. "Cultural variations in emotions: A review". Psychological Bulletin; 112, 1992. pp 179-204.

Meeren H, Heijnsbergen C, Gelder B. "Rapid perceptual integration of facial expression and emotional body language". Procedings of the National Academy of Sciences of USA, 2005; 102(45): pp 16518–16523.

Nogueiras A, Moreno A, Bonafonte A, Mariño JB. "Speech emotion recognition using hidden markov models". In *Proceedings of Eurospeech*, Aalborg, Denmark, 2001.

Parkinson B, Colman AM. Emotion and Motivation. Longman, London, UK, 1995.

Planalp S. Communicating Emotion: Social, Moral, and Cultural Processes (Studies in Emotion and Social Interaction). Cambridge University Press, 1999.

Plutchik R, Kellerman H. "A general Psychoevolutionary theory of Emotion, in Emotion Theory, Research, and Experience". Academic Press, 1990; 1. pp 1980-1990.

Plutchik R. The nature of emotions. American Scientist, 2001; 89. pp 344, 2001.

Picard RW. "Affective Medicine: Technology with Emotional Intelligence". In Future of Health Technology, R. G. Bushko ed. OIS Press, 2001.

Ravindra De Silva P, Bianchi-Berthouze N. "Modeling human affective postures: an information theoretic characterizatino of posture features". Computer Animation and Virtual Worlds, 2004;15. pp 169–276.

Salovey P, Mayer JD. "Emotional Intelligence", Imagination, Cognition and Personality 1990; 9. pp 185-221.

Scholesberg H. "Three Dimensions of Emotions", Psychological review, 1954.

Short J, Williams E, Christie B. The social psychology of telecommunications, Toronto, ON: Wiley, 1976.

Selvarajah K, Richards D. "The use of emotions to create believable agents in a virtual environment",.In Proceedings of the Fourth international Joint Conference on Autonomous Agents and Multiagent Systems-AAMAS'05, 2005.

Willyard CH, McCLees CW, ""Motorola's Technology Roadmap Process", Research Management , pp 13-19, Sept.-Oct. 1987.

Yu F, Chang E, Xu YO, Shum HY. "Emotion Detection From Speech To Enrich Multimedia Content", in the *Second IEEE Pacific-Rim Conference on Multimedia,* October 24-26, 2001, Beijing, China.

CULTURAL DETERMINANTS OF CREATING MODERN ORGANISATIONS – THE ROLE OF TRUST

33

W. M. Grudzewski
Warsaw School of Economics, Collegium of Business Administration
Correspondent Member of Polish Science Academy, POLAND
w.grudzewski@orgmasz.pl

I. K. Hejduk
Warsaw School of Economics, Collegium of Business Administration, POLAND
ihejdu@sgh.waw.pl

A. Sankowska
Warsaw University of Technology, Faculty of Production Engineering, POLAND
e-mail: amsankowska@wp.pl

M. Wańtuchowicz
Warsaw University of Technology, Faculty of Production Engineering, POLAND
e-mail: monika.wantuchowicz@wp.pl

The virtual form of organisation is the answer for turbulent and highly competitive environment and rising demands of customers. However, the theory of virtual organisation (VO) is still evolving and being systematized, similarly to its practice. Therefore, there is a focal quest to determine the conditions and circumstances favourable to creating VO. It appeared in the author's research that trust in general and trust management particularly plays the significant role in VO. The article explores the cultural determinants of VO and provides the examples of Swedish and American culture.

1. INTRODUCTION

The twentieth-first age requires adapting new organisational forms for cooperation. This is the consequence of continuous changes in turbulent and competitive environment as well as more and more demanding clients (Grudzewski, Hejduk, Sankowska and Wańtuchowicz, 2007). Many authors underline the significant role of trust in relations based on cooperation (e.g., Casson 1991, Dasgupta 1988, Gambetta 1988, Handy 1995, Lorenz 1988, Ring and Van de Ven 1992). By researchers, trust is perceived as the focal point for further discussion on components that contribute to the success of modern organisations (different forms of collaboration, e.g.: strategic alliances, and partnering networks of small- and medium-sized companies).

Virtual organisation (VO) is frequently in the centre of attention among theoreticians and practitioners of management. Currently the coherent theory is being built. Therefore, there appear many questions that still need to be answered. One of them is of focal meaning: *what are the conditions necessary for creating VO?* Cultural determinants are believed to be crucial. Hence, it is not surprising that

Please use the following format when citing this chapter:

Grudzewski, W.M., Hejduk, I.K., Sankowska, A. and Wańtuchowicz, M., 2008, in IFIP International Federation for Information Processing, Volume 283; *Pervasive Collaborative Networks*; Luis M. Camarinha-Matos, Willy Picard; (Boston: Springer), pp. 323–332.

VOs are present and active in some countries, cultures more often that in others. The United States of America and Sweden has been carefully selected to illustrate the case of VO's cultural determinants. *Nota bene*, Swedish organisations are said to be the most trustworthy all over the world (Edelman Trust Barometer, 2007). This fact is meaningful because trust is nowadays recognized as crucial and economically measurable value (Lewicka-Strzałecka, 2003). At this juncture we shall ask: *how Swedish organisations achieve so high level of trust?* And *why American organisations having similar cultural determinants are confronted by growing trust deficit?* Finally, we can infer a conclusion of great worth for other organisations all over the world - crucial for their further functioning and development. This paper is supporting the following thesis: **trust management applied in practice allows to improve the performance of organisation, above all the performance of VO**.

In this paper, we explore the cultural determinants and its importance for creating modern organisational forms – VOs in Sweden and the US. The starting points are results of our research as well as opinions of four authorities in cultural management - Charles Hampden-Turner, Fons Trompenaars, Geert Hofstede and Gert Jan Hofstede. The implication is that national culture characterizes the attitude to the category of trust.

The analysis of our results will consequently but also indirectly give the answer for the following question: *what kind of culture stimulates and fosters creating as well as functioning of modern organisations, most notably VOs?* Firstly, we will explore the specific features of both cultures – American and Swedish ones. Secondly, on the basis of our results, we will discuss the critical success factors (CSF) for creating and functioning VOs in the context of cultural determinants. We will present the visible and invisible impact of culture and culture dimensions on creating VOs in particular. In our empirical and theoretical discussion we will bring forward different opinions on the superiority of information and communication technologies (ICT) over culture with reference to VO functioning.

2. SWEDISH CULTURE *VERSUS* AMERICAN CULTURE

2.1 Organisational culture and trust management

Culture determines the patterns of behaviors, defines situations and their perception. It diversifies the view of the world and actions taken by individuals (organisations). Among theoreticians as well as practitioners there is disagreement about the importance of technology and culture. On the one hand, technology is considered as the hard core of every organisation. On the other hand, technology and its products are said to contribute to any fundamental value changes. However, we strongly believe that culture creates the context for technology. Organisational changes rather refer to applied practices (Hofstede and Hofstede, 2007, p. 25). In those circumstances, exploring culture in VO is well-grounded and required (see Figure 1).

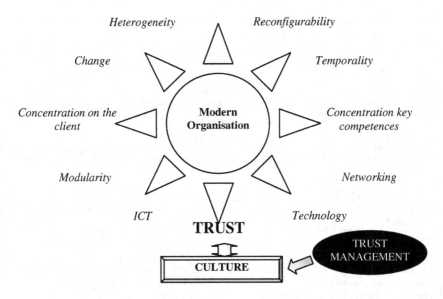

Figure 1 - Characteristics of modern organisation *via* culture

There are at least eleven features of the modern organisation (see Figure 1). Trust determined by culture is an unambiguous characteristic of virtual collaboration in the light of existing theory as well as empirical results from real VOs (see e.g.: Handy, 1995, Grudzewski, Hejduk, Sankowska and Wańtuchowicz, 2007). Therefore, there is no doubt about the rising role of **the most recent management method – trust management** – initiated and disseminated in management sciences by Grudzewski, Hejduk, Sankowska and Wańtuchowicz (2007, 2008).

2.2 Characteristic of Swedish and American cultures

According to French sociologist Pierre Bourdieu culture is collective programming of the mind that allows to distinguish members of one specific group or category of people (Hofstede and Hofstede, 2007, p. 17). Culture profile is similar in Sweden and the USA. The wealth hoarding system is based on universalism, analysis, individualism, external controllability, gained status, equality and sequentiality. Swedish culture is bearing a close resembling to American one in six from seven categories. The only difference is in control location: internal or external. External controllability of Swedes is coming from their strong dependence on nature, severe climate and export.

In principle, Swedish and American cultures are two most similar cultures in comparison to other cultures (Hampden-Turner and Trompenaars, 2006/1993). Table 1 presents the wealth building values in Sweden, the US and other countries according to Hampden-Turner and Trompenaars[1] (2006/1993):

---

[1] Different classification was proposed by Hofstede: power distance (from small to large), collectivism – individualism, femininity - masculinity, avoidance of the uncertainty (from weak to strong).

Table 1 – Seven dimensions of culture in different countries according to Hampden-Turner and Trompenaars

INDIVIDUALISM	COLLECTIVISM
personal freedom, human rights, competitiveness	social responsibility, harmonious relations, collaboration
The United States, Sweden	**France, Japan, Germany**
SEQUENTIALITY	**SYNCHRONOUSNESS**
keeping with scheduled course	tasks coordinating
The United States, Sweden	**Japan, France**
GAINED STATUS	**ASCRIPTIONS STATUS**
what we did, our results	who we are, our potential, connections
The United States, Sweden, Germany	**France, Japan**
UNIVERSALISM	**PARTICULARISM**
rules, codes of law and generalization	exceptions, special conditions, unique relations
The United States, Sweden, Germany	**France, Japan, Germany**
FRAGMENTATION	**ENTIRENESS**
atomization, reduction, analysis, objectivism	holism, polishing, synthesis, relation ability
The United States, Sweden	**France, Japan, Germany**
INTERNAL CONTROLLABILITY	**EXTERNAL CONTROLLABILITY**
conscience and internal beliefs	patterns and factors influencing from outside
The United States, France, Germany	*Sweden*, **Japan**
EQUALITY	**HIERARCHY**
The United States, Sweden, Germany	**France, Japan**

Individualism characterizes individuals that build loose relationships, concentrating on themselves and their families (Hofstede and Hofstede, 2007, p. 88). Swedish individualism is very unique and differs a lot from American one. Swedes are individualistic, aware of their own identity, exceptionality, freedom, aspirations and values and in the same time they are modest and aware of their social duties. They emphasize that source of their own satisfaction and destinies are support and help in development of others. They perfectly deal with dilemma of bringing together individualism with social duties. Moral rights are understood like voluntary agreement denominating rules of conduct and cooperation. Hampden-Turner and Trompenaars (2006/1993) call this socialized individualism.

Swedes and Americans represent sequential culture. It means a race against time. Tasks need to be done faster and faster, using high-tech machines and production lines. In this context, VO - *ad hoc* form of collaboration created dynamically, in short period of time – beyond doubt is the best solution.

Logic of building virtual collaboration is founded on equality of partners. It is assessed *via* its results, using category of achievements. **Universalism** warrants acceptance as well as dissemination of framework of reality view, regardless of situation and particular interests - which in new alliances secure acknowledgement of rules and norms as binding - and recognizing all collaborants equally regardless of their group affiliation. As a consequence, activities become more predictable. Rejecting hierarchy, injecting equality are promoting trust in accordance with theory of "liking those who are similar to ourselves" (Grudzewski, Hejduk, Sankowska, Wańtuchowicz, 2007) what was confirmed in the last survey by Edelman in 2007. **Particularism** interprets activities differently according as groups to which individual belongs to. Furthermore, it conduces to building trust in small group to which belongs individual (e.g.: family, mafia, organisation clique) and mistrust towards individuals from other groups. Social trust originates from universalism while particular trust from particularism (see Figure 2).

Equality between collaborants is crucial issue for building trust atmosphere. Employees tend to trust people similar to themselves rather than CEO. Simple worker are granted higher level of trust than CEO. Outsiders, for instance: financial analysts, scientific and didactic workers, win high level of trust (Edelman, 2007). It has focal meaning when building effective leadership, internal as well as external communication plan.

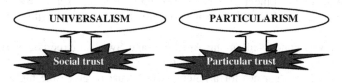

Figure 2 – Two different types of trust induced by universalism and particularism

It becomes visible that Americans and Swedes belong to different cultures which are characterized by high level of trust. They can be described as **trust cultures** – *in society there are common rules that impose to recognize trust and reliability as values, trust in others and meeting the obligations as norms of appropriate conduct* (Sztompka, 2007). In other words, we can generally trust others.

Trust is believed to be the critical success factor in the opinion of Swedish and American experts according to research by Grudzewski, Hejduk, Sankowska and Wańtuchowicz in 2006 and 2007 (see Figure 3). The most important CSFs are: honesty and clearness of communication (Swedish experts) and trust (American experts). At first glance the results seem to be totally disparate. Nevertheless, careful analysis leads us to *modus vivendi* between those two indications. Honesty and clearness of communication is the focal element of trust building process, precondition of trust atmosphere between collaborating parties (more details: Grudzewski, Hejduk, Sankowska and Wańtuchowicz, Zarządzanie zaufaniem w organizacjach wirtualnych, 2007 and Trust Management in Virtual Work Environments: A Human Factors Perspective, 2008). *Trust management* (Grudzewski, Hejduk, Sankowska and Wańtuchowicz, 2008, p. 37) *covers the activities of creating systems and methods that:*

1. Allow relying parties to make assessments and decisions regarding the dependability of potential transactions involving risk
2. Allow players and system owners to increase and correctly represent the reliability of themselves and their systems.

The highest rank was given to communication issues from strong deprootedness of trust in Swedish culture. Swedish culture belongs to the one of the most trusting cultures all over the world. It is corroborated by for example the roots of word *trust* that is probably of Scandinavian origin, akin to the Old Norse *traust* (Grudzewski, Hejduk, Sankowska and Wańtuchowicz, 2008, p. 22).

2.3 Critical success factors ranking by Swedish and American experts

Hence, we can ascertain that trust is part of Swedish culture foundation. In the same time, in American culture trust is derived from trust to law institution. Therefore, we assume that the best patterns of trust can be drawn from Scandinavian culture where trust is rather a culture norm than a law norm. Furthermore, it probably influenced penal code that we lighter compared with other countries. In cultures with law-rooted trust the first factors stopping from breaking the law are harshness and inevitability of a punishment. It is not surprising that the last survey by Edelman in 2007 announced that Swedish organisation are the most trustworthy all over the world.

A survey was conducted among American and Swedish experts experienced in intercollaboration. From 48 initial factors that are believed to impact the decision to select or not select a partner for a potential VO, trust received the highest sum of ranks given by experts. Each factor could receive 44 points maximally. Trust was ranked highest among 10 critical success factors for VOs with the highest sum of ranks.

The experts' survey (see Figure 3) allows us to indicate rare supplies based on the ranking of the CSFs. Moreover, we concede that American and Polish cultures are characterized by the scarcity of trust comparing to Swedish one. Consequently, it is rare supply in economy[2].

Ranking position	Critical success factors by Swedish experts.		Ranking position	Critical success factors by American experts.
1	**Honesty and clearness of communication**		1	**Trust between collaborators**
2	Communication via Internet		2	Respecting all verbal agreements
3	Security of ICT systems		3	Communication *via* Internet
4	Meeting deadlines by collaborators		4	Shared access to databases
5	**Trust between collaborators**		5	"Win-win" attitude between partners
6	Ability to communicate in foreign languages		6	Meeting deadlines by collaborators
7	High throughput and transfer rate of communication systems		7	Each collaborators focus on its core competences
8	Communication via fixed phone		8	Collaborators' openness to cooperation
9	Communication via mobile phone		9	Accuracy of feedback between collaborators
10	Collaborators' openness to cooperation		10	Willingness of collaborators to exploit a market opportunity quickly

Figure 3 - The significance of specific VO critical success factors by Swedish and American experts (Grudzewski, Hejduk, Sankowska and Wańtuchowicz, 2007, 2008).

---

[2] Trust is indicated as the most important when building collaboration between enterprises in IT Polish sector (see: Grudzewski, Sankowska and Wańtuchowicz, 2005).

2.4 Trust culture *versus* other elements of culture

At this point, we can raise the following question: *how trust is related with other elements of culture?* Trust is understood as a "bet" (belief and, based on it, activity) that future activities of other people or functioning of the devices or institutions will be advantageous to us (Sztompka, 2007, p. 99). It is a new type of specific, unique and precious capital that influences the economic performance of organisations and societies. Trust predisposes to the role of the strategic supply in organisation because it easily undergoes the following tests: (Grudzewski, Hejduk, Sankowska and Wańtuchowicz, 2008, p. 21): **value test** (trust helps organisations adapt to dynamic changes in turbulent environments), **rarity test** (high levels of trust are nontangible assets in only some organisations), **ownership test** (interpersonal trust is seen as specific "employee's corporation" because it can be observed in a certain employee), **imitation test** (trust is highly resistant to imitation or automatic copying), **resistance test** (when creating trust with time, there is a tendency to trust growth), **substitution test** (trust cannot be replaced with other utilitarian value because it is the driving force for new culture norms), **competitiveness test** (trust can form the basis for the highly competitive action strategy), **formalization test** (trust cannot be created through administrative regulations and codified organisation rules), **organisation test** (trust practically contains all aspects of enterprises' functioning).

Scientific attitude to problem solving is linked with trust between people (Bjerke, 2004/1999). It is the result of universalistic attitude of science to encountered problems and then it secures predictability of activities and reactions. Traditional attitude results from lack of trust (see Figure 4). Forasmuch, trust and science coincide with each other. Consequently, their synergetic effect conveys generous benefits. Further on, VO - that is always grounded on trust – notwithstanding its dynamic form can solve rational problems. Therefore, **VO can exist only in cultures that value trust greatly**. In other cultures traditional attitude to problems solving denies VO.

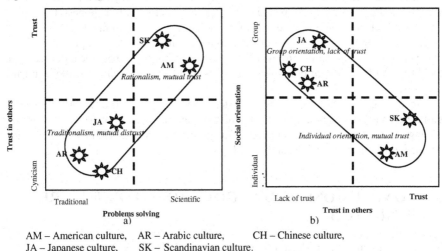

AM – American culture,   AR – Arabic culture,   CH – Chinese culture,
JA – Japanese culture,   SK – Scandinavian culture.

Figure 4 - Direct and permanent dependences between level if trust and: a) methods of solving problems b) types of social orientation (Bjerke, 2004, p. 258-259)

Individualistic social orientation means that people trust in each other (Bjerke, 2004/1999, p. 257). It is remarkable fact that group orientation is followed by lack of trust in other group members. In practice, it implies that the role of equal chances and social agreement appreciating individualism grows in societies and environments. Strong equality can be seen in almost everything, and this has made it easier to create less formal, more delegating styles of management in Swedish organisations. The interpersonal friction between managers and workers is reduced all employees expect to have a say and Swedish organization itself is seen as an organism for creativity and innovation and the learning process is highly appreciated. In the same time, position in hierarchy, strong sense of duty and sometimes consensus are highly valued in societies and environments oriented on group like Sweden.

We commit a mistake presuming that individualism supporters do not take care about the society development, e.g. Americans founded more voluntary associations than any other nation (Trompenaars and Hampden-Turner, 2004/1993). Therefore, we profess our opinion that individualistic societies can create VO because there is no distrust, no negation against strangers and consequently higher ability to sign new agreements.

People from culture with high level of trust do deal perfectly in the situation of uncertainty or lack of order (Bjerke, 2004/1999, p. 261). It is said that trust is a strategy of dealing with uncertainty. Hence, it is not surprising that Swedes are famous for low *uncertainty avoidance index* (UAI). Avoiding uncertainty describes the level of threat perceived by members of certain culture in the face of new, unknown situation (Hofstede and Hofstede, 2007/2005, p. 181). Culture of mutual cynicism, mistrust entail formal legal remedies.

Trust is a value and determines the success of transaction in trust cultures. It is a stimulator of human activities. In such cultures we can observe social well-being and economic growth in the opinion of Fukuyama (1995). In cynicism cultures those who trust are said to be naive. They often are victims of dishonest behaviors. Cynicism induces the increase in transactional costs and limits the freedom of activity, collaboration, cooperation, communication, it divides people. Trust does not perform its functions in cynicism culture because it becomes depreciated. Doubtless VO as form of collaboration can be more common and prevalent in trust cultures.

According to IBM survey by Hofstede and Hofstede (2007/2005) Swedish culture characterized the lowest masculinity index all over the world. Therefore, it belongs to so-called feminine cultures. This culture is distinguished by sensitive and protective values and care about the quality of life.

3. CONCLUSIONS AND SUGGESTIONS FOR FUTURE RESEARCH

The role of trust in modern organisation especially in VO is enormous. This generates the need for trust management. It is crucial issue for every organisation nowadays. Our research confirmed the thesis about focal role of trust for creating VO. This cultural determinant was denoted by American and Swedish experts.

Discussion about the cultural dimensions favorable for creating VO can be conducted not only on the national level but also on organisational level. The knowledge about the influence of certain culture dimensions can be the guideline on creating cooperation suitable for modern virtual collaboration. It can be the implication for organisation building trust that improves its results. The importance of trust in cooperation is crucial for enterprises, especially in dynamic sectors. Alarming is lower trust in CEO comparing to line workers. This is a signal that there is a need to rebuild cognizant and carefully directed leadership.

Multicultural enterprises where employees have different cultural background meet a particular challenge. There is a tendency to place trust and consequently high asymmetry in attitude to trust. Finally, in order to build VO and trust on macro (national) level and micro (organisational) level, we need: socialized individualism, universalism in work processes and operational rules, equality, scientific attitude to problem solving, law level of avoiding the uncertainty, clearness of activities.

4. REFERENCES

1. Bjerke B. Kultura a style przywództwa. Zarządzanie w warunkach globalizacji. Oficyna Ekonomiczna, Kraków 2004.
2. Casson M. The economic of business culture: Game theory, transaction cost, and economic performance. Oxford: Claredon 1991.
3. Dasgupta P. *Trust as commodity*, [in:] Gambetta D. (ed.): Trust: Making and breaking cooperate relations, Oxford: Blackwell 1988.
4. Edelman Trust Barometr 2007.
5. Fukuyama F. Trust: The social virtues & creation of prosperity, The Frez Press, New York 1995.
6. Gambetta D. Trust: Making and breaking cooperate relations. Oxford: Blackwell 1988.
7. Grudzewski WM, Hejduk IK, Sankowska A, Wańtuchowicz M. Zarządzanie zaufaniem w organizacjach wirtualnych, Difin, Warszawa 2007.
8. Grudzewski WM, Hejduk IK, Sankowska A, Wańtuchowicz M. Trust Management in Virtual Work Environments: A Human Factors Perspective, Series: Ergonomics Design & Mgmt. Theory & Applications Volume: 2, Taylor & Francis CRC Press, 2008.
9. Grudzewski WM, Sankowska A, Wańtuchowicz M. *Virtual Scorecard as a decision-making tool in creating Virtual Organisation*, [in:] Camarinha-Matos L. M., Afsarmanesh H., Ortiz A. (eds.): *Collaborative Networks and Their Breeding Environments*, series International Federation for Information Processing (IFIP), the Kluwer Academic Publishers - Springer, USA-Norwell, 2005, pp. 293-300.
10. Hampden-Turner Ch, Trompenaars, A. Siedem kultur kapitalizmu, USA, Japonia, Niemcy, Francja, Wielka Brytania, Szwecja, Holandia, Oficyna Ekonomiczna, Kraków 2006.
11. Handy Ch. Trust and virtual organization, Harvard Business Review, May-June 1995.
12. Hofstede G, Hofstede GJ, Kultury i organizacje, Polskie Wydawnictwo Ekonomiczne, Warszawa 2007.
13. Lewicka- Strzałecka A. Zaufanie w relacji konsument –biznes, Prakseologia, nr 143, s. 195-207.
14. Lorenz EH. *Neither friends nor strangers: Informal networks of subcontracting in French industry*, [in:] Gambetta D. (ed.) Trust: Making and breaking cooperate relations. Oxford: Blackwell 1988.

15. Ring PS, and Van de Ven AH. Structuring cooperative relationships between organizations, Strategic Management Journal, 13(7), 1992, pp. 483-498.
16. Sztompka P. Zaufanie. Fundament Społeczeństwa, Znak, Kraków 2007.
17. Trompenaars F, Hampden-Turner Ch. Siedem wymiarów kultury, znaczenie różnic kulturowych w działalności gospodarczej, Oficyna Ekonomiczna, Kraków 2002.

34

SQUEAK, AN INVISIBLE LABORATORY FOR TEACHERS AS LEARNERS

Luís Valente
IEC, University of Minho, valente@iec.uminho.pt
António José Osório
IEC, University of Minho, ajosorio@iec.uminho.pt
PORTUGAL

In this paper we highlight the empowerment of fresh developers challenged to create their own virtual laboratories of learning in Squeak's World. We suggested to a large group of teachers, from all school levels in Portugal, the use of Squeak as a multimedia system, an interface development environment, or simply as a programming language, in order to create new virtual worlds or simulated environments. They were challenged to exploit such a tool, knowing that school and schooling are fine, assuming that we aim to make it better, even if we do not always know what that means.
Keywords: Virtual worlds, children, simulation, creativity, Real Life, invisible laboratory.

1. CURRENT CONTEXT OF INFORMATION AND COMMUNICATION TECHNOLOGY (ICT) IN PORTUGUESE EDUCATION

1.1 Context

The last PISA report (Pinto-Ferreira et al, 2007) about the scientific competences of Portuguese students, published by GAVE[1], denotes that students with worse academic results are also those who have more difficulties in the utilization of ICT. Governmental initiatives to provide better ICT access to all students are based on that observation. A recent initiative named Schools, Teachers and Laptops (STL), started by the end of 2006, provided schools above primary level with a technological kit containing fourteen laptops for students' use and ten laptops for teachers, and adding to those a multimedia projector and a wireless access point. And, as a consequence of the Technological Plan for Education, established in 2007, all teachers and 10th grade students got the opportunity to acquire, in financially worthwhile conditions, a laptop with mobile Broadband Internet access.

However, the plans for ICT integration in the curricular activities continue to suffer huge limitations due to the difficulty that schools have in the process of implementation of new activities or because of their own cultural paradigms and

---

[1] GAVE – Ministry of Education's Bureau of Educational Assessment - a free translation of "Gabinete de Avaliação Educacional do Ministério da Educação"

Please use the following format when citing this chapter:

Valente, L. and Osório, A.J., 2008, in IFIP International Federation for Information Processing, Volume 283; *Pervasive Collaborative Networks*; Luis M. Camarinha-Matos, Willy Picard; (Boston: Springer), pp. 333–340.

practices of classroom organisation. Very often, computers are installed in laboratories and ICT activities are referred to as computer software lessons. This makes computers become the subject of study instead of becoming instrumental conditions for learning.

1.2 Barriers to ICT adoption

From our experience in monitoring the schools' ICT integration process, we find considerable difficulty in the adoption of strategies for the use of new technologies.

The Ministry of Education's recent initiative seems to be insufficient to change the situation and it is clear to us the inability to attract teachers into adopting ICT in teaching. Year after year, the Portuguese teachers had training in technology areas, but the assessment structures and the career progression mechanisms do not sufficiently value the professional training in areas that are not specific to the teaching specialization.

Moreover, the technocentric perspectives refuted by Seymour Papert are commonly adopted. We commonly verify that ICT activities are simply the ones proposed by ICT curriculum teachers, and often other teachers assume they do not have enough knowledge or skills to use ICT in their teaching.

From our point of view, this lack of confidence and low self-esteem could be overcome with more eclectic policies for the integration of technologies.

1.3 Resistance to change

The main resistance to the change of paradigm relies on a poor reflection about how technology may help to improve the students' academic development. From our observation, sharing knowledge, resources and strategies is also difficult. But, to be fair, we cannot ignore that education in our country has experienced a large uncertainty in terms of guidelines in recent years. The reforms and counter-reforms have succeeded at such high a rhythm that we have had 12 different Education ministers in the past twenty years.

Resistance is a chronic feature of our society and the direct relation of students' success with the teacher's performance led teachers to ignore the most constructivist methodologies in favour of more traditional practices in which they feel safer. Associating the uncertainty factor to which we referred to the constant agitation in Portuguese education, we can understand why the less entrepreneur ones tend to adopt less risky projects and practices. When the most entrepreneur teachers do not get the expected success, they become easy targets for the most sceptical and conservative ones and the education system does not protect them either.

1.4 Reprinting the analog model

Despite the recognition by all of those responsible for education that new technologies require new methodologies, the inability to innovate and the lack of research lead to the replication of the analog model when designing and implementing the use of ICT in education. This attitude is feeding a certain disinterest in the students who are fascinated by the novelty of console games, the interactive features of mobile devices and the engaging activities offered by many online sites.

While teachers are adopting static electronic presentations, for example, or are using primarily the e-learning platforms as repositories of teaching notebooks (Valente and Moreira 2007), students are succumbing to the offers from Real Life (Osório 2007) which is taking them into immersion and into performance roles that the school does not encourage or tolerate. They become winners, clever and creative individuals outside school.

The reward of success denied by the school is easily obtained through the online services available on 3G mobile phones or in the cybercentres right in front of schools.

In a pseudo-attitude of innovation and commitment to change the paradigm, the school has systematically ignored, for decades, research evidence from the most remarkable educational researchers on the field of technology integration in education. Seymour Papert, for example, has been insatiable in alerting to the dangers of technocentric teaching; Alan Kay proposes creative and innovative approaches for children to learn with computers (Dynabook), since the 1960s. Nicholas Negroponte has partially jumped into the reality of a dream world where each child can have his/her own computer and Allison Druin (Druin and Inkpen 2001), using a paraphrase of the Papertian idea of computers' invisibleness, suggests that they need to be "seamlessly infused into the school's environment, activities and culture", while Kirschner, Sweller and Clark (Kirschner, Sweller et al. 2006) agree on the lack of minimal guidance learning with ICT. Yet the school continues to show arrogance regarding the most creative proposals it is offered.

1.5 Computers as curriculum contents

Our consultancy activity in the area of ICT enabled us to note, for example, a very strong tendency to focus the learning on the physical resources; schools often promote activities more related to equipment than to strategies for their use. Learning Moodle or doing PowerPoint are very common expressions in the projects for ICT integration. It is not unusual to find exploration activities focused on the technical characteristics of the computers or other technical resources. The main rules for the use of equipment and ICT spaces are sometimes genuine obstacles to their use, ignoring its advantage to value learning. In some cases the aim seems to be to preserve the computer at any cost as if one were preserving a rare book by not touching or opening it.

It is a frequent concern of the Heads of schools to lock the computers they have in rooms, misnamed laboratories, in which they are then subject to regulations that exclude the computers' natural and spontaneous use. In the STL initiative we mentioned before, any teacher was enabled with sufficient resources to use ICT in any subject. However, in many cases, schools have stuck these computers in a room/laboratory, inhibiting healthy ICT adoption by the educational community as suggested, among others, by Alison Druin (Druin and Inkpen 2001). In many cases, the importance of having certain equipment seems to be more valued than the concern related to taking advantage of it.

In such a context, but believing that we are in the vanguard of technology, a pro-active attitude towards the use of information and communication technologies in education seems to be necessary. We approached these issues by studying, translating and developing the Squeak system for the conception and construction of virtual laboratories for learning.

As stated by Sussman & Wisdom (2002), we are concerned with the use of computers not purely as an aid to the visualization or numerical computation but as a programming tool in "a functional style to encourage clear thinking. Programming forces one to be precise and formal, without being excessively rigorous" (p. 2).

2. THE SQUEAK SYSTEM

Squeak is a system for object-oriented programming, developed at Apple and tested in Disney. It combines the capabilities of the SmallTalk language with the easiness of an environment based on the visual metaphor of drag and drop. Perfectly suitable to inexperienced users, Squeak begins to make sense to us, with the contributions of various communities of users encouraged by Alan Kay through the Squeakland portal and the interest drawn by the initiative OLPC (One Laptop per Child).

Squeak is the implementation of a proposal on how we can use computers to interact with information, to create our own knowledge, emphasizing the importance of the principles from the Dynabook's ideas that Alan Kay advocates.

In an interview granted to "The Book and the Computer", Alan Kay explains his Dynabook concept: "a portable interactive personal computer, as accessible as a book". This device, that could connect to a network and provide its users with text, viewing of images, video and audio, is considered to be the first draft of the personal computer and laptop, but only still a dream.

While a multimedia system, by allowing kids programming their own play, the Squeak Etoys developed by Kay's team at ViewPoints Research Institute, opens a world of possibilities for exploration and experimentation within all areas of knowledge, exceptionally visible in models' simulation and representation, as stated by Allen-Conn & Kim Rose (2003) in the book *Powerful Ideas in the Classroom*.

However, our difficulty to abandon the traditional models and interfaces often prevents us from seeing the world of Squeak beyond the blank screen.

3. THE *SQUEAKLÂNDIA* PROJECT AND COMMUNITY

3.1 The Squeaklândia project

Squeaklândia (http://www.squeaklandia.pt) is the first community of Squeak users in Portugal, emerging from an academic project at the University of Minho. Aiming to enable its use by a large number of teachers and students we have translated the English version of Squeak into Portuguese, because we found in Squeak the possibility to profit from the use of open software. Behind this option is the additional value brought about by Web 2.0 features such as the final user's ability to reconfigure the interface. Our reflection about prior observations and experiences with teachers and schools made us propose the use of Squeak as a multimedia system, an interface development environment, or a programming language to create and to design virtual learning laboratories.

In the summer of 2007, in collaboration with seven schools and two teacher training centres, we provided a Squeak Free Course to the community. Consequently, we also developed a virtual community (web site plus Moodle instance) of virtual laboratories' developers where the software is available for download and where we want to provide some examples of projects made with Squeak.

3.2 Squeak Online Course

The enthusiasm shown by teachers while programming their first "toys" in Squeak made us build a learning space in our Web site. In late December 2007, we began to accept registrations for the first fully online course on Squeak. This is a self-supported training course built up in Moodle using video lessons, tutorials and discussion forums. In a week 280 candidates signed up to join it.

In this course we present the system and teach some principles on programming with Squeak, mainly by working with movement scripts. The contents are the most basic characteristics of the system: learn how to create and save a project in Squeak; learn to get objects in motion and control them with a virtual joystick; learn how to use simple conditioned events.

The course is organized in modules that are supported by diverse information documents, such as manuals for download in PDF format, resources' sequence in HTML format created in the e-learning platform and videos explaining the necessary procedures for doing small projects.

The modules are designed to allow self-learning and respecting a gradual increase in difficulty. Support is given to students through discussion forums and a system of pre-scheduled online chat. The contents are presented once every two weeks and at the end of the course the trainees should upload a project on which what their learning is implemented.

Then the projects available in a database's internal platform are evaluated by the course teacher, and are made accessible to all other participants in an attempt to promote the sharing of ideas and resources. Likewise we created a system to collect suggestions for new projects which we expect to be a birthplace for future Squeak projects.

We also proposed a space to gather project ideas by using an HTML form, trying to encourage all participants, in a kind of online brainstorming activity, to share their ideas.

3.3 Teachers as learners

Since the community is completely open, it is not possible to accurately characterize its members, but in the beginning of the course we asked the participants to fill in a short questionnaire that allowed us having a clearer idea of who is interested in Squeak.

By the time we are writing this paper only 133 participants have answered the questionnaire. From this information we can see that the majority of the participants are female (52%) and that the most expressive age group is from 46 to 50 years, as follows: 4% are under 30 years old, 17% are between 31 and 35 years old, 22% are between 36 and 40 years old, 19% are between 41 and 45 years old, 23% are between 46 and 51 years old and 17% are over 51. 5% of the participants are teaching in higher education or not teaching at all.

In spite of there being a minority of pre-school teachers (1%) and primary school teachers (9%), there are teachers belonging to all groups of the Portuguese education system with special emphasis on ICT teachers (17%) who form the largest group.

3.4 Reasons given for having signed up

One of the questions we asked the participants is their reason for signing up. Although we still did not perform a proper statistical treatment, we noted that 25% refer reasons related to the desire to learn, 17% say that they have signed up by curiosity, 21% state they are looking for new things, 23% affirm having signed up because they are concerned with providing their students with new opportunities for learning and 11% declared having signed up because they like technology.

Perhaps we can realise here a concern with the quality of professional performance and discover some very important proactive attitudes to reach the success through new approaches in education, but the short time during which the experience is running does not give us the basis we need to go deeper in our assessment.

4. SQUEAK ACTIVITIES

4.1 Proposed exploitation

In the online course participants were taken to explore the potential of Squeak related to the movement and its control through scripting. The aim was not exactly to explore practical applications but to highlight the easiness of the programming, associated with the learning potential of Squeak. It is worth to mention that at an earlier trial workshop on Squeak, held a few months ago, we were confronted with the observation that the word "programming" stated at the activity title was discouraging for candidates seeking information before subscribing.

The tasks of this first course imply designing and building a virtual laboratory, even incipient or embryonic, allowing learning how to program without even using the terms and concepts associated with traditional programming.

The students of this course were required to submit a draft project at the end of the course to show their achievements.

4.2 The first Squeak projects

As the projects were being transferred to the platform we found they do not vary all that much from the general application suggested in the course contents, but there are some attempts to use creativity which bring us high hope on the impact of the course.

Thus some projects are combining the movement of rotation with the linear displacement of everyday life objects, verifiable for instance in cycling, in the movements of joggling in circus (see Figure 1), in the handling of the solar system's elements and so on. Other projects try to represent the movement of animals in nature such as birds, fish and domestic mammals and motorized transport vehicles, such as boats and aircraft.

The use of a kind of joystick to control movement was also already submitted, applied to most common examples as car circuits or to discover the pathways in fictional labyrinths or an animal's tracks in nature. Another proposal encouraged the representation of fables' elements: *The Tortoise and the Hare*.

A number of projects can be included in the category of "testing" learning achieved in other environments, such as healthy food and the sorting out of domestic waste.

We have projects in which the user interaction is reduced to acting in a start/stop button or to the exploitation of curriculum contents. One of such projects simulates a voyage discovering Brazil and another shows the movement of the sails of a windmill, for example.

Figure 1- Squeak projects presented for assessment

Initially, as they did not have enough experience, participants showed a tendency to replicate the projects which were presented to them as examples, but later they started trying more complex and interesting simulations. We detected this feature in the work of participants that had several projects, and in those cases, the first projects were always less creative and denoted less personal investment than the subsequent ones.

In all projects participants tried to simulate curriculum content issues, using Squeak as an invisible laboratory. While learning at their pace, independently, trying new activities and discovering the basics of programming with Squeak, these teachers highlighted many of the thoughts valued in education.

5. CONCLUSION

The greatest difficulty in learning how to use a new system such as Squeak seems to be directly connected to the learner's ability (or inability) to explore available documents and to understand and deconstruct them. Very often the help requested to the course trainer consisted in solving small problems, such as the upgrade of plug-ins in common Web browsers or the location of downloaded files.

We found that those participants, who take longer than most to reach the features, capabilities and the appropriate way to use the software, express some rejection attitudes towards Squeak. Firstly, they start comparing the final "products" they get from Squeak with the products they get from other systems they are already used to, such as "PowerPoint" or "Flash" clips, ignoring the added value features brought about by the new tool.

Most of these teachers have a critical perspective of Squeak, close to that described by Seymour Papert in the paper "Computer Criticism vs. Technocentric Thinking", meaning that they expect something from Squeak but not what they can do with Squeak.

It is worth to mention that many of the enrolled participants in this community have an evident interest in computers and technology but low expertise in operating it or in its educational use, which gives them a perspective clearly different from the perspective that Papert defends. We also noted that "insecurity sometimes makes a technical object loom too large in their thinking... their intimidation and limited technical understanding often blind to the fact that what they see as a property of 'the computer' is often a cultural construct".

However, some participants are beginning to ask questions related to situations not yet tested, using a hypothetical-deductive language: *if I use the "x" characteristic can I get the "y" effect?* As they progress in the acquisition of knowledge and understanding the way Squeak language works, Squeak learners seem to discover original, different features allowing us speculating that they are starting to realize Squeak's power.

Most recently we reached a way to embed the Squeak project as a multimedia filter in the Moodle platform, and we hope this development can improve Squeak's and Moodle LMS's integration. Moodle is a strong trend in Portuguese Schools and this advance gave us the possibility to create a database functionality that launches automatically every Squeak project into a web plug-in.

Even though we are at an early stage of our study, we are gathering indicators (the high number of course participants, the participation level in online activities and discussions, the questions posted to the trainer, the participants' concern with design) pointing to the development of a research attitude in our *Squeaklândia* community participants. Therefore we will continue to maintain our Squeak project visible aiming to enable Portuguese teachers to learn, experiment and research in invisible programming laboratories.

6. REFERENCES

Allen-Conn, B. J. and K. Rose (2003). Powerful Ideas in the Classroom. Glendale, Viewpoints Research Institute, Inc.

Druin, A. and K. Inkpen (2001). "When are Personal Technologies for children?" Personal and Ubiquitous Computing 5(3).

Kirschner, P. A., J. Sweller, et al. (2006). "Why Minimal Guidance During Instruction Does Not Work: An Analysis of the Failure of Constructivist, Discovery, Problem-Based, Experiential, and Inquiry-Based Teaching." Educational Psychologist 41(2): 75–86.

Osório, A. J. (2007). Real Life. Personal communication. Braga.

Papert, Seymour (1987). Computer Criticism vs. Technocentric Thinking. Educational Researcher 16 (I)

Pinto-Ferreira, C., A. Serrão, et al. (2007). PISA 2006 – Competências Científicas dos Alunos Portugueses. Lisboa, GAVE - Gabinete de Avaliação Educacional.

Sussman, G., Wisdom, J. (2002). The Role of Programming in the Formulation of Ideas. AI Memos (1959 - 2004). MIT - Artificial Intelligence Laboratory. http://hdl.handle.net/1721.1/6707

Valente, L. and P. Moreira (2007). Moodle: moda, mania ou inovação na formação? – Testemunhos do Centro de Competência da Universidade do Minho. Challenges 2007, Braga, Centro de Competência da Universidade do Minho.

PART 11

VIRTUAL TEAMS AND SOCIAL PROTOCOLS

35

MODELLING MULTITHREADED SOCIAL PROTOCOLS WITH COLOURED PETRI NETS

Willy Picard
Department of Information Technologies
Poznań University of Economics
ul. Mansfelda 4, 60-854 Poznań, POLAND
picard@kti.ae.poznan.pl

Support for human-to-human interactions over a network is still insufficient, while important in the context of Web 2.0. Many works have to be done to provide both theoretical and practical knowledge to this field. The model of social protocols has been formerly presented as a model of human-to-human interactions. In this paper, an enhanced version of social protocols supporting multithreaded collaboration and based on coloured Petri nets is presented.

1. INTRODUCTION

The development and the wide adoption of Wikis, blogs and the concept of folksonomies have led to a generation of Web-based communities (also known as *virtual communities*) and hosted services referred by the term *Web 2.0*. The goal of the Web 2.0 hosted services is to support creation and sharing of contents among members of a given community.

The Web 2.0 is based on the idea that the Web should be not only a set of isolated information sources, but also a network of interrelated *services* providing users with various but complementary features. Examples of such services are Google Maps (Google Maps, 2008) for maps-based services, Del.icio.us (Del.icio.us, 2008) for storing, sharing and discovering Web bookmarks, and Flickr (Flickr, 2008) for photo sharing services.

The Web 2.0 is *participatory* as it involves the users in the production of the contents, instead of being based on the classical separation of roles between producers and consumers of contents. The Web 2.0 is *collaborative* as the contents are produced by a community of users instead of isolated users. Probably the most famous participatory and collaborative Web 2.0 site is the encyclopaedia Wikipedia[5] in which anyone may create or edit articles..

To summarize, the definition of the Web 2.0 that we are using in this paper is the following one:

> *The Web 2.0 is a network of interrelated services, used mainly by a large number of small communities which create contents in a participatory and collaborative way.*

Please use the following format when citing this chapter:

Picard, W., 2008, in IFIP International Federation for Information Processing, Volume 283; *Pervasive Collaborative Networks*; Luis M. Camarinha-Matos, Willy Picard; (Boston: Springer), pp. 343–350.

In the Web 2.0, collaboration is a mean for community members to create *contents*. Interactions among community members are limited by the *collaboration protocols* ruling a given service. A collaboration protocol defines various roles and interactions among members playing these roles. As an example, most blog providers, e.g. (Google Blogger, 2008) or (Wordpress.com, 2008), define the roles of author, friend and anonymous. Authors may publish and modify posts on their blog, manage their list of friends, and set their blog as public or private. On a public blog, friends and anonymous users may read and comment any post, while on a private blog, only friends may read the blog and publish comments. Currently, collaboration protocols are not easily modifiable by the service providers nor community members as collaboration protocols are "hard-coded" in the code of the Website providing the service. Following on the previous example, the addition of a new role, such as editor, or the addition of new interactions, such as the possibility for a friend to invite new friends would lead to important changes in the code of the Website providing the service to be modified. A solution to this problem is the separation of collaboration protocols from the rest of the code of Website. Such an approach to collaboration has its root in workflow management systems in which the definition of the workflow is orthogonal to the implementation of the tasks to be performed during the workflow runtime.

Currently, many research works focus on Business Process Modeling and particularly Web services and associated standards: high-level languages such as BPEL or WS-Coordination take the service concept one step further by providing a method of defining and supporting workflows and business processes. However, most of these actions are directed towards interoperable machine-to-machine interactions over a network. Support for human-to-human interactions over a network is still insufficient and many research works have to be done to provide both theoretical and practical knowledge to this field. Emerging standards, such as (BPEL4People, 2007) and (WS-HumanTask, 2007), aim at providing better support for activities performed by humans in the BPEL framework. However, these two standards do not directly address human-to-human interactions but rather propose a formal definition of human activities and potential inclusion of these tasks within a BPEL process.

The insufficient support for human-to-human interactions over a network is a strong limitation for a wide adoption of *professional virtual communities (PVCs)*. As mentioned in (Camarinha-Matos, 2005), "professional virtual community represents the combination of concepts of virtual community and professional community. Virtual communities are defined as social systems of networks of individuals, who use computer technologies to mediate their relationships. Professional communities provide environments for professionals to share the body of knowledge of their professions [...]". According to (Chituc, 2005), little attention has been paid to the social perspective on Collaborative Networks (CN) business environment, including obviously professional virtual communities in which social aspects are of high importance.

This paper is an attempt to provide a model for human-to-human interactions within professional virtual communities. The proposed model enhanced the former model of *social protocols* proposed by (Picard, 2005) by allowing members of a given community for a *multithreaded collaboration*. It should however been kept in mind that the results presented here are a work in progress and therefore they are not claimed to be neither sufficient nor exhaustive.

In this paper, the concept of multithreaded social protocols is proposed as an answer to the issues pointed above. In Section 2, the requirements for social protocols for professional virtual communities are presented. Next, coloured Petri nets, on which the proposed model for multithreaded social protocols is built, are briefly introduced. Then, a model for multithreaded social protocols is formally presented. In Section 5, an example illustrates a potential application of the proposed model for the collaborative building of a Frequently Asked Question list (FAQ). Finally, Section 6 concludes the paper.

2. REQUIREMENTS FOR SOCIAL PROTOCOLS FOR PVCS

In the context of professional virtual communities, the concept of social protocols has been proposed (Picard, 2005) as a model of interactions among collaborators within a given sub-community.

The following requirements for social protocols as a model of interaction among collaborators has been identified:

> *reusability:* a given social protocol should be reusable to rule the interactions within various sub-communities; A social protocol aims at modelling a set of collaboration processes, in the same way as a class models a set of objects in object-oriented programming. In other words, a social protocol may be seen as a model which instances are collaboration processes;

> *separation of tasks implementation from social protocols:* a social protocol should model potential interactions among collaborators, however the interactions should decoupled from implementation of the tasks performed by collaborators. As a consequence, tasks of a given social protocol may be implemented in various ways, using various technologies, or various locations/hosts;

> *support for social aspects in collaboration:* interactions are strongly related with social aspects, such as the role played by collaborators;

> *strong mathematical foundations:* social protocols model a complex situation of potential interactions among humans. Therefore, strong mathematical foundations are required as a mean to check properties such as structural validity, reachability, liveness and boundedness;

> *multithreading:* within a given sub-community, it is quite frequent that collaborators work on many topics at the same time. Therefore, social protocols should allow collaborators to work in a multithreaded way, i.e. to work simultaneously in many subprocesses.

The model of social protocols presented in (Picard, 2005) addresses the four first requirements. The fifth requirement is not answered by the formerly proposed model which is single-threaded, as based on Finite State Machines.

In this paper, an enhanced model of social protocols addressing the five requirements presented above is presented. The enhanced model extends the former one by replacing Finite State Machines by Coloured Petri Nets.

3. COLOURED PETRI NETS

Petri Nets were invented by (Petri, 1962) as part of his dissertation, *Kommunikation mit Automaten* (communication with automata) as mathematical representations of discrete distributed systems. Application of Petri Nets to workflow management have been studied by (Aalst, 1998) with the conclusion that "many features of the Petri net formalism are useful in the context of workflow management".

A classical Petri net consists of *places, transitions* and *directed arcs* between places and transitions. Places may contain *tokens*. The set of tokens, potentially spread in many places is called a *marking*. A marking may change when a transition is *fired* (or triggered). The firing of a transition *t* is possible iff all places *p* for which a directed arc from *p* to *t* exists (*input places*) contain at least one token. Where a transition *t* is fired, tokens from the input places are consumed, an action is potentially performed, and new tokens are placed in *output places* (i.e. places to which a directed arc from transition *t* leads).

An example of a classical Petri net is presented on Figure 1. The presented Petri net consists of 5 places (represented by circles) and 2 transitions (represented by rectangles). All input places of the left transition contain at least one token, therefore the left transition may be fired. The state of the Petri net before the firing of the left transition is presented in Figure 1a), while the state resulting from the firing of the left transition is presented in Figure 1b). Tokens in the left places are removed and a token is placed in the central place. Then, the right transition may be fired. After the right transition has been fired, tokens are placed in the output places of the right transition, as presented in Figure 1c). Now the left transition can not be fired because only the top-left place contains a token and the bottom-left place which is required to fire the left transition does not contain any token.

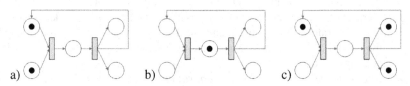

Figure 1 - a) an example of a Petri net; b) after firing the left transition;
c) after firing the right transition

Coloured Petri nets (Jensen, 1996) has been proposed as an extension to classical Petri nets. Coloured Petri Nets (CPN) incorporate the concept of data structuring which was missing in Petri's original works. In a CPN, each token has a value often referred to as '*colour*'. Coloured token may be used to represent objects in the modelled system. A coloured token may for instance represent a post or a comment in a blog. The colour of a token may be used in directed arcs to specify 1) the type of data that a given transition requires and processes, 2) the type of data that a transition produces.

An example of a coloured Petri net based on the former example of Petri Net is presented on Figure 2. Tokens, as well as directed arcs, are now associated with data types. The left transition requires tokens associated with data types *a* and *c*. When this transition is fired, the token associated with the data types *a* and *c* are removed and a new token associated with data type *d* is placed in the central place.

An important feature of Petri nets, and by extension an important feature of CPNs, is the possibility to model multi-threaded systems as Petri nets. Indeed, an important principle of Petri nets is the principle of locality: the behaviour of a transition exclusively depends on its locality, i.e. its input and output places. As a consequence, various transitions may be simultaneously enabled (i.e. they can be fired) if the marking contains tokens in all input places of these transitions.

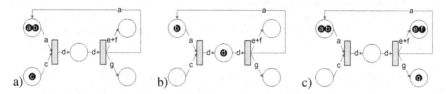

Figure 2 – a) an example of a coloured Petri net; b) after firing the left transition;
c) after firing the right transition

4. A MODEL FOR MULTITHREADED SOCIAL PROTOCOLS

4.1 Single-threaded social protocols

The model of multithreaded social protocols proposed in this paper is an extension of the model of social protocols presented in (Picard, 2005). "A social protocol aims at modelling a set of collaboration processes, in the same way as a class models a set of objects in object-oriented programming. In other words, a social protocol may be seen as a model which instances are collaboration processes. Social protocols model collaboration at a group level.".

The former model consists of a finite state machine (FSM) modelling potential interactions within a group. In these finite state machines, transitions are labelled by roles and are associated with actions. "In a social protocol, collaborators – as a group – move from state to state via the transitions. A transition may be triggered only by a collaborator labelled with the appropriate role. A transition is associated with the execution of an action. Execution of an action means the execution of remote code. SOAP or CORBA are examples of technologies that may be used to such remote code executions."

The first three requirements presented in Section 2 are clearly addressed by the former model. Mathematical foundations are in the theory of automata. Additionally, an algorithm for structural validation of social protocols has been presented in (Picard, 2007). However, the fifth requirement, i.e. multithreading, is not supported by the former model as finite state machines are not well-adapted to model multithreaded systems. The main contribution of this paper is the replacement of FSMs by CPNs in social protocols to support multithreaded processes.

4.2 Formal model for multithreaded social protocols

A ***multithreaded social protocol*** *Π-net* is a coloured Petri net consisting of (P, T, A, C, I, R, f_A, f_{TI}, f_{TR}, M_0) where

> ➢ P is a finite set of places,

> T is a finite set of transitions, such that $P \cap T = \varnothing$,
> A is a finite set of arcs, such that $A \cap T = A \cap P = \varnothing$,
> C is a finite set of data types, also called colour sets,
> R is a finite set of roles,
> I is a finite set of interfaces to actions,
> f_A is the arc function defined from A to $P \times T \times C \cup T \times P \times C$, defining arcs as triples (place, transition, colour set),
> f_{TI} is the interface function from T to I, associating transitions with interfaces,
> f_{TR} it the role function from T to R, associating transitions with roles,
> M_0 is the initial marking.

A multithreaded social protocol consists of places and transitions. Places and transitions are connected with directed arcs which are associated with colour sets. Transitions are associated with an interface of an action to be performed if the transition is triggered by a collaborator playing the associated role. Finally, the initial state of a multithreaded social protocol is defined by its initial marking.

A *token* is a pair (p, c) where $p \in P$ and $c \in C$.

A *marking* is a set of tokens.

A *multithreaded social process* is an instance of a multithreaded social protocol. A multithreaded social process consists of (Π-*net*, U, f_{UR}, M) where
> Π-*net* is a multithreaded social protocol,
> U is a finite set of users,
> f_{UR} is the role-user mapping function from U to R, associating users with roles,
> M is the current marking.

When a multithreaded social protocol is instantiated, roles have to be attributed to existing users and M is initialized to M_0. Next, users trigger enabled transitions, modifying the current marking.

A *transition* $t \in T$ *is enabled* for (may be triggered by) user $u \in U$ iff:
> $f_{TR}(t) = f_{UR}(u)$, i.e. user u plays the role r associated with transition t,
> $\forall a \in A \ \exists (p,c) \in P \times C$ such that $f_A(a) = (p,t,c)$, $(p,c) \in M$, i.e. for all arcs leading to transition t, there exists at least one token of the corresponding colour sets in the current marking.

The *firing of a transition* $t \in T$ is performed in the following way:
> $\forall a \in A \ \exists (p,c) \in P \times C$ such that $f_A(a) = (p,t,c)$, $M = M - (p,c)$, i.e. for all arcs leading to transition t, tokens of the corresponding colour sets in the current marking are removed from it.
> $f_{TI}(t)$ is executed, potentially using the removed tokens as arguments,
> $\forall a \in A \ \exists (p,c) \in P \times C$ such that $f_A(a) = (t,p,c)$, $M = M + (p,c)$, i.e. for all arcs coming from transition t, tokens of the corresponding colour sets are added to the current marking.

5. AN EXAMPLE OF MULTITHREADED SOCIAL PROTOCOL

The example of multithreaded social protocol which is presented in this section is oversimplified for readability reasons. It is obvious that social protocols modelling real-world collaboration processes are usually much more complex. The same example has been presented in its single-threaded version in (Picard, 2006).

The chosen collaboration process to be modelled as a multithreaded social protocol is the collaborative authoring of a "FAQ" document. Some users (denoted by the letter "u" in transitions) only ask questions, while others, referred as "experts" (denoted by the letter "e" in transitions) may answer, remove or comment on questions. Other users, referred as "managers" (denoted by the letter "m" in transitions), may interrupt the work on the FAQ document. The work on the document may terminate either by a success (the document is written and the manager estimates that its quality is good enough to be published) or by a failure (the manager estimates that the work on the FAQ should be interrupted). On arcs, the colour "start" refers to the initial token, "q" to a question, "a" to an answer, "r" to a removed question, "c" to a comment, "failure" to the final state of the collaboration when the FAQ is not published, and "success" to the final state of the collaboration when questions, answers and comments are published. One may notice that some colours are prefixed with the negative sign "-": in this case, the token in the input place is removed when the transition is fired, else the transition is enabled iff the token exists but it will not be removed.

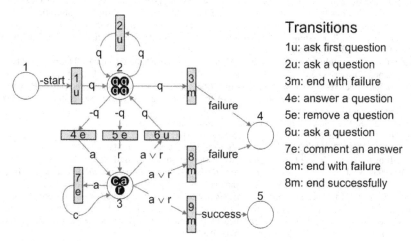

Transitions

1u: ask first question
2u: ask a question
3m: end with failure
4e: answer a question
5e: remove a question
6u: ask a question
7e: comment an answer
8m: end with failure
8m: end successfully

Figure 3 – Example of multithreaded social protocol for FAQ list building

In the situation presented in Figure 3, four questions are waiting for answers or removal, one question has been answered and commented, one question has been removed. The multithreaded aspect of the presented social protocol is visible in the current situation as many transitions, e.g. "2u", "4e", and "7e" may be performed concurrently: a user may ask a new question ("2u"), while an expert answers an existing question ("4e") and a second expert comments on the formerly answered question ("7e").

6. CONCLUSION

While many works are currently done on modelling collaboration processes in which software entities (agents, web services) are involved, modelling collaboration processes in which mainly humans are involved is an area that still requires much attention from the research community. The model presented in this paper is an attempt to provide a formalized model of human-to-human interactions.

The main innovation presented in this paper is the extension of the social protocol model by replacing FSMs by CPNs so that multithreaded processes are supported. Additionally, the strong mathematical foundations of Petri nets, with the existence of many analysis techniques, ensure that powerful analysis capabilities may be added to information systems supporting multithreaded social protocols.

The next steps will include modification of our technique for the adaptation of single-threaded social protocols to multithreaded social protocols, allowing collaborators to modify a multithreaded social protocol at runtime.

7. REFERENCES

[Aalst 1998] W.M.P. van der Aalst, "The Application of Petri Nets to Workflow Management", The Journal of Circuits, Systems and Computers, 8(1), pp. 21 – 66, 1998.

[BPEL4People, 2007] WS-BPEL Extension for People (BPEL4People), Version 1.0 June 2007, https://www.sdn.sap.com/irj/sdn/go/portal/prtroot/docs/library/uuid/30c6f5b5-ef02-2a10-c8b5-cc1147f4d58c , accessed on March 2008.

[Camarinha-Matos 2005] L.M. Camarinha-Matos, H. Afsarmanesh and M. Ollus, "ECOLEAD: A Holistic Approach to Creation and Management of Dynamic Virtual Organizations", In L. Camarinha-Matos, H. Afsarmanesh and A. Ortiz, Eds, *Collaborative Networks and their Breeding Environments*, Proceedings of the 6th IFIP Working Conference on Virtual Enterprises (PRO-VE 2005), Valencia, Spain, September 26-28, 2005, Springer, pp. 3 – 16, 2005.

[Chituc 2005] C.M. Chituc, A.L. Azevedo, "Multi-Perspective Challenges on Collaborative Networks Business Environments", In L. Camarinha-Matos, H. Afsarmanesh and A. Ortiz, Eds, *Collaborative Networks and their Breeding Environments*, Proceedings of the 6th IFIP Working Conference on Virtual Enterprises (PRO-VE 2005), Valencia, Spain, September 26-28, 2005, Springer, pp. 25 – 32, 2005.

[Del.icio.us 2008] Del.icio.us, http://del.icio.us/, accessed on March 2008.

[Flickr 2008] Flickr, http://www.flickr.com/, accesses on March 2008.

[Google Maps 2008] Google Maps, http://maps.google.com/, accessed on March 2008.

[Google Blogger 2008] Google Blogger, http://www.blogger.com/, accessed on March 2008.

[Jensen 1996] K. Jensen. *Coloured Petri Nets. Basic concepts, analysis methods and practical use.* EATCS monographs on Theoretical Computer Science. Springer-Verlag, Berlin, 1996.

[Petri 1962] Petri, Carl A. "*Kommunikation mit Automaten*". Ph. D. Thesis. University of Bonn. 1962

[Picard 2007] W. Picard, "An Algebraic Algorithm for Structural Validation of Social Protocols", Proceedings of the 10th Int. Conference on Business Information Systems, Lecture Notes in Computer Science, 4439, Springer, pp. 570–583, 2007.

[Picard 2006] W. Picard, "Computer Support for Adaptive Human Collaboration with Negotiable Social Protocols". In A. Witold and H.C. Mayr, Eds, *Technologies for Business Information Systems*, Proceedings of the 9th Int. Conference on Business Information Systems in cooperation with ACMSIGMIS, Klagenfurt, Austria, May 31 – June 2, 2006, Springer Verlag, pp. 193 – 203, 2006.

[Picard 2005] W. Picard, "Modeling Structured Non-monolithic Collaboration Processes", In L. Camarinha-Matos, H. Afsarmanesh and A. Ortiz, Eds, *Collaborative Networks and their Breeding Environments*, Proceedings of the 6th IFIP Working Conference on Virtual Enterprises (PRO-VE 2005), Valencia, Spain, September 26-28, 2005, Springer, pp. 379 – 386, 2006.

[Wordpress.com 2008] Wordpress.com, http://www.wordpress.com/, accessed on March 2008.

[WS-HumanTask 2007] Web Services Human Task (WS-HumanTask), Version 1.0, June 2007, https://www.sdn.sap.com/irj/sdn/go/portal/prtroot/docs/library/uuid/a0c9ce4c-ee02-2a10-4b96-cb205464aa02 , accessed on March 2008.

36 VIRTUAL TEAM WORKING: CURRENT ISSUES AND DIRECTIONS FOR THE FUTURE

Aisha Abuelmaatti and Yacine Rezgui

Built and Human Environment Research Institute, University of Salford, Salford, UK.
a.m.t.abuelmaatti@pgr.salford.ac.uk *and* y.rezgui@salford.ac.uk

Value networks underpinned by global and localised virtual teams are believed to have high potential for SMEs. Yet, the successful migration to value-added alliances is blended in the right combination of organizational, legal, economic, socio-cultural, and technical factors, and requires further research into innovative business models. These models should leverage existing SME competences and transcend existing virtual collaboration barriers and limitations. Grounded in state-of-the-art literature, the paper identifies current insight for the deficient research in virtual teams and presents them in the form of open research questions.

1. INTRODUCTION

Virtual team working is a concept that has matured through a long evolutionary process (Maznevski and Chudoba, 2000; Carmarinha-Matos and Afsarmanesh, 2005). While organisations emerge and claim to have adopted the modus operandi of virtual teams, the reality is that conventional face-to-face modes of operation will remain the organisational norm for some time to come (Arnison and Miller, 2002). Yet, the rapid pace of globalisation, the increasing need for agility, and the fast development of Information and Communication Technologies (ICT) will force organisations to embrace virtual collaboration to enhance their competitiveness (Arnison and Miller, 2002; Rezgui, 2007; Workman, 2007).

Small and Medium Sized Enterprises (SMEs) form a large proportion of organizations in Europe. While large enterprises have the advantage of taking on mass tasks, the size of SMEs tied to their limited resources prevent them from sustaining their competitiveness with larger organizations. However, SMEs exhibit advantages compared to large enterprises, in particular when it comes to adapting to changes and adopting technology (Rezgui, 2007).

Sustainable competitive advantage is interwoven with innovation (Barrett and Sexton, 2006). In this context, value-added alliance formation can be seen as an innovation and is essential in the current dynamic business environment (Helling et al., 2005). While a number of requirements emerge to support the migration of SMEs from traditional organizations to empowered alliances, a number of barriers hinder this migration. These include factors related to culture, organizational structure, decision making processes, perceptions in relation to change, shared

Please use the following format when citing this chapter:

Abuelmaatti, A. and Rezgui, Y., 2008, in IFIP International Federation for Information Processing, Volume 283; *Pervasive Collaborative Networks*; Luis M. Camarinha-Matos, Willy Picard; (Boston: Springer), pp. 351–360.

responsibility management, liability, copyright and confidentiality issues, trust, employee-manager relationships, management strategies, and ICT maturity and capability (Rezgui 2007).

Barrett and Sexton (2006) define the process of innovation as a cyclical process of diagnosing, action planning, taking action, evaluating and specifying learning. It is vital to note that when operating in global markets, the criteria for competitiveness change continuously. A value network or alliance cycle starts with sensing an opportunity or need to innovate in response to competitive conditions. In particular, the SMEs' motivation to innovate is not solely to grow, but can be directed at competing with larger enterprises. A Value network underpinned by virtual team working is not an end in itself but can be a means to achieve sustainable competitiveness. In fact, SMEs consider virtual teams as (a) innovations with the potential to respond to complex business environments (Workman and Kahnweiler, 2001); (b) provide purported benefits (Rezgui and Wilson, 2005), and (c) create opportunities that are not found in traditional teams (Barrett and Sexton, 2006). Despite the rapid growth of virtual team innovations, their performance is far below their potential. Although research has helped to speculate success, global SME virtual teams face significant organisational, economic, legal, socio-cultural and technical challenges (Kayworth and Leidner, 2000; Zigurs, 2003). It seems easy for academics to research and develop virtual team solutions, yet the reality of deployment and adoption is complex given the numerous types of challenges faced by the virtual team.

In order to reach the optimal level of virtual team functioning, given the complexity of this phenomenon as well as the lack of research to date, further research into innovative business models that leverage existing SME competences and transcend current organisational, economic, legal, socio-cultural and technical barriers and limitations is therefore an important prerequisite. The paper identifies a gap in formal theories, structure, modelling, and life cycle behaviour of virtual teams and alliances. Grounded in state-of-the-art literature, the paper identifies current barriers, limitations and insight for the deficient research in virtual teams and expresses these in the form of open research questions. Moreover, virtual team working challenges are reviewed by integrating recent literature in response to the growing awareness of the need for formal business models for SMEs. On the basis of this current literature review, a proposition for future direction is presented.

2. METHODOLOGICAL CONCEPTUAL FRAMEWORK

A comprehensive literature review has been carried out targeting virtual team research. The conceptual framework underpinning the review is illustrated in Figure 1, while the key references organized by conceptual area are given in Table 1.

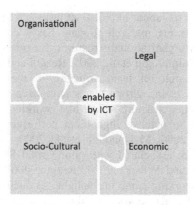

Figure 1 – Research Conceptual Framework.

Table 1 – Key references

Organisational	*Socio-cultural*
Zigurs, 2003	Zigurs, 2003
Kürümlüoglu et al., 2005	Kayworth and Leidner, 2000
Rezgui and Wilson, 2005	McDonough et al., 2000
Kaiser et al., 2000	Arnison and Miller, 2002
Kaywoth and Leidner, 2000	Workman et al., 2003
McDonough et al., 2000	Kürümlüoglu et al., 2005
Workman, 2001	Rezgui and Wilson, 2005
Vakola and Wilson, 2004	Rezgui, 2007
Rezgui, 2007	Wiesenfeld et al., 2000
Pawar and Sharifi, 2000	Hoefling, 2001
Barrett and Sexton, 2006	Mezgár, 2006
	Arnison and Miller, 2002
Legal	Pawar and Sharifi, 2000
Shelbourn et al., 2005	Yukl, 2002
	Connaughton and Daly, 2004
Economic	Walters, 2000
Walker, 2000	
Arnison and Miller, 2002	
Lipnack and Stamps, 2000	
Franke, 2001	
Coulson and Kantamneni, 2006	
Alsakini et al., 2007	
Helling et al., 2005	

3. ORGANISATIONAL DIMENSION OF VIRTUAL TEAMS

Virtual team working relies on the wide use of ICT, nevertheless handling the barriers and limitations of organizational structure, decision making, and perception in relation to change are fateful. This section addresses apiece respectively.

3.1 Structure

Collaboration gives rise to the fundamental requirements of labour division into tasks and the coordination of these tasks. The structure of an SME is reflected in the ways in which it divides its labour into distinct tasks and then achieves coordination among them. Virtual teams research to date has focused on the necessity of restructuring traditional organisational structures to exploit the fast development of ICTs (Zigurs, 2003; Kürümlüoglu et al., 2005; Rezgui and Wilson, 2005). In review of the substantial research on team structure in the traditional environment, coordination difficulties facing virtual teams have been found uncounted for. The literature relating to the structure of virtual working has put forward some suggestions attempting to achieve high team performance (Kaiser et al., 2000; Kaywoth and Leidner, 2000; McDonough et al., 2000; Workman, 2001). Yet, as managerial structures are associated with poor virtual SME alliance performance (Zigurs, 2003; Vakola and Wilson, 2004; Rezgui, 2007), the lack of structures handling virtual team working came under light. As such, the nature of the virtual SME alliance requires fresher approaches, thus providing fertile grounds for future research.

Further research should address: *what structural work arrangements are best suited to the work that must transcend geographical boundaries and time? How SMEs effectively enforce these structures? What are the necessary abilities of the manager to facilitate communication among team members to create clear structures and foster role clarity to improve collaboration? Are there other strategies that SMEs can implement to improve virtual team working performance?*

3.2 Decision making and perception in relation to change

SMEs find themselves in an almost constant state of change as they strive to respond to the pressure of the increasingly globalised and competitive environment. Thus, quick decision-making and innovation activity in response to rapidly changing conditions and demands is necessary (Pawar and Sharifi, 2000; Barrett and Sexton, 2006). The creation and operation of the SME alliance is regarded as a change initiative within the participating SMEs. Its members are likely to experience lifecycle problems– set up, operation, and winding down, where each of these different phases is likely to involve change in staffing, tasks, objectives and resources (Rezgui and Wilson, 2005). While most research in this area has been unable to break away from the traditional models, Rezgui and Wilson (2005) thoroughly reviewed the barriers and argued for a fresher approach. Future research in this area poses the questions of: *what tasks enable perception, awareness, and preparedness to change? Do traditional managerial change mechanisms remain applicable in the virtual SME alliance environment? Either wise, what are the most appropriate change mechanisms? What business and organizational methods offer innovative and sustainable services along the collaboration? What formulas, depending on the nature and scale of the SME changes, are effective for decision-making? What is the necessary vision and systemic thinking required to manage the change lifecycle?*

4. LEGAL DIMENSION OF VIRTUAL TEAMS

A typical process in the virtual team working is the removal or inclusion of participants. Virtual teams involve cooperation between legally independent SMEs.

The fact that a virtual team has a legal identity does not mean that claims cannot be addressed directly towards the members. However, claimants will probably suffer some difficulties in determining the exact identity of the different members because of the appearance of the SME alliance as one enterprise (Shelbourn et al., 2005). To this end, attention should be paid to liability sharing and distribution.

SMEs use of "virtual teams" arises unanswered legal questions. The legal status still has to find a coherent framework and has not yet been adequately discussed. To ensure that SMEs are efficiently supported along their virtual collaboration path to delivering innovative solutions requires addressing the following issues: *How to manage intellectual property rights and cope with copyright and confidentiality issues? How to manage responsibility? How to share and distribute liability? How to monitor these throughout collaboration? How shared responsibility by means of rights and ownership of outcomes is identified? How these foundations can be blended together to generate the basic building block to deliver sound legal entity?*

5. ECONOMIC DIMENSION OF VIRTUAL TEAMS

The rapid pace of ICT has transformed the traditional economy into a smart new economy (Walker, 2000; Arnison and Miller, 2002). Pressures are forcing SMEs to become more adaptive and agile in their tasks and adopt innovative approaches. As a result, virtual teams have the potential to improve quality and performance and leverage capabilities (Lipnack and Stamps, 2000). Economic activity in this context means the cooperation of production ingredients to achieve competitiveness and maintain good cooperation between members of the SME alliance (Franke, 2001; Coulson and Kantamneni, 2006; Alsakini et al., 2007).

While a number of studies (Lipnack and Stamps, 2000; Walker, 2000; Franke, 2001; Arnison and Miller, 2002; Coulson and Kantamneni; 2006; Helling et al., 2005; Alsakini et al., 2007) discussed the collaborative networks' economic dimension, the complex business environment poses persistent problems to SMEs. From the economic standpoint, achieving competitiveness and maintaining good cooperation cannot depend solely on mutual faith. Research is needed to devise *how to share profits and losses in the context of an SME alliance? How to ensure that the collective financial gain of the SME alliance outweighs the individual profits of associated member SMEs? How SMEs evaluate and determine the right economic costing in a consistent manner across the network?*

6. SOCIO-CULTURAL DIMENSION OF VIRTUAL TEAMS

Socio-cultural barriers and limitations of maintaining virtual working teams are highlighted by integrating present literature on trust, social cohesion, team member structure – user / manager relationships, influences on the management and strategies.

The core of research arguments on trust centers on a belief that only trust can prevent the geographical boundaries and time zones of virtual team members from becoming psychological distances (Zigurs, 2003). Several suggestions to manipulate trust are present (Kayworth and Leidner, 2000; McDonough et al., 2000; Arnison and Miller, 2002; Workman et al., 2003; Kürümlüoglu et al., 2005; Rezgui and Wilson, 2005; Rezgui, 2007). Yet, such trust albeit swift is known to be fragile (Wiesenfeld et al., 2000; Hoefling, 2001; Zigurs, 2003; Mezgár, 2006).

Research suggests that face-to-face interaction has a direct impact on team performance through building team trust and enabling team members to exchange valuable socio-cultural information (Arnison and Miller, 2002; Rezgui, 2007). Research stresses the need for initial face-to-face meeting to provide the grounds for a worthwhile ICT collaboration (Kürümlüoglu et al., 2005). Extending this idea even further, research suggests that virtual team members conduct periodic face-to-face meetings (Kürümlüoglu et al., 2005; Rezgui, 2007).

It is essential that team managers play a pivotal role in favour of relationships (Kayworth and Leidner, 2000; McDonough et al., 2000; Pawar and Sharifi, 2000; Arnison and Miller, 2002; Yukl, 2002; Connaughton and Daly, 2004; Kürümlüoglu et al., 2005; Rezgui and Wilson, 2005). Relationship management ought to influence a strategy that identifies and maintains relationships which in turn ensures that objectives meet expectations (Walters, 2000). Rezgui (2007) accentuated this issue calling for a certain shift in the leadership approach identifying the need for essential attributes.

Seeing the decades of traditional team working, the legitimate question posing itself here is *whether virtual teams can function effectively in the absence of frequent face-to-face communication? Further research should address what facts pave the way to foster swift trust? How is trust maintained? What working infrastructures utilized by teams attempt to foster trust? Which, if any, team training accustoms expert team members in their fields to the particular requirements of virtual working? What can relationship management do to foster teams of mixed experiences? How would members relate and identify themselves to their manager in a virtual context? What are the qualities that a virtual team manager ought to have to cope with the complexity resulting from non-collocation and virtual collaboration including trust, lack of cohesion and resolving issues? In the worst case scenario, what requirements the team needs to benefit from the diversity and dispersion regardless of trust?*

The fact remains that the organisational culture is a critical factor to hold virtual teams. What remains unclear are *how team members in a virtual context build, sustain and strengthen culture in the absence of frequent face-to-face interaction? How often should the team members communicate to remain glued? How to foster a culture of extensive collaboration? What behaviours inhibit a team's ability to develop a shared culture? What behaviours raise a team's ability to develop a shared culture? What current SMEs culture circumstances hinder team effectiveness in the virtual environment? Can a set of cultural attributes that promote effectiveness of teams be identified? How can these attributes be effectively enforced in virtual teams to ensure that members remain glued?*

7. TECHNOLOGICAL DIMENSION OF VIRTUAL TEAMS

A technological solution in the context of virtual teams has to support the central business processes; allow integration of systems and interoperability between disparate applications; and the management of interactions between individuals and teams (Rezgui, 2007). A number of researchers have proposed to adopt approaches that federate services from various non-collocated organisations and software houses and making the applications they offer available via ubiquitous web browsers. This is commonly known as service composition.

As largely reported in the literature, web service composition is a very complex and challenging task. A number of key issues emerge from the literature as essential to support effectively service composition in favour of virtual team working, including: Coordination (to manage interaction between services and coordination of sequences of operations, to ensure correctness and consistency); Transaction (to manage short-duration / atomic and long running business activities); Context (to adjust execution and output to provide the client with a customised and personalised behaviour: may contain information such as a consumer's name, address, and current location, the type of client device, including hard- and software that the consumer is using, or all kinds of preferences regarding the communication); Conversation modelling (to facilitate service discovery and dynamic binding, service composition model validation, service composition skeleton generation, analysis of compositions and conversations and conversation model generation); Execution monitoring (involves either centralised or distributed execution of composite web services). On the other hand, existing web service engines are ill-suited to support the dynamic and changing nature of service environments. The paper argues that a number of key limitations emerge, which hinder full exploitation of web services as a promising middleware technology to support virtual team working, including:

- Existing service description and Web Service flow languages are ill suited when addressing the dynamics and non-functional characteristics of distributed business processes. The current Business Process Execution Language (BPEL) version does not support run-time alterations to address unforeseen problems, such as the replacement or addition of a new Web Service. In order to manage this uncertainty, BPEL processes need to have the ability to be extended to meet unforeseen post-deployment requirements and user needs.

- Web service flow engines, such as the ones implemented to support BPEL, lack execution monitoring functionality to manage the running process. These can help debug processes during development stage, with monitoring, and even be driven by agents at production stage. It is possible, for example, to embed, without modifying the engine implementation, a planner on the top of the latter. From events triggered by a monitor, this planner can take actions to avoid any disruption and to adjust the process. Such a tool can be useful particularly for long running processes.

- Web service composition methodologies have a focus on syntactic integration and therefore do not support automatic composition of web services. Semantic integration is crucial for web services as it allows them to (a) represent and reason about the task that a web service performs, (b) explicitly express and reason about business relations and rules, (c) understand the meaning of exchanged messages, (d) represent and reason about preconditions that are required to use the service and the effects of having invoked the service, and (e) allow intelligent composition of web services to achieve a more complex service.

Also, long running virtual team processes are subject to evolutions and change of different nature: process model evolution due to change in the environment (change in the law, change in the methodology), process instance evolution (or ad-hoc evolution) due to specific events occurring during a given process execution (delay, new available or lack of resources) or partnership evolution at execution time having an impact on part of the process. These shortcomings require essential advances and improvements.

The research suggests that new forms of software licensing are needed to provide a better software service that includes configuration, maintenance, training and access to a help-desk to ensure that SMEs are efficiently supported along their path to engage effectively in virtual teams.

8. CONCLUSION

Original motivation of the analysis in this paper was to review present virtual team working research. However, the lack of present research made additional research questions equal focus of the paper. The characteristics of SMEs suggest that in researching, developing, and evaluating potential virtual teamwork solutions, the human and organisational aspects require close attention. This means that social and, ultimately, economical considerations have to be made rather than concentrating the development process on the technology alone as has been traditionally the case.

Given current limitations of virtual team research, the paper contributes to existing knowledge by raising a number of research questions related to (a) clarifying and defining the nature of teamwork that takes place amongst SMEs, (b) specifying the technological, regulatory and socio-organisational environment to support team working effectively; and (c) researching into factors that facilitate virtual team adoption and use across SMEs and more generally in relation to any organization. Also, while existing research has provided little formalization of working procedures and managerial structures of virtual teams, the paper calls for further research in (a) technology maturity and software provision models, (b) organisational and process settings, and (c) social, including socio-emotional considerations, adapted to the needs of SMEs. It is hoped that the paper will trigger further research that will contribute to develop a holistic understanding of the complex theme of Virtual Teams.

9. REFERENCES

1. Alsakini W, Kiiras J, Huovinen P. "Competitive Virtuality among Construction Management Services Company". In Encyclopaedia of Networked and Virtual Organizations, Goran D. Putnik, Maria M. Cunha, eds. Information Science Reference, 2006
2. Arnison L, Miller P. Virtual teams: a virtue for the conventional team. Journal of Workplace Learning 2002; 14: 166-173.

3. Barrett P, Sexton M. Innovation in small, project-based construction firms. British Journal of Management 2006; 17: 331-346.
4. Carmarinha-Matos LM, Afsarmanesh H. "Base concepts". In Virtual Organizations Systems and Practices, Luis M. Camarninha-Matos L, Hamideh Afsarmanesh, Martin Ollus, eds. New York: Springer Science, 2005.
5. Connaughton S, Daly J. Identification with leader: a comparison of perceptions of identification among geographically dispersed and co-located teams Corporate Communications: An International Journal 2004 9: 89–103.
6. Coulson and Kantamneni, Virtual corporations: the promise and perils. DC Press: 2006; www.dcpress.com/jmb/virtual.htm: last accessed 27/12/07
7. Franke, UJ. Virtual web organizations & market conditions. The electronic journal of organizational virtualiness: 2001; 3: 43-64.
8. Helling K, Blim M, O'Regan B. An appraisal of virtual networks in the environmental sector. Management of Environmental Quality: An International Journal 2005; 16: 327-337.
9. Hoefling T. Working Virtually: Managing People for Successful Virtual Teams and Organisations. Stylus Publishing, 2001.
10. Kaywoth T, Leidner D. The global virtual manager: a prescription for success. European Management Journal 2000; 18: 183-194.
11. Kaiser P, Tullar W, McKowen D. Student team projects by internet. Business Communication Quarterly 2000; 63: 75-82.
12. Kürümlüoglu M, and Nøstdal R, Karvonen I: "Base concepts". In In Virtual Organizations Systems and Practices, Luis M. Camarninha-Matos L, Hamideh Afsarmanesh, Martin Ollus, eds. New York: Springer Science, 2005.
13. Lipnack J, Stamps J. Virtual Teams: People Working Across Boundaries With Technology. New York: John Wiley & Sons, 2000.
14. Maznevski ML, Chudoba KM. Bridging space over time: global virtual team dynamics and effectiveness. Organisation Science 2000; 11: 473-492.
15. McDonough EF, Kahn KB, Barczak G. An investigation of the use of global, virtual and collocated new product development teams. The Journal of Product Innovation Management 2000; 18: 110-120.
16. Mezgár I. Integration of ICT in Smart Organizations. Idea Group Inc, 2006.
17. OASIS, BPEL specification, http://www.oasis-open.org/committees/tc_home.php?wg_abbrev=wsbpel last accessed 05/02/08.
18. Pawar KS, Sharifi S. Virtual collocation of design teams: coordinating for speed. International Journal of Agile Management Systems 2000; 2: 104-113.
19. Rezgui Y, Wilson I. "Socio-organizational issues". In Virtual Organizations Systems and Practices, Luis M. Camarninha-Matos L, Hamideh Afsarmanesh, Martin Ollus, eds. New York: Springer Science, 2005.
20. Rezgui Y. Exploring virtual team-working effectiveness in the construction sector. Interacting with Computers 2007; 19: 96-112.
21. Shelbourn M, Hassan T, Carter C. "Legal and contractual framework for the VO". In Virtual Organizations Systems and Practices, Luis M. Camarninha-Matos L, Hamideh Afsarmanesh, Martin Ollus, eds. New York: Springer Science, 2005.
22. Vakola M, Wilson IE. The challenge of virtual organization: critical success factors in dealing with constant change. Team Performance Management 2004; 10: 112-120.
23. Walker JW. E-leadership?. Human Resource Planning 2000; 23: 5-6.
24. Walters D. Virtual organizations: new lamps for old?. Management Decision 2000; 38: 420-436.
25. Wiesenfeld BM, Raghuram S, Garud R. Communication patterns as determinants of organizational identification in a virtual organization. Organization Science 2000; 10: 777-790.

26. Workman M.   Collectivism, individualism, and cohesion in a team-based occupation. Journal of Vocational Behavior 2001; 58: 82–97.
27. Workman M, Kahnweiler W, Bommer W. The effects of cognitive style and media richness on commitment to telework and virtual teams. Journal of Vocational Behaviour 2003; 63: 199-219.
28. Workman M. The effects from technology-mediated interaction and openness in virtual team performance measures. Behaviour and Information Technology 2007; 26: 355-365.
29. Yukl G. Leadership in organizations. Englewood Cliffs, NJ: Prentice-Hall Inc, 2002.
30. Zigurs I. Leadership in virtual teams: oxymoron or opportunity?. Organizational Dynamics 2003; 31: 339-351.

37

FRAMEWORK FOR OPEN, DISTRIBUTED AND SELF-MANAGED SOCIAL PLATFORMS

Juliana Mitchell-Wong, Suk Keong Goh, Mohan Baruwal Chhetri,
Ryszard Kowalczyk, Bao Quoc Vo
Centre for Information Technology Research
Swinburne University of Technology
Hawthorn, Victoria, AUSTRALIA
{jmitchellwong, sgoh, mchhetri, rkowalczyk, bvo}@ict.swin.edu.au

At present there are no digital social platforms that are open, distributed and self-managed. The openness enables end-users to customize their interactions through their selection of relationships and applications; and application developers to customize an interface for end-users with existing or new services. The distributed architecture ensures the scalability of content and entities, and the resilience to abuse. The self-managed platform provides the entity with control over its relationships; applications with control over the services it provides; and end-users with control over their interactions. These requirements led to the design of the social platform framework described in this paper. The key features of the framework are its modular design, use of open standards, distributed architecture, and policy-based management.

1. INTRODUCTION

A digital social platform is an environment that provides social entities with digital connectivity to other entities, and interactivity with other entities through digital applications. These entities represent individuals, communities, or organizations; and they each have a social network consisting of related entities. The mesh of all entity relationships forms the social ecosystem.

Digital social platforms are often associated with the development of web-based social ecosystems. However, the platform can be used to develop any social system where digital entities interact with others such as a supply chain management system. In this paper, the layers and modules of the social platform framework are abstract and applicable to all social ecosystems but the technologies and examples discussed are specific to web-based social ecosystems.

The paper is structured as follows. Section 2 presents background information on existing social platforms, followed in Section 3 with the motivation for the proposed platform framework. The framework along with the technologies for online communities is presented in Section 4; and the prototype implementation and validation of the framework is described in Section 5. A summary of the features for the proposed platform concludes the paper in Section 6.

Please use the following format when citing this chapter:

Mitchell-Wong, J., Goh, S.K., Chhetri, M.B., Kowalczyk, R. and Vo, B.Q., 2008, in IFIP International Federation for Information Processing, Volume 283; *Pervasive Collaborative Networks*; Luis M. Camarinha-Matos, Willy Picard; (Boston: Springer), pp. 361–368.

2. BACKGROUND

In recent years, a number of social platforms have emerged such as Facebook[1], Bebo[2], Elgg[3] and Krawler[4]. They each have different characteristics including open or closed platform source; centralized or distributed connectivity architecture; ecosystem specific or federated identity; direct, indirect, or group relationships; central or self defined profile access control; and application programming interface (API) or ecosystem specific application development.

Most social platforms are closed source and used to create an open ecosystem of entities such as Facebook and Bebo. There are also platforms for closed ecosystems, such as an organization's intranet, that are also closed source such as Krawler. These closed source platforms have led to the widespread walled garden ecosystems because their platforms are incompatible with one another. Open source social platforms such as Elgg enable social ecosystems to be compatible and integrable.

The architecture of most existing platforms is central where content is stored and managed from a single location. The limitations of this architecture include scalability of content and entities, and resilience to abuse. The distributed architecture addresses these limitations and some new platforms are moving in this direction such as Krawler.

Traditionally, the identity of entities is ecosystem specific. However as platforms move towards a distributed architecture such as Elgg, standards for federated identities are emerging such as OpenID[5]. Federated identities enable entities to use the same identity across garden walled ecosystems. This is a step forward towards enabling an entity to integrate its presence in multiple existing ecosystems, and eventually the integration towards a single ecosystem.

Federated identity is also important when entities form relationships across ecosystems of type direct, indirect or group. Direct relationships are those the entity can discover on its own; indirect relationships are those that require assistance from an existing relation such as in the Elgg platform; and group relationships are those that cluster existing relations. Direct relationship is the main type of relationship an entity forms in an ecosystem; group relationships are common in most ecosystems for organizing relationships; however many shy from indirect relationships because of the difficulty in maintaining the privacy and security of entities.

Privacy and security issues also arise in the access of content such as an entity's profile. In a web-based social ecosystem, it is commonly self-controlled, while intra-network social ecosystems such as those based on the Krawler platform are often controlled centrally. The central manager of an intra-network social ecosystem typically has the trust and agreement of its entities from the real world to publish their profile, and it is held accountable for breaching this trust.

Thus far the platform characteristics that support the end-user are described. Application development is a characteristic that affects developers. Since the launch of the Facebook API, it has been popular with both end-users and application developers. It enabled end-users to customize their interaction environment, and

---

[1] http://www.facebook.com/
[2] http://www.bebo.com/
[3] http://elgg.org/
[4] http://www.krawlernetworks.com/
[5] http://openid.net/

third party developers to develop applications. However Facebook is proprietary, which led to the development of Google's OpenSocial[6]. It was launched as an open API that is compatible across ecosystems that are developed based on the OpenSocial platform. Unlike Facebook that requires applications to be stored on its server, OpenSocial enable application developers to host their applications on their own server or with Google. Not too long after OpenSocial was released, Bebo released its Open Application Platform. It is open and based on the Facebook API because Bebo wanted to utilize the numerous existing applications developed for Facebook. Before these APIs, applications were custom developed for the ecosystem which was often inadequate to meet all the needs of the end-users. End-users overcame these inadequacies by forming their social networks in multiple ecosystems for the different applications they offer.

3. MOTIVATION

Existing platforms demonstrate a wide range of characteristics. However, there is no platform that is open, distributed and self-managed. The openness benefits both the end-user and application developer. End-users are able to customize their interaction environment through their selection of relationships and applications, independent of their community or organization membership; whilst application developers are able to customize an interface for end-users using existing or new services. The distributed architecture of a platform ensures the scalability of content and entities, and its resilience to abuse. The self-management in the platform provides entities with control over their relationships; applications with control over the services they provide; and end-users with control over their interactions.

These requirements led to the proposed platform, VastPark's openSocial[7]. The platform is open source, has a distributed architecture, uses federated identities, supports direct, indirect and group relationships, provides the user with control over their own profile, and has an open API for application development. Open source enable different ecosystems to be developed on the same platform, thus facilitating interactions between these ecosystems. The distributed connectivity architecture enables entities to interact independent of garden walled ecosystems. The federated identity management provides a unified profile, authentication, and authorization of an entity across garden walled ecosystems. The proposed platform enables the entity to define any type of relationships: direct, indirect and group. The privacy and security issues of these relationships are managed through self-defined policies for incoming and outgoing interaction access. Finally, applications are developed using an open API so that developers can create applications for multiple ecosystems and to manage their own service. Table 1 provides a characteristic comparison of the existing and proposed platforms.

---

[6] http://code.google.com/apis/opensocial/
[7] http://www.opensocial.com. Note that VastPark's openSocial is unrelated to Google's OpenSocial.

Table 1 – Characteristic comparison of existing and proposed social platforms.

	Facebook	Bebo	Elgg	Krawler	openSocial
Platform source	Closed	Closed	Open	Closed	Open
Connectivity architecture	Centralized	Centralized	Centralized	Distributed	Distributed
Identity management	Platform	Platform	Platform, federated	Platform	Federated
Supported relationship	Direct, group	Direct, group	Direct, indirect	Direct, group	Direct, indirect, group
Profile control	Entity	Entity	Entity	Platform	Entity
Application development	Closed API	Open API	Platform	Platform	Open API

4. PLATFORM FRAMEWORK

The framework of the platform in Figure 1 is designed as layers and modules. Layers separate the different areas of the framework whilst modules separate the different features within the layers. The layers are connectivity, social relationship, social tool, end-user application, management policy, and end-user or software agent. An interface connects the different layers and modules, thus eases the development and maintenance of the platform such that existing technologies are used and future technologies can replace the old. To enable the replacement of a module without affecting the others on the platform, a specification for the interfaces of the modules are required.

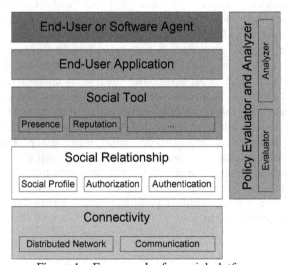

Figure 1 – Framework of a social platform

The connectivity layer form links to other entities on the web for interaction. It consists of two modules: distributed network and communication. The distributed or peer-to-peer (P2P) network is where entities discover and form links to other entities on the web. Discovering and linking entities at this low-level removes the dependence on applications. Some existing P2P protocol include Kademlia (Maymounkov, 2002) and Tapestry (Zhao, 2004). Communication between entities at the network level is commonly Transmission Control Protocol (TCP)[8] or User Datagram Protocol (UDP)[9]. Other available protocols include the Datagram Congestion Control Protocol (DCCP)[10] and the Stream Control Transmission Protocol (SCTP)[11].

The social relationship layer establishes relationships with other entities. It consists of three modules: social profile, authentication, and authorization. The social profile defines its direct, indirect and group relationships. This profile is stored locally or by a third party. The authentication and authorization modules verify the identity and acknowledge the relationship of an entity. Relationships are mostly formed in a centralized architecture where authentication and authorization are performed by a central authority. However as relationships begin to form in a distributed architecture; open standards for authentication and authorization have emerged such as Security Access Markup Language (SAML) for the exchange of authentication and authorization between entities; and OpenID for the authentication of identities.

The social tool layer consists of tools that utilize relationships to obtain information. Presence and reputation are two examples of such tools. Presence is a tool that determines the state of a user represented by an entity on the web. The simplest presence tool has two user states: online and offline. In recent years, the eXtensible Messaging and Presence Protocol (XMPP)[12] also known as Jabber has gained popularity as the protocol for presence awareness. The reputation of an entity is the aggregated observations from other entities. It has been used effectively on the web in centralized communities where observations are reported to the central authority, such as e-Bay[13]. In distributed models, observations are obtained from other entities as required. Existing distributed reputation models include PeerTrust (Xiong, 2003) and Trust Model for Mobile Agent Systems Based on Reputation (TRUMMAR) (Derbas, 2004).

Applications provide end-users with their interaction environment interface. They are custom made for the ecosystem, or developed by a third-party. Custom made applications are often proprietary. However, if open technologies such as Internet Message Access Protocol (IMAP) are used, interactions can cross ecosystems. Applications can also be a mashup (aggregation) of services or widgets (small applications), making it easier for users to create their own application. Bebo's Open Application Platform and Google's OpenSocial are two APIs that enable third-parties to develop applications for use across different platforms.

The policies in the social platform controls access authorization to resources, and sets obligatory actions which can be a reward, penalty or neutral action when specified conditions are met. These policies are specified and evaluated against a request in a language such as Ponder (Damianou, 2001), Rei (Kagal, 2002) and

---

[8] http://tools.ietf.org/rfc/rfc793.txt
[9] http://tools.ietf.org/rfc/rfc768.txt
[10] http://tools.ietf.org/rfc/rfc4340.txt
[11] http://tools.ietf.org/rfc/rfc4960.txt
[12] http://www.xmpp.org/
[13] http://www.ebay.com/

eXtensible Access Control Markup Language (XACML)[14]. The completeness and consistency of policies are often analyzed using logic. The two most common types of logic for this are description logic (DL) and logic programming. They are both mature research areas, thus either representation of the policy leads to readily available analysis tools such as Selected Linear Without contrapositive clause Variants (SLWV) a theorem prover for logic programming (Pereira, 1993), and Pellet a DL reasoner (Sirin, 2007). There are three types of resources: entity, application, and user interaction. The entity's policy controls access to its profile that consists of relationship and personal information, and its policy that explicitly specifies its access control. This policy is used for organizing the entity's relationships. The application's policy controls access to its profile that consists of service and attribute information, and its policy that explicitly specifies its access control. This policy is used for managing the application's quality of service. The user's interaction policy controls the access of incoming and outgoing messages according to the sender's relationship and the application used. This policy is used for managing user-to-user interactions.

The end-user initiates an action or responds to the action of others according to its interaction goals. Its interaction behavior is based on its knowledge of the relevant policies of its own, other users, and applications. When a planned action conflicts with a policy, the user decides if it is willing to bear the consequences of performing the planned action or to change its plan. The framework enables software agents to be used for automating the user interactions according to a specified goal. Existing agent toolkits include Java Agent DEvelopment (JADE)[15].

5. IMPLEMENTATION AND VALIDATION

VastPark's openSocial prototype is implemented according to the platform framework with basic functionality for each layer as shown in Figure 2. Although the modules are basic, they illustrate the benefits and validate the framework.

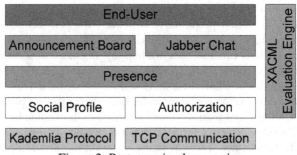

Figure 2: Prototype implementation

Two modules of the connectivity layer are implemented: distributed network and communication. The distributed network module is implemented with the Kademlia P2P protocol for discovering and linking entities in the social ecosystem and the

---

[14] http://www.oasis-open.org/committees/xacml/
[15] http://jade.tilab.com/

communication module is implemented with TCP to provide reliable in-order delivery of messages which is suitable for file transfer but not for streaming video. One problem the prototype faces with the distributed network is the prevention of incoming connections to systems behind different organization's firewalls. This is one of the problems that policy-based management of interactions aims to alleviate by providing the option to manage based on relationships rather than applications.

The social relationship layer consists of the entity's profile and authorization of other entities. The profile is managed locally by the entity and includes information on its relationships and personal details such as age and interests. The local management of the profile provides a single point for information about the entity. However, it requires the entity to be always present to respond to requests. The use of federated identity providers will eliminate this limitation. The authorization of other entities depends on the relationship policies of the entity.

The social tool layer consists of the presence tool which has been custom designed for the prototype. It compiles the status information of users by querying the entities directly or by receiving the information from a common relation.

The application is an announcement board that enables end-users to chat using Jabber. The application enables users to post announcements to the social ecosystem. This action utilizes the presence tool to determine the status of its relations, and their connectivity and communication channel. To respond to the announcements, users use the Jabber service. The announcement board is an application which integrates an external service and a custom built service.

The management policy is specified using the XACML language for controlling interactions to and from the entity and end-user. Authorizing interactions to and from the entity involves forming relationships whilst for the end-user it involves satisfying relationship and application conditions. The policies enable the entity and end-user to self-manage their incoming and outgoing interactions.

The end-user manually interacts with other users through the application interface with constraints set by the relevant policies it defines. This user to user interaction can be automated with software agents in the future.

The layers and modules of the framework such as the connectivity layer enable the replacement of the P2P or communication protocol module without affecting other modules as the interface between layers and modules have a specified format. Furthermore, it simplifies the development of each layer and module.

The prototype validates the framework and a summary is presented in Table 2. To find a plumbing service, an end-user customizes its interaction environment by establishing an interaction network consisting of entities that are plumbers and the application announcement board. This application is composed of a customized messaging service and the Jabber chat service. The entities are represented by peers in a P2P connectivity network; and they each manage their own profile and policy locally on their peer and not on a central server. Policies are used to manage an entity's relationship, the application's services and the end-user's interactions. Unlike other platforms where policies can only be written with conditions based on pre-defined attributes, the policies of this framework have the flexibility to be written with multiple conditions consisting of attributes defined by different sources. For example, the policy can combine the entity's trust measure of an entity with the number of announcements it receives a day as measured by the announcement board application to determine the result of the request.

6. CONCLUSION

Although the prototype implemented is rather basic, it still illustrates the characteristics of the platform framework: connectivity and communication between entities in a distributed network, relationship organization, aggregation of information from relations, aggregation of services or widgets to form an application, and self-management of relationships, applications and interactions.

The proposed framework combines the best characteristics for achieving an open, distributed and self-managed platform which no previous platforms have done. The key features are its modular design, use of open standards, distributed architecture, and policy-based management. The modular design eases the development and maintenance of the framework such that existing technology can be easily replaced with newer technology, and the failure of one component does not lead to the collapse of the system. Open standards ensure interoperability and widespread adoption and uptake of the platform because they are developed publicly by the collaboration of users and developers. The distributed architecture ensures scalability in content and entities, and resilience to abuse. The policies can be used to selectively share information rather than adhering to a fixed mechanism. This offers the entity, application, and end-user a more complete control over its information and interaction.

There are still research problems to tackle before the end-user's web-based social network reflects those in the real world, and are accepted by end-users. Among them are the monitoring and enforcement of policies, and integration of policies between entities such as those between an individual and a community. These are some current work of our group.

7. ACKNOWLEDGEMENTS

This work has been supported by the Agent-Enabled Social Networks project in collaboration with VastPark under the Australian Research Council's Linkage funding scheme (ARC Linkage Project LP0562500).

8. REFERENCES

1. Damianou N, Dulay N, Lupu E, Sloman M. The Ponder Policy Specification Language. In Proceedings of the Workshop on Policies for Distributed Systems and Networks 2001; 1995: 18-39.
2. Derbas G, Kayssi A, Artail H, Chehab A. TRUMMAR – A Trust Model for Mobile Agent Systems Based on Reputation. In Proceedings of the IEEE/ACS International Conference on Pervasive Services 2004; 113-120.
3. Kagal L. Rei: A Policy Language for the Me-Centric Project. HP Labs Technical Report 2002.
4. Maymounkov P, Mazieres D. Kademlia: A Peer-to-peer Information System Based on the XOR Metric. In Proceedings of the 1st International Workshop on Peer-to-Peer Systems 2002; 53-65.
5. Pereira LM, Caires L, Alferes J. SLWV – A Theorem Prover for Logic Programming. In Lecture Notes in Computer Science 1993; 660/1993:1-23.
6. Sirin E, Parsia B, Grau B C, Kalyanpur A, Katz Y. Journal of Web Semantics 2007; 5(2): 51-3.
7. Xiong L, Liu L. A Reputation-Based Trust Model for Peer-to-Peer E-Commerce Communities. In Proceedings of the IEEE International Conference on E-Commerce 2003; 275-284.
8. Zhao BY, Huang L, Stribling J, Rhea SC, Joseph AD, Kubiatowicz JD. Tapestry: A Resilient Global-Scale Overlay for Service Deployment. IEEE Journal on Selected Areas in Communications 2004; 22(1): 41-53.

PART 12

COMPLEX ADAPTIVE SYSTEMS

38

TOWARDS A COLLABORATIVE MODEL FOR WIRELESS SENSOR NETWORKS

Lina M. Pestana Leão de Brito, Laura M. Rodríguez Peralta
and Maurício D. Luís Reis

Laboratory for Usage-centered Software Engineering (LabUse),
Centro de Ciências Matemáticas (CCM), Mathematics and Engineering Department (DME)
University of Madeira (UMa), Campus da Penteada 9000-390 Funchal, Madeira,
PORTUGAL.
{lina, lmrodrig, m_reis}@uma.pt

Collaboration is crucial to Wireless Sensor Networks (WSNs) as a result of the typical resource limitations of wireless sensor nodes. In this paper, we present a model of collaborative work for WSNs. This model is called Wireless Sensor Networks Supported Cooperative Work (WSNSCW) and was created for these specific networks. We also present the formalization of some entities of the model and its properties. This is a generic model that is being used as a basis for the development of a 3D awareness tool for WSNs.

1. Introduction

A Wireless Sensor Network (WSN) consists of a large number of wireless sensor nodes that are, typically, densely deployed. These nodes collect data in the environment surrounding them. Then, data is sent to the user via a sink node, in a multi-hop basis (Alkyildiz et al., 2002).

Taking advantage of wireless communications, WSNs allow for a wide range of applications: environmental monitoring, surveillance, health, traffic monitoring, security, military, industry, agriculture, catastrophe monitoring, etc.

However, wireless sensor nodes are intended to be small and cheap. Consequently, these nodes are typically resource limited (limited battery, reduced memory and processing capabilities). Moreover, due to short transmission range, nodes can only communicate locally, with a certain number of local neighbours. Consequently, wireless sensor nodes have to collaborate in order to accomplish their tasks: sensing, signal processing, computing, routing, localization, security, etc. Thus, WSNs are, by nature, collaborative networks (Gracanin et al., 2006).

At the moment, there are several works regarding collaboration in WSNs, but they refer to a specific type of collaborative task. Until now, the only work that presents a model for cooperative work in sensor networks has been proposed by Liu et al. (2006). However, this model does not consider the particularities of WSNs.

In this paper, we present a model of cooperative work designed for the specific case of WSNs, named Wireless Sensor Networks Supported Cooperative Work

Please use the following format when citing this chapter:

Leão de Brito, L.M.P., Peralta, L.M.R. and Reis, M.D.L., 2008, in IFIP International Federation for Information Processing, Volume 283; *Pervasive Collaborative Networks*; Luis M. Camarinha-Matos, Willy Picard; (Boston: Springer), pp. 371–380.

(WSNSCW). So, it considers the specific requirements of WSNs. It allows not only for the modelling of collaborative work (based in CSCW concepts), but also for the modelling of all the entities that can constitute a WSN. This model is being used in the development of a 3D awareness tool for WSNs.

This paper is organized as follows. In section 2, we briefly describe the related work. In section 3, the WSNSCW model is defined, formalized and exemplified. Section 4 provides some conclusions and perspectives of future work.

2. Related Work

Even though there are several works concerning collaboration in WSNs, they only focus a specific type of collaboration, which is associated with the accomplishment of a certain task, such as: sensing (Wang et al., 2005), signal processing (Ramanathan et al., 2002), computing (Iftode et al., 2004), routing (Chen et al., 2006), localization (Dardari et al., 2004), security (Chadha et al., 2005), task scheduling (Sanli et al., 2005), heuristics (Reghelin et al., 2006), calibration (Bychkovskiy et al., 2003), resource allocation (Giannecchini et al., 2004), time synchronization (Hu et al., 2005), transmission (Krohn et al., 2006), etc. Usually, these collaborations simply intend to improve some parameters of the network (energy cost, coverage, transmission cost, processing cost, delay, etc.).

There are also works regarding collaboration between wireless sensor nodes and other devices (heterogeneous groupware collaboration) to support some specific applications (for e.g., collaboration between sensor nodes and PDAs, in a fire fighting scenario (Cheng et al., 2004)).

The only work found in literature that presents a model for collaborative work in sensor networks, to date, has been proposed by Liu et al. (2006). It is the SNSCW (Sensor Networks Supported Cooperative Work) model. It is a hierarchical model that divides cooperation in sensor networks in two layers. The first one relates to cooperation between humans and sensor nodes (user-executor relationship, being initiated either by the user or by the sensor node), and the other layer relates to cooperation between the sensor nodes (considers two main subtypes of cooperation: peer-to-peer and master-to-slave).

This model was designed for sensor networks. However, it does not consider the specific requirements of WSNs, for instance: its scale, its self-configuration and self-maintenance requirements, the resource limitations of wireless sensor nodes, etc. Also, it only allows for modelling of collaboration itself.

3. The WSNSCW Model

In this section, we present a model of collaborative work for the specific case of WSNs, named Wireless Sensor Networks Supported Cooperative Work (WSNSCW). As WSNSCW is a model of collaborative work created specifically to WSNs, it considers the particular requirements of WSNs. It is, essentially, a graph-based model; nevertheless, it includes other objects in order to make the modelling of all the entities of a WSN possible, which is fundamental to completely represent a WSN.

The SNSCW model (Liu et al., 2006) only focuses the different types of cooperation that can occur in a WSN. Our model not only allows for the modelling of cooperation within the network, but also for the modelling of the entire WSN and all its entities (different types of nodes, relationships, base stations, clusters, etc.). Regarding collaboration, the model includes some fundamental CSCW (Computer Supported Cooperative Work) concepts and properties.

Moreover, WSNSCW is a generic model, in the sense that it can be applied to any type of wireless sensor nodes, regardless of its size, its hardware characteristics, the types of signals it can measure, etc. It can also be applied to any WSN despite of its specific application. However, in this paper we are going to illustrate the application of this model to the specific case of an environmental monitoring application.

3.1 Definitions

We define *entities* as all the components that might exist in a WSN. Table 1 shows the symbol, the concept and the description of all the entities included in the proposed model.

A WSN can have different types of nodes: ordinary wireless *sensor nodes*, *anchor nodes* (which support the sensor nodes in the localization process), one or more *sink nodes* (also known as base stations, which are responsible for sending data to the gateway) and a *gateway* (responsible for sending data to the user, through the Internet). If nodes are grouped in *clusters*, one of the members of each cluster becomes the *cluster head*. In this case, all nodes have to send data to the cluster head (usually, the most powerful node of the cluster), which, in turn, is responsible for sending data to a sink node.

If two nodes collaborate, a *relationship* is established between them. This relationship can be based on: localization of the nodes (proximity), common cluster, phenomenon to monitor, hardware characteristics of the sensor node, etc. Associated with a relationship there is always an exchange of data, which corresponds to the *data flow* entity. Collected data (temperature, humidity, light, etc.) can be sent to other nodes using one or more types of signals (radio, acoustical, etc.). *Obstacles* may obstruct the line-of-sight between nodes, influencing the relationships created.

Several collaborative *sessions* can be established when monitoring a WSN, and they can exist simultaneously or not. Basically, new sessions may be established based on new goals (type of phenomenon to monitor, geographical area to monitor, monitoring time, etc.).

As *battery* is the most critical resource of a sensor node, it is really important that the user knows the state of the battery of each node. Thus, the battery is also an entity of our model.

3.2 WSNSCW Formalization

Using both first-order logic and graph theory, we formalize the main properties of only some of the entities of the model: sensor node, network (WSN) and sink node.

Table 1 - Definition of the entities can constitute a Wireless Sensor Network.

Symbol	Concept	Description
○	Sensor node	Wireless sensor nodes, typically with limited resources. These nodes can be either stationary or mobile. Also, they can be in one of two possible states: active or inactive (sleep mode) in order to save energy.
S_K	Sink node/ Base Station	Node to which data collected by ordinary nodes is sent; being responsible to send data to the gateway. If there is more than one sink node, data may be sent to any sink node and, in this case, sink nodes must be able to communicate to each other.
Ⓐ	Anchor node	Node with known localization.
⬡	Cluster	Group of nodes, created according to: geographical area, type of sensor, type of phenomenon, task, etc.
CH	Cluster Head	Sensor node to whom all sensor nodes in the cluster send the collected data; it is responsible for sending the received data to the Sink node.
Ⓐ ➔ Ⓑ	Relationship	The arrow represents a relationship between nodes A and B. It also represents and adjacency relation between nodes A and B (see section 3.2); nodes A and B are neighbours. A relationship can be established based on: localization, phenomenon, type of sensor node, etc.
{TypeOfSignal.Data} ➔	Data flow	This label identifies both the type of signal being used (radio frequency, ultrasound, acoustical or light) and the type of data being transmitted between nodes (temperature, humidity, light, sound, video, internal voltage, etc.).
▨	Gateway	Device responsible to send the data to the user, through the Internet.
◈	Obstacle	An object (building, tree, rock, etc.) which obstructs line-of-sight between two or more nodes, not allowing for direct communication between them.
⬭	Session	In a certain moment, there may be several collaborative sessions in a WSN. A session can be established based on the objective (type of phenomenon to monitor, geographical area to monitor, etc.) of the WSN.
▮	Battery	It represents the percentage of the sensor node's remaining battery.
人	User	Person that interacts with the WSN, querying the network, visualizing data, etc. The user customizes the work of the sensor nodes; the data collected by sensor nodes is used by the users' application.

Definitions

We can formulate the sensor network as a graph $G(V, E)$. V (vertices) represents the set of sensor nodes, and E (edges) describes the adjacency relation between nodes. That is, for two nodes u, v ∈ V, (u, v) ∈ E if and only if v is adjacent to u.

An arrow between two nodes represents a relationship between them. The arrow represents a producer-consumer relationship. Considering, for example, two nodes: A and B; the arrow Ⓐ ➔ Ⓑ means that node A transmits data to node B. So, node B consumes information from node A. The transmission of data between both nodes follows the format *TypeOfSignal.Data* ({TypeOfSignal.Data} ➔), verifying the consumer-producer property.

Assuming Nr is the total number of sensor nodes that constitute the WSN, let $\mathcal{N}$ = {1, 2, ..., Nr}. Let's represent a wireless sensor node by N_i, with i $\in$ $\mathcal{N}$.

The WSN has a limited lifetime, which can vary from some hours to several months or years. Denoting by LT the lifetime of the network (in seconds), let $\mathcal{T}$ = {1, 2,..., LT} and t_j represent the jth second of life of the network, with j $\in$ $\mathcal{T}$.

Sensor Node (N_i)
A sensor node (N_i) is defined by: N_i = {TS, CM, R, B, L, TM, S, I_D, Ty}. Table 2 defines and formalizes the properties that characterize the entity Sensor Node (Ni).

Table 2 - Definition of the properties of the entity Sensor Node (N_i).

	Properties	Description / Formalization
Sensor Node (N_i)	Types of sensors (TS)	A sensor node (N_i) can have several types of sensors, each one measuring a different phenomenon: Light (Li), Temperature (Te), Humidity (Hu), Sound (Sd), Internal voltage (Iv), Etc. So, TS (N_i) $\subseteq$ {Li, Te, Hu, Sd, Iv, ...}
	Communication modality (CM)	A number of communication modalities can be used, such as: Radio (RF), Light (Li), Ultrasound (US), Acoustical (Ac), Hybrid (Hy). So, CM (N_i) $\subseteq$ {RF, Li, US, Ac, Hy}
	Transmission Range (R)	The nominal transmission range of a radio signal is typically a function of its transmission power level (P_t). Let P_t be the nominal transmission power of a node. $P_R; j \leftarrow i$ is the received power of a signal propagated from node i to node j. A received power $P_R; j \leftarrow i$ above a given threshold P_{th} will provide sufficient SNR (*Signal to Noise Ratio*) in the receiver to decode the transmission. The nominal maximum distance for successful communication can be defined as (Krohn et al., 2006): R = P_t/P_{th} Note that the range can vary between $r=(1-\varepsilon).R$ and R, $\varepsilon > 0$.
	Battery (B)	The lifetime of a sensor node (N_i) is limited by its battery, depending on its capacity and type. The battery can be defined by: • Type of battery -T_B, with T_B (N_i) $\in$ {lithium, alkaline, li-ion, AA, external power supply, solar cells, electromagnetic and piezoelectric transducers, etc.} • Capacity (voltage) - C_B (N_i) [V] • Remaining capacity at time t_j - P_{BNi} (t_j) [%] B_{Ni} (t_j) = {T_B (N_i), C_B (N_i), P_{BNi} (t_j)}
	Localization (L)	Let L_{Ni}(t_j), with i $\in$ $\mathcal{N}$ and j $\in$ $\mathcal{T}$, denote the location of node N_i at time t_j. The type of deployment affects important properties of the network (node density, node locations, etc.). The deployment of sensor nodes may be: • Random (ad hoc deployment, for e.g. dropped by an aircraft). In this case, the localization of a node is unknown: L_{Ni} (t_j) = (x, y, z), where x, y, z $\in$ $\mathbb{R}$ are unknown. • Manual: sensor nodes are deployed in pre-determined positions. In this case, the localization of a node is well-known: L_{Ni} (t_j) = (a, b, c), where a, b, c $\in$ $\mathbb{R}$ are known.
	State (S)	Depending on its power mode, the node N_i can be in one of two states (S): Active (Ac) – Node which is in the active state. Inactive (In) - Node which is in the sleep mode, in order to save energy. So, S (N_i) = Ac or S (N_i) = In

○	Properties	Description / Formalization
	Type of Mobility (TM)	A sensor node (N_i) can be: ■ Stationary (St): $L_{Ni}(t_1) = L_{Ni}(t_2) = \ldots = L_{Ni}(t_{LT})$ ■ Mobile (Mb): The period of mobility can be occasional or continuous: • Occasional (Oc), when long periods of immobility occur: $\exists\, j, l \in \mathcal{T}: L_{Ni}(t_j) \neq L_{Ni}(t_l)$, and $j \neq l \;\wedge\; \exists\, r, s \in \mathcal{T}: L_{Ni}(r) = L_{Ni}(r+1) = \ldots = L_{Ni}(s)$, and $s \gg r$ • Continuous (Cont): $\forall\, j \in \mathcal{T} \setminus \{LT\}\; L_{Ni}(t_{j+1}) \neq L_{Ni}(t_j)$ Mobility can still be classified in: ■ Incidental (Inc), for e.g., due to environmental influences $\approx$ Occasional ■ Desired (Des), whether active or passive, which can be applied to any period of mobility (occasional or continuous). So, TM (N_i) $\in$ {St, {OcMb, Inc}, {OcMb, Des}, {ContMb, Inc}, {ContMb, Des}}
	Identifier (I_D)	Each sensor node has a unique identifier (I_D) $I_D(N_i) = i$, $i \in N$
	Type (Ty)	Alphanumeric that identifies the manufacturer and model of the sensor node. Ty (N_i) = {Manufacturer (N_i), Model (N_i)}

Sink Node (S_K)

Only the properties that differentiate the sink node from the ordinary sensor nodes are described and formalized in Table 3, distinguishing between two cases: Stationary Sink Node (StS_K) and Mobile Sink Node (MbS_K).

Table 3 - Definition and formalization of some of the properties of the entity Sink Node (S_K).

S_K	Stationary (StS_K)		Mobile (MbS_K)	
	Properties	**Description/ Formalization**	**Properties**	**Description / Formalization**
Sink Node (S_K)	Localization (L)	Defined by L_{StSK}, the localization of a stationary sink node is well-known and independent of time.	Localization (L)	Defined by L_{MbSK}, the localization of a mobile sink node varies as it moves along the network.
	Type of Mobility (TM)	TM (StS_K) = St	Type of Mobility (TM)	• Continuous: TM (MbS_K) = {ContMb, Des} • When necessary (the sink node can move in order to allow for other sensor nodes to communicate with it): TM (MbS_K) = {OcMb, Des}
	Power supply (PS)	■ Battery (B) ■ Solar cells (SC) ■ External and unlimited power supply (VDC) ■ Etc. PS (StS_K) $\subseteq$ {B, SC, VDC, etc.}	Power supply (PS)	■ Battery (B) ■ Solar cells (SC) PS (MbS_K) $\subseteq$ {B, SC}

Network (WSN)

A WSN is defined by: WSN = {To, M, H, Nr, A, C, D, Hi, NS$_K$, NA, LT}. Table 4 defines and formalizes all the properties that characterize the entity Network (WSN).

Table 4 - Definition of the properties of the entity Network (WSN).

	Properties	Description / Formalization
Network (WSN)	Topology (To)	The WSN can have different topologies (To): Single-hop, Star, Networked stars, Tree, Graph and Grid. So, To $\in$ {Single-hop, Star, Net-Stars, Tree, Graph, Grid}
	Mobility (M)	There are some different possible scenarios, regarding mobility of sensor nodes: • All nodes are stationary: $\forall$ i $\in$ $\mathcal{N}$, $\forall$ j, l $\in$ $\mathcal{T}$ $L_{Ni}(t_j) = L_{Ni}(t_l)$ • All nodes are mobile: $\forall$ i $\in$ $\mathcal{N}$, $\exists$ j, l $\in$ $\mathcal{T}$: $L_{Ni}(t_j) \neq L_{Ni}(t_l)$, and j $\neq$ l • Only some nodes move: $\exists$ i $\in$ $\mathcal{N}$, $\exists$ j, l $\in$ $\mathcal{T}$: $L_{Ni}(t_j) \neq L_{Ni}(t_l)$, and j $\neq$ l $\wedge$ $\exists$ p $\in$ $\mathcal{N}$: $L_{Np}(t_1) = L_{Np}(t_2) = ... = L_{Np}(t_{LT})$

	Homogeneity (H)	A WSN can be:
		• Homogeneous (Ho), when it is composed by homogeneous devices, which means that sensor nodes are mostly identical from a hardware and a software point of view.
		   • Ho: $\forall$ i, p $\in$ $\mathcal{N}$, Ty (N$_i$) = Ty (N$_p$) and i $\neq$ p
		• Heterogeneous (He), when it is composed by heterogeneous devices, which means that sensor nodes are mostly different from a hardware and a software point of view, for e.g., in type and number of attached sensors (TS).
		   • He: $\exists$ i, p $\in$ N : Ty (Ni) $\neq$ Ty (Np)
		So, H = Ho or H= He

	Number (Nr)	Total number of sensor nodes that constitute the WSN, which may vary from a few nodes to thousands of sensor nodes. Nr $\in$ N
	Area (A)	Area of deployment (m^2). A $\in$ R$^+$
	Coverage (C)	A WSN can have different types of coverage: • Sparse (Sp), when the network coverage is much smaller than its deployment area. • Dense (De), when the network coverage coincides with its deployment area, or comes close to it. • Redundant (Re), when multiple sensors cover the same area. So, C $\in$ {Sp, De, Re}
	Density (D)	Network density can be defined in terms of number of nodes per nominal coverage area (Bulusu et al., 2001): $D = (Nr \times \pi \times R^2) / C_A$, where C_A is the area that is covered by the whole network. C_A (m^2) $\in$ R$^+$ Note that the coverage area (C_A) may be different from the deployment area (A).
	Hierarchy (Hi)	Clusters may be created according to: geographical area, type of sensor nodes, type of phenomenon to monitor, etc., providing the WSN with a hierarchical structure. All clusters must have a cluster head (CH).
	Number of sink nodes (NS$_K$)	A WSN has one or more sink nodes. A sink node can be stationary (StS$_K$) or mobile (MbS$_K$). NS$_K$ < Nr
	Number of anchor nodes (NA)	Anchor nodes are nodes with known location. They can be stationary or mobile: • Stationary anchor node (StA) • Mobile anchor node (MbA) NA < Nr
	Lifetime (LT)	Deployment may be: • One-time activity. In this case, LT = K with K $\in$ N

	Properties	Description / Formalization
		▪ Iterative (continuous) process. In this case, LT ≈ ∞

3.3 Example Scenario

We validate the WSNSCW model by applying it to the specific case of an environmental monitoring application. This work was developed in the context of an European project, named FORESMAC (Project INTERREG III B, 05/MAC/2.3/C16). The purpose of this project is to create a WSN in order to accomplish environmental monitoring of forests.

So, let's consider the example of a forest monitoring WSN. As Figure 1 illustrates, there are 3 simultaneous collaborative sessions. These sessions where initiated by the user, with three different objectives: to monitor the temperature of area A1 (CS1), to monitor the light of area A2 (CS2), and to monitor the humidity of the same area (CS3). So, nodes were deployed in an ad hoc manner, in two different geographical areas of a forest CS2 and CS3 represent exactly the same area; hence, exactly the same nodes). There are 2 sink nodes, 4 anchor nodes and 20 wireless sensor nodes. Within each area, clusters have been created; there are 2 clusters in Area A1 and 2 clusters in area A2; hence, there are 4 cluster heads (CH).

As this scenario relates to an environmental monitoring application, it is very important to correlate collected data in space. So, anchor nodes had to be deployed. The nodes that belong to a cluster are in the active state, as they need to monitor the phenomenon. The remaining nodes are in the sleep mode. The user is typically far away from the forest being monitored. So, he monitors it through the Internet.

Any changes that might occur on this scenario (new collaborative sessions, new clusters, nodes changing from sleep mode to the active state or vice versa, nodes moving, etc.) can be represented by a sequence of figures analogous to Figure 1.

So, by using the WSNSCW model to represent a WSN, it is possible to easily identify the different components of the network and its operation.

3.4 Awareness Tool

We are developing a 3D awareness tool, based in the WSNSCW model that will allow for an interactive navigation in the map of the network. The 3D representation of the network is very important for an awareness tool, so the user can have a more realistic view of the network; it is more appropriated for representing a WSN deployed in different types of terrains (flat, mountainous, etc.), different types of rooms, which obstacles might interfere with the collaboration established between nodes, etc.

Besides allowing for the visualization of all the components defined in the model (different types of nodes, relationships between them, different clusters, data flows, etc.) and its properties, this tool will allow for the visualization of the network hierarchy and, also, for the visualization of different granularities: fine-grain (sensor nodes), middle-grain (clusters) and coarser (sessions) modeling level.

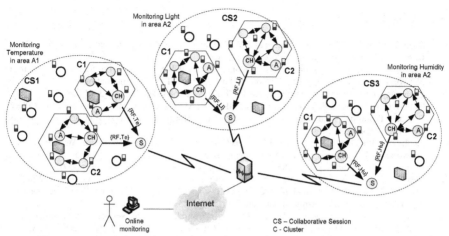

Figure 1 - Applying the WSNSCW model to the specific case of a forest environmental monitoring.

4. CONCLUSIONS AND FUTURE WORK

In this paper we presented the WSNSCW model, which is based in the CSCW methodology and specifically designed for WSNs. The great advantage of this model lies in the fact that, besides modelling collaboration, it also allows for modelling the entire WSN, all its entities, properties, relationships, states, etc., which is fundamental to completely represent a WSN.

This model allows for the representation of the network hierarchy (from the collected data to the user), as well. Moreover, it allows for the representation of each state of the network and its evolution.

In this paper, we applied this model to the specific case of a forest environmental monitoring application. However, it is a generic model that can be applied to an heterogeneous network (any type of sensors and any type of application). So, it is possible to use the entities defined in the model to represent a certain scenario of any application (monitoring a forest, a vineyard, a volcano, a museum, etc.).

Regarding collaboration, the model includes some CSCW concepts (such as: session, relationship, data flow and groups) and properties (such as: connectivity and flow control). In the near future, we intend to include more CSCW concepts. We also intend to complete the formalization of this model using graph theory.

The WSNSCW model is being used as a basis for the development of a 3D awareness tool, which aims at giving the user a more realistic view of the network.

5. REFERENCES

1. Akyildiz, I., Su, W., Sankarasubramaniam, Y., Cayirci, E., "A Survey on Sensor Networks", IEEE Communications Magazine, Aug. 2002, pp. 102-109.
2. Bulusu, N., Estrin, D., Girod, L., Heidemann, J., "Scalable Coordination for Wireless Sensor Networks: Self-Configuring Localization Systems", Proc. of the 6th International Symposium on Communication Theory and Applications (ISCTA'01), Ambleside, UK, July 2001, pp. 1-6.
3. Bychkovskiy, V., Megerian, S., Estrin, D., Potkonjak, M., "A Collaborative Approach to In-Place Sensor Calibration", 2nd International Workshop on Information Processing in Sensor Networks (IPSN'03), April 2003.
4. Chadha, A., Liu, Y., Das, S., "Group Key Distribution via Local Collaboration in Wireless Sensor Networks", 2nd Annual IEEE Communications Society Conference on Sensor and Ad Hoc Communications and Networks (SECON 2005), Santa Clara, California, USA, Sep. 2005.
5. Chen, G., Guo, T.-D., Yang, W.-G., Zhao, T., "An improved ant-based routing protocol in Wireless Sensor Networks", International Conference on Collaborative Computing: Networking, Applications and Worksharing (CollaborateCom 2006), Nov. 2006, pp. 1-7.
6. Cheng, L., Lian, T., Zhang, Y., Ye, Q., "Monitoring Wireless Sensor Networks by Heterogeneous Collaborative Groupware", Sensors for Industry Conference (Sicon/04), New Orleans, USA, Jan. 2004.
7. Dardari, D., Conti, A., "A Sub-Optimal Hierarchical Maximum Likelihood Algorithm for Collaborative Localization in Ad-Hoc Networks", 1st Annual IEEE Communications Society Conference on Sensor and Ad Hoc Communications and Networks (IEEE SECON 2004), Oct. 2004, pp. 425- 429.
8. Giannecchini, S., Caccamo, M., Shih, C.-S., "Collaborative resource allocation in wireless sensor networks", in Proc. of Euromicro Conference on Real-Time Systems (ECRTS'04), June/July 2004, pp. 35–44.
9. Gracanin, D., Adams, K., Eltoweissy, M., "Data Replication in Collaborative Sensor Network Systems", in Proc. 25th IEEE International Performance, Computing, and Communications Conference (IPCCC 2006), April 2006, pp. 389-396.
10. Hu, A., Servetto, S., "Algorithmic Aspects of the Time Synchronization Problem in Large-Scale Sensor Networks", Mobile Networks and Applications, 10, 2005 Springer Science + Business Media Inc., 2005, pp. 491-503.
11. Iftode, L., Borcea, C., Kang, P., Cooperative Computing in Sensor Networks, Handbook of Sensor Networks: Compact Wireless and Wired Sensing Systems, Mohammad Ilyas (ed.), CRC Press, July 2004.
12. Krohn, A., Beigl, M., Decker, C., Riedel, T., Zimmer, T., Varona, D., "Increasing Connectivity in Wireless Sensor Network using Cooperative Transmission", 3rd International Conference on Networked Sensing Systems (INSS), Chicago, USA, May/June, 2006.
13. Liu, L., Ma, H., Tao, D., Zhang, D., "A Hierarchical Cooperation Model for Sensor Networks Supported Cooperative Work", in Proc. of 10th International Conference on Computer Supported Cooperative Work in Design (CSCWD'06), May 2006, pp. 1-6.
14. Ramanathan, P., Saluja, k., Hu, Y., "Collaborative Sensor Signal Processing for Target Detection, Localization and Tracking", in *Proc. of 23rd Army Science Conference*, Dec. 2002.
15. Reghelin, R., Fröhlich, A., "A Decentralized Location System for Sensor Networks Using Cooperative Calibration and Heuristics", in Proc. of 9th ACM international symposium on Modeling Analysis and Simulation of Wireless and Mobile Systems (MSWiM'06), Torremolinos, Spain, 2006, pp. 139-146.
16. Sanli, H., Poornachandran, R., Cam, H., "Collaborative Two-Level Task Scheduling for Wireless Sensor Nodes", in Proc. of IEEE Communications Society Conference on Sensor and Ad Hoc Communications and Networks (SECON 2005), Santa Clara, USA, Sept. 2005.
17. Wang, K.-C., Ramanathan, P., "Collaborative Sensing Using Sensors of Uncoordinated Mobility", *International Conference on Distributed Computing in Sensor Systems (Lecture Notes in Computer Science)*, Marina del Rey, USA, June 2005, pp. 293-306.

39

SUPPORTING COMPLEX ADAPTIVE PROCESSES WITH LIGHTWEIGHT PLATFORMS

I.T. Hawryszkiewycz
Department of Information Systems
University of Technology, Sydney, AUSTRALIA
igorh@it.uts.edu.au

This paper begins by describing the evolving environment towards greater adaptability in today's business processes and the limitations of current methodologies in providing ways to support such processes. Support systems require ways to integrate social connectivity and interactivity into business processes in ways that enable the process to be dynamically changed. The paper describes models that identify requirements for such systems and convert the models to lightweight implementations that support flexibility. It uses ideas from complexity theory and social patterns to create the models.

1   INTRODUCTION

Dynamic changes in the execution of many current processes are placing greater and greater emphasis on designing systems to support users to make process changes. Such agile business processes must integrate all process components into one manageable entity and provide ways to easily and quickly change the process structure to respond to changing needs.   This paper refers to such processes as complex adaptive processes based on the definition of complex adaptive systems (CAS), (Holland, 1995) as made up of many agents (which may represent cells, species, individuals, firms, nations) acting in parallel, constantly acting and reacting to what the other agents are doing.

The control of a CAS tends to be highly dispersed and decentralized. The overall behavior of the system is the result of a huge number of decisions made every moment by many individual agents.. This paper addresses ways to model CAS and show ways to convert these models to computer system architectures that support knowledge workers. In this sense, process complexity is where the process emerges in that it changes as the situation evolves. Knowledge complexity is where new knowledge must be created as a process proceeds. Thus transaction processing, as for example payroll processing, has a well defined structure and knowledge that is relatively stable. Product development, on the other hand, is where the process can change as a product evolves and new knowledge must be continually developed. For example, the requirements a new product must be defined, and refined as new ideas come up and feedback is received from potential users. Each such new input will lead to some new task or action as determined by the product developers. The paper focuses on supporting processes where process and knowledge complexity is high and ways to support the workers in such systems. Workers in complex adaptive processes are often known as knowledge workers (Davenport, 2005, Chen,

Please use the following format when citing this chapter:

Hawryszkiewycz, I.T., 2008, in IFIP International Federation for Information Processing, Volume 283; *Pervasive Collaborative Networks*; Luis M. Camarinha-Matos, Willy Picard; (Boston: Springer), pp. 381–388.

Edgington, 2005). The work of knowledge workers is characterized by greater emphasis on connectivity and interactivity, autonomy and quickly changing practices that require changes in connectivity and interactivity. As a rule they do not follow prescribed processes and efforts to reengineer the work of knowledge workers into prescribed forms have proven unworkable (Davenport, 2005).

The paper will first define the special properties of complex adaptive systems and their impact on modelling and design. It will then propose ways to model such systems. The paper will then describe modeling methods for complex adaptive processes and describe their implementation in lightweight technologies, which allow knowledge workers to change their working relationships and comprehend, and assimilate new technologies in their work (Swanson, Ramiller, 2004).

2   WHAT ARE THE NEW DESIGN CRITERIA?

Complex adaptive processes are currently not well-defined in any formal manner. Our challenge is to define the special characteristics of adaptive processes and provide ways to design them.   A more theoretical approach is provided by complexity theory (Merali, McKelvey, 2006) and that of complex adaptive systems (Holland, 1995). The criteria here include:

- The ability to self organize at local levels in response to a wide variety of external changes,
- The creation and quick establishment of self contained units that address well defined parts of the environment,
- Loose coupling between system elements and a control system to reorganize the structure to respond to external change,
- Ability to organize connections between units and support the changed connections and interactivity.
- Aggregate smaller units into larger components with consequent changes to the connectivity and interactivity,
- Realization of simple interfaces between model components.

Our contribution will be to develop modeling methods that support the special characteristics of complex adaptive systems and convert the models to support systems, which facilitate the work of knowledge workers in complex environments.

3   IMPACT ON MPODELLING AND DESIGN

The impact of this trend is two fold, namely:

- Design methodologies must be able to cater for the dynamic nature of processes and include specific criteria in modeling that emphasize such dynamic nature, and
- Create technical solutions that support user driven change, which are referred to as lightweight technologies in this paper.

There has been work on support for small groups (Sutcliffe, 2005) on complex tasks but there are few widely accepted systematic methods to develop large complex adaptive processes. Many current designs often attempt to re-engineer what are predominantly open systems. However, it is increasingly noted that social relationships are important in knowledge processes such as for example medical systems (Zhang, 2002), where greater emphasis is needed on user analysis and communication. Thus rather than developing systems that provide prescriptive processes, what is needed are infrastructures and the services that can be quickly brought into the process to serve an unanticipated need.

4 MODELLING METHODS FOR COMPLEX ADAPTIVE SYSTEMS

The proposal here is that models of adaptive systems be made up of the three components shown in Figure 1. These are:

- business activities, which must be modeled as loosely connected and the connections can change over time and which can be easily reorganized,
- social networks that model the people relationships, and
- knowledge as that keep track of the connectivity and interactivity in the social and work networks.

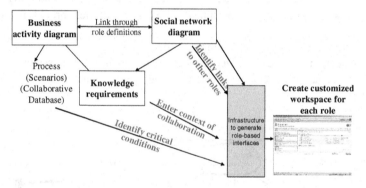

Figure 1 - The blueprint for modelling adaptive information systems

The models must combine the business activities with work and social networking as an integral part of the systems and seeing it as a link between the different activities. The knowledge requirements go beyond simple transaction databases but include records of social interactions integrated into the activities. They will be focused on the knowledge needs of roles within the social structure.

The model components will then be mapped to technologies, in most cases workspaces. The goal here will be to develop an infrastructure that can be used to generate workspaces specific and furthermore to change these dynamically as a situation evolves. Our goal is to show that these three components can indeed model adaptive systems and that there are systematic ways to go from the model to an implementation as the form and function in Gregor and Jones (2007) and develop constructs that provide the dynamic capabilities within this blueprint and constructs to realize architectures based on the blueprint.

One important aspect of this research is the evaluation of any new proposed modelling constructs. The relative novelty of complex adaptive processes precludes an analytic evaluation and suggests a more descriptive approach to evaluation

(Hevner, 2004). At the same time we will draw on existing theories and social structures (Gregor, 2007) to form the evaluation criteria.

4.1   Modeling Business Activities

The business activity models are based on a conceptual model for collaborative systems (Hawryszkiewycz, 2005). The main concepts are activity, role, participant, and artefact. Figure 2 illustrates one instance of such model for evaluating an idea for a new product. Here there are four activities shown as clouded shapes. There three roles shown by Figures and four artifacts shown by the disk shapes. Any number of participants (not shown in this simplified diagram) can be assigned to each role. The model shows that the client and marketing manager interact in activity 'analysis of marketing needs' to develop a market report. Figure 2 illustrates the most fundamental parts of the model with more details found in (Hawryszkiewycz, 2005). The additional detail include various discussion or interaction artifacts and ways to initiate events in one activity that are passed to roles in other activities. The model semantics support dynamic changes to the model and the special characteristics of CAS as:

- They allow activities to be reorganized through changes to roles, and artifacts,
- New activities can be set up and linked to existing activities through roles and artifacts,
- The activities are loosely coupled through their roles,
- New connections can be organized through events or shared discussions,
- Higher level activities can be created to aggregate the activities of existing activities.

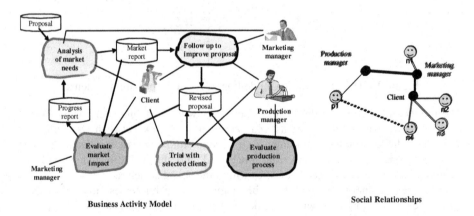

Figure 2 – Business activity diagram

4.2   Modeling the Social and Work Relationships

The social relationships diagram in Figure 2 identifies the interplay between processes, people and technology. It shows people as taking different roles in different activities and thus ensuring the sharing of knowledge. In the social relationships diagram in Figure 2 the roles are shown as black dots. The faces are individuals, who take on these roles. Thus n2 is a client and p1 is the production manager. The thick lines between the roles indicate work connections, which define the essential communication paths for the participants. The dotted lines show informal connections. For example p1 and n4 have an informal connection, which is not part of the work process.

A Practical Example

Figure 3 illustrates the model for outsourcing. It shows three parts, namely:

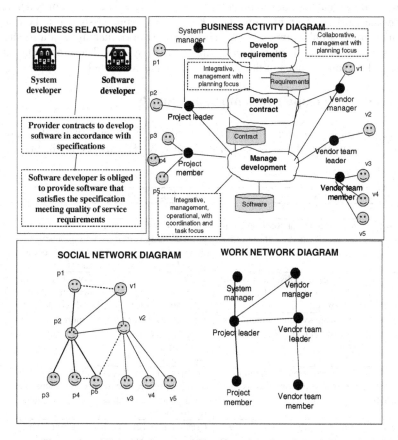

Figure 3 – A Model that combines functional and Social Analysis

- The business relationships that shows that a system developer contracts with a software developer to develop software modules,
- The business activity diagram shows the kind of activities that take place in the relationship. It shows the activities by the clouded shapes, the roles by the black dots and artifacts by the disk shaped figures. The participants are shown as faces. Only the broad level activities are shown. Thus for example the contract development involves the project leader and the vendor manager. Currently p2 is the project leader and v1 is the vendor manager. It should be noted that one

person can take more than one role. A scenario would describe the actions that take place. The activities include:

- Develop requirements, where the system manager and the project leader decide what is to be outsourced and develop the requirements,
- Develop contract, where the project leader and vendor manager
- Manage system development, where the teams work together to create the software.
- The work network is derived from the business activity diagram. It shows the interactions that are required as part of the business activity. For example there is a link from the vendor manager to the project leader as they take part in the same activity, namely, develop contract. The social network diagram is derived from the work diagram by showing links between people assigned to the roles. Thus there is a link from p1 to p2. The social network diagram can also show many of the informal interactions within such a system. These are often the result of personal contact or the fact that people are collocated.

4.3 Catering for open system requirements

The modelling method supports the earlier defined special characteristics of adaptive systems. The way they do so is shown descriptively (Hevner, 2004) in the table below.

Special characteristics	Modeling technique
The ability to self organize at local levels in response to a wide variety of external changes,	Adding roles, participants and new artifacts to an existing activity. Creating a new discussion to include a distant member to provide new expertise to an activity.
The defining and quick establishment of self contained units that address well defined parts of the environment,	Creation of new activity. For example quickly creating a new team from existing members to address a special problem.
Loose coupling between system elements and a control system to reorganize the structure to respond to external change,	People assigned to roles in more than one activity. Events in one activity can be received in other activities, with new events added as required.
Ability to organize connections between units and support the changed connections and interactivity.	Set up events to pass notifications between activities. Share documents and discussions as for example contract development and requirements..
Aggregate smaller units into larger components with consequent changes to the connectivity and interactivity,	Create a new activity that shares artifacts with existing activities.
Realization of simple interfaces between model components.	This is achieved by defining role based interfaces that provide easy links to other roles and activities.

Process emergence here can include creation of new business relationships as for example extending the service to another client, or setting up a transient team to identify the cause of a complex fault.

5 REQUIREMENTS OF TECHNOLOGY INFRASTRUCTURE

Returning to Figure 1 the social network identifies the kind of platforms needed. The business activity model provides guidelines on the kind of activities and their connectivity and interactivity between them. Each platform however has to be adaptable and match the communication practices on the activity. These are often referred to as lightweight platforms (Hawryszkiewycz, 2007). We have identified four level of platform for lightweight communication. These are:

- lightweight exchange, which provides the kind of support needed to support exchanges typically found in offices,
- lightweight collaboration, which supports joint work on artifacts or in informal coordination and planning activities,
- lightweight workflow where on one-off process is followed requiring some monitoring and reporting, and
- process management, which is support for repetitive workflow processes that may result as processes mature.

We have also developed a prototype to demonstrate how technology can support open requirements. The prototype supports the concepts and semantics of the business activity model, and includes ways to support social structures. These can be supported as groups of individuals. Particular individuals or entire groups can be assigned to roles in the business activities. A typical interface is shown in Figure 4.

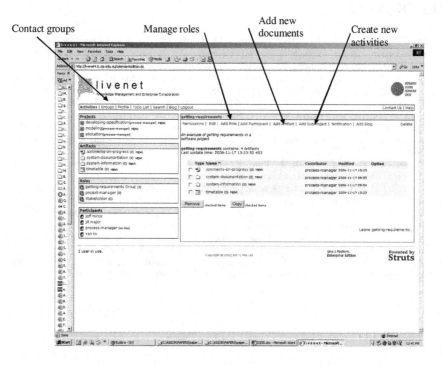

Figure 4 – Workspace for developing requirements

The commands provided though such interfaces satisfy the open system criteria.

- Process emergence with ability to grow by providing dynamic capability to create new groups or activities,
- Dynamic linking between new and existing elements either through people taking roles in the different activities or through an event and notification structure,
- Self-organizing ability for local relationships by allowing changes to workspace participants, new documents, or roles changed,
- Support for communication and collaboration through the addition of new social software as for example discussion systems

6   SUMMARY

The paper described the special requirements that must be met by the increasing number of information systems that are complex and must adapt to emerging business environments. It stressed the need to include work social networks as part of an analysis process and their integration into business activity modelling. The models produced in this way can then be used to create lightweight platforms that support work practices in such environments. The paper illustrated one way to model such systems and convert the model to an implementation that dynamically supports system change.

REFERENCES

1. Chen, A., Edgington, T. (2005): "Assessing Value in Organizational Knowledge Creation: Considerations for Knowledge Workers" MIS Quarterly, Vol. 29, No. 2, June 2005, pp. 279-309.
2. Davenport, T. (2005): "Thinking for a Living" Harvard Business School Press.
3. Gregor, S., Jones, D. (2007): "The Anatomy of a Design Theory" Journal of the Association of Computing Machinery, Vol. 8, Issue 5, pp. 312-335.
4. Hawryszkiewycz, I.T (2005): "A Metamodel for Modeling Collaborative Systems" Journal of Computer Information Systems, Vol. XLV, Number 3, Spring 2005, pp. 63-72.
5. Hawryszkiewycz, I.T. (2007): "Lightweight Technologies for Knowledge Based Collaborative Applications" Proceedings of the IEEE CEC/EEE2007 Conference on E-Commerce Technology, Tokyo, July 2007, pp. 255-264.
6. Hevner, A. March, S.T., Park, J., Ram, S. (2004): :"Design Science in Information Systems Research" MIS Quarterly, 28(1), March, 2004, pp. 75-106.
7. Holland, J. (1995): "Hidden order: How adaption builds complexity" Cambridge Perseus Books.
8. Morgan, G. (1986): "Images of Organization"., SAGE Publications, Beverly Hills, California.
9. Merali, Y., McKelvey, B. (2006): "Using Complexity Science to effect a paradigm shift in Information systems for the 21st. century" Journal of Information Technology 21, pp. 211-215.
10. Sutcliffe, A. (2005): "Applying Small Group Theory to Analysis and Design of CSCW Systems" Human and Social Factors of Software Engineering, May, 2005, St. Louis, Missouri.
11. Zhang, J., Patel, V., Johnson, K., Smith, J. (2002): "Designing Human Centered Distributed Information Systems, IEEE Intelligent Systems, September/October, 2002, pp. 42-47.

40

SOFTWARE AGENTS IN VIRTUAL ORGANIZATIONS: GOOD FAITH AND TRUST

Francisco Andrade[1], Paulo Novais[2], José Machado[2] and José Neves[2]

[1]*Escola de Direito, Universidade do Minho, Braga, PORTUGAL*
[2]*DI-CCTC, Universidade do Minho, Braga, PORTUGAL*
fandrade@direito.uminho.pt, {pjon, jmac, jneves}@di.uminho.pt

Virtual organizations tend to play an ever more part in electronic commerce, as well as software agents, here understood as the building blocks of the methodology for problem solving that is being subscribed. Indeed, one of the issues that have to be addressed is the capability of such entities to rationally and autonomously "think" and decide. The behavior of these agents may go more and more unpredictable; they will choose their own strategies and define their own planning where are faced to a problem, being possible that they may act with good faith or with bad faith. This leads us to the absolute need of considering the major issue of trust in software agent's environments.

1. INTRODUCTION

It must be anticipated the possibility of software agents to play a determinant role in corporate bodies, in virtual enterprises ("temporary alliances of organizations that come together to share skills or core competencies and resources in order to better respond to business opportunities" (Camarinha-Matos and Afsarmanesh, 2004), in Dynamic Virtual Organisations ("...a VO that is established in a short time to respond to a competitive market opportunity, and has a short life cycle" (Camarinha-Matos and Afsarmanesh, 2004). This, intervention intends interactions based on contracts and relations of trust (Teubner, 2001). But agents operate without the direct intervention of human beings and "have some degree of control over their actions and inner states" (Weitzenboeck, 2002). Indeed, it can be can assumed that agents behave upon mental states, that is to say their behavior is a product of reasoning processes over incomplete or unknown information (Andrade et al, 2007). In this sense, agents do make options and their behavior can not be fully predicted.

Thus being, considering open distributed systems and autonomous agents that "act and interact in flexible ways in order to achieve their design objectives in uncertain and dynamic environments", is it possible to trust agents in electronic relations? Trust is mainly a belief in the honesty or reliability of someone ("a belief an agent has that the other party will do what it says it will…given an opportunity to defect to get higher payoffs"). It is clearly a requisite of the utmost importance to consider when deciding on "how, when and who to interact with" because it can not be assumed in advance whether or not agents will behave according to rules of

Please use the following format when citing this chapter:

Andrade, F., Novais, P., Machado, J. and Neves, J., 2008, in IFIP International Federation for Information Processing, Volume 283; *Pervasive Collaborative Networks*; Luis M. Camarinha-Matos, Willy Picard; (Boston: Springer), pp. 389–396.

honesty and correctness. This issue leads us to consider the possibility of agents acting with good or bad faith. But also it forces us to view that ways of ensuring a high degree of reliability of electronic relations participants are required, namely the "need for protocols that ensure that the actors will find no better option than telling the truth and interacting honestly with each other". But trust can be perceived in different ways, from an individual perspective ("an agent has some beliefs about the honesty or reciprocities nature of its interaction partners"), or from a social or systemic perspective ("the actors in the system are forced to be trustworthy by the rules of encounter (i.e. protocols and mechanisms that regulate the system").

At the individual level, trust arises from learning (agents do learn from experience), from reputation (a view "derived from an aggregation of members of the community about one of them") or from socio-cognitive models (mainly the belief that someone is competent or willing to do something).

At the system level, trust can be ensured by constraints imposed by the system, either by using protocols that prevent agents from lying or colluding, or by making the system itself spreading agent's reputation as being truthful or liar, or even by using a system "proof" or "guarantee" of reliability "through the references of a trusted third party".

All these will be important elements to consider within open systems where agents with quite different characteristics may "enter the system and interact with one another", offering different services with different levels of efficiency. And this is of the utmost importance in considering the participation of agents in Virtual Organisations.

2. VIRTUAL ORGANISATIONS

The notion of "consortium" is quite well known in commercial law for a long time, but VE certainly enhance its use in the commercial arena. But the main characteristics of "consortium" remain in virtual enterprises. Here, the main characteristics of commercial societies simply do not exist: there is really not an entity different from the participating companies; there is not an autonomous patrimony; there are no common profits (as an own patrimony) to be distributed among partners (Abreu, 2004). But the "consortium" is valid for itself, as a way to enhance the possibilities of commerce development for its participants.

A virtual enterprise must be regarded as a legal unity based in an organization of informatics means, an autonomous instrument for the production of immaterial goods (or services) only exchangeable through Internet, in a market without any physical, local or time constraints (Abreu, 2003). But it may also be understood as an assemble of enterprises legally and economically autonomous, connected through telematic means temporarily cooperating in the fulfillment of a project or economic activity (Abreu, 2003). Authors tend to assume VE as a "temporary alliance between globally distributed independent companies working together to improve competitiveness by sharing resources, skills, risks and costs" (Camarinha-Matos et al, 2007, Crispim and Sousa, 2005), that is to say a "consortium" – two or more different entities (natural or corporate) "get obliged to undertake certain activities or assuring certain contributions in order to make it possible to achieve certain material or legal acts" (Abreu, 2004). Yet, it may as well be considered the possibility of

Virtual Organisations Breeding Environments, understood as "an association or pool of organizations and their related supporting institutions that have both the potential and the interest to cooperate with each other, through the establishment of a "base" long-term cooperation agreement" (Camarinha-Matos et al, 2005). A With respect to the computational paradigm it were considered extended logic programs with two kinds of negation, classical negation, ¬, and default negation, not. Intuitively, not p is true whenever there is no reason to believe p (close world assumption), whereas ¬p requires a proof of the negated literal. An extended logic program (program, for short) is a finite collection of rules and integrity constraints, standing for all their ground instances, and is given in the form:

$p \leftarrow p1 \wedge \ldots \wedge pn \wedge not\ q1 \wedge \ldots \wedge not\ qm; and$

$?\ p1 \wedge \ldots \wedge pn \wedge not\ q1 \wedge \ldots \wedge not\ qm,\ (n,m \geq 0)$

where ? is a domain atom denoting falsity, the pi, qj, and p are classical ground literals, i.e. either positive atoms or atoms preceded by the classical negation sign ¬ (Binmore and Fun, 1992). Every program is associated with a set of abducibles. Abducibles can be seen as hypotheses that provide possible solutions or explanations of given queries, being given here in the form of exceptions to the extensions of the predicates that make the program.

In terms of a VO one of their building blocks or predicates may be given by predicate *vo*, that stands for a particular entity or organisation, which in abstract terms may be given in the form (Figure 1 and Figure 2).

$vo(\ldots).$

$\neg vo(\ldots) \leftarrow$ /The closed word assumption is being softened/

   $not\ vo(\ldots) \wedge$

   $not\ exception_{vo}(\ldots).$

$?\ (\ vo(\ldots,Y) \wedge Y \geq 0 \wedge Y \leq 1\ ).$ /This invariant states that *vo* takes accuracy values on the interval $0\ldots1/$

$?\ (\ (exception_{vo}(\ldots, X,Y) \vee exception_{vo}(\ldots,X,Z)) \wedge \neg (exception_{vo}(\ldots,X,Y) \wedge exception_{vo}(X,Z))).$

/This invariant states that the exceptions to the predicate *vo* follow an *exclusive or*, and that the last two attributes of *vo* (i.e. (X,Y) and/or (X,Z)) state that there exists a functional dependency between (X,Y) and/or (X,Z) and the remaining attributes of *vo*/.

Figure 1 - The extension of predicate *vo* that stands for a particular company or organisation.

Anyway, "the concept of virtual organization (VO)", as a special kind of consortium for electronic commerce, appears as "particularly well-suited to cope with very dynamic and turbulent market conditions" and "this is largely due to the possibility of rapidly forming a consortium triggered by a business opportunity and specially tailored to the requirements of that opportunity. Implicit in this is a notion of agility, allowing rapid adaptation to a changing environment", with its content being object of a process of optimization, as it is described in (Neves et al, 2007) (Figure 3).

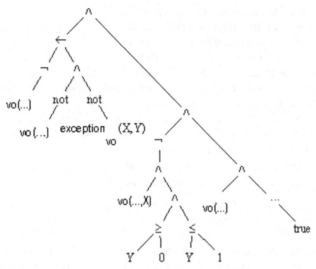

Figure 2 – The evolutionary logic program for predicate *vo*.

There might be legal issues on the use of virtual companies, since they imply cooperation agreements and might restrain concurrence between partners and or between these and third parties (prevented from accessing the agreement) which might have implications in the field of concurrence law (Abreu, 2003). Yet, these agreements may be totally legal, provided the non existence of restrictions to concurrence and the non elimination of concurrence in a substantial part of the market. These virtual enterprises may be quite interesting for the electronic commerce and software agents may certainly play an important role in it. Besides the question of the legal consideration of the electronic agents (are these mere tools used by the participants - natural or legal persons - in the "consortium", it is anyway unavoidable to consider the issue of the behaviour of agents by itself). And it is quite important that agents "know The Law" and social standards of behavior and abide to its rules. But is it possible to have agents abiding with legal and social norms? (Brazier et al, 2002).

3. SOFTWARE AGENTS AND GOOD FAITH

Software agents are computational entities with a rich knowledge component, having sophisticated properties such as planning ability, reactivity, learning capabilities, cooperation, communication and the possibility of argumentation. It is also possible to build logical and computational models having in consideration The Law norms (i.e., legislation, doctrine and jurisprudence). Agent societies may mirror a great variety of human societies, such as commercial societies with emphasis to behavioral patterns, or even more complex ones, with pre-defined roles of engagement, obligations, contractual and specific communication rules. An agent must be able to manage its knowledge, beliefs, desires, intentions, goals and values.

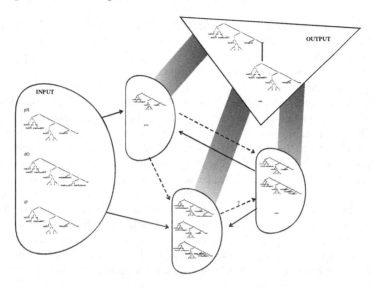

Figure 3 - A blended (i.e. INPUT) of the extensions of the predicates vo, ... whose evolution leads to an optimal Virtual Organization setting (i.e. OUTPUT).

Good faith is related to the ideas of fidelity, loyalty, honesty and trust in business (Lima and Varela, 1987). Good faith may be understood both in a psychological subjective sense and in an ethical objective sense (Lima and Varela, 1987). In the objective sense it consists "in considering correct behavior and not actor's mental attitudes" (Rotolo et al, 2005). It refers to both social norms and legal rules (Rotolo et al, 2005). In the subjective sense it has to do with knowledge and belief. "It regards the actor's sincere belief that she/he is not violating other people's rights" (Rotolo et al, 2005)

Good faith arises from general objective criteria related to loyalty and cooperation between parties. Good faith is an archetype of social behavior; loyalty in social relations, honest acting (Antunes, 1973), fidelity, reliability, faithfulness and fair dealing "and it comprises the protection of reasonable reliance" (Weitzenboeck, 2002).

Acting in bad faith in business may either "lead to the invalidation of some of the contract clauses or of the whole contract" (Rotolo et al, 2005) or even originate liabilities (Antunes, 1973).

The issue is not to wonder whether or not software agents may act in good faith or in bad faith; the question at stake is to consider that software agents acting in business relations will presumably negotiate and perform their acts according to certain standards of behavior. Yet, according to (Russel and Norvig, 2003) "an agent's behavior can be based on both its experience and the built-in-knowledge used in constructing the agent for the particular environment in which it operates", but autonomous systems will produce a behaviour "determined by its own experiences". Furthermore, agents may be "able to act strategically by calculating their best response given their opponents possible moves" (Binmore and Fun, 1992).

Good faith criteria relate to "objective standards of conduct" (Rotolo et al, 2005) that will help determine "whether the agent has observed reasonable commercial standards of fair dealing in the negotiation and performance of the contract" (Weitzenboeck, 2002).

"The form given to the correctness rules allows to impose both positive and negative requirements to be fulfilled" (Rotolo et al, 2005).

Important issue is the one related to the attribution of the acts: should the acts of the electronic agent be attributed to the user who activated it, considering the electronic agent just as an instrument or tool at the disposal (and control??) of the user? Or should the volition of the agent be autonomously considered, since the user may not have been directly involved or consulted and may not even be aware that the agent acted at all (Weitzenboeck, 2002)? Either we assume or not the possibility, in a near future, of any sort of legal personality for software agents, the truth is that we probably should not rely on a legal fiction of attribution of the acts of agents to humans and, at least, it must be considered the autonomous will of the agent for purposes of good faith, bad faith, error on declaration and divergences between will and declaration. And the fact that an agent acts on good or bad faith will surely be of the utmost importance for all those (software or humans) who have to deal with it. Trust will thus become an unavoidable question for agents contracting.

3. TRUST AND SMART CONTRACTS

Trust is intimately related to beliefs. "Trust is a belief an agent has that the other party will do what it says it will (being honest and reliable)" (Ramchurn, et al, 2004). As (Rotolo et al, 2005) put it "agent x thinks that agent y not only is able to do certain actions but that y is willing to do what x needs" (formalization of a "Normative version" of Good Faith"). We can distinguish different levels of trust, the individual level ("an agent has some beliefs about the honesty or reciprocities nature of its interaction partners") and the system level ("the actors in the system are forced to be trustworthy by the rules of encounter (i.e. protocols and mechanisms) that regulate the system" (Ramchurn, et al, 2004).

At the system level it will assume the most relevance special protocols made in "such a way that they prevent agents from manipulating each other (e.g. through lies or collusion) so as to satisfy their selfish interests" (Ramchurn, et al, 2004).

At this system level it will be interesting to focus our attention in the figure of "smart contracts" which are seen as a "set of promises, specified in digital form, including protocols in which the parties perform on these promises" (Szabo, 1996). These contracts are really program codes imposing by itself an enforcement of the contract (the "terms of the contract are enforced by the logic of the program's execution", turning the breach of the contract, at least, quite expensive) (Miller and Stiegler, 2003). Indeed, one of the most relevant and difficult issues about inter-systemic electronic contracting is the one related to enforcement. Enforcement may be seen at two different levels, "publicly, through the court system, and privately, largely through reputation" (Friedman, 2000). The perspective of smart contracts tries to escape these difficulties - "Instead of enforcement, the contract creates an inescapable arrangement" (Miller and Stiegler, 2003).

Smart contracts can thus enhance the trust in electronic contracting. An interesting idea of this model is to use contracts as games. These games have rules - either fixed ones or sets of rules the players will choose (Miller and Stiegler, 2003) - which have to be followed in order to play the game. This is the upcoming of a new and much more reliable form of "adherence contract", in which the contract is seen as an electronic game, managed or arbitrated by a board manager (a trusted third party)(Miller and Stiegler, 2003), which does not itself play the game but only allows the parties to make legal moves. And of course the board manager may be either a human or a software agent. Here, the contract may contain contractual clauses embedded in the software "in such a way to make breach of contract expensive (if desired, sometimes prohibitively so) for the breacher" (Szabo, 1996). In this model, trust is enhanced "by virtue of the different constraints imposed by the system" (Ramchurn, et al, 2004). As far as electronic contracting is concerned we may well consider that "public enforcement will work less well and private enforcement better than for contracts in real space at present" (Friedman, 2000). In cyberspace, reputation will turn to be a key issue and trusted third parties or Networks of Trust (widely trusted intermediary institutions or entities) must play an important role (Miller and Stiegler, 2003). Trust at the system level is based upon different possibilities, that is to say that it might be dependent on special interaction protocols (as is the case with the referred smart contracts), reputation mechanisms and security mechanisms. Reputation mechanisms are thus unavoidable to be considered as instruments required to foster the trustworthiness of electronic interactions (as it was referred already in our previous work (Andrade et al, 2005).

As far as security mechanisms are intended, we must refer the importance of authentication by trusted third parties, that is to say that information about the actors in the system specially delivered by trusted third parties may lead participants (human or software) to act upon what they think is trustable information. That is a special domain for trust and security in electronic relationships – here, as it happens with electronic signatures and time-stamp, the intervention of a trusted third party will be determinant for establishing participant's trust. Of course, this by itself will not be enough to "ensure that agents act and interact honestly and reliably towards each other. They will only represent a barrier against agents that are not allowed in the system".

In the end, trust will be highly dependent on the existence of social networks and on the traceability of past interactions among the agents in the community. This will be a fundamental issue for the existence of virtual organizations and of assuring a minimum reliability for the intervention of agents in it.

4. CONCLUSIONS

A traditional figure of commercial law, "consortium" will be highly enhanced in electronic commerce through appearance and acting of Virtual Enterprises, Virtual Organizations and Virtual Breeding Environments. These will highly depend (or its activities will be strengthened) by the use of software agents. Autonomy is a main advantage of software agents since they will act without any human intervention. Yet, the autonomy of software agents brings along several issues concerning their behavior and the legal consequences of it. One important issue has to do with good faith. Autonomous agents may act with good faith or bad faith, may comply or not with certain standards of behavior. In this sense it is important to understand if agents do comply with social or legal norms. Upon the activities and behavior of software agents engaging in business, it will be built a certain "image" of the agent and trust will be a mandatory requirement for commercial dealings. Trust may be considered both at the individual or system level. At this level, it may become quite interesting to consider the issue of smart contracts as a way of enhancing trust and of achieving enforcement in electronic contracting.

Acknowledgments

The work described in this paper is included in Intelligent Agents and Legal Relations project (POCTI/JUR/57221/2004), which is a research project supported by FCT (Science & Technology Foundation – Portugal).

5. REFERENCES

1. Abreu, J.C., Empresas Virtuais, i"Estudos em Homenagem ao Professor Doutor Inocêncio Galvão Telles", vol. IV – "Novos Estudos de Direito Privado", Almedina, 2003 (in Portuguese).
2. Abreu JC., Curso de Direito Comercial, Almedina, 2004 (in Portuguese).
3. Andrade F., Neves J., Novais P., Machado J., Abelha A., Legal Security and Credibility in Agent Based Virtual Enterprises, in Collaborative Networks and Their Breeding Environments, Camarinha-Matos L. Afsarmanesh H., Ortiz A., (Eds), Springer-Verlag, ISBN 0-387-28259-9, pp 501-512, 2005.
4. Andrade F., Novais P., Machado J., Neves J., Intelligent Contracting: Software agents, Corporate Bodies and Virtual Organizations, in Establishing the Foundation of Collaborative Networks, Camarinha-Matos L. Afsarmanesh H., Novais P., Analide C., (Eds), Springer-Verlag, Series: IFIP International Federation for Information Processing, ISBN: 978-0-387-73797-3, pp 217-224, 2007.
5. Antunes Varela J.M., Das Obrigações em Geral, Almedina, 1973, (in Portuguese).
6. Binmore, K., Fun and Games: A Text on Game Theory. D. C. Heath and Company, 1992.
7. Brazier, F., Kubbe, O., Oskamp, A., Wijngaards, N., Are Law-Abiding Agents Realistic? Proceedings of the workshop on the Law of Electronic Agents (LEA02), 2002.
8. Camarinha-Matos L, Afsarmanesh H, Ollus M. ECOLEAD: A holistic approach to creation and management of dynamic and virtual organizations, Collaborative Networks and Their Breeding Environments, Camarinha-Matos L. Afsarmanesh H., Ortiz A., (Eds), Springer-Verlag, ISBN 0-387-28259-9, pp 501-512, 2005.
9. Camarinha-Matos, L., Afsarmanesh H., The Emerging Discipline of Collaborative Networks. Virtual Enterprises and Collaborative Networks 2004: 3-16
10. Camarinha-Matos, L., Oliveira. A., Ratti R., Demsar D., Baldo, F., Jarimo, T., A Computer-Assisted Vo Creation Framework. Virtual Enterprises and Collaborative Networks 2007: 165-178
11. Crispim J, Sousa JP. A multi-Criteria support system for the formation of collaborative networks of enterprises, Collaborative Networks and Their Breeding Environments, Camarinha-Matos L. Afsarmanesh H., Ortiz A., (Eds), Springer-Verlag, ISBN 0-387-28259-9, pp 501-512, 2005.
12. Friedman, D., Contracts in cyberspace, American Law and Economics Association meeting, May 6, 2000.
13. Lima, Fernando Andrade Pires de / Varela, João de Matos Antunes : "Código Civil Anotado", vol. I, Coimbra Editora Limitada, 1987 (in Portuguese).
14. Miller, M., Stiegler, M., The digital path: smart contracts and the third world, Markets, Information and Communication. Austrian Perspectives on the Internet Economy Routledge 2003.
15. Neves J., Machado J., Analide C., Abelha A., Brito B. The Halt Condition in Genetic Programming. in Progress in Artificial Intelligence, Neves J., Santos M. and Machado J. (eds), Lecture Notes in Artificial Intelligence 4874 Springer, ISBN 978-3-540-77000-8, pp 160-169, 2007.
16. Ramchurn, SD., Huynh, D., Jennings, N., Trust in multiagent systems, The Knowledge Engineering Review 19 (1) 1-25, 2004.
17. Rotolo, A., G. Sartor, and C. Smith., Formalization of a 'Normative Version' of Good Faith. In A. Oskamp and C. Cevenini (eds.), Proc. LEA 2005. Nijmegen: Wolf Legal Publishers, 2005.
18. Russel S., Norvig P., Artificial Intelligence: A modern approach, Prentice-Hall, 2nd Ed., 2003, IBSN: 0-13-103805-2.
19. Szabo, N., Smart contracts: building blocks for digital markets, 1996. (http://szabo.best.vwh.net/smart.contracts.2.html)
20 Teubner G., Das Recht hybrider Netzwerke, ZHR, 2001.
21. Weitzenboeck, E., Good Faith and Fair Dealing in the Context of Contract Formation by Electronic Agents", Proceedings of the AISB 2002 Symposium on Intelligent Agents in Virtual Markets, 2-5 April 2002, Imperial College London.

PART 13

NETWORK ANALYSIS AND STRATEGIC PROCESSES

41 NETWORK STRUCTURE ANALYSIS FOR MULTICULTURAL INDUSTRIAL CNO

Michel Pouly, Mario Greber and Rémy Glardon
Ecole Polytechnique Fédérale de Lausanne (EPFL)
Laboratory for Production Management and Processes, Station 9, 1015 Lausanne,
SWITZERLAND
michel.pouly@epfl.ch,
Mario.greber@epfl.ch, remy.glardon@epfl.ch

Emerging countries like China offer low wages, large production capacities and a huge potential market. Large Western companies already took advantage of these opportunities by opening their own factories in China to build up local supply chains and address this new market, but this solution is not adapted to SME having very limited human and financial resources. Therefore new business models must be developed for them.

This paper presents a multicultural collaborative network of industrial SME including Swiss and Chinese partners. We will first describe the collaboration goals and context, identify the cultural differences affecting the choice of the Chinese network type, analyse the strengths and weaknesses of possible solutions and finally present the realized one.

1. INTRODUCTION

New industrial countries like China offer low work costs, large production capacities and a huge potential market. Large Western companies already took advantage of these opportunities by opening their own factories in China to build up a local supply chain and address this new market, but this solution is not adapted to SME having very limited human and financial resources. Therefore new business models based on collaboration must be developed for them.

This paper presents the results of a recent research project aiming at creating a multicultural collaborative network of industrial SME including Swiss and Chinese partners. We will first describe the collaboration goals and context, identify the cultural differences affecting the choice of the Chinese network type, analyse the strengths and weaknesses of possible solutions and finally present the realized one.

2. COLLABORATION GOALS AND CONTEXT

Swiss Microtech (SMT) is a network of seven independent SME active in the screw machining industry (Pouly et al., 2002). They produce parts for the automotive, medical, space and telecommunication sectors and export 90% of their production. Swiss Microtech has always wanted to be proactive and be prepared to address the current market needs by adding further production capacities in a fully flexible way and outsourcing parts that can no longer be produced in Switzerland in order to survive in a very fierce competitive environment. SMT also wanted to be able to

Please use the following format when citing this chapter:

Pouly, M., Greber, M. and Glardon, R., 2008, in IFIP International Federation for Information Processing, Volume 283; *Pervasive Collaborative Networks*; Luis M. Camarinha-Matos, Willy Picard; (Boston: Springer), pp. 399–406.

"follow" important customers in China through local production and to address the Chinese market, which is considered by the financial analyst community as one of the main future global players.

As the parts produced by Swiss Microtech often require the collaboration of different partners bringing specific technologies and know-how and because of the results reached by the network in Switzerland (Pouly et al., 2005), the creation of a partner network in China looked like a very promising solution with real win-win content:

- SMT could outsource the parts, which cannot be produced in Switzerland for price or capacity reasons to the Chinese network, which would get new orders and profit from the worldwide sales organization of SMT
- SMT could "follow" an important customer to China with the partner network acting as a local proxy. In this case, most parts will be produced in China, some others in Switzerland, but all parts will be delivered by the Chinese network. Swiss Microtech would then be able to produce in China without having to invest all the necessary resources to plan, install, start and operate an own local factory, resources which are beyond the possibilities of small SME like the SMT members.
- Actual and future Chinese markets will be addressed by the local Chinese network that would sell its own parts but also some special parts it is not (yet) able to produce locally and that can be made by SMT.

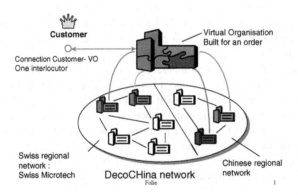

Figure 1 – The DecoCHina network

3. CULTURAL KEY FACTORS FOR CHINESE CNO'S

First of all, we will evaluate the cultural differences, which will influence the choice of the best suited type of network and the way of communication with Chinese companies (Greber, 2006).

3.1 Trust issues

In China, the definition and perception of "trust" is not the same like the one in western countries, where we are used to be open and to trust everybody under certain circumstances. Such a relation in China is mainly limited to family members or close friends of the family. A trust relation in China is much more complicated and very difficult to obtain between two companies as there are three different forms of trust, of which mostly the last one appears in business relations:

Path trust

Path trust is based on an individual's understanding of how another person will act in a certain situation. The feeling of having a common "path" relates each other and creates trust. As it is strongly linked to individuals, it isn't long lasting between companies, especially with the high employee turnover in China.

Situation trust

Situation trust is created when people do an activity based on common interests, hobbies or habits. In the process of doing this activity, the involved people shape a shared psychology, which is the foundation of trust among individuals. As this trust can be of relatively short duration, it is delicate for long-term relations between companies.

Family trust

Family trust is a strong trust among family relatives, which is tied by blood and is strengthened by mutual social connections. It is a very valuable and efficient trust system in the early development stage of enterprises. It facilitates the common interests among company members and helps them to reach an agreement on management goals. It is by far the main trust system in China's small and medium size companies (up to 1000 employees). Foreigners are of course not considered as family members.

3.2 Tendency to hierarchy

Due to China's history, people are used to live within clear hierarchical structures. This is also reflected in the relations within a network where usually one of the members grows much faster than the others and takes automatically the leader's position. In this situation the leader will develop itself further, while the other's growth will be naturally damped and it's very rare to see balanced relations between companies. Without this leadership of one of its members, the structural organization of the network would be difficult, especially if the network should be developed out of suppliers-customers relations, as it is hard to bring all the members on the same level. In some situations, the smaller companies of the network even prefer to stay under the protection of the biggest, for example in case of requests from foreign customers. Their English language skill level is often low and it would take a big effort to assure a direct communication between the small network members and the foreign customers.

3.3 Immediate profitability

Usually, business relations in China are much stronger linked to a direct profit than in Switzerland. The motivation for collaboration can almost only be created with an important order as a start point. The companies have to feel that they can take profit of this order by joining the network. The time between an investment and its revenue has to be very short. It is doubtable whether a cost reduction by commonly buying machines or material and sharing information about suppliers or technical issues is enough "profit" to raise their motivation. The duration of the motivation is also much shorter than in Switzerland. As soon as the direct profit is over, the relations would break. A feeling of togetherness based on a passed common business does usually not exist in China.

3.4 Interest larger than competences

In China, an order can easily be subcontracted 3 or 4 times. The companies take an order even if it is out of their competences and then they will find a partner for subcontracting. This partner itself may subcontract it again. It does not only slow down the request for quotation process but it also shows that it's extremely difficult to evaluate the real competences of a company. Furthermore, the traceability of an order is very difficult to maintain. Within a peer-to-peer network this could be a very difficult point if many companies want to take the same order.

3.5 Importance of the prestige (face)

The good image of each person and of their companies is very important and its loss must be avoided under any circumstances. If something is going wrong, it will probably not be spoken about. That means that not receiving any news does not necessarily mean that everything is running well. Face keeping is also important in the relation between people and attention has to be paid that a question should never risk affecting the other's prestige. For persons who don't have any experience with the Chinese culture, it can be very difficult to estimate the credibility of an answer.

3.6 Communication

Beside the cultural differences, the language is often a communication barrier. The average English language skill level in Chinese SME is rather low. In Chinese local companies it is not an exception that nobody has a sufficient level for technical discussions. Very often a translation by a third person is needed. As the cultural and technical references are quite different, *explicit communication* must be used as things, which are evident for Swiss companies, are not for Chinese ones and vice versa.

4. CHOICE OF THE NETWORK STRUCTURE

We will compare three potential solutions with the help of SWOT (Strengths, Weaknesses, Opportunities and Threats) analysis. In the first solution we don't have a network structure and sporadic subcontracting relations between companies can be formed. The second solution is a hub-and-spoke network, where close relations between the members and the central company are formed but not between the members themselves. In the third solution we find a peer-to-peer network structure, where all member companies are strongly linked to each other.

Advantages of virtual networks are largely discussed in the literature (Bruetsch et al.,1998). In the following SWOT analysis we focus on the compatibility to the Chinese environment and on a future collaboration with SMT. The goal is to find out if one of the two network structures is well adapted or if traditional subcontracting relations are the only solution. The main criteria for the following analysis are:
- Trust issues

- Tendency to hierarchy
- Direct profitability
- Rapid change of motivation
- Competences estimation (partner selection)
- Communication
- Legal issues

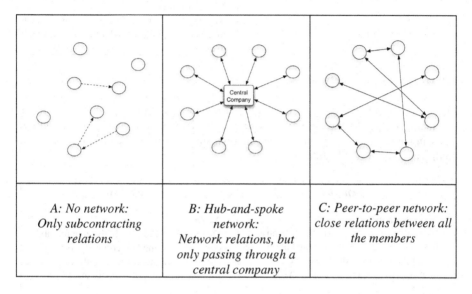

| A: No network: Only subcontracting relations | B: Hub-and-spoke network: Network relations, but only passing through a central company | C: Peer-to-peer network: close relations between all the members |

Figure 2 – Network forms

4.1 Only subcontracting relations

This classical solution is based on sporadic outsourcing relations when a need occurs. Partners must be chosen among a very large base of companies and as everything changes very quickly in China, past experiences may be not relevant.

Strengths	*Weaknesses*
Trust: No deep trust relations needed for collaboration. **Tendency to hierarchy:** Clearly defined structure during the collaboration. **Direct profitability:** Each collaboration leads directly to a financial profit. High motivation of Chinese companies. **Rapid change of motivation:** No long-term bonds and therefore no consequences if the motivation of a partner changes.	**Communication:** Very difficult communication with Chinese companies due to low language levels and cultural differences. Contact to many companies not possible. **Legal aspects:** Especially for foreign customers, very low legal protection because of direct collaboration with Chinese companies. **Choice of partners:** **Difficulty to select a reliable partner**

Opportunities	*Threats*
Simplicity Simple customer-supplier relations	**Competences estimation:** Difficulties for customers to know if a supplier is able to fulfill the requirements, or if it will further subcontract. **Local support:** No support at all, the foreign company must monitor the quality and delivery schedules itself

4.2 Hub-and-spoke network

This solution is based on a very centralized network of suppliers where the hub is the main contact to the foreign company. The hub is responsible for selecting, assessing and continuously monitoring its own suppliers as well as for the respect of quality and delivery schedules.

Strengths	*Weaknesses*
Legal aspects: Protection of foreign customers because the orders are given only to the hub and because of the high pressure on the member companies due to follow-up orders. **Communication:** Existence of an intermediate element between foreign customers and local Chinese companies. This allows an access to a higher number of suppliers **Direct profitability:** From the beginning on the member companies feel the profit in form of direct orders. Important point to increase the motivation. **Tendency to hierarchy:** Clear organization because of hierarchic structure. **Rapid change of motivation:** If one member company jumps off, the motivation of the others is not affected. **Local support:** Strong local support as only the hub is responsible for the orders	**Trust:** Difficult to build trust between a member company and the hub company, if they are not family-related (does not affect a foreign customer of the network.)
Opportunities	*Threats*
Competences estimation: Customers have access to information about member's competences due to the experience of the hub company.	**Rapid change of motivation:** The hub company is the centre of the network. A loss of its motivation would have drastic consequences.

4.3 Peer-to-Peer Network

Peer-to-peer networks are based on the collaboration of independent companies on the same level of hierarchy. As there is no central power, the decisions must be negotiated between the members and an acceptable consensus must be found.

Strengths	*Weaknesses*
	Legal aspects: Especially for foreign customers, very low legal protection because of direct collaboration with all member companies. **Communication:** Very difficult communication with Chinese companies due to low language levels and cultural differences. Contact to many companies not possible. **Direct profitability:** Direct financial profit in form of orders after a long initialization period of the network. In the beginning only economies of scale. **Trust:** Very difficult to build trust within a group of companies which are not family related.
Opportunities	*Threats*
	Competences estimation: Large and similar core competences between members. Leads to conflicts during the order distribution. **Tendency to hierarchy:** Difficulties to obtain a structural organization, as all companies are on the same level. Risk that the stronger companies wouldn't respect the weaker ones anymore. **Rapid change of motivation:** If one member company jumps off, the motivation of the others can be negatively affected.

5. CONCLUSIONS

The message received during the discussions (among others with the Dongguan University of Technology and our industrial partners) was clear: Chinese companies are not yet ready to form peer-to-peer networks, even if this structure is widely seen as the most performing type of network. For the moment, the best solution in terms of cultural compatibility and intercontinental customer relations is the hub-and-spoke type, with a strong and trustful company in the centre of the network.

As an example, the DecoCHina extended network has been created in 2007 with Swiss Microtech and a local Chinese company located in the Province of Guangdong and having both local and Western management as the hub that also brings its own network of around ten local companies (Pouly et al.,2008). This hub company is for the moment the only contact of Swiss Microtech and it takes also the responsibility of its own suppliers. First commercial activities involving both partners are currently on the way.

6. ACKNOWLEDGEMENT

The authors would like to thank Mr. Xu Bing from Dongrui Ltd in Dongguan, Professor Mo and Professor Quan from the Dongguan University of Technology (DUT) for their commitment and support. The authors would also like to thank the Dongguan Bureau for Science and Technology and the Commission for Technology and Innovation of the Swiss federal government, which funded this research.

7. REFERENCES

1. Bruetsch D. et al., Virtuelle Unternehmen, v/d/f Hochschulverlag an der ETH Zürich, 1999
2 .Greber M.; Master thesis, Optimization of the business processes within a Swiss–Chinese collaborative network and development of an assessment methodology for new members, EPFL; 2006
3. Pouly M. , Glardon R, Huber C. , Competitor based strategic networks of SME, in Knowledge and Technology Integration in production and Services, pp 149-156, edited by V .Marik, L. Camarinha-Matos, H. Afsarmanesh, Kluwer Academic Publishers, 2002
4. Pouly M., Greber M., Glardon R., Huber C., Beeler J., DecoCHina: A Swiss Chinese Industrial Collaborative Network of SME, to be presented at the IEEE CSCW08 Conference in Xian, China
5. Pouly M., Monnier F., Bertschi D. , Success and Failure Factors of Collaborative Networks of SME, in Collaborative Networks and their Breeding Environment, pp 597-604, edited by L. Camarinha-Matos, H. Afsarmanesh, A. Ortiz, Springer, 2005

42   STRATEGIC INFORMATION SYSTEM (SIS) OF VIRTUAL ORGANIZATION (VO)

Brane Semolic[1], Jure Kovac[2]

[1] Project & Technology Management Institute, Faculty of Logistics,
University of Maribor, Slovenia, brane.semoli@siol.net
[2] Faculty of Organizational Sciences, University of Maribor, SLOVENIA
jure.kovac@fov.uni-mb.si

In the modern business world, the networked organizational connections tend to become prevailing organizational form. However, virtual organizations represent a special form of network organization. The backbone of virtual organization is its information system. To obtain successful and efficient operating of virtual organization, its strategic information system is of key importance. Strategic Information System (SIS) is a type of Information System that is aligned with business strategy and structure. SIS is designed to support and increase the competitive strength of a VO. We have upgraded Anthony's paradigm, and taken into consideration the changes in the field of organization and management of modern network companies. This includes also the aspect of assuring the suitable information support to corporate management, which has to provide, at different levels and areas of operation, successful and effective management of corporate business processes in virtual environment. In the paper the aspect of defining possible fields of application of the SIS and the study of their characteristics are discussed. The theory is supported and illustrated by the LENS (Laser Engineered Net Shaping) Living Laboratory case study.

1. INTRODUCTION

If we want to develop a competitive strength of our company, it often turns up that despite using our knowledge, capacities and other resources we are still not able to reach the desired goal. In modern business environment, the companies will establish and maintain their competitiveness not solely by optimizing their own potentials, but more often by being able to use also the resources of the others and by interconnecting them into an overall process of creating a new value. The need to connect organizations and to unite the resources has its origins in the demand posed by the global market to remain competitive concerning prices, time and quality. This is why the companies tend to be increasingly specialized and develop only those key areas that enable them to remain competitive on the global market (Milberg, Schuh, 2002, p. 21; Prahalad, Ramaswamy, 2004, p. 96). The networked organizational design is becoming the prevailing organizational form of the 21st century.

The virtual organization's information system represents one of the key success factors. In developing an efficient virtual organization's information system, a special place belongs to the strategic information system. In this contribution, a dimension of the virtual organization's strategic information system on the example of the Living Lab case study is presented.

Please use the following format when citing this chapter:

Semolic, B. and Kovac, J., 2008, in IFIP International Federation for Information Processing, Volume 283; *Pervasive Collaborative Networks*; Luis M. Camarinha-Matos, Willy Picard; (Boston: Springer), pp. 407–414.

2. DEFINITION OF VIRTUAL ORGANIZATION

One of the first contributions in dealing with the topic of virtual companies was a book by title "The Virtual Corporation" by William H. Davidow and Michael S. Malone, published in 1992. Yet, the dematerialization of the products, processes and workplaces in the organization was brought into focus of the field experts already in 1985 (and in 1987, 1994) by Abbe Mowshowitz. On the basis of established frameworks, the authors Venkatraman and Henderson in 1998 developed three gradual models of business virtuality. According to their views, virtual organizations differ from other organizations by specific abilities and by their "virtual attitude of thinking". The mentioned abilities and virtual attitude of thinking are expressed by:

- products and services that are presented to the customers "virtually", or are "virtually" consumed ("virtual encounter");
- supply processes among the organizations and by the processes inside the organizations, where the continuous processes of searching the synergistic links are carried on ("leverage-effects" and "virtual sourcing");
- knowledge in possession of the organization or among the organizations who, at different levels, connect in a flexible and non-bureaucratic way ("virtual expertise") (Venkatraman, Henderson, 1998).

Virtual organizations represent co-operation between formally disconnected organizations or persons who establish vertical or horizontal links and present themselves to the customers of their products or services as a single association. Besides this, in professional literature concerning virtual organizations there is also an obvious emphasis given to the information and communication technology as well as to the absence of the central control functions. Added to this, the time limitation of the concerned association and the geographical dispersion of the virtual organization's members are also stressed (Moldaschl, 1998, p. 19; Mohrman, Galbraith and Lawler III., 1998, p.77; Dessler, 2001, p. 230; Pettigrew and others, 2003, p. 8; Vahs, 2005, p. 507).

As indispensable precondition for the functioning of the above mentioned organizational connectedness the authors quote timely adjusted co-operative processes, organizational development, space dispersion and use of modern communication technology to master the processes of co-operation (Rohde, Rittenbruch, Wulf, 2001, p. 2).

In the literature, the companies are often described as network of companies (i. e. organizations – boundary-less firms or boundless organizations) and by this it's frequently meant a considerable number of dynamic organizations, connected in a network - i. e. virtual companies – that are linked together on a basis of interorganizational information system and guided by the aim to be successful in the area of the given projects.

3. STRATEGIC INFORMATION SYSTEM (SIS)

3.1 Definition of SIS

In theory as well as in practice, different definitions of information systems in a company are at disposal. By information systems we understand primarily the IT supported systems in companies. The most frequently used designation in the Anglo-Saxon world is "Management Information System" which is based on the business operations model developed in 1965 by R. Anthony ("Planning and Control Systems: A Framework for Analysis"), known also as "Anthony's Paradigm". Anthony's Paradigm could be represented in the form of a pyramid indicating the correlation and interdependence between the processes of strategic planning and managerial and operative control. By notion of managerial control are meant the procedures by which company assures successful and efficient use of its resources, whereas the operative control refers to a follow-up of the planned work execution. Five years after the publication of Anthony's Paradigm, W. Zani ("Blueprint in MIS") presented his concept of MIS, based on the latter's starting points, which should support the process of strategic planning and that of the managerial and operative control. In accordance with the nature of work and the needs of MIS users finding themselves at different levels of Anthony's pyramid, Zani speaks of two types of information system. The first one refers to the automation of business procedures, and the second one to providing information to managers for the needs of their decision making. On the basis of this original definition of MIS many different interpretations have appeared.

The next big step in development of the IT supported management information systems offering assistance to the management of a company was made in the early seventies of the previous century, when A. Gorry and M. Scott-Morton ("A Framework for Management Information Systems") presented their idea of Decision Support Systems (DSS). They defined DSS as an information system intended to support inadequately structured decision making, strategic planning, and managerial and operative controls. On these starting points later developed the concept of Executive Information System (EIS) that superstructures DSS.

In this paper, we have dealt with the concept of "Strategic Information System" (SIS), which is based on the above described findings. Its starting points were set by C. Wiseman ("Strategy and Computers - Information Systems as Competitive Weapons"), according to whom the SIS is an information system designed to support and increase the competitive strength of a company. We extended and adopted his concept to the needs of a virtual dynamic organization, where we have alliances of organizations that come together to share skills, core competences and resources in order to better respond to business opportunities. We have a set of temporary business activities which are initiated, organized and led by partners of such an organization. The VO's SIS should cover information needs of participating organizations, projects consortia, VO organizers, involved PVCs etc.

The findings of the authors dealing with the SIS, and the results of our research concerning the characteristics of contemporary corporate management have led us to the conclusion that the SIS should be considered from two aspects, i.e.:
- the aspect of defining possible fields of application of the SIS,
- his characteristics and interrelations, and
- the aspect of searching the fields of application which would, in a real case, help involved organizations to increase their competitive strength.

In our paper, we have limited ourselves to the aspect of defining possible fields of application of the SIS related to virtual dynamic organizations.

To Anthony's paradigm, which served as the starting point for the definition of the field of application of classical managerial information systems, we have added the paradigm of networked organizations that should be present in successfully operating contemporary companies. In this way we have got a modified Anthony's paradigm, shown in Figure 1.

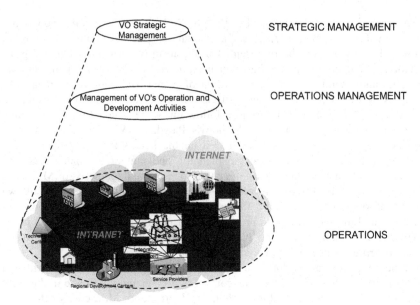

Figure 1: Modified Anthony's paradigm.

Anthony's definition of administration levels we extended on the needs of virtual dynamic organization. Through an analysis of the modified Anthony's paradigm we have reached the definition of the basic fields of application of the SIS which should provide data, information and the corresponding IT tools for the:
- implementation needs of VO's business processes,
- needs of management of VO's business activities, and
- needs of VO's executives.

According to Anthony's paradigm, it is possible, in a company, to identify three characteristic levels of decision making - the executive (top management) level, which is responsible for strategic management of a company, the medium management level, which is responsible for individual SBUs, and the business functions, projects and operations management level, which is responsible for the performance of business activities. Individual levels are interrelated, yet relatively independent in their decisions and planning.

As the business processes on the operations' level are determined, the decision processes can be structured in advance, too, and they are in this way easy to manage. There is quite a different situation on the remaining two management levels. The more we approach to the top management, whose task is strategic management of a company, the more the decision processes grow stochastic, or they can be only partly structured or not structured at all. Manager "plays" several roles. In the role of "liaison" and "leader," manager collects information which is relevant to him or her. In the role of "liaison," manager contacts people apart from his or her field of activity, and in different other ways collects information relevant to him or her. As "leader", manager collects information from his subordinates (and superiors). In the role of "monitor," manager systematically searches the environment in order to identify problems and sense opportunities. The information collected in this way is by rule communicated to the superiors - the manager plays the role of "spokesman" - to the subordinates - the manager plays the role of "disseminator" - or he or she uses

this information alone, in one of the following four managerial roles of decision maker: as "disturbance handler", "entrepreneur", "resource allocator" and "negotiator". Information technology influences all these roles; however, its influence on the role of manager as decision maker is the strongest. The versatility of decision situations, which managers or those preparing expert ground for decisions have to face, dictates different modes and scopes of application of information technology. Contemporary manager or operations analyst has at his disposal a range of information technologies which form a Decision Support Systems Group (DSSG). These are:
- Decision Systems (DS),
- Decision Support Systems (DSS),
- Expert Systems (ES),
- Group Decision Support Systems (GDSS).

The central part of DSSG represent Decision Support Systems (DSS). In practice, the notions of DSS and EIS (Executive Information Systems) are often confused. Thus, sometimes, the first or the second notion is interchangeably used for the same system. Nevertheless, the DSS and the EIS are two different systems, and they should be treated separately, as each of them is intended for different users, and they also have different purposes and modes of application.

The DSS are primarily intended for managers and experts who prepare the grounds for executive management's decisions. They help solve problems to which the solutions are not structured in advance. Usually there are several different ways to the solution of these problems. The user of such systems sets different possible scenarios of solution by using the logic "What if..." and the method of "Goal Seeking Analysis". The basis of DSS is a "model-data" combination by means of which relations between the data of the operations field in question are described. Systems should be simple and provide access to various data that make possible to form models which are basis for the performance of the said analyses.

VOs' managers need in the first place the following information:
- key (actual) problems and possible reasons,
- the most important indicators of success and effectiveness of temporary consortia in the form of planned and real values and deviations,
- financial situation in VO's operations and projects,
- key indicators of operations by areas of responsibility (e.g. by projects, activities, etc.), and
- various (consolidated) reports produced by the criteria and in the way dictated by the actual situation.

All these information refer to the success and effectiveness of the operations, adaptation and development business processes.

4. CASE STUDY – LENS LIVING LAB

4.1 What is LENS Living Lab

Lens Living Lab is a real-life research and operational laboratory with the focus on a Lens new technology applications development and operational use. The LENS Living Lab creates a base for inventing, testing, prototyping and marketing of new LENS technology applications. The major advantage of virtual organization's LENS Living Lab is creation of pools of innovative organizations and experts from different research and end user areas who are collaborating and cooperating in this virtual environment.

The areas of LENS Living Lab application research and operations are: Tool making and niche machines production, Automotive, Aeronautics and Medicine.

The participating organizations are divided in following groups: Material science, Mechanical Engineering, Laser and Electronics, End Users, IT and Networking Technologies.

They have been involved in three operational and research frameworks as follow (Table 2): Technological and Innovative Centre (TiC LENS), LENS Living Lab and Laser Collaboration Platform (AA LaseR).

Table 2: Co-operation and Collaboration Frameworks

Framework	Role	Partners
TiC LENS	LENS Operations	LENS Consortia
LENS Living Lab	LENS Application Research and Use	Membership
Laser Collaboration Platform	Wider laser community collaboration	Open

The Figure 2 is illustration of LENS Living Lab business model. The LENS Living Lab members are business partners who have long term interest for such a co-operation. Those organizations and individuals are from research and industrial sector.

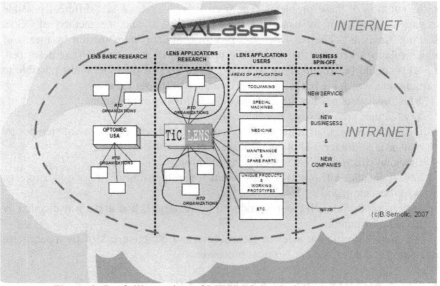

Figure 2: Draft illustration of LENS Living Lab business model

4.2 Organization and Co-Ordination of LENS Living Lab

The LENS Living Lab is an open network organization having three levels of inter-organizational co-operation and coordination (see Figure 3). The first level deals with the strategic business issues. At this level, the participating partners sign the long-term co-operation agreement. This agreement defines the areas of cooperation and management of LENS Living Lab. The second level deals with the inter-organizational issues (joint and support operation and project management). This level is related to the coordination of agreed business activities and connected organizational processes. The third level of co-ordination is related to the definition of IT and telecommunication platform of co-operation.

Figure 3: Levels of co-ordination in LENS Living Lab

4.3 The Third Level of Co-Ordination ICT Tools

The basic collaboration is usually based on phone, fax, and email communication. Although much work has been done to improve the collaborative ability among SMEs and research organizations, most of them still require suitable instruments supporting collaboration of the organizational as well as on data flow level. The lack of suitable instruments lies in the complex nature of collaboration. On the one hand, it is a question of having the right ICT tools. On the other hand, it is a question of organizational structure to allow seamless information processing as well as correct internal competencies to execute the collaborative processes typical of dynamic electronic marketplaces.

In the LENS Living Lab we are recognizing five groups of ICT tools:
- CRM (TCS portal, Tool East Solution, Video-cluster, etc),
- e-collaboration platform (Share Point, Skype, etc.),
- e-project management & project office (Open Sourced SW),
- LENS Living Lab specific functional ICT tools (Tool East Solution, etc.) and
- LENS Living Lab Executive SW Tools (not developed yet)

The LENS Living Lab project is in progress and all decisions about the ICT tools are not finalized yet. We are using the Slovenian Toolmakers Cluster portal as the basic e-platform to build up the LENS Living Lab SIS. We are planning to use the open sourced Tool East solution to support CRM, as well as development and production processes within the network of LENS Living Lab. The Tool East solution will be operational this year. This SW has been developed by the EU consortia (partners form Slovenia, Germany, Italy, Slovakia, Bulgaria).

5. CONCLUSIONS

Virtual organizations are a special form of network organizations based on the modern information and communication technology and having various configurations. This is why we can hardly imagine a successful and efficient virtual organization's operating without a modern information and communication technology. A Living Lab is an environment in which researchers, developers and users cooperate with the common objective of delivering a tested product, solution or service respecting the users' requirements and in a shortest time possible. We used the case study of LENS Living lab to present described concept in praxis. The LENS Living Lab is an open network organization having three levels of inter-organizational co-operation and coordination.

The key success factor in operating virtual organizations, as well as Living labs is their information system. One of the most important parts of it is SIS. In our concept we are using upgraded Anthony's paradigm, shown as SIS application from point of view of networked virtual organizations. For introduction of such a system into reality, the use of proper ICT tools is needed. We have grouped the tools in five specific groups.

6. REFERENCES

1. Beck TC. Cooperation bei der Nexwerkorganisation, IO Mangement, No.6, Zürich, BWI–ETH, 1998.
2. Bullinger HJ, Warnecke HJ, Westkamper E. Neue Organisationsformen im Untermehmen. Berlin: Springer Verlag, 2003.
3. Byrne J, Brand R, Port O. The Virtual Corporation, Business Week, (8.2.93), New York, 1993.
4. Davidov WH, Malone MS.The Virtual Corporation, New York: Harper-Collins, 1993.
5. Dessler G. Management, New Jersey: Prentice Hall Inc., 2001.
6. Eriksson, Mats; Niitamo, Veli-Pekka; Kulkki, Seija; Hribernik, Karl A. Living Labs as a Multi-Contextual R&D Methodology. In: Proceedings of the ICE Conference, 2006
7. Hesselbein F, Goldsmith M, in Beckhard R. The Organization of the Future, San Francisco: Jossey-Bass, 1997.
8. Kelly K. New Rules for New Economy, New York: Viking Penguin. 1998.
9. Korine H, Gomez PY. The Lap to Globalization, San Francisco: Jossey-Bass, 2001.
10. Malone WT. The Future of Work, Boston: Harvard Business School Press, 2004.
11. Milber J, Schuh G. Erfolg in Netzwerk, Berlin: Springer Verlag, 2002.
12. Mohrman AS, Galbraith JR, Lawler III.E. Tomorrow's Organization, San Francisco: Jossey-Bass, 1998.
13. Moldaschl M. Kultur-Engineering und Kooperative Netzwerke, IO Mangement, Nr.6, Zürich: BWI – ETH, 1998.
14. Pettigrew A, Whittington R, Melin L, Runde CS, Bosch FAJ, van den Ruigrok W, Numagami T. Innovative forms of Organizing, London: Sage Publications, 2003.
15. Prahalad CK, Ramaswamy V. The Future of Competition, Boston: Harvard Business School Press, 2004.
16. Rohde M, Rittenbuch M, Wulf V. Auf dem Weg zur virtuellen Organisation, Heidelberg: Physica-Verlag, 2001.
17. Semolic B, Virtual and Living Laboratories, INOVA Consulting, 2006,
18. Semolic B, MIS Integration , Faculty of Business Administration and Economic, University of Maribor, 1992,
19. Semolic B, LENS Living Laboratory Project, INOVA Consulting, TCS, 2007,
20. Semolic B, AA LaseR Collaboration Platform, INOVA Consulting, TCS, 2007,
21. Semolic B, Jannicke Baalsrud Hauge, Ali Imtiaz, Richard Stevens, The Tool East Solution for Industrial Clusters in Eastern Europe, IPMA Project Management Practice, ISSUE 4, IPMA, Nijkerk, 2008
22. Semolic B and Co, LENS Living Lab Project, FP 7 project proposal, P&TMI, Faculty of Logistics, University of Maribor, 2008
23. Vahs D. Organisation, Stuttgart: Schaffer-Poeschel Verlag, 2005.
24. Venkatraman N, Henderson JC. Real Strategis for Virtual Organizing, Sloan Management Review, 1 (40), MIT, 1998.

43

PROACTIVE MANAGEMENT
OF BUSINESS CHANGE

Mamadou Camara , Lyes Kermad, Abderrahman El Mhamedi

IUT de Montreuil- Université de Paris 8.
140, rue de la Nouvelle France
93100 Montreuil Cedex, FRANCE
E-mail: mamadousamba_c@yahoo.fr

This paper addresses enterprise performance problems that can occur after Business Process Reengineering (BPR) project as consequence of business change. The general idea is to lean a Bayesian network from past BPR projects and use this model for prediction in future restructured processes. The role of Bayesian network will be to measure influence of business process structural changes, quantified by structural change metrics, and the increasing or decreasing of process performance, quantified by operational variation metrics. The paper's focus is interoperable structural change metrics definition using process ontology, and operational variation metrics definition. Bayesian prediction model learning, application and result interpretation are discussed in (CAMRA, et al., 2007). The method we propose is for use for the validation of enterprise restructuration, more precisely in the validation of business processes restructuration's.

1. INTRODUCTION

The Business Process Reengineering method (BPR) is described by Hammer and Champy as 'the fundamental reconsideration and the radical redesign of business processes, in order to achieve drastic improvement of current performance in cost, services and speed   (Hammer, et al., 2003). Information technology like ERP (Enterprise Resource Planning) is a critical enabler of this change (García Díaz, 2004). The risk that users can not answer the changes is one of the most important problems in BPR projects (Tatsiopoulos I. P., 2003) which suffer from low rate of success.

Looking at the research done on risk management in BPR projects, we can find that there is a lack of quantitative methodologies to manage risk related to business change. Mostly, final users' dissatisfaction face to the deepness of change is just cited in risk factors and change management is recommended in success factors (Bernard J., 2002) (Hammer, et al., 2003) (García Díaz, 2004) (Kermad L., 2003) (Bernier, et al., 2003). Some author's like Anderson (Anderson, 2001) have addressed organizational change's impact in BPR projects using quantitative method. His proposition is a Bayesian prediction of the impact of potential changes in organization structure, senior leadership, and strategic vision variables on the decision marking variables. We think that his variables are too global because he is working at the level of the whole enterprise. He also uses a questionnaire to measure

Please use the following format when citing this chapter:

Camara, M., Kermad, L. and Mhamedi, A.E., 2008, in IFIP International Federation for Information Processing, Volume 283; *Pervasive Collaborative Networks*; Luis M. Camarinha-Matos, Willy Picard; (Boston: Springer), pp. 415–422.

variables, with the consequence that the variables will not be completely quantitative and completely objective. In (Tatsiopoulos I. P., 2003) also, the application of Monte Carlo simulation is presented for risk related to time, and the author says that a similar approach is proposed for risk related to organizational change without presenting that. We consider that the transposition of this method can not be done automatically because its application varies according to what is analyzed. We've chosen to work in business process level because, according to Garcia (García Díaz, 2004), the unit of analysis in BPR is the business process as opposed to departments or functional areas.

For Bernard (Bernard J., 2002) , the business change problem's causes are the gap between as-is and to-be business processes and consequences are deacrese of employes productivity. We propose to define structural change metrics which measure this gap which is the result of change operated on business processes during the BPR. Structural change metrics are extracted from information on processes registered on the process modeling tolls databases. To ensure interoperable metrics not depending on modeling tool, we will use business process ontology to represent our processes. We also define operational variation metrics which represent performance variation between the executions of as-is process and executions of to-be process. A Bayesian model is learned from historical data obtained from past BPR projects. The Bayesian network is a measurable influence relation and prediction model between process performance variation and process structural change. Our contribution is not in the Bayesian network formalism but rather in the definition of the entries of the Bayesian network and the interpretation of the prediction results. The method we propose is for use, as additional criteria, in the validation of the enterprise restructuration, more precisely in the validation of business processes restructuration. Actually, validation criteria are Business/IT alignment and/or performance indicator resulting from simulation of the newly designed process. The paper's focus is interoperable structural change metrics definition using process ontology, and operational variation metrics definition. Bayesian prediction model learning, application and result interpretation are discussed in (CAMRA, et al., 2007).

2. BUSINESS CHANGE MEASUREMENT

2.1 Change metrics definition and data collection

The structural change metrics we define on business processes are combination of structural metrics (Tjaden, 2001) (Aguilar, et al., 2006A) (Aguilar, et al., 2006B) defined in Business Process Structural Analysis and change metrics (Demeyer, 2000) (Gokhale, et al., 1997) defined in software engineering. Structural metrics are quantification of static properties of business processes (Tjaden, 2001) and represent process structural complexity. In software engineering, Demeyer (Demeyer, 2000) defines change metrics by comparison between successive versions of object-oriented software systems source code. Structural change metrics are extracted by comparison between the AS_is and the To-be version of the business process. This comparison determinates how many units are added and removed for every significant element or relation in the model. To avoid redundancy of data we choose to focus the metric definition on the relations between the elements of the process rather-that on the elements themselves. For example for the Relation "Responsible" (An organizational Unit is Responsible of a Function) two metrics are defined. Rmv_Res and Add_Res represent respectively the percent of Removed (only in as-is process) and Added (only in to-be process) relations of type Responsible.

$$\bullet \ \ Rmv - Res = \frac{\text{Number of Responsible Relations only in As-Is Model}}{\text{Number of Responsible Relations in As-Is Model}} \times 100$$

$$\bullet \ \ Add - Res = \frac{\text{Number of Responsible Relations only in To-Be Model}}{\text{Number of Reresponsible Relations in As-Is Model}} \times 100$$

We illustrate change metric calculation through an order processing business process model taken from (Scheer, 1998) in which it is described before and after BPR. These two versions of the business process are depictured in figure2 and figure3. We have for example, one removed relation of type "Responsible" (Plant-OrderPlanning) in a total of three relations of this type. Then the metrics Rmv_Res for this process takes the value 1/3 or 33 %.

2.1 Business Process Ontology and change metrics interoperability

Business process ontology defines the concepts that constitute a business process and the relationships among them (Jenz, Business Process Ontologies: Frenquently Asqued Questions, 2003B). As such, the business process ontology defines structure. A knowledge base is the result of instantiating ontology, i.e. populating ontology with data (Jenz, 2003A). As such, a knowledge base contains structure and data. Ontology provides terminology interoperability which is the capability to recognize that two pieces of data are talking about the same thing, even though different terminology is being used (Jenz, 2003A). Business process ontology is a machine-readable representation which allows ease and automatic comparison, validation querying and transformation of processes. Business process ontology would describe all concepts related with a business process. In particular it would define entity types such as business activity, business document, business object, business event, business rule, role, resource, and control flow (Jenz, 2003B). Several approaches, techniques and methods have been used to develop enterprise or business process ontology. The best-known are:

- TOVE : Toronto Virtual Enterprise (Kim, 1999)
- Enterprise Ontology (Uschold, King, Moralee, & Zorgios, 1998)
- BMO Business Management Ontology (Jenz, 2004)
- BPMO Business Process Modeling Ontology (Dimitrov, et al., 2007)

We are interested particularly in BMO (Jenz, 2004) because it is available for free download and is editable using Protégé-OWL. Protégé-OWL (Stanford, 2008) provides a graphical and interactive ontology-design and knowledge-base development environment. Metrics interoperability means in this study that the definition and the extraction of structural change metrics can be performed independently of the business process modeling tool or specification language. To ensure this interoperability we propose the use of business process ontology, the

BMO as intermediate representation. For example we can have to constitute a dataset with processes (As-is ad To-be versions) created using ARIS and other processes (As-is ad To-be versions) created using ADONIS. Each concept, and each relation, in the BMO structure (figure 1) have an equivalent class or relation in ARIS and ADONIS meta-models. We translate these process models in process ontology form using two deferent java programs. A third java program will perform the extraction of metrics on all ontological process models in the same manner. For example each function in a process modeled with ARIS will be represented by an instance of the class PrivateProcessTask. We use java because of the existence of Jena java API (Sourceforge, 2008) which enable to handle Protégé-OWL ontology.

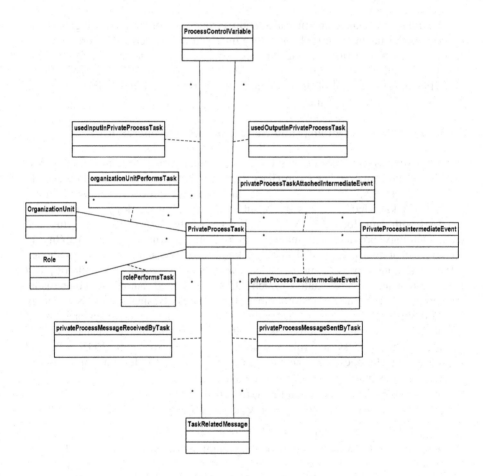

Figure 1BMO structure

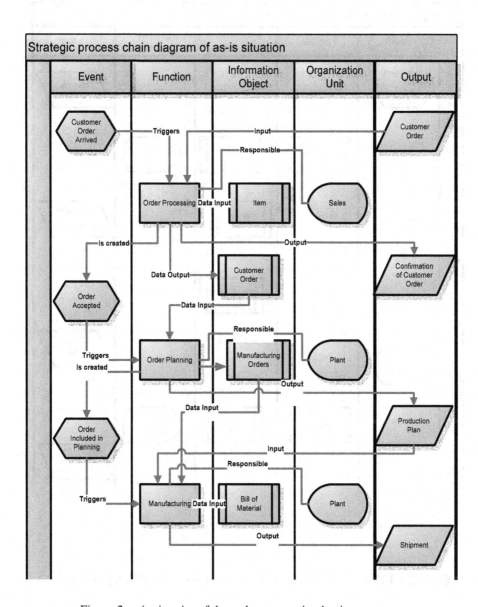

Figure 2 as-is situationof the order processing business process

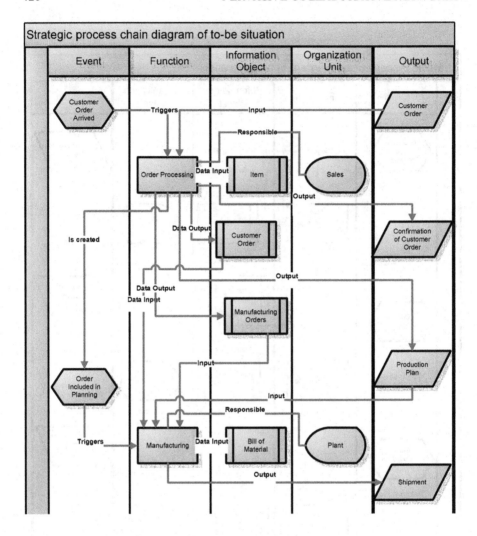

Figure 3 to-be situationof the order processing business process

3. OPERATIONAL VARIATION METRICS DEFINITION

Operational variation metrics are also defined; they should represent the process performances variations between the executions before and after BPR. We can find in the literature the following operational metrics:

- Percent manufactured correctly (Tjaden, 2001), fraction (Florac, 1999) or proportion (Baillargeon, 2004) of nonconforming (defective) used in control charts for variables; Average proportion of nonconforming used in control chart p for attributes (Baillargeon, 2004).

- Process Mean time (Aguilar, et al., 2006A) (Tjaden, 2001), Processing time (Kock, 2001), Cycle time (Kock, 2001), Average time elapsed (IBM, 2008)
- Process cost (Aguilar, et al., 2006A) (Scheer, 1998), average cost of execution (IBM, 2008)

For operational variation metrics extraction the following steps are performed for every process to register in data collection:

1. The As-is process is monitored using BAM (Webmethods, 2006) techniques during a given period
   a. Average time elapsed (ATE) metric is calculated
   b. Average cost execution (ACE) metric is calculated
   c. Fraction nonconforming metric (FNC) is calculated if the characteristic is measurable
   d. Average proportion of nonconforming (APNC) metric is calculated if the characteristic is an attribute
2. The To-be process is monitored using same techniques and for a similar period : 1.a, 1.b and 1.c or a.d are performed for the restructured process
3. Operational variation metric are calculated as following

   a. Variation on ATE : $V\_ATE = \dfrac{ATE_{as-is} - ATE_{to-be}}{ATE_{as-is}} \times 100$

   b. Variation on ACE : $V\_ACE = \dfrac{ACE_{as-is} - ACE_{to-be}}{ACE_{as-is}} \times 100$

   c. Variation on FNC : $V\_FNC = FNC_{as-is} - FNC_{to-be}$

   d. Variation on APNC : $V\_APNC = APNC_{as-is} - APNC_{to-be}$

Our proposition consists to the construction of mathematical model using data-collection processes and the application of this model for prediction on other processes. For data-collection processes, structural change metrics and operational variation metrics are extracted. In reality this type of historical data can be held for example by a consulting company having taken part in several BPR projects where it capitalized these data. For processes on which the model is applied only structural change metrics are extracted, in the same way as for data-collection processes, and operational variation metrics are predicted using the model.

4. CONCLUSIONS

We propose prediction model to evaluate impact of structural change on process performance, in order to validate process redesign. The principal contribution of this study is structural change metrics and operational variation metric's definition and their use. We've show how business process ontology can help to create interoperable structural change metrics. The final objective of this work is the application of the proposition with a real data set collected on real company processes.

5. REFERENCES

Aguilar E., R. et Ruiz F., Garcia, F., Piattini, M., Evaluation measures for business process model [Conférence] // Symposium on Applied Computing (SAC). - 2006A. - pp. 1567-1568.

Aguilar E.,A. et Ruiz F., Garcia, F., Piattini, M., Applying Software Metrics to evaluate Business Process Models [Revue]. - [s.l.] : CLEI electronic journal, 2006B. - Vol. 9.

Anderson R., D., Lenz, R., T., Modeling the Impact of Organizational Change: A Bayesian Network Approach [Revue]. - [s.l.] : Organizationnal Research Methods, 2001. - 1 : Vol. 4.

Baillargeon G. Statistique Appliquée et Outils d'Amélioration de la Qualité [Livre]. - [s.l.] : SMG, 2004.

Bernard J. Rivard S., Aubert B., Evaluation du risques d'implémentation de progiciel [Rapport] : Gestion intégré des risques / rapport du projet réalisé dans le cadre de l'entente entre Hydro¬Québec, VRQ (Valorisation Recherche Québec) et CIRANO . - 2002.

Bernier C et Roy V. L'évolution des rôles dans la gestion des projets TI : le cas des ERP [Revue]. - [s.l.] : Revue Internationale de gestion, 2003. - 2 : Vol. 28.

CAMRA Mamadou, KERMAD Lyes et EL MHAMEDI Abderrahman PROACTIVE MANAGEMENT OF ORGANIZATIONAL CHANGE USING BAYESIAN NETWORKS [Conférence] // MITIP 2007. - Florence 6-7 September : [s.n.], 2007.

Demeyer S., Finding Refactorings via Change Metrics [Conférence] // the 15 th ACM SIGPLAN conference on Object -Oriented Programming, systems, languages, and applications, 2000.

Dimitrov Marin [et al.] A BPMO Based Semantic Business Process Modelling Environment SBPM 2007.

Florac W., A., Carleton, A., D., Measuring the Software Process: Statistical Process Control for Software Process Improvement [Livre]. - [s.l.] : Addison Wesley Professional, 1999.

García Díaz Martha Liliana A METHODOLOGY TO FACILITATE CONTINUOUS IMPROVEMENT IN THE SERVICES PROVIDED BY THE FACILITIES DEPARTMENT AT UPRM [Rapport]. - 2004.

Gokhale S., S. et Lyu M., R., Régression Tree Modeling for the Prediction of Software Quality [Conférence] // ISSAT'97. - Anaheim, CA : [s.n.], 1997.

Hammer Michel et Champy James Le Reengineering [Livre]. - Paris : Dunod, 2003.

IBM Documetation IBM Websphere Business Modeler Advanced // publib.boulder.ibm.com. 2008.

Jenz D., E., Business Management Ontology (BMO) [Rapport]. - 2004.

Jenz, D. E. (2003A). Business Process Ontologies: Frenquently Asqued Questions. Jenz & Partner GmbH.

Jenz, D. E. (2003B). Business Process Ontologies: Speeding up Business Process Implementation. Jenz & Partner GmbH.

Kermad L. Roucou P., El mhamedi A., Les conditions de succès d'un projet ERP [Conférence] // 5ème Congrès International de Génie Industriel. - Québec : [s.n.], 2003.

Kim, H. M. (1999). Representing and Reasoning About Quality Using Enterprise Models. Enterprise Integration Laboratory University of Toronto.

Kock Ned Changing the focus of Business process redisgn from activity flow to information flow [Revue]. - [s.l.] : Defense Aquisition Review Journal, 2001.

Scheer A., W., Aris - Business Process Modeling - [Livre]. - New York : Springer Verlag, 1998. - pp. 16

Sourceforge. (2008). Jena A semantic Web Framework for java. Récupéré sur jena.sourceforge: http://jena.sourceforge.net

Stanford, u. (2008). protégé. Récupéré sur protege.stanford.edu: http://protege.stanford.edu

Tatsiopoulos I. P. Panayiotou N. A., Kirytopoulos K, Tsitsiriggos K., Risk management as a strategic issue for the implementation of ERP systems: a case study from the oil industry [Revue]. - [s.l.] : International Journal of Risk Assessment and Management, 2003. - 1 : Vol. 4.

Tjaden G., S., Business Process Structural Analysis [Rapport] / Georgia Tech Center for Enterprise Systems. - 2001.

Uschold, M., King, M., Moralee, S., & Zorgios, Y. (1998). The Enterprise Ontology. The Knowledge Engineering Review Vol 13 .

Webmethods Business Activity Monitoring (BAM) The New Face of BPM [En ligne]. - June 2006. - http://www1.webmethods.com/PDF/whitepapers/BAM-The_New_Face_of_BPM.pdf.

PART 14

QUALITY, GOVERNANCE AND LEGAL ISSUES

44

ON QUALITY ISSUES IN NETWORKED VALUE CONSTELLATIONS

Novica Zarvić[*], Roel Wieringa, Pascal van Eck
Information Systems Group, Department of Computer Science,
University of Twente, THE NETHERLANDS
{n.zarvic, r.j.wieringa, p.a.t.vaneck}@ewi.utwente.nl

One of the main purposes of collaborative networks is to satisfy specific consumer needs, which one company cannot satisfy alone. With the opening of the internet in the 1990s the number of companies that collaborate by means of computer networks increased rapidly. As far as one of our main foci is the consideration of value object exchanges between the involved business actors, we refer to such collaborative networks as networked value constellations or value webs. The business requirements of networked value constellations need to be enabled and operationalized by means of functional and quality requirements at the IT level. Our paper aims to build a sound understanding of how to plan quality related issues by considering distinct perspectives, namely the business perspective and the information systems perspective. Each perspective requires multiple quality-related considerations. From a business perspective, we have (a) to consider the quality perceptions by the end consumers, (b) to plan the quality of the value objects to be produced, and (c) to plan the quality of the value objects to be transferred. From an information systems perspective we need (d) to plan the quality of the software-intensive systems. The last quality issue, (e) structural properties of the network, has to be applied to both mentioned perspectives. In this paper we provide a framework for discussing and addressing the described quality issues and suggest several techniques in doing so. We point out where these techniques can e used as such and where additional research is required.

1. INTRODUCTION

A value web or a networked value constellation represents an inter-organizational business setting by considering value exchanges between independent business actors. e^3-*value* models (Gordijn, 2001; Gordijn, 2003), as a graphical representation form of value webs, are based on principle of economic reciprocity. This means that for every value exchange, something of value is expected in return. The e^3-*value* approach was introduced in a time when many dot-coms failed financially, because many companies wished for a 'slice of the cake' without assessing the economic sustainability of the business idea as a whole. In recent work, we have shown how to check functional alignment between value models and the supporting IT functionality (Zarvić, 2008). We are of the opinion that, next to the financial assessment of possible future success and pure functional alignment, also diverse

[*] Supported by the Netherlands Organisation for Scientific Research (NWO), project 638.003.407 (Value-based Business-IT Alignment)

Please use the following format when citing this chapter:

Zarvić, N., Wieringa, R. and van Eck, P., 2008, in IFIP International Federation for Information Processing, Volume 283; *Pervasive Collaborative Networks*; Luis M. Camarinha-Matos, Willy Picard; (Boston: Springer), pp. 425–432.

quality issues play an important, if not crucial, role in the overall success. In this analytical work, we discuss important quality-related considerations that arise during the business-IT alignment task of networked value constellations, of which some are resolved and some not. Thereby we distinguish between two different perspectives, namely the business perspective and the information systems (IS) perspective. In section 2 we present our alignment framework, a conceptual framework showing the main relation between the perspectives, before we present an illustrative e^3-value example. On the basis of this example we discuss in the remaining sections the identified quality issues along the two perspectives, suggest several techniques for this setting, and point out how they are related, before we draw our conclusions.

2. CONSIDERING QUALITY IN E-BUSINESSES

2.1 Quality issues and the alignment framework

The design of a system that supports a business need is a complex process with many different stakeholders involved. For managing this complexity, researchers apply multi-perspective approaches. In this paper we distinguish the business perspective and the IS perspective. The two are interrelated and their main relationship is a "put into operation" relation (Gordijn, 2003), which means that the IS perspective enables the previously stated business requirements.

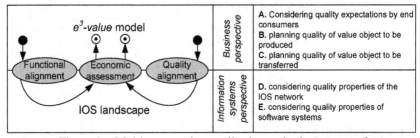

Figure 1 – Multi-perspective quality issues in the context of
Networked business-IT alignment

Figure 1 shows the two perspectives under consideration and represents on the left our alignment framework for value webs. Firstly, on the basis of the value-based business requirements, designers need to elicitate the functional requirements of the underlying IS level. This process might reveal the need for completely new systems that need to be build or even bought by the respective business actors. Of course such investments must subsequently be considered in the profitability calculations. Secondly, we need to identify at what level of quality the business requirements captured in e^3-value models should be enabled. If we have implemented an e-payment mechanism, and this mechanism is neither secure nor fast enough, we cannot assume this leading to a business success story. Quality is defined by ISO 8402 to be "the totality of characteristics of an entity that bear on its ability to satisfy stated and implied needs" (ISO, 1994). Taking this general definition, we can identify in our alignment framework on the right of Figure 1 several locations along the two perspectives, where we deal with such quality characteristics:

A. quality expectations of end consumers (business perspective),
B. quality planning during value object composition/production (business perspective),
C. quality properties of the business network (business perspective),
D. quality properties of the IOS network (information systems perspective),
E. quality properties of software systems (information systems perspective).

The elicitation of quality requirements in the context of networked value constellations is, to the best of our knowledge, insufficiently addressed in the literature. Derzsi (2007) addresses scalability issues in value webs by relating the number of value object transfers to the number of invocations in an UML deployment diagram, but there exists no work that encompasses and structures the distinct quality issues between the two perspectives in a value web context, like done in this paper.

2.2 An example business case

In the following we will introduce the e^3-*value* modeling notation, before we treat in the coming sections each quality issue separately. Figure 2 shows an e^3-*value* model, in which end consumers purchase a value object a, which satisfies their needs, from a retailer, but the retailer will not work for free and expects something of value in return, i.e. value object b.

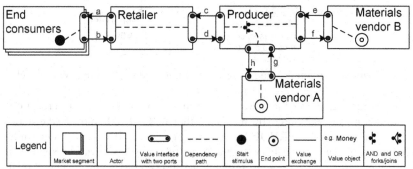

Figure 2 – Educational example of an e^3-*value* model.

O'Sullivan (2002) describes this as the obligation to pay for a service. Such a refundment obligation does not necessarily consist of money or fees in the classical sense, but it can be any object of economic value. The retailer gets the value object from a producer, who is composing/producing the value object by combining value objects, as the ingredients of the object to be produced, from diverse vendors.

The concepts used are: an *actor* is a participant in the value web and an independent, rational economic entity. A *market segment* is a group of actors that share the same needs. Actors exchange *value objects* with each other. A value object is anything that is of value for at least one actor or market segment, such as money, a service, a product, or an experience. The e^3-*value principle* of economic reciprocity is hereby assumed, so that a transfer of a value object is always coupled to a reciprocal value transfer. Value objects are transferred through *value ports*. *Value interfaces* are groupings of value ports. A *value exchange* between two actors, then, connects two value ports with each other and represents an atomic trade of value objects between value ports. *Value activities* can be assigned to actors and represent a collection of operational activities, which must yield profit. To show which value exchanges are needed to fulfill a consumer need, we can draw a *dependency path*, which is a set of connected line segments that starts with a filled circle (representing the occurrence of a the consumer need) and ends in a double lined circle (representing the boundary of our model). *AND/OR* elements can be used for merging and splitting parts of a dependency path.

3. QUALITY ISSUES AT BUSINESS LEVEL

3.1 End Consumer Quality Expectation of Value Object Consumption

Quality issue A, the *expectations of the end consumers* on the quality of the value object to be consumed is one of the most important locations to look at while planning inter-organizational business constellations, because a value web exists by definition for satisfying complex needs of end consumers.

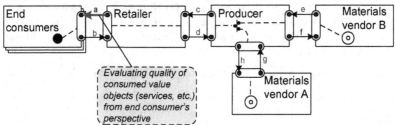

Figure 3 – Planning End Consumer Quality Perception in a Value Web

In the service marketing literature end consumer expectations and perceptions on service quality are measured by means of the SERVQUAL model (Parasuraman, 1985). The original SERVQUAL model considers 10 quality determinants, including well known quality attributes as reliability, security, responsiveness, understandability, etc. In previous research we showed the main conceptual relations of these determinants to software quality characteristics as suggested by the ISO 9126 standard (Zarvić, 2007). SERVQUAL considers quality to be the difference between customer expectations and perceptions, and is considered to be a measure of how well the service level delivered matches customer expectations. For determining this difference, the so-called SERVQUAL questionnaire, a 22-items likert scale, is used. By considering quality as the difference between expectation and perceived delivery, the results of this analysis are mainly usable in the context of business re-engineering, because the complete approach assumes the existence of a service (otherwise there is no notion of perceived delivery). This is at first sight not useful for the exploration and design phase of a value web, but certain elements of the SERVQUAL instrument are usable. In Figure 3 for instance value object *a* represents the service under consideration. In case business planners are interested in meeting end customer expectations of service quality, the first questionnaire dealing with the customer expectations builds a sufficient basis. Possible end consumers, like e.g. internet surfers, are asked to state subjectively their qualitative expectations on a potential business service. The results of this questionnaire build an essential basis for meeting quality expectations at the end consumption point in networked businesses. Note that the SERVQUAL instrument stems from a time when most business services were traditional services like a haircut or a taxi drive. With the advent of the internet, thus of commercial IT services, many slightly altered SERVQUAL versions have been introduced, like for example E-S-QUAL (Parasuraman, 2005) or IS-SERVQUAL (James, 2002), which take the new internet environment into account.

3.2 Planning Quality Properties of Value Object Production/Composition

The second quality issue B, the *qualitative planning of value object production/composition,* is also an important quality issue with respect to networked value constellations. e^3*-value* models often only show trading path of value objects, but sometimes a value object needs to be composed or produced at one of the actors. In figure 4, the AND join at the producer indicates that the producer composes out of value objects *e* and *g*, a new value object *c,* which is later transferred further to the retailer.

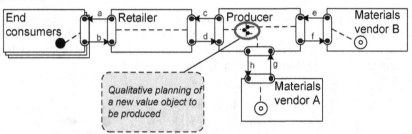

Figure 4 – Qualitative Planning of Value Object Production

The e^3*-value* developers state that a value object can be a good, a service, or even an experience (Gordijn, 2001). In case it is a physical good, the quality function deployment (QFD) tool, sometimes also called the House of Quality, can be used for planning in a qualitative way. QFD originated in the early 1970s in Japan in the automotive industry (Hauser, 1988). Its usage was fast expanded to quality planning of other tangible goods than automobiles and is generally applicable to this category. The next category, services, also profits from QFD, since its usage was adapted in the late 1990s for qualitative service design (Ermer, 1998). The last category, experience, is somehow fuzzy, as far as it can indicate to experience something new or to be satisfied for whatever reason. In some cases this experience is not semantics, like for instance music. We do not consider this fuzzy category implementable in terms of information technology.

3.3 Planning Quality Properties of Value Object Transfer

Every value object transfer has to be planned also in a qualitative way. Considering the value object transfers in the figure below, we can assume that value objects *b*, *d*, *f*, and *h* represent money or fee in terms of the obligation to refund a value object. It is clear that such payments need to be secure, reliable and fast. Apart from that, we are not aware of any technique that deals with the quality of value object transfers, so that this represents an unresolved problem. Again, QFD seems a good candidate for performing this task. In future research we will investigate its usage and define heuristics with respect to planning qualitative value object transfers. SERVQUAL-like approaches might also be good candidates, as the transfer of a value object is itself a service.

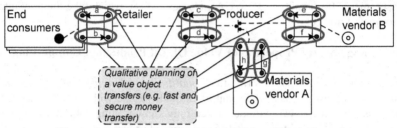

Figure 5 – Qualitative Planning of Value Object Transfers

4. QUALITY ISSUES AT BOTH LEVELS

In e^3-*value* we represent a business network as a graph, where we indicate which business node delivers which value objects to whom and what it gets in return. The IOS landscape of a networked value constellation is usually also represented as a graph, connecting the information systems with each other.

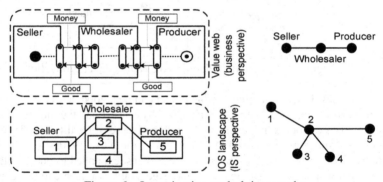

Figure 6 – Investigating underlying graphs.

There exists many situations that can lead to changes of the business network, thus of the underlying graph. For instance, after some time of existence one business actor in the networked value constellation decides to outsource certain activities to a new business actor. As a consequence, one business actor node has to be added to the representation, which means in turn that we are dealing with a new graph. Changes of networked value constellations are also conceivable during the e-business exploration phase, while deconstructing and reconstructing value models. Kumar and van Dissel (1996) argue that inter-organizational dependency patterns, previously identified by Thompson (1967), are as such to be reflected by the design of IOS. Figure 6 shows that this is not a one-to-one mapping or derivation, which is reflected by the underlying graphs on the right. The wholesaler hosts for instance three information systems. Current work (Zarvić, 2008b) gives evidence that it is important to consider structural properties of the underlying graphs as indicators of certain quality aspects that arise while opting for one network constellation or another. In one of our case studies, we showed that an outsourcing option has lead on the one hand to a less complex network, but on the other hand also to a less reliable constellation (Zarvić, 2008b). Take for instance figure 6, where we deal with a *chained* pattern style at the business perspective, but at the IS perspective we have a combination of *chained* and *pooled* pattern style. For the discussion of complexity and reliability issues, our simple approach, which is based on basic properties from graph theory, has to be applied to both perspectives.

5. QUALITY ISSUES OF UNDERLYING SOFTWARE

Quality issue E, namely the *quality of software-intensive systems* (IS perspective), is a well researched area, where we can make use of many existing software quality models, or even change and update them for fitting our purposes (Lauesen, 2002). In figure 7 the six sets of characteristics, including subcharacteristics, of the ISO 9126 quality model are shown. ISO 9126 is not only useful for the evaluation, but also for the specification of quality (Stefani, 2008). As far as the functions/services of software products are the artifacts that enable and support value object transfers, the external metrics suggested by ISO 9126 could be used as the technical means for analyzing the quality of value object transfers at IS level (see Section 3.3). This is a clear interrelation and represents a part of the described future research in section 3.3.

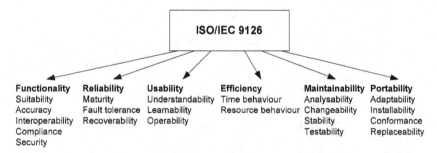

Figure 7 – Characteristics and sub-characteristics of ISO 9126.

6. SUMMARY AND CONCLUSIONS

We have presented a conceptual framework for business-IT alignment that includes next to functional also quality issues. More precisely, these quality issues were situated along the business perspective and the IS perspective, tools for dealing with them were allocated, and interrelated. Thereby we indicated which issues represent resolved and which unresolved problems. Next to the fact that we described the need for quality during the planning and alignment process in a comprehensive way, it should be noted that solely two perspectives were considered. This means that other conceivable perspectives, like e.g. a process or workflow perspective or even a hardware perspective, were not considered in this paper. Summing up, quality issues A, B and D are not unresolved issues, as far as existing techniques can be used to tackle them. However, quality issues C and E are highly interrelated and represent unsolved research problems that we aim to approach in future research. Also other instruments like the goal-question-metric (GQM) are conceivable in this context, but they do not offer a possibility to prioritize technical means as e.g. QFD does. However, this is not decreasing the value of the present work, as far as it represents, to the best of our knowledge, the first systematic attempt to view and analyze quality from a total quality management (TQM) point of view for the respective perspectives. In future work we aim to further investigate the QFD approach and its applicability to the value web context. In particular we intend to define heuristics for its usage with respect to qualitative value object transfers and their realization at the software level by considering software characteristics and metrics as suggested by ISO 9126.

7. REFERENCES

1. Derzsi Z, Gordijn J., van Eck P. "Assessing Feasibility of IT-enabled Networked Value Constellations: A Case Study in the Electricity Sector". In Proceedings of 19th International Conference (CAiSE 2007), Trondheim, Norway, Springer LNCS 4495: 66-80, 2007.
2. Ermer D, Kniper M. Delighting the customer: Quality function deployment for quality service design. Total Quality Management 1998; 9(4&5): 86-91.
3. Gordijn J, Akkermans H. Designing and Evaluating E-Business Models. IEEE Intelligent Systems 2001; 16(4): 11-17.
4. Gordijn J, Akkermans H. Value-based requirements engineering: exploring innovative e-commerce ideas. Requirements Engineering Journal 2003; 8(2): 114-134.
5. Hauser J, Clausing D. The House of Quality. Harvard Business Review May-June 1988; 63-73.
6. ISO 8402. Quality Management and Quality Assurance - Vocabulary. International Organization for Standardization, April 1994.
7. ISO 9126. Information Technology – Software Quality Characteristics and Metrics (ISO/IEC 9126-1 and ISO/IEC 9126-2). International Organization for Standardization, June 1995.
8. Jiang J, Klein G, Carr CL. Measuring Information System Service Quality: SERVQUAL from the other side. MIS Quarterly 2002; 26(2): 145-166.
9. Kumar K, van Dissel H. Sustainable Collaboration: Managing Conflict and Cooperation in Interorganizational Systems. MIS Quarterly 1996; 20(3): 279-300.
10. Lauesen S. Software Requirements – Styles and Techniques. Addison Wesley 2002.
11. O'Sullivan J, Edmond D, ter Hofstede A. What's in a Service? Towards Accurate Description of Non-Functional Service Properties. Distributed and Parallel Databases 2002; 12: 117-133.
12. Parasuraman A, Zeithaml VA, Berry L. A Conceptual Model of Service Quality and Its Implications for Future Research. Journal of Marketing 1985, 49: 41-50.
13. Parasuraman A, Zeithaml VA, Malhotra A. E-S-QUAL: A Multiple-Item Scale for Assessing Electronic Service Quality. Journal of Service Research 2005, February, 213-233.
14. Stefani A, Xenos M. E-commerce system quality assessement using a model based on ISO 9126 and Belief Networks. Software Quality Journal 2008, 16:107-129.
15. Thompson JD. Organizations in Action. McGraw-Hill 1967.
16. Zarvić N, Wieringa RJ, van Daneva M. "Towards Information Systems Design for Value Webs". In Proceedings of Workshops and Doctoral Consortium of CAiSE 2007, Trondheim, Norway, Tapir Academic Press, 453-460, 2007.
17. Zarvić N, Wieringa RJ, van Eck P. "Checking the Alignment of Value-based Business Models and IT Functionality". In Proceedings of 23rd Annual ACM Symposium on Applied Computing, Fortaleza, Brazil, (accepted for publication) 2008.
18. Zarvić N. "Considering Structural Properties of Inter-organizational Network Fragments during Business-IT Alignment". (submitted) 2008.

45

DEVOLUTION IN A
VIRTUAL ENTERPRISE

Muhammad Kashif Farooq, Shafay Shamail, Mian M Awais
LUMS, DHA, Lahore, PAKISTAN
{kashiff, sshamail, awais}@lums.edu.pk

E-Government as a virtual enterprise, having many vertical portals, works in collaborative network to deliver e-services. The decentralization in e-governance depends on how much a governance structure decentralizes its political, fiscal and administrative powers. E-governance devolution areas may be planning, business process re-engineering, change management, enterprise architecture, networks, portals, back-offices, e-services, etc. Improper devolution in e-governance may affect cost, implementation, manageability, trust, outsourcing and localization. In this paper, we analyze a centralized web portal with its outcomes and derive a framework for devolution in e-governance. We propose an extension in the Soufflé theory of decentralization to calibrate suitable degree of devolution in e-governance. At the end we explain our approach by applying it to a real scenario.

1. INTRODUCTION

Devolution is a very common mechanism for establishing a decentralized stable governing structure. It may be categorized as political, fiscal and administrative devolution (Yulian, 2004). These can further be defined as transfer of political, fiscal and administrative powers to sub-national level (Janssen, 2005). Devolution with its various types has been implemented in many countries (Work, 2002). Decentralization and devolution are dominant themes in the contemporary discussion of e-governance policy throughout world, and are becoming very popular in many developing countries. Devolution is more institutionalized and is extensive form of decentralization (Janssen, 2005). It means the central government transfers authority like political, decision making, finance and management to local governments through constitutional provisions and legally recognized jurisdiction to provide legal mandate for the local authority to exercise the delegated powers.

Collaboration theory defines two viewpoints, coordination effect and self-organizing. Su and Zhu (2007) discussed these viewpoints in e-government perspective and emphasized that e-government is a collaborative network of government agencies to provide services to citizens and business concerns (Su and Zhu, 2007).

Now e-governance or e-government is gaining key position in every level of government structure and involves in 360 degree services like Government to Citizen (G2C), Government to Business (G2B), Government to Government (G2G) and Government to Employees (G2E) (Lee et. al., 2007). A central e-government is also needed to be decentralized as traditional government decentralizes in the form of political, fiscal, or administrative manners (Janssen, 2005). This new type of decentralization or devolution is becoming a challenge for policy makers.

In this paper we are focusing on devolution in e-governance with respect to other devolutions (political, fiscal and administrative) and identify relational constants

Please use the following format when citing this chapter:

Farooq, M.K., Shamail, S. and Awais, M.M., 2008, in IFIP International Federation for Information Processing, Volume 283; *Pervasive Collaborative Networks*; Luis M. Camarinha-Matos, Willy Picard; (Boston: Springer), pp. 433–440.

from Soufflé theory (Parker, 1995). The Soufflé theory of decentralization explains the role of political, fiscal and administrative devolutions and their result. We extend it for devolution in e-governance.

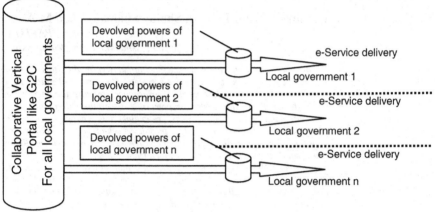

Figure 1 – Vertical Portal Having Devolved Powers

2. DEVOLUTION IN E-GOVERNANCE FOR COLLABORATIVE APPROACH

E-government structure is very complex and needs to be analyzed that how many administrative components or how much power should be centralized and how much decentralized. It all depends on recourses, manageability trust and quality of services. Generally there are two approaches of devolution for stable governing structures: devolution among multilevel governments, and devolution among institutions. These types are discussed below.

2.1. e-Government Devolution among Multilevel Government Structure

Many governments use strategy of centralized e-government initiatives, portals and services to reduce cost and integration issues. They share technical, financial and HR resources. In federated structure, federal government becomes the owner of the project and lower governments with their agencies become the collaborative partners of that project. So, federal government has to plan a detailed policy about devolution. In multilevel government structure, a centralized portal providing services to all levels of governments may be named as vertical portal. Figure 1 shows the relationship between a central vertical portal and the power devolved as a result of decentralization. In such cases one centralized G2C portal provides services to all local governments. Portal of a particular government agency that has no vertical (multi level government) structure, such as foreign and defense office, the portal may be named as horizontal portal. Centralized virtual office and backend offices are the most optimum structure in which a centralized virtual office provides services to multiple backend offices (Homburg, 2002). In this form of devolution the governing structures should select institutions to be devolved among different levels of governments such as health and education. Where as institutions such as defense and foreign office need not to be decentralized

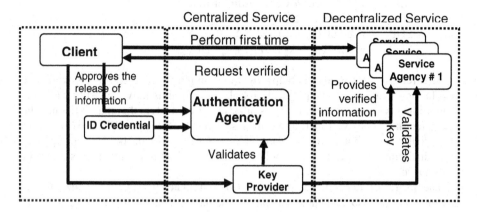

Figure 2 – Collaboration of Centralized and Decentralized Services

2.2. Institutional Devolution/Collaboration for e-Government

Many governments use strategy to integrate many services related to different agencies on one portal. It is much more convenient for end user to access one portal that provides all services from birth of a citizen to death. For this purpose many agencies or departments have to be collaborated on one portal. A decentralization or devolution plan among different agencies at same government level or among different decentralized government levels is required for this portal. Figure 2 shows collaborated services among different agencies (Adam et. al.,2005, Kolsaker, 2005, Ho , 2002, Chun et. al., 2002, Homburg, 2004, Lee, 2005, Hu et.al., 2006). For example to provide centralized authentication, an agency can provide verification service to all decentralized agencies, such as to health agencies of all local governments. The trust in inter-organizational relationships is similar across most of such cases. Tolbert et al (2003) conclude that higher trust levels lead to lower costs. Political approaches and institutional analyses also have shown that trust is an important factor in governance mechanism across organizations. But these structural approaches do not account for how trust develops (Tyworth and Sawyer, 2006).

3. PROPOSED MODEL FOR DEVOLUTION IN E-GOVERNANCE

Governance is a complex structure and depends upon many variables. Given that it is devolved into political, financial and administrative sections, the overall impact of governance can be measured by individually measuring the impact of each of these. Devolution of e-governance is not an independent term; it is a relative term and we can safely say that "the sum of Devolution Powers (DP) of e-governance is directly proportional to the sum of Devolution Powers related to Political, Financial and Administrative factors". This can be represented in the following form:

DP_{eGov} = Devolved Power of e-governance
DP_{Pol} = Dev olved Power of Political
DP_{Fin} = Devolved Power of Financial

DP_{Adm} = Devolved Power of Administration

$$\Sigma DP_{eGov} \; \alpha \; (\Sigma DP_{Pol} + \Sigma DP_{Fin} + \Sigma DP_{Admin}) \tag{1}$$

$$\Sigma DP_{eGov} = k \; (\Sigma DP_{Pol} + \Sigma DP_{Fin} + \Sigma DP_{Admin}) \tag{2}$$

$$\Sigma DP_{eGov} = k_1 \Sigma DP_{Pol} + k_2 \Sigma DP_{Fin} + k_3 \Sigma DP_{Adm} \tag{3}$$

The relation given above helps us in defining the degree of e-governance devolution in terms of its political, fiscal, and administrative constituents. The proportionality constant k incorporates other empirical factors that may influence the integrated and cohesive functioning of these three constituents. When divided over individual constituents, the proportionality constant k can be broken up into individual contributions for each political, fiscal, and administrative constituent of governance.

The factor $k1$ depends on political will to initiate and institutionalize the e-governance. It also depends on public demand. The factor $k2$ depends on transparency and Business Process Re-engineering (BPR) in financial structure. It also depends on how much local government is answerable to its citizens about its financial affairs. The factor $k3$ depends on need or priority to achieve e-governance for command, control and planning. It also depends on e-readiness of local government. In order to identify these parameters, we study Soufle theory of decentralization [16] and extend it for application in the e-governance devolution.

4. PROPOSED EXTENSION IN SOUFFLE THEORY FOR E-DEVOLUTION IN GOVERNANCE

4.1. Soufle Theory

Parker (1995) presented a conceptual model – named as "Souffle" Theory of decentralization - that explains the role of political, fiscal, and institutional decentralization as they relate to rural development outcomes. Like a souffle that needs just the right combination of milk, eggs, and heat to rise, a successful program of decentralization must include just the right combination of political, fiscal, and institutional elements to improve rural development outcomes.

4.2. Extension in Soufle Theory

In this paper, an extension in Souffle Theory is being suggested to define e-governance devolution. Possible areas of devolution in e-governance and outcomes of that system have been derived. Then further more system results and development impact of this devolution have also been derived. Proposed extension is described in Table 1 extended from (Parker, 1995). Scale of devolution depends upon the size of the country, its resource base, human capacity and governance style. Large countries with a federated structure might begin with a decentralized approach and then bring in standardization and coordination though a central agency. Table 2 shows the magnitude of $k1$, $k2$, and $k3$ with respect of decentralized choices for devolution in e-governance. The effect of k can be formulated as given in equation (4).

$$k= \# \text{ of powers to be devolved / total decentralized choices} \tag{4}$$

Table 1 – Soufflé Theory and Proposed Extension

Source: Adapted from Parker, A. N. Decentralization: The Way Forward for Rural Development?
Policy Research Working Paper 1475, The World Bank, Washington, D.C. 1995.

The Soufflé Theory of Decentralization

Decentralization Choices	System Outcomes	System Results	Development Impact
Political • Civil Liberties • Political Rights • Democratic Pluralistic System	▪ Political Accountability ▪ Political Transparency ▪ Political Representation		
Fiscal & Financial ▪ Fiscal Resources ▪ Fiscal Autonomy ▪ Fiscal Decision-making ▪ Subnational Borrowing	▪ Resource Mobilization ▪ Resource Allocation ▪ Fiscal Capacity ▪ Subnational Indebtedness	▪ Soft/hard Budget Constraint ▪ Moral Hazard ▪ Macroeconomic Instability ▪ Responsive Services ▪ Effective Services ▪ Efficient Services ▪ Sustainable Services	▪ Increased Incomes ▪ Increased Productivity ▪ Increased Literacy ▪ Decreased Mortality ▪ Growth of Civil Society etc.
Administrative • Administrative Structures and Systems • Participation	▪ Administrative Capacity ▪ Admin. Accountability ▪ Admin. Transparency		

Extension of e-Governance Devolution

e-Governance			
▪ Shadow Enterprise Architectures ▪ Business Process Re-engineering ▪ Change Management ▪ Development ▪ Cyber Laws ▪ Operations	▪ Localization ▪ Bridging the Digital Divide ▪ Capacity Building ▪ Access for all	▪ Affordable and Secure e-Services ▪ Innovative Services	▪ Informative Society ▪ Cyber State

CHANGE FACTORS

TIME

Table 2 – Decentralized choices verses political, financial and administrative devolved powers

Devolution Powers	EA	BPR	CM	Cyber Laws	Development	Operations
Pol	High	High	Medium	Medium	Low	Low
Fis	High	High	Medium	Medium	Medium	Low
Adm	High	High	High	Medium	Medium	Medium

5. DEGREE OF DEVOLUTION ISSUES: A CASE STUDY

In this section we study a case of centralized solution for the local governments and departments. The Provincial Government initiated a centralized web portal through an IT agency of provincial government to represent 35 local governments and 40 provincial departments. The IT agency trained personnel from portal partner departments and local governments to update contents.

5.1. Issues

11 Local governments and 11 departments launched their independent websites with the passage of time. After detailed interviews with these 22 portal partners, following facts have been concluded.

Portal partners wanted 1) their own graphic design to represent their specific cultural, geographic and professional themes, 2) multi language interface, 3) local news highlights, 4) independent URLs, 5) innovative ideas, 6) more administrative authority than just content updating and 7) more dynamic pages, database access and interactivity. However these portal partners lacked the authority and skill to handle these issues.

5.2. Solution: Degree of devolution for a virtual enterprise

Degree of devolution in this centralized initiative can be devised as per corresponding point as mentioned above. Each department and local government should have right and skill to design their own theme or template to represent their specific cultural, geographic values and professional areas. These independent themes or templates can be chosen from independent URL access or template selection utility. We have tested our framework for degree of devolution on three selected local governments A, B, and C. These local governments launched their own websites and came out from the sphere of centralized portal. We estimated capability maturity of these local governments by analyzing their websites and estimating how much devolved powers have been exercised in the area of political, fiscal and administration. These estimates are shown in Table 3. By using Tables 2 and 3, we derived suitable decentralized choices for the selected local governments. These are shown in Table 4. By using equation (5), giving weight to High, Medium, and Low, k values based on equation (4) are calculated and are shown in Table 5. For example, for a virtual enterprise, out of a total number of decentralized choices of 6, if 4 are devolved then k comes out to be equal to 0.67.

k= # of devolved powers that exercised / total decentralized choices   (5)

These numbers indicate the relative degree of devolution that these three local governments can exercise if they implement the proposed decentralization choices.

Table 3 -Political, fiscal and administrative strengths of selected local governments

Local Govt.	Political	Fiscal	Administrative
A	High	High	High
B	Medium	Medium	High
C	Medium	Medium	Medium

Table 4 -Suitable decentralized choices (from Tables 2 and 3)

Local Govt.	Powers to be devolved
A	All
B	CM, Cyber Laws, Development and Operations
C	Cyber Laws, Development and Operations

Table 5 – Assignment of $k1$, $k2$ and $k3$ for selected local governments

Local Govt.	Political k_1	Fiscal k_2	Administrative k_3
A	1	1	1
B	0.67	0.67	1
C	0.67	0.67	0.67

6. CONCLUSION

Devolution is the need of every enterprise governing structure. In this paper, we have proposed and discussed a framework to assess the degree of devolution in e-governance. It is analyzed that degree of devolution in e-governance is proportional to other devolutions (political, fiscal and administrative). Proper degree of devolution is important for effective e-services. We have also proposed the extension in Soufflé theory and verified that it also supports the devolution in e-governance. We have applied our proposed framework of devolution in a virtual enterprise in the background of devolution in e-Government and calculated the relative degree of devolution in terms political, fiscal, and administrative strengths.

7. REFERENCES

1. Adam, N. R., Atluri, V., Chun, S. A., Fariselli, P., Hopper, J. C., Bojic, O., Stewart, R. T., Fruscione, J., and Mannochio, N. Technology transfer of inter-agency government services and their transnational feasibility studies. In Proceedings of the 2005 National Conference on Digital Government Research (Atlanta, Georgia, May 15 - 18, 2005). ACM International Conference Proceeding Series, vol. 89. Digital Government Research Center, 225-226.
2. Bhatnagar, S. "Egoverment: Lessons from Implementation in Developing Countries", Indian Institute of Management, Amedabad – 380015 , Published in Regional Development Dialogue, Vol. 24, UNCRD, Autumn 2002 Issue.
3. Chun, S. A., Atluri, V., and Adam, N. R. Dynamic composition of workflows for customized eGovernment service delivery. In Proceedings of the 2002 Annual National Conference on Digital Government Research (Los Angeles, California, May 19 - 22, 2002). ACM International Conference Proceeding Series, vol. 129. Digital Government Research Center, 1-7.
4. Ferro, E. Cantamessa, M. and Paolucci, E. 2005. Urban vs. Regional Divide: Comparing and Classifying Digital Divide, Lecture Notes in Computer Science, Volume 3416/2005. Springer Berlin / Heidelberg New York, 81-90.

5. Heeks, R. "The Core-Periphery Approach to Management of Public Information Systems" IDPM, University of Manchester, UK, 1999, Published in: "Government IT"
6. Ho, A.T. "Reinventing Local Governments and the E-Government Initiative" Iowa State University, "Public Administration Review" July/August, Vol. 62, No. 4, 2002.
7. Homburg, V. and Bekkers, V. "The Back-Office of E-Government, (Managing Information Domains as Political Economies)", Proceedings of the 35th Hawaii International Conference on System Sciences – 2002.
8. Homburg, V. E-government and NPM: a perfect marriage? In Proceedings of the 6th International Conference on Electronic Commerce, (Delft, The Netherlands, October 23-27, 2004). ICEC '04, ACM International Conference Proceeding Series, vol. 60. 547-555.
9. Hu, P. J. Cui, D. and Sherwood, A. C. "Examining Cross-Agency Collaborations in E-Government Initiatives", Proceedings of the 39th Hawaii International Conference on System Sciences – 2006.
10. Janssen, M. Centralized or decentralized organization? In Proceedings of the 2005 National Conference on Digital Government Research, (Atlanta, Georgia, May 15-18, 2005). ACM International Conference Proceeding Series, vol. 89. Digital Government Research Center, 247-248.
11. Janssen, M., Kuk, G., and Wagenaar, R. W. A survey of e-government business models in the Netherlands. In Proceedings of the 7th international Conference on Electronic Commerce (Xi'an, China, August 15 - 17, 2005). ICEC '05, vol. 113. ACM Press.
12. Kolsaker, A., E-Government: Towards Electronic Democracy, chapter: Third Way e-Government: The Case for Local Devolution, Lecture Notes in Computer Science, Volume 3416/2005. Springer Berlin / Heidelberg New York, 70-80.
13. Kostopoulos, G. K. e-Government in the Arabian gulf: a vision toward reality. In Proceedings of the 2003 Annual National Conference on Digital Government Research (Boston, MA, May 18 - 21, 2003). ACM International Conference Proceeding Series, vol. 130. Digital Government Research Center, 1-7.
14. Lazer, D. and Binz-Scharf, M. C. Managing novelty and cross-agency cooperation in digital government. In Proceedings of the 2004 Annual National Conference on Digital Government Research (Seattle, WA, May 24 - 26, 2004). ACM International Conference Proceeding Series. Digital Government Research Center, 1-2.
15. Lee, S. M., Tan, X., and Trimi, S. Current practices of leading e-government countries. Communications of the ACM 48, 10 (Oct. 2005), 99-104.
16. Luna-Reyes, L. F. Cresswell, A. M. and Richardson, G. P. "Knowledge and the Development of Interpersonal Trust: a Dynamic Model", Proceedings of the 37th Hawaii International Conference on System Sciences – 2004.
17. Parker, A. N. Decentralization: The Way Forward for Rural Development? Policy Research Working Paper 1475. The World Bank, Washington, D.C. 1995.
18. Su, F., Zhu, H., in IFIP International Federation for Information Processing, Volume 252, Integration and Innovation Orient to E-Society Volume 2, eds. Wang, W., (Boston: Springer), 2007, 390-396.
19. Tolbert, C. and Mossberger, K. The effects of e-government on trust and confidence in government. In Proceedings of the 2003 Annual National Conference on Digital Government Research (Boston, MA, May 18 - 21, 2003). ACM International Conference Proceeding Series, vol. 130. Digital Government Research Center, 1-7.
20. Tyworth, M. and Sawyer, S. 2006. Organic development: a top-down and bottom-up approach to design of public sector information systems. In Proceedings of the 2006 international Conference on Digital Government Research (San Diego, California, May 21 - 24, 2006). dg.o '06, vol. 151. ACM Press.
21. Work, R. Overview of Decentralisation Worldwide: A Stepping Stone to Improve Governance and Human Development, 2nd International Conference on Decentralisation, (Manila, Philippines, July 25–27, 2002).
22. Yulian, E. L. "Decentralization, deconcentration and devolution: what do they mean?" Interlaken Workshop (Interlaken, Switzerland April 27 – 30, 2004).

Piotr Stolarski[1], Tadeusz Tomaszewski[1]

[1] Poznan University of Economics, Department of Information Systems, al.
Niepodleglosci 10, 60-967, Poznań, POLAND
{P.Stolarski, T.Tomaszewski}@kie.ae.poznan.pl

In this paper we describe a legal framework for simple tax status detection of transaction parties as a part of a hybrid eCommerce information system. We also focus on one, in our view more interesting point encountered during the model setup which is the case of legal knowledge modeling in such a way that it is immune to fast-pace changing of jurisdiction. This kind of quality is especially important in the tax and commerce law domain as regulations connected to those two branches are characterized by a high volatility.

1 INTRODUCTION

Recent years witnessed an intense development of eCommerce and its technologies. Although the eBusiness systems market seems to mature yet with still emerging technologies but it is certain that we are still merely on the brink of the true revolution promised by web semantics or web services. So far the undisturbed expansion of electronic economy was in fact due to projected potential and common policy yet this progression may not for long be without any threats. As long as the whole industry was at its startup stage it was left mainly unnoticed by institutions. However as eMarkets are becoming a major source of profits and centers of added value in the global economy landscape, they (and their participants) have been recognized as vital objects of interest of stakeholders from different countries and different legal systems. Additionally it has to be taken into consideration that while institutions of national authority work on a local basis, the eCommerce performance is worldwide. These should generate a growing need for the eCommerce world combined with legal knowledge systems capable of interpreting the eCommerce matters with regard to and in context of the applicable legal recognition.

Constructing the general framework has also another advantage over creating a hardcoded built-in rules-based system as the model approach enable the use of similar specific solutions in different jurisdictions and by larger group of entities including on-line stores, eMarkets themselves, on-line auctions systems and individual contractors as well as different tax institutions. In the paper we delimit ourselves to address the issues of sale of finished product domain only.

The paper is divided into five main sections which are as follow: 2. Legal Models, eBusiness & Taxes – is the general introduction to the legal knowledge models, together with an ontology definition, additionally we give a general overview of the knowledge sources subject to analysis during conceptual work on the tax ontology; in 3. Domain-specific Cases section we demonstrate selected

Please use the following format when citing this chapter:

Stolarski, P. and Tomaszewski, T., 2008, in IFIP International Federation for Information Processing, Volume 283; *Pervasive Collaborative Networks*; Luis M. Camarinha-Matos, Willy Picard; (Boston: Springer), pp. 441–448.

examples of problems specific to the legal and tax domain description. 4. Putting that all Together – binds the gathered experiences into a comprehensive model proposition whereas 5. is the sum of Lessons Learned.

2 LEGAL MODELS, eBUSINESS & TAXES

2.1 Legal Ontologies

Legal knowledge modeling is a vigorous research discipline. Currently two main directions may be pointed out, namely: Automatic argumentation and ontological representation. While the first branch is more focused on legal discourse and active use of the model, the latter one create an inevitable background providing legal-specific notion of understanding the domain terms which has to be somehow represented in any legal-aware system.

The legal ontologies are specific ones on account of the difficulty of proper representation of often very subtle nuances among terms, highly-specialized corpuses used to incorporate knowledge from – being mostly formal documents with language of particular features. Moreover, there are also some extended expectations formulated towards such knowledge models connected to their use. A concise description of works related to legal ontologies may be found for instance in [1].

In our works we utilize the definition of ontology similar to the one taken from [2]. This definition is compatible with most ontology description languages (OWL, WSDL) [3, 4].

According to Gangemi [5] such knowledge models may be useful in the legal domain in a number of contexts: 1) For knowledge validation; 2) Classification of instances or facts; 3) As helpers for information extraction; 4) For automation of planning; 5) For formalizing case abstractions within a general framework; 6) Advance reasoning in rule-based systems.

As it will be showed later at least the first, second, third as well as the last one are within the scope of creation of framework for tax analysis.

EBusiness is the conduct of automated business transactions by means of electronic communications networks [6]. In comparison to the above definition the eCommerce is being defined as a process of focusing on buying and selling products and services via Internet. It is therefore regarded to be the narrower term to eBusiness. As mentioned earlier, the efforts of creation of legal ontologies are intensified for last decade and there exist a rather large resource of those containing and dealing with a general legal vocabulary [7]. We perceive a lack of oriented models describing more precisely matters of a concrete branch of law, a statute or even only some specific regulations. It is certain that with new opportunities of use arising and with demand form the software systems for facilities enabling easy to (re)use dedicated expert knowledge which additionally will be change-proof the specific ontologies will be of great value. It is however a very hard task to develop a knowledge model which will embrace all the mentioned needs and other constraints (i.e. security concerns) thus the intense ongoing research effort in this track is essential. For the same reason also in the tax law not much work has been done in recent years although the requirement for a concise tax ontology together with a suggested outline has been addressed by Melz and Valente in [8] since their work no essential progress was reported. It is also important that their proposition was based on the U.S. law. A vocabulary concerning taxes is also enclosed in large projects such as LegalRDF [9]. It is however a general approach focusing on taxonomical representation.

The interesting fact is that the necessity of supplying the comprehensive tax knowledge model seems commonly recognized in practice by the many authors of the ontologies from eCommerce domain[1].

2.2 Tax Regulations - EU Context

The EU policy states that the tax regulations are the issue of national sovereignty and therefore the harmonization efforts are limited only to ensuring that some very general rules are applied. The regulations then aim to provide compatibility between systems of the Member States without immediate integration. Thus the regulations in the legislation of EU may be found mainly in high-level, general documents[2]. Yet as early as in 2000 the EU authorities regarded eCommerce as the international issue rather than a local one [10].

2.3 Polish Taxation System

Polish tax law is an independent branch of law it utilizes many institutions from the civil law yet because of its character it is much more related to the administrative part of legal system. From the point of view of the sources of regulations the three parts may be distinguished, namely:

- The Tax Ordination statute [11] – introducing all the common and important general norms.
- A group of tax-specific statutes – bringing institutions specific to the given type of tax.
- Regulations delegated form the statutes – lower level acts.

The Tax Ordination is a large about 45000 words document divided into 10 Divisions that actually instantiate the taxation system. On the other hand the statute does not establish any tax itself. According to the Polish Constitution [12] "[...] imposition of taxes, as well as other public imposts, the specification of those subject to the tax and the rates of taxation, as well as the principles [...] shall be by means of statute" which means actually - by the mentioned tax-specific bills.

Another important aspect of tax law especially in Poland is the level of turbulence and incorporated amendments. For instance the bill of Civil Deeds Tax was changed 17 times, the Tax Ordination 53 and the Personal Income Tax bill 148 times[3]. Therefore even this demonstrates the great need to take into account altering regulations in the modeling effort.

---

[1] Semantic content search engine Swoogle returns about 125 result documents with the keyword „tax"; an essential part of them being the eCommerce related ontologies.

[2] See for instance Articles 90 and next of the Treaty Establishing the European Community

[3] Basic statistics available on Polish Parliament's legal acts database: http://www.sejm.gov.pl/prawo/prawo.html

3 DOMAIN-SPECIFIC CASES

Let us consider the following case. We assume that we are able to deliver the legal knowledge representation of the actually valid part of the tax law connected to matters of eCommerce which may be done using the developed ontology stub. The actual validity means that the model reflects the state of the law for – let say – 31 January 2008. The very fragment of such representation is visible on Fig. 1.

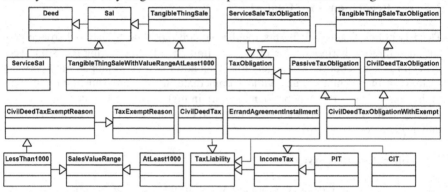

Fig. 1 Fundamental concepts of the tax ontology.

It has to be clarified that the above model brings in a major simplification – it assesses the instantiation of tax obligation independently for any subject.

Let us consider the consequences of it if in our system we commence to analyze some specific transactions dated 18 December 2006. It is important to bear in mind that in case of the bill of Civil Deeds Tax the last amendment came into force with the beginning of year 2007. As a result it means that we have to cope with the common legislation problem meaning addressing changes in regulations which in turn yields or may yield particular modification of the real-life scene (or at least statuses of their actors). We will take a closer look at this problem now.

ECommerce transactions are commonly stored, for the sake of retrospective examination, in some kinds of databases or logs. The unofficially emerging standard may be the one proposed by Google – the ELF/ELF2[4]. Such sets of data are the source of indeed valuable information also when it comes to tax investigation and categorization. This simple format contains information about each separate transaction and any item being the object of the transaction. In our modeling case it may look like this:

```
!36530 123.123.123.123 [18/Dec/2006:11:31:45 -0800] - -
1000.99 - - Warsaw - 23452 PL "Mozilla" ""

36530 123.123.123.123 [18/Dec/2006:11:31:45 -0800] "LG LCD
Display 17in" - 1000.99 1 - "Mozilla" ""
```

The first two lines describe the whole transaction whereas the next two represent the sole item of the transaction. We should also note, that it seems – that that particular format does not support any information about the currency of transaction.

If we extract interesting facts from the log we may represent it in the form of a

---

[4] https://secure.urchin.com/helpwiki/ELF_%26_ELF2_Log_Formats

semantic net like the one presented on Fig. 2.

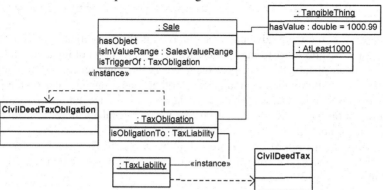

Fig. 2 Simple representation of the presented example.

The same information may be transformed into OWL and integrated with our tax ontology. Yet, as our tax legal knowledge model reflects so far the legislation state dated the end of January 2008, after applying a reasoner we get the result that on the side of the seller there exist the TaxObligation and it is a plain CivilDeedTaxObligation which would be correct supposing that the analyzed transaction had taken place under the ruling of the amended bill of Civil deed Tax. Unfortunately it did not.

This example excuses enough for introducing some kind of ontology evolution or versioning system. There is a number of works on the topic of ontology version tracking, for example [13]. The one method most close to our needs is proposed in [14]. Unluckily the application of model of Eder and Koncilia has disadvantages (mentioned in the referred paper). The authors, however do claim that apart from presented "OWL standard employing" approach there should be other approaches possible to attain similar (or better) results – amongst them the "Meta-ontology" one – which we developed in our model.

The authors of the model assert that "main advantage of this approach is that any ontology description language [...] can be used to define the different ontology versions" which suggest that they mean to use some external resources to describe the ontologies which is not a necessity. It seems that there is a simpler possibility – to employ the OWL Full features in order to extend meta-classes, meaning owl:Class and owl:ObjectRelation. Below we present a short OWL Full code which shed a light on how it may be achieved – however a detailed description is out of scope of this paper.

```
<owl:Class rdf:ID=" VersionedClass">
  <rdfs:subClassOf rdf:resource="&owl;Class"/>
    <rdfs:subClassOf><owl:Restriction>
    <owl:onProperty
rdf:resource="#hasPreviousVersion"/>
    <owl:someValuesFrom
rdf:resource="#VersionedClass"/>
    </owl:Restriction></rdfs:subClassOf>
  </rdfs:subClassOf>
</owl:Class>
```

```
<owl:Class rdf:ID="VersionedObjectProperty">
 <rdfs:subClassOf rdf:resource="&owl;ObjectProperty"/>
 . . .
```

In this solution the main advantage we perceive is the theoretical[5] possibility of use of any standard reasoner to make inference on both meta-ontology and ontology levels. This means that it should be possible to check the consistency of the ontology also against its versioning description layer. Another improvement relies on the fact that we allow to identify classes not only by their validity dates but also by explicit enumeration of their predecessors and ancestors which resembles more the evolution description in comparison to "weak" versioning.

After discussing the improvements we will return to our initial case. If we sum up the initial knowledge model with the meta-ontology versioning solution we will get a result similar to Fig. 3.

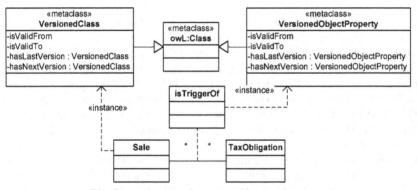

Fig. 3 Introduction of meta-level into tax legal ontology.

Now in contrast to the earlier analysis we are able to obtain a proper result - on the side of the seller there is no TaxObligation – at least not of type CivilDeedTaxObligation (which does not exclude that other side of transaction will be the subject of such obligation or that other type of taxes: VAT and PIT will become applicable). There is still also an issue of incorporating knowledge about conditions of utilizing different branch versions (parts) of the time-dimension cast of the knowledge model.

4 PUTTING THAT ALL TOGETHER

The example from the previous section represents a single important but not the only issue connected with the tax law knowledge representation. In fact we introduced only a very simple case with a number of simplifications. More to that we actually dealt with merely one type of tax (only mentioning others) – featuring relatively small number of norms and concise regulation. However the studying of a larger resource of legal acts of the domain and additional other source texts (professional press materials and legal advises) we came to formulate a number of assertion about

---

[5] Unfortunately, there is no reasoner that fully support all OWL Full features – for the list of most common OWL reasoners, see http://www.w3.org/2001/sw/WebOnt/impls#Implementations

prospect system of tax legal status analysis for the eBusiness. On the basis of these assertions we are able to view an outline of model representing the structure of such a system. The model is shown on Fig. 4.

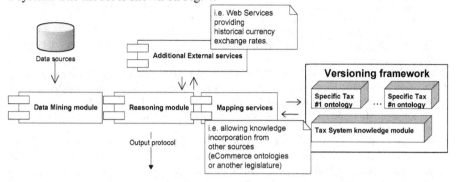

Fig. 4 Outline of tax analysis system model.

Though it is a sketch rather, we are certain that the model may well serve as a reference in most of the solution for a wide range of tax-issues tackling.

5 LESSONS LEARNED

In the paper besides short introduction to the field of legal knowledge modelling putting stress to legal ontologies and tax knowledge representation we portrayed the general assumption of Polish tax law. We also added an international context as we recognize its importance in the eCommerce and eBusiness world. On the top of that we presented a specific case pointing out difficulties that should be addressed by the system of eCommerce tax analysis. Then we described an outline of model of such system in order to solve more general problems than those given in the example. On the other hand we referred to the model of ontology evolution showing its new realization (in comparison to the authors' original one) via the extension on the meta level.

As the consequence we came to formulate the following postulation as the future recommendations: 1) Turbulent legal environments produce a requirement for versioning in real-life legal knowledge models; 2) We acknowledge the earlier formulated need for creating comprehensive highly specialized tax domain ontologies; 3) In order to come up with effective solutions a number of obstacles have to be overcome; 4) The suggested solution of utilizing the meta-classes to describe ontological elements' evolution is another interesting and particularly hopeful approach; 5) This approach may be successfully used in eBusiness tax analysis infrastructure.

REFERENCES

1. Benjamins R., Casanovas P., Breuker J., Gangemi A., (Eds.) Law and the Semantic Web.

Legal Ontologies. Methodologies, Legal Information Retrieval, and Applications. Springer Verlag, LNAI 3369, Berlin, 2005.

2. Maedche, A. & Staab, S., Measuring Similarity between Ontologies. In: Proc. of the European Conference on Knowledge Acquisition and Management - EKAW-2002, Madrid, Spain, LNCS/LNAI 2473, Springer, 2002.

3. Knublauch H., Musen M. A. & Rector A. L.. Editing Description Logic Ontologies with the Protégé OWL Plugin. International Workshop on Description Logics (DL2004), Whistler, Canada, 2004.

4. www.wsmo.org/TR/d37/v0.1/20080125/d37v0.1_20080125.pdf (read on 17-02-2008).

5. Gangemi A., Design patterns for legal ontology construction, Proceedings of LOAIT '07 II Workshop on Legal Ontologies and Artificial Intelligence Techniques, 2007.

6. Papazoglou M. P. & Ribbers P., e-Business. Organizational and technical Foundations, Wiley & Sons, 2006.

7. Breuker J., Boer A., Hoekstra R & van den Breg K., Developing content for LKIF: Ontologies and frameworks for legal reasoning, in T.M. van Engers (editor) Legal Knowledge and Information Systems. Jurix 2006, IOS Press 2006.

8. Melz E., & Valente A., Modeling the Tax Code in R. Meersman (editor) On the Move to Meaningful Internet Systems 2004: OTM 2004 Workshops, Springer Verlag, LNCS 3292, Berlin 2004.

9. http://www.hypergrove.com/legalrdf.org/inventory.html (read on 17-02-2008).

10. http://ec.europa.eu/publications/booklets/move/17/txt_en.pdf (read on 17-02-2008).

11. Ustawa z dnia 29 sierpnia 1997 r. - Ordynacja podatkowa. Dz.U. 1997 nr 137 poz. 926.

12. http://www.sejm.gov.pl/prawo/konst/angielski/kon1.htm (read on 17-02-2008).

13. Flouris G., On the Evolution of Ontological Signatures, Proceedings of BIS 2007 Workshops on Ontology Evolution (OnE'07), Poznan 2007, ISBN-13: 978-83-916842-4-5.

14. Eder J. & Koncilia Ch., Modelling Changes in Ontologies, in R. Meersman (editor) On the Move to Meaningful Internet Systems 2004: OTM 2004 Workshops, Springer Verlag, LNCS 3292, Berlin 2004.

PART **15**

COLLABORATION INFRASTRUCTURES

THE ECOLEAD COLLABORATIVE BUSINESS INFRASTRUCTURE FOR NETWORKED ORGANIZATIONS

47

Ricardo J. Rabelo[1]; Sergio Gusmeroli[2]

[1] *Federal University of Santa Catarina, BRAZIL, rabelo@das.ufsc.br*
[2] *TXT e-solutions, ITALY, sergio.gusmeroli@txt.it*

This paper points out the need of advanced collaborative business ICT infrastructures (CBI) for CNOs, the requirements for the development of CBIs, and the technologies and trends considering CNO issues. The CBI devised in the ECOLEAD Project is also presented, showing how most of these requirements and emergent ICTs have been incorporated in it. This CBI – called *ICT-I* – is a distributed, open and security-embedded infrastructure, and it relies on the service oriented architecture paradigm. Its services are to be used under the on demand and pay-per-use models. The assessment of ICT-I, some conclusions and challenges are presented in the end.

1. INTRODUCTION

The adoption of the Collaborative Networks Organizations (CNO) paradigm by organizations imposes deep changes on the way they operate, both at intra and inter-enterprise levels. In resume of what several authors have presented recently (e.g. Camarinha-Matos et al., 2005), it could be said that these changes are related to three essential pre-conditions necessary to support the realization of the CNO concept. The first one is that working as a CNO requires *collaboration* among partners at a level far beyond sending e-mail messages. The second one is *trust*, considering that partners shall rely on each other. The third one is that *all* the transactions within the CNO should be digital, made via computer networks.

One of the several issues that have to be tackled to support this scenario is related to the required supporting *collaborative business infrastructures* (CBI). In essence, a CBI for CNOs should enable networked organizations to agilely define and set up relations with other organizations seamlessly, and to be adaptive according to the business environment conditions and current organizations' autonomy levels (Camarinha-Matos and Afsarmanesh, 2004).

Despite the complexity the development of such kind of CBI represents, the fact is that current software solutions neither attend these requirements at all nor offer an integrated support to several CNO-related business processes.

This paper aims to present the CBI implemented in the ECOLEAD project, which is called *Plug and Play Horizontal ICT Infrastructure (ICT-I)*. ICT-I is a SOA/web-services-based open platform for CNOs, comprising a set of integrated tools, and that was devised to be easy-to-use and also affordable to SMEs.

This paper is organized as follows. Chapter 1 highlights the need of CBIs for CNOS. Chapter 2 presents general requirements for that as well as some obstacles

Please use the following format when citing this chapter:

Rabelo, R.J. and Gusmeroli, S., 2008, in IFIP International Federation for Information Processing, Volume 283; *Pervasive Collaborative Networks*; Luis M. Camarinha-Matos, Willy Picard; (Boston: Springer), pp. 451–462.

towards the development of advanced CBIs. Chapter 3 presents the ICT-I. Chapter 4 describes the implemented services of ICT-I. Chapter 5 makes a general analysis of ICT-I, pointing out its features, innovative aspects and limitations.

2. REQUIREMENTS FOR A CBI TO CNO

CNOs have a different sort of business processes that is not handled by B2B and EIA solutions. Actually, CNO processes *complement* the processes managed by such solutions. CNO processes use to be interactive/user-centric, asynchronous and not necessarily well structured or defined a priori. Their main focus is on flexibility and adaptability, rather than on execution efficiency. Figure 1 lists just some CNO-related processes (at application level) involved in the life cycle of a CNO of type Virtual Organization (VO), which should then be supported by CBIs to CNOs.

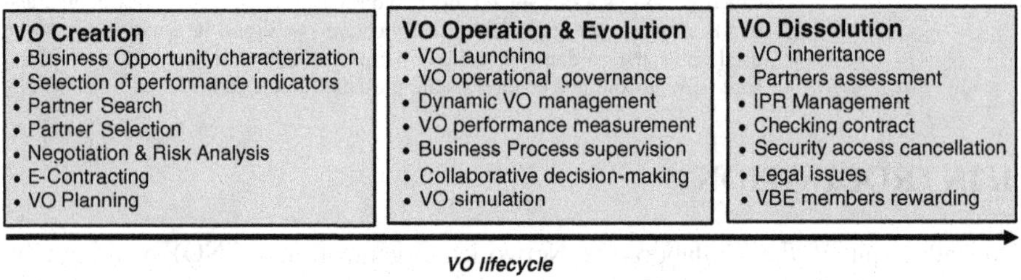

VO Creation	VO Operation & Evolution	VO Dissolution
• Business Opportunity characterization • Selection of performance indicators • Partner Search • Partner Selection • Negotiation & Risk Analysis • E-Contracting • VO Planning	• VO Launching • VO operational governance • Dynamic VO management • VO performance measurement • Business Process supervision • Collaborative decision-making • VO simulation	• VO inheritance • Partners assessment • IPR Management • Checking contract • Security access cancellation • Legal issues • VBE members rewarding

VO lifecycle

Figure 1 – Example of CNO-related collaborative processes

As it can be realized, a CBI for CNOs is much more than a platform for CSCW. Ideally, a CBI for CNOs should provide functionalities for enabling[1]: *people* to collaborate and negotiate; *systems / services* to execute and adapt; *knowledge and information* (at *all* levels) to be exchanged and retrieved; *computing and human resources* to be discovered and shared; *processes* to be interconnected and synchronized. Managing this with high efficiency, cleverness and transparency is one of the toughest challenges to be faced by advanced CBIs.

From the technological point of view, the consideration of emerging business models and ICTs in the design of advanced CBIs is of paramount importance as they represent elements that will increasingly be incorporated into the next generation of eco-systems, which are implemented in a diversity of platforms, equipments and ubiquitous devices. Figure 2 resumes an interpretation on the NESSI roadmap[16], compared to the general nowadays' reality. This aims to characterize past and future values in terms of CBIs for CNOs, where the aspects of collaboration flexibility and human intervention start to be as important as process efficiency and full automation. This reflects a scenario where compound and autonomous modules of software – deployed in several repositories, and seen *services* and as *utilities* (SaaS + U) – can act with cleverness and flexibility to solve problems and to adapt themselves to changes in the business environment, having the human being as the centre of actions and decisions.

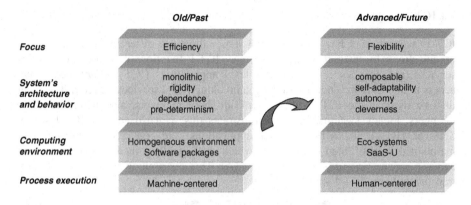

Figure 2 – Shift on the focus of collaborative business ICT infrastructures

3. DEVELOPED CBI: THE ECOLEAD ICT-I

The conception of ICT-I tried to follow the vision presented in Figure 2. Nevertheless, developing a completely transparent, fully interoperable and totally reliable CBI to cope with all CNO requirements is not possible considering the limitations of current ICTs and a good number of related research problems. Moreover, CNO is an emergent area and many related issues are still gaining ground, which means the existence of several open questions. In this sense, the strategy adopted in ICT-I was to design a generic/reference architecture and flexible framework in way it can evolve as long as newer CNO models and ICTs are introduced and open questions are solved.

The essential idea of ECOLEAD ICT-I is based on the vision of a *plug & play* infrastructure. This means that any CNO member is provided with adequate tools to be *"plugged"* into the ICT-I / CNO community and to *"play"* (i.e. to collaborate with other organizations) in a secure, on-demand and pay-per-use ways. In direction to cope with this need, ICT-I has been fully developed based on open and platform-independent specifications and ICT standards.

Regarding its features and potentialities, ICT-I applies the Service Oriented Architecture (SOA) approach, and *web-services* (WS) is the core technology that has been used to implement ICT-I. Following SOA principles, and aiming at supporting the desired flexibility, ICT-I has been designed as a *distributed* open bus composed of many (distributed) services which are accessed on demand to support CNO members in doing businesses and collaborating.

It is important to point out that ICT-I is *not* a framework for SOA-based developments (like IBM *WebSphere*[2], SAP *NetWeaver*[3] or Oracle *Fusion*[4]), nor an integrated CSCW/Groupware package (like *Lotus*[5] or *PHPCollab*[6]), nor another B2B middleware (like Microsoft *BizTalk*[7]), and nor a proprietary services-based platform (like *DBE*[16]). Actually, any of these SOA frameworks could be used to develop (web-)services (WS) for CNOs. In ECOLEAD, all the developed services have utilized *AXIS*[8] framework, which is robust, open-source, non-proprietary and compliant to the W3C recommendations (www.w3c.org).

3.1 ICT-I Scope

ICT-I acts as a CNO collaborative bus, allowing different and distributed organizations to interact with each other. ICT-I functionalities are modeled as services (see next sections) and high-level applications (ICT-I *clients*) can have access to them via web portals and/or via invoking ICT-I services directly. ICT-I can then be used as the ICT "glue" to link all those elements, also including CNO members' legacy systems. Figure 3 illustrates this scenario and the ICT-I scope. Services (ICT-I and services-based applications) are registered, deployed and maintained in distributed repositories, which are logically joined in a common area called *Services Federation* (see section 3.4). This distribution is, however, totally transparent to the ICT-I's clients.

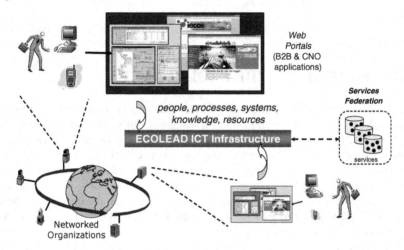

Figure 3 - General ICT-I usage scenario

3.2 Interoperability

Interoperability plays an essential role in any infrastructure where CNO actors and their applications are distributed and heterogeneous. In this context, Interoperability is seen as the ability of a system or a product to work with other systems or products without special effort from the customer or user[9].

Interoperability is a very wide area, comprising since low-level sensors integration till higher levels of inter-organization collaboration. Regarding the core focus of ECOLEAD ICT-I, interoperability aspects are covered only at its essentials, i.e., interoperability issues are tackled by each ICT-I service according to its very specific needs, also benefiting from existing software and approaches.

An extremely important enabler for interoperability is the use of standards. Large international initiatives (e.g., OMG, OASIS, W3C and TeleManagement Forum) have been creating specifications with large acceptance by software developers and vendors worldwide. Therefore, to mitigate interoperability problems, the ECOLEAD ICT-I has been fully developed based on ICT standards, independent of computer platforms. Yet, all the current available ICT-I services have been formally specified independent of technology, using the UML methodology, meaning that they can be implemented in several languages and environments. ICT-I services have been implemented, however, as WS, which is a particular technology. On the other hand, WS is considered the standard *de facto* for implementing SOA-based systems.

Another relevant aspect to support the ICT-I vision is the possibility of invocation/interaction among WS deployed in different B2B frameworks. In this sense, WSIF standard[10] is a strategic element. Thanks to it, collaboration can be much enlarged as any company can put available and share its services with CNO members seamlessly if services are prepared for that (Piazza and Rabelo, 2007).

3.3 SaaS & Utility Models

In order to provide an affordable and 'made to fit' ICT-I for companies, ICT-I applies some principles of the *SaaS-U* (Software-as-a-Service / Utility) model[11]. In the *SaaS* model, software access is subscription-based, remotely hosted, and delivered over the Internet, without the need of complex implementations and IT infrastructure. This also means to allow on-demand services from large-scale and ubiquitous environments, where services can be accessed from everywhere and can be composed according to business rules and models. All this means that ICT-I doesn't require any local deployment. Its services are accessed remotely, upon request, paid-per-use, based on a contract (SLA – service license agreement) for hosting, managing and providing access to its services, no matter where the services providers are and how services have been deployed in the given WS frameworks.

3.4 Services Federation

A fundamental concept in the ECOLEAD ICT-I is the so-called *Services Federation* (see figure 3). This concept was adapted from Sun (Sun, 1999) to be used in the ICT-I environment, meaning that CNO-related services can belong to a virtual logical entity, the Services Federation. This federation comprises *all* services that can be reached, used and shared among CNO members, involving the ones related to: i) the ICT-I lifecycle; ii) the supporting services for high-level applications (i.e. the ICT-I itself); iii) the CNO life cycle (comprising VBE, PVC and VOM vertical services [see Chapter 4]); and iv) legacy / (intra-organization wrapped) systems services.

This is however transparent to users and applications. From the ICT-I point of view, services are invoked, searched, discovered and properly executed no matter which web services are needed to support a collaborative transaction, where they are, how they should be executed, and which technologies have been used in their implementations. Providers of such services can be both CNO members and independent software providers/vendors, having their own policies and rules to manage the services repositories. This means that *ICT-I clients* involve not only CNO client applications, but also CNO services providers.

ICT-I is evolving as the Services Federation is to be a dynamic and self-manageable entity, with new members and services being incorporated to (or modified) and others being withdrawn from it. A given service may have different implementations available over the network.

3.5 Security Framework

Security is a crucial issue in CNOs as several sensible information need to be accessed to guarantee the adequate management of CNOs. Organizations are often very skeptic to share information, and this is worse when there is a need to collaborate with unknown partners. Part of the problem is related to the lack of trust, both between organizations and in their systems. Therefore, security is a must to reinforce trust building and, as such, it should be managed properly.

Managing security is very complex. Considering that most of organizations in a CNO are composed of SMEs and that Virtual Organizations (VO)[12] are per definition a unique business, the security mechanisms to support the sharing and information access should be flexible and easily configurable, also considering the possible different laws each partner's country has. This aims at allowing a quick visibility setup of companies' information according to each VO needs and of the partners' roles in every VO. Ideally, this should be dynamically made and adjusted as long as business processes are executed and hence the information access by the involved partners can be controlled accordingly. Besides this functional complexity, other problems create tremendous difficulties for this envisaged scenario.

Aiming at filling this need, a security framework to cope with CNO requirements has been devised (Sowa et al., 2007). It supports AAA (*Authorization, Authentication and Accounting*) mechanisms and secure authenticated channels, allowing SMEs to configure the security levels and mechanisms for *each* VO they are involved in. The main element of the security framework is DRACO (*Dynamic Responsibility Authorization for Collaborative Organizations*) (Sowa et al., 2007).

The security framework is embedded in the ECOLEAD ICT-I. This prevents CNO users both from dealing with the usual complexity to deploy security systems locally, and from knowing security aspects in details. DRACO development has focused on handling CNO requirements. Other necessary security elements came from other reference international initiatives in the security area, namely *WS-Federation*[13], *Liberty Alliance*[14] and *WS-Trust*[15].

Another facet of the developed security framework is on how security is used by client / CNO applications. Instead of embedding security cares in the software code, DRACO uses a declarative approach to support security transparency. This means to move main security aspects to the server level, avoiding applications and web pages to have any code about security into them. This approach provides means for selecting the security functionality that is effectively required by a given application / service. Once a given service is chosen and VO roles are assigned to by the VO manager, the information access rights configuration is dynamically and automatically set up, and the required security mechanisms can be used.

4 ICT-I SERVICES

In order to provide an open and scalar model, ICT-I has a Reference Architecture *(ICT-I-RA)* from which instances-of it can be derived for different CNOs. In theory, it comprises "all" the possible classes of services than can be useful for any kind of CNO manifestation. This generalization has considered the three kinds of CNOs tackled in ECOLEAD: *Virtual organization Breeding Environment (VBE), Virtual*

Organizations (VO) and Professional Virtual Communities (PVC). The ICT-I-RA goal is to be the base for a globally coherent *derivation* of particular CBIs for given CNOs; in this case, it was used to derive the ICT-I (Rabelo and Sesana, 2008).

4.1 The ICT-I Reference Framework

Figure 4 shows reference framework derived from ICT-I-RA. Actually, this represents *one* vision in terms of which concrete services could be derived from the ICT-I-RA's abstract classes. For instance, the abstract class "human collaboration services" is seen as a *CSCW* issue (for further implementation), which in turn has been thought as *groupware, officeware* and *product development* supporting services. It is up to the system designer and developer to implement his view about e.g. the groupware service (for example, including services like mailing, blog, video-conference, etc.). The other boxes represent the equivalent derivations from the other abstract classes.

Despite the performed derivation, only some of these services have been indeed *implemented* in ECOLEAD. Services in grey scale represent the developed services, whereas the black ones are supported only at a basic level. Services in white represent those that were not implemented but that can be further added to the framework in the future. Anyway, the implemented services support several of the most relevant requirements for CNO activities.

ICT-I services are positioned at different layers. *Horizontal* services are the ones independent of any specific type of CNO. For example, knowledge search service can be useful both to VBE and VO management. *Basic* services are domain-independent and are essentially used by other services – mainly by horizontal services – to support the complete and correct execution of a collaborative transaction. *Platform Specific Services* is a layer to cope with the fact that, in practice, services (both Basic and Horizontal) require specific tools and/or services when deployed. Therefore, they are intrinsically dependent on the services' implementation. Finally, *Legacy system* services are the ones that provide information about activities inside a given company to satisfy CNO needs. They use to be implemented in heterogeneous platforms and native front-ends, typically representing ERP systems and corporate databases. It shall be pointed out that legacy system services don't belong to ICT-I, but they may belong to the services federation.

In ECOLEAD, web-services technology and other associated standards (e.g. SOAP, UDDI and WSDL) have been chosen for implementation. Although this technology particularization, the specification of the services are made using UML methodology, which in turn makes the services specification independent of platform and, as such, they can be implemented using other technologies (e.g. web-services without SOAP or UDDI) and supporting tools (either open-source or COTS), depending on the envisaged CNO to support.

In resume, and considering the requirements stressed in chapter 2 and the features described in chapter 3, a CBI derived from the ECOLEAD ICT-I-RA - and hence that it was derived for the ECOLEAD project - is defined as *an open, distributed, scalable, transparent and security-embedded collaborative service-oriented infrastructure, tailored to support CNOs in the modeling and execution of collaborative tasks, accessed on-demand and paid-per-use.*

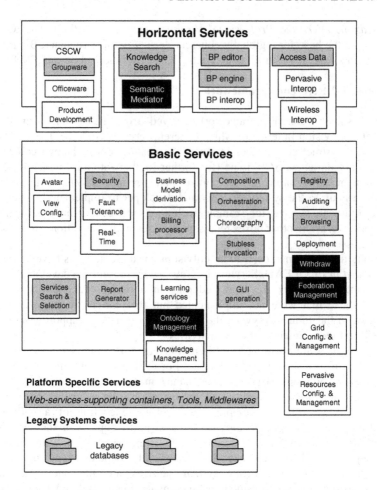

Figure 4 – ICT-I Reference Framework

4.2 Implemented Services

This section explains in very general terms the implemented services.

Horizontal Services

- CNO Actors On-Demand Collaboration Services. For supporting *human collaboration*: mailing, chat, task list, file storage, notification, calendar, wiki, forum, voice and syndication.
- CNO Knowledge Search Services. For supporting *knowledge sharing*, empowering the management of distributed and heterogeneous bodies of knowledge exposed by CNOs. Proper ontology and reconciliation rules are used for bridging some semantic gaps among knowledge repositories, allowing seamless retrieval of information.
- Interactive, user-centered BP Management Services. For supporting *business process interconnection*, on top of an existing open-source BPM environment (modeling module and execution engine), ICT-I provides support to task-

oriented, interactive decisional activities to be performed by CNO actors. The forthcoming *BPEL4PEOPLE* standard can also be used for that.

- CNO Data Access Services. For supporting *systems interoperability*, ICT-I offers services to support an easy and secure access to CNO members' databases, which includes a support for their definition and configuration and for the information that has to be shared.

Basic Services

- ICT-I Security Services. These services support confidentiality, integrity, availability and authentication in the communications. This includes the log-in and user management service.
- ICT-I Billing Services. They allow the implementation of different billing models to support the pay-per-use and on-demand service provision.
- ICT-I Services Composition. This service provides facilities to define and execute composed services, preferably using BPEL standard for services composition.
- ICT-I Reporting Services. For supporting the generation of reports to other services (e.g. "detailed billing usage", "services bill summary"), using pre-defined templates in well known formats (e.g. pdf, XML, HTML).
- ICT-I Services Registry and Discovery. For supporting the publishing of the web services in a UDDI repository as well as the search and browsing of services. These services also include the management of the ICT-I life cycle, involving services associated to its deployment, plugging, use, maintenance, unplugging and undeployment.

ICT-I services can be accessed via the ECOLEAD portal, from which users can have access to the ICT-I UDDI. This UDDI is so far centralized and it has a link to each individual service. Actually, so far this UDDI represents the Services Federation. As services have been developed by different partners, the UDDI makes the automatic link between the client application and the site where the invoked service is physically deployed.

The very detailed specification and implementation model of each implemented service is presented in Ratti and Rodrigo (2007). Some services are to be transparent to the users / clients, whereas other services are designed to assist end-users in some tasks. Figure 5 shows a graphical interface of an Editor of iBPM service (Ratti and Gusmeroli, 2007), which is one of the developed services. This editor allows the combination of human tasks and interactions with BPEL processes, creating a so-called collaborative business process.

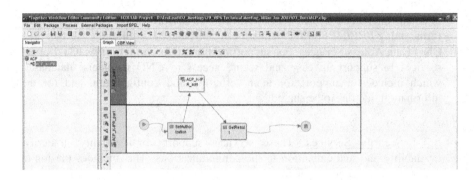

Figure 5 - iBPM editor

5. CONCLUSIONS AND GENERAL ASSESSMENT

This paper has presented the Collaborative Business ICT infrastructure (ICT-I) that was developed in the ECOLEAD Project for supporting CNOs in collaborating and doing businesses more effectively. It has been conceived based on the service oriented architecture paradigm / web-services technology, providing organizations with a transparent (mostly), platform-independent, easy-to-use, secure-embedded, lean, distributed, scalar, on-demand and pay-per-use ICT-I. Its conception and features are in line with some relevant initiatives, like NESSI[16] and ATHENA[8].

Supporting CNOs imply in a different set of functionalities, meaning that ICT-I complements B2B functionalities Thanks to the ICT-I framework flexibility and strong utilization of standards, all these functionalities can be integrated in the same computing environment (web portals, for instance) so that users do not need to see them as separate systems.

From the technological point of view and following current trends, ECOLEAD ICT-I has as main features:

- It is a web-based integrated platform devoted to CNOs, meaning that users should only have a browser and internet access. No local deployments;
- Services are accessed on demand This means having almost an 'a la carte' environment to fit each organization's needs.
- Services are paid per use, respecting variable and flexible business models;
- It is open and flexible to embrace new services without any interference in the use of the infrastructure, also meaning that ICT-I is scalable;
- As most of the ICT-I services are web-based and can be accessed via portals (*portlets*), they can also be accessed through mobile devices;
- Services & data access are dynamically controlled by a flexible security system.

These features cope with requirements for an effective usage of this by SMEs. Actually, regarding its CNO orientation and other features stressed along the paper, it is believed that ICT-I is unique and it clearly goes towards supporting several requirements of Web 2.0 and Enterprise 2.0.

However, so far there is no support in terms of wider methodologies to guide a derivation process (e.g. using Model Driven Architecture approach), and to assist companies to overcome interoperability problems (e.g. ATHENA roadmap).

At the individual services and implementation level one can say that there are some equivalent services available in the Internet that offer equivalent functionalities. Yes, indeed. Actually, all the developed services made use of open source software available in a way to avoid the "re-invention of the wheel" and to add value on top of them when both integrating them in a common and relatively user-friendly (for an infrastructure) environment, and adapting them to some CNO requirements. Other more global issues are foreseen only at the conceptual and very generic level, such as fault tolerance mechanisms, services federation management, mobile access, etc. No support, or only very basic, is offered for issues like these.

Its validation has been so far achieved non-formally and partially. Non-formally because any supporting derivation methodology has been developed to guide the creation of particular business infrastructures for given CNOs. It is assumed that it is validated by the simple fact that a concrete business infrastructure (the ICT-I) was successfully implemented, i.e. it was possible to create a given instance of the ICT-I Reference Architecture following formal specifications of the derived services. Partially, because every single ICT-I service couldn't be exhaustively tested in many scenarios and real case situations. So far they were only tested in some trials and take-up-based scenarios. In terms of performance, level of transparency, *plug & play* effectiveness, etc. of the ICT-I services, a detailed but preliminary analysis is provided in Ratti and Rodrigo (2007).

From the conceptual point of view, ICT-I is similar to what *Salesforce.com*'s platform[17] does. The difference is that this offers only CRM-related (web) services, which are physically centralized at the Salesforce company and whose services are provided by itself. Customers usually pay a fee monthly or pay according to the number of users a company has. ICT-I offers CNO supporting services independent of domain, and it is totally open and scalar, where providers can be any organization, including CNO members.

Web-service technology, despite its potentialities and increasing acceptance, has some drawbacks (e.g., it is stateless) that should be managed depending on the desired business process's behavior. Dealing with large-scale fault-tolerance platforms is still an open and very complex topic of research so it is expected that future outcomes of this can be incorporated in the ICT-I. Another complex issue is the management of the services federation. Each service provider can determine its own operational and security rules besides having different levels of computing infrastructures to run services, which can create serious troubles and to lead to other class of interoperability problems when several providers were established. Moreover, the operational policies should deal with the different life cycles of each service that is made available, which is also complex. Services should be easily discovered and immediately integrated/bound to workflow or orchestration systems mechanisms, but this bumps into the different ways and semantics the diverse providers have registered the services, on how the services interfaces (WSDL) are expressed, and if context awareness has to be considered.

All these difficulties represent challenges in the web-related community in spite of several ongoing works. Two interesting research projects that can be mentioned and that are dealing with some of those problems are DBE[18] and ABILITIES[19], but their results are still not at a level for being now used. These problems are essentially related to the *technological* perspective of the difficulties and impacts the adoption of the CNO paradigm by companies and the use of such kind of CBI to support their collaboration tends to provoke. Other perspectives, e.g. organizational, cultural, financial, among others are also extremely relevant and must be dealt with for the successful realization of the CNO paradigm. These perspectives are, however, out of scope of this paper.

5.1 Acknowledgments

This work was mostly supported by the European Commission under the project IST FP-6 IP ECOLEAD project (www.ecolead.org). The Brazilian participation was also supported by the Brazilian Council for Research and Scientific Development – CNPq (www.cnpq.br) in the scope of IFM project (www.ifm.org.br).

6. REFERENCES

1. Camarinha-Matos, L. M.; Afsarmanesh, H.; Ollus, M.; 2005. Virtual Organizations: Systems and Practices, Springer.
2. Camarinha-Matos, L. M.; Afsarmanesh, H.; 2004 . Towards Next Business Models. In Collaborative Networked Organizations: a research agenda for emerging business models, Kluwer Academic Publishers, pp. 3-6.
3. Piazza, A.; Rabelo, R. J.; 2007. An Approach for Seamlessly Interoperation among heterogeneous web services-based B2B Frameworks [in Portuguese], Proceedings 8th Brazilian Symposium on Intelligent Automation, pp. 451-458.
4. Rabelo, R.; Sesana, M.; 2008. Technical Report (Deliverable) D61.1d – ICT-I Reference Architecture and Framework for CNOs, in www.ecolead.org.
5. Ratti, R.; Rodrigo, M.; 2007. Technical Report (Deliverable) D64.1d – ICT-I Services, in www.ecolead.org.
6. Ratti, R.; Gusmeroli, S. (2007). Interactive User-Centered Business Process Management Services, in Proceedings PRO-VE´2007 - 8th IFIP Working Conference on Virtual Enterprises, in Establishing the Foundation of Collaborative Networks, Springer, pp. 487-494.
7. Sowa, G.; Sniezynski, T.; 2007. Technical Report (Deliverable) D64.1b – Configurable multi-level security architecture for CNOs, in www.ecolead.org.
8. SUN - JINI Technology Architectural Overview, http://www.sun.com/jini/whitepapers/architecture.html, Jan 1999, in 30/01/2008.

---

[1] This is essentially based on the Companion Roadmap: www.companion-roadmap.org
[2] www-306.ibm.com/software/websphere/
[3] www.sap.com/platform/netweaver
[4] www.oracle.com/applications/fusion.html
[5] www.ibm.com/developerworks/lotus/products/notesdomino/
[6] sourceforge.net/projects/phpcollab/
[7] www.microsoft.com/biztalk/default.mspx
[8] ws.apache.org/axis/
[9] www.atena-ip.org
[10] ws.apache.org/wsif
[11] http://www-304.ibm.com/jct09002c/isv/marketing/saas/index.html
[12] A Virtual Organization is a virtual and temporary grouping of organizations which is formed to attend to a given business opportunity.
[13] www.ibm.com/developerworks/library/specification/ws-fed
[14] www.projectliberty.org
[15] docs.oasis-open.org/ws-sx/ws-trust/v1.3/ws-trust.html
[16] NESSI Strategic Research Agenda - Framing the future of the Service Oriented Economy. Version 2006-2-13 (http://www.nessi-europe.com/documents/NESSI_SRA_VOL_1_20060213.pdf); ICT for Enterprise Networking (http://cordis.europa.eu/ist/directorate_d/en_intro.htm).
[17] www.salesforce.com
[18] www.digital-ecosystem.org
[19] services.txt.it/abilities

48

WEB SERVICES-BASED COLLABORATIVE SYSTEM FOR DISTRIBUTED ENGINEERING

A. Pawlak, P. Fraś, P. Penkala

Institute of Electronics
Silesian University of Technology
Gliwice, POLAND
Adam.Pawlak@polsl.pl

Design of complex electronic systems requires often collaboration of engineers who work in remote locations. This collaboration enabled by the network needs to be supported by seamless and secure integration of distributed design tools.

The paper presents a web services-based environment enabling integration of distributed design tools. It is based on TRMS (Tool Registration and Management Services) which are scalable, easily accessible, secure, and available on different platforms due to their implementation in Java.

1. INTRODUCTION

Collaborative engineering for distributed product development is a new paradigm of engineering work that has become feasible due to dynamic progress in information and communication technologies. This new engineering paradigm can be enabled with innovative infrastructures, collaborative working environments, net-aware engineering tools, and new design methodologies based on re-use of globally accessible resources, as well as application of advanced security of network operations and distributed tools management.

Many research efforts were directed during recent years towards new infrastructures and collaborative working environments (CWE, 2006), like projects CoSpaces, and eCoSpace. New design methodologies, like SoC (System-on-a-Chip) design based on globally accessible IP components, are proliferating into engineering practices (Brglez, 2001), (Saucier, 2007).

The paper addresses the selected topic of collaborative engineering, namely integration of distributed engineering tools that is relevant for distributed CWEs. The authors with the approach presented in the paper aim at supporting SMEs that operate in collaborative networks. Available for SMEs distributed collaborative engineering environments do not support adequately integration of tools of dispersed design groups, and do not consider distance-spanning related issues, like: firewalls, security (including user authorization, data and transfer encrypting), distributed inter-organization workflows, and remote administration of users and tools.

Please use the following format when citing this chapter:

Pawlak, A., Fraś, P. and Penkala, P., 2008, in IFIP International Federation for Information Processing, Volume 283; *Pervasive Collaborative Networks*; Luis M. Camarinha-Matos, Willy Picard; (Boston: Springer), pp. 463–472.

Although these problems have been partially solved in large global enterprises that are able to pass designs between their branches around the globe, SMEs still have major problems in entering outsourced design contracts due to a lack of affordable collaborative infrastructures.

The paper presents the new web services-based realisation of Tool Registration and Management Services (TRMS). TRMS has originally been developed within the EU E-Colleg project (*www.ecolleg.org*) (Bauer, 2001) (Schattkowsky, 2004). The solution presented in the paper is a result of R&D work conducted during the EU MAPPER project (*mapper.eu.org*) (Johnsen, 2007). The new TRMS environment (also referred to as TRMS2), offers to dispersed engineers some innovative features that enhance existing distributed collaborative engineering infrastructures with new services. TRMS has been originally developed as a stand alone application (Fraś, 2004) but as a result of deployment experiments, and especially due to new requirements concerning its interoperability with other collaborative environments, its architecture has been based on web services.

The paper presents requirements, justification and an outline of the new architecture of TRMS based on web services, as well as its application in integration of engineering tools for electronic systems design. This work constitutes a part of the MAPPER collaborative framework (Johnsen, 2007) that comprises also other relevant for inter-enterprise engineering collaboration elements, like: collaborative workspace used in our applications for supporting design specification refinement (CURE, 2008), engineering use of visual knowledge models (Pawlak, 2007), and participatory design methodologies (Johnsen, 2007). Other important for TRMS issues, like the use of ontologies for tools integration have been presented elsewhere (Szlęzak, 2007).

The paper is organized as follows. Firstly, new requirements on TRMS are shortly explained; secondly, the overall architecture and TRMS services-based functionality are described. Finally, we conclude on the experiences relevant to the web services-based architecture of TRMS deployed to a distributed design of an electronic component.

2. CHALLENGES AND REQUIREMENTS

2.1   Challenges in collaborative design

Current trends in global engineering (Radeke, 1998), mass-customisation and increased competition are leading industry towards collaborative networks of design engineering and manufacturing organisations. Increasingly, products must be rapidly adapted to customer needs, leading to faster innovation cycles and more complex collaborative engineering. The core problems and challenges in the area of faster and more flexible design and manufacturing concern:
- Concurrency in all operations, increasing efficiency and decreasing time-to-market.
- Quick and inexpensive formation of networked design organisations.
- Processes and products that can be rapidly reconfigured to accommodate diverse and changing needs and opportunities. Collaborative product, process

and service engineering must thus be managed and performed across networked organisations.

- Integration of tools of remote groups of engineers isn't supported adequately in terms of: security, distributed inter-organization workflows, and remote administration of users and tools.

Design engineering in collaborative networks constitutes a new engineering paradigm that needs to be supported with new design methodologies, tools and practices. Although collaborative engineering has been advocated for already more than a decade, in practice, it remains typically restricted to engineering groups from large global companies, but even there support for collaboration between dispersed company's sites proves to be limited.

It has been observed (Ranta, 1999) that automobile industry was usually a source of innovation in terms of new production paradigms and the best practices in manufacturing industry. However in categories of management and control of demand-supply chain and industrial structures, electronic industry sets new paradigms through creation of global collaborative (engineering) networks (Salminen, 1997). This enables the partner companies to compete against others in terms of time to market, product flexibility and shared knowledge.

2.2 Requirements

The main requirements on TRMS have been formulated already in (Fraś, 2004). During R&D work conducted in MAPPER and TRMS deployments in distributed design scenarios, e.g. (Fraś, Kostienko, 2004) and (Siekierska, 2006) additional requirements have been identified and formulated. Below they are enumerated and shortly explained:

- services supporting interoperability with advanced collaborative environments
- access to particular TRMS services,
- support for secure work in the networks with NAT and firewalls,
- support for long task execution and operation tolerating Internet connection breaks,
- simple client application for common users, and
- multi-user access to invoked tasks.

As original TRMS has been developed as a stand-alone application its integration with other collaborative systems, like workspaces was a demanding task. With web services-based architecture selected services are available from outside and the system is easily integrateable using common services platforms.

Access to a particular service like user authentication is very useful in larger collaborative environments with numerous components, e.g. synchronous and asynchronous communication, and collaborative workspaces. If user authentication service can be shared among system components, the user will need to be verified once only. Further examples of use of TRMS services that should be accessed by external CE components are: tool invocation, tasks and workflows management, as well as users' management.

Secure work in collaborative environments is a must in industrial settings that use firewall systems and filters which control contents of transferred data. Network address translation systems (NAT) constitute an additional obstacle for a direct communication with machines of an internal network.

Some remote tasks, like simulation of certain components may take long times (hours or even days). Thus, supporting of such practical cases by letting a user to initiate the remote task only without a need to maintain the connection is very useful.

Supporting users with various versions of clients depending on their role, needs and experiences simplifies the use of the system.

As tasks are often shared among dispersed users, e.g. designers working in different locations, it is very useful that each of them may monitor and control their progress

3. TRMS ARCHITECTURE

A general architecture of TRMS comprises three basic components: Global Tool Lookup Server (GTLS), Tool Server (TS), and the Client application.

GTLS manages the TRMS environment whereas Tool Servers enable remote tool invocation. The Client application allows a user to control the environment and tool invocation. Each instance of the TRMS environment must comprise one GTLS server and an arbitrary number of Tool Servers and Client Applications. A quantity of Tool Servers depends on a number of installed tools that are expected to be accessible over the network. Each computer running such a tool needs an operational Tool Server.

The TRMS environment uses for communication the standard https or http protocols. Communication among components of the environment is synchronous and conducted always in a direction „to GTLS". The GTLS server never initiates alone a connection to a Tool Server, neither to a user who uses a Client Application. The connection is initiated by the Client or TS. Tool invocation on TS is done indirectly. Firstly, a user sends a request to GTLS and from there an appropriate Tool Server takes information on its task. This mechanism allows usage of the environment in networks protected by firewall systems or using NAT. In such networks the Client application and the Tool Server operate from a security perspective, like a common browser, i.e. invoke a remote resource on a server beyond the protected network.

3.1   GTLS – Global Tool Lookup Server

The main component of TRMS is the GTLS server. It is responsible for management of elements of the environment. GTLS is also responsible for the security policy of the whole environment, registration of user activities and of access to tools, maintaining statistics, identification of an intruder attack. GTLS, as the only component of the TRMS environment should be accessible from the Internet. In such case, GTLS plays a role of a broker and a temporary repository in a communication between a Client Application and Tool Servers.

A relational data base is used as the main data repository for GTLS. DB contains information on users and their privileges, TSs, registered tools, and workflows.

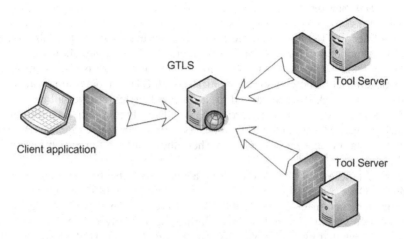

Figure 1 - General architecture of the TRMS environment

GTLS has been implemented as a set of web services (Apache AXIS). Selected web services have been shortly characterised below.

Administration
The administration services are responsible for registration and modification of data on users and their privileges, elements of the system, as well as, information on accessible tools and machines that make them available.

User and Server Authentication
Login to GTLS is the first task a user is expected to do upon invocation of the Client Application. User authentication is performed then. As soon as the user (designer) logs in, a new session is created and the user receives its session key which later on is used for authorisation. Tool Servers are authenticated automatically upon their invocation.

Task Management
Each tool that is expected to be accessible over the network needs to be registered and placed in the task queue. Registration involves determination of necessary data for tool invocation, like: tool name, complete path to tool location, and information on the Tool Server on which the tool resides (as well as additional data on the tool: its description, author, creation date). Registration can be conducted by a user with appropriate privileges. The task queue constitutes a set of refined task instances that comprise in addition to information on the tool, also data on the particular refinement (status and information on messages that result from tool invocation, like *std output, std error*).

Workflow Management
A workflow constitutes a set of tasks that are in the task queue. The current implementation supports sequential workflows, i.e. a new task is invoked if the

previous one has been completed. It is the GTLS server that controls a sequence of tasks invocations.

3.2   Tool Server

The Tool Server (TS) is responsible for controlling users' access to tools. A client invoking a tool does it through the Tool Server. The Tool Server allows for sharing of the particular tool through the Internet. Its additional task is brokerage in user authentication. The Tool Server communicates with GTLS in order to update its task queue. If a new task has been added to the queue then TS retrieves all required for tool invocation (e.g., parameters, input data) data. The task is executed in the following, and all input data are returned. As soon as, the tool completes its work, all result data are sent back to GTLS, where they wait for retrieval by the Client Application.

It is not necessary that TS remains available all the time, although this is preferred. Once a user tries to invoke a tool on TS that is off-line, information on this trial remains on GTLS until this Tool Server becomes available again. The Internet access isn't required as well during the tool invocation. In such case, messages generated by the invoked tool are buffered by the Tool Server, and with the subsequent connection to the network will be transmitted to GTLS.

3.3   Client application

The Client application has a simple GUI that enables login to the system, its administration and usage of available tools. It enables a full control over the environment, management of users and tasks. Each task needs to be registered by the Client application. Registration of a workflow will be possible as well. Upon an invocation by a user, information on a particular task is placed in a task queue on GTLS and awaits there for its retrieval by an appropriate Tool Server.

Figure 2 presents the client application with a workflow comprising six design tasks that are performed by an engineer during design task realisation. These design tasks are related to: service of design data repository, compilation, simulation and synthesis. They are explained in the following section.

GUI enables invocation and termination of a task, or even a complete workflow. Once a workflow is invoked, subsequent tasks are invoked automatically by GTLS. The application enables monitoring of each invoked task status. Messages that are generated by the invoked tool (*std output*), as well as error messages (*std error*) are available as well.

Many users may concurrently control a particular workflow. They have access to all information on executed tasks and may mange all tasks. A user may anytime switch off the client application without loosing any data, as all information on the invoked task and messages generated by the task are buffered on the GTLS server. Upon a new login step the client application will fetch from GTLS all data that appeared when a user wasn't present in the system.

An applet version that may be invoked through a browser has been developed as well.

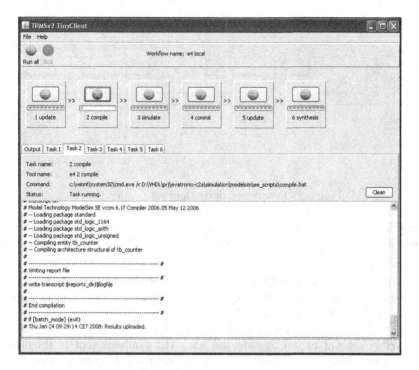

Figure 2 - Client application

3.4 Security measures

TRMS enables secure data transfer with authentication and authorization of users, as well as it includes security management mechanisms that allow an administrator to monitor users' activity and to execute a proper security policy. Invocation of each web service requires user authorisation which is realised using a session key. TRMS uses as default the HTTP SSL channel for communication between components what assures confidentiality of transferred data. Use of the standard Internet protocol is useful for networks protected by firewalls, e.g. corporate networks.

4. DEPLOYMENT OF TRMS

An experiment on distributed collaborative design and verification between two remote branches of one company – IP (virtual) electronic component design house has been performed as a part of the MAPPER project activities. It comprised the following tasks: *code development, synthesis, change notification, FPGA implementation, error handling,* and *notification of task completion.*

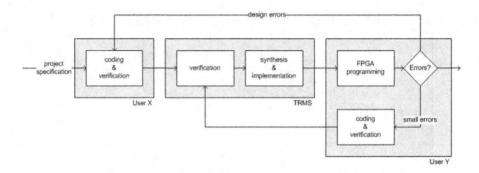

Figure 3 - Distributed design and verification flow

Code development: A designer X in Gliwice location prepares a RTL code and synthesis scripts using the text editor. The files are uploaded into CVS (using a local CVS client).

Synthesis: The designer X in Gliwice launches the following tasks in TRMS:
– Upload of the source code from the CVS repository to the remote machine where the synthesis tool is installed.
– Execution of compilation and simulation of a design and subsequently the synthesis script on the remote machine. The synthesis tool is installed in location Gliwice on the machine other than the designer's one with the TRMS Tool Server running. The designer can control the progress of the synthesis process (it can be stopped any time, e.g., when a designer notices that something goes wrong).
– Commitment of the synthesis result files into the CVS repository.

Change notification: The designer X in location Gliwice and a designer Y in location Bielsko get an e-mail notification about changes in the CVS repository. In addition, any designer (from Gliwice or Bielsko) can log into the TRMS system and check the status of the synthesis process.

FPGA implementation: The designer Y in location Bielsko downloads from the CVS repository (using a local CVS client) the implementation results needed for programming an FPGA chip.

Error handling: In case of design or implementation errors one can identify the following cases:
a) Errors that can be handled by the engineer in Bielsko (e.g., FPGA pin assignment):
   In this case the engineer in Bielsko fixes these errors, uploads modified files to the CVS repository and uses the TRMS remotely to re-run synthesis on the machine located in Gliwice (the tasks described in synthesis).
b) Errors that have to be handled by engineers in Gliwice (e.g., more serious design bugs):
   The engineer in Bielsko notifies the engineer in Gliwice that a serious error has been found, and from now we return to code development.

Notification of task completion: If there are no new bugs the design verification is completed.

The experiment has demonstrated that TRMS can accelerate designers' activities in case of sequential operations. A workflow solution enables automation of selected design tasks. Another advantage of using TRMS is the ability provided to engineers located in Bielsko to invoke tools which are installed in the Gliwice branch of the company. Upon installation of TRMS they can work with remote tools smoothly.

Main restrictions of the current TRMS version that have been pointed to by the application engineers are:
- TRMS technology for workflow definition and design tasks automation in general, requires training before a novice engineer can apply it efficiently,
- TRMS can invoke command line scripts only,
- The workflow engine of TRMS supports currently sequential workflows without decision blocks and loops only.

5. CONCLUSIONS

The presented TRMS architecture and its functionality fulfil requirements for a secure collaborative infrastructure. The TRMS infrastructure supports tool integration and management. In our opinion, TRMS is a solution for distributed cooperating engineers and gives them a possibility for a simple invocation of distant tools. Distributed engineering work will become much easier if engineers are able to cooperate in larger networks with many registered tools. Their work will be accelerated and thus work costs will be reduced. A registered tool will provide a service to distributed design engineers. It is expected that the overload due to tool installation and configuration processes may be reduced substantially. Additionally, encrypted and digitally signed messages assure a high level of security in sensitive design information exchange. TRMS constitutes the infrastructure well tailored to distance-spanning engineering collaboration in complex distributed product design.

The TRMS architecture based on web services has the following advantages:

- Enables easier integration with other collaborative environments,
- The use of the standard HTTPS protocol enables control of the network traffic,
- GTLS as a communication broker enables use of tools that are installed in local networks on machines that are not visible from outside,
- The new architecture supports also tools that require long computation times,
- The environment is robust enough for transient problems in accessing the network,
- It reduces demand for a broad bandwidth in accessing the network, and speeds up the overall the environment.

Basing the TRMS architecture on web services opens it for further improvements that will be due to forecasted new standardisation initiatives related to collaborative services (MAPPER D13, 2008).

Further R&D related to TRMS includes enhanced workflow management system and improved support for engineering teamwork with both synchronous and asynchronous collaboration.

5.1   Acknowledgments

Authors would like to acknowledge collaboration with Szymon Grzybek and Wojciech Sakowski from Evatronix SA on TRMS deployment in the distributed design and verification of the USB transceiver virtual component.

6. REFERENCES

1. Bauer M., *et al.*, "Advanced Infrastructure for Pan-European Collaborative Engineering". In: Stanford-Smith B; Chiozza E: E-work and E-commerce, Novel solutions and practices for the global networked economy. IOS Press / Ohmsha, Berlin, 2001.
2. Brglez F., E-Design Concepts and Practice: An Overview, IP SoC Grenoble, 2001.
3. CoSpaces IP project 1st Annual Conference, 26-28.09.2007, Leiria, Portugal.
4. CURE - Collaborative Universal Remote Education, http://cure.sourceforge.net/
5. CWE, 1st Conf. on Collaborative Working Environments for Business and Industry (CWE'06), Brussels, 10-11.05.2006, Conference Report.
6. eCoSpace project Newsletter Nb. 3, June 2007.
7. Fraś P., Kostienko T., Magiera J., Pawlak J., Penkala P., Stachańczyk D., Szlęzak M., Witczynski M. "TRMS Deployment in Distributed Engineering Applications", Proc. CCE'04, Tatranska Lomnica, Slovakia, April 18-21 2004 (ISBN 91-975604-0-5).
8. Fraś P., *et al.*, "Collaborative infrastructure for distance - spanning concurrent engineering". PRO-VE'04, in Luis M. Camarinha-Matos (Ed.) "Virtual Enterprises and Collaborative Networks". 5th IFIP Working Conf. on Virtual Enterprises, Toulouse, Kluwer Academic Publishers, 2004.
9. Haake J., Schümmer T., "Supporting Effective Collaborative Engineering". Proc. Workshop on Challenges in Collaborative Engineering, Krakow, 11-13.04.2007, Lecture Notes in Informatics (LNI), Vol. 120, GI - Gesellschaft für Informatik, Bonn, 2007.
10. Johnsen S., *et al.*, "Model-based Adaptive Product and Process Engineering". New Technologies for the Intelligent Design and Operation of Manufacturing Networks, Rabe, M.; Mihók, P. (eds), Stuttgart, Fraunhofer IRB Verlag 2007.
11. MAPPER D13 "Standardisation Activities Report", Feb. 2008, http://mapper.eu.org/miug/.
12. Pawlak A., Jørgensen H., Penkala P., Fraś P., "Business Process and Workflow Management for Design of Electronic Systems- Balancing Flexibility and Control". as [8].
13. Radeke E., "GEN - Global Engineering Networking". Proc. Conf. on Integration in Manufacturing, 1998, Goteborg.
14. Ranta, J., "Globalisation of manufacturing – A new paradigm emerging from electronics industry". IST99, European Conference on Information Society Technologies, Helsinki (Finland).
15. Salminen V., Buckley E., Malinen, P., Ritvas, J., Silakoski S., Sauer, A., "Global engineering networking – Turning engineering knowledge into an accessible corporate asset". Proceedings of the 11th Conf. on Engineering Design (ICED'97), Tampere (Finland), vol. 25, p. 165-172.
16. Saucier G., "IP website as a catalyst of IP industry". Proc. Conf. on IP Based Electronic System, Grenoble, 5-6th Dec. 2007.
17. Schattkowsky T., Mueller W., Pawlak A. "Workflow Management Middleware for Secure Distance-Spanning Collaborative Engineering". In L. Fischer (ed.) The Workflow Handbook 2004, WfMC, Lighthouse Point, USA, 2004.
18. Siekierska K. *et al.* "Distributed collaborative design of IP components in the TRMS environment". Microelectronics Reliability, Elsevier Journal, vol. 46, 2006, 5-6.
19. Szlęzak M., Pawlak A., Wojciechowski K., "Markup Language Based Design Tool Integration Method Supporting Collaborative Engineering". Pre-Proceedings of CollABD'07, 1st Workshop on Integrated Practices for the 21st Century: Collaborative Working Environments, (G. Carrara and Y. Kalay (eds), Sapienza Univ., Rome, 13-15.12.2007.

49

DISCOVERY AND SELECTION OF CERTIFIED WEB SERVICES THROUGH REGISTRY-BASED TESTING AND VERIFICATION

Dimitrios Kourtesis[1], Ervin Ramollari[1],
Dimitris Dranidis[2], Iraklis Paraskakis[1]

[1] *South East European Research Centre (SEERC),*
Research Centre of the University of Sheffield and CITY College
Mitropoleos 17, 54624, Thessaloniki, GREECE
dkourtesis@seerc.org, erramollari@seerc.org, iparaskakis@seerc.org

[2] *Computer Science Department, CITY College,*
Affiliated Institution of the University of Sheffield,
Tsimiski 13, 54624 Thessaloniki, GREECE
dranidis@city.academic.gr

Reliability and trust are fundamental prerequisites for the establishment of functional relationships among peers in a Collaborative Networked Organisation (CNO), especially in the context of Virtual Enterprises where economic benefits can be directly at stake. This paper presents a novel approach towards effective service discovery and selection that is no longer based on informal, ambiguous and potentially unreliable service descriptions, but on formal specifications that can be used to verify and certify the actual Web service implementations. We propose the use of Stream X-machines (SXMs) as a powerful modelling formalism for constructing the behavioural specification of a Web service, for performing verification through the generation of exhaustive test cases, and for performing validation through animation or model checking during service selection.

1. INTRODUCTION

Reliability is a fundamental prerequisite for establishing collaboration within a network of peers, be them human or machines, and issues such as trust management and evaluation of trustworthiness are significant challenges in Collaborative Networks research. Collaborative business processes built on top of service-oriented infrastructures in networked organisations are typically realised as compositions of autonomous but trustworthy Web services provided and consumed across intra- and inter-organisational boundaries. The individual Web services that a collaborative business process comprises are discovered and composed at design-time on the basis of some specification that is meant to explicate the functional or non-functional properties of each service.

The *formality* of this specification may vary depending on the employed service description framework, and the degree of ambiguity or rigour in the description determines the extent to which a specification can be amenable to automated

Please use the following format when citing this chapter:

Kourtesis, D., Ramollari, E., Dranidis, D. and Paraskakis, I., 2008, in IFIP International Federation for Information Processing, Volume 283; *Pervasive Collaborative Networks*; Luis M. Camarinha-Matos, Willy Picard; (Boston: Springer), pp. 473–482.

processing. The *correctness* of the implementation with respect to its corresponding specification may also vary, due to modelling inconsistencies that may be intentional or unintentional. In highly dynamic and loosely coordinated environments, service specifications are especially likely to become outdated and unreliable sources of information due to Web service implementations becoming modified or replaced, or due to other changes in infrastructure. To avoid making design-time decisions based of inaccurate information and incurring the associated cost of run-time errors, special care must be taken to ensure that service specifications are reliable, i.e. that they correspond to the actual service implementations they are meant to describe.

This paper introduces a novel approach towards extending the capabilities of a service registry with additional *functional testing* and behavioural verification functionality that can serve as a basis for overcoming the aforementioned challenge. We propose the use of Stream X-machines (SXMs) (Laycock, 1993) (Holcombe and Ipate, 1998) as a modelling formalism for constructing the behavioural specification of a service at the provider-side, and generating test cases at the registry-side to verify that the actual service implementation conforms to the specification. A significant advantage of Stream X-machines compared to other behavioural modelling and testing formalisms is in their associated testing method, which is guaranteed to reveal all inconsistencies among an implementation under test and an advertised specification (Dranidis, Kourtesis and Ramollari, 2007). The Web service test set that is generated by the registry is represented as a sequence of operation invocations with appropriate inputs and expected outputs. By applying the generated set of tests to a Web service implementation and evaluating its responses, the registry can conclude if it is behaviourally-equivalent to its associated specification. The registry acts as a *certification authority* for service specifications and as a trusted third party that service consumers can rely on for design-time *discovery*.

An additional feature of the proposed approach that sets it apart from other solutions in the literature is that the SXM specification and the generated test sets can be used not only for registry-side *verification*, but also for consumer-side *validation* after discovery and during service *selection*. Service consumers can validate the behaviour of every certified candidate service that the registry returns as a match to their needs, in order to select the most appropriate one. Validation can take place either by executing the SXM specification with an X-machine animator and visually inspecting its behaviour, or by performing model-checking to assert desirable or undesirable properties described by temporal logic formulae. This allows service consumers to essentially simulate the service behaviour and evaluate it without having to perform real testing with the associated overhead for both service consumer and service provider.

The rest of this paper is organised as follows. Section 2 presents a summary of related work in the domain of model-based Web service testing and verification. Section 3 provides an overview of the Stream X-machine modelling formalism that this paper suggests as a suitable means to model the behaviour of stateful Web services. Section 4 provides an overview of the proposed holistic approach for discovery and selection of certified services through registry-based testing and verification, presenting the approach from the perspectives of the provider, the registry and the consumer, and emphasising on their associated activities. Section 5 concludes the paper by summarising the main points of the presented work and suggesting directions for future research.

2. RELATED WORK

A number of approaches have been proposed for the verification of Web services by employing model-based testing. In (Sinha and Paradkar, 2006) a method is proposed for annotating a WSDL document with concepts from an OWL ontology representing inputs, outputs, preconditions and effects, and automatically translating the resulting WSDL-S specification into a semantically-equivalent extended Finite State Machine (EFSM) model. A set of manual or automated techniques for generating test cases based on the EFSM model is also provided. The techniques vary in terms of adequacy criteria, coverage and completeness.

The use of an EFSM modelling formalism for describing the dynamic behaviour of a Web service is also proposed in (Keum, Kang and Ko, 2006), where a manual procedure is suggested for deriving the EFSM model from a WSDL description. The proposed EFSM model is an FSM extended with memory, predicate conditions and computing blocks for state transitions. With proper tool support the EFSM model can be used for automatically generating Web service test cases with increased test coverage that includes both control flow and data flow. The authors provide experimental results showing that their method has the potential to find more faults compared to other methods, but notably without completeness guarantees.

The number of research works proposing the incorporation of Web service model-based testing and verification functionality in service registries is rather limited. The addition of a lightweight verification mechanism to UDDI service registries was first proposed in (Tsai et al, 2003). The key idea was to attach so-called "test scripts" to Web service specifications for both service registry and service consumers to use. Before publishing a service advertisement at the service registry or before consuming a service the associated test scripts could be used to test the actual service and verify its behaviour. The proposed approach is very abstract and does not prescribe the use of a specific formal or informal method of representing service behaviour, nor one for generating the test scripts.

In (Bertolino et al., 2005) the authors propose a framework with an enhanced UDDI registry that generates test cases for Web services, executes them, and monitors the interactions between the service under test and other services already registered with the framework in order to verify conformance to the published specification. Emphasis is placed on verifying that a Web service is interoperable with other registered services, and the framework is called an "audition framework" in the sense that a Web service undergoes a monitored trial before being admitted. The authors suggest that the behavioural service specification should be expressed as a UML 2.0 Protocol State Machine (PSM) diagram that can be semi-automatically transformed into a Symbolic Transition System (STS) on which existing automated test generation methods can be readily applied. The utilisation of the proposed behavioural specification formalism for matchmaking among service advertisements and requests is left undefined. Discovery is assumed to be supported by the typical means available in UDDI, i.e. keyword-based search and categorisation.

In (Heckel and Mariani, 2005) the authors propose a "high-quality service discovery" approach that incorporates automatic testing and verification of Web Services before allowing their registration to the service registry. The authors propose Graph Transformation (GT) rules as the modelling formalism to be used for constructing behavioural service specifications. Conformance test cases are to be automatically generated from the provided specification and executed against the target Web Service. If the test is successfully passed, the service can be registered. Apart from testing and verification the GT-based service specifications can be also used for matchmaking among services and service requests that have been also expressed via GT rules. The proposed approach does not prescribe the use of UDDI or any other specific service registry specification as the technical infrastructure to support the approach.

A significant drawback in the above model-based verification approaches is that the test case derivation methods they employ cannot guarantee completeness in testing of the service implementations. In contrast, the Stream X-machine testing method on which our approach relies is proven to generate a complete set of test cases that can reveal all inconsistencies among an implementation under test and an SXM specification (Ipate and Holcombe, 1997). Moreover, a novel proposition in our approach is the use of the behavioural service specification by service consumers to perform validation after discovery, during the phase of service selection, through model animation or model checking. Validation is an important utility for service consumers, since it can assist them in selecting the most appropriate services from a list of candidates, regardless of the matchmaking and discovery method that was used to deliver this list.

3. MODELLING SERVICES AS STREAM X-MACHINES

Stream X-machines (SXMs) are a computational model capable of representing both the data and the control of a system. SXMs are special instances of the X-machines introduced in 1974 by Samuel Eilenberg (Eilenberg, 1974). They employ a diagrammatic approach of modelling control flow by extending the expressive power of finite state machines. In contrast to finite state machines, SXMs are capable of modelling non-trivial data structures by employing a memory attached to the state machine. Moreover, transitions between states are not labelled with simple input symbols but with processing functions. Processing functions receive input symbols and read memory values, and produce output symbols while modifying memory values. The benefit of adding the memory construct is that the state explosion is avoided and the number of states is reduced to those states which are considered critical for the correct modelling of the system's abstract control structure. A divide-and-conquer approach to design allows the model to hide some of the complexity in the transition functions, which are later exposed as simpler SXMs at the next level.

A Stream X-machine is defined as an 8-tuple, $(\Sigma, \Gamma, Q, M, \Phi, F, q_0, m_0)$ where:

- Σ and Γ is the input and output finite alphabet respectively;
- Q is the finite set of states;
- M is the (possibly) infinite set called memory;
- Φ, which is called the type of the machine SXM, is a finite set of partial functions (processing functions) φ that map an input and a memory state to an output and a new memory state, $\varphi : \Sigma \times M \rightarrow \Gamma \times M$;

- *F* is the next state partial function that given a state and a function from the type *Φ*, provides the next state, $F : Q \times \Phi \to Q$ (*F* is often described as a state transition diagram);

- q_0 and m_0 are the initial state and memory respectively.

Apart from being formal as well as proven to possess the computational power of Turing machines (Holcombe and Ipate, 1998), SXMs offer a highly effective testing method for verifying the conformance of a system's implementation against a specification. Stream X-machine models can be represented in XMDL (X-Machine Definition Language), a special-purpose markup language introduced in (Kapeti and Kefalas, 2000). XMDL has served as a common language for the development of numerous tools supporting Stream X-machines (Kefalas, Eleftherakis and Sotiriadou, 2003). An extension of XMDL to support an object-based notation was suggested in (Dranidis, Eleftherakis and Kefalas, 2005). The object-based extension, called XMDL-O, enables an easier and more readable specification of Stream X-machines.

In order to model the behaviour of a Web service using a Stream X-machine, the modeller must perform data-level and behaviour-level analysis to derive the appropriate SXM modelling constructs. Parallels can be easily drawn among a stateful Web service and a Stream X-machine, since they both accept inputs and produce outputs, while performing specific actions and moving from one internal state to another. SXM inputs correspond to SOAP request messages, outputs correspond to SOAP response messages, and processing functions correspond to Web service operation invocations in specific contexts (an operation invocation may map to more than one processing functions because of the potentially different input data parameters values provided). In addition, the modeller has to define the memory structure, not only as a substitute for internal state, but also to supply sample test data that can become part of the generated test sequences. SXM-based modelling is applicable in the context of complex conversational Web services where the result obtained from invoking a Web service operation depends not only on the consumer's input, but also on the internal state of the service.

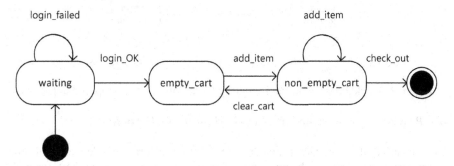

Figure 1 – Example of Stream X-machine model for a shopping cart Web service

Figure 1 illustrates an example SXM model of a simple Web service that provides the backend functionality of a shopping cart to Web-based client applications. The service comprises four operations (login, addToCart, clearCart, and checkout) allowing customers to perform authentication, add items to the shopping cart, clear the cart, and proceed to checkout. The SXM modelling constructs depicted in Figure 1 are the states belonging to set Q, the names of processing functions belonging to set Φ, and the state transition diagram corresponding to F. A fully-detailed description of this modelling example, including a complete definition of all processing functions, inputs, outputs and memory is provided in (Dranidis, Kourtesis and Ramollari, 2007).

4. ROLES AND ACTIVITIES IN THE PROPOSED APPROACH

The approach that we put forward in this paper involves all three types of stakeholders in a SOA environment, i.e. service providers, service registries, and service requestors (consumers). As depicted in Figure 2, the role of each stakeholder is associated with a number of activities. In brief, we propose that the behaviour of a Web service should be formally modelled at the provider-side, in order to facilitate registry-side verification at the time of service publication and consumer-side validation at the time of service selection. In the following three sections we present an overview of the activities performed by each stakeholder in the scheme.

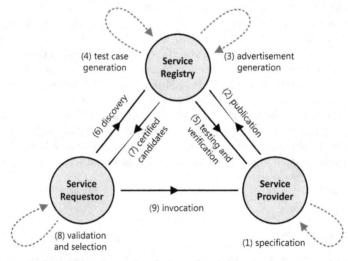

Figure 2 – Stakeholder roles and ordering of activities in the proposed approach

4.1 Provider-side construction of a behavioural specification

The objective of the service provider is to construct a formal model reflecting the behaviour of the service to be published (activity 1 in Figure 2) using the Stream X-machine (SXM) formalism as described in section 3. The SXM model must be encoded in XMDL-O and stored in an external document that must be subsequently "linked" with the service's WSDL document. The association among the two document artefacts can be established by employing the SAWSDL (Semantic Annotations for WSDL) (Farrell and Lausen, 2007) specification and its mechanism for annotating Web service descriptions with pointers to externally maintained semantically-rich specifications. In order to indicate the association between the two documents an SAWSDL *modelReference* annotation pointing to the URL of the SXM specification document must be placed within the *wsdl:portType* definition of the service's WSDL document.

The process of constructing an SXM model from a WSDL description can be automated to a great extent by modelling inputs, outputs, preconditions and effects (IOPE) as concepts in an OWL ontology and then pointing to them from within a WSDL document through SAWSDL annotations. The description of an approach for modelling Web service inputs and outputs in an OWL-DL ontology and then creating semantically annotated service descriptions using SAWSDL is provided in (Kourtesis and Paraskakis, 2008). The method has been extended for modelling preconditions and effects in an OWL-DL ontology and for capturing the IOPE semantics of Web service interfaces through SAWSDL annotations. An algorithm has been also defined for the semi-automated transformation of the resulting SAWSDL specification into an SXM specification, but the presentation of these extensions is beyond the scope of this paper. Modelling of IOPE semantics in the aforementioned manner would not only assist in increasing the automation of the SXM model construction process, but would also serve as a basis for performing semantically-enriched matchmaking and discovery for high-precision retrieval of services, as discussed in (Kourtesis and Paraskakis, 2008b).

Regardless of the method used to construct the SXM specification, manual or semi-automated, as soon as the semantically annotated WSDL document is complete, the provider must submit it to the service registry for processing and publication (activity 2).

4.2 Registry-side generation of test cases and verification

The objective of the service registry is to verify that the service implementation is functionally conformant to its advertised specification, and if this holds, provide a certification for the service advertisement. All activities within the service registry are automated, and their ordering is as follows. Firstly, the registry processes the incoming SAWSDL description and creates a service advertisement with a status of pending certification (activity 3). Secondly, the attached SXM specification is used for deriving a complete set of test cases that can reveal all inconsistencies in the service implementation to be verified (activity 4). Lastly, the executable tests are run by the registry's SOAP testing engine and if the results are successful (i.e. if the produced outputs match the expected ones) the service advertisement obtains certification status (activity 5).

The benefit of performing this procedure at the registry-side and at the time of publication, as opposed to performing it on the consumer-side at the time of service selection, is that it needs to be performed only once, by a trusted third party that assumes the responsibility of certification and can be held liable for its decisions. Since only successfully tested services receive certification status by the registry, consumers can be sure that the specifications of the services they discover are reliable sources of information.

As already mentioned, the SXM testing method that serves as the foundation of our approach is guaranteed to generate a complete, finite set of test cases that can reveal all inconsistencies among an SXM specification and an implementation under test. This is an important criterion for entrusting the process of verification and certification to the registry. The SXM testing method is a generalization of the W-method (Chow, 1978) and works on the basis that both specification and implementation could be represented as Stream X-machines with the same type Φ (i.e. both specification and implementation have the same processing functions), where Φ satisfies two fundamental design for test conditions: (i) completeness with respect to memory – all processing functions can be exercised from any memory value using appropriate inputs, and (ii) output distinguishability – any two different processing functions will produce different outputs if applied on the same memory/input pair. More details about the derivation of the test sequences are provided in (Dranidis, Kourtesis and Ramollari, 2007).

For our testing approach to be applicable, we assume that the operations of the Web service under test follow the request-response message exchange pattern, i.e. they accept a request message from the consumer and return a response message. This makes it possible to fulfil the condition for output distinguishability, and also enables the testing engine to understand which processing functions have been activated during an execution path based on responses of the service. We do not consider this restriction important or unrealistic, since the request-response message exchange pattern is currently the typical way of engineering Web services.

4.3 Consumer-side validation and service selection

The next activity in the process is for the service consumer to formulate a discovery query and submit it to the service registry (activity 6). The registry will perform some form of matchmaking based on the available advertisements and the specified request, and return the results (activity 7). The discovery and matchmaking method by which the candidate services will be derived is independent from the rest of the approach, and can be based on any existing method. A semantically-enhanced service matchmaking method such as the one described in (Kourtesis and Paraskakis, 2008) would however by strongly encouraged, since it is free of ambiguity, takes more information into consideration, and has the potential of resulting in more accurate matches. In any case, if the registry returns more than one certified services as matching candidates, the consumer must go through a service selection process (activity 8).

As already discussed, the SXM specification that is associated with each of the certified candidate services can be used not only for registry-side verification, but also for consumer-side validation during service selection. A method that enables behavioural validation is model animation through appropriate tools. During animation the consumer feeds the SXM model with sample inputs while observing the current state, transitions, processing functions, memory values, as well as outputs. The sample inputs to be provided for driving the animator can be the actual test data that were generated and used by the service registry at the phase of verification. This would relieve the service consumer from the burden of re-generating the data from the SXM specification.

The animation process can be readily supported by existing tools. X-System (Kapeti and Kefalas, 2000) is a Prolog-based tool supporting the animation of Stream X-machine models, while a Java-based graphical user interface on top of X-System is also available. In addition to animation, model checking techniques can be employed on the SXM model to check for desirable or undesirable properties specified with temporal logic formulae. Research on X-machines already offers a model-checking logic, called XmCTL, which extends Computation Tree Logic (CTL) with memory quantifiers in order to facilitate model-checking of temporal properties in X-machine models (Eleftherakis, Kefalas and Sotiriadou, 2001).

5. CONCLUSIONS

The contemporary IT infrastructure landscape is changing rapidly, and SOA-based solutions are becoming dominant. Collaborative business processes layered on top of SOA infrastructures are typically realised as compositions of autonomous Web services that are discovered and composed on the basis of some specification explicating their functional or non-functional properties. In highly dynamic and loosely coordinated environments service specifications can easily become outdated and dissolve into unreliable sources of information. To avoid making design-time decisions based of inaccurate information and incurring the associated cost of run-time errors we propose a registry-based testing and verification approach that can be used for ensuring that service specifications are reliable, i.e. that they correspond to the actual service implementations they are meant to model.

The approach that we put forward in this paper involves all three types of stakeholders in a SOA environment, i.e. service providers, service registries, and service consumers. The service registry becomes a trusted third party and certification authority that undertakes the responsibility of testing a service's implementation to verify that it conforms to its advertised formal specification. We propose the use of Stream X-machines (SXMs) as a powerful modelling formalism for constructing the behavioural specification of a Web service at the provider-side, in order to facilitate registry-side verification at the time of service publication and consumer-side validation at the time of service selection.

The particular strengths of the presented approach compared to other works in the literature can be summarised in three points. Firstly, a significant advantage of Stream X-machines compared to other behavioural modelling and testing formalisms is in their associated complete testing method, which is guaranteed to reveal all inconsistencies among a specification and the implementation under test. Secondly, the SXM specification and the generated test sets can be used not only for registry-side verification, but also for consumer-side validation after discovery and during service selection. Thirdly, the proposed approach can be readily supported by a number of existing tools for SXM modelling, test case generation, verification, and validation, as well as an existing open source service registry implementation for performing semantically-enhanced publication and discovery of services. The main objective for future research is the consolidation of existing techniques, methods and tools into a comprehensive application framework and the development of the connecting components and user-friendly interfaces that would be required in order to yield an all-inclusive solution with industrial applicability.

6. ACKNOWLEDGMENTS

This research work was partially supported by FUSION (Business process fusion based on semantically-enabled service-oriented business applications), a research project funded by the European Commission's 6th Framework Programme for RTD under contract number FP6-IST-2004-170835 (http://www.fusion-strep.eu/).

7. REFERENCES

1. Bertolino A., Frantzen I., Polini A. and Tretmans J. Audition of Web Services for Testing Conformance to Open Specified Protocols. *Architecting Systems with Trustworthy Components*, Springer LNCS 3938, 2006, pp. 1-25.

2. Chow T.S. Testing Software Design Modelled by Finite State Machines. *IEEE Transactions on Software Engineering, Vol. 4*, 1978, pp. 178-187.

3. Dranidis D., Eleftherakis G., and Kefalas P. Object-based Language for Generalized State Machines. *Annals of Mathematics, Computing and Teleinformatics (AMCT), Vol. 1, No. 3*, 2005, pp. 8-17.

4. Dranidis D., Kourtesis D. and Ramollari E. Formal Verification of Web Service Behavioural Conformance through Testing. *Annals of Mathematics, Computing & Teleinformatics (AMCT), Vol. 1, No. 5*, 2007, pp. 36-43.

5. Eilenberg S. *Automata, Languages and Machines, Volume A*. Academic Press, New York, 1974.

6. Eleftherakis G., Kefalas P., and Sotiriadou A. XmCTL: Extending Temporal Logic to Facilitate Formal Verification of X-machines. *Analele Universitatii Bucuresti, Matematica-Informatica*, 50:79-95, 2001.

7. Farrell J. and Lausen H. (Eds). *Semantic Annotations for WSDL and XML Schema (SAWSDL)*. W3C Recommendation, August 2007.

8. Heckel R. and Mariani L. Automatic Conformance Testing of Web Services. In Cerioli M. (Ed.): *FASE 2005*, LNCS 3442, Springer-Verlag Berlin Heidelberg 2005, pp. 34-48.

9. Holcombe M. and Ipate F. *Correct Systems: Building Business Process Solutions*. Springer Verlag, Berlin, 1998.

10. Ipate F. and Holcombe M. An integration testing method that is proved to find all faults. *International Journal of Computer Mathematics, Vol. 63*, 1997, pp. 159-178.

11. Kapeti E. and Kefalas P. A Design Language and Tool for X-Machine Specification. *Advances in Informatics*, Fotiadis D. and Nikolopoulos S. (Eds), World Scientific, 2000, pp. 134-145.

12. Kefalas P., Eleftherakis G. and Sotiriadou A. *Developing Tools for Formal Methods*. In Proceedings of the 9th Panhellenic Conference in Informatics (PCI 2003), November 2003, pp. 625-639.

13. Keum C., Kang S. and Ko I.Y. *Generating Test Cases for Web Services using Extended Finite State Machine*. In Proceedings of the 18th IFIP International Conference on Testing Communicating Systems (TestCom 2006), Springer, 2006, pp. 103-117.

14. Kourtesis D. and Paraskakis I. Web Service Discovery in the FUSION Semantic Registry. In Abramowicz W. and Fensel D. (Eds.): *BIS 2008*, LNBIP 7, Springer-Verlag Berlin Heidelberg 2008, pp. 285–296.

15. Kourtesis D. and Paraskakis I. Combining SAWSDL, OWL-DL and UDDI for Semantically Enhanced Web Service Discovery. In Bechhofer S. et al.(Eds.): *ESWC 2008*, LNCS 5021, Springer-Verlag Berlin Heidelberg 2008, pp. 614–628.

16. Laycock G. *The Theory and Practice of Specification-Based Software Testing*. PhD thesis, Department of Computer Science, University of Sheffield, UK, 1993.

17. Sinha A. and Paradkar A. *Model-based Functional Conformance Testing of Web Services Operating on Persistent Data*. In Proceedings of Workshop on Testing, Analysis and Verification of Web Services and Applications (TAV-WEB'06), July 2006, pp. 17-22.

18. Tsai W.T., Paul R., Cao Z., Yu L., Saimi A. and Xiao B. *Verification of Web Services using an Enhanced UDDI Server*. In Proceedings of 8th IEEE International Workshop on Object-oriented Real-time Dependable Systems (WORDS 2003), January 2003, pp. 131-138.

PART 16

SERVICE-ORIENTED APPROACHES

50

AN E-SERVICE SOA MODEL FOR VIRTUAL SERVICE ENTERPRISES

Christian Zirpins and Wolfgang Emmerich

Computer Science Department, University College London, UK
(C.Zirpins|W.Emmerich@cs.ucl.ac.uk)

Economic theory defines services as customisable, interactive processes that providers have the potential to carry out together with clients that benefit from their effects. It is understood that service transactions are best organised by means of virtual collaborative networks, where ICT allows configuring multiple providers and processes on a per-request basis. Existing conceptual models for virtual service enterprises propose service virtualisation to allow for flexible and agile regulation and enforcement of coordination between multiple providers and clients. In this paper, we present an approach for realising business service virtualisation based on software service technology. In particular, we propose a SOA model for representing virtual business service processes as e-services. E-service models specify interactions between multiple providers and clients of virtual service enterprises by means of patterns and allow for flexible regulation and enforcement of their coordination.

1. INTRODUCTION

Services make up a growing industry of intangible goods. It has been argued that organisational requirements to provide configurable, interactive and immaterial service processes are best met by virtual organisation [Picot and Neuburger 1998]. Respective virtual service enterprises are temporal organisational networks that abandon institutionalised network management in favour of information and communication technology (ICT). This allows for dynamic identification, initiation, negotiation operation and liquidation of service networks on a per-request basis.

As an important aspect of ICT support for virtual service enterprises, regulation and enforcement of coordination rules for cooperative activities of service client(s) and providers in temporal service networks need to be enabled in a flexible and agile manner. In earlier work, we have shown, how this can be archived by virtualisation of services themselves [Zirpins and Emmerich 2008b]. We have presented a conceptual reference model that explains how to coordinate a virtual production network (VPN) for services by means of planning and control production of virtualised business services (VBS). The latter procedures can be effectively supported by ICT. We showed that respective technology includes representations of virtual service processes (e-services) as well as structured methods for their planning and control (e-service management). Moreover, we presented evidence for the fitness of software service technologies [Papazoglou and Georgakopoulos 2003] and Web Services [Alonso et al. 2004] in this respect. Software service abstractions showed potential to represent virtual business service processes in a way that service oriented development life-cycle methodology could be adopted to regulate and enforce coordinative rules in virtual business service production networks (VBSPN).

Please use the following format when citing this chapter:

Zirpins, C. and Emmerich, W., 2008, in IFIP International Federation for Information Processing, Volume 283; *Pervasive Collaborative Networks*; Luis M. Camarinha-Matos, Willy Picard; (Boston: Springer), pp. 485–492.

In the PARIS research project (**P**attern-based **AR**chitectures for **S**ervice **I**nteraction – see http://www.cs.ucl.ac.uk/staff/c.zirpins/paris/), we have developed an approach to realise e-service technology by means of service-oriented software architecture (SOA) for e-services and service-oriented development life-cycle methodology for e-service management. In terms of e-services, we propose a general SOA model that defines how virtual business service processes (VBSP) according to our conceptual model are to be represented by software service abstractions. More explicit, we provide a formal e-service metamodel in UML that defines concepts of workflow, software service interaction processes as well as business service interaction underlying our e-service abstraction. The metamodel underlies the definition of a domain specific graphical modelling language for e-services that can be used to design and execute e-services in the course of planning and control of VBSPs.

In this paper we focus on the PARIS e-service metamodel and its SOA for representing VBSPs. Section 2 introduces the software architecture model that has been developed to realise e-services. This includes an informal systems model as well as a formal metamodel that defines structure and semantics of e-service design in UML. The paper closes with related work and a summary and outlook in sections 3 and 4.

2. SERVICE-ORIENTED ARCHITECTURE FOR E-SERVICES

Service virtualisation technology builds on realisation of virtual service processes. These VBSPs essentially act as interaction programs to flexibly regulate and rapidly enforce coordination of cooperative activities between members of virtual service networks. To archive this, VBSPs substitute interactive aspects of conventional service processes by ICT. The goal is for representations of communication endpoints and interaction process patterns to allow for formal specification and automated enforcement of interaction and coordination between operative information systems of network clients, providers and brokers. This ability shall then be used to integrate systems of network participants into temporal cooperative information systems for control of service production that we refer to as *e-service systems*. Generally, we refer to the integrative core of such a system as *e-service*. Furthermore, we distinguish regulation of composition logic by means of *e-service schemas* from enforcement of composition logic by means of *e-service instances*.

Our general concept is to leverage service-oriented software technology to realise e-service systems in general and e-services in particular. More precisely, we adopt SOA for e-services and service-oriented development life-cycle methodology for e-service management. In this paper, we focus on SOA for e-service instances and on design of e-service schemas as SOA models. In the following, we will first outline a specific *service-oriented software model* that explains the roles, functions and software service abstractions involved in the life-cycle of e-service systems. We will then present an UML-based *e-service metamodel* that gives a detailed description of SOA for e-service instances and builds the foundation of a graphical language for e-service schemas.

2.1 A Basic Model for Service-Oriented E-Service Systems

Service-oriented computing (SOC) is a paradigm for building and operating software application systems by means of service abstractions and architecture, utilising service development life-cycle methods and methodology. The paradigm is fundamentally described by "service-oriented models" (SOM) like that of [Papazoglou and Georgakopoulos 2003]. SOMs specify roles (e.g. client, provider, broker, aggregator, operator) and their functions (e.g. description, publishing, discovery, selection, access, coordination, composition, marketing, support etc.) with respect to service development on various abstraction levels (basic, composed, managed). In our approach to realise VBS by means of SOC technologies, we propose a SOM refinement for the case of managing e-service-systems. Our SOM corresponds to the PARIS VBSPN model and we refer to it as *PARIS SOM (PSOM)*. PSOM refines service abstractions, roles and role functions in order to match the requirements for service virtualisation in the PARIS conceptual model.

Firstly, PSOM refines software service abstractions for business service process virtualisation. The PARIS model defines *demands*, *assets* and *capabilities* as the main concepts of VBSPs. In PSOM, we map these concepts to refined software service abstractions. Demands and assets represent endpoints of clients and providers that handle interactions for consumption of service content. We map both concepts to refinements of atomic service abstractions referred to as *demand* and *asset service*. Demand and asset services are formally specified by service description languages and automatically controlled by means of service access mechanisms. We require specification and automation of service interaction steps by means of operational interfaces. Further specifications might include conversations or semantics.

Capabilities represent interaction process patterns of providers and brokers. They regulate and control an administrative procedure to access service content. We map this concept to a refinement of composite services referred to as *capability services*. Capability services are formally specified by means of service coordination protocols and automatically controlled by means of service composition schemas. We require specification and automation of service interaction processes by means of functional process structure, roles and implementation. Further specifications might include non-functional aspects. As regards concepts of flexible planning, we require specification of protocol patterns and their automated resolution into executable orchestration schemas. Such technologies are beyond current SOC state-of-the-art, but we propose a solution in our e-service metamodel. With respect to the structure of VBSPs, asset services are associated with local capability services that regulate and enforce interactions with demand services to access service contents. Furthermore, global capability services regulate and enforce interactions between local capability services to combine service content of various providers in a service network.

Fig.1 shows the refined service abstractions of PSOM and their relationships. Furthermore, it indicates the refinement of SOM roles and functions to match the roles of the PARIS conceptual model and their responsibilities of VBS production planning and control. Here, client- and provider roles of PSOM are both refinements of SOM service providers, as they provide atomic demand- and asset services. The coordinator role is a refinement of the SOM service aggregator, as it provides composite capability services. The abstract coordinator role is assigned to the concrete roles of broker and provider as regards global and local capability services.

In the pre-contact phase of VBS, PSOM roles are responsible for specification and mutually adjusting their services. Providers describe asset- and local capability services and publish them in repositories of brokers that are accessible within and outside of the service network. Outside of the network, clients query the repository to discover asset services and capability services. In turn, they specify their demand services and likewise publish them in a repository. Inside the network, brokers discover demand services as well as asset services and related local capability services. They specify global capability services that combine asset services with respect to demand services by composing respective local capability services.

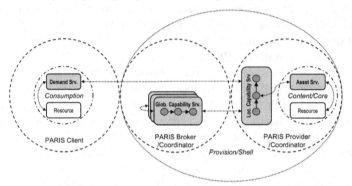

Figure 1 – Service-oriented Model of Business Service Virtualisation in PARIS

In the contact phase of VBS, roles of PSOM execute their services to automate control of business service processes. Brokers rapidly optimise and implement global capability services with respect to non-functional requirements of client requests. All other services can be implemented and deployed in the pre-contact phase. In turn, execution of global and local composite capability services automatically enforces the planned regulation of interactions in the business service process.

Finally, in the VBS post-contact phase, PSOM roles analyse service interaction logs that were monitored in the contact phase. With respect to the results, they might evolve specific aspects of the service specifications to optimise effectiveness or efficiency of the VBSP. They re-publish these changes for future service transactions.

2.2 Service-Oriented Software Architecture for E-Services

PSOM gives an overview of business service process virtualisation by means of software service abstractions. However, a more precise specification is needed in order to realise the indicated role functions of VBS transactions. Planning functions require a specification language that enables formal design, analysis and adjustment of all e-service parts. Control functions require a software architecture framework as well as executable languages to construct and run all e-service components. We provide a basis for both by means of a service-oriented metamodel for e-services that we refer to as *PARIS E-Service Metamodel (PSM)*. Classes and relationships defined in the metamodel translate to components and relationships of a service-oriented software architecture for e-services as well as syntactical elements and semantics of an UML-based language for e-service design.

PSM is as agnostic as possible with respect to specific SOC standards and technologies. Our conception aims at clear abstraction layers of platform independent e-service models and platform specific software service models that are precisely mapped to conform to service virtualisation requirements. PSM architecture does not define technology platforms to implement platform specific service models. The rationale is to define a generic framework architecture that is applicable to multiple existing SOC standards and technologies and to uncouple architectural concepts from their fast evolution cycles. Concrete mappings need to be defined from platform specific software service models onto concrete ones.

In order to represent process organisation of service provision, PSM defines a process-driven SOA. Abstracting from specific technologies, PSM builds on a generic notion of *working process* [Kosiol 1962]. In organisation theory, working processes involve performers that carry out associated activities of structured methods for the sake of transforming inputs into outputs. In PSM, we adopt these generic concepts for both business service processes and software service interaction processes and we base their mapping upon these common roots. Technically, we use a workflow metamodel to formalise working processes and define metamodels of software service interaction and e-services as stepwise refinements.

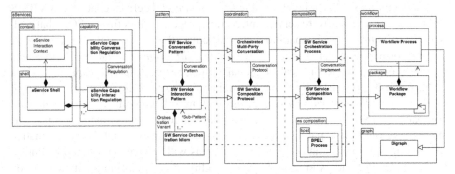

Figure 2 – Overview of the PARIS E-Service Metamodel (PSM)

Fig.2 shows an overview of PSM in terms of UML packages and key classes. The foundation is a *graph metamodel* that introduces *directed graphs (Digraph)* as a basis for higher-level process descriptions. In turn, PSM defines a graph-based *workflow metamodel*. Its main ingredients are workflow process and package elements defined in respective sub-models. *Workflow processes* refine and extend digraphs as regards concepts of general working processes including participants, applications, data and structured activities. *Workflow packages* offer a further structuring principle that allows defining multiple workflow processes with a shared scope.

On the next level, PSM refines and extends workflow elements as software service interaction processes. They either serve as coordination protocols to regulate service interactions or as composition schemas for automated enforcement of these regulations. Composition schemas are defined in the *composition metamodel* for services. It refines and extends workflow processes as *software (SW) service orchestration processes*. They are structured within *software service composition schema* containers that refine workflow packages. Coordination protocols are defined in the *coordination* metamodel as generalised perspective on service interaction processes. Here, orchestration processes are refined as *orchestrated multi-party conversations* that focus on fewer elements of service interaction with respect to coordinative regulation. Conversations are aggregated into *software service composition protocols*, which represent observable choreography in the course of service composition.

Beyond schemas and protocols, PSM defines an abstraction of interaction process pattern to capture multiple variants of interaction that are equivalent in terms of functional effects but different in terms of non-functional properties. Interaction patterns are defined in the *pattern metamodel* for service interaction. It refines and extends orchestrated multi-party conversations as *software service conversation patterns*. Conversation patterns allow flexible non-deterministic description of orchestrated conversations that are part of interaction patterns. *Software service interaction patterns* refine composition protocols as non-deterministic choreography protocols. They aggregate sets of interaction sub-patterns whose conversation patterns together comprise typical interaction situations with multiple implementations. Each sub-pattern can be root of an individual interaction pattern. Interaction patterns also contain a set of *software service orchestration idioms* that each represent one possible transformation of non-deterministic service conversation patterns into deterministic orchestrated multi-party conversations and service orchestration processes.

On the topmost PSOM level, the *eService metamodel* defines concepts of VBSPs and relates them to software service interaction processes. It defines a SOA that realises assets, demands and capabilities. In particular, the metamodel refines software service conversation patterns as *eService capability conversation regulations* that capture provision logic of local or global virtual business service capabilities in a flexible non-deterministic way. eService capability conversation patterns are part of *eService capability interaction regulations* that are refined software service interaction patterns. eService capability interaction regulations specify interaction patterns that involve multiple capability conversations of sub-patterns and define alternative coordination protocols and orchestration schemas with varying non-functional properties. Brokers/providers in charge of a capability are responsible for its interaction regulation and all related conversation regulations of sub-patterns. Multiple capability interaction regulations are composed into an *eService shell* that represents a holistic VBSP. It also contains eService roles (brokers, providers, clients) and endpoints of involved assets and demands including message data formats that are defined within a common *eService interaction context*.

From a top-down perspective, PSM concepts define how the design of a VBSP is to be structured, how its structural parts are to be specified by means of interaction patterns and how these specifications are to be implemented by software service interfaces and composition schemas. The successive layers correspond to platform independent and specific parts of a modelling hierarchy that can be extended and mapped to various concrete software service technology platforms. We have defined one such refinement in terms of Web Service composition. Here, the *ws composition metamodel* defines extended concepts of Web Service architecture like WSDL-based interface descriptions. From this model, we have defined a mapping onto BPEL software service composition descriptions that can be deployed and executed within BPEL-compliant software service composition middleware platforms.

The PSM modelling hierarchy encourages stepwise development of e-services by means of structured design, verification and transformation methods. Such methods are at the heart of our e-service management approach as they allow meeting agility and flexibility requirements of VBS transactions. As a basis for such methods, PSM sub-models define elements of a graph-based process specification language for VBSPs and software service interaction processes [Zirpins and Emmerich 2008a].

4. RELATED WORK

The focus of this document is on utilising pattern-based, process-driven SOA for flexible modelling of service-oriented collaborative information systems that represent coordinative regulations of business service processes and allow for their rapid adaptation and enforcement. In terms of related work, we will first discuss examples of VO modelling approaches that build on service federation concepts and then look at exemplary approaches to flexible modelling of interaction-based software architecture for collaborative information systems.

Service federation emerged as a paradigm for modelling VO structures and realisation of ICT infrastructure by means of SOC [Camarinha-Matos 2005]. Exemplary projects adopting the service federation paradigm include *Fetish-ETF* [Camarinha-Matos et al. 2001]. It follows a peer-to-peer type VO approach for service providers of a tourism industry cluster. A *promoter node* utilises service market mechanisms for virtual enterprise initiation and promotes services either in *atomic* form or as *value added services* that build on general distributed business processes. A second example is the *WebBIS project* [Benatallah et al. 2000] that employs a service model with rule-based coordination concept. It introduces *virtual enterprise services* that specify and enforce their individual coordination logic by means of ECA rules. They group in *communities* that resemble a peer-to-peer type VO. Our approach shares the adoption of a service federation approach. It differs in its focus on virtual service enterprises and its adoption of pattern-based SOA for increased flexibility.

Pattern-based modelling of flexible software architecture is tackled by several other approaches. Pattern-based modelling of process-driven SOA is proposed by [Zdun et al. 2007]. They introduce *software patterns* to capture best practises and identify their building blocks as *pattern primitives* that can be used for individual SOA models. An approach for context-aware adaptive workflow applications is proposed by [Modafferi et al. 2006]. The approach builds on a methodology for development of *context-sensitive business processes*. It includes language primitives to model context-sensitive regions of a process by means of *context change patterns* and transformation rules to construct BPEL processes. Udupi and Singh introduce a modelling approach for service interaction that includes pattern concepts [Udupi and Singh 2008]. They focus on agreement and enactment of *service engagements* based on *commitments* of autonomous parties. Commitments are combined as (virtual) *organisations* that include policies of involved participants and determine their interactions. Specification is guided by design-patterns. The main distinguishing factor of our work is the federated characteristic of our service interaction patterns and in particular the structuring of interworking software service orchestrations.

5. SUMMARY AND OUTLOOK

In this paper we have introduced a SOA model for virtual service enterprises. In particular, we have proposed an UML-based SOA metamodel for realisation of e-services that represent virtual service processes. Planning of virtual service processes by means of e-service modelling provides means to regulate coordination of cooperative activities in a service network. Concepts of service interaction patterns allow for flexibility of coordinative regulations as well as their rapid enforcement

For demonstration and evaluation, we have conducted a case study experiment in the area of computational chemistry e-science. It is based on polymorph prediction research, where benefits were expected from virtualisation of e-science labs. In PARIS, we have examined virtualisation of polymorph prediction labs as virtual scientific service production networks [Zirpins and Emmerich 2008a].

Our current work concentrates on e-service management technology. We are adopting enterprise architecture to integrate e-service-management into the wider context service enterprises. The resulting framework defines an engineering approach to run virtual service enterprises by means of e-service technology. We are developing a service-oriented development methodology and implementing a tool set demonstrator for our e-service SOA that includes a model-driven development tool chain as well as an execution platform based on OGSA and BPEL.

7. REFERENCES

[Alonso et al. 2004]   G. Alonso, F. Casati, H. Kuno, et al. *Web Services - Concepts, Architectures and Applications.* Springer, 2004.

[Benatallah et al. 2000]   B. Benatallah, B. Medjahed, A. Bouguettaya, A. Elmagarmid, et al. Composing and Maintaining Web-based Virtual Enterprises. In *VLDB Workshop on Technologies for E-Services, Cairo, Egypt, September 2000*, pages 155–174. Informal Proceedings, 2000.

[Camarinha-Matos 2005]   L. M. Camarinha-Matos. ICT Infrastructures for VO. In L. M. Camarinha-Matos, H. Afsarmanesh, and M. Ollus, editors, *Virtual Organisations: Systems and Practices*, pages 83–104. Springer, New York, 2005.

[Camarinha-Matos et al. 2001]   L. M. Camarinha-Matos, H. Afsarmanesh, E. C. Kaletas, and T. Cardoso. Service Federation in Virtual Organizations. In George L. Kovács, Peter Bertók, and Géza Haidegger, editors, *Digital Enterprise Challenges: Life-Cycle Approach to Management and Production*, IFIP Conference Proceedings 205, pages 305–324. Kluwer, 2001.

[Kosiol 1962]   E. Kosiol. *Organisation der Unternehmung.* , Wiesbaden, 1962.

[Modafferi et al. 2006]   S. Modafferi, B. Benatallah, F. Casati, and B. Pernici. A methodology for designing and managing context-aware workflows. In *Mobile Information Systems II; IFIP International Working Conference on Mobile Information Systems, (MOBIS) Leeds, UK, December 6–7, 2005*, volume 191/2005 of *IFIP*, pages 91–106. Springer Boston, 2006.

[Papazoglou and Georgakopoulos 2003]   M. P. Papazoglou and D. Georgakopoulos. Service-Oriented Computing: Introduction. *Communications of the ACM*, 46(10):24–28, 2003.

[Picot and Neuburger 1998]   A. Picot and R. Neuburger. Virtuelle Organisationsformen im Dienstleistungssektor. In M. Bruhn and H. Meffert, editors, *Handbuch Dienstleistungsmanagement*, pages 513–534. Gabler, Wiesbaden, 1998.

[Udupi and Singh 2008]   Y. B. Udupi and M. P. Singh. Design Patterns for Policy-Based Service Engagements. Technical Report TR-2008-3, Department of Computer Science, North Carolina State University, 2008.

[Zdun et al. 2007]   U. Zdun, C. Hentrich, and S. Dustdar. Modelling Process-Driven and Service-Oriented Architectures Using Patterns and Pattern Primitives. *ACM Transaction on the Web*, 1(3):14:1–14:44, 2007.

[Zirpins and Emmerich 2008a]   C. Zirpins and W. Emmerich. Service-Oriented Modelling and Design of Virtual Business Services. Research notes, University College London, Dept. of Computer Science, 2008.

[Zirpins and Emmerich 2008b]   C. Zirpins and W. Emmerich. A Reference Model of Virtual Service Production Networks. *Service Oriented Computing and Applications*, (Special Issue on: Service Intelligence and Service Science), 2008.

51

A SERVICE ORIENTED FRAMEWORK FOR MOBILE BUSINESS VIRTUAL COMMUNITIES

Julien Subercaze[1], Pierre Maret[1],
Jacques Calmet[2], Pravin Pawar[3]

[1]INSA-LYON, LIRIS (CNRS UMR 5205), FRANCE, julien.subercaze@liris.cnrs.fr,
pierre.maret@liris.cnrs.fr,
[2]University of Karlsruhe (TH), GERMANY, calmet@ira.uka.de
[3]University of Twente, THE NETHERLANDS, P. Pawar@utwente.nl

The rise of the availability of a variety of mobile devices in the personal and professional domains leads to an increased need of middleware and organizational structures. Due to the recent improvement of the computing power of mobile devices, mobile users may now also act as service providers. We design a service-oriented architecture to introduce mobile virtual communities enabling mobile devices to be used also as service providers.

1. INTRODUCTION

The growing market of mobile devices, along with the ubiquitous availability of wireless and broadband access networks has opened a new era of market solutions. The sale of internet compatible devices is growing exponentially in recent years. For example, the sale of PDA units has reached the 17.7 million mark in 2006[1], a 25.4% increase over 2005. Also, the manufacturer *Research In Motion*, that dominates the market of PDA devices with its Blackberry line of products, announced a 76.5% jump of sales in the first quarter of 2007[2][3].

Simultaneously, the world of sensors is experiencing dramatic changes. For example, prices of imaging sensors since the introduction of CMOS sensors[4] are falling sharply while their quality is increasing[5], and medical sensors prices also follow the same trend. As a *Research and Marketers* report noticed, "*With the (actual) price of medical sensors (...), low cost and high volume sales have become the key to remaining competitive in the disposable sensors market*"[6].

---

[1] http://www.m-travel.com/news/2002/02/pda_sales_incre.html
[2] http://www.rim.net/investors/pdf/2007rim_ar.pdf
[3] http://www.computing.co.uk/computing/news/2193170/blackberry-sales-double
[4] http://www.instat.com/abstract.asp?id=161&SKU=IN0703690MI
[5] http://www.purchasing.com/article/CA6499634.htm
[6]http://www.researchandmarkets.com/reports/365353/world_market_for_sensor_opportunities_in.pdf

Please use the following format when citing this chapter:

Subercaze, J., Maret, P., Calmet, J. and Pawar, P., 2008, in IFIP International Federation for Information Processing, Volume 283; *Pervasive Collaborative Networks*; Luis M. Camarinha-Matos, Willy Picard; (Boston: Springer), pp. 493–500.

Location sensors, i.e. GPS sensors, when not already embedded in mobile devices, are also available at much lower prices than only two years ago. A recent survey[7] shows a demand of mobile users to have an integrated GPS in their next mobile phone. Professional users are also fully concerned with these new tendencies. In the medical field, the use of specific external and internal non-intrusive sensors to treat patients, and the general use of mobile devices by healthcare providers are growing rapidly.

All of these changes show that we are witnessing the development of three trends in parallel: firstly, an increasing processing capability of mobile devices; secondly, an ever growing ubiquitous connectivity and thirdly, the widespread availability of sensors which can be interfaced to mobile devices respectively. These current trends assessed together result in the emergence of new user behaviors and open new opportunities for software products that will take full advantages of these features.

In this paper we describe our approach for mobile business virtual communities (MBVC). It follows the principles of service-oriented architecture that extends for business application our previous definition of virtual knowledge communities (Maret, 2008). Section 2 of the paper investigates related work on virtual organizations and communities, mobility and middleware support for web services. Section 3 describes the service-oriented features, while section 4 describes the mobile virtual communities platform architecture, this extends an off the shelf open source community software to include our service oriented architecture. In section 5 we present an example of MBVC based on this architecture. Finally we present some concluding comments in section 6.

2. RELATED WORKS

Current investigations on virtual communities and virtual organizations focus often on the service oriented architecture. (Baglietto 2005) presents such an architecture implemented in the case of cargo and transport business area.(Shan 2006) defines a high level visual language for the description of service compositions in virtual organisations for non expert users. None of these architectures take the mobility feature into account.

Web services can be embedded on mobile devices, using mobile middleware such as those proposed in (Pratistha, 2003), (Srirama, 2006) or (Pawar, 2007). In our work, we rely on the middleware developed by Pawar (2007), which was initialy implemented for the remote patient telemonitoring in the mobile health domain.

Virtual enterprises have been defined as "a temporary consortium of autonomous, diverse and possibly geographically dispersed organizations that pool their resources to meet short-term objectives and exploit fast-changing market trends" (Davulcu, 1999).

Creation of virtual enterprises has to be made through a contract. Contracts could take into account business and/or legal issues. (Metso, 2005) proposes a B2B web service based middleware to set up business level contracts between the different

---

[7] http://www.itnews.com.au/News/67338,gps-to-boost-mobile-phone-sales.aspx

actors. (van den Heuvel, 2003) proposes an architecture that coordinates web-service based organizations with contracts, focusing on business and legal issues.

Mobile virtual communities are introduced in (El Morr, 2007) and (Kawash, 2007). However, interfacing mobile virtual communities with service oriented architectures for virtual enterprises has not been fully explored. The aim of this paper is to combine virtual communities' facilities and middleware support for mobile web services. We use also contracts and negotiations tools for SOA, which lead then to the creation of MBVC.

3. SERVICE ORIENTED ARCHITECTURE

In service oriented architecture (SOA), the different entities taking part in the system (also called actors) are either 'service providers' or 'service consumers'. This is not exclusive: actors can also be both providers and consumers.. A service is a unit of work which can be done by a service provider to achieve desired end results, for a service consumer. In SOA, mobile devices usually play the role of service consumers. Due to the evolution of the computing power, connectivity ability and storage capacity, the role of mobile devices has to be reconsidered. Indeed, we use mobile devices also as service providers. We will now first present the architecture for SOA mobile business virtual communities and then analyze the creation process and the use of a virtual community within the SOA.

A service federation approach has been identified in (Camarinha-Matos, 2005).The partners are service providers, they form a community of providers and the resulting enterprise is a complex composition and orchestration of their services.

We propose a so-called Community Platform, based on the principles of SOA and using open source community software. Two types of actors are fundamental to this platform. The first ones are *actors providing services* and willing to propose them for the creation of Mobile Business Virtual Communities (MBVCs). They form the community of Providers. The providers could be fixed as well as mobile. The second type of actors is composed of the *end-users* (or service consumers), using MBVCs, i.e. using some of the proposed services. End-users form the second community.

Combining both communities (Providers and End-users) into one platform leads to some valuable advantages: The community platform considers the user profiles and actions, as well as the user's rights, and then selects the most appropriate service for this user. This is clearly of interest for business applications, but it can also be implemented towards medical assistance for instance (Pawar, 2008). Since our architecture includes also mobile devices as service providers, end-users can invoke these mobile services (Fig.1).

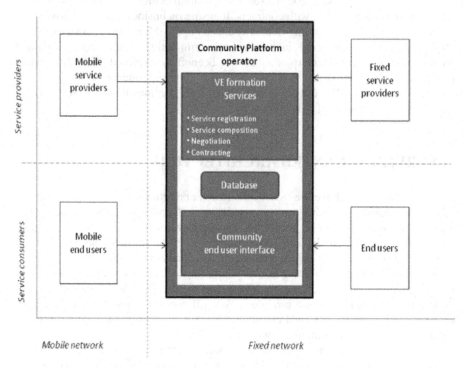

Figure 1: Fixed and mobile service providers and consumers around the community platform.

4. MOBILE BUSINESS VIRTUAL COMMUNITIES

4.1 Creation of Mobile Business Virtual Communities

The creation of the MBVC (fig. 2) is organized by the community platform operator (CPO); the first step is the registration of the services on the platform. Any user could register as a service provider. The next step consists of the partners' aggregation. This is controlled by one of the partner, using profile information, history and all other data it can find. Partners finalize their engagements in the contracting step. The Virtual Enterprises (VE) is then published.

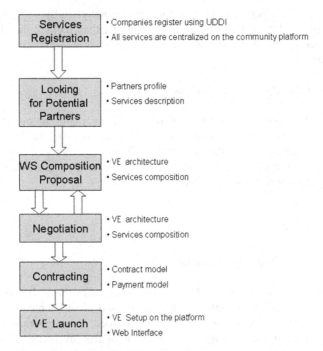

Figure2 : VE Creation Diagram

The community platform operator (CPO) provides the facilities to the service providers to create virtual enterprise within the platform. Revenue sources of the CPO are decided during the contract step. Revenues of the CPO may be for example calculated on a percentage on transactions, or on the duration of the community or on any agreed upon procedure.

The list of VE is presented on the community platform. End-users decide then to act as members of a given VE. Members can use fixed or mobile devices and they can participate using fixed or mobile services in sharing data and documents within the communities. On the platform, several communities are identified. The service providers form the community of providers. On the other side, end users are also forming a community. Then around the VE formed by the service providers, several communities (MBVC) involving the end users are made up. We demonstrate those communities in the next section.

4.2 Implementation

Our implementation is based upon an off-the-shelf open source community platform. The platform Dolphin[8] was tuned to fulfill the requirements of the Service Oriented Architecture. We select to use Web Services technologies for this implementation and we rely on the PHP-based library NuSoap[9] to interface Dolphin

---

[8] http://www.boonex.com/products/dolphin/
[9] http://sourceforge.net/projects/nusoap/

native PHP with Web Services. The VE formation is not yet fully implemented, so it remains controlled by the CPO. VEs are created and they include mobile services. Users can become members of these communities; they can participate and make use of the services.

4.3 Problems related to mobile devices

The use of mobile devices involves numerous problems regarding connectivity and quality of service. Problems of connectivity are solved by using the Mobile Service Platform (MSP) middleware (Pawar 2007). MSP exploit multi-homing support for the resource constrained and handheld mobile devices and integrates a *QoS context source* to take QoS issues into account.

5. USE CASES

5.1 Content server within communities

User generated content is one of the growing business in the web economy. This generates a considerable amount of traffic, composed of the content generated by user. This content production is usually not rewarded. They provide storage and sharing facilities and the contents are generated for free by users, although those websites generate subsequent revenue through displayed advertisements. Using our platform, providers of pictures or videos register as content providers. The proposed service is in this case the access to pictures or videos. Members of this MBVC can send requests to the mobile service in order to get some pictures or videos. Members could be both content consumers and content producers. The community platform guarantees that content producers are rewarded according to the traffic generated by their provided content. End-users are thus encouraged to provide original contents.

The design of this MBVC encompassing mobile services matches our platform architecture. It consists of 1) the basic Virtual Communities features 2) the content provider service and 3) the billing service (fig. 3). Notice that the billing service is part of the platform because it is shared by all MBVCs. Others services can be added to the communities, such as the file storage service, the video encoding service and context advertisement service. Providers can be companies specializing in either fixed or mobile services or in both of them.

This business case enabled by our architecture is a win-win situation. Users earn money from the content they provide and the file storage and video encoding companies. High quality contents are also encouraged and this is also valuable for all: end-user, content providers, service providers and platform operator.

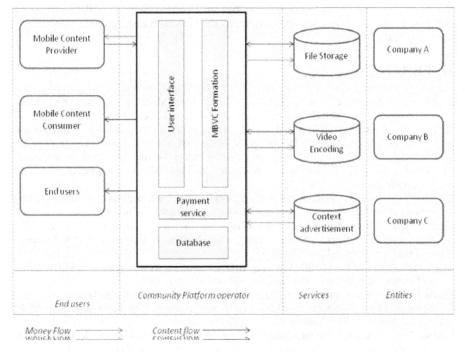

Figure 3: Use-case "Video sharing"

5.2 Decision making support within communities

Employees of a company form a community centered on its activity. Knowledge management into companies is a strategic issue, especially when decisions must be taken with limited time and incomplete knowledge.

Models and implementations of decision making processes have been proposed in several trivial or complex forms. (Yang 2007) gives an example of a service that makes decision with uncertain knowledge based on Bayesian networks.

Let us imagine a company's employee loading a decision making process as a service on her/his mobile device. Once this device is recognized within the company's community on the community platform, the service (decision making process) can be declared and then be used as a mobile service.

6. CONCLUSION

In this paper we introduce mobile virtual business communities based on a service-oriented architecture. We design an architecture centered upon the community platform operator. This platform supports the creation of virtual communities based on a service federation approach. Relying on an adequate middleware we integrate mobile devices as services providers and include them as active resources shared within virtual communities. We outline the architecture and our first use case considers mobile service provider in a service federation approach organization.

Future works will concentrate on the creation process of communities providing composed services and interfaces to create easily web based business community using mashups[10] editors.

REFERENCES

P. Maret, J. Subercaze, and J. Calmet , Peer-to-Peer Model for Virtual Knowledge Communities, Proc. of *AIKED 2008*, Cambridge, UK, 365-370, 2008.

C. El Morr, J. Kawash. Mobile virtual communities research: a synthesis of current trends and a look at future perspectives. *IJWBC , 3*, 386-403, 2007.

Jalal Kawash, C. El Morr . A novel collaboration model for mobile virtual communities. *IJWBC* , 427-447, 2007.Pierpaolo Baglietto, Massimo Maresca, Andrea Parodi, and Nicola Zingirian.

Stepwise deployment methodology of a service oriented architecture for business communities. *Information & Software Technology*, 47(6):427–436, 2005.

César Garita, Ulises Agiiero, Lorenzo Guadamuz, *Network-Centric Collaboration and Supporting Frameworks*, chapter Areito: A Development Platform For Virtual Learning Communities, pages 323 – 332. 2006.

Janne Metso and Lea Kutvonen. Managing virtual organizations with contracts. In *Workshop on Contract Architectures and Languages (CoALa 2005)*, 2005.

Pravin Pawar, Bert-Jan van Beijnum, Arjan J. H. Peddemors, and Aart van Halteren. Context-aware middleware support for the nomadic mobile services on multi-homed handheld mobile devices. In *ISCC*, pages 341–348. IEEE, 2007.

I. Made Putera Pratistha, Nicholas Nicoloudis, and Simon Cuce. A microservices framework on mobile devices. In Liang-Jie Zhang, editor, *IWCS*, pages 320–325. CSREA Press, 2003

Baohua Shan, Yanbo Han, and Hongcui Wang. Enabling virtual organizations with an agent-mediated service framework. In *CSCWD*, pages 626–631. IEEE, 2006.

Satish Narayana Srirama, Matthias Jarke, and Wolfgang Prinz. Mobile web service provisioning. In *AICT/ICIW*, page 120. IEEE Computer Society, 2006.

Willem-Jan van den Heuvel and Hans Weigand. Coordinating web-service enabled business transactions with contracts. In Johann Eder and Michele Missikov, editors, CAiSE, volume 2681 of *Lecture Notes in Computer Science*, pages 568–583. Springer, 2003.

Lai Xu and Paul de Vrieze. Fundaments of virtual organization E-contracting. In Luis M. Camarinha-Matos, Hamideh Afsarmanesh, Paulo Novais, and Cesar Analide, editors, *Virtual Enterprises and Collaborative Networks*, volume 243 of IFIP, pages 209–216. Springer, 2007.

Yang Yi, *A Framework for Decision Support Systems Adapted to Uncertain Knowledge*, PhD Dissertation Karlsruhe University, 2007.

Hasan Davulcu, Michael Kifer, L. Robert Pokorny, C. R. Ramakrishnan, I. V. Ramakrishnan, and Steven Dawson. Modeling and analysis of interactions in virtual enterprises. In *RIDE*, pages 12–18, 1999

---

[10] http://en.wikipedia.org/wiki/Mashup_%28web_application_hybrid%29

DYNAMIC ADAPTATION, COMPOSITION AND ORCHESTRATION OF WEB SERVICES IN VIRTUAL ENVIRONMENTS

52

Peter Bertok
Stephen Reynolds
RMIT University
Melbourne, AUSTRALIA
peter.bertok@rmit.edu.au

To solve interaction and discovery problems, Web services need to be unambiguously described. Existing technologies, such as WSDL describe the functional aspects of Web services, network service end points and interfaces. The semantic aspects are more difficult to handle, as different organizations operate in different ways, and may use different information models and domain specific vocabularies.

This paper explores how ontologies can be used to orchestrate dynamic Web service compositions. A shared ontology is developed that exchanges data and meaning. By adding "smarts" to the service description and not including within the applications' processing of the data, the descriptions are able to move freely between domains. Examples from a bookshop service are used indicate that the proposed method's is well suited to virtual environments.

1. INTRODUCTION

The World Wide Web is shifting from a predominantly information interaction platform operating with HTML documents to a service interaction platform operating with Web services [1], but existing technologies offer only partial solutions [2]. The power of Web services lies in the successful management of the relationships and composition of cooperating business services in a distributed application-to-application (A2A) or business-to-business (B2B) environment. Web service composition is very complex, due to the high autonomy, high distribution, and high heterogeneity of the services involved [3].

Today's Web services are predominantly isolated remote data services. An example is an international online trader that has built an intra-organizational service that operates within a localised environment. Our goal was to build reactive and adaptive Web services that can automatically reason with different business schemas to find a matching service. If a matching service is found, it invokes the service to form a virtual business environment. This happens automatically without user intervention.

At the same time, that most existing Web service composition and orchestration methods are assuming an unknown, but fairly static environment, where once a matching service has been found, invocation and execution is straightforward. The solution proposed here addresses the issue of failures by detecting failed services and invoking replacements.

Please use the following format when citing this chapter:

Bertok, P. and Reynolds, S., 2008, in IFIP International Federation for Information Processing, Volume 283; *Pervasive Collaborative Networks*; Luis M. Camarinha-Matos, Willy Picard; (Boston: Springer), pp. 501–508.

Web service architecture is implemented via the Web Service Technology Stack (Table 1). Data moves up and down through the layers, each layer addressing a separate business problem.

Table 1: The Web Service Technology Stack [2]

Layer	Description
Discovery	Means for consumers to fetch descriptions of providers
Description	Description of the service, contact point and its use
Packaging	Date encoding, serialization and marshalling
Transport	Application-to-application protocols. TCP, HTTP
Network	Addressing and routing

Adaptation and composition of Web services is implemented via the Description and Discovery service layers. In the proposed system, the existing Description and Discovery service layer were extended, to avoid the need to rewrite other parts of the infrastructure because of the specialization of the layers.

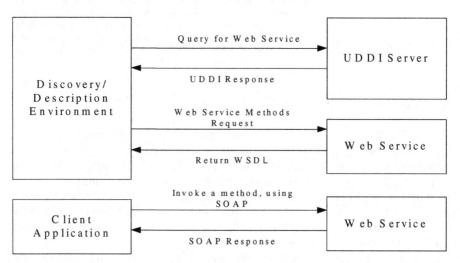

Figure 1: Web Service Technologies [2]

To call a Web service, firstly, a web service has to be discovered by querying a UDDI server. The server returns information about Web services that match the specified requirements and a link to a WSDL document that details the methods exposed by the Web service (Figure 1). The methods and parameters described by the WSDL document are used to build a SOAP request to invoke the web service.

2. PREVIOUS WORK

2.1 Concepts
Carman, Serafini, Traverso [4] propose that the complex problem of Web service composition can be simplified by breaking services into their constitute parts. An

aggregate Web service is composed of *atomic Web services*. An atomic Web service is broken into states, document types and actions that collectively identify it uniquely. Data heterogeneity is resolved by data mapping requirements that decide if data described by one data type can be substituted by another. DAML-S is used to specify schemas that describe the operations (precondition, post conditions), goals and states that are available to the system when it needs to discover and execute service operations. These schemas would semantically describe data types and enable other Web services to automatically interpret and match data types.

Sirin, Hendler, Parsia [5] present a prototype for *semi-automatic binding* of Web Services based on service constraints. They enhanced the business process flow representation of BPEL4WS with semantics to enable runtime discovery of Web Services and to resolve inter-service dependencies during dynamic binding of Web process flows. Business constraints were captured in the DAM-S ontology technology, a Semantic UDDI module was to discover the services and a dynamic binder and invoker was used. However, the Web services and their inter-dependencies still had to be known at design time.

For *composition,* Korhonen, Pajunen, Puustjärvi [6] propose that a Web service compositor should select the most appropriate available service based on policies and regulations that match the caller's organizational requirements. They describe Web services via syntactic, semantic and pragmatic (contextual), properties. They also introduce the concept of "conversation" to identify all the business documents that compose a business model. While the solution allows designers to choose Web service providers that meet organizational goals, it may be too complicated to achieve business goals.

The WebTransact framework by Tosic, Pagurek, Esfandiari and Patel [7] is a centralized approach to the *management* of distributed Web services. It enables structurally and semantically different services to work together to achieve the same business goal via composition and by integrating semantically equivalent remote services. It coordinates the sequence of service invocation within a Web service composition and manages the data flow between the services.

Automatic orchestration of services has been addressed in static environments only [11].

2.2 Related Technologies

Collaboration protocol profiles (CPPs) have been defined for ebXML, which describe the transport, security, communication protocols and business processes an organization recognizes to set up an ebXML relationship. These protocols and processes specify syntax and enable communication, but interoperability for message content, including invocations, has to be provided by additional methods. Our solution goes further by providing information for service invocation, and defining a pluggable architecture that does not need additional, connecting elements.

A number of ontological modeling and description methods are available for Web services, such as WSMO, SWSO, OWL-S, which address the same space. Some of them also have associated reasoners. Our implementation uses OWL-S markup language constructs to describe Web service capabilities and properties.

3. PROPOSED SOLUTION

3.1 Outline and Contribution

We describe a framework for automatic Web service orchestration: for dataflow management and to manage the execution of atomic units. The Web services share a stateful context to support distributed transactions, and a compensation process is available to respond to failure conditions, in particular in case of long-running transactions. The description of the services allows them to remain mobile and independent of the deployment environment. Our main contribution is the last part, dynamic orchestration that addresses issues related to the composition of services external to the choreographer, and an ability to respond to failure conditions.

3.2 Web Service Description

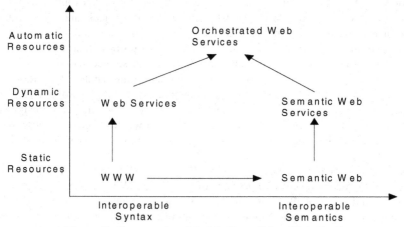

Figure 2: Convergence Models Describing Web Services

Approach

Web service description is used to compose Web services into units of work that accomplish definite goals, e.g. fulfilling a single order of a series of parts from a buyer to different suppliers. A Web service is unambiguously described by its type, and is defined by the messages exchanged between its service partners. Web service type description includes functionality as well as business semantics.

Figure 2 adapted from [8] shows that by converging the syntactic and semantics models the WWW moves from a static resource environment to a machine-processable, automatic resource environment, where functional and semantic information is described, and relationships are published and available for discovery. Figure 3 (adapted from [10]) illustrates the associated information that needs to be published to enable a collaborative Web Service Environment.

Active Information Management

In order to be able to move freely between domains, data needs to be classified and rules applied so each domain can understand not only the data, but also their relationship. XML only provides syntactic interoperability, and we added semantic information in the form of "smarts" to the data, rather than include it in the application's processing of the data [9].

To achieve Active Management of Data we use four properties [9]: XML documents for a single domain, XML documents composed from multiple domains, XML documents that can describe relationships, and Trust Relationships.

After applying all the above, the data is application-independent, composable and classifiable. The data is tagged with information that is machine-understandable and can be extended to form an ontology.

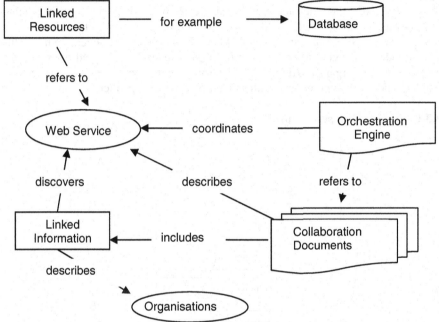

Figure 3: Advanced Web Service Model

Business Profiles

Profiles help organize and apply rules and properties of Web services within diverse application environments. To support discovery of services, Web services are abstracted to a set of high-level specifications that allow for description of profiles and a means of associating them to Web services. The profile lists the technical information needed to do business electronically, i.e. which XML schemas to use, security rules etc, and describe the relationship and dependencies between services. The profiles exist as independent documents to enable them to be composed in unique combinations and need to be accessible online.

Web Service Orchestration

To compose Web services into a structured workflow, an implementation neutral standard vocabulary (structured protocol) script is used, together with an orchestration engine to implement the process descriptions. This script is compiled into runtime scripts that are executed by the orchestration engine. The script provides syntax for describing business workflow logic, sequences and logic, and description of public and private business protocols.

Web Service Description
We describe a Web service as an ontology, so Web service profiles become syntactically interoperable, and terms can be mapped between the participating Web services. This adds a representation and inference layer on top of the Web's current layers and enables Web services to play the different roles, such as information brokers, search agents, information filters and intelligent information integrators.

Because of using an ontology language, Web services possess knowledge representation and can behave like plug-in sockets when connecting the user to *virtual business environments*. We can also use ontological reasoners both at edit-time (model construction) and at run-time (system execution), and Web service compositors can organise individual Web services into aggregated Web services by matching business requirements with suitable Web service partners.

3.3 Capturing Web service profiles

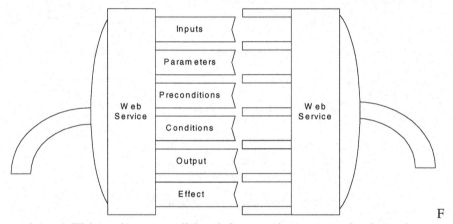

F

igure 4: Web services externalising their properties to create plug-in services

To externalise a Web service, it is viewed as a black box with properties, such as preconditions, input, output etc, as shown in figure 4. The rich description of Web services enables them to connect and form virtual business environments (figure 5).

Web service workflow
The composite service workflow is described by first defining each atomic service, then by describing the composite services that aggregate the cooperating atomic services into a structured workflow. An example is ItemBuy, a composite Web service that uses the following atomic services: LocateItem, PutItemInCart, SignIn, CreateAcct, CreateProfile and LoadProfile. The Web service parameters and service workflows are stored in a repository.

3.4 Implementation

Our prototype extends the Description Layer (Web Service Technology Stack) by adding an upper ontology layer to describe the Web services and service properties unambiguously. The advantages of this approach are:

- It complies with the Web Service Technology Stack, which is universally available.
- Existing Web service technologies such as WSDL and UDDI can be used to combine the syntactical discovery of Web services (via an UDDI registry) with the semantic description of a Web service profile Ontology.

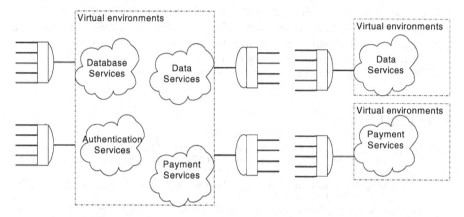

Figure 5: Web services creating business virtual environments

The profile matching is transparent to the requester. A Service Broker provided the functionality of discovering suitable Web services, by querying syntactic Web service information via the UDDI registry and semantic information via the semantic repository. The results of the queries are combined and presented to a Reasoner that mediates between various Web service profile ontologies by applying rule reasoning. This approach also provides limited fault-tolerance, and service failures result in the initiation of a new discovery process.

The combination of semantic and syntactical querying enabled service providers to publish their services via the UDDI server. The UDDI service was extended with an OWL classification identifier that also contained links to associated OWL-S documents. The Service Broker queries the UDDI server to obtain the OWL classifier, downloads the associated OWL-S document links and sends the links to the Reasoner. The Reasoner uses the links to query the services profile, identify the service types and discover if the service types are compatible. This reasoning is automatic. The rules defined were simple "is a" or "has a" rules which can be extended. The service providers must plan ahead when they publish their services by adding this special classification.

4. CONCLUSION

Web service compositions often involve external services that are outside the control of the orchestrator. This raises the problem of matching services syntactically and semantically, and responding to failures.

In our solution, automatic service discovery and composition was achieved via modelling the services property types and their messages as an ontology, which enabled a reasoner to mediate between services. To discover matching services, machines automatically query and reason the data, arbitrate between descriptions and then choose the most appropriate service, based on a given set of rules.

After detecting service failures or unavailability of services, the framework can initiate a new service discovery to readjust execution, and provide limited resilience.

A prototype model was built that combines a UDDI registry service with a semantic framework. By enhancing the WSDL descriptions, a Web service is unambiguously identified via its type. Using ontologies enabled reasoning by querying the data to identify type and its relationships. The prototype demonstrated that services could understand not only their data types but also other services' data types that they had no prior knowledge of or relationship with.

5. REFERENCES

1. Paulo F. Pires, Mário R. F. Benevides, and Marta Mattoso *"Building Reliable Web Services Compositions"*. Computer Science Department. COPPE - Federal University of Rio de Janeiro, Brazil, 2002
2. James Snell, Doug Tidwell and Pavel Kulchenko *"Programming Web Services with SOAP"*. O'Reilly, ISBN: 0-596-00095-2, January 2002
3. Vladimir Tosic, Bernard Pagurek, Babak Esfandiari, Kruti Patel. *"On Various Approaches to Dynamic Adaptation of Distributed Component Compositions"*. OCIECE-02-02, June 2002.
4. Mark Carman and Luciano Serafini and Paolo Traverso, *"Web Service Composition as Planning"*, carman,serafini,traverso@irst.itc.it, http://www.zurich.ibm.com/pdf/ebizz/icaps-ws.pdf
5. Evren Sirin, James Hendler, and Bijan Parsia, *"Semi-automatic Composition of Web Services using Semantic Descriptions"*, University of Maryland, Computer Science Department, College Park MD 20742, USA evren@cs.umd.edu, University of Maryland, MIND Lab, 8400 Baltimore Ave, College Park MD 20740, USA hendler@cs.umd.edu, bparsia@isr.umd.edu
6. Jarmo Korhonen,Lasse Pajunen and Juha Puustjärvi, *"Automatic Composition of Web Service Workflows Using a Semantic Agent"*. Software business and Engineering Institute,Helsinki University of Technology, {jarmo.korhonen,lasse.pajunen,juha.puustjarvi}@hut.fi, Proceedings of the IEEE/WIC International Conference on Web
7. Vladimir Tosic, Bernard Pagurek, Babak Esfandiari, Kruti Patel, *"On the Management of Compositions of Web Services"*. Network Management and Artificial Intelligence Lab, Department of Systems and Computer Engineering, Carleton University, Ottawa, Ontario, Canada {vladimir, bernie, babak, kpatel}@sce.carleton.ca
8. The Semantic Web, A guide to the Future of XML, and Knowledge Management, Micheal C. Doaconta, Leo J Obrst, Kevin T. Smith, Wiley Publishing. Inc, 2003
9. Michael C. Daconta, Leo J. Obrst,Kevin T. Smith, Wiley Publishing, Inc. *"The Semantic Web-A Guide to the Future of XML, Web Services, and Knowledge Management"* ISBN: 0471432571.
10. Tim Berners-Lee, Original Web proposal to CERN, http://www.w3.org/History/1989/proposal.html
11. Dyaz, G.; Cambronero, M.E.; Pardo, J.J.; Valero, V.; Cuartero, F. *"Automatic generation of Correct Web Services Choreographies and Orchestrations with Model Checking Techniques"*, Telecommunications, 2006. AICT-ICIW apos;06. International Conference on Internet and Web Applications and Services/Advanced International Conference on Volume , Issue , 19-25 Feb. 2006 Page(s): 186 - 186

53

AN APPROACH FOR ESTABLISHING TRUST RELATIONSHIPS IN THE WEB SERVICE TECHNOLOGY

Diego Zuquim Guimarães Garcia, Maria Beatriz Felgar de Toledo

Institute of Computing, University of Campinas, BRAZIL
{diego.garcia,beatriz}@ic.unicamp.br

Some solutions have been proposed to deal with the establishment of Web service relationships. For instance, a consortium has developed the Web Services Trust Language (WS-Trust) that offers a trust model for Web services. However, trust is one aspect in a set of aspects involved in Web service security that includes, for instance, privacy preservation. Based on this fact, the goal of this paper is to propose a trust approach for Web services. The approach integrates WS-Trust with standards for policy and ontology, which are used to preserve privacy.

1. INTRODUCTION

In the current market, organizations depend on getting involved in collaborations with other organizations for responding to some market opportunities. Significant progress has been done towards making the Web service technology a suitable solution for supporting such collaborations. For example, the interoperability among software systems is an important benefit of this technology. However, there are still open issues hindering this, including the lack of suitable mechanisms to support trust management.

A base for collaborations among organizations is the trust among them (Msanjila and Afsrarmanesh, 2007). This paper deals with technical aspects for the establishment of trust relationships. It focuses on trust relationships among entities in the Web service technology. Thus, the proposed approach is suitable for the establishment of trust relationships among software systems representing organizations in the dynamic Web service environment.

Some solutions have been proposed to deal with trust management in Web services. Among them, the Web Services Trust Language (WS-Trust) (Nadalin et al., 2007) deserves special consideration. At present, it is an OASIS (Organization for the Advancement of Structured Information Standards) standard. It defines a Web service trust model. However, trust is just one aspect involved in Web service security and some security aspects have relationships among them (Geuer-Pollmann and Claessens, 2005).

The goal of this paper is to propose an approach for trust relationship establishment that, differently from the current approaches, integrates WS-Trust with the Web Services Policy Framework (WS-Policy) (Bajaj et al., 2006). This

Please use the following format when citing this chapter:

Garcia, D.Z.G. and Felgar de Toledo, M.B., 2008, in IFIP International Federation for Information Processing, Volume 283; *Pervasive Collaborative Networks*; Luis M. Camarinha-Matos, Willy Picard; (Boston: Springer), pp. 509–516.

paper deals specifically with policies for privacy preservation and uses the Platform for Privacy Preferences (P3P) (Cranor et al., 2002).

The use of WS-Policy may restrict relationships among interoperable services. In order to overcome this limitation, a privacy ontology in Web Ontology Language (OWL) (Patel-Schneider et al., 2004) is used for annotating policies. This semantic information is used to verify if providers and consumers have compatible policies.

The rest of the paper is organized as follows. Section 2 presents basic concepts. Section 3 describes the proposed approach for trust establishment. Section 4 discusses related work. Finally, Section 5 closes the paper with conclusions.

2. BASIC CONCEPTS

2.1 Web Services and Policies

In the Web service technology, organizations (providers) provide Web services to other organizations (consumers). An organization can take both roles. A Web service is an electronic service identified by a URI (Uniform Resource Identifier). XML (eXtensible Markup Language) standards are used to specify service interfaces and to invoke services through the Web. The Web service technology comprises three basic standards (Alonso et al., 2004):

- Web Services Description Language (WSDL): a format for describing the functionality of a service;
- Universal Description Discovery & Integration (UDDI): a registry that supports service publication and discovery;
- SOAP (formerly Simple Object Access Protocol): a protocol for message exchange among services.

Additional standards are under development. One example is WS-Policy (Bajaj et al., 2006). It provides a model for expressing service properties as policies. Policies can be associated with XML elements, as defined in the Web Services Policy Attachment (WS-PolicyAttachment) specification. A policy is a collection of alternatives and each policy alternative is a collection of assertions. An assertion is defined as an individual requirement, capability or other property. Assertions specify characteristics that are critical to service selection and use, for instance, Quality of Service (QoS) attributes.

2.2 Web Service Security

In Web services, mechanisms to protect SOAP messages are defined in the Web Services Security (WS-Security) standard (Nadalin et al., 2006). They include digital signature, to protect against inappropriate message alteration, and encryption, to deal with incorrect message disclosure.

Services have to exchange security tokens to secure their communications. A security token is a collection of claims. A claim is a statement made by an entity, for instance an identity or capability statement. However, each service needs to determine if it can trust the other one, that is, to accept as true the claims in the token sent by the other service. This can be accomplished directly or by means of a third party. WS-Trust (Nadalin et al., 2007) defines extensions that build on WS-Security mechanisms to broker trust relationships.

There are standards for other aspects of Web service security (Zhang, 2005). However, the Web service technology still lacks a standard for privacy preservation. There is a privacy standard for the Web. P3P (Cranor et al., 2002) is a World Wide Web Consortium (W3C) Recommendation for a Web privacy framework. It defines a privacy vocabulary. The developing P3P Version 1.1 includes a mechanism that can be used to employ P3P with other protocols and applications, beyond HyperText Transfer Protocol (HTTP) transactions, including XML applications.

3. WEB SERVICE TRUST ESTABLISHMENT

In the approach, to interact with a service, consumers must send policies that satisfy the service policy. Consumers that try to interact with services, but do not possess the trusted tokens required by the services, are rejected. The approach is illustrated in Figure 1.

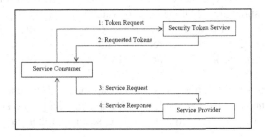

Figure 1 – Approach for Web service trust

Sometimes, consumers do not possess suitable policies to satisfy service policies. In this case, the consumer uses a Security Token Service to obtain the necessary tokens (Step 1 in Figure 1). Security Token Services are trusted third-party authorities defined by WS-Trust that issue tokens. Tokens are included into WS-Policy policies and are signed to guarantee that they have been issued by Security Token Services. After receiving a policy with the necessary tokens from the Security Token Service (Step 2), the consumer uses it to interact with the service to which the policy applies (Step 3). The service verifies the consumer policy in order to confirm that the consumer satisfies its requirements. After the verification, the service responds the consumer request (Step 4).

A proof-of-possession token received by the consumer along with a security token can be used to indicate that it has the right to use the security token.

Security Token Services are Web services and define policies. Thus, consumers must provide suitable tokens to use Security Token Services. After verifying that the tokens received from a consumer have been issued by Security Token Services and that the tokens can be used by the consumer, the Security Token Service issues the requested tokens.

Two messages are used for issuing tokens. The *RequestSecurityToken* message is used for requesting the issuance of tokens. The *RequestSecurityTokenResponse* message is used for returning issued tokens.

The *RequestSecurityToken* message is prepared by the consumer as follows:
1.   The message is signed by the consumer with its private key;
2.   Then, it is encrypted using the public key of the Security Token Service.

After receiving the *RequestSecurityToken* message, the Security Token Service sends a *RequestSecurityTokenResponse* message. This message includes policies with the requested security tokens and the associated proof-of-possession tokens. The Security Token Service performs the following steps to create a security token:
1.   The Security Token Service generates a symmetric key;
2.   It encrypts the key using the public key of the service, which the consumer wants to use, and includes the encrypted key into the security token;
3.   Then, it includes the requested claims into the token;
4.   Finally, it signs the token using its private key.

The Security Token Service creates a proof-of-possession token as follows:
1.   It encrypts the symmetric key using the public key of the consumer and includes the encrypted key into the proof-of-possession token;
2.   Then, it signs the token using its private key.

After receiving the *RequestSecurityTokenResponse* message, the consumer sends the token together with the service request. This message is prepared as follows:
1.   The symmetric key from the proof-of-possession token is decrypted by the consumer;
2.   Then, the service request is signed using the symmetric key;
3.   The signed service request is encrypted using the public key of the service;
4.   Finally, the service request and the security token are included into the request message.

After receiving the request message, in order to execute the requested operation, the service performs the following steps:
1.   The service verifies the claims in the token;
2.   Then, it decrypts the symmetric key from the security token;
3.   Finally, the service decrypts the service request.

3.1 Trust Brokering

In addition to token issuance, that is, the creation of a security token and its proof-of-possession token, Security Token Services are responsible for other actions:
- Validation: the authenticity of an issued token is evaluated;
- Renewal: a new validity period is defined for an issued token whose validity period has expired;
- Cancellation: the use of an issued token is terminated.

These actions are performed using the same messages used for issuing tokens. These messages are specified below.

The *RequestSecurityToken* message includes the following attributes and elements:
- *Context*: a context identifier to enable the correlation of the request and the subsequent related messages;

- *RequestType*: the requested action (token issuance, validation, renewal or cancellation);
- *TokenType*: the type of the requested security tokens;
- *Lifetime*: the desired validity period for the security tokens;
- *AppliesTo*: the service, which the consumer wants to use and to which the security tokens apply;
- *ProviderPolicy*: the policy of the service with the required tokens that the consumer does not possess;
- *ConsumerPolicy*: the policy of the consumer with tokens that are necessary for the execution of the requested action;
- *IssuedTokenPolicy*: a policy with tokens to be validated, renewed or cancelled.

The *RequestSecurityTokenResponse* message includes the following attributes and elements:

- *Context*: the context identifier from the associated *RequestSecurityToken*;
- *Lifetime*: the lifetime of the returned tokens, which can be different from the requested validity period;
- *RequestedSecurityToken*: a policy with the requested security tokens;
- *RequestedProofToken*: a policy with the proof-of-possession tokens associated with the security tokens included in the message;
- *RequestResult*: an indication of the result of the requested action.

3.2 Privacy Policies for Supporting Trust Establishment

In the approach, the establishment of trust relationships is controlled using policies. Policies are used during different phases of the Web service life cycle:

- At design time, service providers define policies describing privacy preservation properties of their Web services and tokens that must be presented and proved by consumers;
- At runtime, service consumers define policies stating their tokens and privacy preservation properties that should be offered by Web services.

The provider and consumer policies are intersected to compute the effective privacy policy. This policy indicates the interoperability between the participants in terms of privacy preservation.

The basic structure of policies is compliant with the WS-Policy normal form, which is shown in Figure 2.

01	<p:Policy>
02	<p:ExactlyOne>
03	(<p:All>
04	(<Assertion ...> ... </Assertion>)*
05	</p:All>)*
06	</p:ExactlyOne>
07	</p:Policy>

Figure 2 – Basic policy structure

In Figure 2, *p* is a prefix for the WS-Policy namespace URI. In addition to the components included into the normal form, other general-purpose components can facilitate policy manipulation. A policy includes the following components:

- *Policy*: the root element that indicates a policy;
- *Name, Id*: two kinds of policy identification may be used. Either the policy is associated with an absolute URI, using the *Name* attribute, or it is associated with a reference within the enclosing document, using the *Id* attribute;
- *PolicyReference*: the *PolicyReference* element may be used to include the content of a policy into another policy;
- *Service*: a provider policy includes a *Service* element to describe details of the service implementation for which the policy has been specified. A consumer policy includes this element to specify details of the service type to which the policy applies;
- Operators: in a policy, policy alternatives are grouped into an *ExactlyOne* operator. The *All* operator represents a policy alternative and groups the alternative assertions;
- Assertions: policy assertions are elements that represent consumer privacy requirements and service privacy capabilities. A policy assertion may contain nested assertions and a nested policy.

It is in the assertion components that a policy is specialized. Policy assertions use concepts from a privacy ontology based on the P3P vocabulary. The ontology supports a high abstraction level for dealing with privacy preservation goals. The elements defined in the privacy ontology are described in Table 1.

Table 1 – Privacy ontology elements

Privacy Element	Description
Data items	Data items required to use services
Recipients	Entities that receive data items directly or indirectly
Use purposes	Purposes for which data items are used
Availability duration	Retention time for data items

Policy operations defined by WS-Policy may be used for processing privacy policies. For example, the intersection operation is used to determine providers whose privacy policies are suitable for a given consumer policy.

4. RELATED WORK

Some studies in the area of Web services that use WS-Trust are presented below.

Fang et al (Fang et al., 2004) and Wang (Wang, 2006) describe conversation establishment protocols.

Dini et al (Dini et al., 2005) propose an extension to WS-Trust for supporting self-adaptable trust based on past relationships between services.

Semantics for the main mechanisms of WS-Trust and protocols based on WS-Trust are developed in (Bhargavan et al., 2007).

Most of the work deals with trust in an isolated manner. Relationships among different aspects of security are not considered. Policy management, for instance, may be integrated into the WS-Trust trust model.

Work on Web service policies (Mukhi and Plebani, 2004) offers contributions to trust management. For example, mechanisms such as policy merge and intersection can be applied to manipulate security tokens. The same happens with work on QoS semantics. The approach of using ontologies for specifying QoS is employed in studies on some aspects of security. Kagal et al (Kagal et al., 2004) use the Semantic Web technology to handle authorization for Web services. Shields et al (Shields et al., 2006) propose an approach for the specification of access control policies.

Trust management using policies can employ a similar approach. An ontology may be used to capture semantic information about policy assertions. This information improves policy intersection, since intersection considering only the syntax of policies may not identify all compatible policies. In this case, trust relationships are not restricted by the verifications of characteristics performed during their establishment. In this work, this is accomplished by extending WS-Policy with the use of OWL and integrating it into WS-Trust.

5. CONCLUSIONS

The Web service technology still lacks facilities to deal with security. Particularly, the lack of suitable support for trust management is hindering its wide deployment. In the Web service architecture, the WS-Trust standard offers a framework for trust management. However, the current approach does not offer a mechanism for integrating trust and privacy policy management.

This issue has to be addressed in order to make the Web service technology a suitable solution for supporting collaborations among organizations. Trust is a base for such collaborations (Loss et al., 2007) and privacy is an important concern in this area (Masaud-Wahaishi et al., 2007).

In this paper, an approach that combines WS-Trust, WS-Policy and OWL was introduced to support the establishment of trust relationships with privacy preservation in the Web service technology. Policies are used to control security token exchange and privacy compatibility verification. A P3P-based ontology helps specifying semantics-enriched policies, which describe privacy requirements and capabilities of service consumers and providers.

The main contribution of this paper is extending the trust management approach for Web services with the use of semantic policies to enable service participants to establish trust relationships in conformity with privacy policies.

Future work includes investigating the possibility of extending the proposed approach with the inclusion of components of other privacy approaches, such as the approaches of rights management (Kenny and Korba, 2002) and pseudonym technology (Song et al., 2006). Moreover, the integration of the proposed approach and solutions for other aspects of Web service security may also be considered (Geuer-Pollmann and Claessens, 2005). Finally, a case study may be used to evaluate the benefits of the approach. Future work may be developed on these issues in order to support the applicability of the proposed approach in scenarios with different security constraints.

Acknowledgements

This project is supported by FAPESP.

6. REFERENCES

1.   Alonso, G., Casati, F., Kuno, H., Machiraju, V. Web Services: Concepts, Architectures and Applications. Springer. 2004.
2.   Bajaj, S., et al. Web Services Policy 1.2 - Framework. W3C, April 2006. http://www.w3.org/Submission/2006/SUBM-WS-Policy-20060425/, accessed on 02/2008.
3.   Bhargavan, K., Corin, R., Fournet, C., Gordon, A. D. Secure Sessions for Web Services. ACM Transactions on Information System Security. Vol. 10, No. 2, pg. 8, 2007.
4.   Cranor, L., Langheinrich, M., Marchiori, M., Presler-Marshall, M., Reagle, J. The Platform for Privacy Preferences 1.0 (P3P1.0) Specification. W3C, April 2002. http://www.w3.org/TR/2002/REC-P3P-20020416/, accessed on 02/2008.
5.   Dini, O. A., Moh, M., Clemm, A. Web Services: Self-adaptable Trust Mechanisms. In Proceedings of the Advanced industrial Conference on Telecommunications/Service Assurance with Partial and intermittent Resources Conference/E-Learning on Telecommunications Workshop (AICT-2005), pg. 83-89, Lisbon. July 2005.
6.   Fang, L., Meder, S., Chevassut, O., Siebenlist, F. Secure Password-based Authenticated Key Exchange for Web Services. In Proceedings of the Workshop on Secure Web Services (SWS-2004), pg. 9-15, Fairfax. October 2004.
7.   Geuer-Pollmann, C., Claessens, J. Web Services and Web Service Security Standards. Information Security Technical Report. Vol. 10, No. 1, pg. 15-24, 2005.
8.   Kagal, L., Paolucci, M., Srinivasan, N., Denker, G., Finin, T., Sycara, K. Authorization and Privacy for Semantic Web Services. IEEE Intelligent Systems. Vol. 19, No. 4, pg. 50-56, 2004.
9.   Kenny, S., Korba, L. Adapting Digital Rights Management to Privacy Rights Management. Computers & Security. Vol. 21, No. 7, pg. 648-664, 2002.
10. Loss, L., Schons, C. H., Neves, R. M., Delavy, I. L., Chudzikiewicz, I. S., Vogt, A. M. C., Trust Building in Collaborative Networked Organizations Supported by Communities of Practice, in Establishing the Foundation of Collaborative Networks, Springer, pg. 23-30, 2007.
11. Masaud-Wahaishi, A., Ghenniwa, H., Shen, W., A Privacy-Based Brokering Architecture for Collaboration in Virtual Environments, in Establishing the Foundation of Collaborative Networks, Springer, pg. 283-290, 2007.
12. Msanjila, S. S., Afsrarmanesh, H., Towards Establishing Trust Relationships among Organizations in VBEs, in Establishing the Foundation of Collaborative Networks, Springer, pg. 3-14, 2007.
13. Mukhi, N. K., Plebani, P. Supporting Policy-driven Behaviors in Web Services: Experiences and Issues. In Proceedings of the International Conference on Service Oriented Computing (SOC-2004), pg. 322-328, New York. November 2004.
14. Nadalin, A., Goodner, M., Gudgin, M., Barbir, A., Granqvist, H. WS-Trust Version 1.3. OASIS, March 2007. http://docs.oasis-open.org/ws-sx/ws-trust/200512/ws-trust-1.3-os.pdf, accessed on 02/2008.
15. Nadalin, A., Kaler, C., Monzillo, R., Hallam-Baker, P. Web Services Security: SOAP Message Security. OASIS, February 2006. http://oasis-open.org/committees/download.php/16790/wss-v1.1-spec-os-SOAPMessageSecurity.pdf, accessed on 02/2008.
16. Patel-Schneider. P. F., Hayes, P., Horrocks, I. OWL Web Ontology Language Semantics and Abstract Syntax. W3C, February 2004. http://w3.org/TR/owl-semantics/, accessed on 02/2008.
17. Shields, B., Molloy, O., Lyons, G., Duggan, J. Using Semantic Rules to Determine Access Control for Web Services. In Proceedings of the World Wide Web Conference (WWW-2006), pg. 913-914, Edinburgh. May 2006.
18. Song, R., Korba, L., Yee, G. O., Pseudonym Technology for E-Services, in Privacy Protection for E-Services, IGI, pg. 141-171, 2006.
19. Wang, J. A Web Services Secure Conversation Establishment Protocol Based on Forwarded Trust. In Proceedings of the International Conference on Web Services (ICWS-2006), pg. 569-576, Chicago. September 2006.
20. Zhang, J. Trustworthy Web Services: Actions for Now. IT Professional. Vol. 7, No. 1, pg. 32-36, 2005.

PART 17

TRANSPORTATION NETWORKS & MOBILE BUSINESS

IMPACT OF BENEFIT SHARING AMONG COMPANIES IN THE IMPLANTATION OF A COLLABORATIVE TRANSPORTATION SYSTEM - AN APPLICATION IN THE FURNITURE INDUSTRY

54

Jean-François Audy[1] and Sophie D'Amours[2]

1 Doctoral Student, Department of Mechanical Engineering, CIRRELT, FORAC Research Consortium, Laval University, CANADA, jean-francois.audy@cirrelt.ca
2 Professor, Department of Mechanical Engineering, CIRRELT, FORAC Research Consortium, Laval University, CANADA, sophie.damours@forac.ulaval.ca

Transportation has become an increasingly important part of the Canadian furniture industry supply chain. Even when different furniture companies ship to the same regions, the same cities and/or the same furniture retailers, coordination between two or more companies is rare. Recently, interest in collaborative transportation planning to support coordination has intensified as important potential benefits (e.g. cost and delivery time reductions) have been identified. Even though substantial benefits can be realized, the methods for sharing benefits among companies as well as the leadership of the collaboration implementation are key issues in deciding on a logistics scenario for the collaboration. In this paper, the impacts of these two key issues are illustrated using an industrial case study of four Canadian furniture companies shipping to the United-States.

1. INTRODUCTION

With 95-96% of the total export value over the last decades (IC, 2008), the main export market of the Canadian furniture industry is the United States. As neighbouring countries, most deliveries are done by truck over long distances. In 2006, the exportation value was $CDN 3.9 billion, a decrease of 6.9% of the historical peak in 2000, while the total export value of furniture in US rose by 173% (ITA, 2008). Increased competition from countries with low production costs, mainly China, together with escalating fuel prices and environmental concerns have created the need to improve transportation efficiency.

Last year's appreciation of the Canadian dollar against the US dollar as well as the request of furniture retailers to reduce delivery time have also added extra pressure on the Canadian furniture industry supply chain. Efficiency, velocity and flexibility of transportation operations form part of the essential elements in attaining the characteristics of the furniture manufacturer of the future described by (Archambault *et al.*, 2006).

However, even when different furniture companies located in the same region ship to the same market regions, the same cities and/or the same furniture retailers,

Please use the following format when citing this chapter:

Audy, J.-F. and D'Amours, S., 2008, in IFIP International Federation for Information Processing, Volume 283; *Pervasive Collaborative Networks*; Luis M. Camarinha-Matos, Willy Picard; (Boston: Springer), pp. 519–532.

coordination in the transportation operations between two or more companies is rare. In the furniture industry of the Canadian province of Quebec, which employs a third of the work force in the furniture industry in Canada (MEDIE, 2007), the interest in transportation operations coordination by collaborative planning has heightened as significant potential benefits have been identified in two recent internal studies (Audy, 2007) and (Audy *et al.*, 2008).

By exploring different logistics scenarios allowing collaborative transportation planning among a group of furniture companies, cost and delivery time reductions have been identified as well as gain in market geographic coverage. Even though a logistics scenario of collaboration can provide substantial benefits for the group, each company will evaluate a scenario in regard of its own benefits. Some benefits are computed according to a sharing rule which divide among the companies the group benefit, therefore using a given rule instead of another have an impact on the appreciation level of each scenario by each company. Consequently, the implementation of the collaborative transportation planning implies both, a decision on the logistics scenario as well as a decision on the sharing rule(s). In this paper, we study a set of situations in which the leadership of the collaboration is assumes by only one company.

In this paper, we first introduce in section 2 the transportation planning problem studied in the context of the Canadian furniture industry. Then, in section 3, we present a general framework for collaborative transportation planning. We discuss the benefits of collaborative transportation planning and how they can be shared. We also present a set of four logistics scenarios allowing an implementation of collaborative transportation planning in an industrial case study of four furniture companies. In section 4, the numerical results obtained on each of the logistics scenarios are presented. The core of this paper refers to Section 5 in which the impact of different benefit sharing methods as well as the implementation leadership is illustrated and discussed using the case study. Finally, concluding remarks are provided.

2. TRANSPORTATION PLANNING

In the Quebec's furniture industry, most customer orders are less-than-truckload size shipments and are delivered by truck to the furniture retailers. Some companies' ship palletized disassembled furniture while others, such as the companies in the case study, ship assembled furniture inside cardboard boxes. For the latter, the volume of the trailer is the capacity limit rather than the weight. The maximum volume is variable depending on the assorted boxes' dimensions and the skill of the loading staff. In the case study, the limit has been fixed around a conservative volume of 2900 cubic feet and all cardboard boxes of an order must be carried together in order to visit the customer only once.

Even when the furniture company is make-to-stock or make-to-order, furniture companies realize their transportation by a carrier operating mainly according to one of the two following modes.

The first mode is multiple-stop truckload (TL) operations. The TL carrier delivers a trailer to the shipping dock of the furniture company who loads the trailer with many shipments. Occasionally, only one shipment will fill the trailer but, on average, 9 to 21 shipments are needed to do so. Soon after the trailer is loaded, a driver of the TL carrier will leave for the destination of its first customer delivery. Since the shipments are not handled again before their delivery to the customer, the loading of the trailer must respect the 'First In, Last Out' constraint: the sequence of the deliveries of the shipments is the reverse of the sequence of the loading of the shipments in the trailer.

Thus the loading decisions are tightly linked to the truck routing decisions. Efficient planning is a key issue for short delivery time and reduced cost. This planning is commonly done on a weekly basis by the furniture company. Each planned route must respect operational constraints such as the driver's hours of service regulations (i.e. working/driving time daily limits and minimum daily rest time) and the business hours of the customers. The cost of a route is proportional to the total one-way traveling distance (i.e. from the dock of the company to the last customer delivery including all intermediate stops) with specific traveling distance rates by destination zone (i.e. the states of the last customer delivery). A cost by intermediate stop, a cost for customs documentation preparation and a fuel surcharge is also charged on each route.

The second mode is less-than-truckload (LTL) operations. The LTL carrier always keeps a trailer at the furniture company in order to allow the company to load its shipment as it is ready. Each day or so, the carrier comes with a new trailer and leaves with the previous one to collect these shipments and bring them to its terminal. The LTL carrier handles these transportation/consolidation operations with many furniture companies in order to consolidate a large number of shipments at its terminal and in order to achieve truck routing planning several times a week and dispatch drivers regularly. After a shipment has been collected at the company, the LTL carrier guarantees its delivery inside a specific time range by destination zone. The increase of potential damage due to additional orders handled is a disadvantage of the LTL mode.

Without being concerned with the planning, the furniture company is charged on each of its shipments rather than on a route basis. The cost is proportional to the shipment volume, with specific rates by volume range and destination zone. The cost of shipment is subject to a minimum charge in addition to a fuel surcharge. The rate table structure of LTL carrier enables computing the cost of a shipment to the advantage or the disadvantage of the shipper, see e.g. (Klincewicz and Rosenwein, 1997) and (Caputo *et al.*, 2005). The first is applied in the case study as this is the present situation for one of the companies.

When it is really cost-effective and the customer allows it, a furniture company operating with the first mode could use a regional LTL carrier. In this case, rather than planning the shipment delivery up to customer location, the delivery is planned up to one of the regional LTL carrier terminals who offers the service to the customer (e.g. within a radius of 200-300 Km). In the case study, the regional terminals network of the North American carrier USF (www.usfc.com) has been used as a base. The cost charged by a regional LTL carrier is usually proportional to the shipment weight and subject to a minimum charge in addition to a fuel surcharge.

3. TRANSPORTATION PLANNING

Actually, the companies in the case study realize their transportation operations with the carrier/mode they judge to be more beneficial for them. (Caputo *et al.*, 2005) report that although different criteria may influence the selection of a carrier, such as quality of service, schedule reliability (both for pickup and delivery), possibility of negotiating terms and conditions, geographic location and cost, the latter is often the most important as is the case for the four companies. Therefore, the case study focuses on the cost reduction benefit although delivery time is also measured. Meeting delivery time is a critical additional criterion for the companies as well as special requirements related to the handling of assembled furniture (e.g. air ride suspension trailer, careful handling staff).

According to (Cruijssen *et al.*, 2007a), identifying and exploiting win-win situations among companies at the same level of the supply chain in order to increase their performance is about *horizontal cooperation*. We can consider this case study as an example of horizontal cooperation. The literature provides interesting case studies of horizontal cooperation among companies which report cost-savings opportunities, see e.g. (Bahrami, 2002), (Frisk *et al.*, 2006), (le Blanc *et al.*, 2007), (Cruijssen *et al.*, 2007b) and (Ergun *et al.*, 2007). In this paper, when the companies accomplish collaborative planning, cost-savings derive from two coordination opportunities: improved delivery routes and better transportation rates.

By planning together the delivery routes of the four companies' shipments, efficiency improvements could be achieved, such as reduction in traveling distance and increase in the loading rate of the trailer. A savings of 5% by such improved efficiencies with multi-stop delivery routes among half a dozen manufacturing plants are reported by (Brown and Ronen, 1997).

By negotiating their transportation rates together with the carrier rather than individually, the companies obtain at least the better transportation rates of the actual rates of the four companies. (Kuo and Soflarsky, 2003) report discounts in the ranges of 20-45% by negotiate with several carriers, with up to 70% discount from some large firms. The existence of these discounts, but in lower percentages, has been confirmed in our case study by a comparison of the actual rates of the four companies as well as a current quotation study by a consulting firm among the LTL and TL carriers of assembled furniture operating in Quebec (QFMA, 2008).

Along with shipping a greater volume, the companies can more easily use several carriers and therefore, as reported by (Caputo *et al.*, 2005), take advantage of the backhauling practice of the carriers, i.e. usually in a destination zone, a specific carrier will have better rates because he has a significant number of customers inside this zone who allows him to be loaded during the return trip. For the companies in the case study, taking advantages of this practice is more pertinent than ever before. Indeed, the last years' raise in the trucking flow imbalance between Canada and United-States increase the opportunities for the carriers to realize backhauling from United-States to Canada (NATSD, 2008).

3.1 Sharing the benefits of the collaboration

Collaboration brings up the following question. How should the benefits gained through collaborative transportation planning among a group of companies be shared between the companies? First, you have to determine if the benefits can be divided or not among the companies. In the case study, cost-saving can be divided while reduction in delivery time cannot. The total delivery time of each player in the collaboration is computed according to the delivery date of each of its shipments which is already determined by the transportation plan in the logistics scenario. To address the sharing problem, cooperative game theory provides a natural framework.

In cooperative game theory, a situation in which a group of companies can obtain through cooperation a certain benefit (such as a cost-savings) which can be divided without loss between them, can be described in a *n-person game with transferable utility*. Moreover, in such game, a company is named a *player* and a group of companies a *coalition*. As mentioned by (Hadjdukavá, 2006), there are two fundamental questions that need to be answered in such game: (1) which coalitions can be expected to be formed? and (2) How will the players of coalitions that are actually formed apportion their join benefit?

By studying a set of situations in which the decision to implement a logistics scenario is taken by a leading company, we address the first question in a very restrictive way. Indeed, in each situation, we limit to one the number of coalition that can be formed. Specifically, if we disregard external business considerations and focus on cost reduction, the leading company will choose the logistics scenario (including one sharing rule) that will provide it the greatest savings. However, in order to be able to implement the chosen logistics scenario, the leading players must provide enough savings to the other players. How much is enough to convince a player to join the coalition? At the least, the cost allocated to a player must be less than its stand alone cost. However, in practice this issue is much more complex and it is based on negotiation between the companies which goes beyond the scope of this paper, see (Nagarajan and Sošić, 2008) for a review of cooperative bargaining models in supply chain management. (Frisk *et al.*, 2006) address the second question by using a cost allocation method instead of a saving allocation method. In other words, instead of splitting the savings of the coalition among the players, the cost of the collaborative planning is split between the players. Several cost allocation methods exist in literature, an extensive list of papers on cost allocation methods, which are partly based on cooperative game theory such as the *Shapely value* and the *nucleolus*, can be found in (Tijs and Driessen, 1986) and in the literature survey by (Young, 1994). The computing and analysis of some cost allocation methods on a case study in forest transportation with eight companies is presented in (Frisk *et al.*, 2006) as well as a new method called *equal profit method* that provides an as equal relative profit as possible among the players. For the purpose of illustrating the impacts of different cost allocation methods on the leader's collaboration implementation decision, only three cost allocation methods were computed. They are described below.

M1 Proportional equal savings: the cost is allocated in order that each player obtains the same percentage of savings. For the leading player(s), the fairness of the method is the main argument favoring this method. It should however be noted, that the leading player do not always play fair as discussed in (Audy *et al.*, 2007).

M2 Weighted volume: the cost is allocated according to the proportion of the player's shipping volume of the total volume shipped by the coalition. Because transportation costs are often charged on a volume basis, this method was instinctively suggested by the companies and was unanimous. This method is also easy to understand and implement.

M3 Weighted volume according to the transportation plan: this method is similar to method M2 with the difference that the transportation plan is explicitly taken into account in the cost allocation. In this case, for each delivery route, the cost is spread between the furniture companies using the route accordingly to the volume ratio of their shipments to the total volume shipped on the route. Also, for the consolidation operations, a cost is charge to each furniture company for each of their shipments. This method is based on the principle of 'user-pays' that appears, in the present quotation study (QFMA, 2008), to be a standard in the industry.

3.2 Implementation of the collaboration

In the case study, collaborative planning has been explored under four different logistics scenarios.

#1 LTL mode: in this scenario, the coalition outsources to a common LTL carrier the operations of consolidation-warehousing and transportation, upstream and downstream from the terminal. This offers from an asset-based company of multiple and bundled services, rather than just single and isolated transportation or warehousing service refers in the literature to a third party logistics (3PL) provider, see (Selviaridis and Spring, 2007) for a review.

#2 TL mode with terminal at company #1: in this scenario, the coalition outsources to company #1 the operations of consolidation-warehousing at the terminal, which is located at company #1. To avoid possible conflict of interest, the truck routing at the terminal is done by a computer application and company #1 must follow pre-agreed rules in its consolidation-warehousing operations. In a discussion on inter-organizational system, (Kumar and van Dissel, 1996) identify possible risks of conflict and strategies for minimizing the likehood of such conflict. In practice, possible conflict of interest or the appearance of such still remains. Companies #2-4 must accept this risk since in this scenario the company #1 must be consider as a 3PL just as the LTL carrier in scenario #1 but a 3PL without transportation asset. Transportation operations upstream and downstream from the terminal are outsourced by the coalition to a common TL carrier. The shipments of companies' #2-4 are delivered to the terminal during the week using only full truckload delivery except when a partial delivery is necessary on Friday afternoons to clear the shipments inventory at a company. Consolidation is done during the weekends as well as the start of the trip. As the 3PL of the consolidation-warehousing and logistics planning services, company #1 charges companies' #2-4 a cubic foot flat rate on their total shipping volume.

#3 Hybrid TL/LTL mode with terminal at location i: in this scenario, the coalition outsources to a common LTL carrier the operations of consolidation-warehousing and transportation upstream from the terminal, which is at location *i*. The transportation operations downstream from the terminal are outsourced to a common TL carrier. As company #1 in scenario #2, the LTL carrier charges a cubic foot flat rate for its consolidation-warehousing and logistics planning services.

#4 Hybrid TL/LTL mode with terminal at location ii: this scenario is similar to scenario #3 but the terminal is at location *ii* rather than at location *i*.

Figure 1 illustrates the scenarios in a diagram where the numbered squares represent each company, the circle the terminal, and the arrows the oriented flows of furniture. The line at the top of each diagram identifies the service provider (i.e. company #1, LTL or TL carrier) to which the coalition outsources the operations of i) transportation upstream the terminal, ii) consolidation-warehousing at the terminal, and iii) transportation downstream the terminal.

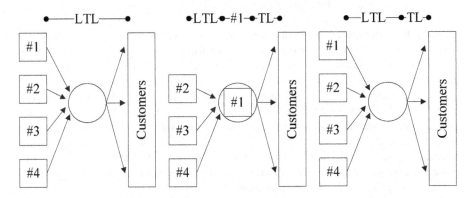

Figure 1 - Diagrams of the logistics scenario #1 (left), #2 (centre) and #3-4 (right)

These scenarios are based on the available realistic option of collaboration implementation for the four companies. The locations of the terminals in scenario #3 and #4 are in the two areas where terminals already exist. The existing terminals belong to LTL carriers meeting the minimum requirements of the companies and therefore, permitting collaboration. Aware of the difficulties of launching a new terminal, e.g. (Heliane Martins de Souza Hilário, 2007), the option to build or rent a terminal has not been considered. In our study, the high investment requirement has been the decisive factor of not acquiring a new terminal. On the other hand, it is the low investment requirement that made scenario #1. In scenario #2, company #1 has enough warehousing capacity and reception/shipping docks to carry out the consolidation. In fact, in the first half of the years 2000, the volume consolidated and shipped by company #1 was greater than the total actual volume of all companies.

Moreover, the common LTL/TL carrier in the scenario should not be considered only as a service provider operating alone. The carrier could belong to a group of collaborating carriers such as World Wide Logistics, an ongoing founding organization of six specialized furniture carriers (Thomas, 2008). With customers across the United-States of America, the coalition could be forced to outsourced several carriers according to exclusive geographic area or to designate a lead logistics provider (LLP). LLP manages on behalf of its customer (here, the coalition) the complex relationships involving multiple providers (Lieb and Miller, 2002). In the literature, the term fourth party logistics (4PL) provider is also use to designate such provider having this coordination capability, see e.g. (van Hoek and Chong, 2001).

4. NUMERICAL RESULTS

The data used in the case study has been collected in the billing system of the four furniture companies on a weekly basis during four consecutive weeks, earlier in the fall. The results are thus based on a comparison of the stand alone cost (delivery time) of each company. Specifically, the cost (delivery time) reduction/loss of each logistics scenario are defined by the difference between the sum of the stand alone cost (delivery time) of each company compared with the cost (delivery time) of the collaborative transportation plan of the logistics scenario. Moreover, the cost-savings of each player is the difference between the player's stand alone cost and its allocated cost (according to one of the three cost allocation methods) in the logistics scenario.

In accordance with the priorities of the four furniture companies and the deployment of the Quebec road network, two regions of the United States have been targeted for the collaborative planning of their shipments. First, all the states on the West Coast and second, the states surrounding the Great Lakes. Figure 2 shows the volume shipped during the four weeks in each ZIP code. The bigger the circle, the more volume was shipped. The different circle colours refer to the four companies (i.e. red: #1; yellow: #2; blue: #3 and green: #4).

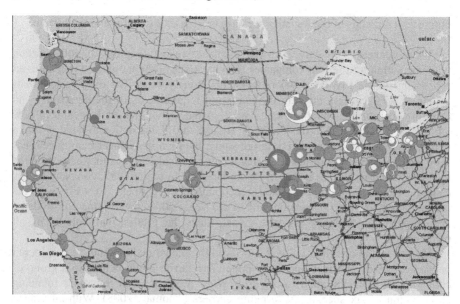

Figure 2 - Shipping volume per companies during the four weeks

The western region is characterized by a wide territory, a small density road network and clustered customers. The Great Lakes region is characterized by a high density road network and scattered customers. The case represents a total of 363 shipments to 256 different customers for a percentage of 44.6% of the total volume shipped in the United States by the companies during these four weeks. No volume was shipping in Montana, Wyoming, South and North Dakota. The representation of the volume shipped during the four weeks compared to the rest of the year has been confirmed by a comparison with the volume shipped during four periods of five weeks distributed in the year 2006-2007.

The furniture companies are uneven in volume shipping. Company #1-4 shipped, respectively, 66.6%, 17.5%, 9.3% and 6.7%, of the total volume shipped while the distribution of the stand alone cost is 59.7%, 21.8%, 10.4% and 8.2%. A significant difference between the two percentages of a company suggests that some companies are more cost-efficient than others.

4.1 Result for all companies

For each of the four weeks, collaborative planning was done for the four scenarios. Table 1 shows the results, in percentages of cost-savings and delivery time, per week and total. The scenario with the higher cost-savings is #2 while scenario #1 is the only one that generates loss. The reason for the loss in scenario #1 is discussed in Section 4.2. The fact that no transportation operations upstream from the terminal are required for company #1, who in addition is the highest volume shipper in the coalition, mainly explains the superior savings of scenario #2 versus scenarios #3-4.

Table 1 - Result in cost-saving and delivery time reduction per scenario

	Cost-savings				Delivery time	
	Scenario				Scenario	
Week	1	2	3	4	1	2 to 4
1	-17,3%	14,3%	9,7%	11,7%	35,3%	22,7%
2	10,9%	26,7%	28,0%	29,4%	12,6%	11,0%
3	-8,1%	17,0%	12,8%	14,3%	33,0%	6,0%
4	-13,9%	-2,8%	-3,7%	-3,0%	14,8%	-6,1%
1 to 4	-9,0%	14,9%	11,8%	13,4%	29,6%	11,6%

All scenarios generated a loss during the fourth week while all scenarios generated a savings in the second week. The weekly variation in scenario #2-4 illustrates the impact of the shipping volume and its geographical distribution on the efficiency improvement that can be obtained in collaborative planning.

All scenarios cut the total delivery time. Scenario #1 has the higher reduction which is very predictable. In scenario 1, several consolidation operations happen during the weeks, allowing gradual departure of trucks for faster delivery, while in scenarios #2-4, consolidation operations are performed only during the weekend, thus delaying the delivery of shipments already at the terminal. This weekend consolidation and the weekend closure of the customers as well as the proportionally short distances between the terminals as regards the average distance to reach the customers, explains why the three terminals have the same performance in delivery time. There is enough 'dead' time to allow a truck starting from the farthest terminal to reach the first customer at the same time as a truck starting from the closer terminal.

4.2 Result per company

Table 2 shows the results in percentage of delivery time reduction per company. Even if globally we have a reduction of the delivery time in all the scenarios, we see that company #2 increases its delivery time in all scenarios and also company #3 in scenarios #2-4. The average increase by shipment is less than 1 day for company #2 in scenario #1 (+0.66 day/shipment) and company #3 in scenarios #2-4 (+0.25day/shipment). Since these two companies have actual delivery performance meeting, and generally bellow, the requirement of their customers, these small increases should not have a significant impact among their customers. However, by extending the delivery time of 3.1 days by shipment on average, the increase in scenarios #2-4 for company #2 is significant. Indeed, for this company who is production-to-order, this increase would likely have an impact among its customers and thus, scenario #1 represents less incertitude and risk than scenarios #2-4.

Table 2 - Result in delivery time reduction per company

Company	Scenario	
	1	2 to 4
1	37,0%	27,0%
2	-15,4%	-72,5%
3	29,5%	-3,4%
4	40,6%	27,6%

Table 3 shows the results, in percentage of cost-savings per company for each of the cost allocation methods. Note that as transportation and consolidation operations are charged individually on each shipment according to the rate table of the LTL carrier, no allocation method has been necessary for logistics scenario 1. Also, note that the absence of shipping volume by some companies during certain weeks explains why the cost-savings percentage is not identical for all companies in each scenario with the cost-allocation method M1. Indeed, as for collaborative planning, the cost allocation methods are computed each week.

Table 3 - Result in cost-saving per company

Company	Scenario and cost allocation method					
	1		2			
	n.a.		M1	M2	M3	
1	-29,3%		14,5%	4,7%	6,8%	
2	19,2%		12,5%	30,0%	28,0%	
3	27,7%		22,1%	26,2%	20,7%	
4	17,3%		15,2%	34,3%	31,6%	

Company	3			4		
	M1	M2	M3	M1	M2	M3
1	10,9%	0,9%	-1,9%	12,4%	2,6%	0,02%
2	10,6%	28,7%	33,4%	11,9%	29,7%	34,2%
3	21,1%	24,9%	25,8%	22,6%	26,3%	27,6%
4	10,7%	30,8%	37,4%	12,5%	32,3%	37,6%

Except for the two losses for company #1 (i.e. -29.3% and -1.9%), all scenarios and cost allocation methods provide a cost-savings to each company. Moreover, the significant loss of company #1 in scenario #1 is the reason behind the global loss of this scenario (i.e. -9.0% in Table1) even if the three other companies obtain a saving. Indeed, among the companies, company #1 is the only one who actually operates using the TL mode. We can see that with high shipping volumes such as company #1, the TL mode is more cost-efficient than LTL mode even with the better transportations rates of scenario #1.

5. DECISION ON THE LOGISTICS SCENARIO BY EACH COMPANY

According to the previous results, we can study all the four situations in which each of the four companies sets the decision on the logistics scenario (including the choice of the sharing rule) to implement.

If the leadership of the collaboration is assumed by company #1, he will implement scenario #2 with the cost allocation method M1. Indeed, this choice provides the greatest cost-saving to company #1 (i.e. 14.5%) and the three other companies obtain interesting cost-savings. However, if company #2 considers the impact of scenario #2 on its delivery time too important, he will not join the coalition. The result of scenario #2 without company #2 must be evaluated by company #1. Scenario #2 demands a high degree of involvement and operation changes for company #1. Therefore, if the result of scenario #2 without company #2 is not considerably profitable for company #1 (e.g. more than 2% savings), it is likely that company #1 will not go along with any collaboration implementation.

There are two alternatives if the leadership of the collaboration is assumed by company #2. If company #2 considers the impact of scenarios #2-4 on its delivery time too great, then scenario #1 will be preferred. In scenario #1, the savings/loss for a company derives from the better/worse transportation rates of the coalition. With a loss in scenario #1, this implementation must be done without company #1. Without the shipping volume of company #1 in the coalition, the transportation rates discount allowed by the LTL carrier will likely be less. However, cost-saving will still be obtained with the high savings of companies #2-4 (i.e. 19.2%, 27.7% and 17.3% respectively).

If company #2 can do with the increase of its delivery times in scenarios #2-4, scenario #4 with method M3 will be implemented as if the leadership is assumed by company #3 or #4. This decision leads to a situation where it is a sub-optimal scenario which is implemented, i.e. optimal scenario #2 generates 1.5% more cost-savings than sub-optimal scenario #4.

However, in a coalition, mainly with few players as in the case study, it is likely that the companies with the greater shipping volume will have a stronger position in a negotiation (Frisk *et al.*, 2006). Therefore, with only 0.02% of savings in scenario #4 with method M3, company #1 will certainly use its stronger position to negotiate a larger part of the cost saving. This larger part could be obtained by modifying the scenario and/or allocation method decision or by using another allocation method which may include the payment to company #1 of a compensation out of the savings of the other companies. Of course, if the negotiation ends with a saving for the leader less than in scenario #1, the leader will decide to implement scenario #1 without company #2. The notion of compensation of a specific player could also be used in other situations by the leader(s), e.g. convince company #2 to join a coalition in scenarios #2-4 even if its delivery time increases. Aware of this business consideration of an uneven negotiating position between the players, it is to the advantage of companies #2-4 to either together or as a pair, take the leadership to increase their position regarding company #2 and thus limit the additional savings to give to company #1 so it will participate in the coalition.

For each company, the cost-savings difference between computing of cost allocation according to the transport plan (i.e. method M3) rather than the total cost (i.e. method M2) as more common cost allocation methods was significant (i.e. difference of 2% or more except for company #2 in scenarios #3-4). Since the principle of 'user-pays' as in method M3 appears to be a prerequisite in the industry for any cost allocation method, it is necessary to think ahead to avoid a situation where a sub-optimal scenario is implemented as in the case study.

6. CONCLUDING REMARKS

It has been demonstrated that collaboration in transportation can provide different benefits. Some of these benefits can be divided among the companies and others not. Using a case study of four Canadian furniture companies shipping to the United-States, it has been shown that the benefits divided among the company as well as the leadership of the collaboration impact the implementation decisions. Some leading company and sharing methods could lead to the implementation of a sub-optimal logistics scenario that does not capture all the potential benefits. Also, even with impressive benefits, if the implementation of a logistics scenario generates only one very significant benefit loss, then a leading company could reject it.

As future research work is concerned, different issues should be studied. New logistics scenarios integrating both the LTL mode and the TL mode should be considered. (Caputo *et al.*, 2005) report attractive savings by using both modes, especially when LTL mode is used to deliver to marginal customers. Considering different types of benefit in the cost allocation methods would also be a challenging problem. In the case study, considerable coverage benefit could be achieved through the coalition, raising the question of how much this is worth.

Typically, the decision on the benefits sharing among the companies is determined simultaneously that the decision on which coalitions can be expected to form (Greenberg, 1994). Few approaches address at once these two issues and they should be investigated, see (Hadjdukavá, 2006) for some approaches. Moreover, in the paper the approach chosen to address these two issues is static, i.e. the coalition is formed according to the leading company best solution and remains unchanged. This approach is justifiable considering the high transaction costs to implement such collaboration. (Macho-Stadler *et al.*, 2006) note that the transaction costs seem much higher the more companies are involved. However, these two issues should be addressed using a more dynamic approach allowing modifications to the coalition as time goes by. Finally, the issues of the optimal size of the coalition, when should one stop adding new company in the coalition? Economics do provide a rich understanding of the fundamentals behind these issues, the next step is to validate the knowledge in fieldwork.

Acknowledgments

The authors wish to thank Philippe Marier of FORAC Research Consortium, Charles Doucet of the Quebec Furniture Manufacturers Association and the project leaders in the four furniture companies of the case study for their contribution to this work. Also, the authors wish to acknowledge the financial support of the Natural Sciences and Engineering Research Council of Canada and the private and public partners of the FORAC Research Consortium.

7. REFERENCES

1. Archambault, G., Carle, D., Caron. M. and R. Vézina, 2006. The furniture manufacturer of the future - executive summary [In French]. FPInnovations – Forintek, Quebec: FPInnovations-Forintek.
2. Audy, J.-F., 2007. Feasibility study for a transportation collaboration project in a network of companies in the furniture industry [In French]. FORAC Research Consortium, Quebec Furniture Manufacturers Association research mandate No. 1. Quebec: FORAC Research Consortium.
3. Audy, J.-F., D'Amours, S. and M. Rönnqvist, 2007. Business models for collaborative planning in transportation: an application to wood products. In: Camarinha-Matos, L., Afsarmanesh, H., Novais, P., Analide, C., eds. IFIP International Federation for Information Processing, Volume 243, Establishing the Foundation of Collaborative Networks. Boston: Springer, 667-676.
4. Audy, J.-F., D'Amours, S. and P. Marier, 2008. Project on the simulation of a collaborative transportation planning in a network of companies in the furniture industry [In French]. FORAC Research Consortium, Quebec Furniture Manufacturers Association research mandate No. 2. Quebec: FORAC Research Consortium.
5. Bahrami, K., 2002. Improving supply chain productivity through horizonal cooperation – the case of cusumer goods manufacturers. In: Seuring, S., Goldbach, M., eds. Cost Management in Supply Chains. New York: Physica Verlag, 213-232.
6. Brown, G.G. and D. Ronen, 1997. Consolidation of customer orders into truckloads at a large manufacturer, The Journal of the Operational Research Society, 48 (8), 779-785.
7. Caputo, A.C., Fratocchi, L. and P.M. Pelagagge, 2005. A framework for analyzing long-range direct shipping logistics, Industrial Management and Data Systems, 105 (7), 876-899.
8. Cruijssen, F., Dullaert, W. and H. Fleuren, 2007a. Horizontal cooperation in transport and logistics: a literature review. Transportation Journal, 46 (3), 22-39
9. Cruijssen, F., Bräysy, O., Dullaeert, W., Fleuren, H. and M. Salomon, 2007b. Joint route planning under varying market conditions. International Journal of Physical Distribution and Logistics Management, 37 (4), 287-304.
10. Ergun, O., Kuyzu, G., and M. Savelsbergh, 2007. Reducing truckload transportation costs through collaboration. Transportation Science, 41 (2), 206-221.
11. Frisk, M., Jörnsten, K., Göthe-Lundgren, M. and M. Rönnqvist, 2006. Cost allocation in collaborative forest transportation. Norwegian School of Economics and Business Administration, Discussion paper No. 15. Bergen: NHH Department of Finance and Management Science.
12. Greenberg, J. 1994. Coalition structures. In: Aumann, R.J., Hart, S., eds., Handbook of Game Theory with Economic Applications. Amsterdam: North-Holland, 1305-1337.
13. Hadjdukavá, J., 2006. Coalition formation games: a survey. International Game Theory Review, 8 (4), 613-641.
14. Heliane Martins de Souza Hilário, 2007. Personal communication through a portugese speaking collegue, Matheus Pinotti Moreira, 30 January 2007, Ms. Martins de Souza Hilário was the manager of the Intersind Central de Fretes
15. IC, 2008. Trade Data Online, requests on NAICS based code #337, data available from 1997 to 2006 [online]. Industry Canada, Government of Canada. Available from: http://www.ic.gc.ca/ [Accessed 25 January 2008]

16. ITA, 2008. TradeStats Express, requests on NAICS based code #337, data from 1997 to 2006 [online]. International Trade Administration, Department of Commerce, United States of America. Available from: http://trade.gov/index.asp [Accessed 25 January 2008]

17. Klincewicz, J.G. and M.B. Rosenwein, 1997. Planning and Consolidating Shipments from a Warehouse. The Journal of the Operational Research Society, 48 (3), 241-246.

18. Kuo, C.-C. and F. Soflarsky, 2003. An automated system for motor carrier selection, Industrial Management and Data Systems, 103 (7), 533-539.

19. le Blanc, H. M., Cruijssen, F., Fleuren, H. A. and M.B.M. de Koster, 2007. Factory gate pricing: an analysis of the Dutch retail distribution. European Journal of Operational Research, 174 (3), 1950-1967.

20. Lieb, R. and J. Miller, 2002. The use of third-party logistics services by large US manufacturers, the 2000 survey. International Journal of Logistics Research and Applications, 5(1), 1-12.

21. Macho-Stadler, I., Pérez-Castrillo, D. and N. Porteiro, 2006. Sequential formation of coalitions through bilateral agreements in a Cournot setting. International Journal of Game Theory, 34 (2), 207-228.

22. MEDIE, 2007. Profile of the Quebec furniture industry [In French]. Ministry of Economic Development, Innovation and Exportation, Government of Quebec. Quebec: Government of Quebec.

23. Nagarajan, M. and G. Sošić, 2008. Game-theoretic analysis of cooperation among supply chain agents: review and extensions. European Journal of Operational Research, 187 (3), 719-745.

24. NATSD, 2008. Tables in section 6: North American Merchandise Trade [online]. North American Transportation Statistics Database. Available from: http://nats.sct.gob.mx/ [Accessed 25 January 2008]

25. QFMA, 2008. [forthcoming]. Consulting firm Logistique CAF, Quebec Furniture Manufacturers Association mandate.

26. Young, H.P., 1994. Cost allocation. In: Aumann, R.J., Hart, S., eds., Handbook of Game Theory with Economic Applications. Amsterdam: North-Holland, 1193-1235.

27. Selviaridis, K. and M. Spring, 2007. Third party logistics: a literature review and research agenda. International Journal of Logistics Management, 18 (1), 125-150.

28. Thomas, L., 2008. Six furniture trucking firms to merge [online]. Furniture Today. Available from: http://www.furnituretoday.com/ [Accessed 30 April 2008]

29. Tijs, S. H. and T. S. H. Driessen, 1986. Game theory and cost allocation problems. Management Science, 32 (8), 1015-1058.

30. van Hoek, R.I. and I. Chong, 2001. Epilogue: UPS Logistics – practical approaches to the e-supply chain. International Journal of Physical Distribution and Logistics Management, 31 (6), 436-468.

55

INTELLIGENT TRANSPORT SYSTEM BASED ON RFID AND MULTI-AGENT APPROACHES

J. C. Q. Dias*, J. M. F. Calado**, A. L. Osório*** and L. F. Morgado***

*UMTE/ISEL – Instituto Superior de Engenharia de Lisboa
**IDMEC/ISEL – Instituto Superior de Engenharia de Lisboa
***GIATSI/ISEL – Instituto Superior de Engenharia de Lisboa
Polytechnic Institute of Lisbon
(e-mail: {jdias, jcalado}@dem.isel.ipl.pt)
(e-mail: {aosorio, lm}@deetc.isel.ipl.pt)
PORTUGAL

This paper presents an Intelligent Information and Communication Technology (IICT) architecture able to cope with the nowadays logistics operators challenges. The aim is to achieve an Intelligent Transport System based on RFID together with Multi-agent systems. Furthermore, the logistical platforms (production or distribution), as nodes of added value of supplying and distribution networks, are proposed as critical points of the visibility of the inventory, where these technological needs are more evident.

1. INTRODUCTION

The supply chain strategic management as a simultaneous local and global ("glocal") value chain is a collaborative/cooperative organization of stakeholders, many times in co-opetition, to perform a service to the customers respecting the time, place, price and quality levels. This complex scenario requires a tighter collaboration among the involved organizations and suggests the need of an innovative collaborative platform for the networked organizations considering they need to participate in collaborative processes (Osório, 2006). The proposal of a breeding environment in (Camarinha, 2004) as preparedness for an agile collaboration among organizations with a diversity of business, management and technological cultures, is strategic applied to a logistic supply chain considering a growing need for multi-modal operations and transports across countries.

In a Supply Chain Management (SCM) (Chen and Paulraj, 2004), planning of demand and supply for commodities in global value chain networks gains increasing importance in the process industry in the context of globalization. Hence, being logistics (Bowersox and Closs, 1996; Dornier *et al.*, 1998) the art and science of managing the flows of goods or products, research on this field should aim to find the lowest cost carrier that provides the highest value, improving the visibility (monitoring and tracing) and velocity of the flow of materials and products and, reducing the amount and cost of carrying inventory or rolling stock, as well as, reducing or completely eliminating stocks in the supply chains interfaces or in other points of the suppliers network (Choi and Hong, 2002) and distribution channels (Dornier *et al.*, 1998). During the last decades, several enterprises have achieved flexibility and increased competitiveness by implementing the "lean" or "just-in-time (JIT)" principles developed at Toyota (Womack and Jones, 1996). Supply chain integration with transparent information flow is one of the key parameters to achieve such an approach. Thus, for logistics, Information and Communications

Please use the following format when citing this chapter:

Dias, J.C.Q., Calado, J.M.F., Osório, A.L. and Morgado, L.F., 2008, in IFIP International Federation for Information Processing, Volume 283; *Pervasive Collaborative Networks*; Luis M. Camarinha-Matos, Willy Picard; (Boston: Springer), pp. 533–540.

Technologies (ICT) is particularly a time and embeddedness issue, providing the logistics operators the ability to cope with the mentioned new challenges. Because of ICT, freight distribution is within a paradigm shift between inventory-based logistics to replenishment-based logistics. Logistics is thus concomitantly concerned by compression distribution costs and time (Christopher, 2000; Dolgui *et al.*, 2005). Time is a major issue for freight shipping as it imposes inventory holding and depreciation costs, which becomes sensitive for tightly integrated supply chains (Hasse and Rodrigue, 2004).

This paper aims at evidence and proposes the use of Radio Frequency Identification (RFID) technologies integrated to an Information and Communication Technologies (ICT) framework. The proposed framework is based on Distributed Artificial Intelligence (DAI) supported by a Multi-Agent System (MAS) approach, as the most value advantage of SCM in cooperative intelligent logistics systems. Furthermore, is proposed that logistical platforms (production or distribution), as nodes of added value of supplying and distribution networks, are the critical points of the visibility of the inventory, where these technological needs are more evident. The paper is organized as follows. Section 2 presents the Logistics as an integrated system that includes transportation operations in a worldwide market and presents the concept of SCM giving evidence that enabling technologies support the flows, specially, information flows. In Section 3 authors argue that ICT is a significant source of competitive advantage in SCM, proposing a multi-agent system approach including RFID to cope with the nowadays challenges of global value chains. Section 4 presents a case study and Section 5 provides some concluding remarks.

2. SUPPLY CHAIN MANAGEMENT CHALLENGES

New modes of production and new operations are concomitant with new modes of distribution, which brings forward the realm of logistics as science of physical distribution and supplying (Hesse and Rodrigue, 2004). Therefore, logistics represents an entire system of space/time/cost interdependencies and respective trade-offs. Freight distribution is now considered with more attention as productivity gains in manufacturing are increasingly derived from efficiency at terminals instead from efficiency of transportation modes (Rodrigue, 1999). Strategic management of the value chain is actually a phenomenon simultaneously local and global ("glocal") because through postponement operations it is possible customize, locally and add value to the inventory. Outbound logistics involves postponement that allows product differentiation and customization to be put off by building inventory as late as possible, that is, orders taken at the no-differentiated semi-finished inventory stage (Dornier *et al.*, 1998). The classic trade theory neglects the role of transport and logistics particularly the fact that transport costs have a fundamental impact on the amount of trade and goods exchange. Hesse and Rodrigue (2004) argue that this perspective is mainly the result of a misinterpretation of role of the transport sector, freight alike, as a derived demand.

A supply chain, providing management of flows, is viewed as a network consisting of two or tree tiers of suppliers, manufacturers, distributors, retailers, and customers in a collaborative/cooperative organization of stakeholders, many times in co-opetition, to perform a service to the customers respecting the time, place, price and quality levels (Figure 1). At the operational level, this network supports three types of flows: *Material flows*, represent physical product flows from suppliers to customers as well as the reverse flows for product returns, servicing and recycling; *Information flows*, represent order transmission and order tracking, and coordinates the physical flows; *Financial flows*, represent credit terms, payment schedules, consignments and title ownership arrangements. The network, in turn, is supported by three pillars: *Processes*, embed the firm capabilities in logistics, new product development and knowledge management; *Organizational structures*, encompass a range of relationships from total vertical integration to networked companies as well as management approaches and performance measurement and reward schemes; *Enabling technologies*, include both process and information technologies. These approaches, in turn, typically lead to new forms of organizational structures (e.g., process orientation) and new forms of inter-organizational collaboration (e.g., outsourcing via third-party service providers or contract manufacturers). This transformation has coincided with the emergence of information and communication technologies (ICT) facilitating closer collaboration and promoting supply chain transparency. Success now hinges on a different set of criteria, where each company is racing to get the right product to the right place (or Just-in-Place, JIP) at the right time (or Just-in-Time, JIT) – and at the right cost. Therefore, real time information provided by ICT is fundamental to achieve the nowadays tasks related to an effective SCM. If a supply chain competes in a competitive environment, the strategic alignment between ICT (Eng, 2006) and business among upstream (suppliers network) and downstream (retailers network) partners will be the key factor for success. Nowadays collaborative logistics models need to be powered by advanced software systems and the Internet, allowing companies to expand collaborative logistic networks on a large scale, to reduce the costs of transportation and lower inventories, eliminating stocks.

3. ICT FRAMEWORK BASED ON RFID AND MAS

The use of an ICT framework based on intelligent multi-agents allows the integration of different supply chain strategies coping with the stocks reduction aim, in lean supply chains. Furthermore, in recognition of the increasing importance of globalization and the resulting need for greater, faster and more flexible communications, a framework is required to allow any company to establish itself in no time, make optimum use of their legacy applications and run efficiently with minimal cost input. Such a framework, very appealing to be based on intelligent multi-agents (Chen *et al.*, 2007) corresponds to an emergent topic called e-logistics. Globalization means that the spatial frame for the entire economy has been expanded, implying the economy spatial expansion, more complex global economic integration and an intricate network of global flows and hubs (Rodrigue, 1999). Also in this context an ICT platform, may based on intelligent MAS, is particularly relevant as it helps strengthen the level of control distributors have over the supply chain. Finally, for many companies globalization is a dominating factor as companies seek to identify the best suppliers of services and products to meet their needs and help drive down costs, but only few have fully integrated and automated all components of their logistics process. However, successful implementation of

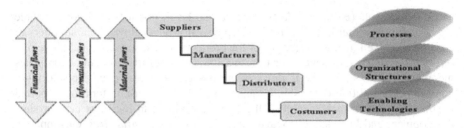

Figure 1 - An integrated model of supply chain.

logistics activities (Bowesox and Closs, 1996) relies heavily on the integration of processes, practices and information to yield meaningful cost and time reductions. Investments on RFID technology will help to leverage reliable and timely RFID (Chao *et al.*, 2007) data to achieve SCM optimal demand and logistics execution. RFID tag data can be tapped to enable complex decision-support with real-time data on supply chain and market conditions. These RFID solutions are designed to facilitate the gathering usage and storage of RFID data.

Taking into account the overall quoted aspects, global value chains in a globalization environment are complex and dynamic processes physically distributed and heterogeneous, where the communication nets among the several parts of the process force a distributed vision of the supply chain. Thus, the use of techniques such as DAI could be a good option to develop an Intelligent Information and Communication Technology (IICT) platform to support the emerging challenges of an effective supply chain management. Namely, methodologies based on MAS may be able to cope with the new challenges concerned with global value chains providing competitive advantages. An agent is a computer system that is capable of flexible autonomous action in dynamic, unpredictable, typically multi-agent domains (FIPA, 2007). In particular, the characteristics of dynamic and open environments in which, for example, heterogeneous systems must interact, span organisational boundaries, and operate effectively within rapidly changing circumstances and with dramatically increasing quantities of available information, like supply chain management, suggest that improvements on traditional computing models and paradigms are required. Thus, the need for some degree of autonomy, to enable components to respond dynamically to changing circumstances, is seen by many as fundamental, providing add value to global chain.

The MAS approach will bring to the supply chain management tasks the following advantages: *Reliability*, MAS are fault-tolerant (FT) and robust (redundant FT agents); *Modularity and Scalability*, instead of adding new capabilities to a system, agents can be added and deleted without breaking or interrupting the process; *Adaptivity*, agents have the ability to reconfigure themselves to accommodate new changes and events; *Concurrency*, agents are capable of reasoning and performing tasks in parallel, which in turn provides more flexibility and speeds up computation; and finally, *Dynamics*, agents can dynamically collaborate to share their resources and solve problems (Wooldridge, 2002).

In large-scale supply chains the supervision and management subsystems are distributed at the nodes of the network, and call for a large number of operators and programs which have to work together to accomplish the overall objectives. So, the need of DAI, and more precisely, the need of agents can be explained by the following topics: Problems are physically distributed; Problems are widely distributed and heterogeneous in functional terms; Networks force a distributed point of view. MAS can thus be seen as serious candidates for the construction of open, distributed, heterogeneous and flexible architectures, capable of offering high-quality service for collective work, without imposing any a priori structure; The complexity of problems dictates a local point of view. Due to the complexity, the processes need the capability to adapt themselves to changes in the context of operations (changes in the operating system, in the database manager or the graphics interfaces, addition of other software and so on). Furthermore, because the distributed nature of MAS, they always assume that reasoning takes place locally, and because they are able to cope with the appearance or disappearance of agents even while the system is functioning, they are architectures especially suitable for providing the capabilities for systems evolution and adaptation; Software engineering is moving towards designs using concepts of autonomous interacting units. The history of software development shows that the creation of computer programs is following a course intended to lead to systems designed as assemblies of entities which will be more and more widely distributed, and making use of components which are more and more individualised and autonomous. MAS have an essential role to play here by acting as possible successors to object-oriented systems and combining local behaviours with autonomy and distributed decision making (Ferber 1999). Thus, the aspects mentioned above are some of the reasons to use DAI (agents) to support the supply chain management tasks, providing an ICT framework able to cope with the emerging challenges concerned with the globalization, giving competitive advantages to the global value chain.

4. CASE STUDY

Due to new corporate strategies, a concentration of logistics functions in certain facilities at strategic locations is prevalent. Many improvements in freight flows are achieved at terminals, distribution points, referred as "logistics platforms" (Aldin and Stahre, 2003). There are many types of structures designed as "logistical" platforms" (Dias, 2005) and, in Europe, there is an association of these platforms named, precisely, "Europlatforms" (Europlatforms, 2007). These infrastructures include the term "logistics" because they add value to the inventory, by many ways: one of them is time compression through cross-docking (Lambert and Cooper, 2000), transhipment, interoperability or intermodality; another through physical operations like inbound modularization and outbound postponement (Dornier *et al.*, 1998); it can be mention, yet, the consolidation of goods, etc. In many cases, literature refers logistics platforms or logistical platforms as an industrial clusters and "distriparks", free zones, "dry ports", trading hubs networks (Europlatforms, 2007) and so on. Thus, in these physical infrastructures is possible find the needs of all relevant factors and sources of competitive advantage of the best value supply chains. It can be mention only the more significant, as follows: Visibility (monitoring, trace and track); Picking and Packing; Demotic and robotized warehousing and factoring; Modularization and postponement operations; Operations optimization; Efficient handling; Transportation management in real time; Interoperability and multimodality; Optimization of transhipment and cross-docking operations; Minimization of impedances; Collaborative suppliers network (ECR; QR/CR – Quick Response/Continuous Replenishment); Time and space compression; Efficient energy management; Orders monitoring and management; Networking connectivity; Real time information sharing; Communications to the front/back offices. These set of significant factors recommend the use of techniques like DAI as a good option to develop an Intelligent Information and Communication Technology (IICT) platform to support the referred emerging challenges in a generic logistical platform as defined by Europlatforms (2007). Namely, methodologies based on MAS approach may be able to cope with the new challenges concerned with global best value chains providing competitive advantages.

In order to investigate and to propose an inductive theory, a field approach was used as methodology, following the recommendations of Eisenhardt, 1989: The current approach is also based on the Grounded Theory, one of the most developed inductive research methods (Glaser and Strauss, 1967). This means that researchers are able to develop theory through comparative analysis because it is possible to look at the same event in different and several settings or situations (Easterby-Smitt *et al.*, 1993). In these conditions the relevant proposition and other conclusions can be presented and applied in a generic case using evidences of several kinds of logistics platforms (case study as a method and strategy of direct research - Mintzbeg, 1979). Multiple sources of evidence (authorities, logistics and transports operators, people responsible for departments of transportation, forwarders, production, distribution, and directors of logistical platforms, etc.) were used, as well the respective methodological triangulation (data, documents, perspectives, key-informants) and the creation of an indispensable chain of evidence (Yin, 1994).

Analyzing several logistical infrastructures, nine case studies, according, so as possible, to the concept referred as "Europlatforms", a conceptual model of an IICT system based on RFID and multi-agents, is depicted in Figure 2. Such an approach has been design for a generic logistics platform and a prototype is currently under development and test. Keeping in mind the growth of the World Wide Web and the rapid trend for e-Logistics to be use by the main logistics operators, in the current approach significant efforts has been done to develop standardised software models and technologies to support and enable the engineering of systems involving distributed computation. These efforts have been creating a rich and sophisticated context for the development of agent technologies.

Hence, a communication standard has been developed, which can be seen in Figure 2 as a Transport Management Service Bus (TMSB). The framework of the current approach is based on the principles of the so-called service-oriented architectures (SOAs) for distributed applications involving the creation of systems based on components, each of which provides predefined computational services (Huhns and Singh, 2005). Interfaces between the different software modules, ensured through a TMSB, can therefore be realised by agents that send and receive messages, while the services themselves are the resources characterised by the functionality provided. Agent technologies provide a way to conceptualise these systems as comprising interacting autonomous entities, each acting, learning or evolving separately in response to interactions in their local environments. Such a conceptualisation provides the basis for realistic computer simulations of the

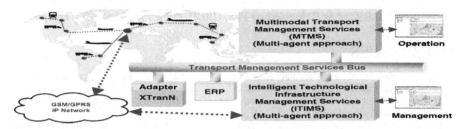

Figure 2 - Conceptual model for an IICT logistics platform.

operation and behaviour of a logistics platform and of design of control and intervention processes (Bullock and Cliff, 2004). However, despite a number of languages, frameworks, development environments, and platforms that have appeared in the literature (Luck *et al.*, 2004), implementing MAS is still a complex task. In part, to manage MAS complexity, the research community has produced a number of methodologies that aim to structure agent development. Even if practitioners follow such methodologies during the design phase, there are difficulties in the implementation phase, partly due to the lack of maturity in both methodologies and programming tools. Further research is needed to move from analysis and design to code. Anyway, an IICT framework based RFID together with a MAS approach will provide great competitive advantages to overall global value chain based in each node of a network of logistics platforms.

5. CONCLUSIONS

It has been observed that the use of RFID technologies will enable a framework for enterprises to collaborate, plan monitor and execute, while optimally adapt in real-time to operate under unplanned occurrences in the extended supply chain. Therefore, Multi-agent systems promise to be a valuable software engineering solution for the development of an ICT framework, able to cope with the emerging challenges intrinsic to the supply chain management tasks, where the complexity and the distribution of the processes ask for new approaches. Furthermore, it has been proposed logistical platforms as nodes of added value of supplying and distribution networks, being the critical control points (track and trace) where the needs of valuable software engineering solution are more evident. In addition, the wide adoption of the Internet as an open environment, the increasing communication capabilities and the increasing popularity, in industry, of machine-independent programming languages, such as Java, make the adoption of multi-agent technology a feasible and a very interesting solution. The supply chain management includes most of the MAS characteristics: supply chains are dynamic, complex and large processes, spatially distributed and changeable in a dynamic, fragmented and global world. Thus, it can be said that the problems related to the supply chain management tasks fulfil the necessary requirements for a successful MAS application, providing competitive advantage to the global value chain.

Acknowledgements. The authors would like to acknowledge the cooperation of several key-informants and other persons in all firms and logistical platforms analyzed. Furthermore, the research work was partially funded by Project POCTI-

SFA-10-46-IDMEC of FCT, funded by POCI 2010, POSC, FSE and MCTES.

REFERENCES

1. Aldin, N. and Stahre, F.. Electronic commerce, marketing channels and logistics platforms - a wholesaler perspective. *Europ. J. Operationalt Research*, 2003; **144 (2)**, pp. 270-279.
2. Bowersox, D. and Closs, D.J.. *Logistical Management, the Integrated Supply Chain Process*. Mc Graw-Hill, International Edition, 1996.
3. Bullock, S. and Cliff, D.. *Complexity and Emergent Behaviour in ICT Systems*. Foresight Report, Intelligent Infrastructure Futures, United Kingdom. http://www.foresight.gov.uk/Previous_Projects/Intelligent_Infrastructure_Systems/Reports_and_Publi cations/Intelligent_Infrastructure_Futures/ComplexityandEmergentBehaviour/, 2004.
4. Camarinha-Matos, L. M.; Afsarmanesh, H.. Supporting Infrastructures for New Collaborative Forms, in Collaborative Networked Organizations, pp. 175-192, Kluwer Acad. Publishers, 2004.
5. Chao, Chia-Chen, Yang, Jiann-Min Yang and Jen, Wen-Yuan. Determining technology trends and forecasts of RFID by a historical review and bibliometric analysis from 1991 to 2005. *Technovation*, 2007; **27 (5)**, pp. 268-279.
6. Chen, I.J. and Paulraj, A.. Understanding supply chain management: critical research and a theoretical framework. *Int. Journal of Production Research*, 2004; **42 (1)**, pp. 131–163.
7. Chen, Mu-Chen, Yang, Taho and Yen, Chi-Tsung. Investigating the value of Information Sharing in Multi-echelon Supply Chains. *Quality & Quantity*, 2007; **41** pp.497-511.
8. Choi, T. Y. and Hong, Y.. Unveiling the structure of supply networks: case studies in Honda, Acura and DaimlerChrysler. *J. Operat. Management*, 2002; **20**, pp. 469-493.
9. Christopher, M.. The agile supply chain competing in volatile markets. *Ind. Marketing Manag.*, 2000; **29 (1)**, pp. 37-44.
10. Dias, J. C Q... *Logística Global e Macrologística*. Ed. Sílabo, 1st ed,, , Lisboa, Portugal, April 2005.
11. Dolgui, A., Soldek, J. and Zaikin, O.. *Supply chain optimisation: product/process design, facilities location and flow control*. Applied Optimization, **94**, Springer, ISBN : 0-387-23566-3, 2005.
12. Dornier, P. P., Ernest, R., Fender, M. and Kouvelis, P.. *Global Operations and Logistics -Text and Cases*. John Wiley & Sons, Inc., 1998.
13. Easterby-Smith, M., Thorpe, R., and Lowe, A.. *Management Research: an Introduction*. Sage: London, 1993.
14. Eisenhardt, K. M.. Building theories from case study research. *Academy of Manag. Review*, 1989; **14 (4)**, pp. 532–550.
15. Eng, T.-Y.. Mobile supply chain management: Challenges for implementation. *Technovation*, 2006; **26**, pp. 682-686.
16. Europlatforms. http://www.eutp.org/download/ClusterPapers/Europlatforms.ppt (site visited 07/7/15).
17. Ferber, J.. Multi-agent systems, An Introduction to Distributed Artificial Intelligence. Addison-Wesley. Harlow, England, 1999.
18. FIPA. The foundation for intelligent physical agents. http://www.fipa.org/, 2007.
19. Glaser, D.G. and Strauss, A. L.. The Discovery of Grounded Theory: Strategies for Qualitative Research. Alding, New York, 1967.
20. Hesse, M., and Rodrigue, J-P.. The transport geography of logistics and freight distribution. *Journal of Transport Geography*, 2004; **12 (3)**, pp. 171-184.
21. Lambert and Cooper. Issues in supply chain management. *Ind. Mark. Manag.*, 2000; **29**, pp. 65–83.
22. Luck, M., Ashri, R. and d'Inverno M.. *Agent-Based Software Development*. Artech House, Inc. Boston, U.S.A, 2004.
23. Mintzberg, H.. An Emerging Strategy of "direct" Research. *Adminis. Science Quarterly*, 1979; **24 (4)**, pp. 582-589.
24. Osório, A. L. and Camarinha-Matos, L. M.. Towards a Distributed Process Execution Platform for Collaborative Networks; 7th IFIP Int. Conf. on Information Technology for Balanced Automation Systems in Manufacturing, proc. published by Springer; Ontario, Canada, 2006; 4-6 September.
25. Rodrigue, J.-P.. Globalization and the Synchronization of Transport Terminals. *J.l of Transport Geography*, 1999; **7**, pp. 255-261.
26. Womack, J. P. and Jones, D. T.. *Lean Thinking: Banish Waste and Create Wealth in your Corporation*. Simon and Schuster, New York and London, ISBN 684810352, 1996.
27. Wooldridge, M.. *An Introduction to Multiagent Systems*. J. Wiley & Sons, Chichester, England, 2002.
28. Yin, R. K.. *Case study research: design and methods*. 2nd Edition, Sage, London, 1994.

Brian G. Keedwell

Integrated Marketing   Brian.Keedwell@telia.com

Making a new market is a challenge. It requires creation of a new form of value and sustainable capture of a fair market share for the new-market makers. The author's mission is to initiate the creation of the Mobile Process Service (MPS) market in the Northern Dimension (ND) that consists of Canada, Nordic/Baltics and North-West Russia – hence NDMPS. Mission, Segmentation, Differentiation and Positioning are to be pre-specified at the NDMPS Board level – only then will Innovation begin. Customized Mobile Process Service will enable multi-nationals that conduct such as selling and delivering of complex products and field services, to operate in a wirelessly enabled, process-oriented manner bestowing high quality and productivity upon those processes. Meanwhile the Smart Business Network (SBN) member vendors will each move up the value chain thus escaping from an increasingly commodity-provider role in this Enterprise Mobility domain.

1. INTRODUCTION

The proposed new market would represent a leap to a conceptually high level. Today's out-of-the-box, generic software-as-a-service (SaaS) mainly automates traditional processes creating little additional value for users. Vendors of advanced technology and services (such as network services) find their evolving technologies applied as incremental improvements rather than as components of systemic innovation. This paper will focus on several innovations which the reader may (or may not) agree are nascent (not yet perceived) needs of customers and vendors alike – satisfaction of which could result in win-win.

Incremental innovations, transformed to systemic innovations by inductive thinking, are to be rapidly diffused. Some examples of such an approach are to be discussed - each example in a separate chapter (numbered 2 to 10):

- Chapter-2 Initiative by a Smart Business Network (SBN): collaboration within a SBN organization, even amongst traditional competitors, can be superior to a hierarchical value chain from both user and vendor perspectives.
- Chapter-3 Cascading innovations: collaboration between Vendors to form a Smart Business Network (SBN) creates the MPS; the PFCN vision for dynamically formed teams at the Customer level depends on MPS.
- Chapter-4 Emphasis on process-orientation: each module of a customized MPS is a service that supports an explicit instance of a defined process.

Please use the following format when citing this chapter:

Keedwell, B.G., 2008, in IFIP International Federation for Information Processing, Volume 283; *Pervasive Collaborative Networks*; Luis M. Camarinha-Matos, Willy Picard; (Boston: Springer), pp. 541–552.

- Chapter-5 Separation of Quality and Productivity: these two aspects are widely confused in definition and practice. Quality and Productivity are usually reciprocally related in S-curve manner.
- Chapter-6 Board guidelines set scene for innovation: goal is to meet functional requirements through simple-to-use solutions. Scientifically derived innovations minimize complication associated with inevitable complexity.
- Chapter-7 Education and research as the means; wealth and welfare of society as the end: The primary end is rapid diffusion of systemic innovation that encompasses processes, organization, software and communication – the two latter are collectively referred to as ICT (information communication technology).
- Chapter-8 Avoiding planning paralysis: Ready-Aim-Fire is to be replaced by Ready-Fire-Aim; aiming can be refined once the 'missile' is in flight. Jumpstart and Pilot can simulate and emulate the commercial condition. We aspire to reach commercialization over the short period of fifteen months that began with Engagement (start Jumpstart) in April 2008, planned to be followed by Conception (launch Pilots) in January 2009 and will hopefully end with Birth (Commercialization) in October 2009. Such a cycle has been started, and postponed several times since 1995 when the vision was articulated, and feasibility demonstrated, at LM Ericsson. (14), (16) and (18).
- Chapter-9 Live demonstration: concurrent with presentation of this paper at PRO-VE'2008 in September 2008, links will be provided to narrated, animated Power-points for those not at the live presentation (11). The targets of the links will be updated from time to time - one is already reachable even though the demonstration has yet to be finalized

Geographically the Northern Dimension is proposed to include Canada, Nordic/Baltics (NORBA) and North-West Russia.

A marketing initiative would bring Task Forces to this region to meet Smart Business Networks that would offer to conduct MPS pilot projects in preparation for global deployment.

**BIRTH OF MOBILE PROCESS SERVICE
IN THE NORTHERN DIMENSION**

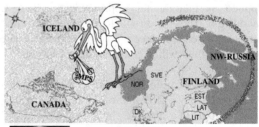

Build it (the MPS Competence Region)
– and they will come
Kevin Costner, Field of Dreams

2. INITIATIVE BY A SMART BUSINESS NETWORK

SMART BUSINESS NETWORK (SBN) ORGANIZATION

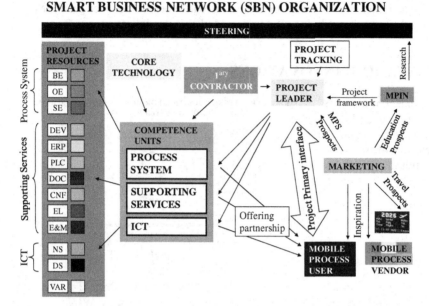

The totally disaggregated SBN organization model has twenty-five objects. PROJECT RESOURCES, COMPETENCE UNITS and MOBILE PROCESS VENDOR can be thought of as cluster objects within which 'generalization' can be described.

Project-resources are sub-contractors to Competence-units. Project-resources are recruited by Competence-units. Project-resources exist in four clusters as follows
<u>Process system cluster</u>: BE=Business engineering, OE=Organization engineering, SE=Software engineering
<u>Supporting services cluster</u>: DEV=Devices, ERP=Enterprise resource planning, PLC=Product life cycle, CNF=Conferencing, EL=E-learning, E&M=E-mail and messaging
<u>ICT cluster</u>: NS=Network service, DS=Data service
<u>Value-added retailer cluster</u>: VAR=Value-added retailer

Without doubt the most important aspect of such an organization is the net-value of the synergy that exists between the role holders in which specialization brings value and cost-to-organize and harmonize off-sets that value.

This organization model is the tip of a massive iceberg in which most synergies are 'under-the water'. Diverse examples of creation- and capture-of-value synergies include that MPIN (Mobile Process Innovation Network) described in Chapter-7 of this paper, provides a common environment for education, research and liaison between customers and vendors concurrent with Industrial Pilot Projects (IPP)

leading to rapid diffusion of education and research to commercialization. Another deeply submerged synergy is that travel costs during marketing, education and research activities are sponsored by airline SBN members – the latter get their pay-off as exclusive carriers during pilot-projects and commercialization.

3. CASCADING INNOVATIONS

Achievement of the MPS mission (make the MPS market) can be considered as a cascade of two innovations:

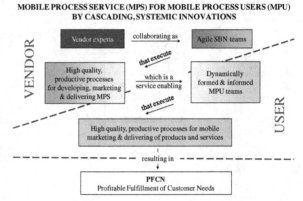

MOBILE PROCESS SERVICE (MPS) FOR MOBILE PROCESS USERS (MPU) BY CASCADING, SYSTEMIC INNOVATIONS

VENDOR & USER WIN-WIN

- VENDOR - an innovation related to how to organize the vendors in a manner that enables developing, marketing and producing a customized MPS for each Mobile Process User (MPU), and
- USER - an innovation related to how the MPU will exploit the MPS to transform its mobile processes.

This has turned out to be a tricky catch-22 in which the MARKETING role, assumed by Integrated Marketing, has attempted to convince both sides that there is a potential win-win.

At time of writing this paper there is a shared interest by a cluster of SMEs in Stockholm to invest in a few days to build a demonstration of how a MPS could enable a single mobile process, and there is interest

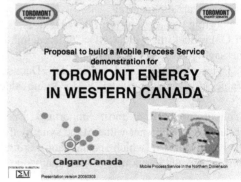

from Toromont Energy in Canada to study such a demonstration seriously if it shall be built. Distinguished Professor Emeritus Don Cowan, University of Waterloo has offered to host and chair a conference at which such a demonstration would be shown and debated. Both Vendors and Users need to see REALITY – a live demonstration.

4. EMPHASIS ON PROCESS-ORIENTATION

According to Ivar Jacobsen: "a PROCESS is a series of activities that produces a result of value – for the Customer".

There is still a wide discrepancy between Business PROCESS Orientation as a way of thinking and Business Process Orientation as a way of working (3).

According to the CAT EMEA Service Process manager (8): "for Caterpillar, PROCESSES, based on long experience, a vision of the business future and superior delivery, are sustainable competitive advantages in the field service business. Capture of that knowledge as models, and creation of subsequent systems from such models, is the route in which we are already engaged and we therefore have a conceptual fit with Integrated Marketing."

So what is the difference between a Product (which could be an out-of-the-box software), Software-as-a-Service (SaaS) and Mobile PROCESS Service (MPS)? MPS is the result of thinking outside the box. The Editor of MobileMonday has a journalist's analogy to a bird, an airplane and Superman (19).

It might be that PROCESS orientation really is still more a way of thinking than a way of working (3). If that is so it's not surprising that there is still no market for a Mobile PROCESS Service – hence our mission to 'Make the Mobile PROCESS Market'. It is our increasing perception that a MPS is a pre-requisite for making Business PROCESS Orientation a way of working (rather than just a way of thinking) – thus we have a classical Catch-22 situation (1).

This Catch-22 situation will ultimately be overcome when true MPS becomes successfully commercialized – but we know how difficult it is to infuse a systemic, as opposed to an incremental, innovation.

Introducing Business PROCESS orientation when the processes are mobile presents an added challenge because data flow between the resources (such as Sales Executives and Service Engineers) are envisioned to act as members of dynamically formed and informed, competent, empowered, self-managed teams.

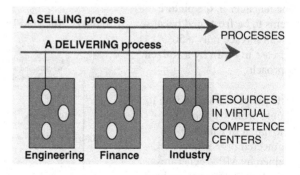

Selling and Delivering of Field Service are highly event-driven suggesting state-flow as a preferred model for MPS (2) and (6). State-flow is essential if 'Human-Assisting' Systems are to be superseded by 'Human-Assisted' Systems (4).

5. SEPARATION OF QUALITY AND PRODUCTIVITY

The difference between dreams, hallucinations and visions is that vision includes a plan to reach the goal.

The mission - namely to 'Make the Mobile Process Service market'- will be accomplished if the PFCN VISION, namely Profitable Fulfillment of Customer Needs (PFCN) is realized.

PFCN vision

IF
B2B, mobile, event-driven processes - such as selling and delivery - are engineered, then conducted by dynamically formed and informed, self-managed, empowered, competent teams

AND IF
agreement can be reached about how to share the created value

THEN
high process Quality and Productivity will result in Profitable Fulfillment of Customer Needs.

Sooner or later the vocabulary MUST be standardized – especially Quality and Productivity. Integrated Marketing has adopted Sohlenius' definitions (21) in which Productivity can be seen as a reciprocal of cost (and time) of conducting the process:

$$\text{EFFECTIVENESS} = f \text{ (Quality, Productivity)}$$

All this is easier understood by considering where Quality and Productivity is manifested in a Profit & Loss statement.
The S-curve notion is easier to explain with Cost of Goods and Services (CG&S) as a variable because it is Cost, rather than Productivity, that appears in a Profit & Loss statement:

PROFIT AFTER KAIZEN OR INNOVATION

		AFTER	AFTER
TODAY		KAIZEN	INNOVATION
100	SALES	100	110
40	CG&S	38	40
-----		-----	-----
60	GROSS PROFIT	62	70
30	M & S	27	30
20	ALL OTHER	20	20
-----		-----	-----
10	NET PROFIT	15	20
-----		-----	-----

The manager in the picture seems to be frustrated because he can foresee only a 50% increase in profit by a Kaizen approach.

With insight he sees a way to double profit by applying innovation in which re-engineered processes, as enabled by MPS, generates a new relationship (curve shape and displacement) between Quality and Productivity.

S-CURVE SHIFTS AFTER KAIZEN OR INNOVATION

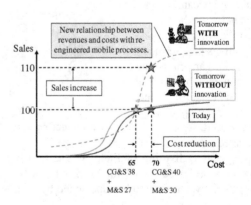

New relationship between revenues and costs with re-engineered mobile processes.

Tomorrow WITH innovation

Sales increase

Tomorrow WITHOUT innovation

Today

Cost reduction

Sales
110
100

65
CG&S 38
+
M&S 27

70
CG&S 40
+
M&S 30

Cost

Getting better Quality without sacrificing today's Productivity

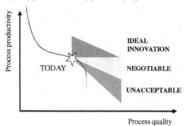

ASPIRATIONS FOR PROCESS QUALITY INNOVATION
Quality gain constrained by productivity requirement

A process innovation, **enabled by MPS**, that shifted the Quality/Productivity curve to the 'Tomorrow with Innovation' shape, would give a wide range of achievable superior qualities with negotiable productivity degradations.

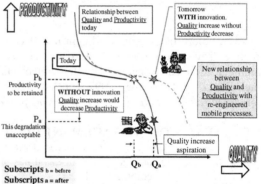

ACHIEVING PROCESS QUALITY BY INNOVATION

Getting better Productivity without sacrificing today's Quality

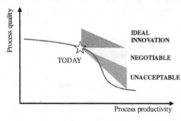

ASPIRATIONS FOR PROCESS PRODUCTIVITY INNOVATION
Productivity gains constrained by quality requirement

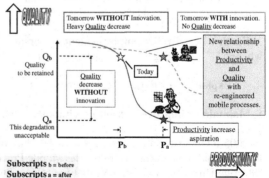

ACHIEVING PROCESS PRODUCTIVITY BY INNOVATION

A process innovation, enabled by MPS, that shifted the Quality/Productivity curve to the 'Tomorrow with Innovation' shape, would give a wide range of superior Productivities with negotiable degradations of Quality.

A 'Draining the Swamp' internal document by Integrated Marketing shows the relevance of the S-curve nature of the Quality/Productivity relationship (17).

6. BOARD GUIDELINES SET SCENE FOR INNOVATION

Constraints on paper length prevent presentation of Systemic Innovation. That subject is published elsewhere (20).

SYSTEMIC MAP OF THE INNOVATION PROCESS

Model World	Model for Dialog with Customer	Functional Model	Product Model	Process Model
Decision World	Customer Needs / Expectation	Functional and emotional requirements	Design parameters / Product	Process variables / Production
Human Competence World	Vision	Goal	Strategy	Activity

Gunnar Sohlenius

However, before Innovation can begin it is necessary for the Board to formulate a directive. This aspect was addressed at a conference hosted by Ericsson Mobile Communication and organized by Integrated Marketing Nordic AB at Memory Hotel, Kista 27 November 1997 entitled *'Exploiting radio communication in engineered field marketing, sales and service processes'* (7).

BETA LAVAL'S TOP MANAGEMENT DIRECTIVE

Acting upon the advice of a strategic business consultant the top management of Beta Laval has formulated a series of directives for the coming fiscal year:

1. Initiate a transition to being a more process-oriented company in which processes shall be identified, engineered and subsequently dramatically improved.

2. **Become a more customer-focused company** in which the needs of each individual customer shall be profitably fulfilled.

3. **Further decentralize empowerment of personnel to plan and implement activities** wherein managers act as enablers and coaches.

4. **Exploit modern technology** by applying inductive thinking.

5. **Maintain or improve current profitability level.**

In 2005 Integrated Marketing suggested (18) that the equivalent of a Top Management Directive will be required to 'Make the Mobile Process Service market'. We called it a 'Steering Directive' and that a Virtual Enterprise, Professor Emeritus Kenny Preiss calls it a Smart Business Network (SBN), might be capable of such a 'Mission Impossible' (12). Such an initiative must have strong leadership from a respected organization that might be a potential Customer, Vendor, Government or Academic unit (a university or institute). The hesitation by either of such organizations has been described (9).

7. EDUCATION AND RESEARCH AS THE MEANS; WEALTH AND WELFARE OF SOCIETY AS THE END

Cooperation with industry & National interest

There are strong forces today suggesting that academics should be more practical-thinking and that business practitioners should be more theoretical.

Cooperation with Industry ....

ACADEMIC INSTITUTION THIRD MISSION
achieved by
ENTERPRISE MOBILITY BEACH-HEAD

Some universities teach in a real-life environment. It is hard to imagine a better lab than a MPS (mobile process service) project at a time when both process and organization engineering are rapidly moving up to debunk the myth that it's all just about technology.

INTEGRATED MARKETING
ΣM

Enterprise mobility beachhead

The power of multi-disciplinary education is emerging fast, but it is essential to also work with sub-sets that overlap for a purpose. In this case the purpose (we call it the MISSION) is Birth of the Mobile Process Service market for the joint benefit of vendors and customers. Conception to Birth concurrent with education is a worthwhile goal. Learn while doing, and do while learning.

MOBILE PROCESS INNOVATION NETWORK
Education, Research & Industrial Pilot Project business unit clusters
with Enterprise Mobility beachhead

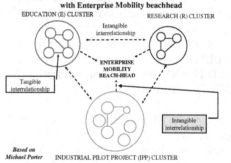

Based on Michael Porter   INDUSTRIAL PILOT PROJECT (IPP) CLUSTER

E, R & IPP transformation period

On the basis that research (R) and industrial pilot projects (IPP) require educated researchers and project managers, it seems that initial attention should be given to MPS-oriented education (E). Eventually researchers and project managers will become educators and the synergy between the three (E, R and IPP) will be repaid as high

SYNERGISTIC ENABLERS OF THE THIRD MISSION
A seven-year transformation period

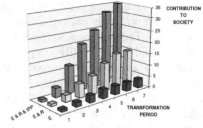

Quality and Productivity of mobile processes.

8. AVOIDING PLANNING PARALYSIS

PATH TO MPS COMMERCIALIZATION

Spear-headed by Tele-Energy and -Medicine demonstrations

| Jumpstart | Pilot | Commercial |

This is a proposal for the commercialization of Mobile Process Service by Autumn/Fall next year – that is by October 2009 (narrated animated reference 16). There would be three phases – JUMPSTART, PILOT and COMMERCIALIZATION. Milestones would be ENGAGEMENT, CONCEPTION and BIRTH. The suggestion is to conduct the JUMPSTART phase in Canada. BUILD DEMO could be completed by August 2008 thus creating a platform for a two-day, multi-national conference to be hosted by University of Waterloo.

At this NORTHERN DIMENSION CONFERENCE, delegates would plan the SEEK PILOTS and MEET PROSPECTS processes. The SEEK PILOTS process, beginning in October 2008, is expected to locate six international end-user PROSPECTS committed to send Task Forces to meet the vendor team Nov/Dec.

The International Institute for Telecommunications (IIT) and/or the Canadian Wireless Telecommunications Association (CWTA) could play Host at the six PROSPECT meetings during which Pilot Projects would be offered. Pilot agreements with three of the six PROSPECTs, has been defined as the CONCEPTION milestone. The three pilot projects could be conducted, in parallel, in Northern Dimension countries as agreed with the three end-user companies – for example one project in each of Canada, Finland and NW-Russia. Alberta Advanced Education & Technology is suggested to consider founding the MOBILE PROCESS INNOVATION NETWORK, possibly through an Alberta Ingenuity award, triggered by an Alberta university, and later other universities and institutes in Canada, the Northern Dimension – or even globally. Each individual pilot project has three stages – Process Simulation, followed by Lab Emulation, followed by Field Emulation. Birth of the Mobile Process Service market occurs with the first commercialization. Conception to birth in nine months – we are only human.
Planning paralysis would end if JUST ONE respected party would engage (15)!

9. LIVE DEMONSTRATION

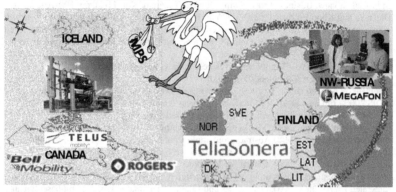

SEPTEMBER 2008 DEMO SCENARIO:
TELE-ENERGY IN CANADA & TELE-MEDICINE IN RUSSIA
ICT Data Centre at TeliaSonera in Nordic/Baltic

Build it
and they will come
Kevin Costner,
Field of Dreams

Any Operator may provide (or outsource)
GSM, CDMA or Mobitex Network Services

It is hoped that the presentation of this paper at PRO-VE 2008 in September 2008 can be supported by a live demonstration FROM CANADA, FINLAND and RUSSIA.

A narrated, animated Power-point story-board of the 'Identify Service Need' process was already available for download in March (13). A corresponding animated Power-point of the Russian 'Identify Diagnosis Need' process, as it applies to medical care, has to be constructed as the demo story-board.

The intention is to start building the demonstrations in Stockholm, for debate at a two-day multi-national conference hosted and chaired by Distinguished Professor Emeritus Don Cowan at University of Waterloo, Canada during August.

Demo construction will be monitored by process-oriented software (5) accessible over Internet by all Smart Business Network (SBN) members. This will impart an understanding of process orientation to all SBN members as they observe Assessing, Building-team and Contact-coordination (ABC) during demo construction process.

10. REFERENCES

1. Andersson T., Bider I., Svensson R. (2005). Aligning people to business processes. Experience report. Software Process: Improvement and Practice (SPIP), Willey, V10(4), 2005, pp. 403 - 413.
2. Andersson, T., Andersson-Ceder, A., and Bider, I. (2002). State Flow as a Way of Analyzing Business Processes – Case Studies. Logistics Information Management, 15:1, MSB University Press, 2002, pp. 34-45.
3. Bider I. (2005). Business Process Orientation: a Way of Thinking or a Way of Working? Industrial Review. Business Process Mngt Journal, Emerald, Vol. 11(1), pp. 100-101, 2005.
4. Bider, I., and Khomyakov, M. (2002). If You Wish to Change the World, Start with Yourself: An Alternative Metaphor for Objects Interaction 2001. In: Piattini, M., Filipe, J., and Braz. J., eds. Proceedings of ICEIS 2002 - the Fourth Conference on Enterprise Information Systems, Vol. 2, ICEIS Press, 2002, pp. 732-742.
5. IbisSoft (2007). ProBis – Lightweight Business Process Support System http://www.ibissoft.se/Download/ProBis.pdf
6. Khomyakov M., and Bider, I. (2000). Achieving Workflow Flexibility through Taming the Chaos. OOIS 2000 - 6th international conference on object oriented information systems. Springer, 2000, pp.85-92. Reprinted in the Journal of Conceptual Modeling, August 2001: http://www.inconcept.com/JCM/August2001/bider.html
7. Integrated Marketing (1998).Abstract from application to European Union for funding (Esprit_1998). http://www.pfcn.mine.nu/im/archive/Esprit_1998.pdf p. 38.
8. Integrated Marketing (2003). Caterpillar Reference. http://www.pfcn.mine.nu/im/archive/CaterpillarReference.pdf
9. Integrated Marketing (2005). Nets, Trees and Chains, an animated Power-point based on an internal communication with Professor Emeritus Kenny Preiss, BenGurion University of the Negev, Israel. http://www.pfcn.mine.nu/im/archive/CanadaNetsTrees&Chains.ppt
10. Integrated Marketing (2008). Demonstration planned for BASYS2008 in Portugal June 2008. PAPER WITHDRAWN http://www.pfcn.mine.nu/im/archive/BASYS2008_Abstract.pdf
11. Integrated Marketing (2008). Link to demonstration to be occasionally updated depending on design progress as the Prove2008 September conference date approaches. http://www.pfcn.mine.nu/im/archive/PROVE2008Demonstration.pdf
12. Integrated Marketing (2005). Professor Emeritus Kenny Preiss, Ben Gurion University of the Negev, Israel contribution to application by Inspiring Mobile Processes (IMP) to Tekes in Finland.http://www.pfcn.mine.nu/im/archive/VARA.Preiss.Kenneth.pdf
13. Integrated Marketing (2008). Demo ambition for Waterloo, Springtime 2008. http://www.pfcn.mine.nu/im/archive/ToromontDemo.ppt
14. Integrated Marketing (1995). Ericsson Mobile Data News 2/95 http://www.pfcn.mine.nu/im/archive/IMConference1995.pdf
15. Integrated Marketing (1998-2005). Funding attempts. http://pfcn.mine.nu/im/archive/EightPastApplicationsForPfcnFunding.ppt
16. Integrated Marketing (2008). Narrated, animated Path to Commercialization 20080508. http://www.pfcn.mine.nu/im/archive/PathToMpsCommercialization_version20080508.ppt
17. Integrated Marketing (2002). Draining the Swamp http://www.pfcn.mine.nu/im/archive/Draining SwampSurrounded.pdf
18. Keedwell, Brian (2005). Mobile Process Service, by an Agile Network, as a Disruptive Operating Innovation. International Conference on Agility, Helsinki Finland July 2005. http://www.pfcn.mine.nu/im/archive/mpsi_icam.pdf
19. Poropudas, Timo (2005). MobileMonday, Helsinki, Finland. "It's a bird, it's an airplane…no it's Mobile Process Service". MobileMonday website 6 January 2005. http://www.mobilemonday.net/mm/story.php?id=4024
20. Sohlenius, Gunnar (2007). The Nature of the Industrial Innovation Process, Coxmoor, UK, ISBN: 978-1-901892-23-9
21. Sohlenius, Gunnar (2005). Systemic Nature of the Industrial Innovation Process, Tampere University, p. 10.

PART 18

REGIONAL MANIFESTATIONS OF CN -1

57

TOWARDS A SUSTAINABLE INNOVATION FRAMEWORK TO ASSESS NEW INDO-SWISS COLLABORATION SCENARIOS

*Myrna Flores, **Mathew Cherian, ***Claudio Boër

*Swiss MTO Network - Swiss Federal Institute of Technology, Lausanne (EPFL)[1]
myrflores@hotmail.com
**Indian Institute of Technology, Madras, Department of Management Studies
mathewch@lycos.ch
***University of Applied Sciences of Southern Switzerland (SUPSI)
Department of Technology and Innovation, Institute CIM for Sustainable Innovation (ICIMSI)
claudio.boer@supsi.ch, SWITZERLAND

The world is "becoming flat" (Friedman, 2005), this means that innovations are emerging thanks to the deployment of new open collaborative frameworks and Information and Communication Technologies that enable the development of new products and services. Additionally, there are two key emerging trends changing the business arena: 1) the fast development of economies, such as China and India that besides low cost opportunities also represent new attractive markets counting together with more than 2 billion people and which at the same time are investing to improve their innovation capabilities and 2) the acknowledgement of the latent worldwide need to care not only about economic returns, but also about the social welfare of human beings, in whichever market they live, and the impact that any type of organisation has on the environment to diminish worries such as global warming, energy consumption and waste. Therefore, the goal of this paper is twofold: 1) propose a sustainable innovation framework that integrates four key enablers and 2) explain how this framework was applied in the SWISSMAIN project to assess and compare seven identified scenarios to enable Swiss and Indian firms to collaborate towards new business opportunities considering economic, social and environmental impacts..

1. INTRODUCTION

In the last years there has been a growing interest on the terms "*Innovation*" and "*Collaboration*". Many authors have given several definitions; but we could say that one word for Innovation is "*change*". Innovation means doing things in a different way, changing the rules of the game to improve the current status quo. The outputs are new products, processes and/or services that have business returns to give firms competitive advantage. What about "*Collaboration*"? In very simple terms it means doing things together, integrating partners inside and outside the organisational boundaries towards a shared strategy.

Even though these two terms seem very fashionable and simple to understand in terms of meaning, for most organisations is difficult to implement them successfully

---

[1] *Dr. Myrna Flores was a visiting researcher as part of the Swiss MTO Network in EPFL during 2007*

Please use the following format when citing this chapter:

Flores, M., Cherian, M. and Boër, C., 2008, in IFIP International Federation for Information Processing, Volume 283; *Pervasive Collaborative Networks*; Luis M. Camarinha-Matos, Willy Picard; (Boston: Springer), pp. 555–566.

in and individual way and even more challenging to apply in real business real scenarios when different organisations collaborate to achieve a common goal.

As a consequence, different approaches have been proposed to motivate and support different organisations to target innovations in a collaborative way. In Europe, the **Breeding Environment** approach emerged due to the success of several FP5 and FP6 EU funded research projects, which follow EU policies that stress the need of companies to collaborate in networks to share risks; competences and knowledge increase their success. One key project for the diffusion of this approach was the FP6 ECOLEAD Project. A Breeding environment represents an association or pool of organizations and their related supporting institutions that have both the potential and the will to cooperate with each other through the establishment of a "base" long-term cooperation agreement and interoperable infrastructure (Camarinha-Matos and Afsarmanesh, 2004).

Another approach to enhance innovation and collaboration is the one followed by the Living Labs Europe Project, which defines a the **Living Lab** as a "city area which operates a full-scale urban laboratory and proving ground for inventing, prototyping and marketing new mobile technology applications. A Living Lab includes interactive testing, but is managed as an innovation environment well beyond the test bed functions. As a city-based innovation resource the Living Lab can take advantage of the pools of creative talent, the affluence of socio-cultural diversity, and the unpredictability of inventiveness and imagination in the urban setting". Even though initially the Living Labs Europe Project targeted mobile applications, the concept is now applied to different sectors towards the creation of city based innovation hubs.

Additionally, the **open innovation** model (Chesbrough, 2006) proposes a broader collaborative approach, not linked to specific regions or partners, where as the author indicates "different partners should take much greater use of external ideas opening their business models". The open innovation approach also considers innovation intermediaries as those external entities that provide support to the innovation process.

Even if these models have made a great progress to enable firms understand and identify the potential new opportunities for innovation carried out in a collaborative way, there are still several uncovered angles. One key issue rarely integrated so far in most collaboration or networking approaches is "sustainability". This term is most of the times confused with the temporal space, in other words, it is being understood as making the innovation "*durable*" and "*successful*" in a long period of time. Nevertheless, the concept to be targeted in this paper goes beyond. Sustainability refers to networks of partners working in a collaborative environment, a living lab or an open innovation model which during the innovation process will consider the integration of the economic, social and environmental aspects of Sustainable Development.

The United Nations World Commission on Environment and Development reached a global consensus on the meaning of Sustainable Development: "development which meets the needs of the present without endangering the ability of future generations to meet their own needs".

The term refers to achieving economic and social development in ways that do not exhaust natural resources. At this point, the following research questions could be drawn:

1) How do networks of partners be mobilised to collaborate for innovation outputs integrating the economic, social and environmental aspects of sustainable development achieving "sustainable innovations"?
2) Is there any framework that enables and guides single organisations and networks to concentrate in key aspects towards innovation and sustainable development?
3) How can partners in developing countries, which usually have another level of conscience about the social and economical aspects, integrate sustainable development, especially when collaborating with western partners?

2. TOWARDS A SUSTAINABLE INNOVATION FRAMEWORK

Sustainable innovation is a process where sustainability considerations (environmental, social and financial) are integrated into company systems from idea generation through to research and development (R&D) and commercialisation. This applies to products, services and technologies, as well as new business and organisation models (Charter M. and Clark T., 2007). Even if the definition seems very simple and clear, still companies and networks struggle to understand how to integrate these concepts in their daily operations.

As a result, organisations which are part of collaborative networks could apply a framework to support a successful integration of the Sustainable Development principles and the development of highly innovative products and services for the global markets. In this regards, an integrated framework has been proposed to integrating four key enablers:

1. **Mass customization (MC)**, relates to the ability to provide customized products or services through flexible processes in high volumes and at reasonably low costs (Da Silveira G., et. al., 2001). One key dimension is to provide sufficient product variety to meet diverse customer requirements, business needs and technical advancements while maintaining economies of scale and scope within manufacturing processes (Huang G., et. al., 2005). The current challenge in regards to a collaborative network is to target mass customisation following the sustainable development guidelines starting from the requirements gathering and design phase, integrating the different partners' competencies.

2. **Sustainable Development (SD)**, targets the business holistic view of economic success taking care of wider environmental and social implications. Some authors argue that even if existing sustainable development policies, plans and programs within firms provide an important foundation on which to build efforts, they don't provide guidance to integrate the Sustainable Development concept in the day to day operations. Rocha, et. al (2007) have proposed a Sustainable Development Management System that integrates seven key elements: stakeholders, resources, leadership, processes, values, objectives and results. Additionally, other authors have stated the relevance of defining and implementing social and environmental performance indicators to follow up the impact in projects and technology life cycles (Brent C., et. al., 2007). Proper training to employees from the different partners of the network and incentives to change their mindsets may be required to achieve the expected results when collaborating.

3.   **Value Network (VN),** considers the need to right partner selection and network creation addressing also the environmental and social elements for sustainable innovation. Key activities under this enabler should focus on expanding the traditional focus on the forward flow of materials, components and products to explicitly address disposal, recycling, reconditioning and remanufacturing of used products (Kocabasoglu C., et. al., 2007). Additionally, different practices of knowledge management should also be addressed enabling different knowledge resources of sustainable development documents and know-how to be accessible by intra and inter-organisational partners to promote practices developed across organizational, professional, and multicultural boundaries to obtain multiplying effects (Wetherill M., et. al, 2007). This is particularly important for disseminating best practices to the network partners located in emerging markets, which usually don't assign sufficient resources to learn and implement Sustainable Development goals in real practice.

4.   **Product and Service Life Cycle** thinking demonstrates an important paradigm shift because it inherently analyses impacts of products and services from cradle to grave, i.e. from resource extraction to final waste disposal addressing also environmental and social challenges. Companies can no longer afford being concerned only with product quality and production efficiency. Practical realizations of life cycle thinking in business strategies are numerous and include life cycle analysis (LCA), which lays ground for design for environment, eco-labelling, and environmental product declarations and environmental management systems (Mont O. and Bleischwitz R., 2007).

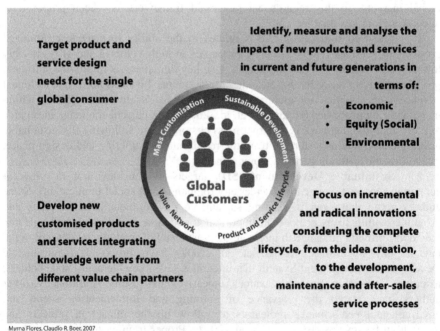

Figure 1. Integrated Framework for Sustainable Innovation
(Source: Flores & Boër, 2007)

The following sections will provide and insight of how the proposed Framework for Sustainable Innovation has been applied in a research project to support Swiss SME's to analyse potential collaboration scenarios in India.

3. THE SWISSMAIN INDIAN PILOT AND THE RESEARCH APPROACH

The SWISSMAIN project is a research project funded by the Swiss Innovation Promotion Agency - CTI International. One key research interest of the industrial partners was to identify new possible business models or scenarios that could enable them to identify business and collaboration opportunities in India considering not only economic but also social and environmental issues.

As a result, the SWISSMAIN Indian pilot was launched with the objective to support Swiss and Indian companies in the machine building sector to identify collaboration opportunities considering sustainable innovation concepts (economic, social and environmental). One deliverable of this Indian Pilot was the development of scenarios to facilitate Swiss firms to identify different potential ways to do business in India to integrate and evolve into new collaborative environments, where not only Switzerland obtains sustainable benefits but also the Indian counterparts.

According to Schoemaker (1995), scenario planning enables managers to identify a big range of possibilities to capture different opportunities in rich detail; Scenario Planning is a disciplined method to imagine different futures that can be applied to greater range of futures simplifying the avalanche of data into a limited number of possible states. Even though the proposed SWISSMAIN scenarios were defined targeting new collaborative environments for Indo-Swiss collaborations, they could also be applied within other contexts.

The current state is the *"AS-IS"* scenario and applying the Scenario Planning research methodology seven different scenarios were identified and analysed after carrying out fifteen face to face interviews to companies both in India and Switzerland during the SWISSMAIN Indian pilot.

To identify, develop, compare and analyse the possible business scenarios among Swiss and Indian entrepreneurs, a questionnaire with both open and multiply choice questions was designed to carry out face to face interviews. This SWISSMAIN survey had as an objective to understand the current business arena from Swiss and Indian entrepreneurs considering their initial (past), current and future collaboration perspectives and integrating a Sustainable Development Framework (Flores, et al 2008). More specifically, the first part of the questionnaire focused on gathering data about: 1) the different reasons of Swiss companies doing business in India or vice versa, 2) the impact, 3) the main challenges and 4) the Critical Success Factors (CSF's). The second part had the objective to obtain information about the experiences of the Swiss companies doing business in India applying the three axes of sustainable development: economic, social and environmental.

Table 1 presents the AS-IS (status quo) and the seven scenarios identified in the SWISSMAIN Indian pilot applying the Scenario Planning research method (Schoemaker, 1995). Figure 2 represents the AS-IS scenario.

AS IS *(status quo)*	Swiss companies are mainly sourcing components from European suppliers but exporting globally. There is currently no collaboration for product development with Indian partners. Furthermore, in regards to product innovation and market introduction in India the presence of Swiss firms is still very low in contrast to German and Japanese competitors.
1	**EXPAND SOURCING AND SELLING TOWARDS PRODUCT CUSTOMISATION** The very first scenario, targets an expansion of current sourcing and selling activities in India and also to increase customisation for emerging markets, considering: • The Swiss company's production/assembly remains in Switzerland • The Swiss firm assesses and selects new Indian suppliers, targeting a more collaborative environment for product design and customisation for India • Starts business collaborations, mainly selling and buying transaction • Swiss finished product(s) are sold to the same markets and/or new markets (including India)
2	**CONCENTRATE SOURCING IN DEVELOPED/DEVELOPING INDUSTRIAL CLUSTERS** The second identified scenario looks forward to motivate and enable Swiss firms to look for business opportunities by collaborating with Indian partners located in established or developing new clusters. In scenario 2 the following is considered: • The Swiss company's production/assembly remains in Switzerland • The Swiss company assesses and selects suppliers located in well established clusters (industrial aggregations) in different locations in India taking advantage of scale economies, networking activities and established infrastructure in the cluster (such a training from local associations and Universities). • New long term Indo-Swiss partnerships are built focusing on new product development or re-design of products with local suppliers and customers
3	**DEVELOP NEW CROSS BOARDER ALLIANCES (CBAs)** • The Swiss company looks for an existing Indian partner in the same or related market for fast entry to Asian/Indian market • Indian and Swiss partner form a new company with a common strategy and vision
4	**FULL OWNERSHIP IN EMERGING MARKET** In this full ownership scenario, the Swiss opens a new production facility in India targeting the local (Indian and/or emerging) market with existing products or customized ones according to the local needs. Based on the different interviews carried out in Swiss companies located in India, this is the most common current scenario of Swiss firms investing in India as for many of them seems less risky due to the fact that business culture is very different and unknown to Swiss counterparts, especially SME's
5	**ACQUISITION IN EMERGING MARKET** In this scenario, the Swiss company searches, selects and performs a due diligence to acquire a successful Indian-own established company in the same or similar industrial sector to facilitate the company entry to that (Indian and/or Asian) market with existing products or customized ones according to the local markets needs.
6	**TECHNOLOGY TRANSFER TO FIRM IN EMERGING MARKET** This sixth scenario considers a Swiss company licensing technology to an Indian firm to produce a finished product not existing in that particular emerging market.
7	**NEW SERVICES PARTNERSHIPS** In this last identified scenario a Swiss company identifies an local firm(s) or organisation(s) that can support delivering new value added services in that particular emerging market. During the research project, both interviewed Indian and Swiss firms, mentioned that this trend is growing.

Table 1. SWISSMAIN Collaboration Scenarios

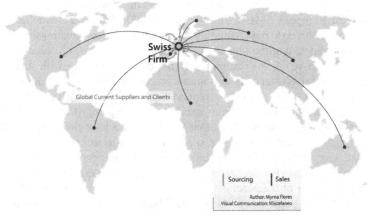

Figure 2. SWISSMAIN AS-IS Scenario

4. APPLYING THE SUSTAINABLE INNOVATION FRAMEWORK TO ASSESS AND COMPARE THE SWISSMAIN SCENARIOS

As observed from table 1, depending on the specific strategy, collaboration intensity, identified risks and business goals, different Indo-Swiss collaborative scenarios could emerge. Nevertheless, the proposed Sustainable Innovation framework (Figure 1) has been applied to assess and compare them. In other words, the proposed Sustainable Innovation Framework can be seen as a Benchmarking tool to compare the AS-IS with the seven identified scenarios. Table 2 provides an insight of the resulting comparison. For each scenario the level of impact has been identified for each of the enablers of the framework. Higher the intensity means that that enabler will be more strongly reinforced to achieve sustainable innovations. As observed, the AS IS scenario is the one that proposes less value or innovation creation to achieve sustainable innovations. This represents the starting point for companies to make decisions to select and further develop another TO BE scenario targeting both the potential collaboration with Indian counterparts integrating sustainable development principles.

In regards to **product customisation**, the seventh scenario "**new services**" can provide Indo-Swiss new collaborations higher impact, especially as the target will be to support the customisation of the local Indian needs with the local Indian skills in key processes such as design and after sales services.

In regards to **sustainable development** enabler, it seems obvious to think that the **"full ownership"** scenario of a Swiss company in India will have a very high impact as it will be "easier" to follow and implement current Environment Health and Safety (EHS) and green supply chain best practices followed in Switzerland in the new owned facility in India. Training to employees and suppliers could be carried out to transfer the EHS and green supply chain skills.

For the **value network**, working with "**specialised industrial clusters**" represents a high opportunity to integrate more rapidly new suppliers and obtain multiplying effects. A cluster is defined as a concentration of 'interdependent' firms within the same or adjacent industrial sectors in a small geographical area (Observatory of European SME's, 2002). Porter (1990) defines a cluster as a set of industries related through buyer-supplier and supplier-buyer relationships, or by common technologies, common buyers or distribution channels, or common labour pools. Therefore, Swiss firms can gain benefits by collaborating with suppliers in specialised industrial clusters, as for instance, consolidating raw materials from different suppliers in the cluster to reduce logistics and benefiting from their proximity to implement Just-in-Time practices reducing logistics costs and lead times. It is also important to highlight that UNIDO has a joint programme with the Indian government to support SME's in special locations to technologically catch-up and improve their manufacturing capabilities to better integrate with global value chains. One very successful case study was identified in Bangalore, where a very well developed cluster of the Machine Tool Making Industry was found. During the SWISSMAIN Indian pilot, the CEO of Ace Micromatic, one of the main Indian OEMs in this sector, was interviewed as he is leading this cluster in Bangalore. The cluster counts with more than 30 Indian partners (both SME's and OEMs) who are sharing best practices to increase their competitiveness. Recently this cluster has started to increase its exports to Asia being considered a very successful cluster project by UNIDO. Additionally, the Indian government has a new programme to develop the following new clusters: Pune, Vododara and Ludhiana (table 3).

Finally, for the innovation considering the complete **product life cycle**, again the "**new services**" services scenario seems a very feasible approach to add value in the complete product life cycle, specially when the Swiss production facility is in Switzerland and it is costly for the company to setup a new office in India only for these services. In fact, the "new services" scenario is currently applied by several companies in the machine tool sector in India with Japanese counterparts to provide maintenance services to products, local training to customers and product re-design according to local specific needs.

	AS IS	Scenario 1 Expand Sourcing for Product Customisation	Scenario 2 Sourcing in Specialised Clusters	Scenario 3 Cross Border Alliances	Scenario 4 Full Ownership	Scenario 5 Acquisition in India	Scenario 6 Tech Transfer	Scenario 7 New Services
Product Customisation	◔	◑	◑	◐	◑	●	◑	◐
Sustainable Development	◑	◑	◑	◑	◐	◕	◔	◑
Value Network	○	○	●	◕	◑	◕	◔	◑
Innovations in Product Life Cycle	◔	◑	◕	◑	◕	◑	◔	●
Impact on SWISSMAIN Scenarios	○ Very Low	◔ Low	◑ Medium	◕ High	● Very High	Source: Myrna Flores, 2007		

(left axis label: Sustainable Development Framework Four Enablers; bottom axis label: SWISSMAIN Scenarios)

Table 2. Sustainable Innovation Framework applied to SWISSMAIN to Benchmark the seven identified scenarios

As the next step of this scenario benchmarking approach, a roadmap can be suggested to start step by step new Indo-Swiss collaborations. In the case of the SWISSMAIN Indian Pilot, two key scenarios are currently being targeted by the industrial project partners for next steps:

Scenario 2: To develop a clear understanding of the Indian clusters' technological and production skills, competences, directory of suppliers and range of prices. Table 3 and Figure 3 show the three main identified clusters which could provide machined components in India to Swiss entrepreneurs.

	Quality	Low Volumes	Price	Guidelines	Specialisation of each cluster
Pune	1	3	3	1	Precision engineering, automotive, machine tools
Vadodara	2	1	2	2	Castings, fabrications, heat treatment, precision machining
Ludhiana	3	2	1	3	Castings, forging, not high precision
	1 best option	2 average	3 worse option		Source: Myrna Flores, 2007

Table 3. Identified Clusters in India for machined components
(Source EDI India, 2007)

Figure 3. Concentrate Sourcing in Developed/Developing
Industrial Clusters (Scenario 2)

Scenario 7: To identify which services could be developed to cover all the value chain. Specific needs from interviewed Swiss companies in India also include vocational training services for technical personnel to operate advanced machinery and maintenance service to customers. Local Universities can also be seen as partners to support the training services and the collaborative product design. Figure 4 presents the Scenario 7 of SWISSMAIN.

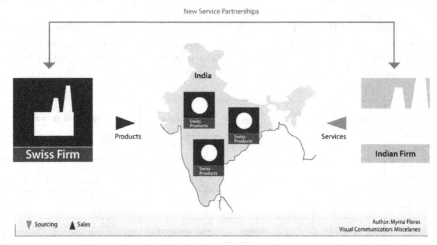

Figure 4. New Services Partnerships (scenario 7)

5. CONCLUSIONS

The current paper proposed a new sustainable innovation framework integrating key concepts such as innovation, collaboration and sustainable development. This framework was used as a guideline and benchmarking tool to compare the seven identified scenarios. It is also important to mention that by applying this framework during the SWISSMAIN Indian pilot, several weaknesses and strengths of each scenario were identified specially for the deployment of sustainable development practices and collaboration to obtain as target result high innovation outputs. Future efforts should concentrate to further develop the framework to develop a methodology consisting of quantitative measures to have proper Key Performance Indicators (KPI's) that can quantify not only qualitatively but quantitatively each enabler to support the comparison and right selection of the best potential TO BE collaboration scenario by Swiss SME's.

6. ACKNOWLEDGEMENTS

The authors would like to thank the Swiss Innovation Promotion Agency – CTI International for the funding provided to realise the SWISSMAIN Indian Pilot. Gratitude is also given to Mr. Duruz from Maillefer and Mr. Voirol from Bosch-Sapal, industrial partners of the SWISSMAIN project, who provided their business requirements to develop the scenarios. We also sincerely thank Prof. L.S. Ganesh, Prof. Srinivasan and Prof. Prakash Sai, from the Indian Institute of Technology in Madras for supporting this Indo-Swiss research project and the 15 Swiss and Indian firms and organisations, which participated actively in the project during the face to face interviews.

A special thank you note is also given to the University of Applied Sciences of Southern Switzerland (SUPSI), for supporting Myrna Flores to lead the SWISSMAIN Indian Pilot while working at the Institute CIM for Sustainable Innovation (ICIMSI) and to Michel Pouly from the Swiss Federal Institute of Technology, Lausanne (EPFL), the project leader of the SWISSMAIN project, who invited Myrna Flores as a visiting researcher in EPFL to develop this research. Last but not least we thank Ana Beatriz Dominguez Organero for her great work in the graphic design of visual information.

7. REFERENCES

Brent C., and Labuschagne C., 2007, An appraisal of social aspects in project and technology life cycle management in the process industry, Management of Environmental Quality, An International Journal, 18: 413-426

Camarinha-Matos L. and Afsarmanesh H., Collaborative Networked Organizations, A research agenda for emerging business models, 2004

Charter M. and Clark T., 2007, Sustainable Innovation Key conclusions from Sustainable Innovation Conferences 2003–2006, The Centre for Sustainable Design University College for the Creative Arts, www.cfsd.org.uk

Chesbrough H., Open Business Models, How to Thrive in the New Innovation Landscape, Harvard Business School Press, 2006

Entrepreneurship Development Institute of India (EDI-India), http://www.ediindia.org

Da Silveira G., Borenstein D., Fogliatto F., 2001, Mass customization: Literature review and research directions, Int. J. Production Economics 72:1-13

Flores M., Boer C., Canetta L., Pouly M., Cherian M., 2008, "Critical Success Factors and Challenges to develop new Sustainable Supply Chains in India based on Swiss Experiences", *To be published in the International Conference of Concurrent Enterprising, ICE Conference Proceedings 2008*

Friedman T., 2005, The World is Flat, Ed. Penguin

Huang G., Simpson T., Pine, B.J. II., 2005, The power of product platforms in mass customisation, Int. Journal of Mass Customisation, Inderscience Enterprises Ltd, 1: 1-13

Kocabasoglu C., Prahinski C. Klassen R., 2007, Linking forward and reverse supply chain investments: The role of business uncertainty, Journal of Operations Management, 25: 1141–1160

Living Labs Project, http://www.livinglabs-europe.com/livinglabs.asp

Mont O. and Bleischwitz R., 2007, Sustainable Consumption and Resource Management in the Light of Life Cycle Thinking, European Environment 17: 59–76

Observatory of European SMEs, Regional clusters in Europe, European Community, http://europa.eu.int/comm/enterprise, (2002)

Porter M., The Competitive Advantage of Nations. Free Press, New York, 1990.

Rocha M., Searcy C. and Karapetrovic S., 2007, Integrating Sustainable Development into Existing Management Systems, Total Quality Management, 18:,83 – 92

Schoemaker, P., 1995, Scenario Planning: A Tool for Strategic Thinking, Sloan Management Review; Winter 1995; 36, 2

United Nations, General Assembly, Brundtland Report: Our Common Future: Report of the World Commission on Environment and Development, available at: http://www.worldinbalance.net/pdf/1987-brundtland.pdf

United Nations Industrial Development Organization (UNIDO) Cluster Development Programme in India, http://www.smallindustryindia.com/clusters/unido/cdp.htm

Wetherill M., Rezgui Y., Boddy S. and Cooper G, 2007, Intra- and Inter-organizational Knowledge Services to Promote Informed Sustainability Practices, Journal of Computing in Civil Engineering, 21: 78-89

ENRICHING COLLABORATION AMONG EASTERN EUROPEAN SMEs THROUGH DEDICATED VIRTUAL PLATFORM
Potentials, Needs, and Research Challenges

58

Ali Imtiaz,
Research Institute for Operations Management (FIR) at Aachen University of Technology,
Ali.Imtiaz@fir.rwth-aachen.de, GERMANY

Jannicke Baalsrud Hauge
Bremen Institute of Industrial Engineering and Applied Work Science
baa@biba.uni-bremen.de, GERMANY

In the wake of Globalization, the Eastern European small and medium size manufacturers (SME) are facing ever-increasing competition from the larger and multi-national players. Collaboration with other companies may be the only economical way to overcome this challenge. In most cases, these communities are formed due to favourable socio-economic conditions found in a specific geographical area. Therefore, a specialized approach needs to be developed to cater the possible interactions for related SMEs in a specific industrial sector; this is only possible through an affordable collaboration platform. This article will present a research approach and the relevant challenges for the development and introduction of a collaboration tool based upon open source capabilities with industry specific business process functionalities.

1. INTRODUCTION

The success of collaboration is not only a matter of finding a partner with the right key competencies, but more a question of having the right ICT tools for seamless information processing and the right people to perform the daily collaboration work as well as on the ability of the participating organisations to act in a dynamic environment [Österle, 2001, COM 2002]. Looking at the supply chain of the manufacturing industry, it is obvious that the Tool-and-Die making workshops play a role as suppliers of knowledge intensive products and services [Auerbach et al. 2006]. Therefore, every change large manufactures do on their supply strategies, leads to a new requirement which a tool and die making workshop has to meet in order to stay as a supplier.

Up to now, the Tool-and-Die making workshops have been able to meet these new requirements with high quality products and services as well as an excellent educated workforce but this isn't possible any more as the non-European competition from other SMEs grows [Semolic et al, 2007]. Furthermore, the one-of-a-kind production results in high costs and risks, since more complex products in terms of functionalities and high quality demands engage more complex and expensive manufacturing technologies. The range of needed manufacturing technologies comprises traditional as well as more innovative and expensive

Please use the following format when citing this chapter:

Imtiaz, A. and Hauge, J.B., 2008, in IFIP International Federation for Information Processing, Volume 283; *Pervasive Collaborative Networks*; Luis M. Camarinha-Matos, Willy Picard; (Boston: Springer), pp. 567–576.

technologies. These are seldom all in-house, so there is need for sharing capacities (machines, materials, machine operator) and knowledge resources (technologies, competences). This leads to a need for tighter collaboration [Scheer, 2002, Sherman, 1996, Frederix, 2003] and to a further development of the existing regional industrial clusters towards virtual enterprise networks not only loosely sharing tools, but actively using a common collaboration platform.

The need of better collaboration requires a faster, more reliable and integrated support system. It is needed to sustain a constructive trend for industrial collaboration among SMEs. Therefore an effective as well as an efficient way of observing, analysing and handling of information is required. A collaborative platform can help to achieve a seamless information flow between the cooperating companies. Furthermore, only implementing a common collaboration platform without developing a common business model will lead to sub-optimal solutions.

2. BACKGROUND

Typically clusters are product-oriented specialized communities [Porter, 1998]. Within clusters, there are companies focusing on different stages of the manufacturing cycle (e.g., treating raw materials, assembling) [Eschenbächer, 2003]. All companies maintain a high degree of specialisation on the final product specific features, which implies that "generic" production capacity is not offered. The situation of company specialisation within clusters historical and cultural reasons. Product know-how has been transferred from one generation of workers to the other, as the strong localisation has prevented work force mobility. In periods of growth, the number of companies have multiplied through spin-offs and outsourcing, spreading the knowledge of products and processes.

Customers of clustered SMEs are medium to large companies selling to final customers world-wide. The customer's expectations from these SMEs are mainly the faster, cheaper and more efficient delivery of the complex tools. Due to the above described features, the cluster is a natural source of specialised production capacity for these companies. Often SMEs do not have resources to response to these requirements alone. It is therefore imperative to form sustainable collaborative networks. Far from being "community leaders", these companies develop opportunistic subcontracting relations with the small manufacturers. Sub-subcontracting is observed frequently, as excess demand is passed on from one small company to the other when an order cannot be fulfilled internally. In most cases, this happens in quite informal and hectic way through a network of relationships nurtured by proximity.

Sharing knowledge, expertise, competences and particularly the lessons learned is very well acquainted inside the tool-shops. So the basic premise for the collaborative work and the sharing culture is well developed [Österle, 2001; Frederix, 2003; Semolic, 2007]. The latter premise, the motivation to share, is pushed by extremely tough market conditions because of the cheap labour force from China and other fast developing countries from the Far East. Tool-makers detected already that their only competitive advantage is continuous innovation in technology and technical solutions. For this reason, they are able to offer high quality and innovative solutions to the most complex problems (tools). The only guaranty is the effective knowledge sharing supported by the management of the innovations.

Looking at different SME clusters, it can be stated that these often have both "technical" and "organisational" problems related to their production management and resource planning, as well as to e-collaboration but also with respect to management of customer relations and e-collaboration in carrying out their day-to-day business.

3. RESEARCH METHOD

Clusters are still trying to find the most efficient organizational model to support interoperability and collaboration in the production of tools. Because of the nature of the small production volume, which is usually individual production, interoperability and collaboration in particular process is still vague. Each project usually includes one or at most two partners collaborating. The rules of interoperation are therefore not yet exploited. Collaborative design, collaborative technology planning and distributed manufacturing are still far from real implementation. The most successful collaboration processes in tool making clusters are seen to be education, marketing activities and some common research projects.

On the level of operation software, the clusters are dependent on their customers. As suppliers, they are usually bonded to the software solutions of their customers. Most used commercial solutions are SAP and BAAN as ERP systems, CATIA and ProEngineer as CAD/CAM systems. They are also using some specific B2B applications and solutions to solve particular specific problems which are mostly connecting one of the partners in the cluster to one of the customer. The figure below shows a typical network of tool and die makers:

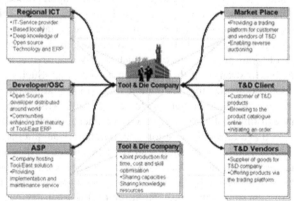

Figure 1: Network of tool and die makers including customers and suppliers

In order to improve the collaboration ability, there is a need among the Tool and Die maker to have a common collaboration platform serving their specific need and reflecting the diversity and different needs and requirements within this industrial sector. This platform must also offer an access to all other stakeholders in the networks (Suppliers, It vendors, etc.)[Meyer, 2004, Baalsrud Hauge, 2004].

Requirements on collaboration tools

Today, the borders of organizations are becoming more transparent and organizations, enabled by ICT, cooperate in changing constellations. Information, services, and products can be offered by sub-units of organizations, by single organizations or by collaborations between companies [Hribernik, 2008a,b]. The Tool and Die-making workshops have the same typical organisational and technical problems as a lot of other SME clusters. Furthermore they are also facing harder competition from the Far East as well as increasing labour costs which reduce their competitive advantage. The effects of these challenges have become dramatically evident in the last years, as many SMEs have been shut down in industrial clusters around Europe. The process will ultimately endanger the competitiveness of the SMEs clusters and of the entire local economy. Therefore, a suitable collaborative platform for this sector must not only provide an ICT-tool, but need to be embedded in a business model decreasing the organisational challenges, too.

Collaboration means, above all, the integration of systems, services and people in order to deliver results. This implies that in order to achieve the optimised result, all stakeholders need to have the ability to support a seamless information flow and to exchange all relevant documents without any interruptions.

Collaborations are complex to handle due to various reasons: different goals among collaborating partners and rapid process changes [Seiter, 2006]. In these dynamic and flexible networks, most partners have not collaborated before, which often results in the lack of trust. In addition, European collaboration networks also need to deal with the culture aspect. The above mentioned problems are relevant for almost all collaborations. These problems can be classified into three categories:

- Interoperability, management and organisational models
- Sharing culture and technology transfer
- Cheap and effective software solutions based on open-source standards

For Tool-and-Die making workshops, the problems are mainly related to their production management and resource planning, customer relationship management, and especially e-collaboration. Collaboration processes represent a key factor in the competitiveness of Tool-and-Die making clusters. By improving these processes, clusters will be able to strengthen their position as suppliers. Such an improvement can be achieved through the implementation of a collaboration platform utilising emerging, innovative technologies at the lowest possible cost. The Tool and Die making industry can only collaborate if they have interoperable IT solutions. Since expensive ERP and Middleware solution are not being an alternative for many companies, the interoperability problem can only be solved if they begin to use a standardised businesses language. One first step in this process is the use of common Enterprise applications which have similar business concepts and common data schemas. In particular electronic collaboration of the industry we studied (and believed to be true for many similar industries) is best facilitated through the provision ERP applications and to integrate existing applications. To enable industrial cluster made up of SMEs to participate in e-collaboration these applications however must be extended with modules specifically created for the particular processes carried out in the cluster which may be different for other industries.

So far the research and work carried out have shown that if small and medium sized enterprises intend to enter into e-business by means of a solution which is integrated into their business processes with their partners, suppliers and customers, it is not enough to look only at the technical infrastructure and to implement a technical solution, but it is also important to look at the interoperability at an organisational level, so that there is a need for a business model supporting the optimisation of organisational structure within in the cluster additional to the collaboration platform.

Collaboration Platforms
Collaboration platforms are inter-organizational application systems for supporting or enabling inter-firm cooperation and collaboration. Over the past years different collaboration platforms have been developed. Such platforms may differ in the services they offers- ranging from only supporting document handling to complex collaboration platforms comprising ERP-, and SRM/CRM functionalities [Bafoutsou, 2002].

Collaboration platforms support or facilitate inter-firm collaboration and electronic integration within inter-organizational arrangements such as supply chains or in virtual enterprises and networks. Collaboration platforms are expected to benefit participants by reducing the costs and increasing the quality of inter-firm information exchange. Information sharing through shared IT-based platforms may reduce companies' required investments in relationship-specific IT assets [Gogolin, 2003; Hieber, 2002]. However, analysis of the use of collaborative platforms shows a progress in its acceptance and is widely used for research collaborations.

There are several commercial collaborative platforms available on the market today. A typical example of such a platform is the BSCW platform. This platform has been used for several years, and supports common file exchange, messaging etc. Another example is also the waste of collaborative platforms established during research projects in order to support the collaboration. Two good examples here are the collaboration platforms of the ECOLEAD and Laboranova projects. Common for many of the collaboration platforms of research projects is that they are in operation during the project run time, mostly kept on a status quo for several years after that. This allows the partners to get access to tools and material also after the project, but most of these platforms are only open for project members. Additionally, these are non-profit platforms, so that little efforts will be put in order to maintain and improve the platforms for new users after finishing the project.

Also the Tool East project has a collaborative platform which is in use during the project period. The Tool-East collaboration platform is an industry specific solution based upon already available open source based ERP solutions. In this way, the costs are kept on a low level but on the same time offer a solution with the needed functionalities and the possibility to integrate this into already existing solution at the company site. By introducing the Tool-East concept, a standardisation process will be induced, which leads to better data exchange with their business partners in electronic format. For the tool and die making clusters this implies that they can take advantage of other e-business tools to support their particular business processes including collaborative engineering, change management, supply chain management, collaborative load balancing among others.

In order to integrate the component into the overall supply chain, as well the SMEs' existing individual back-end enterprise systems, the solution is being augmented with (adaptive) Web Service Modules based on SOAD, allowing fast and flexible, standardised interfacing. Since the Tool-East solution need to be put on top of existing software it is imperative to identify interfaces at an early stage.

Therefore, the process models and the flow diagram were extended with a column for IT application, which the users completed.

However, as the project develops an open source collaboration tool with ERP functionalities it is essential that the industrial partner can continue to use this platform after closing the project, so it is necessary to develop a platform which is easy to maintain and which generates enough benefit and revenue to be proactively driven from the stakeholder also in the future.

Business model

Looking at the current situation among the tool and die makers, it becomes clear that their future competitiveness will be based upon their ability to adapt their organisational structure combined with their ability to take advantage of new collaboration tools. How ever, even though we have set upon an open source solution which is quite cheap to maintain and to develop further, it has been recognized that the Tool-East collaboration tool will still require quite much technical know-how. It cannot be expected that the Tool and Die makers do have this expertise in house, so it is important to develop a business model ensuring that the tool and die makers will get support and the solution will be maintained also in the future.

In this context, a business model, placed on industrial level, provides a framework. It includes all relevant main business processes in a Tool-and-Die industry. The Tool-East model will decrease existing obstacles for seamless collaboration among SMEs. Business model consists of interrelations of three elements business strategy, business organization and ICT usage and together with legal and social environment, competitive forces, customer demand and technological change impact on company's business model definition as described in the figure below. Until recently, research paid only little attention to the aspect of establishing information transfer and sharing among business networks for collaborative efforts supporting SMEs to play a major role in competing with large enterprises, but strategies that reflect toolmakers clusters intentions is under development. It can be characterized by the strategy developed by the cluster TCS from Slovenia (also partner in this proposal). This strategy supports:

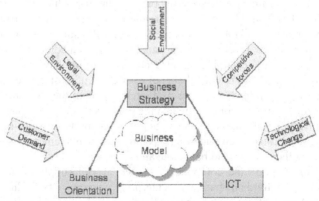

Figure 2: Environment, Business Models, Strategy, Process and Information Systems (Osterwalder, 2004)

- Horizontal and vertical integration of the companies and organizations involved into the tool-making business
- Strategy of a concentric diversification - where the Tool-and-Die technologies are the key competences
- Strategy of internal development on the field of strategic key competences
- Strategy of joint ventures and internationalization

4. FINDINGS

Even though there are several tools available on the market suitable for supporting collaborative work, like advanced SRM/CRM/SCM-tools, most of these are neither affordable for SMEs, nor offer the functionalities required. While adapting and implementing an ERP system for clusters of SMEs, the participating SMEs need to be aware that their business processes belong in the bigger picture of the overall cluster. Therefore, participating SMEs within a cluster must reach the highest level of awareness of the cluster – the realisation that their cluster behaves externally like a single enterprise.

On a high level, the collaboration platform needs to fulfil the following requirements:

- Building-up a platform that bridges the geographic distance between the actors, and creates a virtual mirror-image of their real-world collaboration
- Specifying and developing a secure and trustful plug-and-play environment, that is flexible enough to be adapted to the specific needs of the Innovation Network
- Defining, specifying and developing services and applications supporting characteristic processes in innovation networks, for instance: competence search for network configuration, knowledge exchange among partners, collaborative product development, and setting-up and running virtual laboratories.

The project has decided to develop an open source-based solution, which is quite cheap to maintain and to further develop, but the Tool-East collaboration tool will still require much technical know-how. The Tool and Die-making companies cannot be expected to have the expertise in-house, so the first business considerations have been taken in order to ensure that the platform will be maintained after the finalization of the research project. Therefore, the consortium has emphasized on developing a business model for the post-project time supporting an association between the Tool and Die-making companies and the ICT community. The collaboration will be based on clearly defined roles, strict contracts and management of the various contracts. A proposed structure is developed maintaining a focus on the functional and organisational constraints; briefly presented in the figure below.

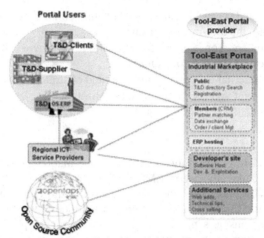

Figure 3: Tool East Solution with the Business Concept

One entity is recommended to run the Tool-East portal with the only public data. The entity will be formed as a virtual organisation of the Tool-East ICT partners representing regional industries. The clients and regional service providers (SPs) have access to the portal and can search and update their profiles. Restricted data is stored and shared between regional SP as a backup of the local setup at the client. A client can access the Tool-East portal through these regional SPs (regional SPs are responsible for data security, maintenance, and training and customized solutions for their regional clients). The Tool-East solution will promote combined development at client level as well as the involvement of open-source community for enterprise level customisations.

The Tool-East collaboration platform has the following logical structure:

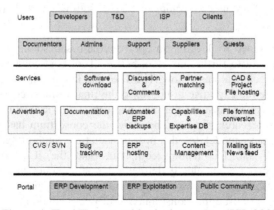

Figure 4: Tool East portal logical structure (JSI, 2007)

The main functionalities are:
- ERP development portal functionalities (source code hosting and versioning system, bug reporting and tracking, file upload / download area through CMS, discussion groups & commentaries (portal database), testing platform (a test installation of an ERP system), news feed (portal))

- ERP exploitation & support functionalities (documentation hosting, program files download area with installation instructions, ERP system testing for evaluation, training and dissemination, ERP system hosting for T&D companies, registration, ERP users directories, public interfaces to link to the ERP system (for public data sharing/gathering, open hosting platform for additional and third party services, automatic software upgrade functionality)
- Public community portal (T&D related news feed with comments and discussion groups, Registration and mailing lists, T&D company directories with their specific knowledge/capability/expertise, Listings, Advertising and business promotion (optionally paid services), Partner matching between clients and T&D companies, Project design file hosting / sharing, Open platform for additional and third party services
- Portal management functionalities (Users management (login, registration, user groups management), Layout management, Editorial function, Contents protection, System and storage management)

5. CONCLUSION

Clearly the European SMEs can only be globally competitive if they manage to organise themselves into clusters and collaborate. To enable industrial clusters, comprising of SMEs, to participate in e-collaboration, ERP based applications must be extended with modules created specifically for the particular processes carried out in the cluster, which may be different for other industries. It is also imperative that they have access to a common collaboration platform not only including common software and the core components of collaborative platforms like messaging and team collaboration tool enabling real-time collaboration and communication but also offering additional services such as training material and a virtual community for information and knowledge exchange. Furthermore, their business processes needs to be aligned and optimised.

The previous research has shown that if small and medium sized enterprises intend to enter into e-business, by means of a solution that integrates their business processes with their partners, suppliers and customers, it is not enough to look only at the technical infrastructure and to implement a technical solution.

The Tool-East virtual collaborative platform will be fairly inexpensive and in addition, offer guidelines and training concepts that assist SMEs in analysing, identifying and finally modifying their business processes through ERP as well as a collaborative e-platform. The solution's modular architecture and the open source approach will not only help SMEs to keep the costs of maintaining and future development low, but also at the same time allow for future technical developments and organisational changes. The implementation of interfaces to standard software used in Tool-and-Die making workshops will also improve the interoperability not only on the organisational level, but also on the data flow level.

For SMEs, an enormous potential can be found in strengthening the open-source initiative in general and particularly in this field of business. The challenge of harnessing the open-source community remains, but the Tool-East project considers it of up-most importance to attempt to leverage the immense power of hundreds of dispersed developers for the development of an integrated business application for

Tool-and Die making enterprises from the very onset to create future sustainability.

ACKNOWLEDGEMENTS. This work has been partly funded by the European Commission through IST Project Tool-East: Open Source Enterprise Resource Planning and Order Management System for Eastern European Tool and Die Making Workshops (No. IST-FP6-027802). The authors wish to acknowledge the Commission for their support. We also wish to acknowledge our gratitude and appreciation to all the Tool-East project partners for their contribution during the development of various ideas and concepts presented in this paper.

6. REFERENCES

Auerbach, M.; Imtiaz, A.; Baalsrud Hauge, J.: Collaboration within tool and die making industry through open-source ERP-solution with integrated CRM-functionalities. In: ICE 2006, 12th Int. Conf. on Concurrent Enterprising: Innovative Products and Services through collaborative networks. Palazzo delle Stelline, Milan, Italy, 26-28 June 2006, Proceedings ICE-Conference 2006, S. 141 – 148

Baalsrud Hauge et al.(2004): Enhancing e-commerce business models of selected SMEs by a multi-mode approach in International Journal of Internet and Enterprise Management, p.122, Vol.2, 2004

Bafoutsou, G., Mentzas, G.: Review and functional classification of collaborative systems, International Journal of Information Management, 22, 2002, S. 281-305.

Porter,M.: Cluster and new economics of competition, Harvard Business review,p.6, 1998

Eschenbächer, J. et al.: Emerging Concepts in E-business and Extended Products, s.15 in Gasòs/Thoben: E-business Applications, p.24 and 28ff, Springer Verlag, Heidelberg, New York, Tokio, 2003

European Commission, COM 2002, 714, Industrial Policy in an Enlarged Europe, Communication from the Commission to the Council, the European Parliament, the Economic and Social Committee and the Committee of Regions

Frederix, F., Cooperation in Dynamic Networked Organizations, p.221 in Gasòs, J. Thoben, K.-D. (Eds.): E-Business Applications – Technologies for Tomorrow's Solutions; Advanced Information Processing Series, Springer, 2003

ECOLEAD project: http://virtual.vtt.fi/virtual/ecolead/

Gogolin, Marcel (2003): Success and Failure of Collaboration Platforms, in: Lechner, Ulrike (Hrsg.), Proceedings of the Tenth Research Symposium on Emerging Electronic Markets 2003, S. 169183, Bremen: University of Bremen, Germany, 2003.

Hieber: R.: Supply Chain Management. A collaborative performance measurement approach. Vdf Hochschulverlag at ETH, Zürich 2002.

Hribernik, K., Thoben, K.-D., Nilsson, M.: Collaborative Working Environments. in: Encyclopedia of E-Collaboration. Idea Group Reference, 2008, pp. 308 – 313 (ISBN: 978-1-59904-000-4)

Hribernik, K., Thoben, K.-D., Nilsson, M.: Technological Challenges to the Research and Development of Collaborative Working Environments. in: Encyclopaedia of E-Collaboration. Idea Group Reference, 2008, pp. 616 – 617 (ISBN: 978-1-59904-000-4)

Laboranova project: http://www.laboranova.com/

Meyer, M.;Lücke, T.; Schmidt, C.:Plug and Do Business – ERP of the Next Generation for Efficient Order Processing in Dynamic Business Networks. In: International Journal of Internet and Enterprise Management 2 (2004) 2, S. 152-162.

Meyer, M.: From Enterprise Resource Planning (ERP) to Open Resource Planning (ORP) – The OpenFactory Project. In: Advanced Manufacturing – An ICT and Systems Perspective. Publisher: Taisch, M.; Thoben, K.-D. Network of Excellence on Intelligent Manufacturing Systems, Mailand and Bremen 2005, S. 324-328.

Österle, H.; Fleisch, E.; Alt, R., Business Networking, Springer Verlag, Berlin, 2001;

Osterwalder, A et. al(2005): clarifying business models;origins, present and future of the concept; http://www.businessmodeldesign.com/publications/Preprint%20Clarifying%20Business%20Models %20Origins,%20Present,%20and%20Future%20of%20the%20Concept.pdf

Scheer, A.-W., Grieble, O., Hans, S., Zang, S.(2002), Geschäftsprozessmanagement – The 2nd wave. In: Information Management & Consulting, 17, 2002 Sonderausgabe, pp. 9-14.

Seiter, M.: Management von kooperationsspezifischen Risiken in Unternehmensnetwerken, Verlag Vahlen, München,2006

Semolic,B, et al: The Tool East Soloution for industrial Clusters in Eastern Europe in: Project Management Practice, Issue 4, Winter 2007/2008, p.3-8.

59	# E-GOVERNMENT IN POLAND AGAINST THE BACKGROUND OF OTHER EU COUNTRIES

Joanna Oleśków-Szłapka
Poznań University of Technology
Institute of Management Engineering, POLAND
joanna.oleskow@put.poznan.pl

Joanna Przybylska
The Poznań University of Economics
Chair of Public Finance, POLAND
j.przybylska@ae.poznan.pl

E-government – the use of information and communication technologies in public administrations, combined with proper organizational change and skills development – has become an explicit component of public sector reform, as an instrument increasing efficiency, strengthen competitiveness and enhance modernization. E-government enhances the delivery of improved public services and supports active democratic engagement.

1. INTRODUCTION

The present digital revolution and increasing competition in Europe and the whole world make electronic administration a more and more important issue both for both the state and the society. Virtualization of public administration is necessary, if only because of the membership in the European Union and obligations it imposes on particular member states. Another reason is related to the changes in the society. The society becomes better educated and hence – more aware of its rights. People begin to claim for improvement of the quality of public services and for the change of old bureaucratic structures. As public expenses continuously rise, citizens, who pay taxes, are more and more interested in their effective use.

The aim of this article is to present the e-government model as a special kind of virtual organization and to compare the processes of e-government implementation in selected European countries. In the conclusion, the authors of this article evaluate the advancement level of the e-government in Poland as compared to other European countries. Apart from that, the authors also indicate the main barriers to implementation of electronic public services in Poland.

Please use the following format when citing this chapter:

Oleśków-Szłapka, J. and Przybylska, J., 2008, in IFIP International Federation for Information Processing, Volume 283; *Pervasive Collaborative Networks*; Luis M. Camarinha-Matos, Willy Picard; (Boston: Springer), pp. 577–586.

2. THE NOTION OF E-GOVERNMENT AND STAGES OF ITS IMPLEMENTATION

2.1 E-government definition

The European Commission defines the notion of e-government as "the use of information and communication technologies in public administrations combined with organizational changes and new skills in order to improve public services and democratic process and strengthen support to public policies"(eEurope…, 2005).

The European Commission defines e-government as more than just a new model of state administration. According to the definition, e-government means a profound reconstruction of business processes of administration, realized on the basis of information and communication technologies, where the aim is to reach the state of transparency and openness of the public sector, which is to be productive, efficient and above all – citizen-friendly. A citizen has a right to expect the state administration to be foreseeable and understandable. A system designed to fulfill these expectations should allow for being controlled by citizens themselves. Such control automatically results in more efficiency on the part of officials, whose work results in the old system were difficult to be evaluated. The essence of e-government is being enterprise-, organization- and citizen-oriented, since nowadays, they all have the right to expect from the state the same quality of services as they receive in the private sector.

E-government is also defined as providing online access to administrative services. According to this definition, it is a way in which public administration uses new technologies in order to provide citizens with services and information customized to their needs and in a much more practical, useful and user-friendly way. As a consequence, public information and services should be available 24 hours a day and 7 days a week (Haltof, Kulągowski, Kulisiewicz, Kuśnierek, Sobczak, 2002).

2.2 Stages of e-government implementation

The development and implementation of e-government involves consideration of its effects on the organisation of the public sector (Cordella, 2007) and on the nature of the services provided by the state including environmental, social, cultural, educational, and consumer issues, among others.

Implementation of e-government into a traditional public office is a multi-stage process (see Figure 1). The first stage – creating the front-office structures – should lead to providing citizens and entrepreneurs with a full access to services. The service area should include the level of "information" and "interaction" (the levels of providing services by e-government are further described in the point 3 of this study). This stage is currently dominant in the EU countries.

The second stage involves reconstruction of structures and inner processes of public offices, according to the needs of users. This should contribute to moving from the level of "interaction" services to the level of "transactions".

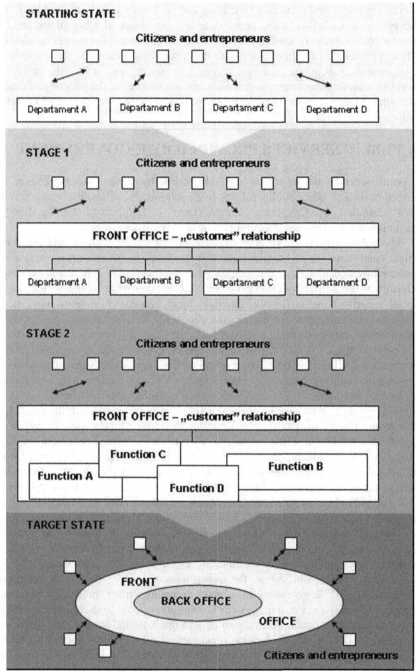

Figure 1 – Exemplary model of e-government implementation

[Authors' study based on J. Florek, Elektroniczny kontakt środowisk lokalnych z urzędem administracji państwowej i samorządowej, Instytut Łączności, Zakład Rozwoju Sieci i Zastosowań Informatyki w Telekomunikacji, Warszawa 2002]

Having integrated particular functional and problem areas (front- and back-office sub-systems), we arrive at the target state and can speak of a completed transition from a traditionally functioning office to e-government. The target model is an office providing full integration of the processes essential for citizens and entrepreneurs, full online customer service, customers' insight into the process and stages of handling their case, supervision and monitoring of the progress of cases by the office's employees and managers, as well as the use of elements of knowledge management (Florek, 2002).

3. PUBLIC SERVICES PROVIDED BY E-GOVERNMENT

Types of services that should be available on-line by the state administration, local governments and other public entities (e.g., schools, hospitals, libraries, etc.) have been classified by Capgemini Ernst&Young and approved by the European Commission (Analiza..., 2002; Online availability ..., 2004).

The public services have been divided into two groups: those addressed to all citizens and those whose recipients are entrepreneurs. In the first group there are: (1) Income taxes (declaration, notification of assessment), (2) Job search (obtain job offerings as organised by official labour offices, no private market initiatives), (3) Social security benefits (obtain: unemployment benefit, child allowance, medical costs and student grants for higher education), (4) Personal documents (obtain: an international passport and a driver's licence for a personal vehicle not for professional use), (5) Car registration (register a new, used or imported car), (6) Application for building permission (obtain a building or renovation permission for a personal building (regular, initial request, i.e. not taking into consideration contesting and appeal)), (7) Declaration to the police (officially declare a theft of personal goods to a local police office), (8) Public libraries (consult the catalogue(s) of a public library to obtain specific information regarding a specific carrier), (9) Certificates (obtain a birth or marriage certificate), (10) Enrollment in higher education (enroll students in a university or another institution of higher education subsidised by an official administrative body in the country), (11) Announcement of moving (announcement of change of address of a private person moving within the country), (12) Health-related service (obtain an appointment at a hospital officially recognised by a national, regional or local authority) (The User Challenge..., 2008).

The public services for businesses are: (1) Social contribution (declare social contributions for employees affected by corporations), (2) Corporate tax (declare corporate tax for income from normal activities of a corporation), (3) VAT (declaration and/or notification for transactions regarding normal activities of a corporation), (4) Registration of a new company (most important registration procedure to start a new company), (5) Submission of data to the statistical office (at least one statistical questionnaire with data to the National Institute for Statistics of the country), (6) Custom declaration (declarations related to the normal activities of a corporation), (7) Environment-related permits (obtain at least one environment-related permit, delivered at the lowest administrative level, concerning the start of a corporate activity (not taking into consideration contesting and appeal)), (8) Public procurement (Tender for public procurement, subject to national public announcement) (The User Challenge..., 2008).

It is worth mentioning that when analyzing public services from the perspective of their implementation, it is assumed that they may be available on one of the four stages of development: Stage 1: the information level - refers to on-line availability of information necessary for starting a process. Stage 2: the one-way level – refers to the possibility of downloading forms from the official website of a public entity, so that after printing a given form, it is possible to start the process related to a given service. Stage 3: the two-way level– refers to the possibility of fulfilling the form on the official website of a public entity (a system of auto-identification necessary). Stage 4: fully electronic transaction system, providing all services online, including the decision-making and -giving. The paper form is unnecessary on any stage of the realization of a service (The User Challenge…, 2008).

4. E-GOVERNMENT IN POLAND COMPARING TO EU

4.1 The actual state of e-government in European Union

European Union constantly monitors e-government developments in member countries. Web-based survey on electronic public services delivered inside EU is held every six months. Member countries are expected to ensure interactivity of basic public services.

On 25th of April 2006, the European Commission adopted the i2010 e-government Action Plan. The action plan defines five priorities: (1) No citizen left behind, (2) Making efficiently and effectiveness a reality, (3) Implementing high-impact key services for citizens and businesses, (4) Putting key enablers in place, (5) Strengthening participation and democratic decision-making.

In this paper we discuss three core e-government indicators: *"online sophistication"* (based on a renewed 5 level model), *"fully-online availability"* (it continue to be measured on the existing 4 level model. This indicator will allow the evaluation on a historical continue basis), and *"user centricity"* (new indicator comprising four sub-indicators: data security, reducing administrative burden, multi-channel access, compliance with accessibility standards).

In UE online sophistication is on average 76%, at the level classified as "transactional". This shows advancement from 2006 where services were classified on average as "two-way interactive". Against the "fully-online availability" indicator Europe has advanced from 50% in 2006 to 58% in 2007. The variance between countries remains important. Austria is located at the top of the EU27+ league table with very impressive ratings at or near 100%. Malta, Slovenia and Estonia again stand out as three of the newer member states that have embraced e-government and achieved continued high levels of online service delivery – well above the average (The User Challenge…, 2008).

With an average of 19% the overall results of user centricity e-service delivery measurement stay modest. Three countries score more then 30% user centricity/ Austria, Norway and Bulgaria (The User Challenge…, 2008).

Citizens and businesses across Europe are discovering the benefits of e-government. A recent Eurostat survey (see figure 2 and figure 3), found that around half of Europe's businesses with internet access now use it to interact with the public authorities, with peaks of 88% and 94% in Denmark and Sweden.

As can be seen from statistics the major lag in EU concerns the usage of e-government by individuals rather than enterprises. Citizens, too, are increasingly visiting government offices on line, rather than queuing outside them. There are still major differences between level of e-government.

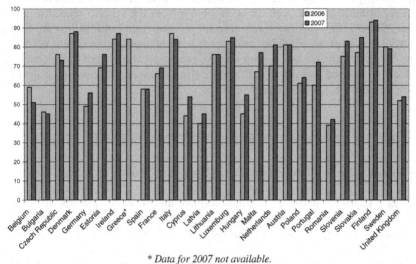

* Data for 2007 not available.
Figure 2 – E-government usage by enterprises[1]
[Authors' study based on Eurostat data]

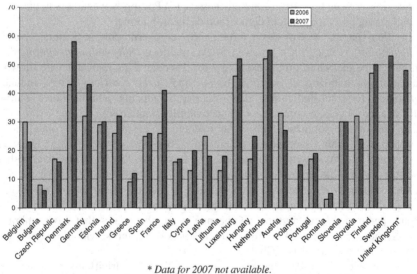

* Data for 2007 not available.
Figure 3 – E-government usage by individuals - total[2]
[Authors' study based on Eurostat data]

---

[1] Percentage of enterprises which use the Internet for interaction with public authorities.
[2] Percentage of individuals aged 16 to 74 using the Internet for interaction with public authorities.

Europe continues to make sound progress on the supply of online public services as a key enabler to deliver the i2010 e-government action plan and Lisbon goals. However much remains to do to serve citizens who are increasingly exposed to and versed in web services (The User Challenge..., 2008).

E-government is progressing at varying speeds in 10 countries that joined EU on 1st of May 2004, where it remains on average less sophisticated than in older Member States. All new members have now established e-government portals that serve as one-stop-shops for citizens and businesses. They have also made significant progress in e-enabling basic public services.

4.2. The development of e-government in Poland

The origins of the first e-government strategies in Poland go back to 2000 when was published a strategy document „Aims and Directions of the Information Society Development in Poland.", edited based on seven opinions prepared on order of State Committee for Scientific Research (Report on e-government..., 2005). One of the strategic objectives consists in using ICT to help establishing open, transparent, citizen-friendly structures of public administration and ensure greater efficiency of the public sector.

The continuation of above concept is the action plan ePoland - The Strategy on the Development of the Information Society in Poland for the years 2001-2006. The plan provides the detail of the actions to implement in order to reach the objectives of the Information Society strategy and of the eEurope+ Action Plan. E-government is one of the main elements of the action plan (ePolska..., 2001).

In Poland as well as in European Union (EU) there is a need to improve access, dissemination and exploitation of public sector information. The development of electronic public services in Poland does not look good when compared to EU Member States.

Poland's *"fully-available online"* indicator has risen from 20% in 2006 to 25% in 2007, which shows modest progress in online service delivery. Poland remains in the lower quartile. The assessment of *online sophistication* of Poland according to the new method shows an average of 53% which is below the EU27+ average. Services for businesses are performing slightly better with 62% against 47% for G2C services. None of the nine defined *pro-active* "stage 5" services attain the maximum score. Thus the user-centric pro-active and automated development of online public services stays in a very preliminary stage in Poland.

Concerning *user centricity*, Poland scores with 13% below the EU27+ average of 19%. Polish entrepreneurs as EU ones are able to run on-line much more errands than citizens. In 2006 in EU percentage of transactions for enterprises on average amounted to 67,8%, for citizens – 36,8%. Whereas in Poland 37,5% and 8,3%. An availability of public e-services is a little, and also a little is usage of already existing on-line services. Poland with 15% of citizens using information or forms from public authorities' websites considerably lags behind the EU average (34%).

Rather high is share of the enterprises that contact with public administration via Internet – in 2007 it reached 64%, what places Poland near to EU-25 average – 66% (Grodzka, 2007; Eurostat).

The development of polish e-government depends on accomplishment of many sectorial and national data communications projects such as: (EU Inclusive e-Government..., 2008): e-PUAP - Electronic Platform for Public Services, Administration to Citizen - A2C, Administration to Business - A2B, Administration to Administration - A2A.

One of main barriers to supply and uptake of e-government is a lack of leaders at central, regional and local level (Goreczna, 2007). Small understanding of e-government issue by politicians is also one of the main obstacles. The other urgent problems related to e-public services development in Poland concerns: legal regulations not adjusted to e-government and knowledge-based economy, underdeveloped ICT infrastructure of households, insufficient funding for development of ICT infrastructure in local public administration, *back-office* infrastructure not prepared to deliver comprehensive eservices, insufficient understanding of e-government and scarce ICT qualifications of public servants.

Local government in Poland is not very much involved in building e-government. It is not interested very much in introducing electronic services. The latter are usually perceived as another task to be fulfilled, not another way of delivering public services that were hitherto accomplished traditionally. Local institutions are predominantly function-oriented, not goal-oriented; basically bureaucratic, that could not "go forward" without instructions "from above"; on the other hand, being resistant to new developments in public sector. Limited access to ICT infrastructure doesn't allow the majority of citizens to experience advantages of Internet therefore – as yet – they don't put pressure on public institutions to develop e-government. Though, citizens are more and more aware of their rights as customers, they expect to be served quickly, effectively and in transparent way.

5. SUMMARY AND CONCLUSIONS

An increasing number of countries and international organizations are realizing the benefits of e-government in the economic, social and administrative sector. The drive to implement e-government has resulted in the formulation of many e-government visions and strategies, driven by their own sets of political, economic and social factors and requirements.

This new vision of e-government encompasses the provision of better public administration, more efficient, transparent, open, and participative governance and the implementation of more democratic political processes. Government in the EU emerges as a tool for better government and, ultimately, for increasing public value. To respond to the challenges posed by these trends, e-government will need to be more knowledge-based, user-centric, distributed and networked.

The future of e-government is very uncertain and requires to be approached by depicting different scenario in which a wide range of contextual factors, such as social, cultural, institutional and economic should be described. Bearing in mind the equal opportunity principle, the common access to e-government services in Poland and other EU countries is conditioned by providing all citizens with Internet access, or at least by establishing a network of public Internet access.

Comparing to EU countries Poland is located in the minority of countries which do not have e-government very well developed and a lot of work must be done in that domain. In 2007-2010 for computerization of public administration is assigned more than 2,5 mld zlotych from the budget, UE funds, Schengen fund and

Norwegian Financial Mechanism (Computerization Plan, 2007). The planned investments shall permit to catch up the other countries in EU.

Actually Poland is in the process of developing a new concept which could rival the use of e-Signatures to access secure public and private on-line services.

The monitoring reports on the implementation of the ePoland Information Society strategy show insufficient progress of the development of electronic services in Poland.

By the end of 2010 twenty public tasks shall be done by means of electronic way. In order to extend current state of e-government, mainly limited to making information available and saving forms from websites, it is essential that to:

- accomplish planned data communications projects,
- amend the law on electronic signature, that enables its implementation and application in wider range,
- simplify and supplement a valid legislation concerning the computerization of administration,
- prepare the infrastructure of the offices,
- provide easy, common and cheaper access to broad-band Internet.

REFERENCES

1. Analiza rozwoju e-usług publicznych w Polsce na tle krajów Unii Europejskiej. Skrócony wyciąg z badań, Cap Gemini Ernst&Young Polska Sp.z o. o., Warszawa, 2003.
2. Computerization Plan for 2007–2010, Journal of Law 2007 no 61, iterm 415.
3. Cordella A., E-government : towards the e-bureaucratic form?, Journal of Information Technology (2007) 22, 265–274.
4. eEurope 2005 Action Plan (http://europa.eu.int/information_society/eeurope/2005/index_en.htm)
5. ePolska, Plan działania na rzecz rozwoju społeczeństwa informacyjnego w Polsce na lata 2001 – 2006, Ministerstwo Gospodarki, 11 września 2001 r., s. 5.
6. EU Inclusive e-Government, national reports supporting policy development for e-Inclusion in the field of ICT and inclusive e-Government, http://countryprofiles.wikispaces.com/EU+Inclusive+e-Government, browsed 28.02.2008.
7. Florek J., Elektroniczny kontakt środowisk lokalnych z urzędem administracji państwowej i samorządowej, Instytut Łączności, Zakład Rozwoju Sieci i Zastosowań Informatyki w Telekomunikacji, Warszawa, 2002.
8. Goreczna M., eGovernment country report for Poland, ASM- Centre of Research, Poland, Warsaw 2007.
9. Grodzka D., E-administration in Poland, Infos no 18, The Seym Analysis Agency, Warszawa 2007.
10. Haltof P., Kuligowski S., Kulisiewicz T., Kuśnierek W., Sobczak A., Raport Administracja Publiczna w sieci 2002 – czy rzeczywiście bliżej obywatela?, Internet Obywatelski, Warszawa, 2002.
11. Online availability of public services: How is Europe progressing? Web based survey on electronic public services. Report of the fifth measurement in October 2004, Capgemini, 2005.
12. Report on e-government in Poland, IDABC eGovernment Observatory, 27 June 2005, s. 5.

13. The User Challenge. Benchmarking The Supply Of Online Public Services. 7th Measurement - September 2007, Capgemini, European Commission Directorate General for Information Society and Media , 2008.

Oihab Allal-Cherif

Grenoble Ecole de Management and LINC Lab
Europole, 12 rue Pierre Semard, BP127, 38003 Grenoble, FRANCE
IRIMA: Institut de Recherche et d'Innovation en Management des Achats
oihab.allal-cherif@grenoble-em.com

Dimitris G. Assimakopoulos

Grenoble Ecole de Management and LINC Lab
Europole, 12 rue Pierre Semard, BP127, 38003 Grenoble, FRANCE
dimitris.assimakopoulos@grenoble-em.com

The deployment and use of electronic marketplaces contrary to expectations still remains marginal in the 'Francophone' business landscape. Even though several major business groups act as champions and invest in them, the vast majority of large and small companies remain wary of these digital inter-company platforms. Despite convincing arguments discussed in the scholarly, professional and trade literature, the credibility of marketplaces is constantly undermined in practice as they have to incessantly fend off rumours about bankruptcy in France and elsewhere. Moreover, the term 'marketplace' can cover a multitude of business relationships and it is currently difficult to compare offers and distinguish across a range of services. The purpose of this paper is therefore to put forward a typology, by identifying, analysing and classifying the about 225 Francophone marketplaces we found in the fall of 2007. The proposed typology enables us to (1) highlight their diversity and types of economic models that underpin their value chain (2) observe that the majority neglects certain high-added value services for which demand is great, and favours services which are hardly cost-effective and for which supply is much higher than demand, and (3) highlight future possible evolutions by examining the collaborative strategies few of these professional virtual communities have been making in the past few years.

1. INTRODUCTION

It seems quite surprising that electronic marketplaces are still struggling to hold sway over the digital networked economy. One would think that the savings vowed by these Internet enabled business platforms would attract hoards of clients eager to make both quick and long-lasting productivity gains. However, commercial success is scarce for the entrepreneurial contenders who embark on the marketplace adventure, and out of the thousands of start-ups that invested in this niche over the last decade or so, only a few hundred in the world actually survived the downturn in 2000. Their number is still dropping today in the aftermath of mergers and

Please use the following format when citing this chapter:

Allal-Cherif, O. and Assimakopoulos, D.G., 2008, in IFIP International Federation for Information Processing, Volume 283; *Pervasive Collaborative Networks*; Luis M. Camarinha-Matos, Willy Picard; (Boston: Springer), pp. 587–596.

bankruptcies of the past few years. And yet, for almost 20 years, experts have agreed that the volume of Business to Business (B2B) commercial exchanges generated by electronic platforms would rise significantly and affect all industries (see, for example, Malone, Yates and Benjamin 1987, 1989).

From the outset, it is not easy to define to what extent companies would be well-advised to steer away or follow this digital hierarchization process. Moreover, given that about 80 percent of the marketplaces created in Europe since 2000 have disappeared, dubiousness reigns. One can still find, however, a countless amount of services whose added value can vary considerably. Marketplaces integrate functionalities that go far beyond the framework of procurement, which is the most common, but not the only domain of expertise. Instability, diversity and fragility do not often facilitate the choice of an e-business solution. Companies liable to use marketplaces need to have a better understanding of their landscape, but it seems almost impossible to obtain a clear vision in such a complex and unstable environment (Grey, Olavson and Shi, 2005). And yet, the stakes are high, because the rise of the Internet in inter-company business dealings has turned optimizing partnerships and customer / supplier management into an important and decisive competitive advantage. It is therefore paramount not to be outstretched by competitors in this domain. Even more so, since strategic positioning is often now built in a global context and the life cycles of products and technologies are becoming shorter, leaving decision-makers little room for hesitation. It seems timely therefore to address the following set of questions:

-   Are marketplaces strictly tools for optimizing costs, or can they be used as strategic tools for collaborative project management, market analysis and intelligence? Or, put it differently, should marketplaces attach more importance in managing transactions, or harnessing information and enabling collaboration and networking as seen in few successful virtual professional communities?
-   Are marketplaces tools for heightening competition, or means for encouraging collaboration among actors that would not otherwise seek to work together in developing new products or services?
-   What is the future of marketplaces? Or, how can we distinguish those which really have a future, from those which are already jeopardized by economic models that are not viable?

To provide some answers to the questions above, we identified about 225 Francophone marketplaces in the fall of 2007 and listed their functionalities (Allal-Cherif, Assimakopoulos and Favier, 2008). This exploratory research yielded an analysis of the Francophone marketplaces within a typology matrix which addressed the type of relations that existed among a broad range of actors. The individual positioning of each of these marketplaces enabled us to observe the strategic positioning of marketplaces in France, and in the French speaking world, as well as speculate about the future of these marketplaces. But before we discuss some of our findings, in the next section we review three distinct views of marketplaces according to the scholarly and professional literature. Furthermore sections 3 and 4 respectively present our research methodology and discuss some of our main findings, including our typology of marketplaces in the Francophone business landscape. Finally, section 5 offers some concluding thoughts looking into a near 'collaborative' future.

2. THREE VIEWS OF MARKETPLACES

Back in 2000, Philippe Nieuwbourg, President of the European Marketplace Association, defined marketplaces as 'virtual spaces for companies to conduct business' (Nieuwbourg and d'Hondt, 2000); Internet sites, where sellers and buyers come together, and make transactions for the purchase of products and services. At least, that is what marketplace managers hoped for, since they would make money easily on this type of activity by charging a commission on each completed transaction among a large number of sellers and buyers. For example, Consumer Packaged Goods, CPGMarket (www.cpgmarket.com) is a marketplace that federates purchases for several major agro-food groups (e.g., Danone, Henkel, Nestlé) from its 7900 suppliers. It completes a huge number of transactions, but this case is exceptional, in the sense that when the industrial giants decide that their transactions will only be made by means of their common marketplace, the suppliers have little choice but to follow suit. Yet an independent marketplace, which simply introduces itself as a new place for buying and selling, and whose only particularity is the fact that it is digital, would hardly be attractive enough to survive.

Commentators have also underlined that a marketplace can be defined 'in the broad sense of the term, as a site of informational exchange about supply and demand, to which the main actors of a given sector or field of activity subscribe' (Rechenmann, 2002). The term 'transaction' has disappeared from this definition: the main aim of marketplaces is therefore shifted from being essentially commercial, to be informational. The decision-makers who visit these marketplaces are, first and foremost, looking for information that will enable them to innovate –generate novel ideas thanks to new economic or technical opportunities that can be consulted on the site – or develop their company thanks to a better understanding of acquired or open market segments. Before aspiring to the title of exclusive purchasing platform of a given sector of activity, i.e. the transactional marketplace, the marketplace must firstly be informational, in other words, federate all of the actors of a professional virtual community and forge itself a solid reputation (Rechenmann, 2002).

The term 'marketplace' is an umbrella term encompassing a number of very different realities because it is used to qualify many forms of inter-company digital relations. These relations essentially exist between companies and their suppliers and range from the simple 'one-shot' purchase, in response to a very specific need, to a long-term partnership, with all associated co-developments, joint investments, projects related to new components, new products, or new technologies. But marketplaces can also facilitate collaboration between companies in competition, be it for buying or selling, or/and, in research and development projects. Marketplaces can therefore position themselves very differently depending on the market they focus on, the way they wish to be remunerated and the role they wish to play with respect to their members. The main advantages of these inter-organisational platforms stem from reducing transaction and coordination costs for all actors, facilitating the search for new suppliers, comparing offers more easily and more comprehensively, eliminating intermediaries, and benefiting from economies of scale. Marketplaces are hybrid organisations between the market itself, where Porter's five forces determine the transactional conditions, and hierarchy, where management sets the standards of acceptable quality, costs and deadlines.

Marketplaces therefore question linear models for circulating goods and capital (Fisher, 1997) and favour the development of networked structures which encourage both competition and collaboration among companies. Even though, the main characteristic of marketplaces is to encourage the circulation of information, therefore to considerably increase the level of transparency within a market (Soh, Markus and Kim, 2006), a better understanding of these tools indicates that the real upheaval will reside in collaboration. Marketplaces constitute a potentially ideal way of coordinating the joint actions of several companies in accomplishing their projects, sharing strategic information and resources, or developing new products and innovative technologies.

Uncertain environments, asymmetry of information and the diverging interests of the marketplace providers and their members assimilate relations between operators, buyers and suppliers to that of an agency relationship (Brousseau, 1993). Such a relationship 'relies on contracts through which two types of organisations (buyers and suppliers) subscribe to the services of a third party (the operator) to accomplish, on their behalf, one or several tasks, in a given decisional domain'. Such a relationship often favours buyers who have the freedom to take initiative and leave suppliers with no choice but to become a member of certain marketplaces chosen for them. Often the founder of a marketplace, and thus its principal shareholder, is a buyer, as it is the case for example in Schneider / SourcingParts. Naturally, this threefold agency cooperation agreement seems skewed, since some interests are easier to be defended than others, and not all stakeholders share the same motivations for belonging to a marketplace. This inequality is undoubtedly one of the main reasons that underlie the unpopularity of marketplaces, because if all parties do not build such relationship based on mutual trust (Pavlou and Gefen, 2004), it is likely that such relationship is going to be under significant strain to deliver in the relatively short term. It may therefore seem meaningful to question such an agency relationship in order to balance out the benefits for each of the parties involved in a marketplace. This rebalancing is not going to take place without a radical change in the underlying economic model, which should no longer be based on cost reductions and optimal transaction management that disadvantages suppliers, but on the added value of a tactical, or even strategic partnership, as opposed to a purely operational one, with these same suppliers. Commentators (e.g., Hartman, 2002) systematically bring the 'cost' dimension of marketplaces to the forefront. However, corporate networks, with several people connecting to the same websites, demonstrate in practice that marketplaces also have a very prominent social dimension. Indeed the economic relations among individuals necessarily entail social relations, such as trust (or the lack of it), that can strongly influence the workings of business practices highlighting how economic action is embedded on social structures and networks (Granovetter 1985; Ratnasingam Pavlou and Gefen 2005, Assimakopoulos 2007).

3. RESEARCH METHODOLOGY

There already exist typologies of marketplaces, but they seldom take into account the type of market or products they deal in. These typologies can hence integrate tools which are not really marketplaces, but on-line e-commerce, auction or price comparison sites. Many terms are used in the academic literature to designate marketplaces, or other phenomena which are similar, yet different. It is difficult indeed to draw a distinction between 'electronic marketplace, electronic market, electronic trades, electronic exchange, electronic hubs, electronic platforms' (Hartmann, 2002). Moreover, increasing integration and convergence of tools make this already confusing situation even worse. For example, ERP systems increasingly integrate more marketplace functionalities, and the marketplaces are integrating more and more ERP functionalities. It is therefore becoming increasingly difficult to distinguish the specific services provided by marketplaces from those commonly offered by other tools. And yet, a number of expectations from companies, which are specific to purchasing and supplier management, come under heavy criticism. These companies would be ready to invest massively if the marketplaces could only offer real long-term solutions to their purchasing problems, not just 'cost killing' options, and news that is only interesting momentarily.

Our research is therefore exploratory in so far as it aims to build a typology of Francophone marketplaces and present a profile of the state of the art of these marketplaces, including services they offer. In the light of such typology we identify opportunities that could lead to the adoption of a different strategy for a better match with expectations of potential clients. In particular, our research followed a four step approach:

The first step consisted in reviewing scholarly and trade literature to draw up an initial list of the most well-known Francophone marketplaces and their principal functionalities. In parallel to this initial inventory, the study of existing marketplace typologies enabled us to determine the criteria by which we could clearly distinguish the composition of this group and its evolution. We shall see below that certain marketplaces are purely operational tools, while others are tactical, others are strategic, and, depending on the case, they offer a broad range of services.

The second step was an Internet search, using search engines to find specialised forums, newsletters and new marketplaces in order to complete the initial list. This was followed by a telephone or mail contact in order to gather a certain amount of detailed information about the functionalities available on each platform. This first-hand information enabled us to build a matrix that associates each of the 225 identified marketplaces to a set of tools offered to its clients.

The third step was based on the previous two and resulted in the drawing of a cognitive map for positioning the functions and service providers along two axes: a horizontal axis measuring the duration of a relationship between the members of a marketplace, and a vertical axis that shows the degree of cooperation between each of the stakeholders. This positioning then led us to structure our typology in four types of services that determine four types of marketplace: e-sourcing, e-procurement, business intelligence and collaborative commerce, with the possibility that one marketplace can cover more than one type of service, or evolve from one type to another.

Finally, the fourth step consisted in putting together a matrix, where the lines show the 225 Francophone marketplaces, and the columns show their functionalities, and precise nature of the services proposed by these marketplaces according to our typology. We could subsequently understand the current situation and draw certain conclusions about the potential and future of these marketplaces.

4. MAIN FINDINGS

The first challenge we encountered in trying to identify and classify all Francophone marketplaces, was a problem of definition, as we've already pointed out above. We accepted a broad working definition that marketplaces can include all the web sites which establish relations of collaboration or competition among companies within the same market. We therefore had sites similar to eBay, a site that supports a great number of companies also in France, claiming the status of marketplace. We also had to go through marketplace referencing directories and the trade press to target all sites that fitted our definition. We completed this initial list with marketplaces selected directly from the Internet, by means of an Internet search and with some additional unreferenced or unregistered marketplaces that had been featured in press articles, or consulting companies' surveys. If these marketplaces could be counted by the hundreds in 2000, it is difficult to list more than a few hundred in France today, all industries included. The last hurdle consisted in comparing their web sites, which despite many points in common, addressed different markets – from the agro-food industry to automotive, to computers, to services, from small start-ups to the subsidiary of one, or several major industrial groups – following different strategies – some buyer-oriented, others supplier-oriented, and others claiming to be independent. By choosing criteria related to the types of relations allowed by the marketplace, as opposed to those related to sectors, or volumes, we focused on the essence of marketplaces, on their 'raison d'être', on what makes them not only attractive to their members, but encourages the loyalty of the latter. In the process we had to identify all types of services likely to be offered by a marketplace and sort them into four broad categories according to the services provided: e-sourcing, e-procurement, business intelligence and collaborative commerce, see Figures 1 and 2.

We define 'e-sourcing' as the search, via Internet based information systems, and over a relatively short period of time, i.e. a few days up to a few weeks, for answers to a commercial inquiry with a view to obtaining the lowest cost and near-immediate cost-effectiveness. It therefore involves finding the best source to respond to a need expressed by a company. This search is accompanied by 'digital negotiations' enabled by new tools such as e-RFIs (electronic Request For Information), forms that allow one to progressively select the top suppliers likely to win a tender, e-RFPs (electronic Request For Proposal), which enable one to finely compare offers, and e-RFQs (electronic Request for Quote/Quotation) which determine the final decision. The e-sourcing process often ends in reverse auctioning to mechanically lower prices and decide between the final suppliers who have passed through all of the prior screening processes. E-sourcing does not really integrate the notion of partnership or of building a long-lasting collaboration between the buyer and the supplier to which it applies. There is therefore an intense and radical sense of competition, the purpose of which is to respond to a punctual need while optimising certain criteria, without considering the quality of the relationship with the supplier in question. Companies, such as HP France or Caterpillar France, regularly revert to auctioning in order to acquire batches of components, or certain volumes of raw materials, needed to manufacture their products. These auctions are organized sporadically with no intention whatsoever of developing further relations with selected suppliers once a transaction has been completed.

'e-procurement' consists in establishing longer term commercial relations compared to 'e-sourcing' between a company and its suppliers thanks to ICT, i.e., it enables the company to structure, record, analyse and optimize the terms and conditions of the products and services provided by these suppliers over a period of a year or so. Suppliers are thus subjected to financial, industrial and technological audits in order to receive an approval needed to belong to a company's partners for a substantial period of time. They can thus benefit from semester or annual purchasing commitments in terms of production volumes from buyers who sign framework contracts which set levels of price, quantity, and above all quality, with penalties in the event of the non-respect of these conditions. The core functionalities of e-procurement systems consist in the consultation of e-catalogues and the issuing of on-line purchase orders. The possibility of saving invoices and analysing data collected by computer tools is an effective means of evolving from the reaction to a "one-off need", to anticipating such need and the implementation of a purchasing strategy that can be examined in more detail through 'business intelligence'. For example, out of the 110 worldwide Thomson sites, the e-procurement application, Hubwoo, is the second most widely-used application after the mail. Managing 1,8 billion euros of purchases in 2004 and roughly 10 000 orders, the use of a purchasing platform generates considerable returns on investment. The example is even more evident with EDF (Electricté de France – the French Electricity company) and its 1 800 agencies in France. e-procurement tools enable EDF to standardize the purchasing processes between the company's agencies and each partner and realize economies of scale. Moreover, given that the EDF agencies know which suppliers they use regularly, they have reduced considerably the number of suppliers in the past few years, and have enabled EDF to focus on those offerings with the best business terms.

'Business intelligence' involves setting up standardisation, globalisation and anticipation solutions with key suppliers, so that a purchasing department can function seamlessly in terms of time and space. Indeed, purchase benchmarking allows the circulation of best practices between countries or continents and between different services. The partnership between buyers and suppliers is particularly close and can involve technological transfers, collaboration on innovative research projects, and support designed to optimize the performance and cost-effectiveness of suppliers. The intervention of consultants or auditing agencies also allows the creation of purchasing procedure certifications. Clients and suppliers are closely interconnected at operational and logistic levels, where manufacturing orders are tracked from the factory to their point of reception. Loyalty is rather strong with these suppliers, who are deeply committed to the success of their client, with whom they share the same risks. For example, the Schneider group, with its solution provider SourcingParts, co-developed a purchasing platform which brings together the functionalities of 'e-sourcing' and 'e-procurement', but more importantly, of 'business intelligence'. The project was implemented to respond to the needs of a large multi-national group for which standardizing the tendering process was fundamental. But the need was also anticipatory: Schneider wished to have the capacity to analyse each of its 4 key markets and 58 purchasing segments in order to optimize the management of its purchase orders, procurement and stocks. Defining performance indicators for the purchasing service per market, segment, country, zone or buyer enables a progressive and continuous improvement not only of cost control, but also of quality, deadlines, technological innovations and purchasing projects.

'Collaborative commerce' is still in its early days in several sectors of the knowledge economy. And yet some companies have begun to develop and sustain cooperation over the mid-to-long term. Collaborative development and co-design consist, for one or several buyers and for one or several suppliers, in sharing resources in terms of knowledge, know-how, equipment or finances in order to create a new product or a new technology. Integrating suppliers into the innovation process offers considerable advantages as for example creating synergies and sharing the same final objectives. For example in the automotive industry, collaborative commerce among partners, who work on successive levels of the value chain, is particularly efficient in the co-design of technical products such as automobile vehicles. Peugeot is one of the few companies in France to have invested massively in this domain in order to develop its own platform, since the potential, in terms of generating competitive advantage, is significant. When we look at the strategic positioning of these marketplaces, we observe that they are concentrated in the 'e-sourcing' quadrangle, and the further we move away from this quadrangle, the fewer there are. Notwithstanding this finding, it is the functionalities of business intelligence and collaborative commerce that are the most popular, and bring most added-value. However they do require greater expertise and trust for companies to join in. Demand is high and even though the investments needed may be significant, there is little supply and great demand for such services.

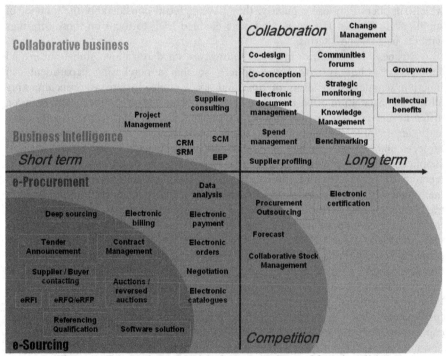

Figure 1: Francophone Marketplaces: typology of functionalities

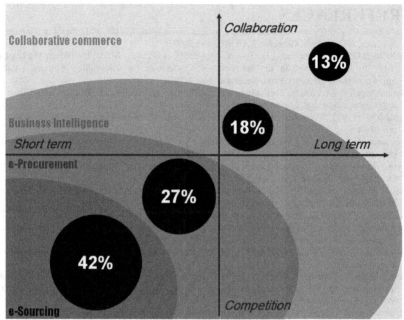

Figure 2: Percentages of the 225 marketplaces according to the 4 types (Allal-Cherif, 2007)

5. CONCLUSION

The analysis the state of the art of marketplaces in France in the fall of 2007 leads us to the conclusion that there is a split between the expectations of companies and the markets their embedded in, and what generally most marketplace providers offer to their clients. Indeed, the majority of marketplaces compete with each other on services related to e-sourcing and e-procurement. Their number (155) and concentration (69%) is high in this quadrangle (see, Figure 2), though they have difficulty when positioning in this quadrangle to being cost-effective and above all they neglect high added value services such us joint project management, product co-design, anticipative purchase analysis and other collaborative services valuable to managers. Having identified this, we can also underline that the concentration of marketplaces leads them to merge or create strategic alliances in order to provide a more comprehensive range of collaborative services and offer solutions that cover all aspects of purchasing and not just the notion of cost control. The choice of a new economic model, which takes into account social relations, such as trust, involved in transactions, would therefore be paramount in making marketplaces more attractive and cost-effective for enabling business intelligence and collaborative commerce. They would thus become true informational platforms and professional virtual communities building tools, federating their resources to reach aims that would otherwise be unattainable without the use of such inter-organisational Internet based systems.

6. REFERENCES

1. Allal-Cherif O. (2007), An economic model for electronic marketplaces, PhD thesis in Management Sciences, University of Grenoble 2, UPMF, may 2007.
2. Allal-Cherif O., Assimakopoulos, D., Favier., M. (2008), A Business Model for French Marketplaces, paper to be presented in the International Conference on Information Systems (ICIS'08, http://www.icis2008.org/), Paris, December 14-17, 2008.
3. Assimakopoulos, D. (2007), Technological Communities and Networks: Triggers and Drivers for Innovation, Routledge, London and New York.
4. Bensaou M. (1999), "Portfolios of buyer-supplier relationships", Sloan Management Review, Summer, pp. 35-44.
5. Brousseau E. (1993), L'économie des contrats, Technologies de l'information et coordination interentreprises, Paris: PUF.
6. Büyüközkan G. (2004), "A success index to evaluate e-Marketplaces", Production Planning & Control, Oct2004, Vol. 15 Issue 7, pp. 761-774.
7. Choi Y. J., Suh C. S. (2005), "The death of physical distance: An economic analysis of the emergence of electronic marketplaces", Papers in Regional Science, 84(4), pp. 597-614.
8. Driedonks C., Gregor S., Wassenaar A., Van Heck E. (2005), "Economic and Social Analysis of the Adoption of B2B Electronic Marketplaces: A Case Study in the Australian Beef Industry", International Journal of Electronic Commerce, 9(3), pp. 49-72.
9. Fisher, M.L. (1997), "What is the right supply chain for your products?", Harvard Business Review, March, pp. 105-116.
10. Gengatharen D., Standing C., Burn J. (2005), "Government-supported Community Portal Regional e-marketplaces for SMEs: Evidence to Support a Staged Approach", Electronic Markets, Dec2005, Vol. 15 Issue 4, pp. 405-417.
11. Granovetter M. (1985), "Economic Action and Social Structure: The Problem of Embeddedness", American Journal of Sociology, 91(3), November 1985, pp. 481-510.
12. Grey W., Olavson T., Shi D. (2005), "The role of e-marketplaces in relationship-based supply chains: A survey", IBM Systems Journal, Vol. 44 Issue 1, pp. 109-123.
13. Hartmann E. (2002), Successful introduction of B2B Projects, an Inter-Organizational relationship Perspective with an Empirical Analysis of the Chemical Industry in Germany, von der Fakultät VIII Wirtschaft und Management der Technischen Universität Berlin zur Erlangung des akademischen Grades Doktor der Ingenieurwissenschaften.
14. Jai-Yeol Son, Tu L., Benbasat, I. (2006), "A descriptive content analysis of trust-building measures in B2Belectronic marketplaces", Communications of AIS, 2006, Vol. 2006 Issue 18, pp. 2-51.
15. Malone, T W, and J Yates and R I Benjamin (1987), «Electronic Markets and Electronic Hierarchies: Effects of Information Technology and Market Structure and Corporate Strategies», Communications of the ACM, 30:6 June 1987, pp. 484-497.
16. Malone, T W, and J Yates and R I Benjamin (1989), "The Logic of Electronic Markets", Harvard Business Review, May-June 1989, pp. 166-170.
17. Mirza B. M., Vipul G., Richard C. C. (2004), "E-marketplaces and the future of supply chain management: opportunities and challenges", Business Process Management Journal, Vol. 10 Issue 3, pp. 325-335.
18. Nieuwbourg P. et d'Hondt H. (2000) – Places de marché sur Internet, Nouvelles règles pour le commerce du XXIéme siècle, Editions BNTP 2000.
19. O'Reilly P., Finnegan P. (2005), "Performance in Electronic Marketplaces: Theory in Practice", Electronic Markets, Feb2005, Vol. 15 Issue 1, pp. 23-37.
20. Pavlou P., Gefen D. (2004), "Building Effective Online Marketplaces with Institution-Based Trust", Information Systems Research, Mar2004, Vol. 15 Issue 1, pp. 37-59.
21. Ratnasingam P., Gefen D., Pavlou P. A. (2005), "The Role of Facilitating Conditions and Institutional Trust in Electronic Marketplaces", Journal of Electronic Commerce in Organizations, Jul-Sep2005, Vol. 3 Issue 3, pp. 69-82.
22. Sharifi H., Kehoe D. F., Hopkins J. (2006), "A classification and selection model of e-marketplaces for better alignment of supply chains», Journal of Enterprise Information Management, Sep2006, Vol. 19 Issue 5, pp. 483-503.
23. Shaw M., (2000), "Electronic Commerce: State of the Art", in Shaw M., Blanning R., Strader T., Whinston A., Handbook on Electronic Commerce, Springer, Berlin, pp. 3-24.

PART 19

REGIONAL MANIFESTATIONS OF CN -2

SCENARIOS TO COLLABORATE WITH EMERGING MARKETS: INITIAL FOCUS INDIA

61

*Myrna Flores, **Mathew Cherian, ***Luca Canetta

Swiss MTO Network - Swiss Federal Institute of Technology, Lausanne (EPFL)[1]
myrflores@hotmail.com
***Indian Institute of Technology Madras, Department of Management Studies*
mathewch@lycos.com
****University of Applied Sciences of Southern Switzerland (SUPSI)*
Department of Technology and Innovation, Institute CIM for Sustainable Innovation (ICIMSI)
& Swiss Federal Institute of Technology, Lausanne (EPFL)
luca.canetta@supsi.ch, SWITZERLAND

Due to competitive pressures in the global business arena, multinational firms have started to migrate to low-cost sources of labour and materials, which are typically located in countries that also represent emerging market opportunities. In the recent years, SME's are also interested in doing business in emerging markets, which represents a bigger effort and risk for them as they have less resources and time to recognize possible ways to start new successful collaborations with these countries and surpass the obstacles that they may encounter when creating new collaborative environments. These collaborations not only imply business opportunities to reduce operative costs or introduce products to those markets, but also innovation opportunities with Universities and Research Centres. Therefore, the objective of this paper is to present different scenarios to support firms to define collaboration strategies to develop new business and innovation opportunities in emerging markets and identify potential risks supporting them to develop new successful partnerships in their current value chain. For each scenario, main potential benefits, risks and critical success factors have been identified.

1. INTRODUCTION

Friedman (2005) describes three key periods of the world's globalization process in his book *The World is Flat*. He states that "Globalisation 1.0" is the time when Christopher Columbus discovered the American continent including the imperialist time of European countries until the late 1800s. Later on, "Globalisation 2.0" is the process when multinational companies are born and start to extend on new markets supported by technological advances of transportation and communication tools up to 2000. Then, the current stage is "Globalisation 3.0" that he calls the "flat world" on the sense that individuals are connected to the internet and can do business where ever they want in a virtual way. In this sense, individuals are the ones that collaborate and innovate using an open innovation model applying technologies such as open source tools which in fact are an output of these collaborative developments. The result is a triple convergence of technology, individuals and organisations skilled enough to take advantage of these new collaborative platforms.

---

[1] *Dr. Myrna Flores was a visiting researcher as part of the Swiss MTO Network in EPFL during 2007*

Please use the following format when citing this chapter:

Flores, M., Cherian, M. and Canetta, L., 2008, in IFIP International Federation for Information Processing, Volume 283; *Pervasive Collaborative Networks*; Luis M. Camarinha-Matos, Willy Picard; (Boston: Springer), pp. 599–610.

Inspired by Friedman, Fung et al. (2008) provide an insight of different business opportunities that may arise in this "flat world" and highlight the importance of Emerging Markets as the markets of the future. Several analysis and researches carried out internationally confirm the importance of these markets in the current business arena. For instance in 2003, Goldman Sachs point out in a landmark study that by the year 2050, the economies of Brazil, Russia, India and China (BRIC) are expected to collectively eclipse those of U.S, U.K., Japan, Germany, France and Italy. Only the US and Japan would be left among the richest six countries. To these original six countries, some have added other markets such as Mexico, South Africa, Eastern Europe and Turkey. This growth will create rapidly new customer demand and changing spending patterns, leading shifts in the demand for different types of products as these markets develop. Global companies, including the SME's, need to be involved or will miss opportunities to grow with these emerging economies.

These last facts seem very promising to attract companies in the western world to invest and think of emerging markets to target new economic growth. Consequently, several questions may arise; especially when firms have not done yet business with these fast growing countries and when it is difficult to identify which is the best possible way to interact with them. At this point, several research questions emerge:

1. *Which different collaboration models or scenarios can be developed to facilitate western companies, both multinationals and SME's, to find business opportunities and be successful in emerging markets obtaining win-win results?*

2. *Besides the economic returns, how can companies in collaborative networks develop and offer products and services considering also social and economic impacts towards a sustainable innovation model?*

Therefore, the goal of this paper is to present the seven scenarios that were developed and analysed during the research carried out by the SWISSMAIN project trying to answer these two previous research questions.

2. THE SWISSMAIN PROJECT AND THE INDIAN PILOT

The SWISSMAIN project is a research project funded by the Swiss Innovation Promotion Agency - CTI International. One key research interest of the industrial partners was to identify new possible business models that can enable them to identify business and collaboration opportunities in India. The two main industrial partners interested in the research, Maillefer and SAPAL-Bosch, highlighted that besides the potential economic benefits that their companies may encounter developing new business relationships with India, social and environmental elements also should be taken into consideration. Both companies are interested to identify potential collaboration opportunities to develop new long term relationships with Indian partners that also pay attention to sustainable development matters such as:

• Adoption of "green" practices at overall production equipment design, manufacturing, use and disposal

• Implementation of Environment, Health and Safety (EHS) procedures increasing the quality of life, working conditions, safety and health of their employees and of the production equipment users.

Therefore, the concept of Sustainable Innovation was applied to develop the scenarios. Sustainable innovation is an emerging and fundamental force for change in business and society (Larson, 2000). Sustainable innovation is a process where sustainability considerations (environmental, social, financial) are integrated into company systems from idea generation through to research and development (R&D) and commercialisation. This applies to products, services and technologies, as well as new business and organisation models (Charter et. al., 2007) According to Rennings (2000) sustainable innovation or eco-innovation is the process of developing new ideas, behaviour, products and processes that contribute to a reduction in environmental burdens or to achieve ecologically specified sustainability targets. As a result, the SWISSMAIN Indian pilot was launched with the objective to support Swiss and Indian companies in the machine building sector to identify collaboration opportunities considering sustainable innovation concepts (economic, social and environmental). One deliverable of this Indian Pilot was to develop scenarios to facilitate Swiss firms to identify different potential ways to do business in India which could evolve into new collaborative environments, where not only Swiss firms obtain sustainable benefits but also the Indian counterparts.

3. RESEARCH METHODOLOGY: SCENARIO PLANNING

Scenario Planning acknowledges that the future is unpredictable and takes that into account by providing a number of different versions of the future. In contrast, most of the other strategic planning tools attempt to predict only one version of the future. It is essential that scenarios are developed in a participative process, sharing perspectives and different points of view. This process in fact requires serious research in the form of data gathering and analysis. Additionally, resulting scenarios should evolve to time, they should be revisited at least annually (Turner, 2002).

According to Schoemaker (1995), scenario planning enables managers to identify a big range of possibilities to capture different opportunities in rich detail; Scenario Planning is a disciplined method to imagine different futures that can be applied to greater range of futures simplifying the avalanche of data into a limited number of possible states. Even though the proposed SWISSMAIN scenarios were defined targeting new collaborative environments for Indo-Swiss collaborations, they could also be applied within other contexts. The current state is the "*AS-IS*" scenario and applying the Scenario Planning research methodology seven different scenarios were developed after carrying out fifteen face to face interviews to companies both in India and Switzerland during the SWISSMAIN Indian pilot.

To identify, develop, compare and analyse the possible business scenarios among Swiss and Indian entrepreneurs, a questionnaire with both open and multiply choice questions was designed to carry out face to face interviews. This SWISSMAIN survey had as an objective to understand the current business arena from Swiss and Indian entrepreneurs considering their initial (past), current and future collaboration perspectives and integrating a Sustainable Development Framework (Flores, et al 2008). More specifically, the first part of the questionnaire focused on gathering data about: 1) the different reasons of Swiss companies doing business in India or vice versa, 2) the impact, 3) the main challenges and 4) the Critical Success Factors (CSF's). The second part had the objective to obtain information about the experiences of the Swiss companies doing business in India applying the three axes of sustainable development: economic, social and environmental.

The economic aspects were covered by collecting data about: production (type of products/components produced, market lifecycle phase, main activities, market focus); logistics (lead-time duration and reliability, transport modes, costs); market (potentiality and profitability, competitive degree), etc. The social aspects considered the cultural differences as well as workforce attitude, organisational behaviour, trust and loyalty. Looking more specifically to the adopted strategies the impact of training (contents, procedures, costs and effectiveness) and management styles (types of ownership, governance models, etc). The environmental axis looked forward to understand how Swiss and Indian companies were sharing green supply chain best practices and how Indian counterparts were adopting them. The role of local universities and research centres to spur innovation in India was also addressed.

3.1 The "AS IS" scenario: Supply chain

Supply Chain Management (SCM) is the total management of a network of facilities and distribution options in a partnership between a consumer, distributor and manufacturer with the purpose of transfer and exchange information and physical goods for the supplier's suppliers to their customer's customers ensuring the right goods in the most efficient manner, reached accurately wherever they are required in a company and beyond (SCOR, 1995).

Within the context of the project, Swiss companies are mainly sourcing components from European suppliers but exporting globally. There is currently no collaboration for product development with Indian partners, furthermore considering product innovation and market introduction in India, the presence of Swiss firms is still very low in contrast to German and Japanese competitors.

3.2 Scenario 1: Expand sourcing and selling towards product customisation

The very first scenario, in terms of lower collaboration complexity, targets an expansion of current sourcing and selling activities in India, considering (table 1):

- The Swiss company's production/assembly remains in Switzerland
- The Swiss firm assesses and selects new Indian suppliers, targeting a more collaborative environment for product design and customisation for India
- Starts business collaborations, mainly selling and buying transactions
- Swiss finished product(s) are sold to the same markets and/or new markets (including India)

In fact, Subramanian, (2007) found that Indian Manufacturing Enterprises, particularly SME's, have been benefited from the large-scale subcontracting of parts and components from Indian and overseas OEMs.

Win-Win Benefits	
For Swiss	**For Indian company**
• Outsource to reduce costs (exports of components) Be more competitive thanks to cost reduction (cost reduction strategy) • Integrate new suppliers for collaborative design	• Increase sales (exports) • Learn procedures and quality standards from Swiss company, especially in regards to environmental procedures
Risks	
For Swiss	**For Indian**
• Increase complexity in Supply Chain in regards to the quality specifications, Indian suppliers not delivering on time. • Loss of local skills in regards to the production know-how of some components • Communication and cultural difference before and during the business transactions	• Not enough experience/knowledge to supply what is requested • Need to strongly invest in technology and training due to the lack of technological competencies which is difficult especially for Indian SME's.
Critical Success Factors (CSFs)	
• Develop a robust suppliers selection methodology • Select the right suppliers • Implement clear procedures and methods for production and quality management • Establish efficient communication channels • Define a supply chain performance scorecard • Collaboration increases with the usage of new Information and Communication Technologies (ICT), especially Enterprise Resource Planning systems that focus on sharing operational information • Study the life cycle of the product and integrate new suppliers for collaborative design for product customisation	

Table 1. *Expand Sourcing and Selling for Product Customisation*

3.3 Scenario 2: Concentrate sourcing in developed / developing industrial clusters

The second identified scenario looks forward to motivate and enable Swiss firms to look for business opportunities by collaborating with Indian partners located in established or developing new clusters (table 2). An Industrial Cluster is defined as a concentration of 'interdependent' firms within the same or adjacent industrial sectors in a small geographical area (Observatory of European SME's, 2002). Porter (1990) defines a cluster as a set of industries related through buyer-supplier and supplier-buyer relationships, or by common technologies, common buyers or distribution channels, or common labour pools. Clustering and networking has helped Indian small and medium enterprises in boosting their competitiveness. India has over 400 SME clusters and about 2000 artisan clusters. Therefore, in scenario 2 the following is considered:

• The Swiss company's production/assembly remains in Switzerland
• The Swiss company assesses and selects suppliers located in well established clusters (industrial aggregations) in different locations in India taking advantage of scale economies, networking activities and established infrastructure in the cluster (such a training from local associations and Universities).
• New long term Indo-Swiss partnerships are built focusing on new product development or re-design of products with local suppliers and customers

- Swiss finished product(s) are sold to the same and new emerging markets

Win-Win Benefits	
For Swiss	**For Indian**
• Win-win attitude • Develop a new collaborative environment to solve targeted problems sharing information • Improve interface with suppliers in the same cluster to improve overall product performance (design and quality) • Reduce costs to manage multiple suppliers within the same cluster Multiplying effects by working with different suppliers within the same location • The Indian government is investing in the upgrade and development of clusters, facilitating companies to find the right partner, especially SME's	• Win-win attitude • Increase quality by learning from Swiss procedures • Faster learning process and product improvement • Economies of scale (share costs for transportation, warehousing, trainings, etc) • The collaboration of suppliers in the cluster maximises the combined competencies of partners to achieve each partner's production order • Faster access of Indian components to the global market increasing their exports
Risks	
For Swiss	**For Indian**
• Not finding the right suppliers in the cluster • Difficulty to orchestrate suppliers in the cluster • Possibility to loose property rights to competition who also source to suppliers within the same cluster • Indian partners do not have the same IT tools for long distance communication	• Usually the OEM orchestrates the New Product Development (NPD) process, SME's have very little decisional power • Swiss partners do not have the same IT tools for long distance communication • Swiss partners do not speak English fluently and existence of cultural differences
Critical Success Factors (CSFs)	
• Identify most advanced clusters in India following a process oriented strategy (potential clusters Pune, Vadodara, Ludhiana for machined parts and components) • Develop a suppliers' selection methodology • Diffuse and implement easy to use information and communication tools (ICT) for information sharing and suppliers management • Co-development of products including customer's and supplier's know-how for local product customisation • Obtain multiplying effects of new competences by collaborating with suppliers in the same cluster	

Table 2. *Concentrate Sourcing in Developed/Developing Clusters* identified benefits, risks and Critical Success Factors (CSF).

3.4 Scenario 3: Develop new cross boarder alliances

A Cross-border alliance can be defined as partnerships that are formed between two or more firms from different countries for the purpose of pursuing mutual interests through sharing their resources and capabilities (Doz et al., 1998). According to Dyer et al. (2001), cross-border alliances (CBAs) aim in bringing in superior competitive position to involved firms. Lorange and Roos (1992) broadly classify strategic alliance as:

1. A formal cooperative venture of two or more independent firms formally working together for their mutual benefits
2. A joint venture to form a separate company of which the founding firms have equity stakes
3. A joint ownership of asset or economic activity to serve interests of partner firms

4. A strategic investment in a partner or share swap as a gesture of working together or a precursor to a merger or to exploit formal ownership rights. Therefore, in this scenario 3:

- The Swiss company looks for an existing Indian partner in the same or related market for fast entry to the emerging Indian market
- The Indian and Swiss partner form a new company with a common strategy and vision

Win-Win Benefits	
For Swiss	**For Indian**
• Faster access to new market (India) taking advantage of the Indian partner knowledge in regards to customer requirements from the Indian counterpart • Lower risk in managing firm in unknown and different business and cultural contexts • Customize design identifying the voice of local customers (VOC) • Increase sales through local known distribution channels and customer contacts	• Acquire new technology and learn best practices from foreign (Swiss) firm • Obtain new technical skills for higher technological products • Increase financial returns based on a product differentiation strategy in domestic market • Provide reduction of raw materials and components costs with local procurement
Risks	
For Swiss	**For Indian**
• Loose Intellectual Property (IP) • Strong cultural differences in doing business and therefore possible emergence of conflicts • Increase the complexity of the supply chain, considering new suppliers and introducing the need to implement new forecasting systems	• Been selected as a partner due to the low cost of labour, thus low collaboration in the new product development process with Swiss partner is limited. Once the foreign partner learns about the emerging market, might want to finish the cross boarder alliance. • Needs to invest in R&D to catch up technologically. This is risky if the Indian company usually doesn't to invest in R&D
Critical Success Factors (CSFs)	
• The right alliance partner selection with clear and aligned long term business strategies • Define and implement the right governance model, identifying the key skills required from both partners to work together in common and new markets with current or customised products • Jointly develop and agree on precise terms and conditions, especially Intellectual property rights • Key processes to develop together as a new partnership integrating knowledge to be stronger at marketing and product development	

Table 3. *Develop New Cross Boarder Alliances* identified benefits, risks and Critical Success Factors (CSF).

3.4 Scenario 4: Full ownership in emerging market

In this full ownership scenario, the Swiss opens a new production facility in India targeting the local (Indian and/or emerging) market with existing products or customized ones according to the local needs. Based on the different interviews carried out in Swiss companies located in India, this was identified as the most common scenario of Swiss firms investing in India, as for many of them seems less risky due to the fact that business culture is very different and unknown to Swiss counterparts, especially SME's. The following table shows the identified win-win benefits, risks and identified CSF's.

Win-Win Benefits	
For Swiss	**For Indian**
• Full control and ownership to take decisions in foreign location (India) • Easier access to new market (India) • Understand more closely the local market needs • Reduce labour and logistic costs • Consider to define and develop projects with local Universities to identify qualified students that can later become employees	• Swiss company will source from Indian suppliers (SME's) integrating them to their local supply chains • Swiss company will provide new jobs and training (when required) to Indian qualified personnel • Swiss Environment, Health and Safety (EHS) practices will be implemented and diffused by Swiss companies in India and its local suppliers
Risks	
For Swiss	**For Indian**
• Failure due to lack of knowledge about market, legal issues, business & working culture • Lack of qualified Indian workforce at the technical and managerial level, therefore need to bring expats to the foreign office • High employee rotation, as many multinationals look continuously for new training personnel in India, which in some occasions is not enough to cover the demand. • Less understanding about Indian regulations	• Not been able to provide high-quality components to Swiss company • Not motivate Swiss companies to increase investments due to bureaucracy, corruption and lack of infrastructure
Critical Success Factors (CSFs)	
• Hire qualified Indian personnel with experience and skills for the different functions of the company in India: marketing, product development, legislations, technical knowledge in regards to product and process • Create new market channels and customer contacts in India as soon as possible • Select the right location in India closer to good sources of knowledge such as clients, suppliers and Universities. Take into consideration where competitors, both domestic and foreign have established their firms in India. Take also in consideration the infrastructure, such as airports, roads and ports. • Take advantage of Special Economic Zones (SEZs) being developed by the Indian government to pay less taxes • In case there is no knowledge about local regulations, consider to hire a skilled consultant • Analyse carefully the market needs and customise products according to local desires	

Table 4. *Full Ownership in India* identified benefits, risks and Critical Success Factors (CSF).

3.5 Scenario 5: Acquisition in emerging market

In this scenario the Swiss company searches, selects and performs a due diligence to acquire a successful Indian-own established company in the same or similar industrial sector to facilitate the company entry to that (Indian and/or Asian) market with existing products or customized ones according to the local markets needs. This is not a very common practice done by Swiss companies, but in contrast there is an increasing trend from Indian successful firms in western countries, which nowadays are buying several successful companies around the world to expand their market horizons. Indian business investors have lately acquired western owned firms from different sectors including steel, pharmaceuticals, automotive components, televisions, such as the recent Jaguar acquisition of the TATA Group from Ford among others. The win-win benefits, risks and identified CSF's are presented in the following table.

Win-Win Benefits	
For Swiss	**For Indian**
• Full control and ownership to take decisions in emerging market (India) • Faster access to a new fast developing emerging market • Capitalise from acquired company knowledge in market business intelligence, distribution channels, suppliers base and customer contacts for product customisation	• Attract foreign capital to India • Merge Swiss competences about high tech products with the knowledge of the Indian acquired company in regards to the market and distribution channels to provide more advanced goods to the final consumers and increase the market share.
Risks	
• Swiss company is not getting profit of acquired Indian acquisition in the expected period of time. Return of investment (ROI) takes more time of the expected • The learning curve is to slow to manage the new acquired company in the emerging market • Not able to diffuse Swiss business culture and procedures in new acquisition • Difficulty to find enough skilled personnel • Current supplier base is not providing the expected quality. Investment will be required to train key suppliers and search for new ones that could supply the requested components • Indian suppliers and employees need training to use the IT systems used in Switzerland	• Indian employees do not have the competences needed by the Swiss company, so some of them may be replaced by skilled employees, in some cases coming from Switzerland • Current supplier base is not providing the expected quality. Some suppliers may be replaced by European known suppliers
Critical Success Factors (CSFs)	
• Retain key personnel from acquired company • Learn fast from Indian partner about distribution channels and the suppliers base • Implement Swiss business strategy and procedures as soon as possible in the new acquisition • Transfer quickly the best business practices to the new Indian acquisition • Understand quickly the market requirements to supply a localised mass customisation strategy for product development • Do joint projects with local Universities to identify smart students to work later on in Swiss firm • Join the local chamber of commerce to learn and understand the emerging market business environment and make new contacts • Visit and evaluate suppliers to understand which improvements could be done in the current supply chain and define actions for improvement	

Table 5. *Acquisition in Emerging market* identified benefits, risks and Critical Success Factors (CSF).

3.6 Scenario 6: Technology transfer to firm in emerging market

This sixth scenario considers a Swiss company licensing technology to an Indian firm to produce a finished product not existing in that particular emerging market. This is one of the most complex scenarios, as it is difficult for a company to select which technology to license to still keep its competitive advantage and access that particular market. Additionally, it required a very high level of trust from the Swiss partner to license the technology to a counterpart in the emerging market to follow all the terms and conditions established and agreed in the technology transfer deal.

For instance, one of the identified case studies under this scenario considered the technology transfer of a mature product which was the first step undertaken by one of the interviewed Swiss companies to establish its presence in India, then the adopted strategy evolved into a full ownership combined with partial local sourcing. The technology transfer scenario was also adopted by an Indian company which established a technological alliance with a South-African counterpart. In this second case study, the technology transfer process was successful and took place in three phases and lasted for seven years. This progressive transition allowed partners to increase their trust and to make affordable the technology transfer being a learning experience for both counterparts.

Win-Win Benefits	
For Swiss	**For Indian**
• Increase profits by selling technology licenses to an Indian firm to introduce a new product to the that particular market • By learning from the experiences done by the Indian firm to sell the products in the domestic market, the Swiss firm can customise the technology to the local needs	• Merge Swiss competences about high tech products with Indian knowledge about the market to provide more advanced goods for the final consumers • Product diversification thanks to the acquisition of Swiss technology with a license • Obtain training for local product manufacturing providing Swiss quality specifications
Risks	
• Indian partner does not respect the license IPR agreement • Do not understand properly Indian laws and regulations	• Indian employees do not have the competences needed by the Swiss company to sell the product in India. Therefore, Indian firm is not selling to the market the right product.
Critical Success Factors (CSFs)	
• Identify the best potential partner in India that already provided a complementary technology to the Indian market • Be able to get financial and business historical data of the potential Indian partner. The Swiss firm should analyse very carefully the reputation of the Indian partner before doing the technology transfer • Involve from the beginning a very skilled lawyer that understands both Swiss and Indian regulations for technology transfer to enable a complete and successful technology transfer process following all term and regulations • It is important to define a common Swiss-Indo strategy for the products to be sold in India by the Indian partner based on the Swiss technology • The technology transfer process requires a detailed plan to transfer the license and product with very clear and defined steps	

Table 6. *Technology Transfer to firm in Emerging Market* identified benefits, risks and Critical Success Factors (CSF).

3.7 Scenario 7: New services partnerships

In this last identified scenario a Swiss company identifies an local firm(s) or organisation(s) that can support delivering new value added services in that particular emerging market. During the research project, both interviewed Indian and Swiss firms, mentioned that this trend is growing. For instance Japanese firms from the machine tool sector are currently developing service partnerships for product design and after sales service, especially because they don't count with the required workforce to provide these services locally.

Win-Win Benefits	
For Swiss	**For Indian**
• Increase additional profits by offering new services in India in collaboration with a local partner(s) • Potential business areas could be: 1. Engineering services, such as product redesign 2. After sales service such as maintenance and training services to clients	• Develop new business partnerships in services • Get new knowledge from new technologies and provide new services to the local market
Risks	
• Indian employees do not have the competences needed by the Swiss company to provide the requested services by the Swiss company in India, therefore training will be required	
Critical Success Factors (CSFs)	
• Identify the best potential partner in India to provide new services • Partners need to define procedures and processes to collaborate in the identified new services for the Indian market • Provide the proper means to stimulate team work and communication among employees of both companies • The top management from the two companies has to be committed and fully support the new partnership • Define clearly Intellectual Property Rights (IPR) terms and conditions	

Table 7. *New Services Partnerships* identified benefits, risks and Critical Success Factors (CSF).

4. CONCLUSIONS

Based on the Scenario Planning methodology carried out during the SWISSMAIN Indian pilot, this paper has provided and insight to different possible scenarios that Swiss companies or other western companies could take into consideration to identify new business opportunities in emerging markets, focusing on India. The scenarios targeted the opportunity identification and risks that both Swiss and Indian partners may encounter. These seven scenarios were developed thanks to the different inputs provided by Swiss (located both in Switzerland and India) and Indian companies, giving highlights of the current business environment in India and sharing information about current risks and opportunities when collaborating with new partners within an Indian context. It should be remarked that despite the opportunities provided by highly collaborative scenarios, most of the times Swiss companies focused on full ownership models. This implies that up to now, the perceived risks are greater than the perceived opportunities to form new types of collaborations. For this reason, a particular attention should be devoted to the development of risk management approaches and a further comprehensive study on each scenario to classify and quantify in more detail the potential risks. This could enable to fully deploy the benefits of an open innovation approach. An interesting perspective is to focus on the last scenario, new services partnerships, because depending on the type of services this can be a favourable arena to develop collaborative practices without incurring in great risks where additionally the investment required is not too high. In every scenario it is important to consider that a common element for success is to define a new shared strategy and business model, where both counterparts look forward to work under an open collaborative framework to obtain win-win benefits implementing in the analysis a sustainable development framework (economical, social, environmental).

5. ACKNOWLEDGEMENTS

The authors would like to thank the **Swiss Innovation Promotion Agency – CTI International** for the funding provided to realise the SWISSMAIN Indian Pilot. Gratitude is also given to **Mr. Duruz from Maillefer and Mr. Voirol from Bosch-Sapal**, industrial partners of the SWISSMAIN project, who provided their business requirements to develop the scenarios. We also sincerely thank **Prof. L.S. Ganesh, Prof. Srinivasan** and **Prof. Prakash Sai**, from the **Indian Institute of Technology in Madras** for supporting this Indo-Swiss research project and the 15 Swiss and Indian firms and organisations, which participated actively in the project during the face to face interviews. A special thank you note is also given to **Prof. Dr. Claudio Boër**, from the **University of Applied Sciences of Southern Switzerland (SUPSI),** for his important advises while Myrna Flores lead the SWISSMAIN Indian Pilot while working at the **CIM Institute for Sustainable Innovation (ICIMSI)** and last but not least to **Michel Pouly** from the **Swiss Federal Institute of Technology, Lausanne (EPFL)**, the project leader of the SWISSMAIN project who invited and supported Myrna Flores as a visiting researcher in EPFL to develop this research during the summer of 2007 in Lausanne.

6. REFERENCES

Charter M. and Clark T., 2007, Sustainable Innovation Key conclusions from Sustainable Innovation Conferences 2003–2006, The Centre for Sustainable Design University College for the Creative Arts, www.cfsd.org.uk

Doz Y.L. and Hamel G., 1998, "The Alliance Advantage: The Art of Creating Value through Partnering" Harvard Business School Press, Boston, MA.

Dyer J H, Kale P and Singh H, 2001, *"How to make Strategic Alliances Work"* MIT Sloan Management Review 2001 Summer Pages 37-43

Dyer, J. H., 1996, "Specialized supplier networks as a source of competitive advantage-evidence from the Auto Industry", Strategic Management Journal **17**(4), pp. 271–292.

Flores M., Boer C., Canetta L., Pouly M., Cherian M., 2008, "Critical Success Factors and Challenges to develop new Sustainable Supply Chains in India based on Swiss Experiences", *To be published in the International Conference of Concurrent Enterprising, ICE Conference Proceedings 2008*

Friedman T., 2005, The World is Flat, Penguin Ed.

Fung V., Fung W., Wind Y., 2000, Competing in a Flat World, Building Enterprises for a Borderless World, Wharton School Publishing, Pearson Power.

Larson A., 2000, Sustainable Innovation through an Entrepreneurship Lens, Business Strategy and the Environment 9: 304–317

Lorange, P and Roos, J (1992) "Strategic Alliance Formation, Implementation and Evolution", Blackwell, Oxford.

India Economic data: http://india.gov.in/business/industry_services/small_medium_enterprises.php

Rennings K., 2000, Redefining Innovation - Eco-Innovation Research and the Contribution from Ecological Economics, Ecological Economics 32, 319 – 332

Schoemaker, P., 1995, Scenario Planning: A Tool for Strategic Thinking, Sloan Management Review; Winter 1995; 36, 2.

SCOR, 1995, Supply Chain Operations Reference Model, www.supply-chain.org

Subramanian, M.H. Bala, 2007, "Development strategies for Indian SMEs: promoting linkages with global transnational corporations" Management Research News; Volume: 30 Issue: 10.

Turner S., 2002, Tools for Success, A Manager's Guide. McGraw Hill.

Observatory of European SMEs, 2002, Regional clusters in Europe, European Community, http://europa.eu.int/comm/enterprise.

Porter M., 1990, The Competitive Advantage of Nations. Free Press, New York.

THE VIRTUAL DEVELOPMENT OFFICE FRAMEWORK FOR BUSINESS NETWORKS: A CASE STUDY FROM THE UMBRIAN PACKAGING DISTRICT

62

Marco Botarelli[a], Paolo Taticchi[b], Luca Cagnazzo[c]

Department of Industrial Engineering, University of Perugia, Via Duranti 67, Perugia, ITALY
[a] *marco.botarelli@unipg.it*
[b] *paolo.taticchi@unipg.it*
[c] *luca.cagnazzo@unipg.it*

The globalization of competition has entailed that organizations of developed countries have to face new kinds of competitors with low labor cost and often advantageous exchange rates (resulting in favorable export selling prices). In such a scenario, innovation and organizational flexibility are becoming fundamental levers to enable enterprises to increase their competitiveness. For this reason, the need arises of an organizational methodology that enables organizational flexibility and capacity of performing innovation. Our recipe consists of the concept of network enterprises, to enable organizational flexibility, and the formalization of the VDO concept – Virtual Development Office – to enable innovation in a collaborative environment.

1. INTRODUCTION

In the current competitive scenario, enterprises competitiveness is not based on company or industry, but on the value creating systems themselves, within which different agents work together to co-create value and build a network (Gadde, Huemer, & Hakansson, 2003). Researches in cooperated systems have contributed to characterize the benefits correlated to the relationship of cooperation between companies (MacCarthy & Golicic, 2002; McLaren, Head, & Y., 2000; Horvath, 2001). These advantages could be particularly important for Small Medium Enterprises (SMEs) given the resource constraints and limitations they work within (Gilmore, Carson, & K., 2001). On the other hand, networking of enterprises entails new organizational problems, such as the decentralization of decision-making process and the horizontal coordination between different business function as well as, outside the firm, between complementary activity performed by suppliers and customers (Ghoshal & Bartlett, 1990). The aim of this paper is to present a new organizational enterprise network model developed within the Italian research project MIGEN[1], during which the authors supported the development of a network from its first steps. Specifically, the paper addresses the following questions: (1) Can

---

[1] MIGEN (the name comes from the Italian acronym for Innovative Models for Enterprises Network Management) is a research project supported by Italian government with the PRIN (Research Project of National Interest) program. The project involved the Universities of Perugia, Florence and Genoa and it focused on the development of specific models and tools for managing networks of enterprises.

Please use the following format when citing this chapter:

Botarelli, M., Taticchi, P. and Cagnazzo, L., 2008, in IFIP International Federation for Information Processing, Volume 283; *Pervasive Collaborative Networks*; Luis M. Camarinha-Matos, Willy Picard; (Boston: Springer), pp. 611–618.

an organizational model be developed which can foster a long term development of a SMEs network? (2) How can the interactions between the network partners be fostered? (3) How can business opportunities and innovation in the network be managed and promoted?

This paper is organized as follows: firstly, a brief description of the contest in which this core study is carried out is described; secondly, based on the case study, a formal conceptual organizational model is offered and its main highlights are discussed.

2. THE GPT CASE STUDY

The scenario in which the presented study has been developed is the district of paper products, printing and publishing in the Centre of Italy. Such a district, composed by over 160 enterprises, is characterized by a high technical-productive specialization due to an historical handicraft tradition in the mechanical and printing field. The competitive potential of the district is severely limited because it lacks the ability to spontaneously aggregate its activities, a situation exacerbated by the absence of leader firms capable of providing direction for the system as a whole.

Through a SWOT (Strengths, Weaknesses, Opportunities, Threats) Analysis, the researchers were able to identify the advantages, the weaknesses, the problems and the possible future turns of the SMEs of the district. One particular outcome from this exercise was the recognition that even those SMEs with good technological knowledge and decisional and adaptive rapidity were constrained by the small business dimensions that put them at a severe competitive disadvantage when compared to larger competitors. This making an entry in the European and international markets difficult; a situation further exacerbated by the absence of an entrepreneurial culture, effective marketing capabilities and the pursuit of preset objectives through defined strategies. In this regard the Umbrian paper mill district can be seen to embody the problems of the Italian Small & Medium Enterprises (SME).

In such a scenario, three firms (Pasqui, Litop and Litograf), characterized by a range of complementary products and by a partnership based on a solid personal knowledge of the entrepreneurs, decided to form a new company: G.P.T., acronym of "Gruppo Poligrafico Tiberino" (that will constitute what the authors introduced in the model with the concept of VDO), with the first intent of integrating the commercial and marketing functions. Since the early stage of its life, GPT perceived the need of expanding its own mission and activities. From 2005 to 2007 GPT grew from the 3 initial partners to the 18 current members, extending its borders from the district localization, to the national territory. Partners are SMEs prevalently belonging to the printing & packaging sector, even if the group growth also involved financial and service companies in order to increase the network competencies and its ability to manage relevant innovative projects. Today's aggregate turnover is about $ 310 million, involving over 700 employees, in 22 establishments, underlining the exponential network expansion. In this direction GPT is today pushing interesting strategies for the consolidation of the Italian market and it now entering the South America and Northern Africa markets.

4. THE ORGANIZATIONAL MODEL OF GPT NETWORK

In order to characterize the organizing scheme of a network we will use the dimensions proposed by Gefferi (1994): (1) a governance structure, namely power relations arising from asymmetries in market base, resources and capabilities that determine how economic surplus is distributed within the chain and how activities are coordinated within and across firms; (2) an input-output structure, or sequence of interrelated value-adding activities, including production design and engineering, manufacturing, logistics, marketing and sales; (3) a geographical configuration, referring to the spatial dispersion or concentration of activities within and across locations; (4) a social and institutional context, formed by norms, value and regulatory frameworks of the various community within which firm operate.

The governance. The governance structure plays a key role not only in the creation and distribution of value, but also in the coordination of networks. From a strategic perspective, the coordination of a network requires some degree of centralization in order to ensure an efficient use of resources, rapid decision making and the emergence of a global vision driving the network. For these reasons management researchers stress the role of the *lead firm* (Jarillo, 1988), continuously engaged in attracting and selecting members, in sustaining network relationships by managing conflicts and learning, in positioning the network in the market and in building the structure and culture of the network (Sydow, 1992). In a network composed by SMEs we can't find a subject that can naturally play the role of lead actor over a long time horizon. In our case, GPT is a formally defined entity that plays the role of a permanent figure (lead actor) operating within an enterprise community that survives the single Virtual Enterprise (VE), defined as a temporary organization of companies that come together to share costs and skills to address business opportunities that they could not undertake individually.

Another important aspect covered by GPT, as a permanent figure inside the network, is the problem of *trust* between partners, which is considered a critical aspect within the network (Jap, 2001), and can result in lower transaction costs, easier conflict resolution, or lower need of formal contracting (Das & Teng, 1998). Trust, while advocated by many authors (Stuart & McCutcheon, 1996), was recognised as needing *time* and care to build (Sobrero & Schrader, 1998) and can be difficultly developed in the typical horizon of a single VE. Similar consideration can be done about *information sharing*. In high level of interdependence environments, in order to manage the complexity of activities, procedures and interfaces have to be precisely defined, and a large investment in time and work is needed. This will result in a large complex system that can be justified only within a long-term strategy of the network (Mrtinez, Fouletier, Park, & Favrel, 2001).

Proposition 1. The definition of a central actor operating on a long-term basis can positively influence some key factors as strategy definition, trust and collaboration, information system management, and goal congruence.

The input-output structure. The main mission of GPT is to manage the organization of the VE when the business opportunity is activated and coordinates the innovation activities according to a long-term strategic decision, through a continuous monitoring of both partner resources and competencies (Teece, Pisano, & Shuen,

1997) and market needs. Once the business opportunity is captured, GPT has to set up the specific virtual enterprise composed by members belonging to the community or even outside the community. One of the main features of GPT is that, even preserving the dynamism of a typical VE in responding to market needs, it allows to centralize and to manage on a long time horizon, some critical "company" activities (i.e. the development of a well-known trademark, a long-term maintenance guarantee), without the limitations of a typical VE (Jagdev & Browne, 1998).

Proposition 2. A constant monitoring of partner competences, technologies, products and processes is a key factor to create business opportunities and design development strategy.

Proposition 3. Giving the growing importance of intangible activities such as understanding customer needs, product development and brand building, the definition of a subject, whose mission is to constantly interact with market, can positively influence network competitiveness.

Proposition 4. Effectiveness of the network is positively influenced by the ability to select specific partner within or outside the community to form a VE and respond flexibly to a business opportunity.

The geographical configuration. One of the current main trends characterizing manufacturing scenarios is represented by the internationalization of production processes; the geographical shape of global production networks results from a combination of local, regional and trans-regional dynamics (Scott, 1996). We could think of the previous as different stages or aspects during the network life cycle; even if the first pool of enterprises participating the network will be probably located in a geographically limited community where those enterprises can already have proactive environment in terms of diffused trust, collaboration, knowledge, etc., the network can be then composed by companies coming from different regions or countries, where each region can be characterized by a specific competence. The same process can be found in the development of GPT, where the geographical closeness, with its advantages in terms of informal links and shared values, has balanced the lack of formalized processes, information technology tools, etc., while its structure allows to strategically manage the link between a VE composed by companies coming from different regions or countries. This has been happening during the GPT expansion, since some partner localization is out of the initial district, but they are distributed in various parts of Italy.

Proposition 5. Even if the geographic closeness can foster the development of a network in its firsts life cycle stages, the structure of the network should allow the participation of companies coming from different countries.

The social and institutional contest. Katz and Darbishire (2000) have shown that country specific labour market structures and institution play a critical role in shaping employment relations systems, although they are affected by the spread of new practices in highly globalized sectors. One of the main advantages of the organizational model proposed is that it can formulate and manage over a single business opportunity a jointly development strategy within the community and drive networks of firms toward continuous improvement and learning. Furthermore, it can interact for the community with institutional subjects as a single entity promoting innovation activity with research centres or the support of financial institutions (banks, government offices, etc.). GPT has in fact good relation with local and national institutions as much as ministries, research centres and prestigious academies, that allow to perform important initiatives and innovative projects.

Proposition 6. Network organization should promote the cooperation between firms and government and research and financial institution to find and efficiently manage resources and competences needed by network for its development.

5. DISCUSSION: THE VIRTUAL DEVELOPMENT OFFICE (VDO) CONCEPT

Considering the attribute previously described, the aim of our work was to define a conceptual organizational model for enterprise networks. In particular we focused on Medium Enterprises (SMEs) that in most cases operate in a dense network or inter-firm relationship given that they represent an important aspect of the European economy. Therefore it's necessary to propose a cooperative model to SMEs to encourage the innovative ability, the innovation and research, to develop technology activity and the quality of the products. Our approach is based on the creation of an independent subject, the VDO (Virtual Development Office) and GPT in the case study, which act as a leading actor, and it has the role of creating, coordinating and managing a community of enterprises. Particularly, it should be the market intelligence of the network, continuously catching business opportunities in the market and positioning the network on it. Moreover, the VDO is the permanent interface to public institutions, financial institutions and research centres. As described before, a proactive collaboration with such subjects is a leverage factor in todays business. The VDO activities presented above are "external" to the network. However, the VDO also has a crucial role inside the network life. First of all, it has the role of maintaining and consolidating the trust of companies involved in the network by generating and promoting a long term alliance. By acting as a central player on respect of the "business ecosystem", it promotes both the willing of cooperation, both the readiness to collaborate each time a "collaboration opportunity" (CO) arises.

The efficacy of this subject, called VDO – Virtual Development Officer, is composed by the following phases:

- Analytic Phase; it involves a continuous monitoring of the environment and the competitive position of enterprises belonging to the enterprise community in terms of resources and competencies. One of the core activities of VDO is the definition of the strategic positioning of the community and the creation/promotion of business opportunities. Moreover it is important that with this approach it is possible to define developmental lines for innovation projects or it is possible to open the community to different actors.
- Planning Phase; after the target definition (business opportunity, new product development project, etc.), the VDO should manage the following activities: (1) plan activities, identifying the necessary resources/capabilities to reach the targets; (2) select the enterprises in the community that will create the virtual

enterprise to satisfy the business opportunity; (3) establish the contribution of every actor in the virtual network and the cooperation rules based on SLA (Service Level Agreement). The last is a very critical activity in the management of the virtual network, given that it requires the definition of organizational models, revenue sharing contracts, transaction costs, etc. i.e. the "rules of the game" that will guide the activities of the single enterprise.

- Operating phase; it implies the control and the monitoring of the quality of the products/services provided (safety, availability, reliability, etc.) and the solution effectiveness; these data represent a fundamental feedback for the analytical phase.

6. CONCLUSION

In this paper we pointed out the increasing importance of an interconnected business environment, especially to foster SMEs competitiveness. After a description of the main current organizational model, we analysed some key dimensions that can be used to classify networks: an input-output structure; a governance structure; a geographical configuration; a social and institutional context. Using these dimensions we proposed a new organizational model based on the figure of the VDO, an institutional subject, acting as a lead actor in an enterprises community.

One of the core activities of VDO is to analysis the market position of the community to establish developmental lines for innovation projects over a long time horizon. Then the VDO, through the different phases we have described (analysis, development and operations), has to manage the specific business opportunity as follows: planning activities, identifying the necessary resources to attain targets; selecting the enterprises in the community that will create the virtual network to meet the business opportunity (the selection can be made by self-nomination or by a VDO selection of the best pool of enterprises that can meet the business opportunity); establishing the contribution of every actor in the virtual network; controlling the execution of the planned activities. The organizational model proposed aim to go over the typical limitations of a VE while maintain its main strength. At the same time it opens a new critical aspect for its management and for the definition of the optimal environment in which the framework should and could be adopted.

7. REFERENCES

Benbasat, I., Goldestein, D., & Mead, M. (1987). The case research strategy in studies of information systems. *MIS Quarterly , September*, 369-386.
Boyacigiller, N. (1990). The role of expatriates in the management of interdependence, complexity, and risk in multinational corporations. *Journal of International Business Studies* (Third Quarter), 357-381.
Chesbrough, H., & Teece, D. (1996). When is virtual virtuous? Integrated virtual alliances organizing for innovation. *Harvard Business Review , 74* (1), 65-73.
Chopra, S., & Meindl, P. (2001). *Supply Chain Management: Strategy, Planning an Operation.* Upper Saddle River, NJ (USA): Prentice-Hall.

Christopher, M. (1992). *Logistics and Supply Chain Management: Strategies for Reducing Cost and improving Services.* London: Financial Times.

Chung, S. (2002). Building a national innovation systems through regional innovation systems. *Technovation , 22*, 485-491.

Cooper, M., lambert, D., & Pagh, J. (1997). Supply Chain Management: more then a new name for logistics. *International Journal of Logistics Management , 8* (1), 1-13.

Czamanski, S., & De Ablas, L. (1979). Identification of industrial clusters and complexes: a comparison of methods and findings. *Urban Studies , 16*, 61-80.

Das, T., & Teng, B. (1998). Between trust and control: developing confidence in partner cooperation in alliances. *Academy of Management Review , 23* (3), 491-512.

Easton, G., & Quayle, M. (1990). Single and Multiple Network Sourcing – Network Implications. *6th IMP Conference*, (p. 474-488). Milan (Italy).

ECOLEAD Project, Deliverable (2004). *Challenges in Virtual Organisations Management Report on methods for distributed business process management.*

Ellram, L. (1990). The supplier selection decision in strategic partnership. *Journal of Purchasing and Material Management , 26* (4), 8-14.

Ernst, D. (1997). From partial to systemic globalization: international production networks in electronics industry. *Berkley Roundtable on the International Economy (BRIE).* Berkley (USA).

European Community. (2004). *Highlights from the 2003 Observatory - Report n. 8.* Observatory for European SMEs.

Fisher, M. (1997). What is the right supply chain for your product. *Harward Business Review , 75* (2), 105-116.

Gadde, L., Huemer, L., & Hakansson, H. (2003). Strategizing in industrial networks. *Industrial Marketing Management , 32*, 357-364.

Gefferi, G. (1994). The organization of buyer-driven global commodity chains: how US retailers shape overseas production networks. In G. Gefferi, & M. Korzeniewicz, *Commodity chain and global capitalism* (p. 95-12). Westport, CT: Greenwood Press.

Ghoshal, S., & Bartlett, C. (1990). The multinational corporation as an interorganizational network. *Academy of Management Review , 15*, 603-625.

Gilmore, A., Carson, D., & K., G. (2001). SME marketing in practice. *Marketing Intelligence and Planning , 19* (1), 31-38.

Goranson, H. (1999). *The Agile Virtual Enterprise.* Westport, CT: Quorum Books.

Gulati, R., Nohria, N., & Zaheer, A. (2000). Strategic networks. *Strategic Management Journal , 21*, 203-215.

Gulati, R., Nohria, N., & Zaheer, A. (2000). Strategic networks. *Strategic Management Journal , 21*, 203-215.

Handfield, R., & Bechtel, C. (2002). The role of trust and relationship structure in improving supply chain responsiveness. *Industrial Marketing Management , 31*, 367-382.

Handfield, R., & Nichols, E. (1999). *Introduction to Supply Chain Management.* Prentice Hall.

Holton, J. (2001). Building trust and collaboration in virtual team. *Team Performance Management: An International Journal , 7* (3-4), 36-47.

Horvath, L. (2001). Collaboration: the key to value creation in supply chain management. *Supply Chain Management: An International Journal , 6* (5), 205-217.

Iansiti, M., & Levien, R. (2004). *The Keystone Advantage: What the New Dynamics of Business Ecosystems Means for Strategy, Innovations and Sustainability.* Harvard Business School Press.

Jacobs, D., & De Man, A. (1996). Cluster, Industrial policy and firm strategy: a menu approach. *Technology Analysis and Strategic Management , 8* (4), 423-437.

Jadjev, H., & Browne, J. (1998). The extended enterprise – a context for manufacturing. *Production planning and control , 9* (3), 216-229.

Jap, S. (2001). Perspectives on joint competitive advantages in buyer-supplier relationship. *International Journal of Research in Marketing , 18* (2), 19-35.

Jarillo, C. (1988). On strategic networks. *Strategic Management Journal , 9*, 31-41.

Johannisson, B. (1990). Community Enterpreneurship – Cases and Concept. *Enterpreneurship and regional development , 2*, 71-88.

Katz, H., & Darbishire, O. (2000). *Converging divergences: wordwide changes in employment systems.* Ithaca, NY: Cornell University Press.

Kochar, A., & Zhang, Y. (2002). A framework for performance measurement in virtual enterprises. *Proceedings of the 2nd International Workshop on Performance Measurement*, (p. 6-7). Hannover (Germany).

Lewis, D. (1990). *Partnership for profit: structuring and managing strategic alliances.* New York: The Free Press.

MacCarthy, T., & Golicic, S. (2002). Implementing collaborative forecasting to improve supply chain performances. *International Journal of Physical Distribution & Logistic Management , 32* (6), 431-454.

McCutcheon, D., & Meredith, J. (1993). Conducting case Studies for operations management research. *Journal of Operations Management , 11* (3), 239-256.

McLaren, T., Head, M., & Y., Y. (2000). Supply Chain collaboration alternatives: understanding the expected costs and benefits. *Internet Research: Electronic Networking Applications and Policy , 2* (4), 348-364.

Mentzer, J., DeWitt, W., Keebler, J., Min, S., Nix, N., Smith, C., et al. (2001). Defining supply chain management. *Journal of Business Logistics , 22* (2), 1-25.

Mrtinez, M., Fouletier, P., Park, K., & Favrel, J. (2001). Virtual Enterprise – organization, evolution and control. *International Journal of Production Economics , 74*, 225-238.

Oliver, R., & Webber, M. (1982). Supply Chain Management: Logistics Catches Up With Strategies. In M. Christopher, *Logistics: The Strategic Issue* (pp. 62-75). Chapman and Hall, London, UK.

Palpacuer, F. (2000). Competence-based strategies and global production networks: a discussion of current change and their implication for employment. *Competition and Change , 4*, 353-400.

Parker, H. (2000). Inter-firm collaboration and new product development process. *Industrial Management & Data Systems , 100* (6), 255-260.

Patel, P., & Pavitt, K. (1994). The nature and economic importance of national innovations systems. *STI Review, OECD*, (p. 9-32). Paris (France).

Porter, M. (1985). *Competitive Advantage, Creating and Sustaining Superior Performance.* New York: The Free Press.

Puto, C., Patton, W., & King, R. (1985). Risk Handling Strategy in Industrial Vendor Selection Decisions. *Journal of Marketing , 49*, 89-98.

Ramsay, J. (2005). The real meaning of value in trading relationship. *International Journal of Operations & Production Management , 25* (6).

Redman, J. (1994). *Understanding state economics through industry studies.* Washington, DC: Council of Governors' Policy Advisers.

Rosenfeld, S. (1997). Bringing business cluster into the main stream of economic development. *European Planning Studies , 5* (1), 1-23.

Sahin, F., & Robinson, E. (2002). Flow coordination and information sharing in supply chain: review implications and direction for future research. *Decision Sciences , 33* (4), 505-536.

Sassen, S. (1991). *The global city: New York, London, Tokyo.* Princeton, NJ: Princeton University Press.

Scott, A. (1996). Regional motors of the global economy. *Futures , 28*, 391-411.

Sobrero, M., & Schrader, S. (1998). Structuring inter-firm relationships: a meta-analytic approach. *Organization Studies - Special Issue: The Organizational Texture of Inter-firm Relations* (Fall), 585-615.

Stuart, F., & McCutcheon, D. (1996). Sustaining strategic supplier alliances. *International Journal of Operations and Production Management , 6* (10), 5-22.

Sydow, J. (1992). On the management of strategic network. In H. Ernste, & V. Meier, *Regional development and contemporary industrial response: extendind flexible specialization* (p. 113-129). London: Belhaven Press.

Teece, D., Pisano, G., & Shuen, A. (1997). Dynamic capabilities and strategic management. *Strategic Management Journal , 18*, 113-129.

Turnbull, P., Oliver, N., & Wilkinson, B. (1992). Buyer-supplier relations in the UK automotive industry: Strategic implications of the Japanese manufacturing model. *Strategic Management Journal , 13*, 159-168.

Voss, C., Tsikriktsis, N., & M., F. (2002). Case research in operations management. *International Journal of Operations & Production Management , 22* (2), 195-219.

Walters, D., & Rainbird, M. (2004). The demand chain as an integral component of the value chain. *The Journal of Consumer Marketing , 21* (7), 465-475.

Westbrook, R. (1994). Action research: a new paradigm for research in production and operations management. *International Journal of Operations and Production Mangement , 15* (12), 6-20.

PLANNING AND INITIATING VIRTUAL COLLABORATIVE NETWORKS FOR SMES IN RURAL AREAS – AN EXAMPLE FROM THE FINNISH ARCHIPELAGO

63

Kristian Packalén

Turku Centre for Computer Science,
Institute for Advanced Management Systems
Research at Åbo Akademi University, FINLAND
kristian.packalen@abo.fi

In an ICT R&D project in the Finnish archipelago, we have come in contact with 17 small business owners, and have gained hands-on information regarding some of the challenges they are facing and problems they have in their everyday work routines. We believe one solution for SMEs in similar settings is to start collaborating more, forming collaborative networks, enabling more effective information sharing, problem solving and also the creation of new value for their customers. The paper presents the challenges and proposes solutions, based on the situation we have observed but presumably also applicable to similar settings.

1. INTRODUCTION

Small and medium-sized enterprises (SME) represent 99 % of all enterprises in the European Union (EU ICT Task Force Report, 2006). Consequently, they play an important role in the economy as well as in society, which is recognized by many authors (see e.g. Thurik and Wennekers, 2004). However, the small businesses often seem to remain small, not reaching their full development potential, recognized by Hadjimanolis (1999). The reason is e.g. limited resources, for example of expertise and money. Hadjimanolis further mention difficultness in answering customers' needs as a problem factor limiting the potentials of SMEs. Other problems facing SMEs in a larger extent than larger organisations is the amount of resources that is consumed by administrative tasks. In Finland this threshold is substantial especially if the SME wants to grow and hire new people, due to the current employment laws and regulations. Hence, much of the small business owners' time goes to administrative and bureaucratic work, leaving little or no time for developing the firm or innovating, i.e. being entrepreneurial in the sense of Schumpeter's (1912) definition of an entrepreneur.

Small businesses in the archipelago face additional challenges that their mainland colleagues and competitors usually do not. SMEs and entrepreneurs in the archipelago spend more resources at finding solutions to communication and logistics problems. Communication problems might exist between the businesses and their customers, in a worst case scenario leading to lost business opportunities. In addition to these aforementioned challenges, many of the SMEs in the

Please use the following format when citing this chapter:

Packalén, K., 2008, in IFIP International Federation for Information Processing, Volume 283; *Pervasive Collaborative Networks*; Luis M. Camarinha-Matos, Willy Picard; (Boston: Springer), pp. 619–628.

archipelago are in the tourism industry, which is, according to Cabrini (2005), becoming more competitive as the tourists' needs are continuously changing. Today's tourists often want full service, with seamless activities, but are also willing to pay for it. The small businesses in the archipelago will need to adapt to these changes in demand, which might be quite difficult for small firms to handle by themselves.

In this paper, collaboration and the use of ICT is proposed, in order to help the small business owners in their endeavors of being entrepreneurial and fulfill the needs of their customers. We see building and participating in Virtual Collaborative Networks (VCN) as a promising solution.

2. THE MobiReal PROJECT

In the Fall 2007, the Institute for Advance Management Systems Research (IAMSR) at the Åbo Akademi University conducted an educational programme in 2 municipalities in the Finnish southwestern archipelago. The project, named MobiReal, was funded partly by the European Social Fund, ESF. The aim of MobiReal was to provide theoretical and especially practical knowledge about new information and communication technologies (ICT) for entrepreneurs and SMEs in the archipelago and also for the employees of the municipalities. Furthermore, the MobiReal project presented new business models for entrepreneurs and SMEs employing ICT solutions foremost within the tourism and hospitality industry. The idea was to demonstrate how ICT could be applied to create new business opportunities.

The general objective of the project was to show how useful services, improving the daily life of the entrepreneur and enabling things previously not possible with existing resources, can be developed using ICT. To measure when such a service has been accomplished, we use the Braudel rule, as presented by Keen and Mackintosh (2001): *"changing the limits of the possible in the structure of everyday life"*. This rule can be seen as the guiding light of this paper.

During the project, we have gotten some insight into the everyday life of small business owners, and challenges they are facing. A small business in the archipelago often has some collaboration in place. However, based on the answers from the post-project questionnaires, we see that most small business owners would like to collaborate more with other companies. The question is then why this is not done in any larger extent, and what could be done to enable more collaboration and whether the collaboration effectively could take place in a virtual setting.

This paper discusses how technology can help small businesses and whether electronic collaboration could be accomplished. We believe technology in itself can be very beneficial for the SMEs, but that even more can be accomplished by the creation and participation in virtual collaborative networks (VCN). We discuss the first steps we have taken to creating such a virtual collaborative setting. Furthermore, we discuss a possible continuation of the learning and collaboration that has been initiated, that is, how the optimal collaborative network for small businesses could look like for SMEs in the archipelago but also more generally.

2.1 Research Objectives and Questions

The research objectives related to collaborative networks for SMEs are based on the Braudel rule, and include finding viable methods by which SMEs can receive support in developing their businesses and find new business opportunities in a resource effective manner. Also, a research objective was to find alternative solutions to maintaining the collaboration between academics and the SMEs as well as internally among the SMEs.

The main research question in relation to these research objectives is:

Could Virtual Collaborative Networks help small business owners become more entrepreneurial?

2.2 Research Methodology

The action research model is chosen for the development, and consequent teaching, of the VCN. Action research is an iterative process, which should incorporate the views and needs of as many stakeholders as possible. Cummings (1989, p. 47) states that action research involves considerable collaboration between the change implementer and the stakeholders the change affects, and that data gathering and diagnosis before action planning and implementation is important, as well as the evaluation of results after the action has been taken. Both before and after the project, we conducted questionnaires, where we asked the participants to grade their computer literacy and also what collaborative tools they use. We aimed at adapting the project, based on these answers and also learn how to improve things based on the post-project questionnaires.

3. COLLABORATIVE NETWORKS – OPPORTUNITIES AND CHALLENGES

A possible answer to the needs and problems SMEs are facing, as we described in the introduction, is according to Taylor (2005) that the SMEs should collaborate with other organisations, by participating in strategic alliances, and then be able to utilize each other's resources and competencies. Recently, we have seen a wide variety of different terms emerging, aiming at explaining various forms of collaborative networks, as e.g. Value Network, Value Web, Virtual Organizations, Virtual Enterprises, Virtual Communities, Collaborative Virtual Laboratories, Communities of Practice, Communities of Interest, and so forth. Although these have some differences, we believe they generally explain quite similar phenomena, and we think it is wise to follow Camarinha-Matos and Afsarmanesh's (2005) recommendation of using the term collaborative network as an umbrella term for these phenomena. Camarinha-Matos and Afsarmanesh (2006) define a collaborative network as "a network consisting of a variety of entities (e.g. organizations and people) that are largely autonomous, geographically distributed, and heterogeneous in terms of their operating environment, culture, social capital and goals, but that collaborate to better achieve common or compatible goals, and whose interactions are supported by computer network."

3.1 Opportunities with collaborative networks

Collaboration is commonly seen as a key enabler of value creation and innovation (see e.g. Martinus et al. 2005). Communities consisting of people with different backgrounds and expertise offer great possibilities to enable innovation and solve problems. Metcalf's law applies, which states that the value of a network grows exponentially in relation to the number of members. This opportunity of gathering collective intelligence (see e.g. Paavola, Lipponen and Hakkarainen, 2002) should be utilized to get better information for example for decision making purposes, and to avoid double labour.

To enable collaboration, we propose building, and participating in, virtual collaborative networks. By virtual we mean that the community should exist on the Internet, being accessible using personal computers or handheld devices and enable electronic collaboration. Quereshi and Keen (2005) define electronic collaboration as "the purposeful use of networking and collaborative technologies to support groups in the creation of shared understanding".

The benefits of collaboration in a virtual setting include that more members can enter the network than is otherwise possible in a traditional off-line setting, that it allows greater disparity of members, enabling a multi-discipline setting, which in turn presumably enables better results. Also, more effective working methods and possibilities to save resources is one of the key opportunities as well as accomplishing economies of scale. When each member can focus on his or her core capabilities, resources can be shared (Camarinha-Matos and Afsarmanesh, 2006).

Zheng et al. (2003) claim that the Internet enables SMEs to benefit from the use of information and communication technology. The Internet presents an affordable and simple way to reach new customers and suppliers. The Internet also creates a global market for companies, but can also be a drawback since the competition is tightened for domestic or local companies. However, it seems that many SMEs do not use these opportunities to their full potential and we ask whether participating in virtual collaborative networks could improve this situation.

3.2 Challenges when planning and implementing collaborative networks

Quereshi and Keen (2005) claim that previous attempts to share knowledge both within and across organizations or entities have often failed. Rutkowski et al. (2002) show the problems that can occur in virtual collaboration, and that you have to take many aspects into mind when designing virtual collaborative environments; aspects regarding technology as well as social aspects. Cultural aspects also play an important role. Hagel and Armstrong (1997, p. 172) recognize that the members are the most important factor of a virtual community, and not the technology. Hence, the development and implementation of virtual communities is not only a technical issue, but rather an organisational one. As we include also virtual communities in our definition of CNs, this applies also in our setting.

To get the SMEs to use the virtual collaborative network, some change management methods will presumably be needed. These change management procedures include for example having good information and persons supporting and encouraging the usage, for example change agents and sponsors. The value of the community must be visible in order to attract users. To accomplish this, education of all stakeholders regarding the actual use and the possibilities should be done. We have given courses in the use of ICT to entrepreneurs in the archipelago, where we have introduced the idea of an electronic collaborative network. The SMEs responded very well to this idea. Whether a CN will appear will depend on a large number of factors, and will presumably entail changing the attitudes and work practices of the entrepreneurs. Information, education, and demonstration of good practices will presumably be needed of the potential members. These are closely related to factors generally seen as change management, which we believe can be adopted also to cases like the presented one. Also resources will be needed to develop the technical functions needed to enable the VCN.

Trust is generally seen as a key factor for accomplishing successful collaboration, especially in a virtual setting (Child, 2001, Rutkowski et al., 2002). The SMEs in the small municipalities studied generally already are collaborating, and know each other from before. It will, then, be interesting to see whether this affects the outcome of the virtual collaboration, and whether the existing relations easily can be transferred to a virtual setting or not. One factor that might be discouraging is that the SMEs we have been dealing with are quite unfamiliar with ICT, as we noticed during the MobiReal project. This may very well mean that virtual collaboration will become difficult to get started. To counter this, further education of the potential users is needed. Another possibility is that face to face collaboration is seen as better, or more easily accomplished. As long as collaboration is taking place, it does not matter in what form it takes, however we believe a virtual setting brings additional values.

3.3 Technologies and Tools for enabling Virtual Collaborative Networks

Lee et al. (2003) describes the existing tools that are used to help build the virtual community by supporting communication. These are for example e-mail, forums, message boards and chat-rooms. Forums are the most common tool used, according to the authors. Forums are used for debates going on for an extended period of time, with discussions regarding topics common to the participants. Chat-rooms enable quick communication, often with shorter messages, also often regarding some common topic. The difference between chat-rooms and forums is that the chats often take place in real time, and that the information entered is perishable. Other, less frequently used tools, are internet broadcasts, telephone-, and video conferencing. Lee et al. question whether these, aforementioned, simple tools really can support knowledge transfer among the participants.

When people talk about technology-mediated collaboration tools, they foremost seem to talk about e-mail, chats and forums. Two examples of this are to be found in the articles by Lee et al. (2002) and Rutkowski et al. (2002). However, wiki has risen as a very important tool for collaboration and a space for collective intelligence. Schaffert et al. (2006) claim that wikis can serve as a knowledge platform for a community of practice, where members of the community can share their knowledge and information with the group, work together or discuss issues. Schaffert et al. also state that a wiki can be used by new members of the community to get informed about the community and its practices. They furthermore regard wiki as a good technology for creating interdisciplinary and intercultural communication environments, where people from different backgrounds can be brought together and discuss a common topic. We believe that this is one of the most powerful features of wiki, and other virtual communication and collaboration means. By bringing together people with different backgrounds, knowledge that otherwise couldn't have been created can be created.

Wiki enables co-authoring of web-sites in a simple manner. It enables whomever to contribute, building a database of information based on the knowledge of a multi-cultural, cross-disciplinary group of people. Lee et al. (2002) claim that there is a lack of tools enabling true knowledge transfer and in-depth sharing among the participants. We believe that Wiki can be an important answer to this request. The strength of wiki compared to forum is the easiness of retrieving information from the knowledge source. For a forum to be effective, the participants often need to follow the forum continuously. Although there often are search functions in forums, it can be difficult to get the whole picture and receive all information regarding a specific topic, or get a general picture about the discussions. With a Wiki, on the other hand, information is usually stored in a way that enables a quick overview as well as helps the participants to get a more profound view of a specific topic.

It is important to stress that accessing the virtual collaborative network should be possible both using web-based and mobile technologies, as they each have their own strengths and weaknesses. Together, these technologies presumably could support the new working methods needed in the archipelago. People usually prefer a personal computer, if it is available, as a personal computer is easier, quicker and more comfortable to use. However, people are often on the move and do not have access to a desktop computer, which seems to apply especially to the people in the archipelago. Then, the ubiquitous nature of mobile devices is needed to allow virtual work on the move (Verburg and Bosch-Sijtsema, 2007).

The technologies used for creating the virtual collaborative network should be easy to use, i.e. be purposeful according to the needs of the users and have good usability, to attract usage rather than discourage it. As for example Davis (1989), with his technology acceptance model, has noticed, it doesn't matter how good a system is, if it is difficult to use. Hence, we aim at the simplicity of the systems. Further on, when collaboration is active, more advanced functions can be introduced upon the users' request.

Even though the technologies used for the creation of virtual collaborative networks are important to study, we believe the challenges when developing the solutions will not as much concern technological issues as organisational and social ones as well as reaching systems with great usability and good content. The value of the content and the functions of the developed products must be apparent to all potential users so that the collaborative network gets enough users and a critical user mass will be reached. If enough users are reached, the community will be living and user-generated content will be developed. This presumably frees up resources and more, better information can be created when the users are enabled to create the content.

Generally speaking, collective intelligence could be gathered through technology enabling user-generated content, and stored in a knowledge repository for later use and revision. Such a knowledge repository is an important part of a VCN.

Information in such a knowledge repository could for example be good practices. The knowledge repository could be built upon wiki-technology, enabling simple co-authoring of information. Tobin (1997) states that knowledge repositories can be used only to capture explicit knowledge but that electronic forums can be used to uncover tacit knowledge. We do not want to go into whether tacit knowledge really can be captured or not, in any case forums are an important part in a virtual collaborative setting.

3.4 Change Management

As is recognized by many authors and practitioners of collaborative networks, accomplishing a working CN is not easy. We have not yet found a solution that would answer this question to its full extent, but believe change management could play an important role in facilitating the function of a CN, especially in the initial phase. We believe this applies to all organizations planning a participation in a CN, also SMEs.

The research methodology of action research that we have used in this case also function as a change management method according to Cummings (1989, p. 47). The action research model is an iterative development process, where collaboration between the change implementers and those that the change affects is vital. Good information flow, as well as input of those affected by the changes, are important features of many change management methods, which we believe is incorporated in the action research model.

4. PROPOSAL: DEVELOPING A COLLABORATIVE NETWORK FOR SMES IN THE SERVICE SECTOR IN THE FINNISH ARCHIPELAGO.

Merging collaboration with digital technologies should result in a basis for a virtual organisation. Especially smaller businesses are expected to gain from the use of ICT by developing and participating in a virtual organization. Knowing that small businesses as a rule have limited resources, ICT can be a relatively inexpensive way to create the basis for a CN and receive many of the advantages that otherwise only larger organisations have. Examples of such advantages are found in marketing, distribution and sales (Botkin and Matthews, 1992, p. 33). We believe that smaller organisations can become more efficient by using ICT and CNs. Thus small businesses will be able to solve many easy problems, dull or time-consuming routine tasks and instead be able to focus on more important, entrepreneurial activities, but also benefit from many of the advantages larger organisations have, for example accomplishing economies of scale.

The planned collaborative network should function as a knowledge repository, harnessing the power of the users and getting network effects. However, we do not yet know how this could be accomplished. It will not be an easy task. As recognized by for instance Hagel and Armstrong (1997, pp. 132-133) and Tickle et al. (2007), building a virtual community is not easy.

A web-based portal will be the core of the planned initial VCN, and will be accessible primarily via personal computers, but also via mobile devices as this is seen important from a tourism perspective. The idea of developing a portal was born in the general lectures held within the MobiReal project, during a discussion and brainstorming session between us, the lecturers, and the participating small business owners. The discussion regarded how the collaboration between the IAMSR and the SMEs could continue also after the end of the project. Also, the idea that the SMEs should start collaborating more with each other electronically emerged. We proposed that an Internet portal could be constructed by the IAMSR in cooperation with some of the participating SMEs. Initially, the portal should have some simple functions, due to the limited scope of the MobiReal project, but also to let the SMEs get familiar with virtual collaboration. The initial functions of the portal include: a knowledge repository, discussion forum, profile pages, document database and groups. The knowledge repository could presumably be based on a wiki, where the participants can co-author for example lessons learned during the project, best practices of the industries, general tips and tricks related to entrepreneurship, etc. The discussion forum is of a traditional type found in almost every virtual community. The profile pages allow for easy presentation of the SMEs, and can function as a substitute for the SMEs' own web-site. The document database, which in the beginning was related to the MobiReal project, can be used to share documents. The groups can be used to have closed virtual communication and collaboration. Additionally, the portal can function as a marketing place for products, presumably web-based, that are related to the archipelago. We hope that such a portal would be used by the SMEs to collaborate and also act as a common face for the small businesses towards their customers, and be an easy way for the SMEs to market themselves and for the potential customers to see the services offered in the two municipalities. The entrepreneurs should take part in the development, and take over the prototype and continue to develop it. This presumably makes them more motivated, plus that they learn how it works from the beginning, which we believe is in the essence of the action research model. However, this takes some resources, since the entrepreneurs need to be educated in the technological aspects of the VCN, in order to maintain it and continue developing it. This knowledge transfer is as important as the actual transfer of a product. Instead of being a one-time event, the knowledge transfer can continue to benefit them in the future. Also, this is vital from a resource perspective as the resources usually are scarce for academics. Furthermore, this may also provide a potential revenue source for the entrepreneurs in the future.

Generally speaking, we would like to see that the collaborative network will have a positive effect on the development of new business opportunities by promoting entrepreneurship and helping individuals in their quest to become entrepreneurs.

The objectives of the planned collaborative network include:

i)   Working as a collaboration platform between SMEs in the service industry, primarily in the Finnish south-western archipelago

ii)   Acting as a common communication channel between the SMEs and their (potential) customers

iii)   Functioning as a collaboration channel between SMEs and external partners, e.g. academics

5. CONCLUSION

We believe that the use of new technologies by the entrepreneurs in the archipelago and more collaboration with other entrepreneurs and with other sectors and organisations would benefit the everyday life in such a degree that they could spend more time to develop their business. We consider developing and participating in virtual collaborative networks, engaging in one form of a virtual organisation, to be a lucrative opportunity for the small business owners. Presumably, collaboration is the only realistic way to tackle many of the challenges these small businesses are facing. During the project in the archipelago, we have seen the need for improved collaboration tools that apply a variety of new technologies. However, due to the limited scope and resources of the project, we have so far only been able to develop applications with limited capabilities.

We recognize that accomplishing a working Virtual Collaborative Network is a difficult task, where technology, although important, only plays a minor role. Hence, accomplishing pervasive collaborative networks requires both persistency, good change management, and a great portion of luck.

Virtual Collaborative Networks offer great possibilities for improved work and communication. Economies of scale can be accomplished when double labour is reduced, and existing information is used more efficiently. The collective intelligence of the members of the community can enable new and better knowledge to be created. The development of virtual collaborative networks should be based on the needs of the users, rather than on technological finesses. If done correctly, the presumed outcomes will provide a substantial value for all stakeholder groups.

6. REFERENCES

1. Botkin, J., Matthews, J. Winning Combinations The Coming Wave of Entrepreneurial Partnerships Between Large & Small Companies, John Wiley & Sons, 1992
2. Cabrini, L. Tourism in the World. A vision for the future, 2nd Congress of Tourism – "To reinvent Tourism, To affirm Portugal", Estoril, Portugal, 4 and 5 July 2005
3. Camarinha-Matos, L. & Afsarmanesh, H. Collaborative networks: a new scientific discipline, Journal of Intelligent Manufacturing, 16, 439–452, 2005
4. Camarinha-Matos, L. and Afsarmanesh, H. Collaborative Networks, Value creation in a knowledge society, In Proceedings of PROLAMAT'06 (Springer), Shanghai, China, 14-16 Jun 2006
5. Child, J. Trust – The Fundamental Bond in Global Collaboration, Organizational Dynamics, Vol. 29, No. 4, pp. 274-288, 2001
6. Cummings, T. Huse, E. Organization Development and Change. Fourth Edition, St. Paul: West Publishing Company, 1989
7. Davis, F. Perceived Usefulness, Perceived Ease of Use and User Acceptance of Information Technology, MIS Quarterly, Vol. 13, No. 3, pp. 319-339, 1989
8. EU ICT Task Force Report, Fostering the Competitiveness of Europe's ICT Industry, 2006
9. Hadjimanolis, A. Barriers to innovation for SMEs in a small less developed country (Cyprus), Technovation 19, 561-570, 1999
10. Hagel, J., Armstrong, A. Net Gain: Expanding Markets through Virtual Communities, Boston, Harvard Business School Press, 1997

11. Keen, P., Mackintosh, R. The Freedom Economy, Gaining the mCommerce edge in the Era of the Wireless Internet, Osborne/McGraw-Hill, 2001
12. Lee, F., Vogel, D., Limayem, M. Virtual Community Informatics: What We Know and What We Need to Know, appearing in Proceedings of the 35th Hawaii International Conference on System Sciences,, pp. 2863- 2872, 2002
13. Lee, F., Vogel, D., Limayem, M. Virtual community informatics: A review and research agenda, Journal of Information Technology Theory and Application, pp. 47 – 61, 2003
14. Martinus, K., Rowe, M., Burn, J., Walker, E. Beyond Clusters – Collaborative Commerce and Clustering, CRIC Cluster conference, Beyond Cluster – Current Practices & Future Strategies, Ballarat, June 30 – July 1, 2005
15. Paavola, S., Lipponen, L., Hakkarainen, K. Epistemological Foundations for CSCL: A comparison of three modes of innovative knowledge communities, In G. Stahl, (ed.), 4th Computer Support for Collaborative Learning: Foundations for a CSCL Community, (CSCL-2002), Boulder, Colorado, pp. 24-32, January 2002
16. Quereshi, S., Keen, P. Organizational Transformation by Activating Knowledge: The Mediating role of Collaboration Technologies, Institute for Advanced Management Systems Research, Research Report 5, 2005
17. Rutkowski, A., Vogel, D., Van Genuchten, M., Bemelmans, T., Favier, M. E-Collaboration: The Reality of Virtuality, IEEE Transactions on Professional Communication, Vol. 45, No. 4, December 2002
18. Schaffert, S., Bischof, D., Bürger, T., Gruber, A., Hilzensauer, W., Schaffert, S. Learning with Semantic Wikis, In: First Workshop SemWiki2006 - From Wiki to Semantics", co-located with the 3rd Annual European Semantic Web Conference (ESWC), Budva, Montenegro, 11th - 14th June, 2006
19. Schumpeter, J., The Theory of Economic Development, Oxford University Press, 1912
20. Taylor, A. An Operations Perspective on Strategic Alliance Success Factors, International Journal of Operations and Production Management (25:5), 2005, pp. 469-490.
21. Thurik, R., Wennekers, S. Entrepreneurship, small business and economic growth, Journal of Small Business and Enterprise Development, Vol. 11, No. 1, pp. 140-149, 2004
22. Tickle, M., Michaelides, R., Kehoe, D. The Challenge of Creating Virtual Communities, Proceedings of the 18:th Information Resources Management Association (IRMA), 19-23 May, 2007
23. Tobin, D. The Knowledge-Enabled Organisation - Moving From "Training" to "Learning" to Meet Business Goals, American Management Association, 1997
24. Verburg, R., Bosch-Sijtsema, P. Guest Editorial – The Limits of Virtual Work, The Electronic Journal for Virtual Organizations and Networks, Vol. 9, Special Issue "The Limits of Virtual Work", July, 2007
25. Zhang, D., Zhao L., Zhou, L., Nunamaker, J. Can e-learning replace classroom learning? Communications of the ACM, 47 (5), pp. 75-78, 2004

64

COLLABORATIVE RESEARCH NETWORKS: INSTITUTE FACTORY OF MILLENNIUM-BRAZIL

Angelita Moutin Segoria Gasparotto

Advanced Manufacturing Center, São Carlos School of Engineering - University of São Paulo
angelita@usp.br
BRAZIL

The contemporary world is structured by means of social and economic relationships, where there is not much room for isolated or particular actions. Therefore, the term "collaborative networks" has been broadly used to describe a system which has agents who try to create synergy in a competitive or non competitive environment. The purpose of this article is to present Brazilian initiatives related to collaborative networks, such as the main projects, researching groups and governmental action programs. It gives special emphasis to the collaborative research network denominated "Institute Factory of Millennium". Topics requiring additional research are also identified.

1. INTRODUCTION

Collaboration is not a recent term. In his book (Williamson, 1975), Williamson already maintained that manufacturing companies could prosper by establishing external partnerships when purchasing goods or services, instead of producing internally. This paradigm was scattered even more through 'outsourcing', now called 'lean organization', where managers reduce the organization spheres by passing them to outsourcing companies, thereby seeking to eliminate inefficient services.

In this context, a collaborative network might be considered an alliance constituted by several entities (e.g.: universities, companies, governmental organs and people) geographically distributed and heterogeneous, regarding their operational, cultural environments, social capital, but which perceives in collaborative work a form to increase revenue and competitiveness, as well as to share resources and acquaintances (Camarinha-Matos & Afsarmanesh, 2008).

Addressed as a class of collaborative network, research networks are also known as teaching, research and development laboratories, where research groups are formed by multidisciplinary teams chosen for essential concerns and competences.

The purpose of this article is to present a study about initiatives that Brazil has undertaken, related to collaborative networks. The article begins with an introduction about collaborative networks and their dimensions. Next, there is a review about networks of collaborative research, denominating them according to their relationship level. A study about Brazil's initiatives in collaborative networks is presented. Special emphasis is given to the collaborative research network denominated Institute Factory of Millennium: a project which is part of the

Please use the following format when citing this chapter:

Gasparotto, A.M.S., 2008, in IFIP International Federation for Information Processing, Volume 283; *Pervasive Collaborative Networks*; Luis M. Camarinha-Matos, Willy Picard; (Boston: Springer), pp. 629–636.

"Millennium Institutes Program", supported by the Ministry of Science and Technology. It is a national scope network which associates 800 researchers in 39 research teams, allocated in 32 colleges and universities.

The following topic discusses the term collaborative research networks and shows the main related classes.

2. COLLABORATIVE RESEARCH NETWORKS

2.1 Introduction

In the last years, an increasing number of research projects have been created and made possible under the forms of collaboration, where different institutions assume specific tasks with the purpose of reaching a determined result.

In this context, the research networks (Weisz & Rocco, 1996) have been typically mentioned as "unphysical" centers, which rely on communications means to promote the interaction of members with complementary qualifications. A network usually counts on multiple sponsors and, frequently, has its duration limited to the time needed for achieving their goals.

2.2 Classes of research networks

Next, the main classes of research networks presented in literature are highlighted.

- *Distributed networks:* is a subtle linking of different research and teaching organizations, related among each other, without the presence of a central agent (Figure 1). In this type of network, each organization member participates and conducts a specific area of their competence. Likewise, responsibilities are equally shared among all participants.

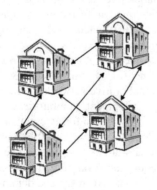

Figure 1 – Example of distributed research networks

- *Networks with a central organization*: in this kind of network, an organization has the role of a leader of their network's activities (Figure 2). The central organization is connected to geographically distributed institutions which act in diverse fields that might have special interests in the research subject. This opportunity probing is performed through the central organization.

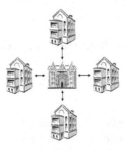

Figure 2 – Example of research network with a central organization

- *Research-and-Teaching Interchange Network:* is a network which congregates different groups and organizations about teaching projects and limited-term researches, in a given interest field (Figure 3). A typical case is one where a research and teaching interchange network sets tasks which are interests of several groups.

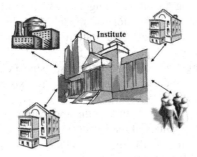

Figure 3 – Example of interchange research network

3. BRAZIL IN A GLOBAL CONTEXT OF COLLABORAIVE NETWORKS

3.1 Introduction

The transformations of global contemporary society have demanded, from companies, universities and research centers, greater dynamism and flexibility when producing their goods and services. Within this context, collaborative networks appear as a way to fulfill these demands with improved accuracy and quality.

Many global manifestations have been shown with regards to collaborative networks (ECOLEAD: htt Many manifestations in a global extent p://virtual.vtt.fi/virtual/ecolead/; CODESNET: http://codesnet.polito.it/; SOCOLNET: http://www.uninova.pt/~socolnet/joomla/), or even efforts to systematize it as a scientific discipline (http://www.uninova.pt/~thinkcreative). The objective of the next topic is to introduce Brazilian initiatives in the setting of collaborative networks.

3.2 Brazilian initiatives about collaborative networks

Brazilian efforts undertaken in the context of collaborative networks are presented next.

- *VIRTEC:* Molded according to the context of virtual organization and based on the trust criterion (Bremer et al., 2001), it was developed at the São Carlos Engineering School Center of Advanced Manufacturing (http://www.numa.org.br) and comprises nine small companies, which offer products and services with a high aggregated value.
- *São Carlos's Cluster of High Technology:* it is the result of an initiative by local companies to establish São Carlos as a technology-reference city, focused on software development, and based on forming collaborative work among companies, assistance agencies, universities and the government (http://www.clustersaocarlos.com.br). Through contracted formal agreements, the Cluster seeks the following objectives:
  - Improving the developing process of softwares for companies, through the definition of models based on better practices for collaborative work and state-of-the-art in management tools for the developing process of softwares;
  - Creating free software solutions, using licenses for the produced artifacts and the integration of pre-existent, publicly available modules;
  - Creating models to enable the application of processes and tools in other companies of the Cluster.
- *VIRFEBRAS:* the Brazilian VO of Tooling Companies (http://www.virfebras.com.br) is an initiative by the University of Caxias do Sul and composed of a group of tool-making companies that work cooperatively, proposing solutions for molds and matrixes.

Concerning research teams in collaborative networks:

- *GSIGMA:* The Manufacturing Intelligent Systems Group was created in 1996, and its objective is to work in research subjects relevant to industrial areas focused on problems associated with the paradigm of organizations in collaborative networks.

- *REDECOOP:* The Cooperation Networks and Knowledge Management Group aims at identifying opportunities and obstacles related to generation, diffusion and knowledge management through inter-organizational networks (http://www.poli.usp.br/pro/networkcoop/), under the context of market globalization and industrial restructuration with the advent of the dry/quick/flexible production paradigm.
- *GEI:* The Integrated Engineering Group (http://www.numa.org.br/grupos.htm) is composed of researchers (teachers, majoring and post-majoring students), whose objective is to develop collaborative projects with other entities in the following topics: product development management, product life cycle, reference architecture for networks, process modeling, quality management, logistics and optimization of production processes.

Concerning governmental support programs in collaborative networks:

- *PIPE/FAPESP:* the Technological Innovation Program in Small Companies exists since 1997 and aims at supporting the development of innovative researches on problems in science and technology, to be performed in companies with up to 100 employees and that have a high potential for commercial or social exchange, enabling them to associate with academic researchers in technological innovation projects (http://www.fapesp.br).
- *CONSITEC/FAPESP:* the objective of the Sectorial Consortium for the Technological Innovation program is to stimulate collaboration by research teams with agglomerated companies, to study relevant subjects and to solve technology problems caused by common undertakings (http://www.fapesp.br).
- *RHAE/CNPQ:* the Development of Human Resources for Strategic Activities, supporting technological innovation, was created in 1988 and its purpose is to promote improvements in companies, stimulating entrepreneurial associations and sectorial technological entities, which in turn develops plans and technological development programs (http://www.cnpq.br).
- *Millennium Institutes:* the Millennium Institutes Program is an initiative from the Ministry of Science and Technology. Its function is to increase the options to finance more comprehensive and relevant projects of scientific research and technological development. Meant for promoting the formation of research networks throughout the national territory, the program seeks scientific and technological excellence in any knowledge field.
- *FINEP:* the Brazilian Innovation Agency (http://www.finep.gov.br/) is a public company subordinated to the Ministry of Science and Technology, with the purpose of promoting and financing innovation, scientific and technological researches in companies, universities, research centers, mobilizing financial resources and integrating instruments to support the country's economic development. Among the main programs, we have:

- *COOPERA*: the Cooperation Program among ICTs (STIs: Science and Technology Institutes) and companies; it establishes financial support for P&D projects and innovation among companies and science and technology institutions.
- *PPI-APL's:* the Research and Local Productive Arrangements Supporting Program establish the financial support for activities developed by the science and technology institutions, facing technological assistance, service rendering and solving these companies' technological problems, creating characteristics agglomerated by local productive arrangements.

4. THE INSTITUTE FACTORY OF MILLENNIUM

4.1 Introduction

Concerning collaborative research networks, the Millennium Institutes Program is a Brazilian initiative from the Ministry of Science and Technology. This program's objective is to increase the options to finance more comprehensive and relevant projects of scientific research and technological developments.

Among the projects approved in the program, we have the Institute Factory of Millennium (http://www.ifm.org.br), whose objectives may be understood as the proposition, development and dissemination of mechanisms to increase competitiveness and scientific and technological knowledge of manufacture industries, especially those dedicated to capital goods, installed in Brazil.

In practice, the IFM is a collaborative research network composed by 800 researchers in 39 research teams allocated in 32 Major Teaching Institutions.

4.2 The IFM Network concerning innovation and learning

One of the main objectives of the research network IFM is to prepare individuals for technological advances, created and systematized by the network. Among these transference mechanisms are:

- *Courses and workshops:* these are specific subjects where the students perform pragmatically inside the project, thus increasing their learning capacity.
- *Assistance:* IFM interventions on companies are different from consultancies, since new concepts are applied, making the company a "storehouse", where new advances are validated.
- *Development of real-time scenarios:* Environments are developed to simulate real companies. Scripts are used to simulate what would happen in real cases of technology application. Roles are defined on these scripts and distributed among the participants. Thus, a real application of new technologies is experienced.

- *Creation of high technology companies around IFM:* the business environment around universities (technology parks and incubators) is used, promoting the generation of undertaking actions.
- *Development of academic/entrepreneurial works:* it enables the development of researches related to practical problems.
- *Self-teaching web environment:* acquirements that are more suitable to capital goods companies are systematized, simplifying their assimilation and usage. It constitutes a free, structured collection of guides, tools, templates, white-papers, case descriptions, on-line courses and evaluations and virtual scenarios.

Since the beginning of its operation, the network has interacted with over 400 companies in the manufacturing sector, resulting in close to 50 university research projects (Master's and Doctorate), becoming effective on solutions for the productive sector. With regards to innovation, the projects linked to MFI have resulted in 17 industrial technology patents, with publication of more than 280 articles in scientific journals, as evidence of the innovative potential of the network and the capacity for improving the productivity of domestic companies.

4.3 IFM Network Research Operation

In order to meet the network objectives, the undertaken actions should be divided as follows:

- *Work Packages:* identified as WPs, they foresee accomplishing actions which integrate the network nodes (entities which are part of the network) proposing solutions for previously identified problems. WP's contemplates:

  - *Subprojects:* identified as SPs, they foresee, one by one, a tasks list which is allocated to one or more researchers to be fulfilled.

The following figure (Figure 4) represents a work package (WP05) with its respective related subprojects (SPs 01 to 06).

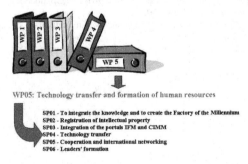

WP05: Technology transfer and formation of human resources

SP01 - To integrate the knowledge and to create the Factory of the Millennium
SP02 - Registration of intellectual property
SP03 - Integration of the portals IFM and CIMM
SP04 - Technology transfer
SP05 - Cooperation and international networking
SP06 - Leaders' formation

Figure 4 – Example of IFM structure

Subprojects might involve surveys, benchmarking, development of sites, laboratorial experiments, machine tests, application of innovations in companies, development of equipments, and many others.

The conception of working with work packages and subprojects results from the experience of IFM's researchers in previous projects, since it:

- Supports integration between network nodes.
- Contextualizes and focuses programmed actions, gathering them around confirmed problems or the ones detected through field surveys in order to bring up the sustainability of the productive chain capital goods.

5. CONCLUSION

This article highlighted the initiatives of Brazil on the collaborative networks. The main projects, research groups and government support programs were described. An emphasis on Collaborative Research Network – IFM was provided, presenting its goals, action models, innovative aspects and contributions. As ideas for further work, there is a need to emphasize that since the economic leverage of Brazil is represented by small and medium-sized enterprises, a point that must be undertaken by the research network includes economic and social aspects of the country. The problems of small and medium-sized organizations help the research network to train human resources with a more realistic view of the market, with a clear understanding of the business itself, possessing information and communications technologies (ICTs) and a greater reach to generate innovations.

6. REFERENCES

1. Bremer, C.F.; Michilini, F.V.S.; Siqueira, J.E.M.; Ortega, L.M. VIRTEC: An example of a Brazilian virtual organization. Journal of Intelligent Manufacturing. 12, pp.213-221, 2001.
2. Camarinha-Matos, L.M, Afsarmanesh, H. Classes of collaborative networks. In: Encyclopedia of Networked and Virtual Organizations. Idea Group, January, 2008.
3. Klen, E.R.; Cardoso, T.O.M.; Camarinha-Matos, L.M. Teaching Initiatives on Collaborative Networked Organizations, Proceedings of 38th CIRP - International Seminar on Manufacturing Systems, Florianópolis-SC, Brazil, 2005.
4. Weisz, J.; Roco, M.C. Research networks and education in engineering in America. Rio de Janeiro: FINEP, 1996.
5. Williamson, O. Markets and hierarchies. New York, NY: Free Press, 1975.

AUTHOR INDEX